The Handbook of
European
Structured
Financial Products

THE FRANK J. FABOZZI SERIES

The Handbook of
European
Structured
Financial Products

FRANK J. FABOZZI

MOORAD CHOUDHRY

EDITORS

WILEY
John Wiley & Sons, Inc.

For general information on our other products and services, or technical support, please contact our Customer Care Department within the United States at 800-762-2974, outside the United States at 317-572-3993, or fax 317-572-4002.

Wiley also publishes its books in a variety of electronic formats. Some content that appears in print may not be available in electronic books.

For more information about Wiley, visit our Web site at www.wiley.com.

ISBN: 0-471-48415-6

Printed in the United States of America

10 9 8 7 6 5 4 3 2 1

Contents

PART FOUR

Mortgage-Backed Securities   411

PART FIVE

Collateralised Debt Obligations   551

About the Editors

Frank J. Fabozzi, Ph.D., CFA, CPA is the Frederick Frank Adjunct Professor of Finance in the School of Management at Yale University. Prior to joining the Yale faculty, he was a Visiting Professor of Finance in the Sloan School at MIT. Professor Fabozzi is a Fellow of the International Center for Finance at Yale University and the editor of the *Journal of Portfolio Management*. He earned a doctorate in economics from the City University of New York in 1972. In 1994 he received an honorary doctorate of Humane Letters from Nova Southeastern University and in 2002 was inducted into the Fixed Income Analysts Society's Hall of Fame. He is the honorary advisor to the Chinese Asset Securitization Web site.

Moorad Choudhry is Head of Treasury at KBC Financial Products (UK) Limited in London. He previously worked as a government bond trader and Treasury trader at ABN Amro Hoare Govett Limited and Hambros Bank Limited, and in structured finance services at JPMorgan Chase Bank. Moorad is a Fellow of the Centre for Mathematical Trading and Finance, CASS Business School, and a Fellow of the Securities Institute. He is author of *The Bond and Money Markets: Strategy, Trading, Analysis*, and a member of the Education Advisory Board, ISMA Centre, University of Reading.

Contributing Authors

Phil Adams	Barclays Capital
Henry Albulescu	Standard & Poor's
Mark J.P. Anson	CalPERS
Adele Archer	Standard & Poor's
Iain Barbour	Commerzbank Securities
Alexander Batchvarov	Merrill Lynch
Ian Bell	Standard & Poor's
Pascal Bernous	Standard & Poor's
Alex Cataldo	Moody's Investors Service
Henry Charpentier	Moody's Investors Servive
Ren-Raw Chen	Rutgers University (New Brunswick)
William H Chew	Standard & Poor's
Moorad Choudhry	KBC Financial Products UK Limited
Alessandro Cocco	JPMorgan Chase
Jenna Collins	Merrill Lynch
Graham "Harry" Cross	YieldCurve.com
William Davies	Merrill Lynch
Andrew Dennis	UBS
Jean Dornhofer	Moody's U.K.
Frank J. Fabozzi	Yale University
Christopher Flanagan	JPMorgan
Anthony Flintoff	Standard & Poor's
Elena Folkerts-Landau	Standard & Poor's
Ronan Fox	Standard & Poor's
Blaise Ganguin	Standard & Poor's
Carole Gintz	Moody's France
Katie Hostalier	Commerzbank Securities
Clayton Hunt	Standard & Poor's
Farooq Jaffrey	CreditTrade
David Jefferds	CreditTrade
Atish Kakodkar	Merrill Lynch
Nikoletta Knapcsek	Moody's Italia
Apea Koranteng	Standard & Poor's

Edmond Leedham   JPMorgan Chase Bank
Barnaby Martin   Merrill Lynch
Oldrich Masek   JPMorgan Securities Ltd.
Miray Muminoglu   JP Morgan
Markus Niemeier   Barclays Capital
Oleg Pankratov   ABN AMRO
Benedicte Pfister   Moody's Italy
Nick Procter   JPMorgan Chase Bank
Hernan Quipildor   Moody's Investors Service
Anant Ramgarhia   ABN AMRO
Edward Reardon   JPMorgan
Everett Rutan   Moody's U.S.
Antonio Serpico   Moody's Investors Service
Arthur F. Simonson   Standard & Poor's
Doreen Tan
Jennifer Thym
Valentina Varola   Moody's Italia
Michael Wilkins   Standard & Poor's

PART

One

Structured Finance and Securitisation

CHAPTER 1

Introduction

Frank J. Fabozzi, Ph.D., CFA
Frederick Frank Adjunct Professor of Finance
School of Management
Yale University

Moorad Choudhry
Head of Treasury
KBC Financial Products UK Limited

Securitisation has been one of the most exciting developments in fixed income markets and illustrates perfectly the dynamic and flexible nature of the market itself. First introduced in the United States domestic market in 1969, it arrived in Europe in the 1980s and has witnessed dramatic growth right from inception. The application of securitisation techniques gives rise to "structured finance" securities, which now encompass a wide class of products, each of which deserves separate treatment in its own right.

In simple terms, securitisation is a procedure by which financial assets such as loans, consumer instalment contracts, leases, receivables, and other relatively illiquid assets with common features that are held on the balance sheet of a bank, financial institution, or other corporate entity are used as collateral backing for a package of securities that are issued to investors. The economic interest in the financial assets are thereby transferred to investors via the securitisation process. At the same time, illiquid financial assets are transformed into liquid securities that trade, to a varying degree, in a secondary debt capital market. While the actual process may be quite complex, involving a number of third-parties such as lawyers, credit rating agencies, insurers, accountants, and trustee service providers, as a concept it is straightforward. It has resulted in an enhanced range of corporate finance options, as well as advanced the process of disintermediation by which the users of capital are brought closer together to the providers of capital.

The motivations behind securitisation are covered in detail in this book, so we need not go into them here. Investors are attracted to such engineered securities mainly because of their desirable investment and maturity characteristics. However, the higher yield is associated with investors bearing some degree of prepayment, early amortisation, credit, and liquidity risk.

THE EUROPEAN STRUCTURED FINANCE MARKET

The first securitisation in the United States market used residential mortgage assets assets. The success of the securitisation process in the residential mortgage markets as a funding source and the acceptance of the derived securities by the investor base led to the application of this technology to other assets, such as credit cards, home equity loans, automobile loans, lease instalment contracts, and manufactured housing loans, to name a few on the ever expanding list of securitisable assets. The first nonmortgage asset-backed security, a computer lease-backed transaction, was issued in March 1985. Later in that same year, the first auto loan-backed securities were issued. Two years later, in 1987, the first credit-card backed security was issued. Since then, the asset-backed market has expanded.

In Europe the first asset classes to be securitised were residential mortgages in the United Kingdom in 1987. Since then, a wide range of assets have been repackaged into structured finance securities, including:

- Commercial mortgages
- Corporate bank loans
- Government assets such as lottery receipts and public sector housing receipts
- Credit card debt
- Car-loan ("auto-loan") receivables
- Corporate assets such as nursing home and funeral home receivables
- Equipment (such as photocopiers and other office equipment) lease receivables
- Consumer loans

The flexibility and applicability of the securitisation concept itself, together with the inventiveness of investment bankers, means that virtually any asset is a candidate for transformation into structured finance securities. The type of asset that is being securitised determines what the issued bond is called. Generally speaking, the structured financial product market is composed of *asset-backed securities* (ABS), *mortgage-backed securities* (MBS), *collateralised debt obligations* (CDO), and *repackaged securities*. As we shall see later, the MBS market is subdivided further into residential (RMBS) and commercial (CMBS) securities, while the CDO asset class also comprises a number of different types too. As a rule of thumb, the nature of the originating institution, as well as the asset class itself, determines what the issued securities are called. Speaking generally, banks originate RMBS and CMBS, while corporates issue ABS. Insurance companies and fund managers issue CDOs.[1]

In Exhibit 1.1 issue volumes for the European market are shown, along with issue volumes in all currencies shown as USD-equivalent. Exhibit 1.2 shows the breakdown of issuance by original asset class. Securitisation has been introduced in a number of countries across Europe, both inside and outside the Eurozone.[2] Exhibit 1.3 shows the issuance breakdown by country, with the largest issuers shown to be the United Kingdom and Italy.

A more recent development in the European market, again following the trend in the United States, was that of CDOs. The CDO market is sometimes considered as distinctly separate from the ABS and MBS

EXHIBIT 1.1 European Issuance Volume, 1996–2003 YTD

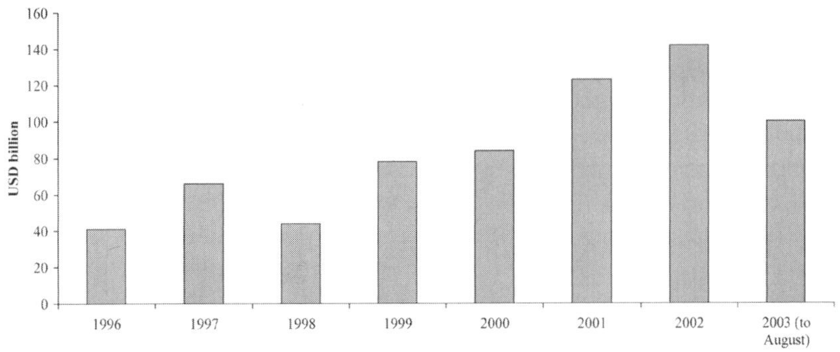

Source: Securitization.Net, JPMorgan Chase Bank.

---

[1] Like all rough rules of thumb, there are exceptions. Bank originators of corporate loans would be issuing ABS, for example, and banks have also been large issuers of CDOs. Government-sponsored issues are usually classed ABS.

[2] During 2003 the newest countries in Europe to witness securitisation were Greece and Poland, while during 2000 Portugal saw its first transaction.

market, but it follows the same principles used for the earlier products. Its growth has been dramatic, given that the first CDOs were only issued in Europe in 1998. Like the other products, it has been introduced in several forms. The main distinction within CDOs has been about the type of assets originated, whether loans (*collateralized loan obligations or CLOs*) or bonds (*collateralized bond obligations or CBOs*), and the motivation behind deal issuance, whether "arbitrage" or "balance sheet." These distinctions are discussed in detail later in this book.

Exhibit 1.4 shows CDO transaction issuance in the European market from 2000. Exhibit 1.5 shows the type of collateral originated during 2002.

EXHIBIT 1.2   Collateral Type During 2002

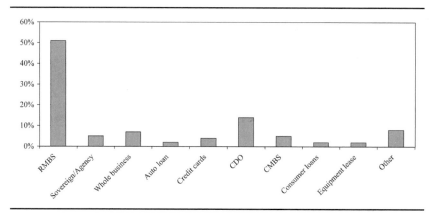

Source: Securitization.Net, JPMorgan Chase Bank.

EXHIBIT 1.3   Origination of Assets in Europe 2002

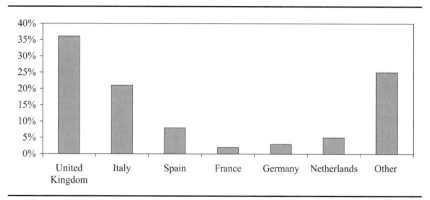

Source: Securitization.Net, JPMorgan Chase Bank.

EXHIBIT 1.4   European CDO Issuance, 2002–2003

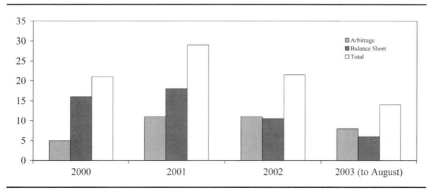

Source: Securitization.Net, JPMorgan Chase Bank.

EXHIBIT 1.5   CDO Collateral Type During 2002

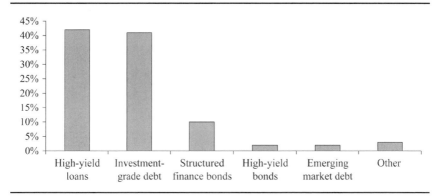

Source: Securitization.Net, JPMorgan Chase Bank.

Part V of this book looks in detail at CDOs, including the newest CDO type known as a *synthetic* CDO, which combines traditional securitisation techniques with credit derivatives.

ORGANISATION OF THIS BOOK

This book is organised into six parts. Part I introduces structured finance products and the concept of securitisation. This includes chapters on the mechanics of a securitisation transaction, as well as separate chapters that analyse structured finance products from the point of view of investors and originators. Included in Part I is a chapter on the various "agency" services required, by investors, in a securitisation deal, and which are provided by specialist banks known as trust banks.

The following parts are split by products. Part II looks at ABS and the various asset classes that have been originated as ABS. It includes chapters on credit card ABS, consumer loan ABS, auto loan ABS, lease securitisations, and mezzanine loan securitisations. There is also a chapter on public sector transactions, which have been dominated by issuance from the Italian government. Information about other types of securitisation backed by trade receivables, corporate stock, and non-performing loans, is also included.

A special type of ABS is whole business securitisations. (A specific example of this type is U.K. pubs). This is covered in Part III.

Part IV focuses on residential and commercial MBS. Because of the size of the Italian RMBS market, a chapter on that market is covered in the book.

In Part V we look at CDOs, both cash and synthetic CDOs. This includes a chapter on valuing CDOs. Because synthetic CDOs make extensive use of credit derivatives, we have included an introductory chapter on these instruments in Part I.

Finally, Part VI looks at structured credit products in the form of credit-linked rates and repackaged transactions. In all parts we have also considered the analysis of structured financial products, primarily credit analysis from the rating agency perspective.

CHAPTER 2

The Concept of Securitisation

Iain Barbour
Global Head of Securitisation
Commerzbank Securities

Katie Hostalier
Head of Structured Finance Research
Commerzbank Securities

Securitisation has become a widely used term to describe many mechanisms through which risks are transferred between various parties. The description encompasses the sale of risk assets in absolute form, as well as the synthetic transfer of specific aspects of risk. This chapter seeks to bring a definition to the word *securitisation*. We seek to define the various contexts in which the word is used, the parties to such contracts, and their motivations. From this high-level background to the market it is apparent that the world of securitisation is still being defined—new asset classes and new mechanisms are being created, with new counterparties coming to the market regularly.

WHAT IS SECURITISATION?

Securitisation is effectively a process through which loans, receivables, and other assets are pooled. The related cash flows and economic values are employed to support payments on related securities. These securities are issued in the public and private markets by or on behalf of issuers, who utilise securitisation to finance their business activities. These securities are generally referred to as *asset-backed securities* (ABS).

9

The investor's risk is therefore linked to the assets which back the securities he invests in. The primary source of interest payments and repayment of principal of the ABS does not rely on the issuer's general revenues, but on the specific cash flows generated by the assets. The investor's credit analysis therefore focuses on a defined pool of assets.

Most securitisation transactions seek to isolate the financial assets that support payment flows on the related ABS. Isolation ensures that payments on the ABS are derived exclusively from the performance of a specific, and often segregated, pool of financial assets.

The pool of assets securitised is frequently enhanced, either by means of internal structural measures or with the help of outside parties, from a credit perspective. Liquidity facilities may provide some credit enhancement, but usually provide a mechanism to streamline cash flows on the transaction, ensuring a smoother flow of payments to investors, especially where underlying payment flows on the securitised assets are subject to some volatility.

This is why ABS are usually issued by special purpose vehicles (SPVs) whose purpose is to hold a specific pool of assets and issue securities against these assets.

The basic concept of securitisation may be applied to virtually any asset which has a reasonably ascertainable value, or that generates a reasonably predictable future stream of revenue. As a result, securitisation has been extended beyond the typical asset classes (see Exhibit 2.1) to less well-known asset classes, including insurance receivables, obligations of shippers to railways, obligations of purchasers to natural gas producers, and future rights to entertainment royalty payments, among many others.

The fundamentals of securitisation are relatively homogeneous, being common to most transaction types. As a result, securitisation structures and the roles and functions of key transaction participants are similar wherever the securitisation concept is applied. This is the case regardless of jurisdiction, despite different regulatory and legal environments. We discuss some generic securitisation transaction features and compare true sale and synthetic securitisation structures later in this document.

Securitisation may therefore be distinguished from other, more traditional forms of debt and equity financing, in which returns to investors are generally derived from the claims-paying ability or profit-making potential of an ongoing business enterprise.

The ABS market can also be distinguished from the corporate debt and equity markets because of the regular return of principal exhibited. ABS require investors to assess the impact of alternative potential future cash flows (including prepayments) in making a meaningful evaluation of a security's yield.

ORIGINATOR CLASSIFICATION

Originators have encompassed many guises. The most common asset originators in the securitisation world are banks, mortgage originators, specialist consumer credit originators, asset managers, and, increasingly, corporates. Exhibit 2.1 summarises most classes of potential originators, the possible range of asset classes they could consider securitising, and their motivations.

The most significant European originators, from a volume perspective, are the banks. Their leading motivation to date has been achieving greater regulatory capital efficiency. However with the proposed changes to the Basel Capital Adequacy Guidelines, this primary motivation is likely to refocus towards liquidity, business growth, prepayment risk transfer, and credit risk transfer.

There are various categories of issuing vehicles for structured transactions, which range from direct issuance by the originators themselves to multiseller conduit structures. These categories can be summarised as follows.

The United States and, increasingly, the European market have seen significant securitisation flows via the conduit market, whereby several originators effectively "club" together under a single sponsored issuance programme. This clearly generates economies of scale for the originators, and is especially efficient for short-dated receivables which are originated by corporates. Additionally, where an originator wishes to preserve some degree of anonymity this can be achieved under some structures. The risk is still transferred to investors, who typically purchase credit-enhanced commercial paper, with credit enhancement either provided by publicly issued securities, or subordinated loans.

In the context of securitisation, these are companies established solely for the purpose of purchasing risk or cash flows from the originator, and routing it to investors. They are often domiciled offshore, and usually bankruptcy remote from the asset originator. This effectively segregates the assets being securitised from the originator's other business assets.

On occasions the originator itself will issue the notes, with the note performance correlated to the performance of specific assets maintained on their balance sheet. Key to the success of such structures is the originator's ability to eliminate other assets from the risk equation. Other occasions where the originator will also act as issuer are where their whole business is being securitised.

EXHIBIT 2.1   Originator Classification, Target Asset Classes, and Motivation

Originator Type	Asset Class	Motivation
Banks	Mortgage loans (residential and commercial); loans (consumer and corporate); bond and credit derivative portfolios; leases	Risk transfer; capital efficiency; new business; liquidity; prepayment risk transfer
Specialist mortgage originators	Mortgage loans (residential—often nonconforming and subprime)	Liquidity; new business; risk transfer; capital efficiency; prepayment risk transfer
Consumer finance providers	Credit card loans; auto finance loans; personal loans; leases	Liquidity; new business; risk transfer; capital efficiency; prepayment risk transfer
Companies	Exports; receivables; inventory; leases	Capital efficiency; liquidity
Leisure and retail operators	Pub receivables; theatre cash flows; retail cash flows; franchise revenues	New business and liquidity; capital efficiency; profit
Real estate developers	Debt finance for offices; hotels; shopping malls; care homes	Capital efficiency; liquidity; term and cost
Municipalities	Social security contributions; taxes; parking tickets; hospitals; specific assets	Capital and balance sheet efficiency; liquidity; term and cost
Governments	Privatisation debt (e.g., PFI in the UK); export credits	Capital and balance sheet efficiency; liquidity; term and cost
Utilities	Receivables; real estate	Capital efficiency; liquidity; term and cost
Projects	Cash flows post completion	Capital efficiency; liquidity; term and cost
Asset managers	Bond, credit derivative and loan portfolios	Risk transfer; capital efficiency; new business; liquidity
Hedge funds and alternative investment vehicles	Bond, credit derivative and loan portfolios; fund of fund structures; structured products	New business and liquidity; capital efficiency; profit
Housing Associations	Real estate portfolios and resultant cash flows	Capital efficiency; liquidity; term and cost
Healthcare	Real estate portfolios and resultant cash flows	Capital efficiency; liquidity; term and cost

Source: Commerzbank Securities.

ORIGINATOR MOTIVATION

Understanding originator motivation and decision-making criteria are fundamental to assessing whether to invest in a structured finance transaction. A successful transaction creates a partnership between originator, servicer, and investor. This partnership must transcend all three parties throughout the life of the transaction, with each ideally understanding each other's motivations.

The key reasons for securitising can be summarised as follow. For banks and corporates, traditional balance sheet risk management requires optimal liability management. Securitisation enables risk capital usage to be optimised, focusing capital utilisation on residual economic risk coupled with allocations for operational and day-to-day business management risks.

Through the effective transfer of credit risk, capacity for incremental credit risk is created, freeing counterparty limits. Two of the most significant constraints on business growth are capital and risk appetite. In optimising capital usage, and reducing credit risk, business capacity is effectively created. One of the most misunderstood motivations. It can be achieved essentially through routing existing revenues, less the cost of the transaction, towards generating a return on the reduced capital allocation.

An added bonus for many is the access to a significant, alternative source of liquidity from an often-new range of investors. For lower rated organisations, securitising selected funded assets possessing an inherently stronger credit quality than their own, this funding may also be less expensive. Furthermore, the liquidity generated may be longer term, and create enhanced matching of assets and liabilities.

We will also discuss later in this chapter some alternative methods of meeting these objectives (outside of securitisation), and contrast these with securitisation techniques.

SECURITISATION TRANSACTION CATEGORIES

As the market matures there are, in our opinion, three broad categories of securitisation transactions. These are described below.

Financing and Capital Management Transactions

Financing and capital management transactions represent the core transaction type in the securitisation arena. In Chapter 6, we present a relative value framework for analysing this transaction type.

Originators generate assets such as loans and receivables which are ultimate payment obligations of their customers (debtors). When securitising such assets (or an interest in these assets), the originator receives liquidity. The issuer in turn uses the assets to collateralise the ABS. The customers will not usually be aware that the assets have been securitised, and that there has therefore been an effective change in control of their liability—the change may in fact not ever be made public, as a synthetic structure may in fact not lead to any change in control, but merely a transfer of risk.

Repackaging for Arbitrage

Repackaging transactions typically take the form of a series of notes issued in the form of an ABS, backed by a portfolio of bonds (including ABS themselves), credit derivatives, loan portfolios, and other forms of credit risk. The arbitrage operates between the yield on the underlying and the required all-in cost of the notes, and success is often measured by comparing the relative costs of holding the assets "on balance sheet" relative to through a securitised structure.

Market-Value Transactions

In market-value-based transactions the asset manager must take specific action, usually selling the collateral, to liquidate assets. This exposes investors to liquidity and market risk.

TRANSACTION FEATURES AND PARTICIPANTS

Securitisation structures appear to be complex; however, there are common features which make them easier to understand, facilitating analysis and comparison.

An *originator* extends finance to a *borrower* to facilitate the *originator's* purchase or use of an asset. This creates a financial asset. Once created, the originator usually continues with the collection and management of the asset, in a consistent manner to ongoing credit and collection procedures. These activities are generally referred to as servicing, and the party performing them is referred to as the *servicer.*

In order to create ABS, the originator conveys the assets to be securitised to another entity (usually a bankruptcy-remote SPV, but also, frequently, a trust)—the *issuer.* The SPV or trust then issues debt securities in the capital markets. The securities are usually purchased by institutional *investors* (including banks, conduits, insurance companies, pension plans, and portfolio managers).

The issuer uses the proceeds from the notes to pay the purchase price of the assets being securitised. The transfer of assets from the originator to the issuer is generally a *true sale*. A true sale removes the assets from what would constitute the bankruptcy or insolvency estate of the originator and legally isolates the assets. Investors therefore look only to the assets themselves for payment, both in the normal course of the originator's business, and also during any potential insolvency or bankruptcy.

The assets are frequently not transferred by true sales in European transactions. In such instances, the originator enters into a credit default swap (or guarantee) with the issuer (and on occasions the investors direct), through which the issuer provides credit protection on the underlying asset pool. These structures are popular in jurisdictions where asset transfer costs are high (usually driven up by stamp duty and other tax or registration costs), as transfer is generally only required if the underlying assets are sold.

Different transactions employ different techniques in order to transfer risk from the originator to investors. Not all of these methods have the effect of creating liquidity. The mechanisms are summarised in Exhibit 2.2.

EXHIBIT 2.2 Risk Transfer Mechanisms

Risk Transfer Mechanism	Action Taken	Balance Sheet Effect
True sale	Originator sells assets to an SPV	Assets usually leave balance-sheet of originator
Sub-participation	Originator "subparticipates" their interests in the asset pool being securitised to an SPV and therefore investors	The assets therefore effectively leave the originator's balance sheet, but in actuality do not—only their risk and rights do
Secured loan	The SPV takes a security interest (usually first priority) over the assets being securitised	The assets do not leave the originator's balance sheet
Credit default swap	The SPV enters into a credit default swap with the originator, effectively agreeing to pay the originator specific amounts in the event that specific credit events occur on the 'securitised' assets	The assets remain on the originator's balance sheet
Guarantee	The SPV guarantees the originator in a similar manner to a credit default swap, however the guarantee may not fall under a jurisdictions credit derivative guidelines, enabling organisations which do not typically enter into such arrangements to enjoy similar benefits	The assets remain on the originator's balance sheet

Source: Commerzbank Securities.

The latter two categories do not in their right generate liquidity for the originator. However, in certain circumstances, the SPV will support its obligations under the guarantee or credit default swap through the issuance of notes, the proceeds of which are, in turn, invested in qualifying notes issued by the originator.

In many consumer finance transactions, and increasingly in European MBS transactions, master trust structures are employed whereby assets are often originated directly into a "master trust," thereby removing the requirement for any further asset transfer.

Assets underlying ABS may bear interest at a different rate to the rate type used for the issuance itself (e.g., fixed-rate assets support floating-rate notes). Furthermore, the underlying assets are often denominated in different currencies from the issuance currency. These differences may cause mismatches in the payment flows. To protect investors from uncertainty, interest rate and currency swaps will typically be engaged in with a swap counterparty.

Credit ratings from one or more of the internationally recognised rating agencies (Fitch, Moody's, and Standard & Poor's are the primary providers) are obtained at issuance for a transaction. Investors rely on independent rating agencies to perform the analysis needed to assess the credit quality, structural integrity, and other attributes of a particular transaction. The rating agencies monitor the performance of the transaction, maintaining and adjusting their ratings accordingly.

The notes issued will often be divided into several classes (or tranches) of debt securities. Through this "tranching," the cash flows can effectively be allocated to different classes in an agreed prioritised order. The different classes may also exhibit different credit, payment, coupon, maturity, and other investment characteristics, to meet the needs and preferences of individual investors.

This role is often performed by the same party, but can be split as the roles are fundamentally separate. The structurer will provide advice and facilitate the efficient structuring of the transaction, whereas the underwriter will play the role of intermediary between an issuer and investors during the distribution process.

These parties will also advise on whether public or private issuance is optimal for the originator/issuer. The decision is dependent on many factors, not least the anticipated transaction size, the level of potential investor interest, and to what extent secondary market trading is required. Public offerings usually cost more and take more time than private transactions (due to securities registration, listing, reporting, legal, accounting, and other fees and expenses that are not present in private offerings), and so public issuance is usually reserved for larger transactions.

Some offerings are structured to comply with Rule 144A under the U.S. securities laws. This enables wider primary distribution, and also access to the highly liquid U.S. market for secondary trading.

It is good market practice for issuers to provide performance data relating to the transaction. The information should typically cover not only information on the performance of the different classes of notes (e.g., prepayment speeds, pool factors, and interest rates), but also extensive underlying asset performance data. In essence, the information should enable an investor to assess the strength of a class of notes from a credit and value perspective in today's terms and compare this data to that forecast by the issuer prior to launch and at various times through the life of the transaction.

CREDIT ENHANCEMENT AND LIQUIDITY FACILITIES

The assets are usually credit enhanced by one or more types of credit facility. Additionally, cash flows may be streamlined using liquidity facilities, which may, in certain circumstances, provide some formal credit enhancement. These facilities are usually generated from the assets themselves, but may be provided, for a fee, by a third party.

There are various forms of credit enhancement available, some internal and some external. We conclude this chapter with a discussion of credit enhancement.

Internal Credit Enhancement

Internal credit enhancement is the most popular form of internal credit support and takes the form of *senior/subordinated notes*. This is technically overcollateralisation and is characterised by the issuance of a senior class of securities protected and supported by one or more subordinated class(es) of notes. Losses are allocated firstly to the subordinated securities and the senior notes are not affected by losses until the subordinate notes are exhausted. The senior notes are usually rated triple-A, with the subordinated (or mezzanine/junior) notes rated between double-A and double-B. There is often a deeply subordinate class of unrated notes which bear the first losses. This is frequently held by the originator, demonstrating their continued credit commitment to the business they originated, and a vested interest in the successful recovery of any assets which underperform.

Overcollateralisation is where the notional amount of notes issued is lower than the available underlying asset pool, and the wider asset pool amount is available for the benefit of investors.

Yield spread is the difference between the coupon on the underlying assets and the security coupon. Where this is available to investors to offset against principal losses, this effectively acts as credit enhancement for a transaction.

Excess spread is the net amount of interest payments from the underlying assets after bondholders and expenses have been paid. Where excess spread is used to cover losses, or is paid into a reserve fund (available to meet future losses) this acts as additional credit enhancement for the transaction.

A *reserve fund* is created by an issuer to reimburse investors for losses up to the amount of the reserve. Reserve funds can be dynamic; they may be built up over time (typically over the first year of a transaction life), replenished through the transaction life, and even decreased as the risk profile reduces.

External Credit Enhancement

A surety bond or guarantee is provided by a rated insurance company to reimburse investors for any losses incurred. The surety is usually provided to enhance investment grade notes to a triple-A level (the rating of the guarantor), and is provided for a margin. The use of a guarantee will depend on the arbitrage between the cost of the guarantee and the consequent lower funding costs achieved. The margin will usually be established at a level attractive to the issuer relative to the all-in cost of structurally enhancing the securities to a triple-A level.

Letters of credit are issued by financial institutions who are paid a fee to stand by with cash to reimburse the issuer for any losses actually incurred, up to the required credit enhancement amount.

These forms of external credit enhancement are rating-linked to the provider of the enhancement. If the provider is downgraded, then the ABS may also be downgraded.

The issuer borrows the required credit enhancement amount and invests this in the highest-rated, short-term commercial paper. In contrast to a letter of credit, this represents a cash deposit—and, therefore, a downgrade of the *cash collateral account* (CCA) provider would not result in a downgrade of the transaction—but may result in the move of the CCA to a more appropriately rated provider.

The collateral invested amount is similar to a subordinated class and is usually purchased by a third-party credit enhancer or securitised as a private placement.

CHAPTER 3

Mechanics of Securitisation

Alexander Batchvarov, Ph.D., CFA
Managing Director and Head, International Structured Credit Research
Merrill Lynch

Jenna Collins
Vice President
Merrill Lynch

William Davies
Assistant Vice President
Merrill Lynch

Structured finance and *securitisation* are usually used as substitute terms, although the former is by definition broader and includes traditional asset-backed securitisations as well as more recent, innovative funding and risk transfer approaches. Such innovations include the future flow (or revenue-based) financing and operating assets (or whole business) securitisation. More recently, a combination of structured finance techniques and credit derivatives has come to create synthetic credit exposures and credit risk transfers, embraced under the generic term synthetic securitisations.

In this chapter, we introduce an analytical credit framework for structured finance bonds in order to make them easier to understand and position in an investment portfolio.

EUROPEAN STRUCTURED CREDIT PORTFOLIOS

It is important to emphasize that securitisation's most "notorious" feature stems from the level of separation of the underlying pool of assets from their originator. For that separation to occur, however, third parties may be introduced and other credit linkages may be created. Hence, the need for a two-dimensional credit plane to populate with structured finance and securitisation credits.

Defining the Credit Space of Securitisation

All fixed income credits can be placed on a credit continuum:

- From credits fully dependent on the operating and payment ability and, hence, bankruptcy risk of the company issuer/originator within the respective industry-specific and market environment.
- Through credits gradually removed from those risks to a point where they are fully separated from the originator and they rely entirely on the performance of the ring-fenced assets, transferred and pledged as bond collateral.

The former, are usually referred to as *plain vanilla unsecured bonds*, while the latter have come to be known as *asset-backed securities*. Between these two well-understood extremes lies a series of credits, which occupy an intermediate position in terms of credit dependence, structural enhancements, legal underpinnings, operating exposure—they have come to be referred to interchangeably as *structured financings* or *securitisations*.

The different types of structured credits occupy a different spot along that credit continuum. The degree of their autonomy from the underlying originator is usually reflected in the gap between the rating assigned to the structured credit and the rating assigned to the related asset originator. The level of dependence on the credit quality of the underlying assets is reflected in the level of credit enhancement, which partially bridges that gap. In an attempt to mitigate the influence of the originator of the assets or the risks associated with the assets themselves on the structured bonds and achieve a higher rating for the latter, additional parties with their own credit risk profiles are introduced. We refer to the latter collectively from here on as third parties or third parties risk. Such third parties may include servicer, insurance provider, swap provider, portfolio manager, property manager, off-takers, and letter of credit provider. Hence, a two-dimensional credit plane is needed to position the universe of securitisations and structured finance credits (see Exhibit 3.1)

EXHIBIT 3.1   Credit Dependence of Securitisation Credits from Originator (Horizontal Axis) and from Third-Party (Vertical Axis) Creditworthiness

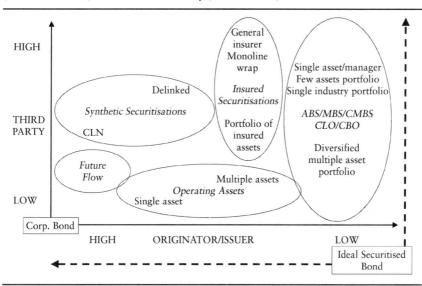

Source: Merrill Lynch.

Understanding the position of any given structured credit within the frame of the credit plane has serious implications for:

- Originators, as they determine the role they play during the life of a given structured credit and related effects on their operating and financial results.
- Investors, as they determine the role of a given structured credit in the overall portfolio management—the portfolio's credit diversification, performance, and monitoring.

Populating the Credit Space of Securitisation

Structured finance or securitisation comprises an array of approximations to debt financing. With a range of options to use, companies can implement variations of any one basic design, depending on their particular needs. With a range of options to choose from, investors can find the best match for their portfolios and portfolio management objectives.

The terms structured finance and securitisation are applied freely to include:

- *Asset-backed securities (ABS) and Mortgage-backed securities (MBS), Collateralised Debt Obligations (CDOs) and Commercial Mortgage*

Backed Securities (CMBS). This is the most fundamental format of securitisation and involves the issuance of off-balance-sheet debt, backed by a homogenous pool of assets. Securitised assets include bank and finance company assets such as credit cards, auto loans, mortgages, leases, corporate loans, real estate loans, and so on, or corporate assets like trade receivables, vendor financing, real estate, and the like. Securitisation in its narrow traditional sense is usually associated with ABS and MBS only.

■ *Future flow (or revenue-based) securitisations*. This type of financing is usually associated with emerging markets and project finance. Assets include revenues generated in the normal course of business of a given company, be it a manufacturer or a property manager—export receivables, fee-based revenues, rental flows, and so on.

■ *Operating assets (or whole business) securitisations*. Viewed as, but not limited to, exit strategies for principal finance and mergers and acquisitions activities; the financing in this case is backed by the core operating assets of a company and the revenues they generate and, typically, has a strong real estate element, which helps put some of these deals in the commercial real estate securitisation and CMBS field.

■ *Insured securitisations*. Any of the above securitisation formats can be subject to a "wrap"—insurance protection against the credit and cash flow risks of a securitised transaction. It allows for the substitution of the credit risk of the assets for the credit risk of the insurance provider.

■ *Synthetic securitisations*. It is aimed at achieving a transfer of the credit risks associated with given assets, while the originator retains them on its balance sheet. Full or partial financing against those assets may or may not be realised. Synthetic securitisations may actually involve many of the securitisation listed so far and it should be viewed more as a form of execution rather than independent securitisation type.

Asset-Backed and Mortgage-Backed Securities

The legal separation of assets from the originator (i.e., a "true sale") ensures that investors in the asset-backed bonds are not directly exposed to credit deterioration or bankruptcy of the originator. This feature fundamentally distinguishes asset-backed securities from unsecured debt issued by the same originator or from other forms of securitisation. Bondholders have no recourse to the originator, except under limited circumstances.

In most cases, the originator remains the servicer of the pool of assets, with a back-up servicer identified at the outset of the transaction in case the originator underperforms or is declared bankrupt during the term of the transaction. Cash flows generated by the underlying assets are used to service the bonds. The credit quality of the asset-backed debt is, therefore, based in the first instance on the credit quality of the legally segregated, ring-fenced pool of assets. However, the ratings assigned to the asset-backed bonds will reflect the extent of internal or external credit support, that is, their credit enhancement.

From investors' point of view "true" securitisation provides credit exposures mitigated through structural, legal, and credit enhancements, generally unavailable in the plain vanilla bond market. The exposures can vary widely and include lots of combinations: numerous obligors—numerous industries portfolio, numerous obligors—single industry portfolio, numerous obligors—single asset, single manager—diversified portfolio, single asset—single manager and so on.

Future Flow (Revenue-Based) Securitisation

In case of the revenue-based securitisation, the well-being of the company generating the assets revenue is of paramount importance for the performance of the securities. The bonds are usually backed by a defined and specific revenue stream generated in the normal course of business of the respective company. These could include fees for services provided to customers; payments due for exported goods, utilisation fees, settlement payments, money transfers, and the like. Bondholders' rights are not limited only to those revenues: in case of default or bankruptcy of the originator, the bondholders have a right to recourse and become general unsecured creditor to the originator.

The credit quality of the revenue-based bonds are generally in line with the credit quality (the unsecured senior debt rating) of the respective originator (representing generation risk for the assets) and the related obligors (representing payment risk for the assets, off-take contacts). Credit support in the structure is achieved through a desired level of debt service coverage, and excess debt service flows are remitted back to the originator or retained in case of adverse events. Covenants may also play an important role.

Investors take full credit exposure to the company and a set of its customers, yet certain other risks (which are inherent in the company's plain vanilla bonds) may be well mitigated (e.g., currency and sovereign risks in case of emerging markets export based deals). They can also have access to areas of credit traditionally reserved for the banks and bank loan market, as is the case with project finance. In the worst case they may be treated as a general nonsecured creditor of the company. Investors' exposure can be defined as multiple obligors—single originator or single obligor-single originator.

Operating Asset Securitisation

An operating asset securitisation quite simply encompasses debt financing backed by a company's operating assets, typically its core assets generating highly predictable income streams given the company's unique position. Under the specific legal structure, known as "secured bond structure," a combination of fixed and floating charges over the assets of the company gives investors the legal right to determine whether to operate or liquidate the company in question in case of default on their debt.

The transaction can be structured with credit enhancement (insurance or credit tranching, or both) and structural covenants to protect investors, just like in traditional ABS. Unlike them, though, operating asset-based securitisations retain a certain level of operating risk. The assets are not typically transferred, only the income from such assets is assigned for the benefit of investors. However, in case of a bond default, investors can choose collectively to run the company or liquidate it (and apply the liquidation proceeds to redeem their principal).

Credit quality of operating asset securitisations does not need to be capped at the level of the operating company, particularly, if the assets can be shown to generate income reliably with little input from the operator and/or to preserve their value in case of company's bankruptcy. Obviously, the credit quality of the underlying obligors (i.e., paying customers of the company, in some cases government or quasi-government bodies) is also an essential feature of the bonds' credit.

Investors gain exposure to companies which otherwise may not issue debt and face full credit exposure to the company in question. They are entitled to a full priority claim against the company with the potential downside in the value of the assets (decline in the market value of the assets) and the timing of the realisation of that value (length of period needed to realise those assets). Credit exposure may take the forms: pool of assets—single industry, single asset—multiple obligors.

Insured Securitisations

Insurance can play different roles in securitisations—it can be applied to the assets in the securitised portfolio, or it can be applied to the securitisation bond in order to enhance its credit quality. Insurance can be provided on the bond level by both general and specialised bond (monoline) insurance companies and on the collateral level by both general and specialised (primary mortgage) insurers.

Through the insurance the risk of the assets or the bonds is shifted to the insurance provider. And the insurers' credit substitutes the credit of the bond or the assets. It is prudent, though, to look through the insurance cover or wrap and determine the risk, to which the insurance provider is exposed and the investor or issuer could be exposed in case of insurers' default.

The application of the "look through" principal require understanding of the process of insurance underwriting, the minimum credit level requirement for the insurance to be applied, the general business of the insurer and the management of the insurers' risk portfolio and overall business. In that respect, the levels of risk should be different and analysed differently for:

- Insurance providers on assets level (e.g., insurers specialising in mortgage insurance who provide coverage on an individual or pool basis) where the securitisation bond is backed by a pool of multiple assets insured on individual or pool basis by one or several insurers.
- Insurance providers on a bond level through specialised bond (monoline) insurers, whereby such insurers take only investment grade risk, manage their risks on a portfolio basis and are tightly monitored by the rating agencies in terms of individual and portfolio risks.
- General insurance providers, for whom bond insurance is just one of the numerous lines of business.

For investors, this is a way of shifting the exposure from the assets and the originator away to another party, yet such exposure to the third party is only to the extent of the credit performance of the underlying bond or pool of assets. In addition, depending on the type of insurance as discussed above, investors exposure to the third party may be viewed as exposures to: a pool of assets, a managed portfolio of risks or a general insurance business.

Synthetic Securitisations

In the case of synthetic securitisation, the assets, usually used for credit reference only, remain on the balance sheet of the respective originator/ issuer. Through a number of mechanisms the originator seeks to shift the risk of those assets to other parties: through a credit default swap to the swap provider or through the purchase of protection from the market, or a combination thereof. Raising financing is of secondary importance, if any, for the seeker of credit protection.

The reference portfolio of assets is clearly defined but remains on the sponsor's balance sheet—the portfolio comprises residential or commercial mortgages, unsecured or secured consumer and corporate loans, real estate. The risks associated with this portfolio and subject to the transfer are defined through "credit events." If bonds are issued, in the case of partially funded or fully funded structures, their credit performance is fully linked to the portfolio and its credit enhancement. In an effort to delink the rating of the bonds from the rating of the issuing bank, the note proceeds may be used to purchase a portfolio of government bonds, mortgage bonds or medium-term notes (MTNs), as collateral for the bonds.

Hence, the credit performance of the bonds depends on the credit performance of the referenced portfolio, the enforcement of credit events, while their cash performance is linked to the cash performance of the collateral portfolio. Unlike conventional ABS or credit-linked note (CLN) structures, the amortization proceeds of the referenced assets are not used to make payments under the structured bonds. Investors only have synthetic exposure to the referenced portfolio, while debt service is met by the yield of the collateral portfolio supplemented by insurance premiums paid by the sponsor in return for credit protection for the referenced portfolio. The purchased collateral is reduced to the extent necessary in order to compensate the sponsor for losses incurred on the referenced portfolio. Ultimately, the collateral is liquidated to meet note holders' principal payments.

Credit exposures are related to the reference portfolio, its credit quality and credit performance related to the definition of credit events and the determination of their occurrence (where the trustee's role is broader than usual). Others stem from the collateral portfolio and its performance—mechanics to protect against its market risk. Credit default swap counterparty is another element in the credit picture. The originator plays a role by assuming the negative carry on the collateral through regular payments made in the form of insurance premiums.

Investors' levels and nature of credit exposure depends on the particular type of synthetic securitisation. In the case of credit-linked bonds, investors' exposure is to both the credit quality of the asset portfolio and the issuer's credit standing. In the case of unfunded or partially funded structures, the exposure is to a diversified assets pool, highly leveraged for the latter. Investors are gaining exposure to the credit risk as defined by the credit events of a diversified and enhanced pool, while the cash flows for debt service are derived from a non-related highly liquid, high credit quality bond portfolio.

Securitisation Credit Space and Investment Portfolio

The stated initial purpose of securitisation was to achieve structured bonds whose credit risk lies with the transferred assets and is entirely delinked from the credit risk of the originator of the assets. The developing the structured techniques and their application to different asset classes and company needs have increasingly lead to introduction of third-party risks or to leaving residual originator risk in the securitisation bonds.

Hence, the need for a credit framework within which to position the securitisation bonds. The proposed framework includes two dimensions to reflect the level of credit (in)dependence of the securitisation bond from the originator and the third parties. The credit risk of the asset itself is a reflection of the risk of the originator and the third party in combination with the credit enhancement as determined by the rating agencies.

In the language of our schematic (see Exhibit 3.1), increasing credit dependence of the securitisation bond from the originator and the third parties would be reflected in moving left on the horizontal axis and up on the vertical axis, respectively. By determining the level of credit dependence of each bond on the originator and the third parties, we can position it in our securitisation credit plane:

- We believe the ideal starting point for full credit independence would be a securitisation bond based on a multiple-asset, geographically well- and industry-diversified amortising portfolio with easily replaceable servicer. In the lower right corner of our credit plane credit dependence is *de minimum*. Such a securitisaton bond should pretty well fit in any portfolio with minimal surveillance.

- Moving left (backwards) on the horizontal axis, the securitisation bonds have an increasing degree of originator risk, that is, risk specific to a given company and a given industry. At its extreme, future flow securitisation bonds offer almost full company risk along with mitigated through structural enhancements certain particularly unpalatable risks. In this case, credit surveillance would require primarily focus on the originator. Intermediary points will include operating assets securitisations based on portfolio of businesses units or a single business.

- Moving up the vertical axis from the ideal starting point, securitisation bonds have an increasing degree of a third party risk to the point of extreme of, say, fully insured by a general insurer single asset transaction with some risk mitigants on the underlying asset. Hence, surveillance is required for the insurance company in question and the associated insurance industry segment. Intermediary points would include on the insurance side: bonds based on a broad portfolio of insured assets, monoline insured bonds, and on the traditional ABS/MBS side multiple industry portfolios, single industry portfolios, decreasing number of assets in a pool down to a single-asset/single-manager situation.

- Moving away from the axes and towards the middle of the credit plane, securitisation bonds would represent different combinations of originator—third parties' credit risks. Different level of monitoring of all the parties involved would then be necessary.

The above three extreme points and the relevant intermediary points should be used as points of reference when building and rebalancing the credit risk of a securitisation bond portfolio.

SECURITISATION FUNDAMENTALS

Despite jurisdictional and structural differences, securitisation transactions share a number of common features, elements, and parties. They are the building blocks of any one securitisation transaction and are crucial to its execution on the one hand and investment analysis on the other.

Structural and Legal Aspects ABS and MBS

The securitisation process features many legal and structural aspects with the main objective of separation of credit risk of the underlying assets from the originator's credit risk. That separation is the necessary prerequisite for achieving a higher credit quality of the asset-backed securities than that of the originator. Other prerequisites include credit and liquidity risk mitigants.

Securitisation Process

Let us look at a very simple schematic diagram shown in Exhibit 3.2 that outlines the main generic structure of securitisation transaction.

The originator, a company or bank, originates assets in the normal course of its business and retains them on its balance sheet. It needs financing, and one way of acquiring it is by monetising the assets it has, selling them to another entity (an SPV) established solely for the purpose of that financing. The SPV (the Issuer) issues securitisation bonds to investors and applies the issuance proceeds to purchase the assets from the asset originator. The SPV's balance sheet now consists of assets—the assets acquired from the originator (as they are no longer on the originator's balance sheet) and liabilities in the form of the bonds issued. The SPV is a shell company, which holds the assets for the benefit of the bond investors. Hence, the need for a company to look after those assets (the servicer). In order to achieve desired credit quality of the bonds issued based on the assets, there is a need for additional supports: credit, structural, and legal enhancements. These are put in place to mitigate the credit, legal, liquidity, interest rate, currency, or other risks associated with the assets and transaction. Hence, the roles of

EXHIBIT 3.2   Generic Securitisation Chart

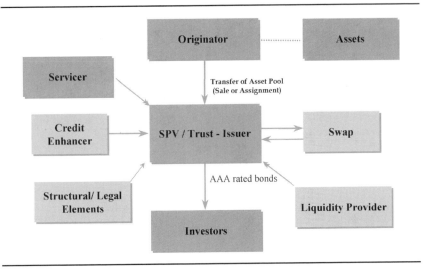

Source: Merrill Lynch.

credit enhancer, liquidity provider, and swap counterparty. The securitisation transaction is structured within a given legal framework in order to achieve the legal separation of the assets from the originator.

The most senior tranches of a securitisation bonds, generally achieve AAA rating. This is an essential aspect of securitisation. Securitisation allows originators with lower credit quality to issue AAA rated bonds. In other words, the originator receives better funding irrespective of its own credit worthiness on a standalone basis.

The legal separation of the assets from the originator, the credit and structural enhancement in the securitisation structure altogether provide for a securitisation bond for highest credit quality (rating).

Key Securitisation Parties

Let us analyse the parties and their role in a securitisation structure (see Exhibit 3.3).

The *originator* is an entity which has funding needs and holds assets that are used as collateral in an asset-backed structure to achieve higher rating and, hence, better funding. The originator could be any entity which has well defined assets on its balance sheet. These assets should generate predictable and stable future cash flows. They should not only be clearly defined, but also be legally transferable by the originator to the issuer.

EXHIBIT 3.3   Key Parties to ABS/MBS Financing

- Assets Originator
  ↓ Entity with funding needs and with assets which can be used as collateral for ABS/MBS funding.
- Issuer of ABS/MBS
  ↓ Entity specifically created for the purposes of the securitisation—Special Purpose Vehicle (SPV) or Special purpose Company (SPC).
- Outside Credit Enhancer
  ↓ Entity providing credit enhancement through insurance, guarantee, or reserve account.
- Servicer
  ↓ Entity which collects and distributes the cash flows from the assets.
- Liquidity Provider
  ↓ Entity that addresses the timing mismatches between the collected cash flows from the assets and the cash flows to be distributed under the structured bonds.
- Rating Agencies
  ↓ Determine the credit strength of an ABS and size the credit enhancement level necessary to achieve that credit strength.

Source: Merrill Lynch.

The *issuer* is a specially created entity for the purposes of the securitisation, known as a special purpose vehicle (SPV) or special purpose company (SPC), or a trust under some Anglo-Saxon jurisdictions. We have to stress the fact that this entity is established only for the purposes of the respective funding and expected issuance of asset-backed securities. Its obligations, hence, should be limited to the satisfaction of this particular purpose. It is an entity structured to be legally different and independent from the originator of the assets. The functions of that entity are limited to the issuance of the bonds (its main creditors are the bondholders) and the acquisition of the assets (thus its main assets are the securitised asset pool). The SPV is not meant to have any other substantial obligations or incur other debt, which could jeopardise its status of a bankruptcy–remote entity.

Outside credit enhancer could be an insurance company or monoline insurer or, in some cases, could simply be a reserve account which is funded with a letter of credit. For most securitisation transactions, however, the credit enhancement is internal to the deal, that is, through subordination or overcollateralisation.

The *servicer* could be an outside party or a party in the structure such as the originator. This is a very important point to understand when analysing asset-backed securities. The servicer is responsible for the assets: the generation of the cash, its collection, pursuing delinquent, and defaulted accounts. This role is crucial because investors rely for their repayment exclusively on the cash generated from the assets, as there is no recourse back to the originator of those assets. If the servicer is the originator, any negative changes that the originator could encounter could affect his role as servicer, influencing the performance and rating of the respective asset-backed securities. As we mentioned earlier, one of the objectives of the securitisation process is to delink the rating of the asset-backed securities from the rating of the pool and the rating of the originator. However, the rating of the originator may continue to have a bearing over the structure and the performance of the deal in its role as a servicer.

The *liquidity provider* addresses only timing mismatches between the cash flows generated in the asset pool and cash flows needed to be paid under the asset-backed security. These timing mismatches may arise because of delays in transferring the money, rising delinquencies, or some technical glitches. It is important to remember that the liquidity provider only covers timing mismatches in the cash flows, not cash shortfalls due to losses in the asset pool.

Important players in the securitisation process are the *rating agencies*. The rating agency in the asset-backed securities and mortgage-backed securities market establishes the credit enhancement levels, i.e., the cushion that investors receive to protect them against losses, according to the desired rating levels. The rating agency has the role of determining the size of the cushion, which ultimately depends on the credit quality of the asset pool and the desired rating of the bonds.

Key Legal Concepts in ABS Securitisation

It is vital to achieve a full separation between the assets and the originator of those assets to obtain AAA rating for the asset-backed securities, so that the assets (and subsequently the bond investors) are not affected negatively by the originator's bankruptcy, which risk could be particularly severe in the case of low-rated originators. There must be a particular structure that allows "absolute" separation in the ownership of these assets from the originator in order to avoid the threat of the assets being consolidated back into the bankruptcy estate of the originator (see Exhibit 3.4).

One of the aspects of the separation is the so called "true" sale of the assets, i.e., ensuring that no creditors of the originator have any claims against the sold assets, and those assets cannot be consolidated in the bankruptcy estate in case of insolvency proceedings against the originator. Furthermore, the sale of the assets is subject to a special agreement between the originator and the SPV.

EXHIBIT 3.4   Key Legal Concepts in Securitisation

Separation of Asset Risk from Originator Risk

- Assets are transferred from the originator to the SPC:
  - ↓ Assets are removed from the bankruptcy estate of the originator who retains no legal and equitable interest in those assets—absolute removal, true sale.
  - ↓ Absolute (true) sale tests: degree of transfer of "risk of loss" away from the originator; degree of retention of ownership benefits by originator; degree of control over the assets after the transfer; accounting treatment of asset Transfer by originator; intent of sale.
  - ↓ Asset transfer results in monetising the assets for cash in consideration of their value—no fraudulent conveyance.
- SPC is structured to be a bankruptcy remote (not bankruptcy-proof) entity:
  - ↓ Its assets are unlikely to be considered part of the assets of the originator in case of the originator's bankruptcy—no substantive consolidation.
  - ↓ Limited risk of bankruptcy filing—voluntary or involuntary.

Source: Merrill Lynch.

The agreement must be an arms-length agreement and the payment must represent fair value of the assets. The originator normally does not retain any control over the SPV nor over the transferred assets. In general, the aim is to fully transfer the assets with their underlying benefits and risks to the SPV.

Another element in the structure is the SPV (issuer), a bankruptcy remote, not bankruptcy proof, entity. The SPV could be structured as a corporate entity or a trust, in all cases independent from the originator. Arrangements are made so that the risk of involuntary or voluntary bankruptcy of the SVP is remote. One way of achieving this is defining explicitly the purpose of the SPV and its obligations towards outside parties. These obligations could be related to the payment of servicing fee of the servicer, fees under the letter of credit provider, amongst others, but its core obligations remain those to the securitisation bond investors. Normally, the SPV should not incur any additional debt.

If there is a swap in the structure, it is important to determine what is the potential termination payment that the SVP could owe to the swap counterparty, and what priority this payment has in the deal's cash flow waterfall. In case of currency swaps, the termination payments could be large and the issuer may face a problem making such a termination payment.

Credit Enhancement

A common feature of all types of securitisation transactions is the use of credit enhancement, that is, a cushion put in place to protect investors against expected losses. The credit enhancement is sized to reflect an expected loss level determined under a series of adverse scenarios that could affect the asset pool during its life.

The credit enhancement for a specific deal is usually a combination of several forms of credit enhancement mechanisms and is a reflection of the specific characteristics of the securitised assets, the goals of the securitisation sponsor and the requirements of the rating agencies.

Credit enhancement is normally sized by the rating agencies to help attain the desired ratings for the securitisation notes. Senior asset-backed notes are usually assigned the highest rating (triple-A).

Internal or external credit enhancement for asset-backed notes is typically complemented with structural investor protection built into the securitisation transaction.

The credit enhancement and the other structural enhancements should amongst them address most of the adverse eventualities that could affect the asset pool and the securitisation bonds. Along with the legal protections they help create bonds which are fundamentally different and more resilient than other fixed income instruments.

Forms of Credit Enhancement

One of the most essential elements in structuring an asset-backed security is establishing adequate credit enhancement levels. The role of credit enhancement is to bridge the credit quality of the assets, which may be B or BB, to the level of the desired rating of the asset-backed security, generally AAA. The credit enhancement is sized to absorb the expected losses that the pool could experience during the life of the asset-backed security, down to a residual level corresponding with the expected losses under the required rating level.

The credit enhancement can be structured in a number of different ways. The main forms of credit enhancement are listed in Exhibit 3.5.

External: Provided by an Outside Party

In the earlier stages of the development of the asset-backed market, the external credit enhancement prevailed. It is called external because it is provided by an outside party, a bank opening a letter of credit (LOC) or an insurance company and a monoline insurer providing a surety bond, or a company giving some other form of guarantee. It would also take the form of a loan provided by a third party and subordinated to the senior asset-backed bonds sold to investors.

EXHIBIT 3.5   Forms of Credit Enhancement

- External—provided by an outside party
  ↓ Bank letter of credit
  ↓ Insurance company surety bond
  ↓ Financial assurance company guarantee
  ↓ Subordinated loans from third party
- Internal—provided by originator or within the deal structure
  ↓ Reserve account/refunded or build up from excess spread
  ↓ Originators guarantee
  ↓ Senior-subordinated structure
  ↓ Excess spread
  ↓ Overcollateralisation
  ↓ Minimum required debt service coverage ratio (DSCR)
- Trigger events

Source: Merrill Lynch.

However, it is important to remember that in the case of external credit enhancement the rating of the security has a direct link with the rating of the credit enhancer, whether it is a bank providing an LOC or an insurance company providing a surety bond. Any rating downgrade, any bad news, any volatility in the quality or performance of the respective credit enhancer will have a direct impact on the performance or the rating of the insured securitisation bond.

Internal: Provided by Originator or Within the Deal Structure

As the market developed, a new type of credit enhancement emerged. This credit support is provided within the structure by the originator or through mechanisms internal to the deal structure (subordination, over-collateralisation, etc). The originator for instance, could provide some kind of a corporate guarantee for the asset-backed securities issued. Such a guarantee is typically attached to the most junior tranches of an asset-backed security for the purposes of improving their rating and improving their distribution in the market place.

The most common form of internal credit enhancement is *subordination. Subordination* or *credit-tranching* means that the cash flows generated by the assets are allocated with different priority to the different classes of notes in order of their seniority. In case of subordination, the face value of the bonds is equal to the value of the assets. The subordinate structures are known as a *senior/subordinated* structure or as a *senior/mezzanine/subordinated* structure. In a simple senior/subordinated structure, the senior tranche is usually rated AAA and it receives the cash flow generated by the assets first, for the purposes of interest and principal payment while the subordinated piece (also called equity piece), receives cash flows second and absorbs the losses first. The priority of the cash flow distribution comes from the top, waterfall like, while the distribution of the losses rises from the bottom.

In case of *overcollateralisation,* the value of the assets exceeds the face value of the notes. For instance, the assets can be purchased at a discount. The level of the discount reflects the level of expected losses to be potentially incurred by the assets, as well as the level of deal expenses.

Another form of internal credit enhancement is the requirement that the cash flows generated by the assets over a specified period of time exceed the debt service requirement of the bonds over the same period by a predetermined factor. The *minimum required debt service coverage ratio* (DSCR) it that factor. The revenue from the assets must exceed the debt service several times, thus allowing for monitoring performance and applying excess debt service to accelerate bond amortisation in case of adverse events affecting the transaction.

Excess Spread Capture Mechanics

There is one additional aspect of credit enhancement, which rating agencies frequently do not take into consideration when they establish the required credit protection level for a given rating. This is the *excess spread.* The assets in the securitised pool generate certain revenue, called *revenue yield* or *gross yield.* The assets generate revenues, associated with the interest charges on the respective debt obligations in that pool. The revenue is used to cover the expenses of the SPV. The expenses are related to the coupon payments under the asset-backed securities to investors and payments to the other parties in the deal (like the servicing fee, the swap counterparty fee or letter of credit fee). Generally, the combination of a coupon payment and servicing fee payment is known as the *base rate* in a structure. The difference between the revenue yield and the base rate or base expenses is known as *net yield.* Exhibit 3.6 provides a numerical illustration of these concepts.

The net yield absorbs one of the main "expenses" in a securitisation, which are the pool losses. The excess spread is an indicator of the credit health of the asset pool since the excess spread moves in the opposite direction of losses and delinquencies. By deducting the losses from the net yield, we get the *excess spread,* also known as *excess servicing fee.* The excess spread generated in each period could be used to cover losses produced in that period or in the next one, if there is any way to capture this excess spread and use it in the future.

EXHIBIT 3.6 Calculation of Excess Spread

☐ Yield–revenue generated by the asset pool from interest payments and other charges–penalties, annual fees, and so on

Minus

☐ Coupon (interest paid under the securitisation bonds) ⎫
                                                                                                                  ⎬ Base rate
☐ Servicing fees (payments made to the servicer)   ⎭

Net yield

Minus

☐ Losses (or charge-offs, lost revenue of the asset pool due to defaults, shortfalls in asset liquidation proceeds, etc.)

☐ Excess spread

☐ Excess spread capture mechanisms

Source: Merrill Lynch.

Generally, the excess spread is remitted back to the originator when not needed. However, many structures have mechanisms in place to build up reserve accounts from excess to be used in case of pool performance deterioration. Thus, the excess spread in each period, or excess spread captured through respective mechanics in a reserve account, provide additional credit support for the asset-backed security. This additional credit enhancement is of particular importance to investors who are focusing on the mezzanine, subordinated and equity tranches.

The *trigger events* in an asset-backed security are structural enhancements in the transaction and are often linked to certain credit events. Occurrence of specified events such as insolvency of originator or deterioration in pool credit quality expressed in increase in delinquency or loss levels or decrease in excess spread, triggers "early amortisation," leading to an accelerated repayment of the notes.

Credit Enhancement Sizing

Credit enhancement is sized by the rating agencies and its amount and process of its determination depends on their rating methodologies (see Exhibit 3.7). We can recall that the credit enhancement is established to absorb expected losses in the performance of the underlying pool of assets. It acts like a loss cushion that is there to absorb the expected losses that the pool could accumulate during the life of the asset-backed security. Consequently, to determine the credit enhancement the rating agencies try to predict the performance of the pool. Its future performance depends on the initial pool quality, general development of the

EXHIBIT 3.7   Credit Enhancement

- Credit enhancement sized to protect against prolonged reductions in cash flow
  - ↓ Modelled on severe stress scenarios, conservative assumptions
  - ↓ Based on a multiple of historical losses
  - ↓ Adjusted for certain structural risks (e.g., commingling, setoff, servicer transfer, cash transfer delays)
  - ↓ Level of enhancement commensurate with desired rating
- Differences in rating approaches
  - ↓ "Weak link"
  - ↓ "Expected loss"
  - ↓ Probability of first dollar loss

Source: Merrill Lynch.

economy, the performance of the originator and the servicer, and the like. In other words, certain assumptions about pool characteristics and how they can be affected by the future developments should be made to size the credit enhancement. One of the best predictive tools available is the scenario analysis based on either probability distribution of scenarios or on certain extreme (stress) scenarios.

The stress scenarios are generally related to the bankruptcy of the originator and assume that the asset pool incurs excessive losses. The bankruptcy of the originator is usually the stating assumption in sizing the credit enhancement; if the originator is also the servicer, the bankruptcy of the former would require the transfer of the servicing function, and this would increase the pool losses. These losses then accumulate during the life of the pool beyond historical averages or extremes. The new line should reflect particular risks at a given pool, for example, the risk of set off, commingling and others. In case of credit cards the originator may issue a credit card to a physical person who also holds deposits with the bank. In case the bank goes bankrupt, these deposits form part of its bankruptcy estate, yet the individual can claim that his debt under the credit card (subject to securitisation) is offset (extinguished) by the deposit he or she holds with the bank (and now held in the bankruptcy estate); thus the credit card securitisation pool incurs a loss equal to that deposit.

Furthermore, if the servicer is the originator, when accumulating the cash flows from the assets transferred to the SPV, these collections, may be comingled or mixed with collections from other assets of the originator. If the originator goes bankrupt it may be difficult to differentiate between the two cash flows, the ones that belong and should be remitted to the asset-backed pool and the others that belong to the bank (and other creditors).

Finally, the credit enhancement level, or the cushion sized to absorb the asset pool losses, should correspond to the required or expected credit rating under the asset-backed securities: the respective rating requires different levels of credit enhancement: highest for AAA, lower for A and even lower for BBB or BB security.

Differences in Rating Approaches

We emphasise that the credit enhancement is determined by the rating agencies, after evaluating the current, historical and future performance of the pool of assets backing the securitisation bond. To establish its size though, the rating agencies use different approaches.

Some of them apply the *expected loss approach*, where they determine the expected losses in the pool under various scenarios. Under this approach, the expected severity of loss to investors as well as their frequency or probability of occurrence is determined. The rating agencies simulate the expected cash flows that the pool could generate, determining the potential losses that it could accumulate. Some go further and link the expected loss to the level of reduction of the internal rate of return (IRR) of the bond: the higher the IRR reduction, the lower the bond rating.

Other rating agencies base their assessment on the so-called *weak link approach*. Under this methodology, the rating agencies look at the confluence of different entities and assets in the structure and determine where the structure could "break," that is, the weakest link in the chain of assets, counterparties and entities. The final rating of the security cannot be higher than the weakest link in the structure. On that basis, the rating agency could determine the probability of first dollar loss.

"Probability of first dollar loss" is another rating approach, which can be contrasted to the "expected loss" approach. Market convention differentiates between the two by stating that the expected loss approach involves a consideration of both probability of default and severity of loss on the liability side of the securitisation, while first dollar loss approach considers only the probability of default, or other words, a missed dollar payment is considered a default regardless of the recovery (may be even equal to 100%) that could follow.

It is also important to understand that more often than not an asset-backed security is rated by at least two rating agencies. Each of them may have a different approach and may focus on different factors or weigh differently the same factors to determine the performance under stress scenarios and related expected loss. The credit enhancement which the respective asset-backed security carries is the highest required by any one of the rating agencies in order to achieve the desired bond rating. In this respect, it is worth investigating any split ratings that exist especially on lower-rated tranches of the securitisation bonds.

ASSET CLASSES AND BASIC SECURITISATION STRUCTURES

The different classes of assets determine the different securitisation structures that are available in the market. Almost any asset type can be securitised if it meets some basic conditions. The broad variety of assets in general fits into two securitisation bond structures: revolving and amortising.

Asset Classes

Let us briefly talk about the asset types that can be securitised. In Exhibit 3.8, one can see a panoply of asset classes ranging from auto loans or credit cards all the way through TV rights, sports and entertainment contracts, exports and workers remittances. We generally talk about traditional and more esoteric, or nontraditional, asset types. But the range of different asset classes that have been securitised basically proves that pretty much any asset type can be securitised if it meets a few basic conditions.

Some of these conditions are related to the ability to transfer the legal ownership or entitlement to the benefits and losses of these assets by the originator to another party for the benefit of the asset-backed investors. These assets should also generate predictable and stable cash flows. Further, rating agencies usually require some historical performance data and performance track record of the respective assets in

EXHIBIT 3.8   Selected Asset Classes

Auto loans	Auto leases
Wholesale auto receivables	Aircraft and computer leases
Credit card receivables	Reinsurance
Home equity loans	Tax liens
Manufactured housing contracts	CBO's/CLO's
Recreational vehicles	Commercial real estate
Boat/truck loans	Credit card voucher receivables
Agricultural equipment loans	Workers' remittances
Student loans	Oil and other raw materials exports
Trade receivables	Project finance
Stranded costs	Sports and entertainment (sales, TV rights)

Source: Merrill Lynch.

order to be able to quantify their credit risk and to size the credit enhancement for the asset-backed deals. To illustrate these points we look at the nature of corporate asset securitisation.

Nature of the Assets Backing Corporate Securitisations

Corporate assets (as opposed to bank ones) present a particular challenge in determining the type of securitisation they are subject to. Corporates have assets of different nature:

- Some of them are existing assets, such as real estate or export receivables, trade receivables, vendor financing, generated based on the performance of certain, often contractual, obligations (goods exported, services performed, products shipped, etc.).
- Others are future assets, such as export receivables, trade receivables, vendor financing, to be generated in the future based on the performance of some, often contracted today, obligations.

The key differentiating factor is whether the obligation has been performed, so that the assets are existing now (current assets), or will be performed, so that the assets will be existing some time in the future (future assets). Hence:

- The current assets will be less dependent on the corporate originator, because it has already performed its obligations and the assets are in existence—now, it is a matter of collection or obligation performance by the counterpart (importer, buyer). So, the linkage with the originator is limited if the originator is also the servicer and to the degree a real servicer replacement is available.
- The future assets will be more dependent on the corporate originator, because it has to perform its obligations in the future in order to generate the assets (export the products, ship the goods, perform the services such as deliver electricity for example). If the originator does not exist in the future, there will be no assets backing the securitisation. So, the linkage to the creditworthiness expressed through the credit rating of the originators is almost 100%. We say "almost" because the credit rating expresses the probability of default on a financial obligation, and not necessarily on a contractual obligation—a company may be in a financial default, but still continue to perform services to clients and thus generate receivables.

Hence, the linkage of the securitisation bonds' rating with the corporate rating of the originator in the second case is much stronger than in the first case. Case in point, EDF transaction in comparison to Cremonini deal (Italian trade receivables deal priced last week).

Another issue is the value of the assets Backing the corporate decuritisation. deals may be structured on the basis of existing receivables (Cremonini), future receivables (EDF) or a mixture of both (Chargeur). A revolving feature added to the existing receivables securitisation does not change their nature—every new purchase of receivables involves existing receivables.

We suggest a simple calculation to determine corporate linkage and exposure: a review whether the corporate receivables' face value is higher, equal, or less than the bonds' face value:

- If the existing receivables' value is higher (bond is structured with over-collateralisation) or equal (bond is structured with subordination) than the bond's face value, then the corporate linkage is low—securitisation bond rating will stand alone dependent more on the credit quality of the receivables, than on the credit quality of the originator.
- If the existing receivables value is less than the bond's face value or the bond is backed by future receivables whose generation depends on the performance of the originator, then the corporate linkage is high—the securitisation bond rating will be almost fully linked to that of the originator.

The above has credit analysis, rating, and pricing implications:

- In the first case, the focus is on the credit quality of the assets and linkage to servicer, hence the pricing should be more independent of the pricing of the originator's standalone bonds.
- In the second case, the focus is on the credit quality of the originator and secondarily on the credit quality of the assets, hence the pricing of the securitisation bonds should be closely linked to the pricing of the corporate's stand-alone bonds.
- Furthermore, the rating of the securitisation bonds in the first case should be fairly independent from the rating of the corporate sponsor, while in the second case it will not only be highly dependent on day one, but will be as volatile during the life of the transaction as that of the corporate.

Basic Structure Types

The different asset classes give rise to different ABS and MBS structures (see Exhibit 3.9). The important element in these structures is to match the cash flows generated by the assets with the cash flows required to

EXHIBIT 3.9   Basic Structure Types

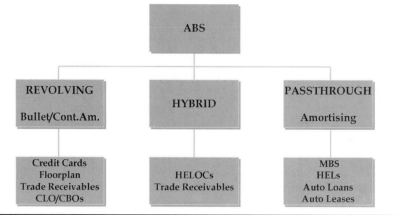

Source: Merrill Lynch.

service the asset-backed security. It is almost like asset and liability matching in a balance sheet situation.

There are two basic asset-backed securities structures: the revolving structures, and the pass-through structure.

Revolving Structures

In most general terms, the revolving structure is applied when a pool of short-term assets is used to back a longer-term asset-backed security. Let us say, a pool of credit cards or trade receivables, which have a life of between 60 and 120 days, is used to back five-year credit card or trade receivables asset-backed notes. The pool of assets generates interest and principal, and how and when the principal is distributed to investors is the main differentiating feature of the respective structure applied. In the case of a revolving structure, the principal generated is used to purchase new receivables during a specified period of time (the revolving period) and is applied afterwards to repay the bonds.

Generally, these revolving structures incorporate two periods. The first period is the *revolving period*. During the revolving period the principal under the asset-backed security remains outstanding in full and the investors receive only interest payments. This reflects the cash flows generated by the assets. The revenue or the yield generated by the assets is used to pay interest to investors (coupon) and all the other expenses we talked about—servicing fee, LOC provider fees, losses. The principal is used to purchase new receivables. This could continue for a number of years, and in our example on Exhibit 3.10, it continues for four years.

EXHIBIT 3.10   Revolving ABS Cashflows

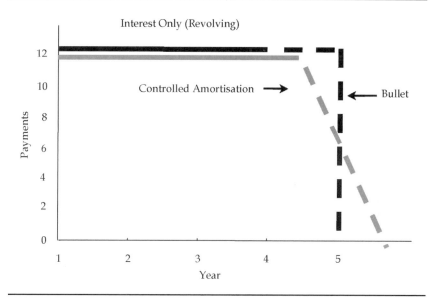

Bullet: one payment at the end of last year.
Controlled Amortisation: 12 equal monthly payments over the last year.
Source: Merrill Lynch.

The question now is, once the revolving period is over, how do we apply principal? One way of using principal is to deposit it into a reserve account, and generally, we refer to this as *principal accumulation period*, an accumulation period. We accumulate principal in a reserve account in order to pay the asset-backed security at its maturity through a soft bullet payment. In other words, we have a *revolving/accumulation/soft bullet* structure.

In other cases, instead of accumulating the principal in a reserve account, we can start paying it out in regular instalments to investors. In other words, a revolving period is followed by controlled amortisation and investors receive their principal back in several regular equal instalments. This is referred to as *controlled amortisation* period. Alternatively, we have a revolving/controlled amortisation structure.

Early Amortisation Triggers

Essential features in these structures are the early amortisation events or triggers. During the revolving period, the principal is applied to buy new receivables. If the originator of those receivables goes bankrupt,

EXHIBIT 3.11   Typical Amortisation (Payout) Events

- Deterioration of net portfolio yield/net excess yield triggers
- Originator/servicer insolvency
- Failure to pay principal on expected payment date
- Minimum seller interest triggers
- Bank breach of representations and warranties
- Failure to transfer funds
- Failure to replace interest rate cap provider in the event of rating reduction below required level

Source: Merrill Lynch.

there will be no receivables to generate and there will be no receivables to be purchased with the principal collected. The solution then is to start passing through the principal to investors. In other words, certain events (or the trigger event), "trigger" the amortisation of the bonds on a pass-through basis. All principal, as collected, is passed through to investors to pay down the asset-backed notes. The early amortisation event could occur at any point in time during the revolving period, the accumulation period or the controlled amortisation period.

Examples of typical amortisation events are shown on Exhibit 3.11. Some of them are related to the originator or the servicer in the transaction, but others are more "economic" in nature, for example, the deterioration of the excess spread below a certain level or the increase of pool losses above a given level.

As we discussed earlier, the difference between the revenue generated by the assets and the expenses needed under the asset-backed security provides excess spread. If this excess spread goes below a certain level, this indicates deterioration in the pool performance. In order to protect investors against further deterioration, an early amortisation of the bond is triggered. The revolving or accumulation period is over, and now principal is passed through directly to investors and they can still benefit from the remaining excess spread generated in the structure.

Just to illustrate this with numbers, let's assume that the trigger is set at 3%. If during the revolving period the excess spread varies between 4% and 6%, the structure is OK. If the excess spread falls below 4%, it signals deterioration and indicates a risk of the excess spread trigger being breached. When the excess spread reaches 3% the trigger is breached and the early amortisation begins. The excess spread trigger is usually set on a three-month rolling average basis, which means that if in any one month excess spread is below 3% and in the other two months of a three-month period it is above 3%, so that the average is above 3%, there will be no early amortisation. This protects against one-off adverse events and seasonal fluctuations.

Pass-Through Structures

On the other side of the structural spectrum is the pass-through structure, where the principal, instead of applied to purchase new receivables, is passed through to investors to repay gradually the outstanding amount of the asset- or mortgage-backed securities. Assets with longer maturities include mortgages, auto loans, and home equity loans. Because they have a longer amortisation horizon, generally they are used to structure longer-term pass-through securities. Again, this is in most generic terms.

Now let us briefly look at the pass-through structures. In the case of pass-through structures, the principal collected from the assets is passed directly through to investors to pay down the bonds. Exhibit 3.12 shows the repayment schedule of a typical pass-through structure (or a typical loan underlying such structure).

You have probably seen this graph in any textbook dealing with mortgage or auto loans, where it shows how such a loan amortises.

In the case of a level pay loan, the borrower makes an equal payment every month, which is split between interest and principal. Usually, in the earlier stages of the life of the loan, more of this payment is allocated to interest and less to principal, and as the loan amortises more payment is

EXHIBIT 3.12   Pass-Through Securities

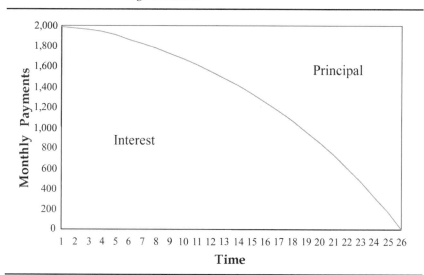

Source: Merrill Lynch.

allocated to principal and less to interest. From the point of view of the borrower, the borrower pays more interest at the beginning and more principal later on, which means that later on the borrower acquires more equity in the asset and has higher motivation to continue paying the loan.

Many of the auto loans and mortgage loans allow borrowers to prepay. One of the main reasons borrowers prepay is because they can obtain a cheaper financing for the respective house or car, which usually happens when interest rates go down or price competition among lenders increases. So, at any stage in the life of a mortgage, the borrower could take a new mortgage and prepay the outstanding amount of the old ones. This is probably all good and clean from the point of view of the borrower. However, from the point of view of the investor in a mortgage-backed security, this means that the investor receives back the principal much earlier than expected. If this happened while interest rates are falling, the investor in a mortgage-backed security would be exposed to higher reinvestment risk and convexity risk.

Hence, a key element in determining the payment profile of such pass-through securities is the determination of the *conditional prepayment rate* (CPR) or speed for the purposes of pricing the security.[1] The CPR states the average speed at which an investor should expect to receive principal back.

The CPR is established as an average over a certain horizon, while in real life the prepayment rate varies from month to month. The monthly prepayment rate could vary due to changes in the interest rate environment, the industry, and to seasonal developments. For example, competition in mortgage lending could force mortgage lenders to lower the price of a mortgage loan and also make borrowers more aware of their refinancing options. That would speed up refinancing of the loans. Specific industry events or tax considerations could introduce definite pattern of seasonal changes. Another factor would be the existence of prepayment penalties and their enforceabilities. Generally, borrowers facing high prepayment penalties are less willing to refinance their loans. However, if the interest rates drop sharply and there are other legal or structural elements in the mortgage, say, reset dates when they are allowed to prepay without penalty, the borrower may consider refinancing the mortgage even if she or he has to pay a prepayment penalty.

Other elements driving prepayments could also be related to the demographics of a given country or people moving from one city to another: in the United States from the East Coast to the West Coast; in the Eurozone, relocating for jobs or other purposes, which has not happened on a large scale yet. In other words, when investors consider buying pass-through

---

[1] The CPR is sometimes referred to as the *constant prepayment rate*.

amortising bonds, (especially if they have fixed rate coupons) investors are facing prepayments risk and have to understand clearly what factors drive prepayment in the underlying assets. To sum up, prepayments are important in determining the maturity of a floating rate pass-thorough securitisation bond, and the convexity and maturity of a fixed rate pass-through securitisation bond.

BENEFITS AND POTENTIAL DRAWBACKS OF SECURITISATION

The most often touted benefits of securitisation are for issuers the ability to raise off-balance sheet financing and to diversify funding sources—and for investors the ability to pick up yield while buying bonds based on credit-enhanced, well-diversified asset pools. However, securitisation can have drawbacks for both issuers and investors if not properly executed or not fully understood.

Securitisation Sponsors

The entities, which get involved in securitisation, are almost as numerous as the assets that can be securitised. Their involvement, though, is often underpinned by different incentives and objectives.

Banks—Consumer and Corporate Loans, Mortgages, Real Estate

Banks are the most obvious candidates for securitisation. They have assets on their balance sheet and want to transfer them to raise funding. In addition, they can transfer the risk associated with these assets through their sale or other means. By doing that, banks release some of the regulatory capital they hold against those assets.

Companies—Trade Receivables, Exports

Companies have assets in the form of trade receivables, export receivables or any other assets (real estate) that could be used in securitisation transactions, for the purposes of financing and streamlining their balance sheet.

Project Finance—Cash Flow Stream Generated Post Completion

After the completion, a project generates sizeable stable cash flows that can be used for the purposes of securitisation. It is also possible early in the construction phase to leverage the cash flows to be generated post completion.

Public Entities—Tax Liens, Social Security Contributions, and Tolls

Municipalities generate stable cash flows and possess certain assets that can be securitised, such as tax liens, social security contributions, parking tickets and taxi medallions. Public institutions may also sponsor specific projects such as toll roads, bridges or hospitals. Municipal assets also can be subjected of securitisation whether they are in the form of existing assets and related cash flows, such as tax liens, social security contributions, and government reimbursements for taxes collected, or assets which will be generated in the future such as fees from crossing a bridge or for using a toll road.

Real Estate Developers—Commercial Real Estate

Real estate developers have commercial real estates, offices, shopping malls, and hotels that generate rental and capital income. Many banks also hold on their balance sheets respective real estate assets. Such assets can be subject to commercial mortgage-backed securities or commercial real estate securitisations.

Countries—Privatisations, Export Credits, External Credits

Countries have export credits, different assets that they may want to privatise as was the case in the UK with the Private Finance Initiative (PFI). These assets could be securitised or the purchase of these assets by another entity, privatisation could be financed through securitisation.

Incentives for Securitisation—The Originator's Perspective

Off-balance sheet financing securitisation allows companies and banks to raise financing off-balance sheet, by monetising their currently existing or future assets. Such financing, especially given its non-recourse nature most of the time, is not recorded as debt and does not affect their financial ratios.

Regulatory Treatment (Regulatory Arbitrage) for Banks

We already briefly referred to the banks' need for regulatory capital relief. When selling assets off-balance sheet, the banks gain off-balance sheet funding (funding against their assets or monetisation of their assets). Also, by transferring these assets or risk associated with them away from their balance sheets, they free up regulatory capital, receiving equity relief. The asset transfer off the balance sheet reduces the leverage and improves the return on equity. In order for securitisation to make economic sense, the cost of securitisation should be less than the cost of equity for the bank. That may or may not be the case, yet there are other benefits from securitisation for the banks.

Alternative Sources of Liquidity and Diversified Funding Mix

Through securitisation banks and companies can access alternative sources of liquidity and diversify their funding mix reducing the correlation between their own financial and the risks of the assets—a point we made earlier. A lower credit quality bank or company, say B or BB, faces very high funding spreads. This issuer may reduce such funding spreads by issuing asset-backed securities, which featuring a AAA rating would be priced much tighter.

Exposure Management

Banks and companies have certain exposure limits or credit lines, specified limits for their credit exposure to different entities. By transferring loans off its balance sheet, or transferring risk associated with some of their loans and other assets, the banks could free their credit lines and avoid breaching their credit limits. They can free up the lines for further lending to the respective sectors or clients.

Removal of Illiquid Assets from Loan Book

Banks and companies can remove illiquid assets from their balance sheets, as is the case with nonperforming or subperforming loans (NPL), and subperforming real estate. Securitisation is often the solution for banks burdened by NPL and an acute need to sanitise their balance sheet. Companies that have accumulated large amounts of real estate may want to focus on their core businesses, but retain use of their real estate assets without burdening their balance sheets. They can transfer those assets through securitisation by selling real estate and leasing it back to their own rise.

Transfer Uncertainties Related to Loan Prepayments to Investors

When finance companies and banks lend for mortgages, they are exposed to the interest risk of those loans, expressed in their prepayment behaviour. Normally, when interest rates fall mortgage borrowers tend to refinance their mortgages, that is, taking a new mortgage with a lower interest rate, and using its proceeds to repay in full the old mortgage loan. This creates prepayment risk for the banks on their balance sheets and requires more active management of their assets. By transferring such assets away, the banks transfer the related prepayments risk, simplify, and improve the maturity management of their balance sheet.

Achieve Better Pricing (Through Higher Debt Rating)

With certain types of structures, like future flow deals (say in the case of exports from emerging markets), highly rated companies in lower-rated countries can raise debt at better terms than the respective sovereign ceiling would allow them to do on a straight corporate bond basis. This is achieved by structuring a deal, where the cash flows are generated by exports denominated in hard currency and captured offshore. The deal can be structured with a rating above the sovereign ceiling of that country, usually at the level of the credit rating of the exporter on a stand-alone basis, and the bond may have much longer maturity that their respective country or exporter would normally get under straight bond funding.

We discussed the different motivations different types of issuers may have to resort to asset-backed financing. We conclude this discussion with a numerical example, which illustrates the effect on securitisation on bank ROE, to describe the benefits for the banks. We show in Exhibit 3.13 a pool of assets that a bank can fund in a traditional way through a bank loan—or innovatively—through ABS. There are two important points to note in the table: the funding cost and the resulting return on equity (ROE) under the two different funding alternatives.

EXHIBIT 3.13   Bank Securitisation—a Numerical Example

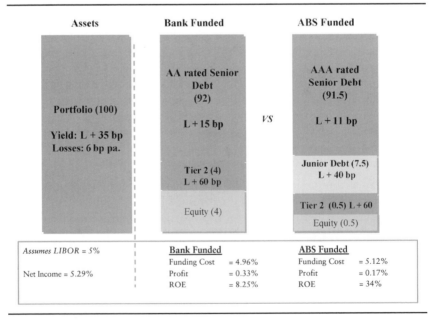

Source: Merrill Lynch.

It is obvious that the asset-backed funding may be slightly more expensive than the bank funding. On the other hand, it results in a much higher return on equity than the bank funding. In this general example, the asset-backed funding achieves an ROE of 34% versus 8.25% in the case of traditional funding sources, that is, ROE increases roughly four times using securitisation. This is a very important issue, in the context of merger and acquisition activities and growing shareholder demands.

Potential Drawbacks of Securitisation

We looked at the incentives banks and companies have to securitise as well as the related derived benefits. Securitisation also has some potential shortcomings and negative aspects.

Retaining the First-Loss Position

In many securitisations the banks or the companies retain the most junior piece in the bond structure. As we discussed earlier, cash flows generated by the pool are distributed from the top, that is, from the senior tranche downwards, whereas the losses are absorbed from the bottom, from the junior tranche upwards. A bank or a company retaining the junior equity piece is in a first loss position and in one small piece, retains the concentrated losses of the large pool of assets it has sold. When an entity relies heavily on securitisation by retaining more equity tranches it increases its effective leverage of the balance sheet. One of the best ways to avoid that is to find a way to sell the equity piece to investors willing to assume the associated risks.

Overreliance on Securitisation

If a company heavily relies on securitisation, it will be determined to maintain high levels of performance of the securitised assets at any cost. Performance of any given asset pool securitisation bond below expectations would make it more difficult for that company to access the securitisation market in the future. To avoid that, the originator may be willing to take some residual risk in the asset pool or to step in to support the asset pool performance. In other words, the originator may indirectly allow for partial recourse, which is not really the stated purpose of securitisation and may provoke regulators' objections.

Asset Risk Transfer Can Be Achieved Through Other Means

Finally, the transfer of risk associated with a given pool of assets could be achieved without selling the assets, but simply by the transfer of that risk through credit default swaps in credit structures, or insuring that risk with an insurance policy for an outside insurer or guarantor. We are referring here to securitisation methods—synthetic and insured structures, different from the traditional securitisation based on asset sale.

ABS/MBS INVESTORS AND THEIR CONSIDERATIONS

It is important to underline the broad range of investors in the securitisation market and the dominant role of banks in that context. The benefits of securitisation relative to other fixed income papers undoubtedly attract ever-increasing number of ABS investors.

Investors in Non-US ABS/MBS

Exhibits 3.14 to 3.17 presents indicative investor distribution for non-US ABS and MBS in 2002. Two features clearly stand out. Firstly, banks continue to be the biggest investors in asset and mortgage-backed securities. Nevertheless, the role of investment advisers and commercial paper (CP) conduits has been growing, representing 20% and 10% of the investor base for new issuance. We have to stress the role of the CP conduits, as in CP conduits we include two different types of entities: the asset-backed commercial paper conduits, which focus exclusively on purchasing bond portfolios and funding them with CP, and the stand-alone securities finance companies, the likes of Beta, Sigma, Centauri, K2, Links, and so on, which also purchase substantial amounts of asset-backed securities.

EXHIBIT 3.14   Tentative ABS Investors Distribution by Country, 2002

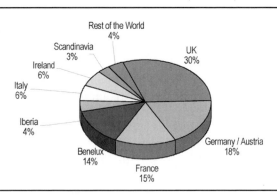

Source: Merrill Lynch.

EXHIBIT 3.15   Tentative Investor Distribution by Investor Type, 2002

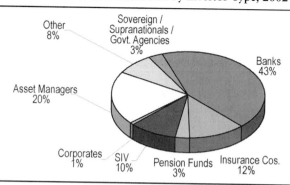

Source: Merrill Lynch.

EXHIBIT 3.16   Tentative Corporate Bond Investors by Country, 2002

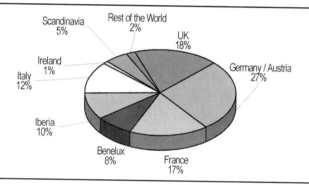

Source: Merrill Lynch.

EXHIBIT 3.17   Title Tentative Corporate Bond Investors Distribution by Investor Type, 2002

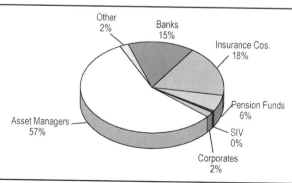

Source: Merrill Lynch.

Two other entities on this pie chart are worth mentioning: the insurance companies and the pension funds. Their share of the purchases of new issuance of asset-backed securities has been gradually growing over the years, and it may also have influenced the structures of the securities issued. Traditionally, asset-backed securities in Europe are issued as floating rate pass-through notes. With the demand of the insurance companies and pension funds for ABS/MBS increasing, more of them are issued as fixed-rate bullet notes, as these are the structures which insurance companies and pension funds tend to buy, given their asset/liability structure.

In terms of geographic distribution of new issuance of non-US asset and mortgage-backed securities, the UK and Irish investors prevail and account for roughly 40% of the placements. The role of German, French, and Italian investors, though, has been growing fast in recent years, while the Benelux countries already have a group of well established sophisticated investors for this type of securities.

We have to emphasise the rapid development of the investor base since the introduction of the euro. As the currencies were eliminated and 11 countries in Europe started functioning as one Eurozone market, investors who traditionally focused on their domestic bonds due to currency considerations are now able to purchase euro-denominated, asset-backed securities from issuers domiciled in any country in the Eurozone. In addition, with the rapid development of securitisation within the Eurozone and the affirmation of the euro as a reserve currency, there is increasing demand for Eurozone ABS and MBS from non-European investors.

Investor Considerations

The investor base for structured finance and securitisation bonds has expanded enormously in the course of the last few years and particularly after the introduction of the euro. Several factors underpin the growing investor interest in ABS.

Attractiveness of ABS Investments

Asset-backed securities are attractive to investors because they give them exposure to a diversified pool of consumer or corporate assets. Instead of buying loans or bonds in a number of industries or geographic areas and building up such a portfolio alone, investors could simply buy into a *collateralised loan obligation* (CLO) which is already such a portfolio. They could also buy into a diversified pool of consumer loans, be it through a credit card, mortgage or auto loan-backed security.

In addition, each of the securities has built-in structural and legal protections we discussed earlier, and are also structured to withstand levels of losses sized under negative future scenarios. This certainly limits the risks, especially for the senior investors in the asset-backed structure. Investors buying into asset-backed or future flow securities from emerging markets are acquiring bonds with reduced currency and sovereign risks.

Diversification Tool

Buying into an asset or mortgage-backed security is definitely a diversification tool when managing a broad portfolio of fixed income instruments. In addition, asset-backed securities generally price wider than comparable corporate bonds, which gives them attractive higher risk adjusted returns.

Rating Stability

Historically asset-backed securities ratings have been demonstrated to be generally stable. There is lower rating volatility in the asset-backed bonds world than in the corporate or bank bonds world. This is to a large degree because these securities already have built in credit and structural enhancements, as discussed earlier.

Relative Spread Stability

The behaviour of traditional assets structured finance bonds on the secondary market has been marked with relatively stable spreads in comparison to other fixed income sectors, such as corporate bonds, high yield bonds, and their derivative products. The lower relative volatility has resulted in lower mark-to-market impact on investors' portfolios.

CHAPTER 4

Credit Derivatives Primer

Frank J. Fabozzi, Ph.D., CFA
Frederick Frank Adjunct Professor of Finance
School of Management
Yale University

Moorad Choudhry
Head of Treasury
KBC Financial Products UK Limited

Mark J.P. Anson, Ph.D., CFA, JD, CPA
Chief Investment Officer
CalPERS

Ren-Raw Chen, Ph.D.
Associate Professor of Finance
School of Business
Rutgers University (New Brunswick)

Credit derivatives are financial instruments that are designed to transfer the credit exposure of an underlying asset or assets between two parties. With credit derivatives, an asset manager can either acquire or reduce credit risk exposure. Credit derivatives include credit default swaps, asset swaps, total return swaps, credit spread options, and credit spread forwards. Certain credit derivatives have been used to create synthetic securitisations whereby the economic risks of financial assets are transferred to another entity without the transferring of ownership of

57

those financial assets. The most commonly used credit derivatives in synthetic securitisations are credit default swaps, total return swaps, and credit-linked notes. We describe credit-linked notes in Chapter 35. In this chapter we will describe the features and investment characterisics of these instruments.[1] We begin with a discussion of the legal documents.

LEGAL DOCUMENTATION

Credit derivatives are privately negotiated agreements traded over the counter. The lack of an exchange-traded product means that in the United States there is very little regulation from either the Securities and Exchange Commission or the Commodity Futures Trading Commission. Instead, credit derivatives are regulated through the content of the individually negotiated contracts. The *International Swaps and Derivatives Association* (ISDA) has recognized the need to provide a common format for credit derivative documentation.

Although the first credit derivatives began to appear on the financial market scene in 1993, it was not until 1998 that the ISDA developed a standard contract to capture these trades. Establishing an industry standard by which to document a derivatives transaction is an important step in the development of any derivative market. It indicates that a critical mass of trading had come together such that all participants in the market recognize the need for a common reference point.

In addition to the definitions of credit events, ISDA developed the *ISDA Master Agreement*. This is the authoritative contract used by industry participants because it established international standards governing privately negotiated derivative trades (all derivatives, not just credit derivatives). The Master Agreement reduces legal uncertainty by providing uniform contractual terms for all derivative participants. It also provides for a reduction in counterparty credit risk by allowing for the netting of contractual obligations. The original Master Agreement was introduced in 1987 and has been revised periodically. The latest version as of this writing is the *2002 ISDA Master Agreement*.

In 1998, ISDA released its contract form for credit derivatives. The documentation is primarily designed for either credit default swaps or total return swaps. In our discussion of the credit default swaps in this chapter, key provisions of the ISDA credit swap contract and other relevant provisions from ISDA publications are covered.

---

[1] For a further discussion of credit derivatives, see Mark J.P. Anson, Frank J. Fabozzi, Moorad Choudhry, and Ren-Raw Chen, *Credit Derivatives: Instruments, Applications, and Pricing* (Hoboken, NJ: John Wiley & Sons, 2004).

Credit Events

The most important section of the documentation for a credit default swap is what the parties to the contract agree constitutes a credit event that will trigger a credit default payment. Definitions for credit events are provided by the ISDA. First published in 1999, there have been periodic supplements and revisions of these definitions

1999 ISDA Credit Derivative Definitions

The *1999 ISDA Credit Derivatives Definitions* (referred to as the "1999 Definitions") provides a list of eight possible credit events:

1. Bankruptcy
2. Credit event upon merger
3. Cross acceleration
4. Cross default
5. Downgrade
6. Failure to pay
7. Repudiation
8. Restructuring

These eight events attempt to capture every type of situation that could cause the credit quality of the reference entity to deteriorate, or cause the value of the reference obligation to decline.

The parties to a credit default swap may include all of these events, or select only those that they believe are most relevant. We describe each below. As explained later, there has been standardization of the credit events that are used in credit default swaps in the United States and Europe. Nevertheless, and this cannot be overemphasized, this does not preclude a credit protection buyer from including broader credit protection.

Bankruptcy   *Bankruptcy* means that a reference issuer either:

1. Is dissolved.
2. Becomes insolvent or unable to pay its debts as they become due.
3. Makes a general assignment, arrangement or composition for the benefit of creditors.
4. Institutes, or has instituted against it, a proceeding seeking a judgment of insolvency or bankruptcy, or any relief under any bankruptcy or insolvency law.
5. Has a petition presented for its winding-up or liquidation.
6. Has a resolution passed for its winding-up, official management, or liquidation.

7. Seeks or becomes subject to the appointment of an administrator, provisional liquidator, conservator, receiver, trustee, custodian, or other similar official for all or substantially all of its assets.
8. Has a secured party take possession of all or substantially all of its assets, or has a distress, execution, attachment, sequestration or such other legal process levied, enforced, or sued on against all or substantially all of its assets.
9. Causes or is subject to any event with respect to it which, under the applicable laws of any jurisdiction, has an analogous effect to any of the events specified in items 1–8.
10. Takes any action in furtherance of, or indicating its consent to, approval of, or acquiescence in, any of the foregoing acts.

In sum, bankruptcy includes any official (court directed) or private action which results in an issuer relinquishing control of its assets, operations, or management. The reference issuer may initiate these proceedings itself, or it may be forced to act by outside parties. Bankruptcy also occurs if the issuer cannot pay its outstanding debts as they become due. Consequently, poor operating performance and lack of short-term financing can force a bankruptcy.

Credit Event Upon Merger   *Credit event upon merger* means that the reference issuer has consolidated, amalgamated, or merged with another entity, or has transferred all or substantially all of its assets to another entity, and the creditworthiness of the resulting, surviving, or transferee entity is materially weaker than that of the reference issuer before the consolidation. For instance, if the combined entity has a lower credit rating after a merger than the reference entity before the merger, a credit event has occurred, subject to a determination of materiality.

Materiality is a term negotiated by the swap parties. Materiality can be defined as a single step downgrade in the issuer's credit rating, or a several step downgrade.

Cross Acceleration   *Cross acceleration* means the occurrence of a default, event of default, or some other similar condition (other than a failure to make any required payment) with respect to another outstanding obligation of the reference entity, which has resulted in the other obligation becoming due and payable before it would otherwise become due and payable. In other words, if the reference issuer defaults on any other bond, loan, lease, or obligation, for purposes of the credit default swap, this counts for a credit event as if the issuer had defaulted on the reference obligation.

Cross Default   *Cross default* is defined similarly to cross acceleration except that the other outstanding obligations are capable of being declared due and payable before such time as they would otherwise become due and payable. The distinction between cross acceleration and cross default is a fine one. For practical purposes a cross acceleration is an actual default event on another outstanding obligation, while a cross default is an event which provides the obligation holder with the ability to declare a default. In this respect, cross default provisions are preemptive—they kick in before the issuer defaults on an outstanding obligation.

Downgrade   *Downgrade* means a reduction in credit rating of the reference entity, or if the reference obligation is no longer rated by any rating agency. The parties to the agreement can specify below what level of credit rating a credit event will occur. Generally, the *specified rating* is set equal to the reference entity's current credit rating so that any downgrade results in a credit event. The parties can also specify the applicable rating agencies, although any nationally recognized statistical rating organization usually qualifies.

Failure to Pay   *Failure to pay* means that, after giving effect to any applicable grace period, the reference entity fails to make, when due, any payments equal to or exceeding any required payment of any outstanding obligation. Failure to pay is a more narrow case of cross acceleration and cross default. Under the latter two conditions, the failure to perform under any loan or bond covenant constitutes a credit event. However, under failure to pay, the lack of a cash payment constitutes a credit event.

Repudiation   *Repudiation* means that the reference entity refutes, disclaims, repudiates, rejects or challenges the validity of, in whole or part, any of its outstanding obligations. Basically, if the reference entity refuses to pay on any of its obligations, the protection buyer may declare a credit event on the reference obligation.

Restructuring   *Restructuring* means a waiver, deferral, restructuring, rescheduling, standstill, moratorium, exchange of obligations, or other adjustment with respect to any obligation of the reference entity such that the holders of those obligations are *materially* worse off from either an economic, credit, or risk perspective. The terms that can be changed would typically include, but are not limited to, one or more of the following: (1) a reduction in the interest rate; (2) a reduction in the principal; (3) a rescheduling of the principal repayment schedule (e.g., lengthening the maturity of the obligation) or postponement of an interest payment; or (4) a change in the level of seniority of the obligation in the reference entity's debt structure. In other words, if the reference entity works out a deal with its creditors on any outstanding obligation where the revised terms of that obligation are *materially* less favorable to the creditors, then the protection buyer may declare a credit event on the reference obligation.

Restructuring is the most controversial credit event that may be included in a credit default swap. The reason why it is so controversial is easy to understand. A protection buyer benefits from the inclusion of a restructuring as a credit event and feels that eliminating restructuring as a credit event will erode its credit protection. The protection seller, in contrast, would prefer not to include restructuring since even routine modifications of obligations that occur in lending arrangements would trigger a payout to the protection buyer.

Moreover, if the reference obligation is a loan and the protection buyer is the lender, there is a dual benefit for the protection buyer to restructure a loan. The first benefit is that the protection buyer receives a payment from the protection seller. Second, the accommodating restructuring fosters a relationship between the lender (who is the protection buyer) and its customer (the corporate entity that is the obligor of the reference obligation).

Because of this problem, the *Restructuring Supplement to the 1999 ISDA Credit Derivatives Definitions* (the "Supplement Definition") issued in April 2001 provided a modified definition for restructuring. There is a provision for the limitation on reference obligations in connection with restructuring of loans made by the protection buyer to the borrower that is the obligor of the reference obligation. This provision requires the following in order to qualify for a restructuring: (1) There must be four or more holders of the reference obligation, and (2) there must be a consent to the restructuring of the reference obligation by a supermajority (66⅔%). In addition, the supplement limits the maturity of reference obligations that are physically deliverable when restructuring results in a payout triggered by the protection buyer.

Consequently, in the credit default swap market, until 2003, the parties to a trade had the following three choices for restructuring: (1) no restructuring; (2) restructured based on the 1999 Definition for restructuring, referred to as "full restructuring" or "old restructuring"; or (3) restructuring as defined by the Restructuring Supplement Definition, referred to as "modified restructuring." Modified restructuring is typically used in North America while full restructuring is used in Europe. When the reference entity is a sovereign, restructuring is often full restructuring.

Whether restructuring is included and, if it is included, whether it is old restructuring or modified restructuring affects the swap premium. Specifically, all other factors constant, it is more expensive if restructuring is included. Moreover, old restructuring results in a larger swap premium than modified restructuring.

2003 ISDA Credit Derivative Definitions

As the credit derivatives market developed, market participants learned a great deal about how to better define credit events, particularly with the record level of high-yield corporate bond default rates in 2002 and the sovereign defaults, particularly the experience with the 2001-2002 Argentina debt crisis. In January 2003, the ISDA published its revised credit events definitions in the *2003 ISDA Credit Derivative Definitions* (the "2003 Definitions").

The revised definitions reflected amendments to several of the definitions for credit events set forth in the 1999 Definitions. Specifically, there were amendments for bankruptcy, repudiation, and restructuring. The major change was to restructuring whereby the ISDA allows parties to a given trade to select from among the following four definitions: (1) no restructuring; (2) full restructuring, with no modification to the deliverable reference obligations aspect; (3) modified restructuring (which is typically used in North America); or (4) "modified modified restructuring." The last choice is a new one and was included to address issues that arose in the European market.

Termination Value and Settlement

The *termination value* for a credit default swap is calculated at the time of the credit event, and the exact procedure that is followed to calculate the termination value will depend on the settlement terms specified in the contract. This will be either cash settlement or physical settlement.

Cash Settlement

A credit default swap contract may specify a predetermined payout value on occurrence of a credit event. This may be the nominal value of the swap contract. Such a swap is known in some markets as a *digital credit derivative*. Alternatively, the termination value can be calculated as the difference between the nominal value of the reference obligation and its market value at the time of the credit event. This arrangement is more common with cash-settled contracts.

Determining the market value of the reference obligation at the time of the credit event may be a little problematic: The issuer of the obligation may well be in default or administration (bankruptcy). The *calculation agent* usually makes the termination payment calculation. The calculation agent is usually the credit protection seller, although both parties to the trade can be joint calculation agents. When used as part of a structured credit product, the calculation agent is usually an independent third party.

Physical Settlement

With *physical settlement*, on occurrence of a credit event, the buyer delivers the reference obligation to the seller, in return for which the seller pays the face value of the delivered asset to the buyer. The contract may specify a number of alternative issues of the reference entity that the buyer can deliver to the seller. These are known as *deliverable obligations*. This may apply when a credit default swap has been entered into on a reference entity rather than a specific obligation issued by that entity (i.e., when there is a reference entity rather than a reference obligation).

Where more than one deliverable obligation is specified, the protection buyer will invariably deliver the one that is the cheapest on the list of eligible deliverable obligations. This gives rise to the concept of the *cheapest-to-deliver*, as encountered with government bond futures and agency futures, and is in effect an embedded option afforded the protection buyer.

Many credit default swap contracts that are physically settled name a reference entity rather than a reference obligation. Upon default, the protection buyer often has a choice of deliverable bonds with which to effect settlement. The broader the definition of deliverable bonds is in the credit default swap documentation, the longer the list of the eligible delivery obligations—as long as the bond meets prespecified requirements for seniority and maturity, it may be delivered. Contrast this with the position of the bondholder in the cash market, who is aware of the exact issue that he is holding in the event of default. Default swap sellers may receive potentially any bond from the basket of deliverable instruments that rank *pari passu* with the cash bond issue—this is the delivery option afforded the protection buyer.

In practice, therefore, the protection buyer will deliver the cheapest-to-deliver bond from the deliverable basket, exactly as it would for an exchange-traded government futures contract. This delivery option has debatable value in theory, but significant value in practice. For instance the bonds of a reference entity that might be trading cheaper in the market include:

- The bond with the lowest coupon
- A convertible bond

■ An illiquid bond
■ A very-long-dated bond

Modified restructuring, described earlier in this chapter, specifically restricts the delivery of long-dated bonds where restructuring is the credit event that triggers a contract payout. When old restructuring is used, a long-dated bond may be delivered and therefore the delivery option does carry value in the market. Similarly for an option contract, this value increases the closer the contract holder gets to the "strike price," which for a credit default swap is a credit event.

Relative Benefits of Cash versus Physical Settlement

In theory, the value of protection is identical irrespective of which settlement option is selected. However under physical settlement the protection seller can gain if there is a recovery value that can be extracted from the defaulted asset; or its value may rise as the fortunes of the issuer improve.

Swap market-making banks often prefer cash settlement as there is less administration associated with it. It is also more suitable when a credit default swap is used as part of a structured credit product, because such vehicles may not be set up to take delivery of physical assets.

Another advantage of cash settlement is that it does not expose the protection buyer to any risks should there not be any deliverable obligations in the market, for instance due to shortage of liquidity in the market—were this to happen, the buyer may find the value of its settlement payment reduced. A final advantage of cash settlement is greater certainty of settlement than the cheapest-to-deliver bond.

Nevertheless physical settlement is widely used because counterparties wish to avoid the difficulties associated with determining the market value of the reference obligation under cash settlement. Physical settlement also permits the protection seller to take part in the creditor negotiations with the reference entity's administrators, which may result in improved terms for them as holders of the obligation.

Conditions to Payment

In order for a payment to be collected by the protection buyer upon the occurrence of a credit event, three conditions must be satisfied:

1. The affected party must deliver a credit event notice.
2. The affected party must deliver a notice of publicly available information.
3. The calculation agent must determine that materiality exists.

Credit Event Notice

A *credit event notice* is an irrevocable notice given by one party to the credit default swap to its counterparty that a credit event has occurred. ISDA allows for the notice to be given in writing or orally, including by telephone, but the parties may negotiate their preferred type of notice.

Notice of Publicly Available Information

A *notice of publicly available information* is a notice that confirms the occurrence of a credit event. This notice must reference a source of "publicly available information" which can include any internationally recognized published or electronically displayed news source such as the *Wall Street Journal*, Reuters electronic terminals, or Bloomberg terminals. Additionally, the parties to the credit default swap can specify a minimum number of publicly available information sources that must confirm the occurrence of a credit event (see the appendix).

Calculation Agent and the Determination of Materiality

The *calculation agent* is the party designated to determine the required payments under the credit derivative transaction. For a payment to occur, the calculation agent must determine that materiality exists.

Materiality is a term that is negotiated by the parties. For instance, if the reference obligation is a high-yield corporate bond, materiality can be defined in terms of a price decline. The parties to the trade can state what dollar or percentage decline in value of the reference obligation is sufficient to qualify as a material credit event. Usually, materiality is stated as a 1% to 5% price decline from the initial price (referred to as the "price decline requirement"). The initial price may equal the reference (strike) price, or the reference price may be set at a different value.

Conversely, instead of a price decline, materiality can be defined in terms of increasing credit spreads. Recall that an increase in credit spreads for a reference issuer means a decline in value for a reference obligation of that issuer. Therefore, materiality can be defined in terms of a minimum credit spread increase (the "spread widening requirement") that must occur before a credit event is recognized.

Materiality, however, is determined by the calculation agent. The calculation agent is usually a point of negotiation in ISDA agreements. Almost always, the dealer who is selling the credit derivative wishes to remain the calculation agent. However, this raises a potential conflict of interest because the dealer/calculation agent might not want to recognize a credit event to prevent its payment obligation to the protection buyer.

Fortunately, ISDA provides for a dispute resolution provision in the contract. In the event that a party to the credit default swap does not agree with a determination made by the calculation agent, the disputing party has the right to require that the determination be made by a disinterested third party that is a dealer of credit derivative instruments. The calculation agent gets to pick the disinterested third party, but only after consultation with the disputing party.

The determination made by the third party is binding on the credit derivative participants unless there is manifest error. The costs, if any, from using the third party are borne by the disputing party if the third party substantially agrees with the calculation agent, and are borne by the nondisputing party if the third party does not substantially agree with the calculation agent. Bottom line: If the disputing party believes that the dealer/calculation agent has not properly recognized a credit event, it can challenge the dealer, but it must be prepared to pay any costs associated with the challenge should its dispute prove unjustified.

The parties can agree to be joint calculation agents. This can alleviate conflicts of interest. However, if the joint calculation agents cannot agree, the same dispute resolution techniques apply.

It is rare for the parties to a credit derivative trade to use an outside calculation agent. The norm is that the broker/dealer is usually the calculation agent; and if there is a dispute, then the parties to the trade turn to an outside calculation agent to resolve the disagreement. This is because it is expensive and time consuming to use an outside calculation agent. Also, the parties to the swap have the best knowledge of the terms of the trade. In contrast, an independent third-party calculation agent is almost always named whenever credit derivative contracts are used as part of structured finance vehicles. Rating agencies such as Moody's specify that a third-party be named to carry out this role. For some structures, a third-party is required only to confirm that a credit event has occurred. Subsequent market valuations are then carried out by the swap dealer. In this case, the third-party is known as a *verification agent* and not a calculation agent.

Upon the occurrence of a credit event, the calculation agent must determine the current market value of the reference obligation to determine if there has been a material decline in value. This is accomplished by obtaining third-party quotes from other dealers and taking the average of the bids, offers, or midmarket quotes. This is just one more check and balance to ensure that the calculation agent performs its determinations in an objective fashion.

CREDIT DEFAULT SWAPS

By far, the most popular type of credit derivative is the credit default swap. Not only is this form of credit derivative the most commonly used

EXHIBIT 4.1   Credit Default Swap

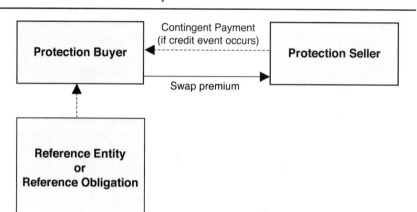

standalone product employed by asset managers and traders, but it is also used extensively in synthetic securitisations.

In a credit default swap, the documentation will identify the *reference entity* or the *reference obligation*. The reference entity is the issuer of the debt instrument. It could be a corporation, a sovereign government, or a bank loan. When there is a reference entity, the party to the credit default swap has an option to deliver one of the issuer's obligation subject to prespecified constraints. So, if the reference entity is Ford Motor Credit Company, any one of acceptable senior bond issues of that issuer, for example, can be delivered. In contrast, a *reference obligation* is a specific obligation for which protection is being sought. Credit default swaps can be classified as follows: single-name credit default swaps and basket swaps.

In a credit default swap, the protection buyer pays a fee, the *swap premium*, to the protection seller in return for the right to receive a payment conditional upon the default of the reference obligation or the reference entity. Collectively, the payments made by the protection buyer are called the *premium leg*; the contingent payment that might have to be made by the protection seller is called the *protection leg*.

In the documentation of a trade, a default is defined in terms of a *credit event*. Should a credit event occur, the protection seller must make a payment. This is shown in Exhibit 4.1.

Single-Name Credit Default Swaps

The interdealer market has evolved to where single-name credit default swaps are standardized. While trades between dealers have been standardized, there are occasional trades in the interdealer market where there is a customized agreement. In the interdealer market, the tenor, or length of time of a credit default swap, is typically five years. The tenor of a swap is referred to as the "scheduled term" because a credit event will result in a payment by the protection seller, resulting in the credit default swap being terminated. Asset managers can have a dealer create a tenor equal to the maturity of the reference obligation or be constructed for a shorter time period to match the manager's investment horizon.

The parties to the trade specify at the outset when the credit default swap will terminate. If no credit event has occurred by the maturity of the credit swap, then the swap terminates at the *scheduled termination date*—a date specified by the parties in the contract. However, the *termination date* under the contract is the earlier of the scheduled termination date or a date upon which a credit event occurs and notice is provided. Therefore, notice of a credit event terminates a credit default swap.

The standard contract for a single-name credit default swap in the interdealer market calls for a quarterly payment of the swap premium. Typically, the swap premium is paid in arrears. The swap premium payment for a quarter is computed as follows:

$$\text{Quarterly swap premium payment}$$
$$= \text{Notional amount} \times \text{Annual rate (in decimal)}$$
$$\times \frac{\text{Actual no. of days in quarter}}{360}$$

Basket Default Swaps

In a basket default swap, there is more than one reference entity. Typically, in a basket default swap, there are three to five reference entities. There are different types of basket default swap. They are classified as follows:

- *Nth* to default swaps
- Subordinate basket default swaps
- Senior basket default swaps

In an *Nth-to-default swap*, the protection seller makes a payment to the protection buyer only after there has been a default for the *Nth* reference entity and no payment for default of the first $(N-1)$ reference entities. Once there is a payout for the *Nth* reference entity, the credit default swap terminates. That is, if the other reference entities that have not defaulted subsequently do default, the protection seller does not make any payout.

For example, suppose that there are five reference entities. In a *first-to-default basket swap* a payout is triggered after there is a default for only one of the reference entities. There are no other payouts made by the protection seller even if the other four reference entities subsequently have a credit event. If a payout is triggered only after there is a second default from among the reference entities, the swap is referred to as a *second-to-default basket swap*. So, if there is only one reference entity for which there is a default over the tenor of the swap, the protection seller does not make any payment. If there is a default for a second reference entity while the swap is in effect, there is a payout by the protection seller and the swap terminates. The protection seller does not make any payment for a default that may occur for the three remaining reference entities.

In a *subordinate basket default swap* there is (1) a maximum payout for each defaulted reference entity and (2) a maximum aggregate payout over the tenor of the swap for the basket of reference entities. For example, assume there are five reference entities and that (1) the maximum payout is $10 million for a reference entity and (2) the maximum aggregate payout is $10 million. Also assume that defaults result in the following losses over the tenor of the swap:

Loss resulting from default of first reference entity   = $6 million
Loss result from default of second reference entity   = $10 million
Loss result from default of third reference entity   = $16 million
Loss result from default of fourth reference entity   = $12 million
Loss result from default of fifth reference entity   = $15 million

When there is a default for the first reference entity, there is a $6 million payout. The remaining amount that can be paid out on any subsequent defaults for the other four reference entities is $4 million. When there is a default for the second reference entity of $10 million, only $4 million will be paid out. At that point, the swap terminates.

In a *senior basket default swap* there is a maximum payout for each reference entity but the payout is not triggered until after a specified threshold is reached. To illustrate, again assume there are five reference entities and the maximum payout for an individual reference entity is $10 million. Also assume that there is no payout until the first $40 million of default losses (the threshold). Using the hypothetical losses above, the payout by the protection seller would be as follows. The losses for the first three defaults is $32 million. However, because the maximum loss for a reference entity, only $10 million of the $16 million is applied to the $40 million threshold. Consequently, after the third default, $26 million ($6 million + $10 million + $10 million) is applied toward the threshold. When the fourth reference entity defaults, only $10 million is applied to the $40 million threshold. At this point, $36 million is applied to the $40 million threshold. When the fifth reference entity defaults in our illustration, only $10 million is relevant since the maximum payout for a reference entity is $10 million. The first $4 million of the $10 million is applied to cover the threshold. Thus, there is a $6 million payout by the protection seller.

Comparison of Riskiness of Different Default Swap [2]

Let's compare the riskiness of each type of default swap from the perspective of the protection seller. This will also help reinforce an understanding of the different types of swaps. We will assume that for the basket default swaps there are the same five reference entities. Six credit default swaps, ranked by highest to lowest risk for the reasons to be explained, are:

1. *$50 million swap portfolio of five different single-name credit default swaps.* For each single-name credit default swap the notional amount is $10 million. Consequently, the aggregate payout if each reference entity pays out its full notional amount is $50 million.
2. *Subordinate basket default swap.* The maximum for each reference entity is $10 million with a maximum aggregate payout of $10 million.
3. *First-to-default swap*: The maximum payout is $10 million for the first reference entity to default.
4. *$10 million swap portfolio five different single-name credit default swaps.* As with the $50 million portfolio, there are five single-name credit default swaps but the notional amount per swap is $2 million instead of $10 million. The aggregate payout if all five reference entities pays out their notional amount is $10 million.
5. *Fifth-to-default swap.* The maximum payout for the fifth reference entity to default is $10 million.
6. *Senior basket default swap.* There is a maximum payout for each reference entity of $10 million but there is no payout until a threshold of $40 million is reached.

Consider first the $50 million swap portfolio comprising of five different single-name credit default swaps. If there are $10 million of losses for each of the references entities, the protection seller for the swap portfolio will have to pay out $50 million. In contrast, the other five

---

[2] The illustration and discussion in this section draws from "*Nth* to Default Swaps and Notes: All About Default Correlation," *CDO Insight*, May 30, 2003, UBS Warburg.

default swaps have a maximum payout of $10 million but their relative risks differ. So the $50 million portfolio swap is the riskiest.

All but the senior basket default swap requires the protection seller to make a pay out from the very first loss reference entity that defaults (subject to the maximum payout on the loss for the individual reference entities). Consequently, the senior basket default swap exposes the protection seller to the least risk.

Now let's look at the relative risk of the other four default swaps with a $10 million maximum payout: subordinate basket default swap, first-to-default swap, $10 million swap portfolio, and fifth-to-default swap. Consider first the subordinate basket swap versus first-to-default swap. Suppose that the loss for the first reference entity to default is $8 million. In the first-to-default swap, the payout required by the protection seller is $8 million and then the swap terminates (i.e., there are no further payouts that must be made by the protection seller). For the subordinate basket swap, after the payout of $8 million of the first reference entity to default, the swap does not terminate. Instead, the protection seller is still exposed to $2 million for any default loss resulting from the other four reference entities. Consequently, the subordinate basket default swap has greater risk than the first-to-default swap.

Now compare the first-to-default swap to the $10 million swap portfolio. The first-to-default swap has greater risk but the reason is not as simple as in the other comparisons made above. To see why the answer requires some analysis assume that the loss of all reference entities defaulting is 50% of the notional amount. This means that for the first reference entity to default, the default loss is 50% of the $10 million for the first-to-default swap, $5 million, and therefore the protection seller for this swap makes a payment of $5 million. No further payments are made. For the $10 million swap portfolio recall that each single-name credit default swap has a notional amount of $2 million. Consequently, the payout is only $1 million (the assumed 50% of notional amount) on the default and since there are five reference entities the total payout would be $5 million. For the protection seller of the $10 million swap portfolio, the only way that there will be a $5 million payout is if all five reference entities default.

The analysis of the relative risk therefore depends on (1) the specific pattern of defaults that is realized and (2) the percentage of the notional amount that results in a loss upon default. For example, suppose that for the first reference entity to default the default loss is 10% of the notional amount. For the first-to-default swap, the payout that must be made by the protection seller is $1 million (10% of $10 million) while only $0.2 million (10% of $2 million for a single-name credit default swap) is made by the protection seller for the $10 million swap portfolio. Should there be either (1) another reference entity that defaults with a default loss percentage that exceeds 40% of the notional amount ($0.8 million = 40% of $2 million) or (2) all four remaining reference entities default with an average default loss percentage that is greater than 10% of the notional amount ($0.2 million per single-name credit default swap and therefore $0.8 million for all four), then the protection seller of the $10 million swap portfolio would pay more than the first-to default protection seller. There are many scenarios that can be evaluated but the likely situations are such that the protection seller in the first-to-default swap would incur a greater payout than the protection seller in the $10 million swap portfolio.[3]

Finally, the $10 million swap portfolio has less risk than the fifth-to-default swap. The reason is that there is only one way the protection seller of the fifth-to-default swap will make a greater payment than the protection seller of the swap portfolio is (1) if all reference entities default and (2) the average percentage default loss for each reference entity is less than the default loss percentage of the last reference entity to default in the fifth-to-default swap.[4]

TOTAL RETURN SWAPS

A *total return swap* is a swap in which one party makes periodic floating rate payments to a counterparty in exchange for the total return realized on a reference asset (or underlying asset). The reference asset could be one of the following:

- Credit-risky bond
- A loan
- A reference portfolio consisting of bonds or loans
- An index representing a sector of the bond market

While these types of total return swaps are more aptly referred to as total return *credit* swaps, they are simply referred to as total return swaps. When the bond index consists of a credit risk sector of the bond market, the total return swap is referred to as a *total return bond index swap* or in this chapter as simply a *total return index swap*.

A total return of a reference asset includes all cash flows that flow from it as well as the capital appreciation or depreciation of the reference asset. The floating rate is a reference interest rate (typically LIBOR) plus or minus a spread. The party that agrees to make the floating rate payments and receive the total return is referred to as the *total return*

---

[3] "*Nth* to Default Swaps and Notes: All About Default Correlation," p. 6.
[4] "*Nth* to Default Swaps and Notes: All About Default Correlation," p. 6.

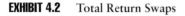

EXHIBIT 4.2 Total Return Swaps

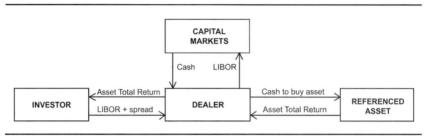

receiver or the *swap buyer*; the party that agrees to receive the floating rate payments and pay the total return is referred to as the *total return payer* or *swap buyer*. Total return swaps are viewed as unfunded credit derivatives, because there is no up-front payment required.

If the total return payer owns the underlying asset, it has transferred its economic exposure to the total return receiver. Effectively then, the total return payer has a neutral position which typically will earn LIBOR plus a spread. However, the total return payer has only transferred the economic exposure to the total return receiver; it has not transferred the actual asset. The total return payer must continue to fund the underlying asset at its marginal cost of borrowing or at the opportunity cost of investing elsewhere the capital tied up by the reference assets.

The total return payer may not initially own the reference asset before the swap is transacted. Instead, after the swap is negotiated, the total return payer will purchase the reference asset to hedge its obligations to pay the total return to the total return receiver. In order to purchase the reference asset, the total return payer must borrow capital. This borrowing cost is factored into the floating rate that the total return receiver must pay to the swap seller. Exhibit 4.2 diagrams how a total return credit swap works.

In the exhibit the dealer raises cash from the capital markets at a funding cost of straight LIBOR. The cash that flows into the dealer from the capital markets flows right out again to purchase the reference asset. The asset provides both interest income and capital gain or loss depending on its price fluctuation. This total return is passed through in its entirety to the investor according to the terms of the total return swap. The investor, in turn, pays the dealer LIBOR plus a spread to fulfill its obligations under the swap.

From the dealer's perspective, all of the cash flows in Exhibit 4.2 net out to the spread over LIBOR that the dealer receives from the investor. Therefore, the dealer's profit is the spread times the notional amount of the total return swap. Furthermore, the dealer is perfectly hedged. It has no risk position except for the counterparty risk of the investor. Effectively, the dealer receives a spread on a riskless position.

In fact, if the dealer already owns the reference asset on its balance sheet, the total return swap may be viewed as a form of credit protection that offers more risk reduction than a credit default swap. A credit default swap has only one purpose: To protect the investor against default risk. If the issuer of the reference asset defaults, the credit default swap provides a payment. However, if the underlying asset declines in value but no default occurs, the credit protection buyer receives no payment. In contrast, under a total return swap, the reference asset owned by the dealer is protected from declines in value. In effect, the investor acts as a "first loss" position for the dealer because any decline in value of the reference asset must be reimbursed by the investor.

The investor, on the other hand, receives the total return on a desired asset in a convenient format. There are several other benefits in using a total return swap as opposed to purchasing a reference asset itself. First, the total return receiver does not have to finance the purchase of the reference asset itself. Instead, the total return receiver pays a fee to the total return payer in return for receiving the total return on the reference asset. Second, the investor can take advantage of the dealer's "best execution" in acquiring the reference asset. Third, the total return receiver can achieve the same economic exposure to a diversified basket of assets in one swap transaction that would otherwise take several cash market transactions to achieve. In this way a total return swap is much more efficient means for transacting than via the cash market. Finally, an investor who wants to short a credit-risky asset such as a corporate bond will find it difficult to do so in the market. An investor can do so efficiently by using a total return swap. In this case the investor will use a total return swap in which it is a total return payer.

There is a drawback of a total return swap if an asset manager employs it to obtain credit protection. In a total return swap, the total return receiver is exposed to both credit risk and interest rate risk. For example, the credit spread can decline (resulting in a favorable price movement for the reference asset), but this gain can be offset by a rise in the level of interest rates.

Total Return Swap Compared to an Interest Rate Swap

It is worthwhile comparing market conventions for a total return swap to that of an interest rate swap. A plain vanilla or generic interest rate swap involves the exchange of a fixed rate payment for a floating rate payment. A *basis swap* is a special type of interest rate swap in which both parties exchange floating rate payments based on a different reference interest rate. For example, one party's payments may be based on 3-month LIBOR while the other parties payment is based on the 6-month Treasury rate. In a total return swap both parties pay a floating rate.

The quotation convention for a generic interest rate swap and a total return swap differ. In a generic interest rate swap, the fixed rate payer pays a spread to a Treasury security with the same tenor as the swap and the fixed rate receiver pays the reference rate flat (i.e., no spread or margin). The payment by the fixed rate receiver (i.e., floating rate payer) is referred to as the *funding leg*. For example, suppose an interest rate swap quote for a 5-year 3-month LIBOR-based swap is 50. This means that the fixed rate payer agrees to pay the 5-year Treasury rate that exists at the inception of the swap and the fixed rate receiver agrees to pay 3-month LIBOR. In contrast, the quote convention for a total return swap is that the total return receiver receives the total return flat and pays the total return payer a interest rate based on a reference rate (typically LIBOR) plus or minus a spread. That is, the funding leg (i.e., what the total return receiver pays includes a spread).

CHAPTER 5

True Sale versus Synthetics for MBS Transactions: The Investor Perspective

Iain Barbour
Global Head of Securitisation
Commerzbank Securities

Katie Hostalier
Head of Structured Finance Research
Commerzbank Securities

Jennifer Thym*

Many mortgage portfolios are now being securitised through synthetic as opposed to true sale structures. This change in structural mechanics creates new factors for investors to consider in their analysis—some beneficial, and others creating additional credit and legal considerations. This chapter compares and discusses these features.

---

* Jennifer Thym was a Senior Analyst at Commerzbank Securities when she coauthored this chapter.

STRENGTHS AND WEAKNESSES OF TRUE SALES VERSUS SYNTHETICS

The positive considerations associated with true sale and synthetic mortgage-backed security (MBS) transactions are summarised in the top panel of Exhibit 5.1. The key weaknesses of true sale and synthetic MBS are identified in the lower panel of Exhibit 5.1. To summarise, a synthetic MBS structure creates a clearly defined risk profile for investors which increasingly mirrors a true sale structure. However in syntheti-

EXHIBIT 5.1   True Sale versus Synthetic
(a) Strengths

True Sale	Synthetic
Transparency of risk assets	Customised risk transfer (e.g., principal only)
Originator bankruptcy- and event-risk remote	Credit events defined (Failure to pay and bankruptcy)
Excess cash flows may form incremental enhancement	Final realised loss structure—cash flow interruption minimised
Contingent servicer and other third parties contemplated at outset	Losses only allocated to compliant risk assets—burden of proof on the originator/servicer
Liquidity facilities cover temporary cash shortfalls or commingling risk	Security transfer and perfection risks minimised

(b) Weaknesses

True Sale	Synthetic
Security transfer and perfection risks	Weak-linkage to CLN collateral
Cash flow interruption possible despite liquidity facility	Correlation risk between the performance of the reference pool and the collateral
Weak-linkage to third parties (currency/interest rate swap counterparty, liquidity provider…)	Information on reference pool tends to be less transparent than in true sale transactions
Degree of correlation risk between third parties involved	Potential junior CDS counterparty risks
Losses are passed-through to investors as they occur	Lack of "excess cash flow" enhancement

Source: Commerzbank Securities.

cally creating a risk profile, incremental risks are created which need to be considered and mitigated. The most significant consideration, from a synthetic MBS securitisation perspective, is the weak linkage (and associated correlation risk) between the primary risk assets and the collateral for the *credit-linked note* (CLN) issued. This risk, as with others created as a direct consequence of synthetic features, is increasingly mitigated through various structural features.

We therefore believe that synthetic MBS structures are becoming increasingly robust from an investor perspective; however for some older synthetic transactions, significant, noncore risks reside within the structures—many of which are not mitigated through structural features. Thus investors in more recent synthetic MBS structures are likely to enjoy increasingly more robust structural features relative to true sale structures.

One key consideration are the rating stability of "sliver" tranches. "Sliver" tranches are usually junior triple-A rated tranches, which will carry higher loss severity in the event that a loss is allocated at the triple-A level. Due to Moody's expected loss approach to rating, we expect that some existing sliver tranches of older revolving synthetic MBS transactions may be subject to marginal downgrade risk even if the reference risks remain stable. We do not expect this consideration to affect Standard & Poor's and Fitch ratings.

GENERIC STRUCTURAL COMPARISON

Exhibits 5.2 and 5.3 summarise, for the same pool of loans (the primary risk assets), a funded true sale and funded synthetic MBS securitisation structure. Whilst variations on both structures exist, these generic true sale and synthetic MBS structures serve to facilitate the comparison, from an investor perspective, of the relative strengths and considerations of each.

True sale structures typically involve the transfer of risk assets from an originator to a special purpose vehicle (SPV) which finances the risk asset purchase through the issue of tranched securities to investors. The securities are secured on the primary risk assets (in this instance loans secured by mortgages over real estate assets) purchased and the cash (or other receivable) flows derived from these risk assets. The cash flows generated by the primary risk assets are used to pay coupons and principal on the securities, as well as the costs of operating the SPV (which are likely to include servicing fees). Various third parties are also normally involved to ensure that extraneous risks are minimised, creating some linkage within the structure to the credit strength of these parties.

EXHIBIT 5.2   True Sale MBS Generic Structure

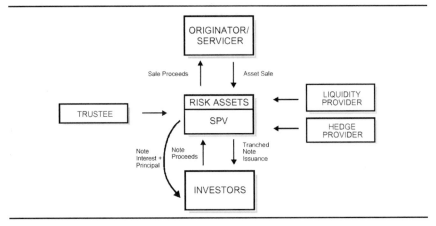

Source: Commerzbank Securities.

EXHIBIT 5.3   Synthetic MBS Generic Structure

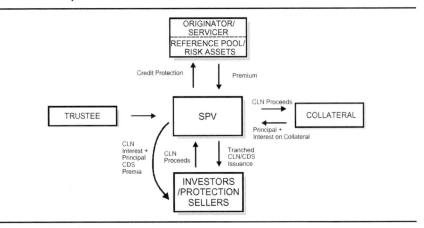

Source: Commerzbank Securities.

Synthetic MBS structures typically involve an SPV issuing securities (CLN) whose credit performance is linked to the performance of a reference pool of primary risk assets (in this instance loans secured by mortgages over real estate assets). Proceeds of the CLN are invested in eligible assets (note that these assets are not the primary risk asset, but become, in essence, a secondary risk asset) and the cash flows derived from these (secondary risk) assets, supplemented by a fee from the primary risk asset originator, are used to pay the coupons, principal, and costs of the CLN and the SPV. The primary risk assets are serviced, typically, by the same entity, which would service them had they not been securitised. This is typically also the case for true sale MBS.

The credit risk of the CLN is effectively weak-linked to the aggregated performance risk for the relevant tranche of risk of the reference pool and the risk profile of the secondary risk assets (or collateral). It is therefore critical for investors to understand not only the immediately apparent aspects of the weak linkage (i.e., which rating is the lower), but also the correlation risks between the risk assets and the collateral.

Some synthetic MBS structures employ credit default swaps (CDS) to transfer some or all of the risk. CDS effectively transfer the risk by replacing the defined credit risk of the risk assets (at the relevant tranche risk level) with the performance risk of the CDS counterparty. This performance risk is likely to entail credit risk which may or may not be correlated with the risk of the risk assets. From an investor perspective however, the risk profile is consistent between a structure employing CLN or CDS; however, if the CDS is at a junior or mezzanine tranche level, the performance risk of the CDS counterparty can become a factor for more senior CLN investors, as failure to perform by the CDS counterparty may, depending upon the legal documentation, create some incremental risk for other investors. Typically, however, such performance risks are written out of CLN documentation; however this example highlights the importance for investors in synthetic (and true sale) structures of understanding documentary risks.

Repayments and prepayments on the risk assets typically cause, either directly in a true sale or indirectly in a synthetic transaction, the bonds or CLN to amortise. Amortisation is typically sequential (i.e., starting with the most senior tranche and ending with the most junior tranche), although various alternative cash flow models can be employed in either structure (for example, fast pay, slow pay, and pro rata to name but two options).

When losses are incurred in the underlying primary risk assets, these will ultimately be passed onto investors according to the specific terms of the structure. Thus for a true sale structure, permanent cash flow interruption will result in a loss being allocated to the most junior investors. There may also be some immediate cash flow interruption whilst security recovery efforts are ongoing unless appropriate liquidity facilities are provided within the structure.

However, for synthetic MBS structures, a loss may only generally be applied to the most junior CLN/CDS outstanding once all recovery efforts have been completed and the defaulted primary risk asset become a realised loss. Thus cash flows are preserved for all investors for as long as possible.

KEY RISK CHARACTERISTICS AND FEATURES COMPARED

Both a synthetic and a true sale MBS structure aim to achieve several common objectives. These include the transfer of credit risk from one or more parties to one or more third parties, typically via a special purpose vehicle (SPV). However there are numerous considerations which should be highlighted when investing in synthetic MBS structures relative to true sale structures—some positive and some negative.

Originator Related Risks

Synthetic MBS structures do not entail the "sale" or transfer of the risk assets to the SPV, removing most risks associated with the sale of assets to be used as security, including perfection and preference risks, and costs associated with the transfer of such assets.

To the extent that the originator becomes insolvent, this is likely to result in the termination of a synthetic MBS structure. Such a termination will typically result in an estimated loss calculation (whereby an expected loss is assessed on loans which are not performing, but equally may not have yet become a credit event) resulting in the application of resultant estimated losses to the most junior notes then outstanding.[1] The secondary risk assets are then typically cancelled (as their terms are usually defined as being identical to the terms of the CLN), with the consequential proceeds used to redeem the CLN outstanding.

Comingling risks are an important factor for true sale investors. To the extent that cash flows are collected by the originator as part of their normal receivable collections, they are frequently "comingled" with other, nonsecuritised, assets. To the extent that such assets are not ring fenced legally, this may create some residual risk to the originator/servicer. This risk does not arise within synthetic MBS securitisations.

Set-off risks are also a consideration, but in this instance for both true sale and synthetics—but for different reasons. In a true sale, the risk that any collateral available to the SPV may be used by the originator to set-off other exposures must be considered; however for synthetic MBS structures, it is important to ensure that the structure uses all available collateral to set-off exposures prior to the allocation of any realised losses.

Liquidity Risks

Temporary cash flow shortfalls rarely create incremental risk for investors in synthetic MBS transactions as only realised losses are typically

---

[1] Note that estimated losses do not typically benefit from synthetic excess spread.

transferred. However shortfalls within true sale structures may lead to immediate cash flow interruption for investors, although liquidity facilities may in turn insulate investors from such risks. Liquidity facility providers, in such circumstances, create an element of weak-linkage for true sale structure investors.

When a risk asset ceases to perform this may lead to cash flow interruption and ultimately a loss being assigned to investors. Losses are typically assigned to the most junior tranche of risk outstanding (although waterfall structures may dictate alternative mechanisms—for example interest costs may be subject to different cash flow priorities relative to principal cash flows). In a true sale structure, payment interruption is typically "bridged" by a liquidity provider, who then ranks senior to bondholders if the relevant risk assets ultimately give rise to a loss. This creates rating linkage risk relative to the liquidity provider who has a potential performance obligation in order to ensure "timely payment of interest and principal" to investors. Losses within a true sale structure arise from many causes—and are not limited to defined credit events, as they are in most synthetic MBS structures.

In the event of originator insolvency, cash flows and security realisation processes may also suffer some interruption due to the temporary (or indeed permanent in some instances) incapacity of the originator.

For the synthetic MBS structure the process is inherently different. Losses are usually applied to investors (again in reverse sequential order) once they become "realised." Thus investors typically continue to receive the payment of principal and interest throughout the period between the event which triggers the realised loss (usually a credit event) and the event translating into a realised loss. This removes the need for a liquidity provider.

In a true sale MBS structure, cash flows derived from the risk assets and cash flows paid to investors are usually "aligned" through the SPV entering into a series of swap arrangements with third parties. These will typically entail coupons (or interest flows) on the assets being translated into equivalent coupons or interest rates (e.g., fixed or floating rate) as on the notes. Additionally, cross-currency risks are absorbed under swap arrangements. Both of these create third party rating linkage for the true sale structure which is not typically relevant to a synthetic arrangement.

Customised Risk Transfer

Synthetic MBS structures transfer "defined" credit risks from one party to another, whereas true sale structures typically transfer the entire credit risk from one party to another. This may result in either marginally more or, more frequently, marginally less credit risk being transferred.

For example, if a borrower on a loan agreement fails to meet a scheduled repayment this may give rise to a loss for the lender. In a true sale structure any permanent cash flow shortfall will result in a loss to the lender and therefore to the most junior ranking investor. In a synthetic MBS structure, however, the mere act of failing to pay may result in a loss passing through to investors. Thus the results should be similar. For residential MBS transactions this is the case, where failure to pay of the borrower (typically an individual) causes almost all defaults.

For commercial MBS, however, a true sale structure may contain other potential causes of cash flow shortfalls. These other causes of default will typically relate to covenant breaches or issues surrounding the real estate title. Such risks are typically not transferred through synthetic MBS structures under which losses can only pass to investors if either a failure to pay or bankruptcy occurs. Synthetic MBS structures can therefore customise the risks to be transferred. In effect, specific risks may be "stripped out" of the structure, enabling only predefined risks to be passed to investors.

Secondary Risks

In a synthetic MBS structure, proceeds of the CLN issued are typically invested in qualifying collateral. This collateral is rated at a level which is sufficient to initially sustain the credit ratings of the CLN at the level justified by the relevant risk profile of the tranche of risk being transferred. However weak-linkage is created. This means that the risk profile of the CLN is not only linked to the relevant tranche of risk, but also to the risk profile of the collateral.

In a true sale structure other forms of secondary risks are incurred. These include swap counterparty and liquidity provider risks. Again, downgrades of the swap and liquidity providers may result in downgrades of the structured securities unless provisions are made to protect investors.

To the extent that correlation exists between the two core risks, then this may cause the relevant CLN to be rated lower then either the rating of the tranche or the rating of the collateral.

It is therefore possible for a specific synthetic tranche to carry a rating below the rating level assigned to that tranche with respect to the primary or secondary risk assets. This is more likely to occur with respect to ratings assigned by Moody's due to their expected loss approach to rating, and the downgrade risk is most acute for tranches where the secondary risk asset and the standalone, primary risk asset CLN ratings are the same, and where the secondary risk asset issuer's business is concentrated in the same assets as the primary risk assets.

There are various options available to insulate investors from secondary risks. These typically include:

- Substitution options, whereby the original secondary risk assets may be substituted if a rating action affecting the secondary risk assets will result in a downgrade of the CLN.
- Top-up provisions, whereby supplementary secondary (or indeed tertiary) risk assets are employed to over-collateralise the initial secondary collateral such that a downgrade of the CLN does not result from a downgrade of the secondary risk assets.
- Par value guarantees, whereby a suitably rated third-party guarantees to repurchase the secondary risk assets at par.
- Replacement swap or liquidity providers, whereby triggers are implemented causing an alternative, suitably rated provider to be found. Alternatively, exposures can be collateralised with appropriately rated collateral.

Loss Severity

When customising the risk to be transferred, probability of default is only one element of the calculation. Severity of loss is also fundamental, and various factors will clearly differentiate true sale and synthetics in this regard.

If an event occurs which results in a potential loss to investors, under a true sale structure any principal outstanding, coupled with interest accruing, and recovery costs will all need to be recovered from any security proceeds forthcoming. Thus the structure is sensitive to the speed of recovery, the prevailing interest rate and the costs incurred, some of which may be beyond the immediate control of the servicer (for example, court imposed costs and taxes).

For a synthetic MBS structure, however, an originator has the opportunity to tailor the risk protection purchased. The protection purchased may be solely on the principal outstanding or may extend to include interest costs (potentially capped) and defined recovery costs.

The best way to understand the loss severity dynamics is to use a worked example.

In our worked example Bank A lends Borrower B a loan in the amount of €80,000 that is secured by a mortgage on a property with an appraised value of €100,000. The origination date *loan-to-appraised value* (LTAV) ratio is 80%. The loan bears interest at a rate of 6% and defaults immediately. Bank A performs the full work-out process and achieves a foreclosure sale price of €85,000 for the property. The process has taken two years, and Bank A has incurred 5% external costs and 1% internal costs (both based upon the recovery value of the property). We assume that the originator has six structural alternatives when securitising their portfolio, and these can be defined as shown in Exhibit 5.4.

EXHIBIT 5.4   Loss Severity Analysis—Scenario Definition

Scenarios	Realised loss components
Scenario One	Synthetic—Principal loss only
Scenario Two	Synthetic—Principal loss and interest loss
Scenario Three	Synthetic—Principal loss, interest loss capped at 4% per annum, and external enforcement costs
Scenario Four	Synthetic—Principal loss, interest loss, and external enforcement costs
Scenario Five	Synthetic—Principal loss, interest loss, external enforcement costs and internal enforcement costs
Scenario Six	True Sale—Principal loss, interest loss, external enforcement costs and internal enforcement costs

Source: Commerzbank Securities.

We assume that in all circumstances the entire loan amount is securitised. The loss severity calculations provide vastly different results and these are illustrated in Exhibit 5.5.

The results become even more divergent if the market value decline increases from the 15% assumed, or equally if the prevailing interest rate increases significantly. It is also worth noting that where structures do not cap interest costs (Scenarios Two, Four, Five and Six in our example) the rating agencies will typically employ significantly higher rates of interest when sizing their credit enhancement requirements. Thus, if investors expect prevailing rates to remain consistently low, then the uncapped interest costs scenarios may prove more robust than those with capped interest costs which will not benefit from incremental enhancement under sustained low interest rate environments.

Alignment of Investor and Originator Interests

In a true sale MBS structure, the entire net cash flow from the risk assets is typically available to meet noteholder obligations. This may create "excess spread" availability for investors, creating additional credit enhancement. In a synthetic MBS structure, excess spread is typically retained by the originator such that credit enhancement is defined at the outset. Furthermore, servicing fees can be subordinated to other noteholder payments, or trigger arrangements put in place in both structure types. To the extent that excess spread (or subordinated servicing fees) is employed, this can successfully align the interests of the originator and investors.

A true sale structure usually employs the entire gross revenues from the loans to meet noteholder obligations and servicing fees (and any

EXHIBIT 5.5 Loss Severity Analysis—Worked Examples

	Scenario One	Scenario Two	Scenario Three	Scenario Four	Scenario Five	Scenario Six
Recovery amount	€85,000	€85,000	€85,000	€85,000	€85,000	€85,000
Principal outstanding	€(80,000)	€(80,000)	€(80,000)	€(80,000)	€(80,000)	€(80,000)
Interest accrual	€0	€(9,600)	€(6,400)	€(9,600)	€(9,600)	€(9,600)
External enforcement costs	€0	€0	€(4,250)	€(4,250)	€(4,250)	€(4,250)
Internal enforcement costs	€0	€0	€0	€0	€(850)	€(850)
Total surplus/(loss)	€5,000	€(4,600)	€(5,650)	€(8,850)	€(9,700)	€9,700
Loss Severity	0.00%	5.75%	7.06%	11.06%	12.13%	12.13%

Source: Commerzbank Securities.

other expenses). Any remaining cash flows are used to create additional reserves to a level sufficient to maintain ratings prior to any distributions to the most junior investors and, potentially, to the originator. Furthermore, triggers are likely to be employed to divert cash flows between investors according to the performance of the transaction.

In a synthetic MBS structure, the cash flows from the risk assets are not directly relevant to the cash flows on the CLN (unless there are payment shortfalls relative to contractual obligations). Therefore, the originator is liable for the guarantee (or credit default protection) payment, but this rarely creates any incremental credit enhancement (although the first synthetic excess spread structures have now been created).

In a true sale structure, a loss in the risk asset(s) will be a loss for investors (in the absence of fraud or other exceptional circumstances, where alternative remedies may exist).

For synthetic MBS structures, a burden of proof exists on the originator/seller and/or the servicer of the assets. The servicer must provide evidence that the realised loss is compliant with the terms and conditions of the relevant risk transfer mechanism. Such conditions are likely to include compliance in all material respects with asset eligibility and servicing criteria.

Thus synthetic MBS may well show some defaulted primary risk assets, which never become eligible for a loss allocation to investors due to their material noncompliance with the original loan eligibility criteria or, equally, if the servicing standards (or lack thereof) are deemed to have contributed materially to the loss allocation.

Operational Risks

Wherever an SPV is employed, the SPV administration must be looked after by appropriate personnel. For both true sale and synthetic MBS structures, these responsibilities have much in common. A servicer will typically manage the primary risk assets day to day; the servicer may or may not be the same party as the originator/seller of the assets. The servicer must ensure that the servicing standards defined in the transaction documentation are adhered to, and must also remain compliant with certain specific criteria relating to their eligibility to fulfil the servicing role. Clearly, therefore, servicer quality is fundamental to risk assessment within a transaction. For synthetic transactions, some servicer risk is removed from the transaction as, if the asset eligibility criteria are not adhered to, then the servicer will typically be unable to make a claim under the structure for a realised loss.

SPVs are typically administered by a trustee. The trustee will work to preserve the interests of investors through the life of the transaction.

Inherently the precise responsibilities differ from transaction to transaction; however if we consider our two generic structures, the core roles become clear. In the true sale structure the core responsibilities can be summarised as follows:

- Ensuring that any reserve funds are maintained by appropriate institutions and to their required levels.
- Ensuring that the key transaction parties continue to meet the criteria for their continued appointment.

For a synthetic MBS structure, the responsibilities usually include all of the true sale responsibilities, plus:

- Ensuring the collateral meets eligibility criteria, as well as being held with an appropriate third party (although these responsibilities may be assigned to a specialist collateral trustee);
- Ensuring that claims under any credit default swap or loss guarantee are compliant with the necessary criteria.

Fundamentally therefore, the trustee will ensure that the SPV is operated in line with criteria established typically at the outset of a transaction. To some extent, their responsibilities overlap with those of the servicer, although we would characterise their role in this relationship as being more supervisory.

Disclosure

When it comes to primary risk asset disclosure, a synthetic MBS structure may be more restrictive. This is because the risk assets are not transferred to the SPV. As such the SPV does not necessarily know the specific details of the primary risk assets purchased and may therefore be restricted in its ability to further transfer specific information concerning the primary risk assets when transferring the risk into the capital markets. For this reason, the extent and quality of disclosure for synthetic MBS are a function of the originator's ability and willingness to disclose.

Leverage Effects

One additional factor which merits discussion in this paper as it relates to all structures is the leverage effect for transactions featuring junior tranches of a specific rating class. For example, where a triple-A tranche is subdivided into two (or more) tranches, where one tranche ranks senior to the other in terms of loss allocation. In these circumstances, the junior tranche of the two triple-A tranches described in this example will exhibit greater loss severity than the more senior tranche(s) and the rating of such junior tranches will therefore be more sensitive to negative credit news than the more senior tranche(s). These circumstances came to the fore initially when cash investors were considering the rating sustainability of junior triple-A tranches, where the senior risk is transferred through senior credit default swaps. Whilst such examples are highly relevant when examining partially or fully funded synthetic MBS structures, they are not unique to synthetics. Indeed many true sale structures feature similar cash flow structures. It is therefore critical in all structured products to evaluate the priorities of payments both pre- and post enforcement of the collateral.

Additional Legal Considerations

The risk that a synthetic MBS structure could be recharacterised as an insurance contract should be considered by investors, as such recharacterisation may make the contracts unenforceable.

SUMMARY

Exhibit 5.6 summarises the key features of true sale and synthetic MBS structures.

EXHIBIT 5.6 True Sale and Synthetic MBS Structural Features Compared—A Quick Comparison

Consideration	Reason	True Sale MBS	Synthetic MBS
Ownership of the securitised assets	Understanding the title to the securitised assets is fundamental to taking effective security interest.	Title is legally transferred to the SPV creating potential perfection risk. However, the SPV owns the primary risk assets, and as such the investors receive a legal interest in the primary risk assets according to the structure created.	The primary risk assets are never transferred creating no transfer risks. Equally ownership of the primary risk assets is usually irrelevant as the owner has purchased protection and thus is focused more on the servicer of the assets rather than their owner. The CLN proceeds are invested in secondary risk assets (eligible collateral) and the ownership of these secondary risk assets must be understood.
Servicing of the assets	The servicer is responsible for the day-to-day management of the assets securitised—their role is therefore critical to the performance of the assets.	The servicer will follow the prescribed procedures for servicing the primary risk asset. However, the remedy for under-performance will be replacement of the servicer in parallel with under-performance of the assets. A loss is a loss in this structure, however small, and will pass-through to investors.	The servicer remains the same as though the primary risk assets had not been securitised; under-performance may result in replacement of the servicer, and under-performance of the primary risk assets. It is most likely, however, to result in the failure of some credit protection claims as the servicer/protection buyer must prove that the claim is valid.
Losses	Understanding what actually constitutes a loss is critical	A loss incurred in the primary risk asset pool will constitute a loss for the issuer, and as such a loss for investors according to the waterfall structure. Thus the rating linkage for the transaction is primarily to the quality of the primary risk assets.	A loss incurred in the primary risk asset pool will translate into a loss for investors to the extent that it is caused by the occurrence of a defined event (typically a credit event). A loss incurred in the secondary risk asset will typically result in a loss to investors. Thus a synthetic MBS structure creates dual rating linkage to the primary and secondary risk assets.
Loss severity	Loss severity is sensitive to recovery rates on any security held on the underlying risk asset, as well as the period to recovery, together with interest and recovery costs accrued.	The issuer will pass on, typically, any ultimate losses (including security recovery costs) to investors. The whole structure also typically benefits from excess spread available on the assets to meet cash flow shortfalls prior to losses being incurred by investors.	Losses are defined, and may include principal, interest and security recovery costs (or combinations of these); furthermore recoveries may be defined. As such a synthetic MBS structure may not be sensitive to the period to recovery (if interest costs are not included in the protection purchased). Excess spread is typically not passed through to investors.

EXHIBIT 5.6 (Continued)

Consideration	Reason	True Sale MBS	Synthetic MBS
Liquidity	Timely payment of principal and interest is essential.	A liquidity facility is typically provided by a suitably rated bank to ensure temporary cash flow shortfalls do not result in payment interruptions to investors. The liquidity facility provider risk creates some weak-linkage in the structure. At some stage the liquidity facility may not be used to meet interest and principal payment shortfalls and as such bondholders may suffer some payment interruption even before the ultimate loss is finally determined.	As the risk is transferred synthetically, liquidity facilities are not required; interest and principal payments continue to be met on the CLN until an actual loss occurs.
Correlation risk	The risk profile of the primary risk assets and the risk profile of the secondary risk assets (or other third party service/hedge providers) may be correlated creating increased risk	The notes issued will represent the relevant tranche risk profile resulting from the primary risk asset quality and structural features. There may be some correlation risk issues to consider depending on the involvement of third parties in the transaction.	To the extent that the risk profile of the primary risk asset and the secondary risk asset coupled with any third parties on whom cash flows are dependent are correlated, this may result in the risk profile of the CLN/CDS being lower than the risk profile of the relevant risk tranche were the structure to be a true sale structure.
Interest rate and currency risks	The interest rate and currency profile of the collateral may not match the interest rate and currency profile of the notes issued creating potential cash flow mismatches.	Interest rate and currency risks are typically hedged through swap arrangements between the issuer and suitably rated counterparty. The structure may therefore become weak-linked to the swap provider(s).	Depending on the protection purchased, these risks may not need to be hedged from a CLN/CDS investor perspective.

Source: Commerzbank Securities.

CHAPTER 6

A Framework for Evaluating a Cash ("True Sale") versus Synthetic Securitisation

Iain Barbour
Global Head of Securitisation
Commerzbank Securities

Katie Hostalier
Head of Structured Finance Research
Commerzbank Securities

The key metrics for evaluating the success of a securitisation transaction present often-conflicting benchmarks. For the decision makers, achieving internal consensus is essential—a consensus that must survive for the many months which inevitably pass from when the transaction is conceived until it is closed. Equally, in creating a harmonious relationship with investors, the originator must articulate its key objectives and build a depth of understanding as to its potential intentions as the transaction moves through its life.

In this chapter we set forth a quantitative model which enables financial institution issuers, as well as investors, to evaluate the relative benefits of various securitisation solutions for risk transfer, specifically focusing on return on equity, return on assets, and business capacity. In our analysis, we compare three securitisation structures and the impact they can make over a similar 6-year period on a hypothetical bank's balance sheet and results. The three generic structures considered are as follows:

- True sale securitisation.
- Partially funded, synthetic securitisation.
- Partially funded, synthetic securitisation involving KfW as an intermediary (i.e., a PROMISE or PROVIDE structure).

We compare the results achieved through the three structures with a base case scenario. This assumes more traditional balance sheet growth supported by new capital generation.

For the purposes of this chapter, we will focus on financing and capital management securitisation transactions and, specifically, on those transactions supported by mortgage (both commercial and residential) and commercial loan transactions for bank originators.

BASE CASE ASSUMPTIONS

For the purposes of the analysis presented in this chapter, we have created a hypothetical bank originator of residential mortgage assets. The model can be applied for most asset classes, although the impact of the various scenarios on some asset classes may be greater than for the worked example employed in this research paper. We assume the opening balance sheet for our hypothetical bank as shown in Exhibit 6.1.

EXHIBIT 6.1   Initial Bank Balance Sheet (Base Case)

Liabilities & Equity	
Tier one	97,500,000
Tier two	135,000,000
Mortgage Pfandbriefe	2,148,750,000
Public sector Pfandbriefe	Nil
MTN Funding	716,250,000
Aggregate	3,097,500,000

Assets	
Mortgage loans	3,000,000,000
Government securities	97,500,000
Aggregate	3,097,500,000

Note: All number in EUR; MTN = Medium Term Note.
Source: Commerzbank Securities.

The core initial assumption is that our hypothetical originating mortgage bank has a target tier one capital ratio of 6.5%, and that all regulatory capital treatment follows Basel 1 guidelines for the period under review. Whilst we would much like to analyse the implications of various securitisation mechanisms under Basel 2, the ongoing uncertainty over the Basel 2 accord vis-à-vis securitisation, limits the value of such analysis for the time being. We assume that tier one capital is invested in "risk-free" securities (in this instance, government bonds), with the risk assets financed using medium term notes (23.875% of the risk asset notional balance at a rate of 25 basis points per annum over the reference rate), mortgage Pfandbriefe (71.625% at a rate of 12 basis points per annum) and tier two capital (4.5% at a rate of 100 basis points per annum).

On the profit and loss account, we assume that the loans generate 75 basis points in revenues over a reference rate. The weighted average annual cost of funding of these loans is assumed to be 19.1 basis points (using the blend of finance discussed above). In addition, we assume servicing (annual) and origination (up-front) costs of 12.5 basis points each, and an annual loss reserve accrual of 10 basis points. Exhibit 6.2 illustrates the hypothetical profit and loss account.

Traditionally, balance sheet growth has been achieved through the reinvestment of retained equity and the origination of new equity to support appropriately leveraged asset investments. Thus, as the asset side of the balance sheet increases, so does the capital base required to support it. The assets are increased, in our example, by the same proportion as would be achievable via a true sale securitisation. If we also compare the return on equity and asset evolution of the traditional balance-sheet growth model, the relatively slow impact of this growth is evident. This is illustrated in Exhibits 6.3 and 6.4, respectively.

We make various generic assumptions for each structural scenario analysis, enabling broad comparisons. These are as follows:

EXHIBIT 6.2   Initial Profit and Loss Account (Year One, Base Case)

Profit and Loss Position	EUR	Bp per Annum
Weighted Income on loans	22,500,000	75.0
Weighted Loss expectation	(3,000,000)	(10.0)
Weighted Servicing costs	(3,750,000)	(12.5)
Weighted Origination costs	(3,750,000)	(12.5)
Weighted Liability costs	(5,719,125)	(19.1)
Gross income on loans after costs	6,280,875	20.9

Note: Servicing costs are assumed to fall to 7.5 bp per annum for incremental loans originated.
Source: Commerzbank Securities.

EXHIBIT 6.3   Traditional Balance Sheet Growth (Base Case)—Without Securitisation

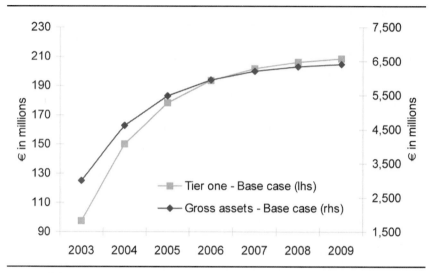

Note: All figures in EUR millions; lhs = left hand side; rhs = right hand side.
Source: Commerzbank Securities.

EXHIBIT 6.4   Return on Equity (Pretax) and Asset Under Traditional Balance Sheet Growth Model (Base Case)

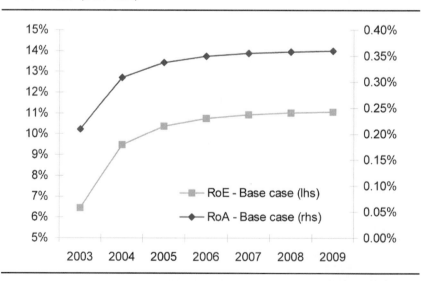

Note: RoE = Return on Equity; RoA = Return on Assets (on balance sheet).
Source: Commerzbank Securities.

- All "available" risk assets are securitised every year (i.e., in year one, €3 billion risk assets are securitised).
- The first loss (reserve fund) position in every securitisation is retained, with one-for-one tier one capital assigned notionally against this position.
- The difference between the aggregate retained first loss positions in the securitisations, and the starting tier one capital position is invested in similar risk assets as efficiently as possible, but either way within 12 months; these assets are in turn securitised the following year.
- All revenue and cost assumptions are the same for newly originated assets as for the original assets; the exception to this is assumed to be servicing costs, where some economies of scale are to be enjoyed—we assume therefore that servicing costs for new assets are 7.5 basis points per annum (as opposed to 12.5 basis points on the original assets).
- The securitisation structure is assumed to be generic in all three scenarios—that is, the credit enhancement required for each rating class is assumed to be constant, and a sequential pay structure employed, with the Class A1 ranking senior to the Class A2 from a loss allocation and repayment flow perspective. Exhibit 6.5 highlights the credit enhancement structure assumed, and the relative funding/protection cost assumptions.
- €1.2 million of up-front expenses are incurred on each securitisation structure plus an additional amount for underwriting, distribution and structuring; these are accrued annually through the expected life of each securitisation. An additional amount is accrued annually to reflect ongoing transaction costs.
- Additionally we assume that at least one securitisation occurs annually, with no minimum volume required for this to become economical.

TRUE SALE SECURITISATION

In the true sale securitisation scenario we assume that all available risk assets at the start of every year are sold to a special purpose vehicle (SPV), which in turn funds the purchase through a securitisation. Aggregate tier one capital is not increased from year to year, but all "released" tier one capital resulting from the securitisations is reinvested in new, similar risk assets.

The "blend" of finance between senior unsecured and senior secured is assumed to remain constant, although the tier-two component increases in percentage terms; this is due to assumed difficulties in repatriating tier two capital due to regulations.

EXHIBIT 6.5 Securitisation Credit Enhancement Structure and Weighted Average Cost Assumptions

Class	Rating	Percentage of total	Amount (EUR)	Cost 1	Cost 2	WA Cost 1	WA Cost 2
Class A1 Notes/Senior CDS	AAA	90.00%	900,000,000	0.065%	0.250%	0.0585%	0.2250%
Class A2 Notes #	AAA	4.00%	40,000,000	0.450%	0.450%	0.0180%	0.0180%
Class B Notes	AA	1.50%	15,000,000	0.550%	0.550%	0.0083%	0.0083%
Class C Notes	A	1.50%	15,000,000	0.900%	0.900%	0.0135%	0.0135%
Class D Notes	BBB	1.50%	15,000,000	1.800%	1.800%	0.0270%	0.0270%
Reserve fund	NR	1.50%	15,000,000				
Aggregate	0	100.00%	1,000,000,000			0.1253%	0.2918%

Note: Cost scenario 1 assumes partially funded synthetic structure; Cost scenario 2 assumes fully funded true sale structure; Class A2 notes # are assumed to be junior from both a loss allocation and a repayment perspective to the Class A1 tranche.
Source: Commerzbank Securities.

Exhibit 6.6 illustrates the pro forma balance sheet of our hypothetical bank, coupled with some ratio analysis.

From Exhibit 6.6 it is evident that the aggregate assets under management rise, whilst the actual balance sheet size falls (assuming appropriate accounting treatment). The benefits are even more apparent when the income and expense statement is examined in Exhibit 6.7.

When viewed graphically (see Exhibits 6.8 and 6.9), and when compared to our base case traditional balance sheet growth scenario, the value achieved through applying true sale securitisation is evident.

Whilst the return on assets is clearly exaggerated by the dramatic decline in on-balance-sheet assets, the impact on the bank's return on equity is significant over the six-year period.

PARTIALLY FUNDED, SYNTHETIC SECURITISATION

In the partially funded synthetic securitisation scenario, we assume that protection is purchased on all available risk assets (as at the start of every year) from a special purpose vehicle (SPV). This SPV then protects its position by issuing credit-linked notes and through entering into a senior credit default swap with a 20% risk-weighted counterparty. Aggregate tier one capital is not increased from year to year, but all "released" tier one capital resulting from the securitisations is reinvested in new, similar risk assets.

Exhibit 6.10 illustrates the pro forma balance sheet of our hypothetical bank, coupled with some ratio analysis. The exhibit illustrates that whilst the aggregate balance sheet continues to rise under a synthetic securitisation, the actual weighted risk assets declines. The benefits are however less dramatic than for the true sale structure already discussed, primarily due to the regulatory capital the originator is required to maintain against the senior credit default swap (CDS) counterparty exposure. This risk-weighted asset creates a drain on the available leverage within the structure.

Exhibit 6.11 illustrates the profit and loss perspective for a synthetic, partially funded structure. The relative lack of growth achieved through this structure is reflected in the marginal increase in return on equity. Clearly the lack of leverage opportunity has a dramatic effect due to the capital allocation to the senior CDS counterparty. When viewed graphically (Exhibits 6.12 and 6.13), and when compared to our base case traditional balance-sheet growth scenario, the marginal value achieved through applying partially funded, synthetic securitisation, under our assumptions, is apparent.

EXHIBIT 6.6 True Sale Securitisation—On- and Off-Balance Sheet Growth

	2003	2004	2005	2006	2007	2008
Residential mortgage loans	3,000,000,000	1,615,384,615	869,822,485	468,365,954	252,197,052	135,798,413
Equity retained in structures	0	45,000,000	69,230,769	82,278,107	89,303,596	93,086,552
Government securities	97,500,000	97,500,000	97,500,000	97,500,000	97,500,000	97,500,000
Aggregate assets	3,097,500,000	1,757,884,615	1,036,553,254	648,144,060	439,000,648	326,384,964
Tier one	97,500,000	97,500,000	97,500,000	97,500,000	97,500,000	97,500,000
Tier two	135,000,000	135,000,000	135,000,000	135,000,000	135,000,000	135,000,000
Mortgage Pfandbriefe	2,148,750,000	1,144,038,462	603,039,941	311,733,045	154,875,486	70,413,723
Public sector Pfandbriefe	0	0	0	0	0	0
MTN Funding	716,250,000	381,346,154	201,013,314	103,911,015	51,625,162	23,471,241
Aggregate liabilities	3,097,500,000	1,757,884,615	1,036,553,254	648,144,060	439,000,648	326,384,964
Net tier one/risk-weighted assets	6.50%	6.50%	6.50%	6.50%	6.50%	6.50%
Net tier one/total capital	41.94%	28.00%	17.31%	10.13%	5.72%	3.17%
Liabilities/total net capital	13.32	9.38	6.35	4.31	3.07	2.34
Asset risk weighting	50.0%	50.0%	50.0%	50.0%	50.0%	50.0%
Target Tier one ratio	6.5%	6.5%	6.5%	6.5%	6.5%	6.5%
Tier one available for securitisation	97,500,000	52,500,000	28,269,231	15,221,893	8,196,404	4,413,448
First loss retained in securitisation	45,000,000	24,230,769	13,047,337	7,025,489	3,782,956	2,036,976
Cumulative capital retained in securitisation	45,000,000	69,230,769	82,278,107	89,303,596	93,086,552	95,123,528
Capital available for reinvestment	52,500,000	28,269,231	15,221,893	8,196,404	4,413,448	2,376,472
% capital released	53.8%	53.8%	53.8%	53.8%	53.8%	53.8%
Loans securitised	3,000,000,000	1,615,384,615	869,822,485	468,365,954	252,197,052	135,798,413
Securitised loans (cumulative)	3,000,000,000	4,615,384,615	5,485,207,101	5,953,573,054	6,205,770,106	6,341,568,519
Risk-weighted assets	807,692,308	434,911,243	234,182,977	126,098,526	67,899,206	36,561,111
Cumulative New Loans	1,615,384,615	2,485,207,101	2,953,573,054	3,205,770,106	3,341,568,519	3,414,690,741
Cumulative Total Loans	4,615,384,615	5,485,207,101	5,953,573,054	6,205,770,106	6,341,568,519	6,414,690,741

Note: All data in EUR unless otherwise indicated.
Source: Commerzbank Securities.

EXHIBIT 6.7 True Sale Securitisation—Income/Expense Statement

Weighted income on loans	22,500,000	34,615,385	41,139,053	44,651,798	46,543,276	47,561,764
Weighted loss expectation	(3,000,000)	(4,615,385)	(5,485,207)	(5,953,573)	(6,205,770)	(6,341,569)
Weighted servicing costs	(3,750,000)	(4,961,538)	(5,613,905)	(5,965,180)	(6,154,328)	(6,256,176)
Weighted origination costs	(3,750,000)	(2,019,231)	(1,087,278)	(585,457)	(315,246)	(169,748)
Weighted liability costs	(5,719,125)	(3,165,316)	(1,790,188)	(1,049,734)	(651,028)	(436,341)
Fixed up-front costs		(710,137)	(1,092,518)	(1,329,231)	(1,565,943)	(1,802,655)
Underwriting costs		(3,660,000)	(1,970,769)	(1,061,183)	(571,406)	(307,680)
Weighted risk transfer cost		(8,752,500)	(13,465,385)	(16,003,092)	(17,369,549)	(18,105,334)
Income after costs	6,280,875	6,731,278	10,633,803	12,704,348	13,710,005	14,142,260
Return on tier one equity (pretax)	6.44%	6.90%	10.91%	13.03%	14.06%	14.50%
Return on assets	0.21%	0.41%	1.13%	2.31%	4.01%	6.18%

Note: All data in EUR unless otherwise indicated.
Source: Commerzbank Securities.

EXHIBIT 6.8   Tier One and Gross Asset Growth: True Sale and Base Case Compared

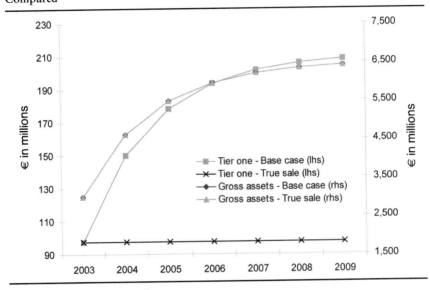

Note: Amounts in EUR million.
Source: Commerzbank Securities.

EXHIBIT 6.9   Return on Equity and Return on Assets: True Sale and Base Case Compared

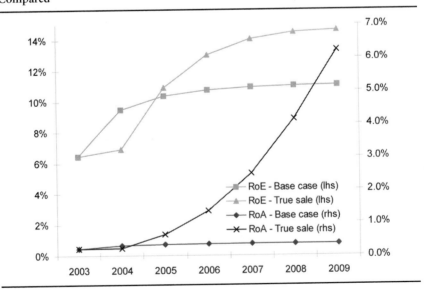

Source: Commerzbank Securities.

EXHIBIT 6.10 Partially Funded, Synthetic Securitisation: On- and Off-Balance Sheet Growth

	2003	2004	2005	2006	2007	2008
Residential mortgage loans	3,000,000,000	3,535,384,615	3,630,930,178	3,647,981,386	3,651,024,370	3,651,567,426
Equity retained in structures	0	45,000,000	53,030,769	54,463,953	54,719,721	54,765,366
Government securities	97,500,000	97,500,000	97,500,000	97,500,000	97,500,000	97,500,000
Aggregate assets	3,097,500,000	3,677,884,615	3,781,460,947	3,799,945,338	3,803,244,091	3,803,832,792
Tier one	97,500,000	97,500,000	97,500,000	97,500,000	97,500,000	97,500,000
Tier two	135,000,000	135,000,000	135,000,000	135,000,000	135,000,000	135,000,000
Mortgage Pfandbriefe	2,148,750,000	2,584,038,462	2,661,720,710	2,675,584,004	2,678,058,068	2,678,499,594
Public sector Pfandbriefe	0	0	0	0	0	0
MTN Funding	716,250,000	861,346,154	887,240,237	891,861,335	892,686,023	892,833,198
Aggregate liabilities	3,097,500,000	3,677,884,615	3,781,460,947	3,799,945,338	3,803,244,091	3,803,832,792
Net tier one/risk-weighted assets	6.50%	4.88%	6.08%	6.42%	6.49%	6.50%
Net tier one/total capital	41.94%	28.00%	24.78%	24.17%	24.06%	24.04%
Liabilities/total net capital	13.32	19.62	21.07	21.34	21.39	21.40
Asset risk weighting	50.0%	50.0%	50.0%	50.0%	50.0%	50.0%
Target Tier one ratio	6.5%	6.5%	6.5%	6.5%	6.5%	6.5%
Tier one available for securitisation	97,500,000	97,500,000	97,500,000	97,500,000	97,500,000	97,500,000
First loss retained in securitisation	45,000,000	8,030,769	1,433,183	255,768	45,645	8,146
Cumulative capital retained in securitisation	80,100,000	94,394,769	96,945,836	97,401,103	97,482,351	97,496,850
Capital available for reinvestment	17,400,000	3,105,231	554,164	98,897	17,649	3,150
% capital released	17.8%	3.2%	0.6%	0.1%	0.0%	0.0%
Loans securitised	3,000,000,000	535,384,615	95,545,562	17,051,208	3,042,985	543,056
Securitised loans (cumulative)	3,000,000,000	3,535,384,615	3,630,930,178	3,647,981,386	3,651,024,370	3,651,567,426
Cumulative New Loans	535,384,615	630,930,178	647,981,386	651,024,370	651,567,426	651,664,341
Cumulative Total Loans	3,535,384,615	3,630,930,178	3,647,981,386	3,651,024,370	3,651,567,426	3,651,664,341
Risk-weighted assets	807,692,308	684,142,012	662,093,036	658,158,142	657,455,915	657,330,594

Note: All data in EUR unless otherwise indicated.
Source: Commerzbank Securities.

EXHIBIT 6.11 Partially Funded, Synthetic Securitisation—Income/Expense Statement

Weighted income on loans	22,500,000	26,515,385	27,231,976	27,359,860	27,382,683	27,386,756
Weighted loss expectation	(3,000,000)	(3,535,385)	(3,630,930)	(3,647,981)	(3,651,024)	(3,651,567)
Weighted servicing costs	(3,750,000)	(4,151,538)	(4,223,198)	(4,235,986)	(4,238,268)	(4,238,676)
Weighted origination costs	(3,750,000)	(669,231)	(119,432)	(21,314)	(3,804)	(679)
Weighted liability costs	(5,719,125)	(6,739,769)	(6,921,915)	(6,954,421)	(6,960,222)	(6,961,257)
Fixed up-front costs	(710,137)	(710,137)	(946,849)	(1,183,562)	(1,420,274)	(1,656,986)
Underwriting costs	(960,000)	(960,000)	(171,323)	(30,575)	(5,456)	(974)
Weighted risk transfer cost	(3,757,500)	(3,757,500)	(4,428,069)	(4,547,740)	(4,569,097)	(4,572,908)
Income after costs	6,280,875	5,991,825	6,790,260	6,738,282	6,534,538	6,303,709
Return on tier one equity (pretax)	6.44%	6.15%	6.96%	6.91%	6.70%	6.47%
Return on assets	0.21%	0.17%	0.18%	0.18%	0.18%	0.17%

Note: All data in EUR unless otherwise indicated.
Source: Commerzbank Securities.

EXHIBIT 6.12   Tier One and Gross Asset Growth: Partially Funded Synthetic and Base Case Compared

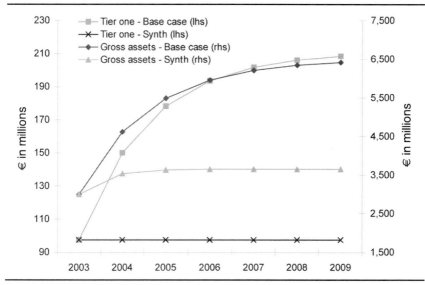

Note: Amounts in EUR million.
Source: Commerzbank Securities.

EXHIBIT 6.13   Return on Equity and Return on Assets: Partially Funded Synthetic and Base Case Compared

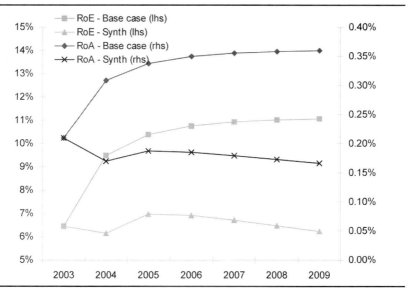

Source: Commerzbank Securities.

PARTIALLY FUNDED, SYNTHETIC SECURITISATION (WITH KFW INTERMEDIATION)

The third securitisation structural alternative we consider is again a partially funded, synthetic structure. However in this instance we place an intermediary, KfW, in between the originator and the ultimate protection sellers.

KfW is assumed to be 0% risk weighted from the originator's perspective due to KfW's status as a German public agency which enjoys an explicit guarantee of its existing and future obligations, pursuant to Article 1A of the KfW Law, by the Federal Republic of Germany. We also assume that any risk asset protection purchased from KfW effectively converts any risk asset into a "qualifying" public sector cover asset for Pfandbriefe issuance purposes. KfW intermediation fees of 6.5 basis points per annum are assumed for the KfW synthetic structure.[1] Bringing KfW into the equation therefore has the immediate benefit of enhancing the regulatory capital leverage opportunity relative to the partially funded synthetic structure employing a 20% risk-weighted counterparty for the senior CDS.

The primary question for an originator is therefore whether the benefit of the 0% KfW risk weighting outweighs the cost of their intermediation. Again we assume that all available risk assets at the start of every year are securitised. Aggregate tier one capital is not increased from year to year, but all "released" tier one capital resulting from the securitisations is reinvested in new, similar risk assets.

Exhibit 6.14 illustrates the pro forma balance sheet of our hypothetical bank, coupled with some ratio analysis. The exhibit emphasises the impact of the leverage achieved as a result of employing a 0% risk-weighted counterparty under the synthetic structure, thus eliminating the "drain" on the available regulatory capital leverage within the structure.

As can be seen in Exhibit 6.15, the profit-and-loss position is more dramatic. The clear value of not only the leverage achieved, but, more importantly, the reduced cost of funding generated through the conversion of mortgage risk into qualifying public sector cover assets is evident. When viewed graphically (see Exhibits 6.16 and 6.17), and when compared to our base case traditional balance-sheet growth scenario, the value achieved through applying the KfW sponsored, synthetic securitisation structure is clearly evident. Whilst the return on assets is clearly exaggerated by the dramatic decline in on-balance-sheet assets, the impact on the bank's return on equity is significant over the 6-year period.

---

[1] This KfW cost is purely illustrative, as we understand KfW's costs are not fixed and may vary according to the precise terms and details of a transaction.

EXHIBIT 6.14   Partially Funded, Synthetic Securitisation (via KfW)—On- and Off-Balance Sheet Growth

	2003	2004	2005	2006	2007	2008
Residential mortgage loans	3,000,000,000	4,615,384,615	5,485,207,101	5,953,573,054	6,205,770,106	6,341,568,519
Equity retained in structures	0	45,000,000	69,230,769	82,278,107	89,303,596	93,086,552
Government securities	97,500,000	97,500,000	97,500,000	97,500,000	97,500,000	97,500,000
Aggregate assets	3,097,500,000	4,757,884,615	5,651,937,870	6,133,351,161	6,392,573,702	6,532,155,070
Tier one	97,500,000	97,500,000	97,500,000	97,500,000	97,500,000	97,500,000
Tier two	135,000,000	135,000,000	135,000,000	135,000,000	135,000,000	135,000,000
Mortgage Pfandbriefe	724,285,441	1,144,038,462	603,039,941	311,733,045	154,875,486	70,413,723
Public sector Pfandbriefe	1,899,286,079	3,000,000,000	4,615,384,615	5,485,207,101	5,953,573,054	6,205,770,106
MTN Funding	241,428,480	381,346,154	201,013,314	103,911,015	51,625,162	23,471,241
Aggregate liabilities	3,097,500,000	4,757,884,615	5,651,937,870	6,133,351,161	6,392,573,702	6,532,155,070
Net tier one/risk-weighted assets	6.50%	2.28%	1.03%	0.51%	0.26%	0.14%
Net tier one/total capital	41.94%	28.00%	17.31%	10.13%	5.72%	3.17%
Liabilities/total net capital	13.32	25.38	34.62	40.83	44.64	46.85
Percentage PS Pfandbriefe finance	61.32%	63.05%	81.66%	89.43%	93.13%	95.00%
Asset risk weighting	50.0%	50.0%	50.0%	50.0%	50.0%	50.0%
Target Tier one ratio	6.5%	6.5%	6.5%	6.5%	6.5%	6.5%
Tier one available for securitisation	97,500,000	97,500,000	97,500,000	97,500,000	97,500,000	97,500,000
First loss retained in securitisation	45,000,000	24,230,769	13,047,337	7,025,489	3,782,956	2,036,976
Cumulative capital retained in securitisation	45,000,000	69,230,769	82,278,107	89,303,596	93,086,552	95,123,528
Capital available for reinvestment	52,500,000	28,269,231	15,221,893	8,196,404	4,413,448	2,376,472
% capital released	53.8%	29.0%	15.6%	8.4%	4.5%	2.4%
Loans securitised	3,000,000,000	1,615,384,615	869,822,485	468,365,954	252,197,052	135,798,413
Securitised loans (cumulative)	3,000,000,000	4,615,384,615	5,485,207,101	5,953,573,054	6,205,770,106	6,341,568,519
Cumulative New Loans	1,615,384,615	2,485,207,101	2,953,573,054	3,205,770,106	3,341,568,519	3,414,690,741
Cumulative Total Loans	4,615,384,615	5,485,207,101	5,953,573,054	6,205,770,106	6,341,568,519	6,414,690,741
Risk-weighted assets	807,692,308	434,911,243	234,182,977	126,098,526	67,899,206	36,561,111

Note: All data in EUR unless otherwise indicated; PS = Public sector.
Source: Commerzbank Securities.

107

EXHIBIT 6.15 Partially Funded, Synthetic Securitisation (via KfW)—Income/Expense Statement

Weighted income on loans	22,500,000	34,615,385	41,139,053	44,651,798	46,543,276	47,561,764
Weighted loss expectation	(3,000,000)	(4,615,385)	(5,485,207)	(5,953,573)	(6,205,770)	(6,341,569)
Weighted servicing costs	(3,750,000)	(4,436,538)	(4,934,294)	(5,221,028)	(5,379,459)	(5,465,780)
Weighted origination costs	(3,750,000)	(2,019,231)	(1,087,278)	(585,457)	(315,246)	(169,748)
Weighted liability costs	(5,719,125)	(5,720,437)	(5,734,572)	(5,744,119)	(5,749,674)	(5,752,770)
Fixed up-front costs		(710,137)	(1,092,518)	(1,329,231)	(1,565,943)	(1,802,655)
Underwriting costs		(960,000)	(516,923)	(278,343)	(149,877)	(80,703)
Weighted risk transfer cost		(3,757,500)	(5,780,769)	(6,870,222)	(7,456,850)	(7,772,727)
Income after costs	6,280,875	10,446,157	13,507,491	15,104,440	15,850,633	16,142,061
Return on tier one equity (pretax)	6.44%	10.71%	13.85%	15.49%	16.26%	16.56%
Return on assets	0.21%	0.22%	0.24%	0.25%	0.25%	0.25%

Note: All data in EUR unless otherwise indicated
Source: Commerzbank Securities.

EXHIBIT 6.16   Tier One and Gross Asset Growth: KfW Synthetic and Base Case Compared

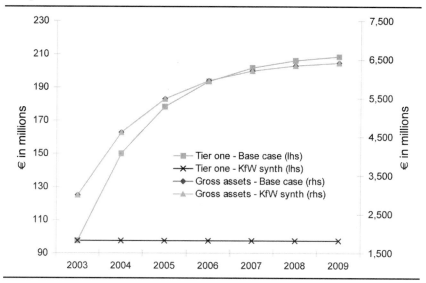

Note: Amounts in EUR million.
Source: Commerzbank Securities.

EXHIBIT 6.17   Return on Equity and Return on Assets: KfW Synthetic and Base Case Compared

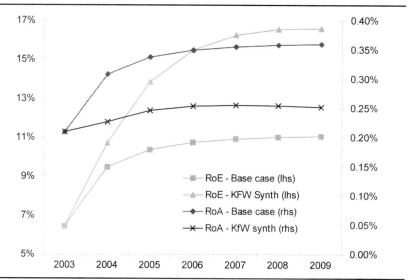

Source: Commerzbank Securities.

CONCLUSIONS

Exhibit 6.18 shows the four options (including the base case) from an asset growth perspective, highlighting the equivalent impact of three of the scenarios relative to the limited overall asset growth achieved through the partially funded synthetic securitisation. However two of the structures (True sale and KfW synthetic) achieve the same asset growth whilst not requiring any incremental tier one capital (see Exhibit 6.19).

Moving on in our analysis to the revenue and profitability parameters, the comparisons assist further in digesting the relative merits of the four options. As can be seen in Exhibit 6.20, from a return on asset perspective the true sale scenario is clearly optimal, reflecting the dramatic reduction in on-balance sheet assets achieved through this structure. From a return on equity perspective, the merits of the KfW synthetic structure are evident in Exhibit 6.21, although the strength of the true sale structure is also clear.

The KfW synthetic scenario does however benefit primarily banks with the ability to issue public sector Pfandbriefe, thus enabling them to reduce their cost of funding significantly. For a bank without the ability to issue public sector Pfandbriefe (or equivalent), the impact is dramatically different, as is illustrated in Exhibit 6.22. From the exhibit it is evi-

EXHIBIT 6.18   Asset Growth Compared (Securitisation Scenarios versus Base Case)

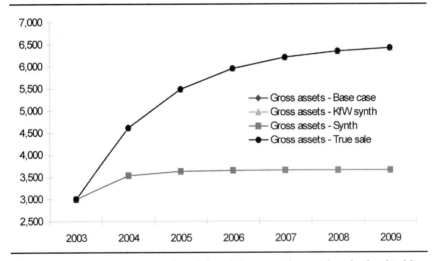

Note: Note that the first, second, and fourth lines overlap, with only the third line (representing the partially funded, synthetic structure) showing a distinct result; amounts in EUR million.
Source: Commerzbank Securities.

EXHIBIT 6.19   Capital Growth Required (Securitisation Scenarios versus Base Case)

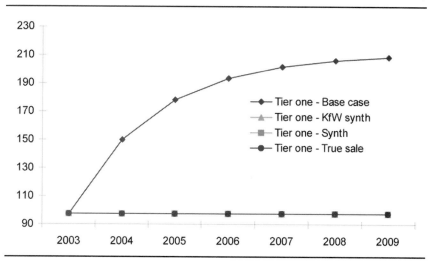

Note: Note that the first, second, and fourth lines overlap, with only the third line (representing the partially funded, synthetic structure) showing a distinct result; amounts in EUR million.
Source: Commerzbank Securities.

EXHIBIT 6.20   Return on Assets Compared (Securitisation Scenarios versus Base Case)

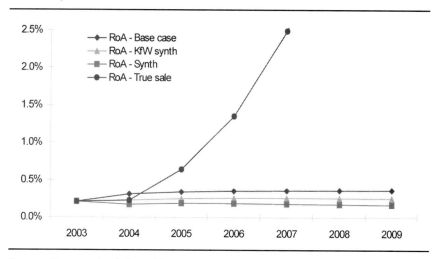

Source: Commerzbank Securities.

EXHIBIT 6.21   Return on Equity Compared (Securitisation Scenarios versus Base Case)

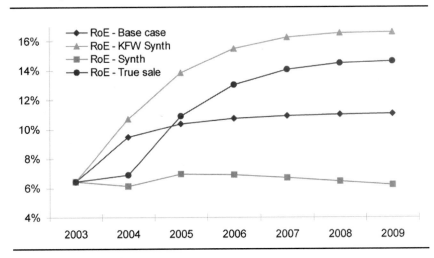

Source: Commerzbank Securities.

EXHIBIT 6.22   Return on Equity Compared (Securitisation Scenarios versus Base Case)

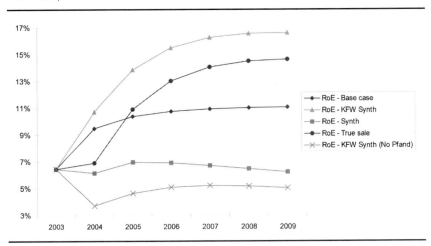

Note: KfW Synth (No Pfand) = KfW partially funded synthetic structure for a non-Pfandbriefe issuer.
Source: Commerzbank Securities.

dent that for most financial institutions, the true sale structure is the optimal from a return on equity perspective. This emphasises, in our opinion, the rationale behind the recently announced true sale initiative in Germany. We have observed that most of the initial sponsoring banks are not natural Pfandbriefe issuers and, indeed, some currently have to bear significantly higher costs of senior unsecured funding than those employed in our model.

Exhibit 6.23 aggregates the results of the model into one simple table that compares the results in year 2009 according to the four quantitative criteria discussed in this chapter for each of the four structures. Coupled with the base case, the relative strengths of the solutions are evident. Clearly the optimal two solutions are the true sale and synthetic KfW structures. However the latter solution only creates real value for those institutions enjoying Pfandbriefe issuing privileges. If, however, the originating bank's cost of senior unsecured funding is reduced by 20 basis points to 5 basis points per annum, the comparison score, as shown in Exhibit 6.24, looks somewhat different. Evident from these results is the sensitivity of the analysis to the originating bank's cost of funds.

Thus for a German Pfandbriefe-issuing bank, as the cost of Pfandbriefe and senior unsecured finance have risen, the relative value of the KfW PROVIDE structures has fallen.[2] Equally, for a German bank not enjoying Pfandbriefe-issuing privilege, the relative value of a true sale structure is clearly evident.

EXHIBIT 6.23   Structural Solutions Compared (Assuming Senior Unsecured Cost of Funds at 25-bp pa)

	RoE	RoA	Asset Growth	Capital Growth	Aggregate
Traditional structure (base case)	3	2	1	5	11
Synthetic—KfW structure with Pfandbriefe	1	3	1	1	6
Synthetic—Not KfW structure	4	4	5	1	14
Fully funded structure	2	1	1	1	5
Synthetic—KfW structure without Pfandbriefe	5	5	1	1	12

Note: Lower score is best.
Source: Commerzbank Securities.

---

[2] To date, mortgage banks have not employed KfW's PROMISE structure given their focus on the real estate finance business as opposed to small- to medium-sized enterprise (SME) lending.

EXHIBIT 6.24   Structural Solutions Compared (Assuming Senior Unsecured Cost of Funds at 5-bp pa)

	RoE	RoA	Asset Growth	Capital Growth	Aggregate
Traditional structure	4	2	1	5	12
Synthetic—KfW structure with Pfandbriefe	2	3	1	1	7
Synthetic—Not KfW structure	5	5	5	1	16
Fully funded structure	3	1	1	1	6
Synthetic—KfW structure without Pfandbriefe	1	4	1	1	7

Note: Lower score is best.
Source: Commerzbank Securities.

EXHIBIT 6.25   Sensitivity Analysis: Asset Retention Costs versus Costs of Senior Unsecured Debt

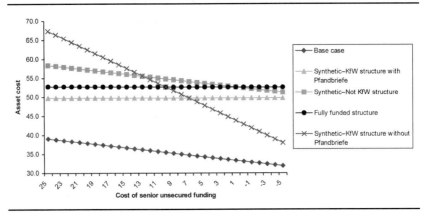

Note: Asset costs include costs of risk transfer, funding and operational costs in 2009 of our scenarios; all other costs are assumed to remain unchanged.
Source: Commerzbank Securities.

From a UK bank perspective, the relative value equation is more marginal. In such circumstances, a comparison between the last two categories shown in Exhibit 6.24 is appropriate, demonstrating that a KfW structure for a UK bank may offer significant value even without Pfandbriefe issuing privilege.

Exhibit 6.25 performs a sensitivity analysis on the various structures, according to various levels of senior unsecured funding costs, emphasising the sensitivity of the all-in asset costs (without any tier one

EXHIBIT 6.26 Sensitivity Analysis: Return on Equity versus Costs of Senior Unsecured Debt

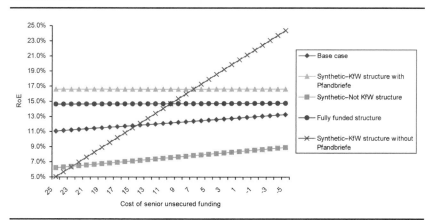

Note: Return on equity (RoE) is assessed as at 2009 in our five scenarios.
Source: Commerzbank Securities.

costs or revenue adjustments) highlighted above. If we examine the scenario results from an alternative perspective—return on equity—the value achieved through securitisation, is evident as can be seen in Exhibit 6.26. Of specific note, is that whilst senior unsecured funding costs are below approximately 10 basis points, the synthetic structure via KfW is the optimal solution for a mortgage originator, be it a Pfandbriefe issuer or not. However, as costs of funding rise above this level, the true sale option becomes more compelling using a return on equity decision-making criteria.

As funding costs tumble further, the equation changes. Indeed at funding levels below about 28 basis points per annum under the applicable reference rate, not securitising may create an optimal solution (although this is unlikely to be the case for a Pfandbriefe issuing bank who will typically continue to enjoy competitive all-in returns through KfW intermediated securitisation).

The conclusion of this analysis is evident: there is no single perfect solution. Depending on how originators rank their objectives from a priority perspective, they are likely to focus on different solutions.

CHAPTER 7

Assessing Subordinated Tranches in ABS Capital Structure

Alexander Batchvarov, Ph.D., CFA
Managing Director and Head, International Structured Credit Research
Merrill Lynch

Jenna Collins
Vice President
Merrill Lynch

William Davies
Assistant Vice President
Merrill Lynch

The analysis of the subordinated tranches of unsecured consumer assets ABS follows the general principles and guidelines of the investment analysis for ABS and their senior tranches. It is or should be, however, more credit intensive—the lower in the ABS capital structure the investors move, the more intensive the credit considerations should become. Analytical methods such as sensitivity and break-even analysis come handy when reviewing payment rates, charge-offs and excess spread. In this chapter we explain how to analyze subordinate tranches.

FRAMEWORK FOR SUBORDINATED TRANCHE ANALYSIS

The framework for credit analysis of subordinated tranches of unsecured consumer loans and credit cards in most generic terms include the following aspects:

- Quality of initial collateral pool and originator's historical pool performance.
- Originator and servicer capabilities and credit standing.
- Structural enhancements (credit enhancement, liquidity facility, reserve accounts, reserve account buildup triggers, early amortisation triggers, etc.).
- Legal enhancement (bankruptcy remoteness of the structure, "true" sale treatment).
- Cash flow "waterfall" and priorities of payment of principal and interest at different subordination levels.

The revolving (substitution) feature of these deals entails changes in the pool composition within the respective eligibility criteria, hence the need to ascertain:

- Tightness of the eligibility criteria.
- Consistency in the underwriting criteria of the originator and ability to manage accounts in accordance with the changing economic and competitive environment.
- Frequency of replenishment and account additions.
- Tightness of economic triggers.
- Ability to build up additional credit support (reserve accounts and excess spread).
- Likelihood of the occurrence of trigger events.

All of the above aspects are relevant to the analysis of both senior and subordinated ABS tranches. With regards to the analysis of the subordinated tranches several additional considerations should be included:

- Excess spread stability or erosion, and, particularly, excess spread variability and determining factors (yield, delinquency, and loss management).
- Originator's pool management capabilities—ability to manage yield, delinquencies, and losses.
- Potential levels of excess spread buildup in an additional reserve account in accordance with the respective triggers.
- Applicability of the reserve accounts.

- Current, historical, and expected losses compared to actual and potential credit enhancement levels.
- Likelihood of servicer bankruptcy/replacement and its effects on pool performance.
- Effects of payment rates on the accumulation of losses and excess spread variability.
- Break-even and sensitivity analysis, and the like.

These aspects are more important to subordinated tranches investors than to the most senior tranches investors given the lower loss cushion protection they have and the higher likelihood of negative consequences of performance volatility. We would discuss those particular aspects in more detail below.

Excess Spread Stability

The main source of loss protection for an investor in the lower tranches of the ABS capital structure is the excess spread. That is, the difference between the revenue from the asset pool (pool yield, which depends on interest rate charged on the underlying accounts, as well as other charges—late payment penalty, annual fees, interchange, etc.) and the expenses under the securitisation (ABS coupon, servicing fees, losses, etc.). Hence, excess spread is a function mainly of the pool yield and pool losses, which both depend on the ability of the originator/servicer to manage the asset pool under different economic scenarios, see below.

A key aspect of the analysis of excess spread is its variability. We are concerned with excess spread variability for a number of reasons:

- It determines the level of the available cushion against loss increases.
- It determines the extent, to which a reserve account can be built up in case of need.
- It determines the likelihood of the occurrence of an early amortisation event, i.e., hitting the economic trigger associated with specified level of excess spread typically on a three-month rolling average basis.

A high volatility of excess spread or its rapid drop may prompt early amortisation without sufficient time to build up additional reserves against future loss increases and depletion of the available protection to the subordinated tranches.

Furthermore, highly volatile excess spread, and especially a steep rapid drop in the levels of excess spread would not allow sufficient buildup of the reserve account (i.e., would limit the available additional cushion against loss increases).

Originator's Underwriting and Servicing

As mentioned above the unsecured consumer loan and credit card deals are usually structured with a revolving period, during which the principal collections from the existing pool are used to purchase new receivables from the original accounts or new accounts altogether. In the case of a master trust, the originator can add new accounts and the associated receivables to the pool on an ongoing basis, which could alter the pool composition and performance over the term of the transaction. Any performance variability would first of all affect the subordinated tranches.

Originator's ability to manage the pool is crucial and depends on a number of factors:

■ Type and purpose of the unsecured loan or credit card, e.g., general credit card or retail credit card, installment consumer loans or revolving unsecured loan facility. For example, one would expect a lower yield and higher first bucket delinquencies for retail cards as compared to general credit cards.
■ Market competition has effects on the way loans are originated and the rates charged (e.g., teaser rates, lower interest rates, annual fees, etc.).
■ Ability to enforce risk-based pricing, thus reflecting the riskiness of the pool.
■ Balance between "convenience users" (borrowers who pay their balances in full every payment date) and "credit users" (real users of the credit facility and payers of interest rate charges)—the effect on pool yield is obvious.
■ Ability to retain good quality accounts, especially among the "credit users."

Likelihood of Servicer Bankruptcy/Replacement

Servicer bankruptcy is not only a trigger event in revolving structures but also could lead to a significant deterioration of the collateral pool performance at least on a temporary basis, for example, an increase in delinquencies and losses, which affects the lower tranches in the ABS structure first.

Overall, the ability to replace a servicer of a credit card pool in the US, for example, is fairly high without much delay, while that may not be the case in Europe. This likelihood, though, should be evaluated against the current creditworthiness of the servicer (usually also the originator)—in Europe all the credit card issuers, for example, are investment grade banks.

In both cases above, originator's ability to manage the pool and a servicer bankruptcy would effect the ability to build-up an additional reserve account among other things.

Applicability of the Reserve Accounts

A key issue for subordinated investors to understand is the applicability of the reserve account, that is, whether it is available to the senior investors or is available only to the subordinated investor, be it the mezzanine or the equity one. It is fairly obvious that a reserve account "reserved" for the subinvestor reduces the amount of losses it can experience. On the other hand, such an account may be providing a false support for the senior investor.

Losses and Credit Enhancement

In order to determine the level of protection provided by the credit enhancement, investors should compare the current, expected and historical portfolio losses to the available credit enhancement at their position in the capital structure.

In this regard, we would like to stress several points:

- When sizing the credit enhancement the rating agencies generally assume zero or negative excess spread.
- In case of amortising assets, the seasoning of the pool with reference to the relevant static loss pool curve becomes crucial in determining the expected loss developments. That should also be valid for revolving pools which allow addition of new receivables, but not of new accounts.
- Pool losses should be adjusted for pool growth. Rapid pool growth could mask loss increases because newly added accounts have initially low losses and delinquencies. In case of an early amortisation, however, no new additions are allowed and then the losses of the underlying pool should increase and test the sufficiency of the available credit enhancement.

Effects of Payment Rates

One of the key variables of the pool performance is the payment rate. Payment rate has potentially different effects on investors:

- On the one hand, it determines how fast the pool pays down, that is, how quickly investors are out of their positions.
- On the other, it determines how quickly the pool quality deteriorates, as the better borrowers tend to pay first.

The combination of the two determines the level of losses that the pool could accumulate—the lower the payment rate, the higher the accumulated losses, the higher the investor exposure.

Waterfall Priorities

ABS capital structure determines the prioritisation of cash flows among different tranches. The senior tranche (usually rated AAA), which usually receives its payments of interest and principal first, is the one that assures that any cash collections first service the senior tranche. As for the subordinated tranches, one should understand how the interest and principal cash payments are distributed, for example:

- Whether interest is paid pari passu or sequentially for the senior and mezzanine tranche.
- Whether principal is paid pro rata or sequentially for the senior and subordinated tranches.
- Whether interest payments for the junior tranches can be subordinated to principal payments for the senior tranches.
- Whether there is some kind of a trigger, which changes the priority of interest or principal distribution during the life of the transaction.

As a rule of thumb, with the risk of stating the obvious, it is best for a subordinated tranche to receive its interest on a pari passu basis and its principal on a pro rata basis.

Likelihood of an Occurrence of a Trigger Event

The trigger events (early amortisation events) in unsecured consumer loan and credit card ABS are associated with two types of negative events—one affecting the originator and/or servicer and their ability to perform their obligations and the others associated with the quality of the asset pool.

The potential negative impact for the occurrence of an early amortisation event is more likely to be greater at the subordinated tranche level than on the senior tranche level. Hence, it is more important for the subordinated tranche investor to evaluate the likelihood of such an event taking place. Their occurrence will lead to changes in the average life of the ABS notes. Depending on the nature of the event, it could have the consequences of increasing volatility in pool performance and rapid reduction in excess spread (reduced cushion against losses and inability to build additional reserves).

Specific Features of Master Trust Structures

When evaluating the credit quality of the different subordinated tranches from series issued by a master trust, several additional aspects come into consideration.

Utilisation of Excess Spread

As discussed in Chapter 8, all master trusts are not the same. They differ in the ways cash flows are allocated and distributed among the numerous series of notes outstanding. In particular, investors should be aware of the ability to allocate excess spread from series with a surplus to others that face shortfalls in their required cash flows.

In that respect a proper question to ask is how the performance of the outstanding series of the trust affect the performance of the particular series held by the investor? The different series in a trust are exposed to the same level of yield and same level of losses and servicing fee expenses, but to different levels of coupon payments, that is, interest expenses and other expenses (swaps, etc.). As a result the servicing shortfall/excess may differ among series. In some cases, the shortfalls (when they are very large) may be shared by all series; in other cases they may be limited to the respective series facing a shortfall. Yet in other cases, excess spread from one series may be redirected to series facing shortfalls.

In addition, the series may have certain specific excess spread capture mechanisms, which require accumulation of excess spreads in a designated reserve account for the benefit of that series or its most junior tranche under certain circumstances. Consequently, the excess spread from that series available to other series in the master trust would be reduced. In most cases of master trust structures, any residual excess spread is released to the originator. One exception is the aircraft master trust structure, where in some cases the excess spread is used to "turbo" the principal repayment of the senior bonds outstanding.

The location of principal from nonamortising to amortising series, or from nonaccumulating to accumulating series.

Utilisation of Principal Collections

Another key point in a master trust structure is the allocation of principal to repay the series, or put differently, the type of amortisation. The principal can be:

- Accumulated in a special account to ensure a bullet payment at expected maturity of the notes (the so-called accumulation structure meant to establish a soft bullet), for example: the CARDS Master Trust.
- Passed-through to investors up to a specified amount (controlled or regulated amortisation structure) such as Arran One MT or fully (rapid amortisation structure, usually a result of the occurrence of a trigger event in all master trusts).

In this regard, it is the level of principal payment rate that determines the speed of accumulation of the principal to achieve the soft bullet structure or the speed of amortisation in case of rapid amortisation. In case of controlled amortisation the required principal payment rate necessary to meet the required controlled principal payment amount is usually much lower than the actual pool principal payment rate.

In a typical credit card master trust structure the revolving period is followed by an amortisation or an accumulation period. In a mortgage master trust structure, the revolving period may be interrupted, to accumulate collected principal and prepayments, and resume upon payment of the soft bullet. Under normal circumstances, in a master trust there are series in a revolving period and in an accumulation/amortisation period. Hence, principal from the revolving series may be re-directed to support series in their amortisation or accumulation periods. Such redistribution mechanism will not work if all series are accumulating or amortising simultaneously.

With regards to the amortisation or accumulation period, a corollary question is related to the speed of amortisation or accumulation. The payment rate becomes important as it determines the likelihood of extension affecting in a domino fashion the senior and the junior tranches.

BREAK-EVEN AND SENSITIVITY ANALYSIS

Many of the issues we discussed above can be put into perspective through cash flow simulations of any given deal. We believe that such simulations are particularly important in the analysis of subordinated tranches. They involve the application of stress scenarios to one key variable of the asset pool in order to determine the effect on cumulative losses for the pool, hence potential losses for investors at different levels of the ABS capital structure.

We use an in-house-developed credit card ABS default model to stress certain key portfolio statistics and determine the break-even loss rate that a hypothetical credit card ABS can withstand before the most junior class loses a dollar of either interest or principal. We illustrate our approach through an example.

We assume a sample capital structure of 10% subordination, hence 90% AAA rated Class A, 6% A rated Class B, and 4% BBB rated Class C. Initially, we assume a base case of 8% payment rate, 6% charge-off rate, no reserve account, and no trapping of excess spread. First, we alternatively stress the payment rate and the charge-off rate to determine loss accumulation and compare it to the available credit enhancement level (excluding excess spread and reserve account). Second, we evaluate the role of the reserve account and excess spread trapping on the cumulative loss levels.

Effect of Payment Rate on Losses

As noted earlier, the payment rate is the percentage of outstanding balances paid (collected) on average monthly. Our first stress test aims to evaluate the impact of fluctuations in the payment rate on principal amortization and cumulative losses. To this end we stressed our base case payment rate of 8% by 50% and 100%. The results are shown in Exhibit 7.1.

Our example reveals that payment rates are inversely related with cumulative losses and length of amortization period. Intuitively as the payment rate increases the time required to make the necessary principal payments decreases and, therefore, investor's exposure decreases as well. Notably, with less outstanding principal exposed to time, cumulative losses decrease. We are left to draw the conclusion that any increase in payment rates is positive for our investor.

Investors in subordinated tranches need to evaluate the factors that could cause the payment rates in portfolios to fluctuate, and in particular slow down. These range from the seasonal (Christmas time, summer holidays) to the fiscal (taxes) and macroeconomic (unemployment, interest rates). For example, in any period of economic slowdown, the subordi-

EXHIBIT 7.1 Payment Rate Analysis

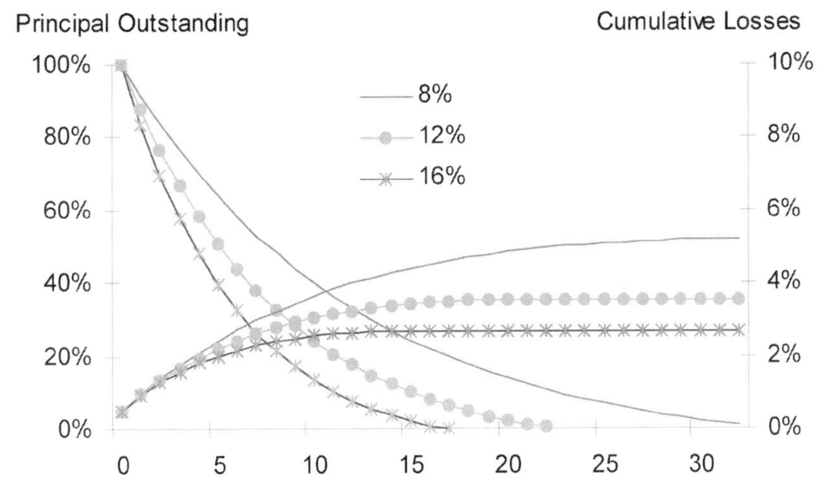

Source: Merrill Lynch.

nated investor must evaluate the extent to which the changing conditions could slow payment rates. Will consumers feeling the pinch slow down repayment, or will they defensively seek to clear debt burdens cutting corners elsewhere? Answering these questions requires an examination of the portfolio's aggregates and understanding consumer behaviour in the respective country. The seasoning of the accounts, the average balances outstanding, the typical utilization of the credit line or credit card, the average interest rate are all factors bearing upon payment rate volatility.

Effect of Monthly Charge-Offs on Losses

In this stress test, we evaluate the extent to which changes in charge-off rates increase cumulative losses. Intuitively we know that cumulative losses will rise. The question, however, is the extent to which charge-offs can fluctuate without compromising the performance of a subordinated piece. To this end, we increased our base case of 6% by 100% and 200% respectively (see Exhibit 7.2).

In all three cases losses wipe out Class C principal in its entirety. In our base case, losses reach Class B principal very near to the transaction's maturity. Increasing our base case by 50% produces a large impact on losses. The first dollar of loss occurs substantially earlier in the transaction (approximately the ninth month). Cumulative losses for the B piece increase to nearly six dollars of principal, essentially eating through the entire piece. Further increasing the stress to double the base case causes losses to eat through both the Class B and C pieces. Class A losses amount to over four dollars of principal.

EXHIBIT 7.2 Charge-Off Analysis

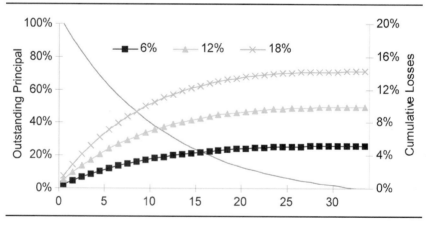

Source: Merrill Lynch.

What is notable in this nightmare scenario is that cumulative losses never increase by the same magnitude as the change in charge-off rates. This is due to the constant amortisation of principal. In a real world example, similar results would hold true accumulation period of a transaction. By extension this suggests that increases in charge-off rates are most damaging to a transaction when they occur during the revolving period, leaving the full principal amount exposed to the increase in loss.

For subordinated tranche investors, the question is whether an increase in charge-off rates is a temporary fluctuation or an indication of erosion of the underlying portfolio's credit quality. In this regard the investor needs to turn to the transaction's performance monitoring for guidance. The investor needs to not only evaluate changes in charge-off rates, but the evolution in the trust's arrears profile. A steady increase of amounts in all arrears bands suggests erosion of portfolio credit quality. No change in the arrears profile suggests a blip.

The investor can look further into the matter by examining the same sort of detail considered for changes in payment rates. However, in this case, the question is not what will cause borrowers to slow down repayment, but cease it all together? As with all forms of default, it is a matter of willingness and ability to pay. Though ability to repay (liquidity) is not captured as a credit card variable, a proxy exists for willingness in the distribution of the portfolio's credit scores.

It is worth emphasizing one more time, however, that this simulation assumes zero excess spread and no reserve account. In a more realistic scenario, the monthly excess spread would dampen the accumulation of losses by absorbing monthly loss fluctuations out of the reserve account. We discuss this issue in the following section.

Reserve Accounts Effects

Our final example seeks to quantify the support that exists beneath a transaction's rated tranches, namely reserve accounts and excess spread. Hitherto our examples have assumed that neither a reserve account nor the trapping of excess spread is in place. For analytical simplicity we will assume the inclusion of a fully funded reserve account sized at 5% of the portfolio's notional amount.

For the first time in our stress testing, our Class C notes emerge with their principal virtually intact. Unlike our base case (where cumulative losses are just over 5%), cumulative losses with the 5% reserve account total 20 bps (see Exhibit 7.3). Clearly, the amount of credit enhancement beneath the "C" piece is key to evaluation of subordinated tranche performance.

EXHIBIT 7.3   Reserve Account Analysis

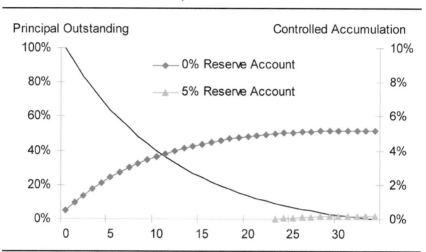

Source: Merrill Lynch.

EXHIBIT 7.4   Sample S&P Reserve Account

3-Month Excess Spread	Required Reserve Amount
> 4.54%	0.00%
4.0% to 4.5%	1.50%
3.5% to 4.0%	2.00%
3.0% to 3.5%	3.00%
< 3.0%	4.00%

Source: Standard & Poor's.

Typically structures that include "C" pieces provide for the provision for charge-offs out excess spread and for an excess spread funded reserve account. As pointed out earlier the level of excess spread in the transactions typically dictates the required funding level of the reserve account. A typical set of requirements is illustrated in Exhibit 7.4. This generally ranges between 0% to the equivalent of 4% of the portfolio's notional value.

With charge-offs met out of excess spread funded reserve account, the majority of capital losses borne by our Class B and Class C notes in our example would not have occurred. Further, had excess spread fallen below zero on a three-month rolling average basis the transaction would have gone into early amortisation.

The risk for investors, however, is a sudden drop in excess spread that prevents full funding of the reserve account and triggers an early amortisation of the transaction. In that respect, comfort with the excess spread volatility of a particular transaction and the adequate management of the servicer of the factors that affect excess spread, as discussed above, become crucial.

An important question for investors is the cause and duration of any changes in excess spread. A one-off drop in excess spread due to accounting adjustment is no cause for concern, while gradual yet rapid decline would create problems. For example, trust excess spread on MBNA International Bank's master trust dropped from 6.65% in November 2000 to 1.41% the following month. The dramatic decline is no cause for alarm— it is the result of an exceptional item resulting from MBNA's implementation of the FFEIC's common charge-off policy. The implementation expedited the charge-off of long term arrears as a one-off item.

Indeed trust excess spread returned to 6.5% during January 2001. Of greater concern would have been a gradual erosion in excess spread from 6.6% to 1.4% over a period of a few months, which would suggest an erosion of portfolio credit quality, diminishing the credit enhancement available beneath the subordinated pieces.

CONCLUSION

ABS capital structure allows investors to assume different risks and achieve different awards by taking a view on the performance of a specific asset pool and its originator/servicer. The lower the investor moves down the capital structure, the more intensive the credit analysis becomes and a more sophisticated cash flow review is required. The a priori understanding of the collateral pool and its expected performance, and the subsequent close monitoring of its actual performance are more time consuming. However, the rewards, as evidenced by the yield pickup when moving down the credit levels, would compensate investors for that.

CHAPTER 8

Key Consideration for Master Trust Structures

Alexander Batchvarov, Ph.D., CFA
Managing Director and Head, International Structured Credit Research
Merrill Lynch

Jenna Collins
Vice President
Merrill Lynch

William Davies
Assistant Vice President
Merrill Lynch

Following its introduction in the mid-1990s, the master trust quickly became the typical structure for credit card securitisations. Since then its applicability has expanded to embrace other asset classes such as unsecured consumer loans, corporate loan obligations, residential mortgages, and so on. As a result, an evolution in the structure has inevitably taken place. We believe that a detailed understanding of such structure is necessary when analyzing the series issued by a master trust, particularly the subordinated tranches, and that is the purpose of this chapter.

BASIC STRUCTURE

Generally, a credit card ABS is issued by a trust as a series of investor certificates and a seller certificate (also known as the *seller's interest*). Certificates give investors undivided beneficial interests in a pool of assets. This element of shared ownership differentiates them from notes, which are typically issued by ABS, and are debt obligations. The use of certificates is intentional as, unlike a discrete trust, master trusts can be used to issue multiple series of notes. The same pool of receivables, generated by the accounts specifically assigned to the trust, secures each series of notes issued. Furthermore, each series of notes has a pari passu claim on the pool's yield, less liability for the trust's costs and delinquencies.

SELLER CERTIFICATE

The seller certificate's primary purpose is to absorb the daily fluctuations in the amount of receivables in the trust. Fluctuations in the amount of receivables are due to many factors, including seasonal effects, returns of merchandise, and the reversal of fraudulent charges. As the amount of receivables outstanding declines (increases) the principal amount of the seller certificate also declines (increases). The minimum amount of the seller certificates for most master trusts is generally around 4–7% of the principal receivables transferred to the trust.

INVESTOR CERTIFICATES

Each series of investor certificates may have several classes. The senior, Class A, is rated AAA while the junior classes, the B and Class C, are generally rated A and BBB, respectively. Prior to the introduction of BBB pieces, issuers used *cash collateral accounts* (CCA) or *collateral investment amounts* (CIA). Though all three methods work to provide the same credit enhancement, they differ in both cash flow mechanics and marketability. For the purposes of our discussion, we will only focus on the Class C structure, which has grown to be the European norm over the past year through transactions by Barclays, Royal Bank of Scotland, and MBNA.

Part of a master trust's appeal for issuers is that it can issue multiple series, thereby spreading the cost across various transactions. Series issued by the same trust can have different characteristics (e.g., coupons, principal amounts, and maturities) despite representing a claim on a common pool of assets. For investors this raises questions as the manner and extent to which cash flows can be allocated amongst the series.

SOURCE AND USES OF CASH

There are four—two major and two minor—sources of cash for monthly collections. The first is the payment of principal. The speed at which this occurs is called the payment rate, which is the percentage of outstanding principal repaid on average each month. The second major source of cash is finance charge income—the interest on the outstanding receivable balances. The two minor sources of cash are any fees payable on the cards and interchange.

Interchange is a payment of fees generated from the usage of credit card networks. Payable to issuers by the networks, interchange is not always included in the definition of income. The sum of interest charges, fees and interchange are the portfolio's income. Dividing income by the total nominal size of the portfolio gives its yield.

Similarly, there are four uses for the cash received. They are ranked in order of priority for disbursement. Foremost is payment for the servicing of the portfolio. Typically the portfolio's seller remains its servicer. Next in priority is payment of the fees for the maintenance of the trust. This covers all expenses from corporate services (accountants, lawyers, etc.) through to trustee fees. The first two uses are administrative and logistical charges. The final two uses represent the actual performance of the transaction, namely the payment of interest and principal. Their treatment is detailed at length below. Any funds left over after meeting all costs is called *excess spread*. Its treatment is also detailed below.

It is important to note that it is convention to express all sources and uses of cash as a percentage of the notional value of the portfolio.

REDEMPTION PROFILES

The first role of cash flow allocation in a master trust is to extend the term the of (mostly) monthly credit receivables to match the term of the notes. Credit card ABS do not contain a static pool of assets. Instead, with each monthly collection by the servicer, existing receivables are individually discharged either in whole or in part depending upon the principal collected. Rather than pass these principal receipts directly on to certificate holders, the trustee uses principal receipts to purchase additional receivables, thereby maintaining the required level of receivables in the trust. "Revolving" asset pools in this manner can create Credit card ABS of varying maturities.

Credit card ABS typically redeem as "soft bullets" in a single repayment of principal. Sinking fund redemptions, however, are possible. A series that has a bullet repayment of principal utilises a controlled accu-

EXHIBIT 8.1 Sample Soft Bullet Redemption

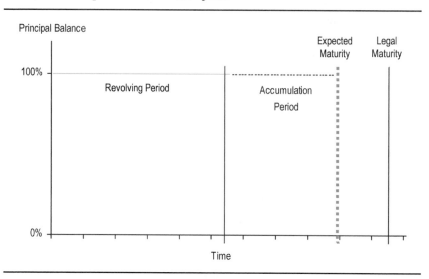

Source: Merrill Lynch.

mulation feature, while a series that has multiple principal payments uses a controlled amortisation feature. The most common revolving-plus-accumulation structure is schematically shown in Exhibit 8.1.

A controlled accumulation structure traps cash received from monthly collections until it has enough collected to repay the principal in full. The cash accumulates in a *principal funding account* (PFA), where it is invested in highly rated short-term or money market instruments. This results in negative carry as cash returns are typically less than the interest rate on the certificates. The time period required to accumulate the required amount of cash depends upon the payment rate of the underlying collateral.

With a controlled amortisation structure, equal installments of principal are passed through to investors over a specified period of time (e.g., 6, 12, or 24 months). This is an attractive feature for issuers since a shorter accumulation period reduces the amount of negative carry experienced by the trust and ultimately the seller/servicer. Common in the early days of credit card securitisation, sinking fund redemptions are now rare.

Key to credit card redemption profiles is the concept of soft maturity schedules. All credit card ABS carry an expected maturity date as well as a legal final maturity date. The expected maturity date is the planned date of the bullet redemption or the final payment under the sinking fund. The trust's ability to meet the payment is a function of the payment rate of the underlying collateral. If payment rates severely under perform from expectations, there is a risk that the trust will have insufficient cash to make the payment. To mitigate this risk, there is a time buffer between the expected and legal final maturity to give the trust an opportunity to accumulate the required cash. Indeed, a transaction's rating typically addresses its ability to repay principal in its entirety by the legal final maturity, not the expected maturity date. Further, missing an expected maturity is not an act of default, though it would understandably be viewed very negatively by the market. The risk that a transaction will not be able to meet its expected maturity date is called *extension risk*.

CASH FLOW ALLOCATIONS

The cash flow derived from the underlying receivables and charged-off amounts are allocated between the seller certificates and each series of investor certificates. The allocation process occurs in stages. At the highest level, the principal balance of the seller certificate and, assuming more than one series has been issued, the aggregate principal balance of the investors certificates are used to allocate cash flow and charged-off amounts. Unless the cash flow allocated to the seller certificate is being used as credit enhancement, or is needed to maintain the seller interest at a specified level, it is released to the holder of the seller certificate.

The next level of allocation occurs among each series of investor certificates. There are three primary methods to allocate cash flow and charged off amounts. These methods are used to distinguish three different types of master trusts, and are illustrated in Exhibit 8.2.

Under the first and second method, the amount allocated to each series depends upon its size relative to the total investor interest. The

EXHIBIT 8.2   Sample Allocation of Excess of Spread

	Method 1		Method 2		Method 3	
	Series 1	Series 2	Series 1	Series 2	Series 1	Series 2
Yield	18%	18%	15%	15%	20%	20%
Expenses	14%	15%	14%	16%	10%	15%
Difference	4%	3%	1%	−1%	10%	5%
Allocated Excess Spread	4%	3%	0%	1%	6%	9%

Source: Merrill Lynch.

trust allocates monthly principal receipts among series based upon a floating percentage during the revolving period and a fixed/floating percentage during any other period (e.g., the accumulation or amortisation period). The trust uses the same formula to allocate finance charge collections (the interest on the underlying collateral) and charge offs amounts. Once allocated to a series, principal collections can be used to purchase new receivables, fund the PFA, or passed-through to investors. Finance charge collections (interest on the underlying receivables) are used to cover coupon payments, charge offs, and servicing fees.

Up to this point the first method and the second method have been the same. They differ in their treatment of excess spread, which represents any excess in finance charge receivable collections. Under the first method (type I master trusts), excess spread is related to either the credit enhancement provider or the seller. The holders of the senior class of any series do not have any rights to the excess spread.

In the second method of allocation (type II master trusts), before excess spread is released to the seller, excess spread for one series is made available to any other series that cannot cover its expenses. Varying coupons of each series issued by the same master trust is the primary reason for different excess spread among series. By allowing the sharing of excess spread, early amortisation risk is reduced for series with relatively high expenses. If the situation continues to deteriorate, however, delaying an early amortisation may expose investors to increased credit risk.

In the third method of allocation (type III master trusts), principal collections are allocated and used in the same manner as the other two methods. The allocation of finance charge receivable collections, however, is quite different. Under the third method, allocation among series depends upon each series' expenses (i.e., coupon, charged off amounts and servicing fees) relative to the combined expenses of all series. By allocating finance charge receivables in this manner, series that have more expenses receive more dollars of finance charge collections. As such, series with relative low expenses are subsidising the series with relatively high expenses. The higher expenses are usually the result of relatively high coupons. Although this allocation method can reduce the credit risk and early amortisation risk for series with relatively high expenses, it increases those same risks for series with relatively low expenses. For example, if the shortfall in one series is very high and the cumulative excess spread of all the other series is insufficient to cover it, all series will face a shortfall to a different degree after the reallocation of the available excess spread.

A final note on the allocation of principal collections, most master trusts allow for the sharing of principal collections. The sharing of principal collections allows a series that is currently in its accumulation or amortisation period to utilise the principal collections allocated to other series that would normally be used to purchase additional receivables from the seller. Recall principal collections allocated to a series are used to purchase additional receivables from the seller when such series is in its revolving period or are allocated principal collections that exceed either their controlled accumulation amounts or controlled amortisation amounts. By sharing principal collections, the receiving series can shorten its accumulation or controlled amortisation period.

Once the cash flow has been allocated to each series, cash flow is further allocated to each class of certificates within a series. Generally, principal payments are made on a sequential basis, with principal payments made to the holders of the Class A then to the holders of the Class B and then finally to the holders of the Class C. Generally, the interest payments on the Class B is pari passu with the interest payments on the Class A and the interest payments on the Class C is subordinated to the interest and principal payments on the Class A and B.

CREDIT PROTECTION

As previously mentioned the credit enhancement for most credit cards ABS consists of the subordination of cash flows and, in certain circumstances, reserve cash accounts. The subordinated cash flows represent excess spread and junior classes.

SUBORDINATION AND RESERVE ACCOUNTS

Generally, excess spread is the amount of finance charge collections remaining after paying for the current period's interest payments on Class A and Class B interest and servicing fee payments and covering the current period's charged off receivables. Excess spread is also used to cover unpaid amounts of interest payments, servicing fees and charged off receivables. In certain structures, excess spread from one series can be shared other series issued by the trust. As discussed above, the method used to allocate finance charge collections determines at what point excess spread will be shared. The amount of excess spread that is not used by investors can either be used to fund a spread account, pay fees to providers of credit enhancement or be released to the seller/servicer.

The junior classes include a Class B and a Class C or a CIA. A Class C is generally structured for institutional investors, while a CIA is structured for traditional bank providers of credit enhancement. As noted, we

EXHIBIT 8.3   Sample Standard & Poor's Reserve Accounts

3-month Excess Spread	Required Reserve Amount
> 4.54%	0.00%
4.0% to 4.5%	1.50%
3.5% to 4.0%	2.00%
3.0% to 3.5%	3.00%
< 3.0%	4.00%

Source: Standard & Poor's.

will be focussing only on the investment merits of the Class C. Cash, if available, is usually deposited into a CCA which supports the Class A and Class B and a spread (reserve) account, which supports the Class C. The CCA is usually fully funded at closing. The spread account may be fully funded, partially funded, or unfunded at the time of issuance. If the spread account is partially or unfunded at the time of issuance and additional deposits are required, such amounts are funded by excess spread. Additional amounts are usually required, if the excess spread is below certain predetermined levels, as the example in Exhibit 8.3 shows.

The amount of credit enhancement depends upon a variety of factors, including the capability of the seller/servicer to manage its credit card business, collateral performance (e.g., defaults, delinquencies, portfolio yield, and payment rate) and the transaction's structure.

As previously mentioned, the reserve account supporting the Class C can either be fully or partially funded, or unfunded at the time of issuance. If it is partially funded or unfunded, the structure will provide a mechanism to trap cash flow in the spread account until it reaches a specified level. The ability to fully fund the spread account will depend upon how quickly the portfolio's credit quality deteriorates. Though excess spread is expected to be able to fund the reserve account during a short period of time, it is susceptible to the risk of a sudden, sharp erosion in portfolio yield. As such there is a risk that the structure might not be able to fund the reserve account to the required levels, thereby weakening the transaction's expected credit enhancement.

Early Pay-out Events

Credit card ABS benefit from structural protections that require the early repayment of principal if certain adverse events occur. These events are classified as either series related or trust related. A series-related pay-out event would result in the early repayment of only the affected series issued by the master trust.

Series related events include the following:

- The average excess spread for any three-month period is less than zero.
- The principal balance of any class of certificates is greater than zero after the expected final payment date.
- Failure by the seller to add receivables when required.
- Failure by the seller/servicer to make required payments.
- Failure of the seller/servicer to cure any breach of its representations or warranties.
- Failure by the servicer to replace any interest rate swap or interest rate cap provider counterparty that does meet the minimum credit rating requirements (in some cases).

Trust related events include:

- Insolvency of the seller/servicer.
- The trust is deemed to be an investment company.

SELLER/SERVICER SUPPORT

Despite the legal separation between seller/servicers and the transaction, most have a strong interest to have their transactions perform successfully. Reasons range from reputational risk to the desire not to compromise future access to the ABS capital markets. This results in an unwritten form of credit enhancement comes in the guise of "moral" support from the transactions's seller/servicer. This consists of providing "support" to credit their credit card ABS, which was not required under the legal documentation. Possible methods include over-collateralising investor certificates or substituting assets of a superior credit quality into the pool.

Though this is yet to publicly occur in European Credit Card ABS market, a US example is First Union, which subordinated its right to receive a servicing fee to ABS holders. For example, Mercantile discounted principal receivables which increased the trust's portfolio yield. Similarly, Banc One (First Chicago) added better performing, seasoned accounts to its trust.

Providing moral support is not without some cost to seller/servicers. By supporting deals after the fact, bank issuers of credit card ABS risk losing their accounting and regulatory off-balance-sheet treatment. Although investors generally prefer deals that do not need support, most investors welcome such support as its maintains the rating of the

ABS. Investors should be aware that at the time of "support" these deals generally trade at a concession to the overall market. Furthermore, though in many cases "support" can be expected, it should never be counted on. This point should be made even more firmly given the recently published second draft of the proposed BIS capital adequacy guidelines. In revolving structures with early amortisation features, for example, triggering early amortisation leaves banks exposed to the need to fund newly generated receivables on-balance sheet (since collections are used to rapidly repay the outstanding securitisation bonds). This could result in liquidity pressures. In addition, there is a potential for reputational damage due to an early amortisation triggered by poor pool performance raising the stakes for the originating bank to find ways to implicitly support the transaction. As a result, the Committee seeks to address these risks by introducing a minimum capital requirement of 10% (or higher, up to 20%) of the notional amount of the off-balance sheet securitised pool of such securitisations.

MASTER TRUST EVOLUTION

Following its introduction in the mid-1990s, the master trust quickly became the typical structure for credit card securitisations. Since then its applicability has expanded to embrace other asset classes such as unsecured consumer loans, corporate loan obligations, residential mortgages, and so on. As a result, inevitable evolution in the structure has taken place. Launched in September 2000, Citibank Credit Card Issuance Trust (CCCIT) represents the latest evolution. The structure is notable for its ability (subject to required credit enhancement levels) to issue the different tranches at individual points in time, rather than all at once. The program debuted in September 2000 with the placement of a $800 million C piece. Over the remainder of 2000, the trust intermittently issued $4.5 billion in Class A and $500.0 million in Class B notes on the back of pre-placed Class C notes.

The structure operates by repackaging certificates purchased from Citigroup's Citibank Credit Card master trust. These certificates are used as the collateral to back the issuance of notes from CCCIT, for which it has a shelf registration. As noted, the CCCIT is able to issue tranches at its discretion, provided that the following credit enhancement levels are available. They are 12.25% below the AAA rated Class A notes, 7.0% below the A rated Class B notes, and the availability of a reserve fund below the BBB rated Class C notes. As with other structures, the required funding level of the reserve account is a function of the amount of available excess spread.

We believe the structure provides a positive model for European transactions for the following reasons.

- *Timing flexibility.* Structured to be MTN-like in its ability to issue on demand, the structure allows the issuer to discriminate between changes in appetite along the credit curve and respond appropriately. This enables an issuer to respond tactically to favourable demand conditions as well as meeting ongoing funding requirements. Further, it reduces the pressure on issuers to place subordinated pieces when attempting to fund during difficult market periods.

- *ERISA eligibility.* Eligible investments for US pension plans is governed by the Employment Retirement Investment Savings Act (ERISA). Understandably, securities enjoy a liquidity benefit from ERISA eligibility. ERISA provides different treatments for equity and debt. Due to their shared ownership properties, ERISA regulations treats certificates as equity not debt. While investment-grade notes may be purchased by funds, pass-through certificates typically must pass the "100 holders rule." Under the 100-holders rule, securities must be held by at least 100 investors to be an eligible investment for pension funds. Though the rule applies to all certificates issued from trust regardless of credit rating, it has historically been hardest for subordinated tranches to pass the test given their relatively small sizes. By issuing all tranches within a series as notes, CCCIT bypasses this issue. In past other issuers have used a second trust to package certificates into notes, but primarily at the BBB level.

- *Application to MBS.* One of the most important innovations in the securitisation of mortgages is the application of the master trust structure, typically associated with credit card ABS, to residential MBS. Pioneered in the UK, it quickly gained favor with the largest mortgage originators and securitisers, leading to the establishment of large securitisation programs with regular multicurrency and multi-tranche issuance.

CHAPTER 9

Trust and Agency Services in the Debt Capital Markets

Nick Procter
EMEA Structured Finance Services
JPMorgan Chase Bank

Edmond Leedham
EMEA Structured Finance Services
JPMorgan Chase Bank

This chapter is an account of trustee and agency services that are required to support proper functioning of the debt capital markets. Specifically we focus on securitisation products, better known as "structured finance" products. A distinction will be made between responsibilities of a trustee and the other services offered by trust banks, known as agency services, to support debt markets structured products. The purpose of this chapter is to give the reader a broad understanding of the work undertaken by trust banks and how these services relate to the structures themselves. It should be noted that whilst many of these services are offered globally, the focus of this chapter is primarily on the European structured finance market.

The term "structured finance" is a generic term. It encompasses bond or note issue transactions involving the securitisation of a pool of assets and taking place under the name of a legal entity known as a *spe-*

The authors would like to thank Paula Jacobsen and Ruth Kentish for review comments and assistance with preparing this chapter.

cial purpose vehicle (SPV). There is a wide range of asset classes that can be securitised. We will discuss the provision of trust and agency services supporting the following types of products: *asset-backed securities* (ABS), *mortgage-backed securities* (MBS), inclusive of *commercial* (CMBS) and *residential* (RMBS) *mortgage backed* deals, *collateralised debt obligations* (CDOs), *asset-backed conduit programs* (ABCP), and *structured investment vehicles* (SIVs). In this chapter we will assume that the bonds under discussion, irrespective of their asset backing, are issued into the Eurozone markets and are international securities clearing in Euroclear or Clearstream.

This chapter is split into two sections. The first section will speak to generic servicing, which is not product specific (though not necessarily applicable to all product types). The second section will speak to specific servicing requirements for the different bond classes.

GENERIC TRUST AND AGENCY SERVICES

We begin with a review of the trustee function and other agency services required for all debt market instruments.

Trustee

The role of the trustee in a Eurobond issuance is to serve as a bridge between the issuer of the bonds and the bondholders throughout the life of the issuance. The scope of duties undertaken by a trustee in connection with any given issuance may vary from structure to structure, but the essence of the trustee's role is to hold and exercise as necessary, and as permitted by the trust documentation, the legal rights of each bondholder in the transaction.

Legal Background

A trust is an invention of common law and is particular to the law of England, the United States, and other countries whose legal traditions have evolved from English law (although a few civil law jurisdictions recognise the concept of a trust in one form or another). The concept of trust flows from the common law construction that ownership rights in property may be divided into two distinct classes: legal ownership and beneficial ownership. A "legal owner" of property holds title to that property and is recognised in law as the owner of such property. A "beneficial owner" of property does not hold legal title to the property, but enjoys some or all of the benefits that normally would be associated with legal ownership of property. The recognition of different classes of ownership rights in common law allows one party to assume legal ownership of a piece of property purely for the purpose of holding that property "on trust" for the benefit of one or more third parties (the very essence of a trust).

A legal owner of property appears to all the world as the actual owner of such property. Thus, the rights of a legal owner in such property cannot be restricted by general operation of law. Where a legal owner holds such property on trust (i.e., as a trustee) for another party, the legal owner's rights in such property must be circumscribed by ancillary means. The common law, as well as statutory law, provides many principles and "default provisions" delineating the division of rights, liabilities and responsibilities between parties to a trust. However, the specific relationship and division of rights between the trustee and the beneficiaries of a trust are regulated largely by the terms of the documentation establishing the trust (normally a "trust deed" under English law).

The terms of trusts created in support of Eurobond issuance are negotiated chiefly between representatives of the issuer (usually the arranger) and the trustee during the deal origination process (although outside parties, such as rating agencies, may have considerable input into the process). As is the case with most trusts, the beneficiaries of such trusts (i.e., the bondholders) have no input into the terms of the trust. However, any party who purchases a bond is deemed upon such purchase to be legally bound by the terms of the trust documentation executed in connection with the issuance. Thus, issuers and trustees are compelled to ensure that Eurobond trust structures meet certain market standards in order to induce investors to purchase the bonds being issued.

Use of Trusts in Eurobond Structures

The concept of trust is particularly well suited to Eurobond issuance because the concept supports an environment in which investors normally hold such bonds anonymously through a clearing system and actively trade such bonds on the secondary market.

The holder of a Eurobond is meant to benefit from a number of covenants, charges, and pledges associated with the issuance. The most basic example of a "covenant" that the issuer would be expected to grant the bondholder is the covenant to repay the debt. A classic example of a "charge" is a "first fixed charge" over assets meant to secure the debt. Such covenants, charges, and pledges must be made in favour of a specific persons or persons to be effective. This is especially important in the case of charges over assets securing the debt. Beneficiaries of such charges must file a copy of the charge with the appropriate registry (which in England is "Companies House") in order to perfect (i.e., ensure the priority of its security interest in such assets against third parties) the security interest granted by the charge.

If the issuer were to grant the rights (e.g., covenants, charges, pledges) underlying such bonds directly to individual bondholders at the inception of the deal, the bonds might not be easily sold on the secondary market without modification of the original issuance documentation. Moreover, modification of the issuance documentation would be impractical in such circumstances because, in addition to cost and time considerations, it would be difficult to verify the identities of the parties to the secondary sale and many investors would not want to reveal their identity to the issuer.

Placing a trustee between the issuer and the bondholders at the inception of the deal eliminates the above problem because the trustee assumes legal ownership of the rights underlying the bonds (e.g., covenants, charges, and pledges) for the benefit of present and future bondholders for the duration of the issuance. Thus, bondholders, as the beneficial owners of the rights attached to the bond which are held legally by the trustee, may freely trade the bonds without the need for modification of the original issuance documents or fear that such transfer would compromise rights underlying the bonds.

A more obvious advantage of placing a trustee between the issuer and the bondholders of a Eurobond issuance is that doing so provides a constant point of contact between the issuer and a set of largely anonymous and often changing bondholders. The bondholders are able to speak to the issuer and other concerned parties with one voice and the issuer is provided a single point of contact with which it can consult as necessary on issues that might arise in the day-to-day operation of the transaction. Such an arrangement is useful not only in default, or potential default, situations, but for disposition of relatively routine or non-controversial matters that might arise throughout the life of the issuance.

Even in far less volatile commercial environments than that in which we now find ourselves, it may be beneficial to all parties to a transaction to modify the terms of issuance documentation and very often time is of the essence. In the absence of a trust structure, issuers would have to convene a meeting of the bondholders to sanction even the most mundane amendment to issuance documentation. Convening such meetings is a costly, time consuming and generally arduous proposition that should only be undertaken when absolutely necessary.

The use of a trust structure in a Eurobond issuance can minimise significantly the need to consult bondholders on certain document modifications. The issuer and trustee typically craft the trust deed to empower the trustee to exercise discretion on behalf of all bondholders within specified parameters. Under current market standards, the trustee is normally permitted to agree to nonmaterial modifications of the terms of a Eurobond issuance and exercise very specific powers, such as the power to appoint or approve replacement agents within defined circumstances and criteria, without consultation of the bondholders. The ability of the trustee to agree to nonmaterial term modifications and exercise certain prescribed powers without consultation of bondholders benefits all parties to the deal both practically and economically because expensive and time-consuming bondholders meetings are not necessary to deal with such issues.

Finally, in cases where convening a bondholder meeting is unavoidable due to the nature of the proposed amendment, the presence of a professional trustee in the structure is invaluable. The trustee, unlike most issuers, has well-established contacts with paying agents and the clearing systems and can play a crucial role in helping the issuer get word of the proposed amendment out to the bondholders and ensuring that the bondholders respond to such proposals. Moreover, an experienced professional trustee can be a useful resource to the issuer who often has no way of knowing in advance of the bondholders meeting whether the bondholders will accept its proposal. Drawing upon its experience, the trustee can advise the issuer of the likelihood of the proposal's success and recommend revisions thereby minimising the chance that the issuer will launch a costly exercise that is doomed to failure from the start.

Note Trustee versus Security Trustee

It is worthwhile to note that in addition to delineating the specific powers and duties of a trustee within a given trust structure, the issuance documentation is sometimes drafted to draw a distinction between the roles of "note trustee" and "security trustee."

A note trustee holds on behalf of the noteholders the issuer's covenant to repay the notes, as well as other related covenants. Accordingly, a note trustee is concerned mainly about whether the issuer is honouring such covenants and whether an acceleration of payment of the notes is in order. A security trustee holds the security interest, usually given in the form of a charge or pledge, granted by the issuer for the benefit of the noteholders and other secured creditors. The security trustee's focus is on enforcement of the security, although it is important to note that normally the security trustee would not enforce the security unless directed to do so by the note trustee.

In most Eurobond structures, the roles of note trustee and security trustee are combined and documented as a single trustee role (i.e., both roles will be documented in a single trust deed). However, some lawyers prefer to document the roles separately, even though each role will be undertaken by the same entity. This is especially common in highly structured deals such as master trusts, where the securitised assets are held by an entity other than the issuer of the overlying notes and the overlying notes are secured by intermediate loans. The logic behind this practice is that even in relatively straightforward structures, the note trustee and security trustee may come in conflict with one another in an enforcement action. (Note that a security trustee often holds the security for the benefit of other secured creditors as well as the noteholders.) Should such a conflict arise, the entity undertaking the roles can simply delegate one role or the other to a neutral third party, thereby eliminating the conflict.

Paying Agent

All debt issuance in the Euromarkets requires a principal paying agent or, in the case of a programme of issuance (for example a Euro-MTN programme), an issuing and paying agent. The responsibility of the paying agent is to provide administrative support to the issuer throughout the lifetime of the issue, the primary one of which is to arrange for payment of the note coupon to investors via the clearing systems. The complete duties of a paying agent are:

- Issuing securities upon demand in the case of a debt programme.
- Authenticating definitive notes.
- Collecting funds from the issuer and paying these out to investors as coupon and redemption payments.
- In the case of global notes, acting on behalf of the issuer to supervise payments of interest and principal to investors via the clearing systems, and in the case of definitive notes, paying out interest and coupon on presentation by the investor of the relevant coupon or bond to the paying agent.
- Transferring funds to subpaying agents, where these have been appointed. For instance, a security that has been listed on the Luxembourg stock exchange must have a local subpaying agent appointed for it.
- Maintaining a bank account of the cash flows paid out on the bond.
- Arranging the cancellation and subsequent payment of coupons, matured bonds, and global notes, and sending destroyed certificates to the issuer.

A paying agent will act solely on behalf of the issuer, unlike a trustee who has an obligation to look after the interests of investors. For larger bond issues there may be a number of paying agents appointed, of which the *principal paying agent* is the coordinator. A number of *subpaying agents* may be appointed to ensure that bondholders in different countries may receive their coupon and redemption payments without delay. The term *fiscal agent* is used to describe a paying agent for a bond issue for which no trustee has been appointed.

Common Depository

The depositary for a Eurobond issue is responsible for the safekeeping of securities. In the Euromarkets well over 90% of investors are institutions, and so as a result issues are made in dematerialised form, and are represented by a global note. Trading and settlement is in computerised book-entry form via the two main international clearing systems, Euroclear and Clearstream. Both these institutions have appointed a group of banks to act on their behalf as depositaries for book-entry securities; this is known as *common depositaries*, because the appointment is common to both Euroclear and Clearstream. Both clearing firms have appointed separately a network of banks to act as specialised depositaries, which handle securities that have been issued in printed note or *definitive* form.

As of February 2003 there were 21 banks that acted as common depositaries on behalf of Euroclear and Clearstream, although the majority of the trading volume was handled by just three banks, JPMorgan Chase Bank, Citibank NA, and Deutsche Bankers Trust. The common depositary is responsible for:

■ Representing Euroclear and Clearstream and facilitating delivery versus payment of the primary market issue by collecting funds from the investors, taking possession of the temporary global note (which allows securities to be released to investors), and making a single payment of funds to the issuer.

■ Holding the temporary global note in safe custody until it is exchanged for definitive notes or a permanent global note.

■ Making adjustments to the nominal value of the global note that occur after the exercise of any options or after conversions in line with instructions from Euroclear or Clearstream and the fiscal agent.

■ Surrendering the cancelled temporary global note to the fiscal agent after the exchange into definitive certificates or a permanent global note—or on maturity of the permanent global note.

A specialised depositary will hold definitive notes representing aggregate investor positions held in a particular issue; on coupon and maturity dates it presents the coupons or bond to the paying agent and passes the proceeds on to the clearing system.

Custodian

The custodian is the party that holds/safekeeps collateral, cash, or other forms of security on behalf of the deal. The custodian takes into custody for safekeeping the assets on behalf of the deal. The securities that a custodian might be expected to take safekeeping of would include, sovereign debt, corporate debt, asset backed securities, corporate loans, equity, distressed debt, repo, cash, and any other form of collateral for which a third-party custodian is required. Given the pan-European and indeed global nature of many structured deals the custodian is often required to offer global capabilities. In order to achieve the required global reach a global custodian will often appoint a subcustodian. The subcustodian will perform the custodial duties for a specific local area.

The custodian/subcustodian is responsible for the following duties:

- Settlement of securities through the applicable exchange.
- Holding securities in clearing account or in physical form, on site.
- Provision of corporate action information.
- Execution of corporate actions such as coupon payments.
- Collection of coupon and principal payments.
- Reclaiming tax on coupons paid net.

Custodial services are often performed by a third party to the deal. This is partly through necessity as in most cases, the deal participants do not have custodial capabilities. Additionally, the third party involvement reinforces the off-balance sheet nature of the deal for the originator and clearly defines those assets associated with the particular deal. Finally, the appointed custodian is generally, although not necessarily, the same entity as the appointed trustee. Hence there is further protection provided to the investor in a default situation as the trustee effectively has control of the assets. This is a source of comfort for investors.

The traditional concept of a custodian as explained above is applicable to those deal types that hold the assets noted. This is usually the case for ABCP programs (although these deals may be set up to fund exclusively trade receivable assets), CDOs, and SIVs. With certain forms of CDO transactions, the proceeds of issued notes are sometimes invested in collateral. This is also held by the deal custodian. In addition, ABS deals may also have a requirement for custodial services. Hence the custodian may be required to take possession of physical deeds and/or pledges. These forms of security will be held in the custodian's vault for safekeeping.

Cash Manager and Account Bank

All structured finance deals have cash movements through the structure. Cash is continuously being generated by the assets, whether they be residential mortgages, credit card receivables, or high yield bonds. Other cash movements may include monies moved through interest rate and FX swaps, third-party fees and expenses such as trustee, rating agency and legal costs, and payment of bond coupon and principal. The responsibility of the movement of the cash, which is distinct from the decision to move the cash, is the role of the cash manager. From a servicing perspective the cash manger does not have discretionary powers— the cash manager only acts on instruction from the originator or deal manager. In this respect the cash manager acts an investment agent, placing funds as directed into designated bank accounts or high-quality assets such as Treasury bills.

Thus there is always a requirement for a cash manger. Crucial to the cash management function is the provision of bank accounts. That is, the deal will necessarily have a requirement for bank accounts (often multicurrency). It should be noted that the cash manager and account bank roles do not necessarily need to be performed by the same entity. Often the cash will be managed by the originator or servicer of the assets but the deal accounts will be held at a separate account bank provider. It is common for one agency provider to be appointed as both cash manager and account bank. Where a different party is appointed for the latter role, the cash manager will be required to liaise with the account bank.

Exhibit 9.1 is the transaction structure diagram for a hypothetical CMBS structure. It illustrates the complex nature of the cash management function. In this example the deal requires management of 21 different cash accounts in multiple currencies. In addition to moving the cash between the accounts in the structure the cash manager may also be expected to maintain ledgers. In the example noted in Exhibit 9.1, the cash movements, including swap and hedge payments, principal and interest collections, interests due on the notes, principal due on the notes, third-party eligible investments (suitably rated money market funds or GIC accounts for example), must all be posted to the appropriate ledger. Given that each SPV in the example may have one or more ledgers, this further serves to highlight the potential complexity of the cash managers duties.

EXHIBIT 9.1 Hypothetical CMBS Transactions Detailing Bank Accounts

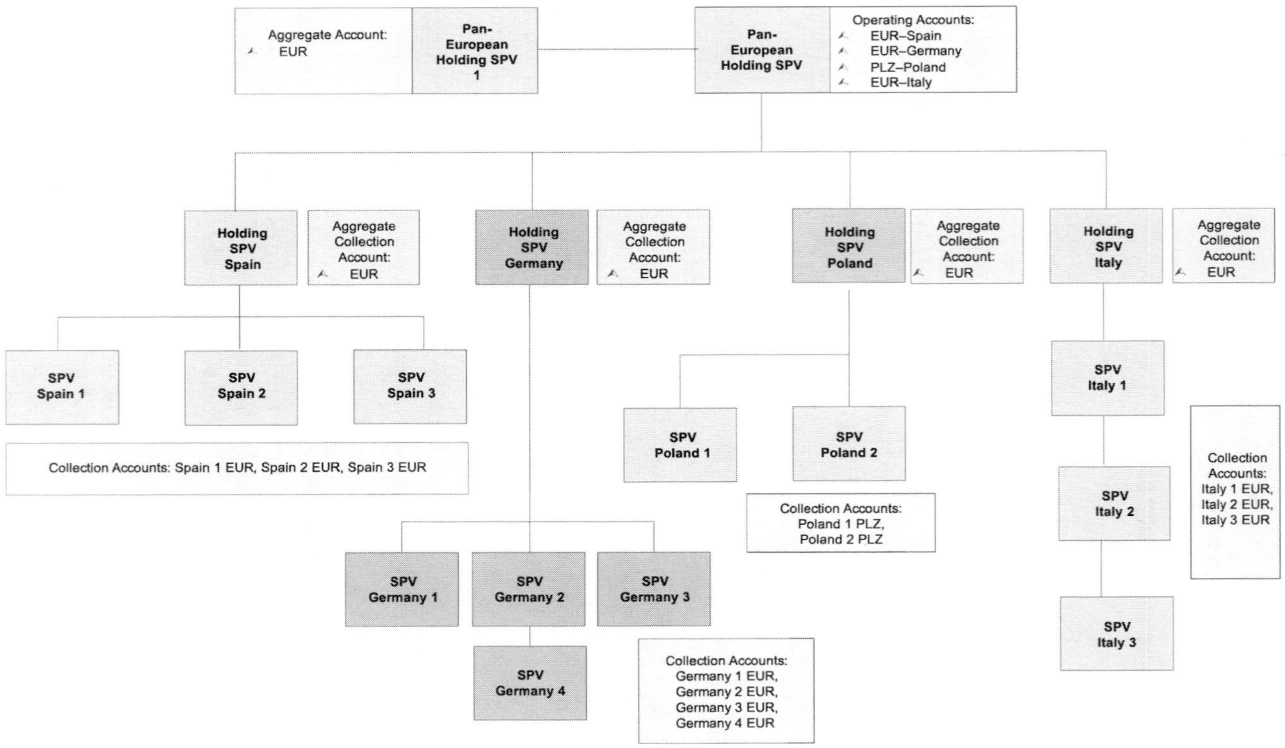

Listing Agent

Increasingly, a requirement for many structured finance deals is to have the issued notes listed on a stock exchange. Listing raises the deal profile and indeed many institutional investors will not invest in a deal unless it is listed. In Europe the Luxembourg Stock Exchange has traditionally been the exchange that European deals have listed on, however the Dublin Stock Exchange is becoming increasingly popular for listing in Europe.

In order to list on an exchange firms use a listing agent. The listing agent facilitates the request to list with the exchange. This will involve:

- Assisting with the completion of the necessary documentation to list.
- Calculation and collection of Exchange fees.
- Submitting the relevant documentation to the exchange.
- Liaising with the exchange to facilitate approval.

Back Up Servicing

The concept of a backup servicer originated in the US market to appease investor and rating agency concerns in the mortgage-backed market. The appointment of a backup servicer on asset backed and mortgage-backed deals in the US market is now widespread. Although the appointment of a backup servicer on ABS and MBS deals is not as prevalent in Europe the markets are increasingly seeking added protection through the appointment of the back up servicer.

The role of the backup servicer is simple in principal. If the servicer of the assets breaches the covenants documented under the servicing agreement and it is deemed that they are no longer fit or able to continue to service the assets, the backup servicer is then responsible for servicing the assets. There are different levels of responsibility depending on what type of backup servicer is appointed:

1. *Hot backup servicer.* The appointment of a hot backup servicer offers the most protection to the deal as the time window in which the servicer is replaced is smallest, usually the hot backup servicer agrees to be servicing the assets within 24 hours.
2. *Warm backup servicer.* A warm servicer ensures that the assets are serviced in the event of a servicer default usually within the period of 5–30 days.
3. *Cold backup servicer.* The appointment of a cold servicer offers least protection to the deal. The cold servicer undertakes to ensure that the assets are being serviced, not necessarily by themselves (most often not themselves), within a specified period, often a period of between 30–90 days.

As one moves down the spectrum from hot to cold the cost of appointing a backup servicer decreases significantly. The reason for this is because a hot backup servicer must effectively mirror the operations of the original servicer in order to be able to start servicing the assets within 48 hours. Depending on the extent of the operation this can be costly both in terms of staffing and technology. The cold servicer on the other hand has time to appoint a servicer capable of servicing the specified assets and assist in managing the hand over to the new servicer.

Although not all backup servicers are rated, increasingly both rating agencies and investor are looking for rated institutions to be nominated as the backup servicer.

The Appendix to this chapter provides a quick reference guide of the trustee and agency roles offer by trust banks to support the structured finance market.

SERVICING FOR CDO TRANSACTIONS

In the second part of this chapter, we consider in greater detail the agency functions performed for specific deal types, beginning with the roles performed by a trustee in a collateralised debt obligation.

Portfolio Administrator

The role of portfolio administrator is critical for those transactions requiring the service. The role is required only for specific transactions such as cash or synthetic collateralised debt obligations (CDOs), conduits and SIVs.

The reporting discipline described later, both in terms of content and complexity, is most rigorous for CDOs. As a result this section will focus on the reporting required for these deal types.

The primary function of the portfolio administrator is to produce the investor reports and the payment date reports for the duration of the deal. The reports enable investors to track the deal, most importantly the performance of the underlying portfolio. The reports are therefore an essential service that enable investors to keep abreast of these complex transactions. In addition the reports are also used by the arranger, portfolio manager and rating agencies. As they are produced by an independent third-party to the deal, portfolio reports are often required by the credit agencies rating the deal. Hence the discipline that the reports enforce also ensures that portfolio managers comply to the strict compliance regulations stipulated in the deal documentation. This is a further comfort for investors.

The disciplines imposed by the reports on the fund managers are part of the terms of the deal stipulating the nature of the underlying portfolio. These terms are evaluated by the rating agencies and must be adhered to at all times if the overlying notes are to retain their ratings. In order to grant the ratings required to place the senior notes (usually AAA) the rating agencies must be satisfied that there is sufficient protection for the senior note holders. Hence portfolio ratings tests are designed and documented, to protect the note holders by providing boundaries in which the fund manager must operate. The performance of the portfolio, and adherence to portfolio tests, is confirmed in the investor report.

Duties

In undertaking the role of portfolio administrator, the agency service provider is responsible for a number of duties. Whilst this will vary depending on the specifics of the deal, the following is a sample of the typical duties undertaken by a portfolio administrator:

- Preparing the investors' report at individual asset level and distributing this to noteholders on a monthly, quarterly, semiannual, or annual basis. The report contains results of portfolio tests and also lists all the assets in the portfolio. Details of each asset are also included, such as coupon payments forthcoming, change of rating, pool factor (if applicable), and so on.
- Undertaking portfolio compliance testing; these are the portfolio tests that dictate the terms and quality of all assets, both at start of the deal and subsequently. The tests are described in the legal documentation describing the deal and may include, for instance, collateral quality tests, concentration limits, coverage tests, weighted average credit ratings, weighted average maturity, geographical concentration, and so on. Tests are as required by the ratings agencies and will be agreed with the issuer. The results are contained within the investor report.
- Preparing the quarterly or semiannual cash flow waterfall calculations; this is in line with coupon frequency and details the cash in the vehicle and shows that all tests have been met and cash flows paid out in accordance with the deal waterfall. The waterfall report is contained within the portfolio investor report.
- Calculating the amounts due on each of the overlying note tranches, and confirming this in the waterfall report.

Varying Degrees of Responsibility

The role of portfolio administrator and the responsibilities associated with the role vary depending on the deal. We describe below the different types of deals with a brief narrative on the most likely level of responsibility assigned to the portfolio administrator:

Managed Cash Flow CDO   Managed deals are the most onerous in terms of work and responsibility for the portfolio administrator. They require the collation and production of investor and payment date reports. (It should be noted that the testing for these types of deals tends to be more detailed and rigorous.) In addition to this, the portfolio administrator also takes responsibility for testing hypothetical trades that the fund manager may want to execute. Given that all tests must be completed to ensure that the deal remains compliant, the time spent undertaking this process can vary and will depend on the number of trades to be tested.

Managed Synthetic CDO   Like a managed cash flow CDO, the portfolio administration responsibilities for a managed synthetic CDO are greater than a static synthetic deal. The managed synthetic deal will generally require a similar level of testing and reporting on the reference portfolio as the managed cash flow deal, although the test will vary slightly. In addition, the portfolio administrator on a synthetic deal is frequently responsible for administrative duties associated with credit default swaps such as verifying credit events, handling cash movements, and acting as auction agent where the default swaps are physically settled.

Static CDOs   Both static cash flow and static synthetic deals do not require the same level of service from the portfolio administrator as the managed deals. As the portfolio does not change in terms of underlying assets, the testing and reporting requirements are less onerous. Additionally there is no hypothetical trading, which further reduces the responsibilities of the portfolio administrator.

Investor Reports

Investor reports are produced on a regular basis, as stipulated in the deal documentation. Typically the reports are produced by the portfolio administrator on a monthly basis, but they may be produced quarterly, semiannually, or annually.

The collation and distribution of the reports is the responsibility of the portfolio administrator; however, it is the responsibility of the fund manager to ensure that all tests detailed in the investor reports pass. Hence the fund manager and the portfolio administrator work together to ensure that all the tests past and the reports accurately reflect the state of the deal at that time.

Investor reports ensure that a level of deal transparency is reached. The reports enable investors to view a snapshot of the deal at a given point in time. Further, they provide boundaries in which the fund manager must operate. The testing that is completed within the reports ensures that the fund manager is remaining compliant with the rules laid down in the deal documentation at the outset. Thus whilst the investment manager is able to trade the portfolio (assuming it is a managed deal), it must trade within the deal parameters.

The deal documentation will stipulate rules governing portfolio characteristics such as par value test, interest coverage tests, diversity test, average portfolio rating, securities sold test, and percent of asset type allowed. All tests must be passing at the time of the report issuance.

The investor reports contain two types of test, quantitative and qualitative tests.

Quantitative Tests

Quantitative Tests break up the portfolio to enable investors to view the composition of the deal portfolio. The quantitative tests are a combination of tests and statistics regarding the composition of the portfolio. The quantitative tests enable investors to review the composition of the portfolio. The test triggers ensure that the composition of the portfolio remains within the deal rules stipulated in the deal documentation. If tests are failing, the portfolio manager usually has some brief period of time when it can try to bring the portfolio back in line with test parameters. This is usually a matter of days. If tests are still failing, the senior notes will start to be paid down to the point where tests are being passed again.

Exhibit 9.2 provides a sample of typical quantitative test. The exhibit details a typical summary page for a CDO, the following pages would present the detailed picture of the CDO and its performance. In this example the quantitative tests nominate the number of bonds, number of loans, and the percent of fixed-, floating-, and zero-coupon issues, as well as the number of upgrades and downgrades.

Qualitative Tests

Whilst the quantitative tests detail the composition of the deal portfolio the qualitative tests endeavor to demonstrate the quality of the portfolio. Hence the qualitative tests reveal the current performance of the deal.

The qualitative test in particular attempt to provide a level of protection to the investors. For example, as detailed in Exhibit 9.2, the tests will ensure that there is sufficient cash flow through the deal to pay principal and interest for the senior notes, that the portfolio is suffi-

EXHIBIT 9.2 Summary Page of Hypothetical Investor Report

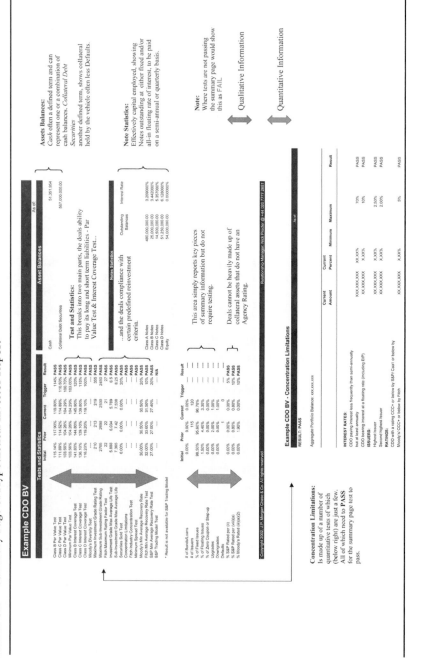

ciently diverse, that the trading restrictions have not been breached (no more than 20% of the portfolio is to be traded for example), and so on.

Once again the test results that are shown in Exhibit 9.2 are the summary of the detail that would be contained in the following pages.

Payment Date Reports

The payment date reports are produced 1–2 days prior to the payment date for a CDO. The majority of structured finance deals pay either quarterly or semiannually. The payment date reports will detail the monies due to be paid out through the deal on payment date—the monies paid out are deal expenses and charges, interest payments, and principal payments.

Given the tranched nature of structured finance deals, the payment date reports enable the holders of various notes to track how the monies through the deal have been applied. It is the responsibility of the portfolio administrator to build a model for the deal payments. The "waterfall" as it is known, is set out in the deal-offering circular. Principal and interest proceeds have different waterfall calculations and are therefore treated separately. Any proceeds that are accumulated within a payment period are run through the appropriate waterfall model.

The payment date report will contain the investor reports, as detailed above, and the waterfall calculations.

The waterfall calculations detail the application of interest proceeds (see Exhibits 9.3 and 9.4) and the application of principal proceeds separately.

Exhibits 9.3 and 9.4 graphically represent the application of proceeds through the CDO as of payment date. Exhibit 9.3 notes the tranched nature of CDOs and identifies that CDOs have a clearly identifiable priority of payments, that is, a waterfall. Exhibit 9.4 then notes in more detail the application of the proceeds through the waterfall. Note that payments of principal and interest are separate, that is, there is a separate waterfall calculation and application of proceeds for interest and principal.

Hypothetical Trade Testing

Managed CDOs allow for a specified level of trading per annum (for example, up to 30% of the nominal value of the portfolio). Any trading that occurs must comply with the rules set out in the collateral administration agreement—that is any trades completed must not compromise the test as represented in the investor reports.

This is the concept of hypothetical testing or "hypo." These are trades which the fund manager hypothetically tests with the portfolio administrator against the deal model (the model from which the inves-

EXHIBIT 9.3 CDO—Application of Proceeds on Payment Date

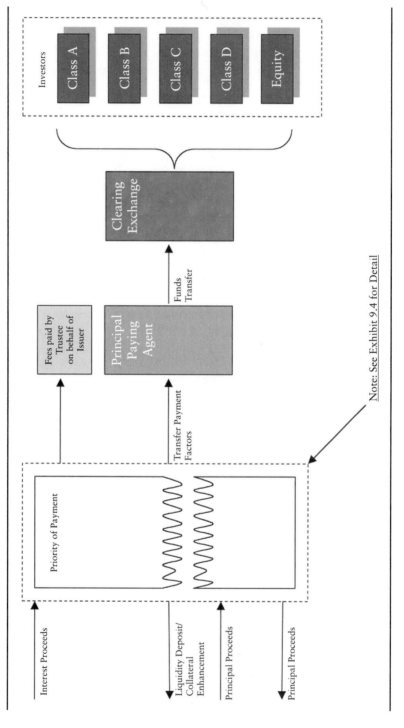

EXHIBIT 9.4   CDO—Priority of Payments

Interest Proceeds Priority of Payments:

Total Interest Proceeds Deposited into the Payment Account on the Business Day prior to the related Payment Date	€XX,XXX,XXX
(A) (i) to the payment of taxes owing by the Issuer accrued in respect of the related Due Period, as notified by an "Authorised Officer" (as defined in the Trust Deed) of the Issuer to the Trustee, if any, save for any value-added tax payable in respect of an	—
(ii) to the transfer to the Interest Account of an amount equal to the Liquidity Cash Reserve Amount for such Payment Date;	XXX,XXX
(B) i) to the payment of accrued and unpaid fees and expenses and other amounts payable to the Trustee pursuant to the Trust Deed (the "Trustee Fees and Expenses") up to an amount equal to €XX,XXX in respect of any Due Period (the "Senior Trustee Expense Cap	XX,XXX
ii) of any unpaid fees payable to the Initial Purchaser pursuant to the Subscription Agreement	XXX,XXX
(C) to the payment of Administrative Expenses (as defined in "The Issuer—Administrative Expenses of the Issuer"), in relation to each item thereof, on a pari passu basis, up to an amount equal to €XXX,XXX in respect of any Due Period (the "Senior Administr	XXX,XXX
(D) to the payment, on a pro rata basis, of any amounts due and payable under any Interest Rate Hedge Transaction (excluding any termination payments)	X,XXX,XXX
and, thereafter, in the event a replacement collateral adviser that is not affiliated with the Collateral Adviser accedes to the duties of the Collateral Adviser, to the payment to such replacement Collateral Adviser of a portion of the Subordinated Colla	—
(E) to the payment, on a pro rata basis, of the Interest Amounts due and payable on the Class A Notes in respect of the Interest Accrual Period ending on such Payment Date;	X,XXX,XXX

Prinicpal Proceeds Priority of Payments:

Total Principal Proceeds Deposited into the Payment Account on the Business Day prior to the related Payment Date	€XX,XXX,XXX
(A) to the payment on a sequential basis of the amounts referred to in paragraphs (A) to (D) of the Interest Proceeds Priority of Payments above, but only to the extent not paid in full thereunder;	0.00
(B) to the payment, on a pro rata basis, of any termination payments due to any Interest Rate Hedge Counterparty (other than Defaulted Interest Rate Hedge Termination Payments) to the extent not paid in full pursuant to paragraph (R) of the Interest Proceeds	0.00
(C) to the payment of the amounts referred to in paragraph (E) of the Interest Proceeds Priority of Payments above, but only to the extent not paid in full thereunder;	0.00
(D) to the payment of the amounts referred to in paragraph (F) of the Interest Proceeds Priority of Payments above, but only to the extent not paid in full thereunder;	0.00
(E) in the event the Class B Par Value Test and/or the Class B Interest Coverage Test is not satisfied on the related Determination Date, to redeem the Class A Notes (on a pro rata basis) and, after redemption in full thereof, to redeem the Class B Notes (on	0.00
(F) to the payment on a sequential basis of the amounts referred to in paragraphs (H) and (I) of the Interest Proceeds Priority of Payments above, but only to the extent not paid in full thereunder;	0.00

tor reports are produced). The fund manager will test a single or basket of trades before they are executed to ensure that when the trades are executed the deal is not compromised. The portfolio administrator reports back on the result of the hypothetical tests; if they have passed, then the fund manager can execute the deal as intended.

CDO Swap Administrator

Swaps have been and continue to be used extensively to manage risk associated with structured finance transactions. Traditionally swaps have been used to manage currency risk where there are currency mismatches between the income generated by the structured assets and the coupons and principal due on the overlying notes. In addition to FX swaps, many transactions also use interest rate swaps to manage interest rate risk where there are interest rate mismatches between the assets and the liabilities of the structure, such as mortgage assets that accrue monthly interest payments, being used as asset backing for note liabilities that are quarterly paying.

The swap contract between the issuing entity and the swap counterparty, regardless of what type of swap it is, will detail the required cash flow and whether it is a one-off payment or a schedule of payments. Once the swap has been agreed, it requires administration. That is, the swap payments between the issuing entity and the swap counterparty must be scheduled, calculated and paid—this is the responsibility of the swap administrator as noted in Exhibit 9.5. Despite the fact that the exhibit details a typical credit default swap (CDS), the duties undertaken by the swap administrator for all swaps as noted above remain the same.

In addition to the traditional use of swaps to manage foreign exchange and interest rate risk, swap technology has also been employed to manage exposure to credit risk, both for individual and groups of

EXHIBIT 9.5   Role of Swap Administration

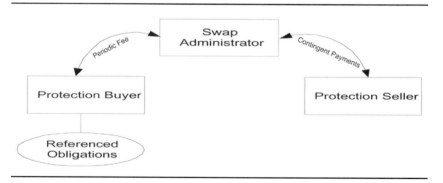

credits. Through the use of CDS and CDO technology, banks were first able to reduce their credit exposure in 1997 when the first synthetic CDO was created. Since then, synthetic CDOs have become an ever increasing part of the CDO marketplace.

In order to obtain protection on a credit or group of credits the protection buyer enter into a CDS through which they pay a premium at agreed intervals. In return for the premium, the swap counterparty (protection seller) provides protection on the credit(s). As can be noted in Exhibit 9.5, the swap counterparty will make payments to the protection buyer when agreed credit events occur on the referenced credit(s). Credit events can include bankruptcy, failure to make interest or principal payments, repudiation, or restructuring of an obligation. Whilst the swap administrator will be responsible for both receipt and payment of funds under the agreement, it is not the swap administrator responsibility to monitor for credit events.

Most recently Europe has seen the launch of several managed synthetics—these are structures in which managers seek arbitrage gain through trading both CDS and *total return swaps* (TRS). In 2001 and 2002, fund managers that originated managed synthetic CDOs included Rebeco, Cheyne Capital Management, BAREP Asset Management, and AXA Investment Management.[1] Given the depth and liquidity of the synthetic credit market, as compared to the cash market, it is expected that managed synthetics will become increasingly prevalent in the CDO marketplace.

ASSET-BACKED CONDUITS

Subadministration

Asset-backed commercial paper conduits are often complex structures which require a variety of services. ABCP structures can take many forms, however they will fall into one of two categories, a single seller conduit (see Exhibit 9.6) or a multiseller conduit (see Exhibit 9.6). It is worth noting the various varieties of ABCP structures as they often reveal the purpose of the conduit and give an indication as to the possible structure.

Despite the variety of structures and purpose of ABCP conduits, many of the servicing requirements are common. The core servicing, which includes custodial services (which are required only for securities

---

[1] Moorad Choudhry, "Combining Securitisation and Trading in Credit Derivatives: An analysis of the managed synthetic CDO," *Euromoney Debt Capital Markets Handbook* (2002).

EXHIBIT 9.6 Different Types of Asset Back Commercial Paper Conduits

Type	Structural Implications	Purpose
Single seller conduit	As the name suggest the issuing/ funding SPV(s) lends money to a single seller SPV which is securitised by a pool of assets held by the seller SPV.	Often set up by banks to fund assets off their balance sheet. Additionally large corporate also use this type of structure as an alternate funding source for their receivables.
Multiseller conduit	Unlike a single seller conduit, a multiple seller will fund multiple pools of assets through multiple SPVs holding separate and discreet pools of assets.	Can be a trade receivables, securities arbitrage or hybrid conduit.
Securities arbitrage conduit	Can be a single or multiple seller conduit.	Set up exclusively to exploit arbitrage gain between revenue generated by assets (such as asset-backed securities, highly rated corporate debt, government securities and high yield bonds) and highly rated commercial paper which is used to fund the asset purchases.
Trade receivables conduit	Can be a single or multiple seller conduit, although they tend to be multiple seller SPV as often they are used to fund assets for third parties, hence asset segregation is required.	Set up usually by banks to offer funding to their clients for their receivables (such as auto loan receivables, property leases and aircraft leases). There are also some large corporate sponsored conduits whose primary purpose is to gain alternative funding sources for their own assets.
Hybrid conduit	Can be a single or multiple seller conduit, although they tend to be multiple seller SPVs as often they are used to fund assets for third parties, hence asset segregation is required.	Set up by banks and large multinationals to fund both security arbitrage asset pools and trade receivable pools.

EXHIBIT 9.7   Servicing Elements Required of an ABCP Conduit

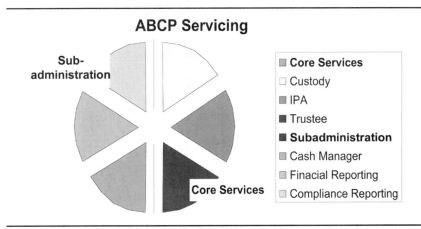

arbitrage of hybrid structures), issuing and paying agency, and account bank servicing, is a crucial part of the servicing required (see the section on "Generic Servicing" for a further explanation of these services). The other crucial aspect to the servicing is the subadministration role.

The subadministration servicing contains a number of elements as can be noted in Exhibit 9.7. It is worthwhile considering the distinction between the role of the conduit manager and the subadministrator. Whilst the conduit manager may undertake many of the duties associated with the role of the subadministrator, and this will vary depending on how the conduit is set administratively, the roles are distinct. The conduit manager is responsible for funding on a ongoing basis, that is managing new issuance and maturing CP, asset purchases, and sales in accordance with the deal covenants, maintaining and renewing liquidity lines, sourcing, and structuring new deals. The primary role of the sub-administrator is to administratively support the conduit and conduit manager. The following section will concentrate the responsibilities and duties of the subadministrator.

Cash Manager

As mentioned previously conduits are often highly complex, this is illustrated perfectly when one consider the cash movements through many of the conduits. It is relevant to consider that the vast majority of conduits have multiple SPVs (even single seller conduits usually have an issuance vehicle, which may be multiple if funding through European and US markets, and a vehicle to hold the assets) and in the case of multiple seller conduits this can number over 20. The assets are often denominated in a variety of currencies. As a result there can be a large number of cash accounts associated with conduits—in some cases this may number over 50.

The types of transactions that the cash manager is required to manage between accounts will include:

- Cash flows associated with issuance and maturity of CP (and in some cases MTNs).
- Loans between issuance SPV(s) and seller SPV(s).
- Repayment of interest and principal of loans between issuing and seller SPVs.
- Payment due under interest rate swaps and FX swaps (inclusive of tracking and calculating swap payments).
- Payment of expenses inclusive of legal costs, one-off structuring costs, trustee fees, conduit management fees, listing fees, and rating agency fees.
- Cash movements to eligible investments inclusive of GIC accounts, highly rated commercial paper, and highly rated money market funds.

Further to the cash movements listed above, the cash manager is responsible for the production of daily cash statements, which are issued to the conduit manager. The cash statements ensure that the accounts are reconciled on a daily basis.

When the cash management function is done by a third party, the cash manager acts under instruction (either dynamic or standing instructions) only.

Financial Reporting

The preparation of accounts is necessary for a number of reason. Foremost the account preparation provides timely information to the conduit manager and sponsor on the performance of the conduit. The information, such as cost of funding and excess spread, clearly speaks to the performance of the conduit at any given period and enable the performance to be measured over time. Whilst the purpose of the reports is obvious the methodology used to calculate the figures differs.

Additionally, the accounts that are produce form an integral part of the annual audited accounts and any tax filings, which must be produced in accordance with deal documentation. Generally, accounts for each of the SPVs are produced on a monthly basis, although they may be completed as infrequently as quarterly or semiannually. The accounts that are produced are P&L and balance sheet for each SPV. When produced by a third party the accounts are distributed to the conduit manager for perusal and comment. The accounts provide a clear indication of the "success" of the conduit.

Portfolio Administrator

Although the discipline of the reporting for conduits is not as rigorous as for CDOs (see the section on CDO—Portfolio Administration), conduits operate under covenants which dictate limits on size and composition of the portfolio. The portfolio administrator is responsible for the completing the test as outlined in the documentation and production of the investor reports. The reports are distributed to the conduit manager, rating agencies and investors. The reports are usually produced on a monthly basis, but can be produced on a quarterly or semiannual basis.

In addition to the production of the reports, the portfolio manager is responsible for the model of the deal. As a result, the portfolio administrator will also be responsible for testing hypothetical trades against the deal model. Prior to purchasing or disposing of an asset, the conduit manager will consult the portfolio administrator to confirm that the deal remains compliant when the trade is executed. See CDO—Portfolio Administration, Hypothetical Testing for a more in-depth analysis of hypothetical testing.

Many conduit managers feel that the disciplines that the portfolio administrator enforces are essential to their day to day operations and consequently perform the functions themselves

Additional Servicing Elements for Conduits

We outline here additional agency services required on conduit structures.

IPA It is worth noting the role of *issuing and paying agent* (IPA) is a far more active one for conduit and SIVs than for other structured finance transactions. This is as a result of the short-term nature of the funding for the structures, namely commercial paper. Commercial paper is short-dated debt and many conduits have limits shorter than the maximum allowable in the market. The assets are often funded for terms much longer than the duration of a single issuance of CP, thus the paper is "rolled." This refers to the practice of issuing new paper in order to pay investors upon maturity of the current CP.

The IPA is responsible for administering the rolling process. This necessitates a degree of diligence on behalf of the PA. In order to fund the maturing CP, the IPA must ensure that there is sufficient new issuance to cover the maturity. Whilst this is relatively simple in the European market, which operates on the $T + 2$ basis, it is far more difficult in the US market, which operates on a similar basis. In the US market the IPA will check for new issuance to cover the maturing CP at 9.00 A.M. If the issuance is not visible, the IPA will immediately contact the conduit manager. The conduit manager will then have a deadline by which funds must be made available to pay for the maturing CP (usually the deadline is no later than 2.00 P.M.). At the time the deadline is breached, the IPA will draw on the liquidity lines. Although the cutoff time is often as late as 4.00 P.M. on the same day the liquidity bank must be given sufficient time to fund. The committed liquidity facilities are in part why the majority of the conduits have a rating of A1/P1. It should be noted that drawing on liquidity is a last resort and rare.

Liquidity Management   As noted above, one of the main functions of the conduit manager is to manage the funding process. Many of the securities arbitrage conduits (or buckets in a hybrid conduit) adopt a policy of "matched funding." "Matched funding," as the name implies, is where the CP issuance is matched to a particular asset purchase. As CP matures the conduit manager is responsible for new issuance to cover the maturity. As part of the calculation, they will include the monies required to cover the maturing CP and any income received from those assets (both principal and interest). Hence the new issuance will be equal to the current issuance redeeming at par less any income (P&I). Though the conduit manager will be managing this process internally, this type of service, often referred to as "liquidity management" is offered as verification to the conduit manager.

Borrowing Base Requirement Verification   When conduits are funding trade receivable assets, there are a number of tests and calculations completed to derive the eligible value of the assets. At inception, the rating agencies and conduit manager agree to the criteria for eligible assets. The result is a number of tests to ensure that only assets of sufficient quality are included in the calculations. (It is often the case that some assets are not included due to failure—this process is known as applying "haircuts.") Once the value of the assets is derived, it is compared to the value of the liabilities to ensure that the structure is sufficient over collateralised. That is, the assets are able to support the liabilities. Whilst the servicer of the assets is generally responsible for running the tests and deriving the borrowing base, the subadministrator will monitor the borrowing base levels to ensure they are not breached. Although to date third parties have not been used to manage borrowing base calculations, eligibility criteria, and liquidity coverage calculations, this is a potential area for third parties to offer assistance to conduit managers in the future.

Structured Investment Vehicles

Although SIV and conduits are often structured quite differently, much of the differences are borne out in the work that the conduit and SIV managers complete as opposed to distinct servicing functions. Essentially Exhibit 9.7, which nominates the servicing functions for conduit, is the same for an SIV with some variations. The core servicing for SIV is the same as is required for a conduit. The differences in servicing required for an SIV is described below.

Capital Adequacy Requirements

A key aspect of the SIV structure is the capital adequacy requirements. SIVs clearly document the capital adequacy requirements and leverage restrictions that must be adhered to. The documentation details the treatment of each asset class and hedge instrument as well as stipulating a reserve. As can be noted in Exhibit 9.8, the limits and test are designed to safeguard investors against the risks noted.

Market Value Risk

SIVs mitigate market value risk through mark-to-market procedures— that is, SIVs are required to mark their pools of assets on a daily basis. The value of the portfolio is used to calculate Net Asset Value (NAV) of the SIV. This in turn is a key element in the capital adequacy model.

Although much of the subadministration duties are performed by the SIV manager, the NAV calculation is a service that may be outsourced to a third-party servicer. As the third party will most often be the custodian, they are often best placed to perform the daily mark-to-market calculations. It should be noted that many of assets held within SIVs prove problematic when trying to retrieve up-to-date pricing. Specifically, the illiquid asset-backed securities that trade infrequently can be difficult to price. Thus, upon purchasing these assets, many of the

EXHIBIT 9.8   Risk Mitigation through Capital Adequacy Requirements for SIVs

The limits and tests that are included in the itemisation of the capital-adequacy requirements are designed to cover the following series of different risks:

- Credit risk associated with each obligor (asset and hedges).
- Potential losses arising from changes in currencies and interest rates.
- Potential default of the SIV for lack of liquidity.
- Marginal cost of liquidating certain assets or hedges.

Note: Due to the intricate and detailed nature of the capital adequacy requirements, both the model and the testing is the responsibility of the SIV manager.
Source: Standard and Poor's Structured Finance—Derivatives Rating.

SIV managers insist that the trading desk provide pricing for the asset on a regular basis.

Upon creation of an SIV, the SIV sponsor invests heavily in the support of these large complex transactions. The SIV manager requires considerable support to build, maintain, and run the capital adequacy model, compliance testing, as well as making the investment decisions. Given the infrastructure that SIV sponsors invest in to support these structures, it is not surprising that the SIV managers, aside from the core servicing, have done much of the servicing work themselves— although with an increasing requirement from both rating agencies and investors to see greater impartiality and separation, the use of third-party servicers may increase in the future.

CONCLUSION

The use of trusts and professional trustees within secured Eurobond issuance serves a number of legal and practical purposes. In the main, however, the essential service the trustee brings to the transaction is stability to the transaction and piece of mind for bondholders and issuers alike. Accordingly, the trustee is an invaluable element of a successful secured Eurobond transaction. Further, to the role of trustee, the trust bank will offer a range of services to support the structured finance market place.

The range of services that the trust bank offers will vary depending on the sophistication and maturity of the trust business. Most, if not all, service providers will offer cash manager, account bank, paying agency, and custodial services in addition to trustee services to support their trust business. Other roles detailed in this chapter such as portfolio administrator and financial reporting may be offered in varying degrees depending on the banks experience and infrastructure.

Although some structures employ different banks to perform various roles in a transaction generally those services that are outsourced are performed by one entity. This is the most preferable solution as confusion regarding duties and responsibilities can arise when there are multiple service providers engaged in one deal. When a single service provider is appointed on all the roles, they simply take responsibility for all the servicing and there is no confusion over responsibilities. Additionally, investors might gain some comfort in the knowledge that the trustee has possession of the deal assets such as cash or securities should they deal default.

Trust banks are also continuing to expand the product offerings to support the structured finance market. Complex transactions such as conduit and SIVs require extensive servicing. Traditionally much of the servicing responsibilities have been borne by the transaction sponsors. In the future, as trust banks become more sophisticated, they may offer greater administrative support to these types of structure, enabling the managers of the structure to focus primarily on trading and structuring decisions. This has the obvious advantages of enabling both parties to be able to concentrate on their strengths.

Also, structures such as CDOs, MBS and ABS transactions are continually being refined and changed as new technologies and structures are employed. This necessitates a degree of flexibility and planning on behalf of the service provider. Those trust banks that aim to excel in the future will need to provide the traditional services as detail above and be nimble enough to foresee the servicing opportunities that are presented by the constantly evolving world of structured finance.

APPENDIX—QUICK REFERENCE GUIDE TO TRUSTEE AND AGENCY SERVICES

Account Bank—Bank with whom accounts are established.

Authentication Agent—Party that signs a security to authenticate the certificate, bond, or note.

Agent Bank or Calculation/Calculating/Reference Agent—This agent is responsible for making and publishing certain calculations that are used to assess security payments, risk determinants, voting rights, and/or to trigger events toward a financial transaction.

Collection/Collecting Agent—Party that receives/consolidates payments. Party may need to furnish reports summarizing activity.

Conversion Agent—Coordinates the surrender of securities by bondholders for the issuance of share certificates in lieu in a convertible bond issue.

Custodian/Subcustodian—Party that holds/safekeeps collateral, cash, or other form of security for the benefit of a client or lender as per underlying documentation

Escrow Agent/Depositary Agent—This agent assumes temporary possession of assets on behalf of two or more parties (one of which may be silent or third party) to a sale, conveyance, or other transaction.

Facility Agent—Party that performs certain rate sets, acts as a conduit of information from a borrower to the lender(s) and vice versa, facilitates payments from a borrower to a lender and vice versa, acts upon majority lender instruction.

Fiscal Agent—The agent prepares and authenticates the securities; arranges, if applicable, an international paying agency network; attends the closing; and delivers the securities to the underwriters as instructed by the issuer. There is no requirement to monitor compliance or pursue remedies upon default, since the agent is acting on behalf of the issuer. However, the agent carries out certain administrative duties such as arranging for security holder meetings and issuing notices.

FX Agent—For the purchase of foreign currency pursuant to instructions from the customer and subject to receipt of funds.

Issuing and Paying Agent—The agent has responsibility for effecting the issuance, primary settlement, and interest and principal payment of short-term and continuously offered long-term instruments (e.g., certificates of deposit, commercial paper, and medium term notes) (see *Paying Agent*).

Paying Agent—The agent arranges the payment of principal and interest to bond holders upon behalf of the issuer. Also ensures that the relevant income tax on interest is withheld pursuant to local tax regulations. For U.S. issuers, the paying agent ensures that the relevant W-8 and W-9 forms are circulated and received in order to withhold appropriately as per U.S. Tax regulations. The paying agent will also facilitate relevant reporting to the IRS in the United States.

Principal Paying Agent—Party primarily responsible to claim funds due on security from an issuer/borrower and disburse same to paying agents, other agents, or investors (see *Paying Agent*).

Reference Agent—See *Calculation Agent*.

Registrar—The agent is responsible for registering exchanges and transfers and for maintaining bondholder records.

Registrar/Transfer Agent—Responsible for issuing and authenticating new securities for securities surrendered for transfer (e.g., as a result of a sale and maintaining ownership records).

Security Agent/Collateral Agent—A private financial institution, typically a bank and often a trustee, that serves as an agent for the credit enhancement provider. It holds and maintains the collateral that is pledged to the trustee to secure the obligations of the credit enhancer under the credit facility. Ensures that the investors/lenders' interest is protected by safekeeping collateral (cash or securities, mortgages, hypothecations, etc.) for the benefit of the "Trustee" who has a fiduciary relationship with the investors/lenders or the investors/lenders directly.

Settlement Agent/Exchange Agent—On a private issue that switches to a registered issue with the Securities and Exchange Commission (a public offering), the agent that coordinates the down-posting of the private issue and issuance of the SEC-registered issue. A settlement agent is also required when a company undergoes restructuring of existing debt (whether in the form of bonds or loans) and receives creditor approval to exchange old debt for new debt and/or shares/options, and/or cash.

Trustee—The trustee has responsibility for any or all of the following roles dependent on the contractual obligations set out in the governing documents including taking a security interest in any and all collateral and assets, and to receive and hold all certifications and/or notifications required from other parties. With regard to any amendments or supplements to the documents, the trustee would determine whether the proposed action is material enough to require noteholder consent; if noteholder consent is required, the trustee would obtain consent from the noteholders. In an enforcement situation, where the deal is in default and must be wound down, the trustee will liquidate the collateral and assets and make payments to the relevant parties, in accordance with the documents. Also, the trustee will generally monitor the activities of the issue to ensure that the spirit of the document is followed and the interests of the noteholders are being looked after.

Warrant Agent—A warrant agent is responsible for the launch of an issuer's warrants (issue/programme) and to advise the issuer of subsequent warrants exercise details of investors. Duty may include calculation of number of shares to be delivered vs. cash for fractional shares, if any.

Asset-Backed Securities

European Credit Card ABS

Markus Niemeier
Manager
Barclays Capital

Credit card ABS (CCABS) constitute one of the most liquid and widely accepted asset classes in Europe and most European ABS investors are likely to hold some credit card securitisations. The purpose of this chapter is to discuss the structural features and investment characteristics of CCABS. The focus is on the UK credit card ABS market, because the vast majority of European credit card transactions are backed by sterling-denominated collateral.

CARD TYPES

Usually, credit cards fall into one of two categories: general purpose cards and private label cards. General purpose cards can be further assigned to the categories standard, affinity, and cobranded. Exhibit 10.1 shows the various types of credit cards.

General Purpose

General purpose credit cards are the most widely issued and accepted; the majority are MasterCard and Visa affiliated. Today, most general purpose credit cards are issued in the form of *teaser rate cards*, which offer a very low or even 0% APR to new cardholders for a limited period, usually up to six months. Such offers are aimed at interest-sensitive borrowers, and

---

The views expressed in this chapter are those of the author and not necessarily those of Barclays Capital.

EXHIBIT 10.1   Types of Credit Cards

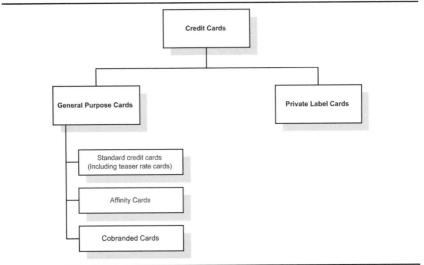

Source: Barclays Capital.

banks have attracted new customers successfully in this way. However, teaser rates on balance transfers (when a customer switches card issuers and transfers the outstanding balance on an existing card to a new card) have encouraged customers to change their card issuers more frequently in order to benefit from the low introductory interest rates. This trend has made it even more important for credit card issuers to build brand awareness and offer additional benefits to keep hold of their customers.

In order to build brand loyalty and increase customer retention, some credit card issuers have started to offer *affinity cards*. In Europe, for example, such cards are issued by MBNA Europe Bank Limited (MBNA EBL), a wholly owned subsidiary of MBNA America Bank, N.A. To be able to issue affinity cards, the company has to identify special interest groups which sign up to an affinity partnership agreement. These could be, for example, associations of medical professionals, fans of auto racing, or college alumni associations. Once an association has established an affinity partnership agreement with a credit card issuer, its members can apply for a credit card which could have a logo of their association, a picture of their favourite driver, or their school seal. This can build brand loyalty and cardholders are less likely to switch to another credit card issuer. MBNA has traditionally been the largest issuer of affinity credit cards. In the United Kingdom, the company has established partnership agreements with various organisations, including Burberrys Limited, the World Wide Fund for Nature, and Manchester United Football Club.

In the case of *cobranded cards*, the bank allies with a company, such as an automobile manufacturer, and the two companies market the card jointly. Such agreements benefit the bank because it can attract additional customers and increase its receivables under management. It also benefits the company through the promotion of its products. For example, in 1993, HFC Bank PLC, a wholly owned indirect subsidiary of Household, Inc. in the United States, introduced the GM Card in the United Kingdom. It has standard credit card features, but customers can also earn reward points for purchases made on the card and redeem them when they buy a new or used Vauxhall car. The agreements for cobranded cards are likely to have different arrangements for sharing expenses and revenues.

Private Label Cards

Private label cards are issued and administered by retailers. Usually, they are given to customers for use in their stores, and their main function is to promote the retailer's products. As a result, credit underwriting may not be as stringent as it is for other types of credit cards. In Europe, as of this writing, there has been only one private label ABS transaction so far. In December 2000, Findomestic Banca S.p.A. securitised credit card borrowings generated through the company's credit card product, Carta Aura.

CREDIT CARD PAYMENT CYCLE

Exhibit 10.2 shows a simplified credit card payment cycle. When a customer buys goods and pays with a credit card, the bank which reimburses the shop owner for the purchase does not forward the full amount to the shop owner but deducts a certain fee called *interchange*. This fee is ultimately shared between the bank, the card association (usually Visa or MasterCard), and the original bank that issued the credit card. So the first bank is paid for processing the payment, the card association for providing the payment and clearing network, and the issuing card bank as compensation for assuming credit risk and offering a grace period on finance charge accrual.

THE EUROPEAN CREDIT CARD ABS MARKET

One of the goals in credit card securitisation, as with the securitisation of other assets, is to remove receivables from the issuing card bank's regulatory balance sheet in order to free up capital. Driven by the need of banks to diversify sources of funding and reduce regulatory capital, the first securiti-

EXHIBIT 10.2   Credit Card Payment Cycle

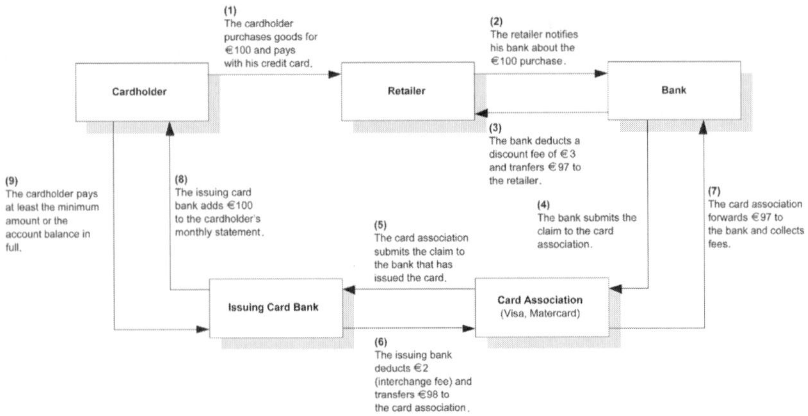

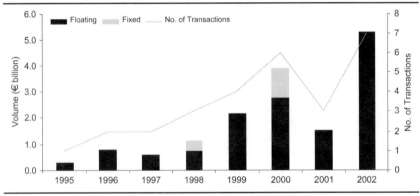

Source: Barclays Capital.

EXHIBIT 10.3   Credit Card Issuance—European Collateral

Source: Bloomberg.

sation of credit card receivables was completed in the United States in 1987. Since then, securitisation has become a favourite source of funding for credit card issuers. Following the US success, MBNA EBL completed the first European credit card securitisation in 1995.[1] Exhibit 10.3 shows the issuance of all rated CCABS backed by European collateral from 1995 to 2002.

---

[1] We define European credit card transactions as those transactions that are backed by credit card receivables that originated in Europe. A US dollar-denominated credit card transaction backed by sterling-denominated receivables would therefore count as a European transaction, while a euro-denominated transaction backed by US dollar-denominated receivables would count as a non-European transaction.

EXHIBIT 10.4   European Credit Card ABS Issuers Ranked by Volume
(1995 to 2002)

Rank	Issuer	Originator	Original Number of Issues	Original Size (€ mil Equiv.)
1	CARDS (MBNA MT 1)	MBNA EBL	12	5,191
2	CARDS (MBNA MT 2)	MBNA EBL	4	2,765
3	ARRAN	The Royal Bank of Scotland	3	2,330
4	Gracechurch	Barclaycard	2	2,026
5	Sherwood Castle Funding	Capital One Bank (Europe)	2	1,321
6	Pillar Funding	Egg Banking	1	793
7	Affinity	HFC Bank	1	633
8	Diners Card Finance	Diners Club Europe (and others)	1	339
	Findomestic	Findomestic Banca	1	311
9	Opus	HFC Bank	1	223
		Total	28	15,598

Source: Bloomberg.

The majority of issues since 1995 have come with floating-rate notes. However, in the latter part of 2000, demand for the asset class was expressed by fixed-rate buyers and MBNA EBL issued two fixed-rate transactions, one euro- and one sterling-denominated. Both issues had 10-year maturities and capitalised on the relatively small supply of consumer asset securitisations available in that sector of the curve. Exhibit 10.4 shows issuers of European CCABS ranked by cumulative issuance.

Since the market's inception in 1995, MBNA EBL has been the dominant issuer of CCABS, both in number of issues completed and total volume of issuance. The company has accessed the securitisation market each year and completed 16 transactions in total. The first 12 transactions, Chester Asset Receivables Dealings (CARDS) 1–12, were issued from the same master trust (MBNA MT 1), which was set up in 1995. In 2001, MBNA EBL created a new master trust "UK Receivables Trust II" (MBNA MT 2) from which four transactions, CARDS 2001-A, CARDS 2001-B, CARDS 2002-A, and CARDS 2002-B, were issued in 2001 and 2002.

The second largest issuer of European CCABS, The Royal Bank of Scotland PLC (RBS), has accessed the securitisation market three times in 2000. Every transaction from its ARRAN master trust has been denominated in US dollars and backed by sterling-denominated collateral. Barclay-card, a division of Barclays Bank PLC, has completed two transactions from its Gracechurch master trust. Notes have also been US dollar-denominated and backed by UK credit card receivables. Capital One Bank (Europe) Limited (COBE), a wholly owned indirect subsidiary of Capital One Bank in the United States, has issued two transactions from its Sherwood Castle Receivables Trust. The first issue is sterling-denominated and the second issue is euro-denominated, which has enlarged the company's investor base to include the euro-denominated investor universe. In both cases, the collateral is sterling-denominated. HFC Bank PLC, a wholly owned subsidiary of Household International, Inc., is the fourth largest issuer of European CCABS. In 1997, the company completed its OPUS transaction, followed by the Affinity 2002-A transaction in 2002. In both cases, notes and collateral are denominated in sterling.

Issuance of European CCABS is clearly dominated by repeat issuers, accounting for more than 90% of total issuance volume. Credit card Issuers that have accessed the securitisation market only once include Findomestic Banca S.p.A. (2000), Diners Club Europe S.p.A. (and others) (2001) and Egg Banking PLC (2002).

From the 28 CCABS transactions shown in Exhibit 10.4, 26 are backed by sterling-denominated credit card receivables and two have euro-denominated collateral. In 2000, Findomestic Banca S.p.A. issued €311 million of notes backed by Italian credit card receivables. In 2001, Diners Card Europe S.p.A. (and other European Diners Club operations) completed its first transaction in a euro-denominated issue. The collateral includes receivables in Italy, Germany, the United Kingdom, Ireland, the Netherlands, and Belgium.

Most credit card transactions completed have usually come with three tranches. The Class A notes, approximately 90% of all European CCABS issued, are usually triple-A rated, the Class B notes, which account for approximately 5%, are usually single-A rated and the most junior tranche, the Class C notes, accounts for approximately 5% and is usually rated triple-B. Exhibit 10.5 shows European credit card issuance by rating since the market's inception in 1995.

STRUCTURAL CHARACTERISTICS

In this section the fundamental structural characteristics of European CCABS are presented. Most of the examples included in this section refer to MBNA EBL's CARDS 2002-A, which was completed in June 2002. The transaction is fairly representative of most other European credit card transactions.

EXHIBIT 10.5   European Credit Card Issuance by Rating

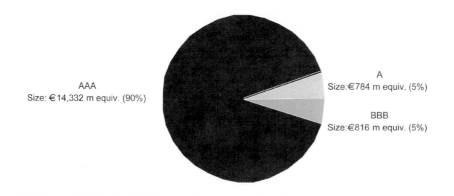

AAA
Size: €14,332 m equiv. (90%)

A
Size: €784 m equiv. (5%)

BBB
Size: €816 m equiv. (5%)

Source: Bloomberg.

Master Trust versus Standalone

In the United States, standalone trusts were the dominant issuance vehicles from 1987 to 1991. An originator designates a specific pool of credit card accounts and sells the receivables and rights to the future receivables arising from those accounts to a discrete trust. The major disadvantage with standalone trusts is that each subsequent securitisation requires the issuer to set up a new trust. This structure was used until 1991 when the master trust became the preferred issuance vehicle.

Master trusts allow issuers to sell multiple securities from a single trust. There is no segregation of any sort between the receivables in the trust and as such, all issues are backed by the same collateral. The master trust structure affords the issuer great flexibility, since the cost and effort associated with issuing a new series from a master trust is lower than for creating a new trust for every issue. For example, an issuer creates a new master trust and sells €100 million in credit card receivables from selected accounts into the master trust and then issues securities backed by these receivables. When more financing is needed, the issuer sells a further €100 million in receivables from more accounts into the same trust and issues more securities. This means that the issuer does not have to set up new master trusts if it wants to securitise new receivables. All securities are issued from the same master trust and backed by the *same collateral.*

A simplified credit card master trust structure is shown in Exhibit 10.6. This particular structure has been developed in the United States and was introduced in Europe with the creation of MBNA's UK Receivables Trust II.

EXHIBIT 10.6   Credit Card Master Trust Structure

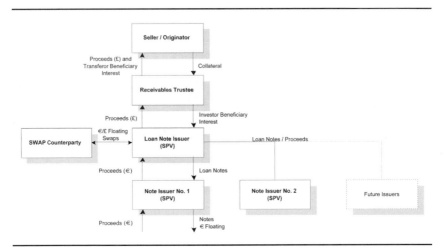

Source: Barclays Capital.

As shown in Exhibit 10.6, the seller or originator transfers receivables from selected accounts to the master trust (receivables trustee) and collects the proceeds from the sale. The seller also retains an ownership interest in the trust (transferor beneficiary interest). This participation performs some crucial functions. The transferor interest absorbs seasonal fluctuations in the credit card receivables balance and is allocated all dilutions (balances cancelled due to returned goods) and ineligible receivables (fraudulently generated receivables or receivables that do not comply with stipulated origination standards). The transferor interest also has the function of aligning the originator's interests with the interests of the investors, that is, if the originator retains an interest in the collateral, the company has a certain interest in servicing the portfolio and making sure that it performs as expected.

In Exhibit 10.6, the loan note issuer, a special purpose vehicle (SPV) acquires the investor interest (investor beneficiary interest) in the trust and finances the purchase by issuing loan notes to the issuer of the notes, a second SPV (note issuer no. 1). If new financing is required, the originator transfers new receivables into the trust and the loan note issuer creates a new investor interest in the trust, which is financed by the issuance of loan notes to a new notes issuer (note issuer no. 2, note issuer no. 3, and so on). The note issuer in turn finances the purchase of these loan notes by issuing notes to investors.

Transaction Structure

The typical credit card transaction structure has three different cash flow periods: revolving, accumulation, and early amortisation. Each period performs a distinct function and allocates cash flows differently. Credit card transactions are usually structured as soft bullets in order to mimic a traditional corporate bond, that is, investors receive monthly or quarterly payments of interest with one single payment of principal on the scheduled redemption date.

During the revolving period, all receipts of principal are reinvested in new receivables. It is the ability to revolve the receivables that provides an issuer with tremendous flexibility in choosing a maturity profile for a securitisation, especially as the average life of credit card receivables is a short five to ten months. A simple amortisation structure in which all principal receipts would be passed through to the investor from day one would result in securities with very short average lives and lumpy, unpredictable principal repayments to investors.

Usually 12 to 18 months before the scheduled maturity date, the accumulation period commences. The length of the accumulation period is determined by the rating agencies (for UK banks that are regulated by the FSA, the length of the accumulation period is determined by the rating agencies together with the FSA) and subject to the monthly payment rate of the receivables pool (discussed in a subsequent section). During this period, principal collections are accumulated in a trust account and invested in short term instruments. On the scheduled maturity date, a bullet payment of principal is made from the trust account to noteholders.

If the portfolio experiences severe asset deterioration, the seller's interest in the collateral falls below a specified level, the notes are not redeemed in full on the scheduled redemption date or, in the case of certain legal problems, the transaction enters into rapid amortisation. During the rapid amortisation period, all principal receipts are, depending on the specific transaction structure, either directly passed through to the investors to amortise the notes or held in a trust account to redeem the notes in full on their scheduled redemption date. Early amortisation triggers are usually found on the trust and series level. If one of the trust's early amortisation triggers is breached, all series issued from the trust enter into early amortisation. If a series early amortisation trigger is breached, only the specific series enters into early amortisation. The following list includes typical trust and series early amortisation triggers.

Trust early amortisation triggers include:

- Events of default, bankruptcy or insolvency by the seller or servicer.
- Seller is unable to transfer receivables to the trust when necessary.
- Seller ceases to be resident for tax purposes.

■ Change of tax law creating a liability for the trustee, other than for stamp duty.

Series early amortisation triggers:

■ Failure to make required deposits or payments.
■ False representations or warranties that remain unremedied for a certain number of days.
■ Three-month average excess spread falls below zero.
■ Seller interest falls below the required level.
■ Servicer default that would have a material adverse effect on the issuer of the loan notes.
■ The investor interest is not reduced to zero on the scheduled redemption date.
■ Early termination of any of the swap agreements if not replaced within a certain number of days.
■ Change of tax law creating a liability for the loan note issuer.

All collections arising from the pool of receivables are split into finance charge income and principal receipts. Finance charges include interest on the receivables, annual fees, late payment fees, overlimit charges, and interchange and are used every month to pay the coupon on the notes, servicing fees, and other expenses. Finance charges are also used to cover receivables that have been charged off. Finance charge income left over after these deductions is called *excess spread* and is usually paid to the seller. Principal receipts are reinvested in new receivables during the revolving period and used to amortise the notes during the amortisation period (or invested in short-term instruments during the accumulation period). Exhibit 10.7 shows a typical soft bullet structure, in which the transaction enters the revolving period followed by the accumulation period.

EXHIBIT 10.7   Amortisation Structure

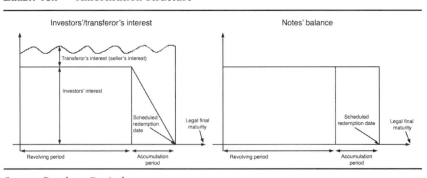

Source: Barclays Capital.

As shown on the left side in Exhibit 10.7, the transaction enters the revolving period immediately following the closing date. During the revolving period, the investor interest remains stable and the seller's interest absorbs any fluctuations in the collateral balance. All principal receipts during this period are reinvested in new receivables. Following the end of the revolving period, the transaction enters the accumulation period. As shown on the right side of Exhibit 10.7, the notes' balance remains constant until the scheduled redemption date, when all principal receipts accumulated in a dedicated trust account are used to redeem the notes in full.

The legal final maturity shown in Exhibit 10.7 is different form the scheduled maturity (also called *expected maturity*). The expected maturity is established when a transaction is being structured and is based on the length of the revolving period and the monthly payment rate of the portfolio. The legal final maturity is the date the rating agencies use when assigning their ratings to the notes. This is the date at which, if full principal were not paid, the issue would be in default. The legal final is typically two years after the expected maturity date. An issue could extend past its expected maturity date if the monthly payment rate (discussed in the next section) fell dramatically during the accumulation period.

Credit Enhancement

A typical issue will feature a triple-A rated tranche, a single-A rated tranche, a triple-B rated tranche and a dynamic spread account. The subordination structure for a typical credit card issue is shown in Exhibit 10.8. In this example, the class A noteholders benefit from the subordination of the Class B and Class C notes, which together provide 12% credit enhancement. The Class B noteholders benefit from the subordination of the Class C notes, which provide 7% credit enhancement. The Class C noteholders benefit from a dynamic spread account.

The amount of credit enhancement for a transaction is determined by the rating agencies and varies by issuer depending primarily on the performance of the underlying collateral. Exhibit 10.9 shows total enhancement levels for three recent transactions completed by different issuers.

The Class C noteholders benefit from a dynamic spread account. If 3-month average excess spread falls below a predetermined level, the spread account builds from monthly excess spread until the target level is reached. In order to fully understand the protection afforded by the spread account we need to assess the degree to which the spread account traps excess spread. Exhibit 10.10 shows excess spread trigger levels and trapping levels for a typical credit card issue.

EXHIBIT 10.8   A Credit Enhancement Structure

Source: Barclays Capital.

EXHIBIT 10.9   Total Credit Enhancement Levels

Issuer	Class A
CARDS 2002-A	12.0%
Sherwood Castle Funding Series 2002-1	16.0%
Affinity 2002-A	15.5%

Source: Offering circulars.

EXHIBIT 10.10   Trapped Excess Spread Levels

Excess Spread (3-month average)	Excess Spread Trapped Up
Greater than 5.00%	0.0%
4.01–5.00%	1.5%
3.01–4.0%	3.0%
Less than or equal to 3.0%	5.0%

Source: Barclays Capital.

EXHIBIT 10.11   Trapped Excess Spread—Slowly Deteriorating Environment

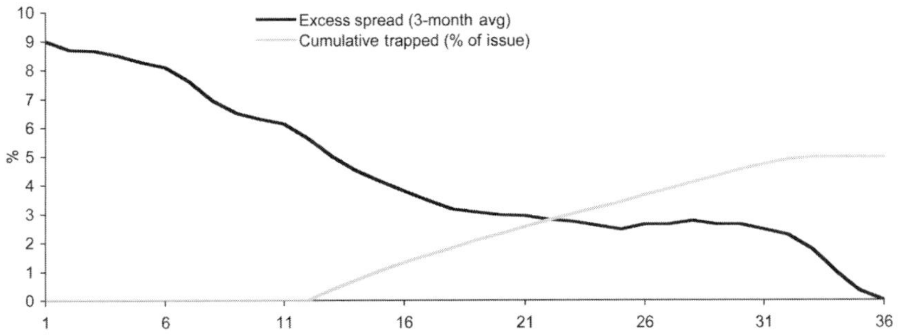

Source: Barclays Capital.

In the following example, the spread account starts to trap excess spread when the 3-month average excess spread level is 5% or lower. As the excess spread level continues to decrease, the level of spread that is trapped increases to a maximum of 5% of the total transaction size.

As the spread account traps excess spread over a period of deteriorating collateral performance, a driving factor in the effectiveness of the spread account is the rate at which the excess spread decreases. If the collateral performance deteriorates slowly, the spread trapping mechanism will most likely be able to trap the maximum amount of spread allowed. However, if there is a rapid deterioration in the collateral performance, the spread trapping mechanism may not be able to trap the maximum allowable amount of spread before the excess spread in the transaction turns negative. Exhibit 10.11 shows a scenario in which excess spread deteriorates from an initial level of 9% to zero over a 36-month period. After 12 months, 3-month average excess spread falls to 5% and excess spread is getting trapped.

In this example, the dynamic spread account builds up to the maximum 5% of the transaction size. The spread account reaches the maximum of 5% in month 33 and then stays at this level. Exhibit 10.12 shows a scenario in which excess spread falls from the initial 9% to zero within 24 months, that is, the same deterioration in excess spread as in the previous example happens over a 2- instead of a 3-year period.

In this example, the dynamic spread account builds up only to approximately 1.6% of the transaction size, which is well below the target level of 5%. These two examples highlight the importance of the originator's ability to service the receivables pool effectively and, as such, avoid a rapid deterioration in the performance of the collateral. An originator that follows strict credit underwriting procedures and has experienced staff servicing accounts that enter a state of delinquency

EXHIBIT 10.12   Trapped Excess Spread—Rapidly Deteriorating Environment

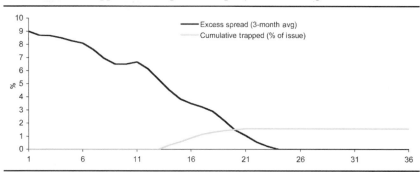

Source: Barclays Capital.

would be in the best position in the event of an economic downturn. The underwriting and servicing abilities of the originator must be analysed and a judgement about its ability to effectively manage any deterioration in the collateral performance must be made to gain comfort with an issuer's Class C notes.

COLLATERAL CHARACTERISTICS

Analysing the collateral characteristics of a credit card portfolio is essential because it tells us how the transaction is likely to perform. The major characteristics we focus on are:

■ Account balance (distribution across various ranges, weighted average).
■ Weighted average credit limit and utilisation.
■ Account age (distribution across various ranges, weighted average).
■ Geographic distribution of accounts.

The distribution of cardholder balances across various balance ranges and the weighted average account balance are both determinants of how well credit risk in the portfolio is diversified. However, it should be noted that although a portfolio with a lower weighted average account balance across all cardholders is preferable to a portfolio with a higher balance, because of the lower loss severity for a single cardholder, lower account balances are generally given to customers with bad credit records. As such, the weighted average account balance of a pool of credit card receivables should always be reviewed in conjunction with the credit card issuer's origination strategy.

EXHIBIT 10.13   Account Age as a Percentage of Total Receivables

	ARRAN 2000-A	Gracechurch No. 1
2 years or less	44.52	12.08
Over 2 to 4 years	37.48	11.90
Over 4 to 8 years	8.00	19.57
Over 8 to 12 years	3.69	12.29
Over 12 to 16 years	3.02	14.12
Over 16 to 20 years	1.42	11.95
Over 20 years	1.87	18.10

Source: Offering circulars.

Furthermore, the weighted average account balance should be analysed in conjunction with the weighted average utilisation of the assigned credit limit. Everything else being equal, we would prefer a portfolio with a lower average utilisation. On average, cardholders with a low credit balance are less likely to default in times of economic downturns than cardholders who have already made full use of the credit given to them.

The composition of a credit card portfolio by account age tells us how the seasoning of the collateral can vary significantly across various portfolios. Exhibit 10.13 shows the initial composition of two credit card portfolios by account age.

The Arran 2000-A portfolio is relatively unseasoned. By the time the transaction was completed, less than 55% of the cardholders in the securitised trust had held a credit card with The Royal Bank of Scotland for more than two years. This is very different from the Gracechurch portfolio, where almost 88% of the cardholders in the portfolio had held a card for more than two years by the time the deal was launched.

Advanced seasoning is a positive attribute for a trust as the portfolio is more likely to exhibit stable collateral performance than a relatively unseasoned portfolio. This is because a pool of new receivables usually experiences increasing losses for the first 18 months after which the losses usually decline and then level out. Over time, positive selection occurs as the lower quality and riskier accounts become charged-off and removed from the pool, leaving the higher quality accounts which should demonstrate more stable performance.

Lastly, it is important to analyse the geographic distribution of accounts. A diverse account base is positive for portfolios of loans as it helps mitigate losses caused by an economic downturn in any one region.

COLLATERAL PERFORMANCE

The key performance indicators for analysing credit card portfolios include portfolio yield, monthly payment rate (MPR), delinquencies, charge-offs, and excess spread. For most European credit card ABS, these performance indicators are published on a monthly basis on Bloomberg. The high degree of standardisation in terms of which performance indicators are published and how they are calculated makes the credit card ABS market very transparent. This also allows us to construct meaningful indices, which help us track the performance of the whole (or a significant part) of the credit card market.

Barclays Capital has developed an index for the European CCABS market, called the Barclays European Credit Card Indicators (BECCI). BECCI includes approximately €12 billion equivalent in receivables held in publicly rated ABS credit card transactions. It covers approximately 85% of the whole European credit card ABS market. Transactions are not included if their performance data is not or not yet publicly available. The various performance indicators are calculated on a weighted average based on the publicly rated notes outstanding.

We will discuss portfolio yield, *monthly payment rate* (MPR), delinquencies, charge-offs, and excess spread as well as *excess spread efficiency* (ESE) and *charge-off coverage* (COC); the latter two are combinations of the first five performance indicators. The various performance indicators will be shown for European and US credit card collateral. We will use our BECCI for European collateral and Standard & Poor's Credit Card Quality Indexes (S&P Index) for US collateral.

Portfolio Yield

Portfolio yield equals finance charges expressed as a percentage of the portfolio's outstanding receivables balance. Finance charges include interest on the receivables, annual fees, late payment fees, overlimit accounts and interchange. Portfolio yield is also driven by the way customers make use of their credit cards. Usually, revolving accounts generate higher finance charges than accounts held by convenience users, that is, customers who usually pay off their balance by the end of each month. Yield also depends on the seasoning of accounts included in the portfolio. If seasoning is low, a substantial proportion of customers may benefit from teaser rates. This proportion falls as accounts are becoming seasoned, which leads to a rise in yield. Exhibit 10.14 shows historical yields for European and US credit card transactions.

EXHIBIT 10.14   Yield, Annualised

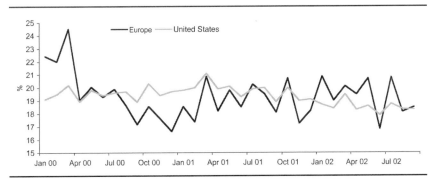

Source: Barclays Capital, Standard & Poor's.

As Exhibit 10.14 shows, yields have fluctuated on a month-on-month basis, both in Europe and in the United States, owing to the different number of days available for collection each month. For example, there was an extra bank holiday in June 2002 in the United Kingdom for the Queen's Jubilee Celebration. As more than 90% of European credit card trusts hold solely UK collateral, the reduced number of collection days in June had a significant impact on our European performance indicators. Cash collections for the master trusts fell by more than a fifth in June with a direct knock-on effect of reducing portfolio yield by almost 20%.

Monthly Payment Rate

The *monthly payment rate* (MPR) includes monthly collections of principal, finance charges, and fees. It is an important variable because it indicates how quickly the receivables base can be liquidated assuming a static pool. As such, with higher MPRs investors can be paid out more quickly during early amortisation. MPR depends on the proportion of convenience customers and is therefore subject to the originator's customer strategy. A high proportion of convenience users, while depressing yield, can lead to a significant increase in MPR.

There is usually a correlation between the MPR and the credit quality of the cardholder. Convenience users are not overextended, while cardholders who make the monthly minimum payment have less flexibility in their budget should an interruption in their income occur. Exhibit 10.15 shows that while fluctuating on a month-on-month basis, monthly payment rates overall were relatively stable between January 2000 and September 2002.

EXHIBIT 10.15   Monthly Payment Rate

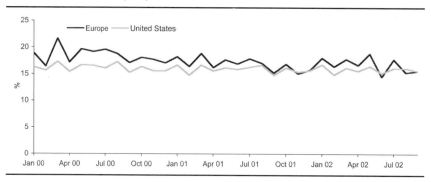

Source: Barclays Capital, Standard & Poor's.

EXHIBIT 10.16   Delinquencies

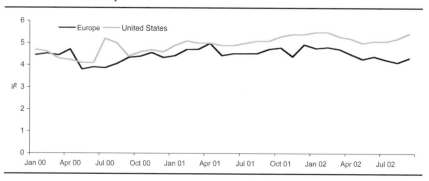

Source: Barclays Capital, Standard & Poor's.

Delinquencies

Delinquencies refer to the number of days that a customer has failed to make payments when due and tends to be a reliable indicator of the (anticipated) trend of charge-offs in a portfolio.

As Exhibit 10.16 shows, delinquencies for European and US credit card collateral basically moved in tandem between April 2001 and September 2002, with figures for Europe consistently lower than those in the United States. In September 2002, the European one-year average stood at 4.53%. This is 76 bp lower than the one-year average for the S&P Index of 5.29%.

When analysing the delinquencies of a particular credit card portfolio, the reported levels should be reviewed on a like-for-like basis, that is, it is important to know about the originator's policies towards delinquencies and charge-offs. Exhibit 10.17 shows receivables that have

EXHIBIT 10.17   30-Day Plus Delinquencies

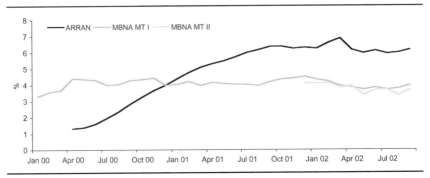

Note: Charge-off policies: ARRAN (365 days), MBNA (180 days).
Source: Bloomberg.

been delinquent for 30 days or more, expressed as a percentage of the total portfolio balance, for three UK credit card master trusts: Arran from RBS and MBNA EBL's two UK master trusts.

At first sight, the Arran portfolio looks inferior to its peers, having experienced a steady increase in delinquencies until October 2001. With more than 6% by the end of September 2002, the Arran portfolio has significantly higher delinquencies than the two MBNA EBL portfolios (below 4%). However, a review of the charge-off policies of the two originators puts this into perspective. MBNA EBL follows the charge-off policy of its parent company, MBNA America, and charges off an account after it becomes 180 days overdue. US companies are required to write off accounts after they have been in arrears for 180 days. There is no policy in the United Kingdom that stipulates writing off debt after a certain time period. Instead, receivables are written off when they are believed to be uncollectable. RBS charges off accounts after 365 days, which is about six months after MBNA EBL's charge-off date. This explains the much higher delinquency ratios revealed by Arran.

Delinquencies are usually reported within delinquency buckets, generally 30–59 days, 60–89 days, and 90 days and more. We developed a model that allows us to estimate like-for-like steady state delinquency levels for different portfolios regardless of the originators' charge-off policies. This model allows us to take 30-day-plus delinquencies which are reported by a company that has a charge-off policy of 365 days and restate these figures assuming a 180-day charge-off policy. Exhibit 10.18 shows actual delinquencies for the Arran portfolio together with two dotted horizontal lines, which represent modeled steady state delinquencies.

EXHIBIT 10.18 ARRAN Delinquency Levels for 180-day and 365-day Charge-off Policy

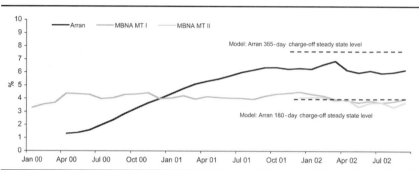

Source: Bloomberg, Barclays Capital.

Assuming a 365-day charge-off policy, *modeled* delinquencies are at 8.91%. Assuming a 180-day charge-off policy, the figure drops to 4.05%. This model does not take recoveries into account and so the difference between *modeled* delinquencies of 8.91% and *actual* delinquencies of 6.06% (average over the six months ending September 2002) suggests that the collections process is effectively reducing the total arrears level by approximately 32% (total delinquencies predicted by the model are 8.91% and actual reported delinquencies are 6.06%. The difference of 2.85% is likely to be due to recoveries and therefore 2.85%/8.91% = 32%).

Exhibit 10.18 shows that on a like for like basis, delinquencies for the Arran portfolio are in line with its peers. Again, the model does not take recoveries into account, and this value may even be considered conservative.

Charge-Offs

Charge-offs are credit losses experienced by the portfolio. Peak losses for credit card accounts are generally observed at about 18 to 24 months of seasoning. Exhibit 10.19 shows charge-offs for the BECCI and the S&P Index.

As with delinquencies, charge-offs for Europe and the United States show similar patterns. However, the significant gap between charge-offs in Europe and the United States shows the relative attractiveness of European credit card collateral compared with US collateral, reflecting the intensity of competition in the US market and the greater tendency to file for individual bankruptcy.

EXHIBIT 10.19   Charge-Offs, Annualised

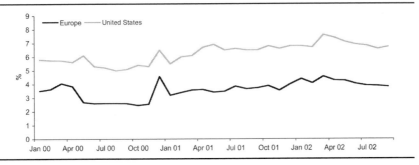

Source: Barclays Capital, Standard & Poor's.

EXHIBIT 10.20   Excess Spread, Annualised

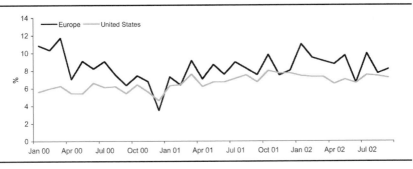

Source: Barclays Capital, Standard & Poor's.

Excess Spread

Excess spread is a particularly important measure of the health of a credit card portfolio and negative excess spread will usually trigger early amortisation. Excess spread is portfolio yield less servicing fees, note coupon, charge-offs, and other costs. Exhibit 10.20 shows 3-month average excess spread for European and US credit card collateral.

Excess spread for European credit card collateral has traditionally been higher than excess spread for US collateral. This is due both to higher portfolio yield and significantly lower charge-offs in Europe.

Excess Spread Efficiency and Charge-off Coverage

Excess spread is important because it is the first line of protection for noteholders in that it absorbs charge-offs. While this is true, two portfolios with similar levels of excess spread can behave very differently in a worsening economic environment. Exhibit 10.21 shows excess spread for two different credit card portfolios.

EXHIBIT 10.21   Performance Statistics

	Portfolio Yield	MPR	Charge-Offs	Excess Spread	Excess Spread Efficiency	Charge-Off Coverage
Issuer 1	16.5%	24.6%	3.5%	5.8%	35.2%	1.66
Issuer 2	24.8%	6.8%	11.2%	5.9%	23.8%	0.53

Source: Barclays Capital.

Although the two portfolios exhibit very similar levels of excess spread, all their other performance indicators are very different. Based on portfolio yield, MPR and charge-offs for the two portfolios, the first portfolio seems to be composed of prime borrowers, while the second portfolio seems to be composed of mid-/subprime borrowers. Whether a portfolio is composed of prime or subprime borrowers impacts the portfolio's performance in a worsening economic environment. Subprime borrowers are usually on a very tight budget with little flexibility for increases in expenses or reductions in income (as expressed in the low monthly payment rate) and as such, a weakening economy could lead to significantly higher delinquencies and charge-offs for the second portfolio. Prime borrowers on the other hand should be in a better position to cope with a worsening economic environment because they often have a higher level of savings. As such, the severity of the change in the performance characteristics of the collateral should be much smaller for the prime portfolio.

However, we are introducing two ratios to help predict the severity of change in collateral performance with a worsening economic environment. The two ratios are *excess spread efficiency* (ESE) and *charge-off coverage* (COC).

The ESE ratio is defined as excess spread divided by portfolio yield; it measures the ability of the servicer to turn yield into excess spread. The greater the ratio, the smaller the predicted impact of a slowing economy on the performance of the collateral. As Exhibit 10.21 shows, the prime issuer (issuer 1) has a much higher ESE ratio than the subprime issuer. The September 2002 ratios for European and US credit card portfolios are 44% and 39%, respectively.

The COC ratio is more a measure of security for the investor as it compares the level of excess spread with charge-offs. The higher the ratio, the greater the ability of the trust to weather a slowdown. Again, the prime portfolio (issuer 1) has a much higher COC ratio than the subprime portfolio (issuer 2). For the prime portfolio, the ratio stands at 1.66, meaning that excess spread would be able to absorb an increase in charge-offs of up to 166%. For the subprime portfolio, current losses could increase by only 53%. The September 2002 ratios for European and US credit card portfolios are 2.15% and 1.06%, respectively.

CONCLUSION

The European credit card securitisation market has grown substantially, both in terms of absolute size and in number of issues. Although the market has traditionally been dominated by sterling-denominated collateral, the securitisation environment in various European countries bodes well for credit card securitisations which should attract banks and specialty lenders looking for alternative sources of funding and effective ways to manage their balance sheets.

The CCABS market continues to be a safe haven for European ABS investors. Especially in 2002, when corporate bonds of various sectors showed increased price volatility and the CDO market experienced a significant number of downgrades, credit card ABS transactions continued to show strong and stable performance. In fact, since the market's inception in 1995, no European CCABS have experienced any downgrades. We believe that CCABS are likely to continue to exhibit strong and stable performance and remain one of the core asset classes for European ABS investors.

CHAPTER 11

European Auto and Consumer Loan ABS

Markus Niemeier
Manager
Barclays Capital

Three types of consumer finance receivables have been securitised in the past: credit card receivables, auto receivables (essentially auto loan and auto lease receivables), and "other" consumer finance receivables, which typically include unsecured personal loans. Credit card receivables are discussed in Chapter 10. The purpose of this chapter is to provide an overview of the European auto and consumer loan ABS markets and review the structural, collateral, and performance characteristics of the two asset classes. We decided to review auto and consumer loan ABS combined in one chapter because of the many similarities between the two asset classes.

THE EUROPEAN AUTO AND CONSUMER LOAN ABS MARKET

Although the first public securitisations of European auto and consumer loan receivables were completed in the early 1990s, issuance in both sectors did not really take off until the mid- to late 1990s. But since then, for lenders of auto and consumer loans alike, securitisation has become one of the favourite sources of funding and an effective way of managing their balance sheets. European auto and consumer loan ABS originators have

The views expressed in this article are those of the author and not necessarily those of Barclays Capital.

traditionally been banks and finance companies. In the case of auto loans, finance companies can be further divided into independent finance companies and captive in-house finance companies owned by an automobile manufacturer. Exhibit 11.1 shows the issuance of publicly rated auto and consumer loan ABS backed by European collateral from 1997 to 2002.[1]

EXHIBIT 11.1   European Auto and Consumer Loan ABS Issuance by Year (1997–2002)

Auto ABS

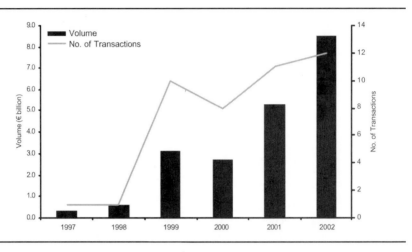

Consumer Loan ABS

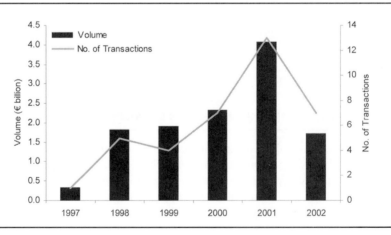

Source: Bloomberg.

---

[1] We define European auto and consumer loan transactions as those transactions that are backed by auto and consumer loan receivables which were originated in Europe.

EXHIBIT 11.2 Top-Five European Auto and Consumer Loan ABS Issuers
(1997–2002)

Auto ABS

Rank	Seller	Issuer	No. of Transactions	Total Issuance (€ billion)
1	Fiat	FIAT, SIAT, ALFA, EAS	4	3,317
2	Banque PSA Finance	Auto ABS Compartiment	2	2,500
3	FCE Bank	Globaldrive	4	2,434
4	Volkswagen Leasing	VCL	3	2,250
5	RCI Banque/DIAC	Cars Alliance	1	1,400
		Total	14	11,901

Consumer Loan ABS

Rank	Seller	Issuer	No. of Transactions	Total Issuance (€ billion)
1	Cetelem	Noria, MasterNoria	6	2,386
2	ABN Amro	Amstel Consumer Loan Securitisation	2	1,624
3	Paragon Group	Paragon Auto&Secured Fin., Paragon Pers.&Auto Fin.	3	1,107
4	Banco Comercial Portugues	Nova	3	895
5	Banco Espirito Santo, Besleasing Mobiliaria	Lusitano	2	700
		Total	16	6,712

Source: Bloomberg.

Traditionally, the two sectors have been clearly dominated by repeat issuers. For example, in 2002, repeat issuers accounted for approximately 75% of all auto ABS issued and 82% of all consumer loan ABS issued (by issuance volume). Exhibit 11.2 shows the top five European auto and consumer loan ABS issuers ranked by cumulative issuance volume from 1997 to 2002.

Auto ABS—Top-Five Issuers

Fiat is the dominant issuer of European auto ABS in terms of total issuance volume. The company has accessed the securitisation market four times, issuing notes from four special purpose vehicles (SPVs), namely First Italian Auto Transaction (FIAT 1), Second Italian Auto Transaction (FIAT 2), Absolute Funding (ALFA), and European Auto Securitisation (EAS). In the case of FIAT 1 and FIAT 2, all receivables are originated in Italy; receivables included in the ALFA portfolio are originated in Germany and those included in the EAS portfolio are originated in France and Spain. For all transactions, notes, and collateral are euro-denominated.

Credipar Group, a wholly owned subsidiary of Banque PSA Finance, which is the captive in-house financing arm of the French PSA Group, has completed just two transactions, but with relatively large issue sizes of €1 billion and €1.5 billion, respectively. The loans in the Auto ABS Compartiment 2001-1 portfolio are originated by Credipar via Banque SOFI (Citroën outlets) and Banque DIN (Peugeot outlets), two wholly owned subsidiaries of Credipar. The Auto ABS Compartiment 2002-1 pool also includes loans originated in Spain by Banque PSA Finance. In both cases, notes and collateral are euro-denominated.

FCE Bank, the captive financing arm of Ford, has completed four EAABS transactions since 1997 (Globaldrive B, C, D, and E), issuing notes under the umbrella of its well-known Globaldrive programme. (Globaldrive 1, the first transaction completed under the Globaldrive programme, is backed by US collateral and as such is not included in Exhibit 11.2.) As one of the earlier and larger auto ABS programmes, Globaldrive is often viewed as a benchmark in the European auto ABS market. The Globaldrive transactions are discussed in more detail below.

Volkswagen Leasing has accessed the securitisation market three times since 1997 under the umbrella of its VCL programme.[2] All transactions are backed by German auto leases and notes and collateral are Deutschmark/euro-denominated.

RCI Banque, the parent company of DIAC, is a 100%-owned subsidiary of Compagnie Financière Renault, the 100%-owned Renault subsidiary in charge of finance and cash management. The company has completed one EAABS transaction, Cars Alliance Funding—Series 2002-1. Notes and collateral are euro-denominated.

Consumer Loan ABS—Top Five Issuers

Among the dominant issuers of European consumer loan ABS is Cetelem, the consumer credit arm of Compagnie Bancaire, which in turn is

---

[2] Two other transaction, VCL No. 1 and VCL No. 2, were completed in 1996 and are two of the first public European auto ABS issues completed. However, Exhibit 11.2 includes only transactions completed since January 1997 and shows only three VCL transactions.

the financial services subsidiary of BNP Paribas. Cetelem has completed six public ABS transactions since 1997, issuing approximately €2.4 billion of notes backed by French unsecured consumer loans. Notes and collateral are French franc-/euro-denominated.

The second largest issuer of European consumer loan ABS is ABN Amro, which has accessed the securitisation market twice since 1997 through its Amstel Consumer Loan Securitisation programme. In each of the two cases the notes are euro-denominated and backed by Dutch consumer loans.

The Paragon Group of Companies has accessed the consumer loan ABS market three times since 1997; once in 2000 under the Paragon Auto & Secured Finance programme and twice in 2001 under the Paragon Personal & Auto Finance programme. In each case, the receivables and notes are sterling-denominated. Although all three pools include some auto receivables, they have been counted as consumer loan ABS for the purpose of this chapter.

Banco Comercial Português has completed three consumer loan ABS transactions since 1997. Nova Finance No. 1, Nova Finance No. 2, and Nova Finance No. 3 were issued in 1998, 2001, and 2002, respectively. Nova Finance No. 1 is Deutschmark-denominated and Nova Finance No. 2 and Nova Finance No. 3 are euro-denominated. All three transactions are backed by Portuguese consumer loans.

Banco Espirito has completed two European consumer loan ABS transactions, Lusitano Finance No. 1 (Portuguese consumer loans) and Lusitano Finance No. 2 (Portuguese consumer loans and leases; the consumer loans are originated by Banco Espirito, the leases are originated by Besleasing Mobiliária). Notes and collateral are euro-denominated.

Issuance by Country

The auto and consumer loan ABS markets are very much pan-European. Exhibit 11.3 shows issuance in 2002 for both markets according to country. Auto receivables have been originated in Austria, Belgium, France, Germany, Italy, Portugal, Spain, and the United Kingdom. Consumer loan ABS have been backed by loans originated in France, Italy, the Netherlands, Portugal, Spain, and the United Kingdom. Exhibit 11.4 shows issuance volume and number of transactions from 1997 to 2002 according to country (transactions are considered to be backed by receivables originated in a particular country if more than 50% of the receivables included in the pool were originated in that country).

Tranching of European auto and consumer loan ABS transactions is much less standardised than, say, European credit card transactions. While most credit card transactions come with three tranches, typically

EXHIBIT 11.3   European Auto and Consumer Loan ABS Issuance by Country (2002)

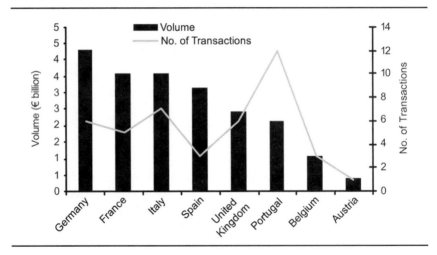

Source: Bloomberg.

EXHIBIT 11.4   European Auto and Consumer Loan ABS Issuance by Country (1997 to 2002)
Auto ABS

rated triple-A, single-A, and triple-B, respectively, auto and consumer loan ABS transactions have come with one, two, three, or even four tranches. The most senior tranche is usually rated triple-A and the most junior tranche is usually rated triple-B. If available, the mezzanine tranche is usually rated single-A and double-A. Exhibit 11.5 shows European auto and consumer loan ABS issuance by rating from 1997 to 2002.

EXHIBIT 11.4 (Continued)
Consumer Loan ABS

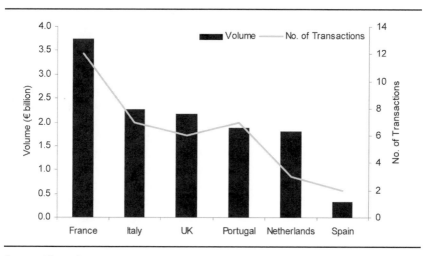

Source: Bloomberg.

EXHIBIT 11.5 European Auto and Consumer Loan ABS Issuance by Rating (1997 to 2002)

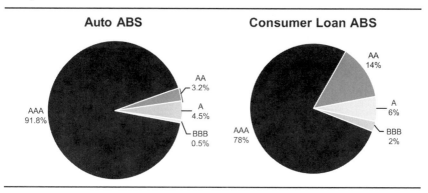

Source: Bloomberg.

STRUCTURAL CHARACTERISTICS

Although auto and consumer loan ABS structures are not very standard-ised, most transactions have a range of structural features in common. The purpose of this section is to provide an overview of typical auto and consumer loan ABS structures.

Transaction Structure

Exhibit 11.6 below shows the structural diagram for a typical auto or consumer loan ABS transaction. Although there have been attempts to create a master-trust like structure for consumer loan ABS, we discuss in this chapter the most common structure used for auto and consumer loan ABS issuance.[3]

Using the transaction structure shown in Exhibit 11.6, a portfolio of auto or personal loans are transferred from the originator of the loans to the issuer (an SPV). Usually, the transfer of the assets is conducted in a manner that results in a "true sale," which effectively removes the assets from the bankruptcy or insolvency estate of the originator. This allows the originator to issue notes with a higher rating than itself. If the issuer were not bankruptcy remote, a double-B rated originator would generally not be able to issue notes with an investment-grade rating. However, through asset securitisation, the same originator would

EXHIBIT 11.6   Auto/Consumer Loan Transaction Structure

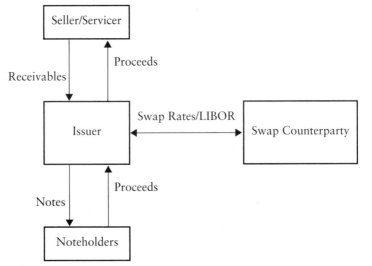

Source: Barclays Capital.

---

[3] For example, the Master Noria transactions are issued from a master-trust type structure. The transactions, backed by unsecured consumer loans, use the concept of an FCC (Fonds Commun de Créances), which may issue different series over time. Master Noria may acquire new eligible loans using both funds from the amortisation of its assets and proceeds from future series issuance.

EXHIBIT 11.7   FIAT 1, Globaldrive B and PPAF 1 Structural Details

	FIAT 1	Globaldrive B	PPAF 1
Issue Size (€ 000 equiv.)	965,000	490,750	279,095
Pricing Date	July 2000	March 1999	June 2001
Original Weighted Average Life (Years)	3.8	3.9	5.0
Length of Revolving Period (Years)	3	3	4
Expected Maturity	March 2005	September 2004	September 2008[a]
Legal Maturity	July 2008	June 2008	June 2021

[a] June 2007, if call-option is exercised.
Source: Bloomberg, offering circulars.

be in a position to issue a tranche of triple-A rated notes (assuming an appropriate securitisation structure and sufficient collateral quality).

Exhibit 11.6 also shows a swap agreement between the issuer and a swap counterparty. A swap agreement is not necessary for all transactions but is generally present to mitigate interest rate risk. The vast majority of auto and consumer loan ABS tranches have traditionally come with floating-rate coupons. If the underlying collateral (or a certain proportion of the receivables in the pool) pays fixed-rate interest, the rating agencies usually require the issuer to enter into an interest rate swap agreement in order to mitigate such interest rate risk.

Auto and Consumer Loan ABS Mechanics

In the following review of some of the fundamental auto and consumer loan ABS mechanics, we will use three transactions as practical examples; two auto ABS transactions, FIAT 1 and Globaldrive B, and one consumer loan ABS transaction, Paragon Personal and Auto Finance (No. 1) (PPAF 1). The FIAT 1 transaction was completed by Fiat in July 2000 and at that time it represented the largest European auto transaction completed. Globaldrive B was completed by FCE Bank in March 1999. PPAF 1 was completed in 2001 by Paragon Finance PLC. In Exhibit 11.7 we outline the structural details for the senior notes of FIAT 1, Globaldrive B and PPAF 1.

Issue Size

Many Participants in the European auto and consumer loan ABS markets tend to be buy-and-hold investors, and so offer-side liquidity in the secondary market may be limited for many issues. However, liquidity tends to improve with larger issue sizes because the size of the transaction impacts the number of investors involved. The FIAT transaction ranks among the largest European auto ABS transactions and is roughly twice the size of the Globaldrive B transaction and more than three times the size of the PPAF 1 transaction. It comes as no surprise that since the closing date, it is one of the few auto issues to have an active secondary market presence.

Revolving Period

In most completed European auto ABS transactions, the senior classes have been structured so that the bonds feature an amortising payment structure with an average life of between 3.5 and 4.5 years; consumer loan ABS transactions tend to have slightly longer average lives, often between four and five years.

Usually included in these structures is a revolving or substitution period during which principal received from borrowers is reinvested in new receivables with the interest paid to noteholders. The revolving period usually lasts for between two and three years, allowing the bonds to have a longer average life than if structured as a straight pass-through. Preset criteria are established regarding the purchase of new collateral during the revolving period that protect investors against a deterioration in the underlying pool of assets.

For example, FIAT 1 benefits from four triggers that measure certain characteristics of the collateral. During the three-year revolving period, new receivables can only be purchased if the eligibility criteria shown in Exhibit 11.8 are met.

The revolving period usually ends on a certain date (e.g., in the case of the FIAT 1 transaction the revolving period is scheduled to last for three years and would therefore end in July 2003) or following the breach of an early amortisation trigger. Exhibit 11.9 shows the three FIAT 1 early amortisation triggers together with the respective maximum trigger levels.

EXHIBIT 11.8 FIAT 1 Collateral Eligibility Criteria

Trigger	Initial Pool	Maximum
Used vehicles in portfolio (%)	17.60	20.00
Borrowers located in South Italy (%)	28.80	40.00
Weighted average remaining maturity (months)	23.30	36.00
Weighted average interest rate (%)	5.31	10.00

Source: Offering circular.

EXHIBIT 11.9   FIAT 1 Delinquency and Write-off Triggers

Trigger	Maximum
2–4-month delinquencies (%, 3-month average)	4.75
5–8-month delinquencies (%, 3-month average)	1.50
Cumulative write-offs (%)	Dynamic calculation: (Quarter number + 1)/12 × 4%

Source: Offering circular.

EXHIBIT 11.10   FIAT 1 Amortisation Structure

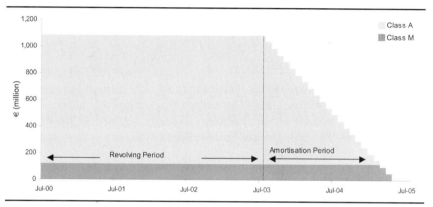

Source: Barclays Capital.

Amortisation Period

Following the substitution period, the transaction typically enters the amortisation period, during which principal collected from receivables is passed through to noteholders. This may lead to a degree of variability in the average life of the security if the borrowers repay their loans more quickly or slowly than the modelled prepayment speed used to price the notes. Exhibit 11.10 shows a simplified paydown structure for the FIAT 1 transaction.

Principal Window

The time period over which principal amortises and is returned to investors is called the *principal window*. The length of the principal window can vary depending on how quickly the collateral is prepaying. As such, cash flows paid to investors during the pass-through period are always subject to a degree of uncertainty. Note also that during this period investors are exposed to reinvestment risk (i.e., the risk that returned principal may have to be reinvested at lower interest rates). The longer the principal window, the greater the investors' exposure to reinvestment risk.

Legal Maturity and Expected Maturity

The legal final maturity is usually different from the expected maturity which is calculated based on the start of the pass-through period and the rate at which the collateral is prepaying. The legal final maturity is the date the rating agencies use in assigning their ratings to the notes. This is the date at which, if sufficient principal were not paid, the issue would be in default. The legal final is typically two to three years after the expected maturity date and depends on assumptions made about the length of repossession or other legal procedures.

Credit Enhancement

A typical auto or consumer loan ABS transaction features one to four tranches, generally rated between triple-A and triple-B. Exhibit 11.11 shows the credit enhancement levels for the FIAT 1, the Globaldrive B, and the PPAF 1 transactions. The three transactions are all structured differently and as such, the senior notes in each issue benefit from different levels as well as types of credit enhancement.

EXHIBIT 11.11 FIAT 1, Globaldrive B, and PPAF 1 Credit Enhancement Structures

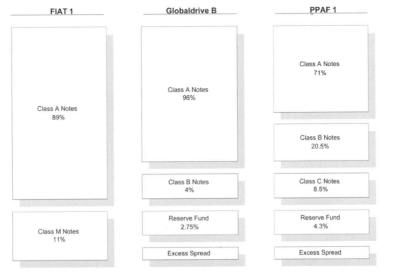

Source: Offering circulars.

The FIAT 1 issue benefits from a credit enhancement level of 11% from subordination of the unrated Class M notes. The Globaldrive B issue benefits from 4% credit enhancement of the Class B notes and a reserve fund, which builds up from 1.8% at the closing date to 2.75% of the balance of the initial pool. Fully funded, the Globaldrive B class A notes benefit from a total credit enhancement of 6.75%. The PPAF 1 issue benefits from a credit enhancement level of 33.3% from subordination of the Class B and the Class C notes (20.5% and 8.5%, respectively) and a cash reserve of 4.3% of the initial notes balance.

For both Globaldrive B and PPAF1 the first layer of protection is excess spread in the transaction, which is the difference between (1) the income received from the pool of receivables, and (2) the coupon due under the notes/payments due to the swap counterparty plus a certain servicing fee. Excess spread that is not used to cover losses on the loans within a certain period is returned to the originator (i.e., excess spread benefits the transaction on a "use it or lose it" basis).

Strictly speaking, the FIAT 1 transaction does not generate excess spread. This explains the high level of credit enhancement from the unrated class M notes (usually, unrated tranches are either privately sold or kept as an equity tranche by the originator). On the closing date, an amount of notes was issued which was equal to the net present value of all future cash payments due from the collateral (as opposed to the principal balance of the collateral). The discount rate used was the fixed rate payable to the swap counterparty (swap rate plus coupon on the Class A notes and all fees associated with the transaction). Structured this way, the receivables always yield the discount rate, leaving no excess spread in the transaction. However, losses on the FIAT 1 portfolio can be covered to a certain degree from interest collections because the structure provides for delinquent principal and defaults to be covered before interest is paid on the Class M notes.

PRODUCT TYPES AND COLLATERAL CHARACTERISTICS

The purpose of this section is to review the most common types of auto and consumer finance products that are offered to customers and that have traditionally been included in ABS transactions. We then describe the fundamental characteristics of auto and consumer loan portfolios and discuss common ways of analysing them.

Product Types

The universe of both auto and consumer loan products offered to customers has become very diverse; products may differ for example in terms of amortisation profile, interest calculation, discounts granted, incentive schemes, or balloon payment terms. The following description of the most common types of auto finance products, namely instalment loans, balloon loans, leases, and long-term rentals shall provide an example.

Instalment Loans

Instalment loans (also called *amortising loans*) are the standard type of auto finance contracts. If customers choose instalment loans, they are required to make the same instalments over the life of the loan, with decreasing interest proportions and increasing principal proportions. Usually, the borrower has to make a certain down payment in the beginning, which is typically about 5–10% of the sales price, but can vary between lenders.

Balloon Loans

Balloon loans allow borrowers to repay the loan in relatively low monthly instalments followed by a single balloon payment at the end (usually up to 60% of the loan). In general, balloon loans are considered more risky than loans with full repayment under equal instalments due to the high residual value (RV) and the possibility that the borrower may not be able to afford to make the final balloon payment. Balloon loans may offer the borrower a set of options before the final payment is due: (1) pay the balloon payment and be released from all future obligations; (2) refinance the final payment by taking on an additional instalment loan; or (3) return the vehicle to the dealer under a repurchase agreement. For example, FIAT 2 is an auto ABS transaction that is partly backed by balloon loans, accounting for approximately 28% of the total initial pool.

Leases

Leases are generally made to commercial parties. Under the lease contract, the lessee makes small monthly payments to the lessor and at the end of the term holds an option to purchase the vehicle for the stated RV. This option is likely to be exercised if the RV is equal to or below the retail value of the car, otherwise the lessee is likely to return the car to the dealer, which can then decide whether or not to take the car. If the dealer also decides not to purchase the car, the lessor takes possession and sells it at its wholesale price. Because of the uncertainty about the realisation of the RV, which can be large relative to the lessee's lease payments, it is important for investors to know if the pool of receivables that backs the transaction comprises only the rental component of the lease contracts or if it also includes the RV component. For example, the five transactions issued under the VCL programme are backed solely by the rental component of the lease contracts.

Long-Term Rentals

Long-term rentals (LTR) have been used only in Portugal. In many aspects, they are similar to lease contracts. A major difference between an LTR and a lease contract is that in the case of the former, borrowers are required to make a cash collateral payment, which may be 30% of the related vehicle value. The cash collateral payment remains untapped over the term of the LTR if the borrower makes timely payments as agreed in the initial contract. In the case of nonpayments, the lender takes possession of the vehicle and the cash collateral payment is used to cover any losses the lender might incur if the price at which the vehicle was sold is below the final contract RV. LTR products have been part of the collateral for the LTR transactions, which were completed in 1999, 2000, 2001, and 2002 by Sofinloc.

Collateral Characteristics

Analysing a portfolio of auto or consumer loan receivables is essential because it tells us how the transaction is likely to perform in the future. The major characteristics we focus on are:

- Term distribution
- Annual percentage rate (APR)
- Geographic distribution
- Seasoning
- Model and make diversification (auto ABS only)
- Proportions of new and used vehicles (auto ABS only)
- Loan-to-value (LTV) (auto ABS only)

Term Distribution

The term of the loan defines the period over which the total amount of principal is repaid. Most auto and consumer loan securitisations allow loans with original terms of 60 months or less. The distribution of loans across the term spectrum is important because losses tend to increase with the term of the loan. For auto loans, this is most likely a result of a slower build up in equity with a longer amortising loan. Exhibit 11.12 shows the amortisation profile for 48-, 60-, and 72-month loans along with a depreciation curve.

The amortisation profiles in this example assume a car sales price of €35,000, a 10% down payment, and an APR of 15%. The most worrying situation is when the amortisation line is greater than the depreciation line; this would imply negative equity in the vehicle and the greatest propensity for default. In this example, the 48-month loan never exhibits negative equity, the 60-month loan experiences some negative equity and the 72-month loan experiences the longest period and the greatest

EXHIBIT 11.12   Generic Principal Amortisation and Depreciation Profiles (auto loans)

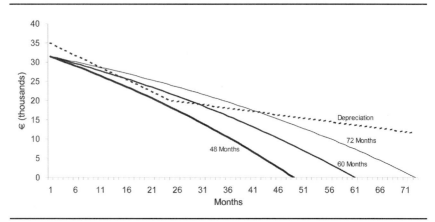

Source: Barclays Capital.

magnitude of negative equity. It is during this period of negative equity that there is the greatest potential for loss on a receivables pool.

Annual Percentage Rate (APR)

Most lenders have models in place that allow them to charge higher interest rates to more risky borrowers. However, it is not appropriate to assess a borrower's credit quality solely based on the weighted average coupon for a pool of collateral. Other considerations include the absolute level of interest rates when the loan was originated and the degree of incentive loans in the pool. Incentive loans carry a below market interest rate, which is typically supported by the manufacturer or the captive finance company in the case of auto loans or the lender or retailer in the case of consumer loans. A pool with a large number of incentive loans may experience a declining amount of interest available as the deal ages. As the borrowers with incentive loans have a below market rate, there is very little reason for them to prepay while those borrowers being charged a higher interest rate may prepay their loans if they have available cash. This lopsided prepayment scenario could leave the pool with a higher percentage of lower yielding loans, and hence lower interest income, as the deal ages.

Geographic Distribution

A pool of collateral should be well diversified geographically to minimise the effect on the pool in the event of a rise in unemployment or recession in any one region. Exhibit 11.13 shows the initial Globaldrive B portfolio, which is geographically well diversified among nine major German regions.

EXHIBIT 11.13 Globaldrive B Geographic Distribution (% of principal balance)

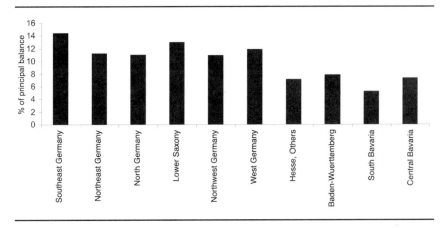

Source: Offering circular.

Seasoning

Advanced seasoning is a positive attribute for a pool of receivables because the portfolio is more likely to exhibit stable performance than a relatively unseasoned portfolio. This is because a pool of new receivables usually experiences increasing losses for the first 18 to 24 months after which the losses are expected to decline and then level out. Over time, positive selection occurs while the lower quality and riskier accounts become charged off and removed from the pool, leaving the higher quality accounts which should demonstrate more stable performance.

Model and Make Diversification for Auto ABS

When assessing a pool of auto receivables, we usually prefer portfolios that are diversified according to model and make. This is because a concentration in one particular brand can expose investors to additional risk if the manufacturer becomes insolvent. A concentration in a particular type of vehicle or model may have negative consequences if customers' tastes change, problems with the particular model emerge or the manufacturer exits the particular market segment.

Model and make diversification are of particular importance if the loans included in the pool have a high RV component, because problems associated with the manufacturer or the car could then lead to depressed sales prices in the used-car market. This in turn could lead to higher loss levels if customers default due to lower recovery values realised by the originator.

New versus Used for Auto ABS

Everything else being equal, we prefer a portfolio that includes only new car loans to a portfolio that includes some used car loans. This is because used vehicles generally experience higher delinquencies and losses than new vehicle loans. Therefore, it is important to pay close attention to the initial share of used vehicle loans in a portfolio, how this share changes over time, and the maximum number of used vehicle loans that can be added to the pool during the revolving period. As Exhibit 11.8 shows, there is a ceiling on the proportion of used car loans that can be added to the FIAT 1 pool during the revolving period. Other auto ABS transactions have similar collateral eligibility criteria.

Loan-to-Value for Auto ABS

The loan-to-value ratio (LTV) represents the size of the loan relative to the sales price of the vehicle. The lower the LTV, the more equity a borrower has invested in the vehicle. The equity in the vehicle should act as an incentive to keep the borrower from defaulting, and thus losing the invested equity. Over time, the amount of the loan will decrease as principal is repaid by the borrower. However, the value of the vehicle will most likely be decreasing as well, based on the vehicle's depreciation curve. This makes it necessary to analyse the rate at which principal is being repaid (amortisation schedule) against the rate at which the vehicle is depreciating in order to determine the borrower's expected equity in the vehicle (see term distribution above).

COLLATERAL PERFORMANCE

The two key quantitative performance indicators for analysing portfolios of auto and consumer loan receivables are delinquencies and charge-offs.

Delinquencies

The performance of a pool of assets is affected by the borrowers' willingness and ability to repay their debt. A key performance characteristic that measures this is the amount of delinquencies in a pool. Delinquencies refer to the number of days that a borrower has failed to make payments when due and tends to be a reliable indicator of the (anticipated) trend of charge-offs in a portfolio.

Additionally, it is important to understand the company's servicing methods and the effectiveness of such methods. The end result of a successful servicing operation is the ability to bring delinquent accounts current and thus minimise charge-offs. Exhibit 11.14 shows total delin-

EXHIBIT 11.14   Globaldrive D Delinquency Rates (%, annualised)

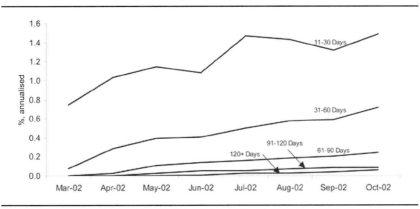

Source: Investor reports.

quencies for the Globaldrive D transaction split up into five delinquency buckets. Globaldrive D was completed by FCE Bank in March 2002.

Delinquencies are usually reported within delinquency buckets and in the case of the Globaldrive transactions, those buckets are 11–30 days, 31–60 days, 61–90 days, 91–120 days, and 120 days and more. The exhibit shows that the figure for 11–30 days delinquencies is significantly higher than the figure for 31–60 days, which, in turn, is higher than the figures for the following three buckets. This result is positive for it shows that FCE Bank is very effective in bringing a proportion of customers in each delinquency bucket current. For example, by the end of September 2002, there were 1,985 loans with a total principal balance of €10,518,858 that fell into the 1–30 days delinquency bucket. By the end of October 2002—30 days later—1,021 loans with a total principal balance of €5,724,505 fell into the 31–60 days delinquency bucket. This means that a significant number of borrowers became current (assuming one loan is made to one borrower). The total number of borrowers who become current is expected to increase further according to the servicer's collection processes, which typically include telephone calls, written reminders, and other measures.

Exhibit 11.14 also shows that delinquencies for each bucket have been rising since the transaction's closing date in March 2002. This trend is entirely expected while the receivables age. By the time the transaction was completed, more than 60% of the receivables (by principal balance) were seasoned for 18 months or less and more than 40% were seasoned for 12 months or less. Therefore, we would expect delinquencies to rise as the receivables age. Exhibit 11.15 shows the same delinquency buckets for the Globaldrive B transaction, which is backed by a much more seasoned pool of auto loan receivables.

EXHIBIT 11.15   Globaldrive B Delinquency Rates (%, annualised)

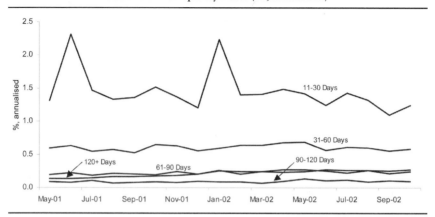

Source: Investor reports.

Delinquencies for each bucket show a high degree of stability (with the exception of the two spikes in the 11–30 days delinquency bucket in June 2001 and January 2002). We generally expect delinquencies to reach steady state levels once a portfolio is fully seasoned, which is usually the case after about 18–24 months. Therefore, we would expect delinquencies for the Globaldrive D portfolio to rise and then plateau after a certain period of time, just as shown in Exhibit 11.15 for the more seasoned Globaldrive B portfolio.

Charge-Offs

Another important performance measure is the default rate. The monthly default curve for auto and consumer loan receivables originated by a generic originator is shown in Exhibit 11.16. The curve is built showing monthly defaults from the number of months since origination of the obligation. The loss curve is minimal for the first year after which there is a fairly sharp spike lasting usually 6 to 18 months. Between the 18th and 24th month, the loss curve reaches a peak and declines fairly rapidly for the life of the receivable. This bell-shaped curve is typical for other auto and consumer loan receivables.

Vintage Charge-Offs

Each originator has its own underwriting and servicing standards. These standards ultimately determine the net loss rate in the originated collateral. It is also important to be aware of the overall health of the economy, for this will affect the performance of the collateral. Collateral that has been originated and serviced in a consistent manner can behave

EXHIBIT 11.16   Charge-Offs (month, %)

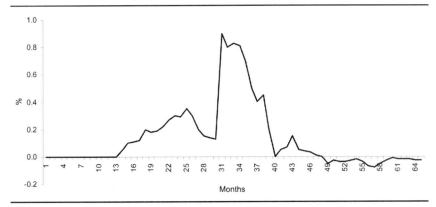

Source: Barclays Capital.

EXHIBIT 11.17   Charge-Offs for Various Quarters of Origination

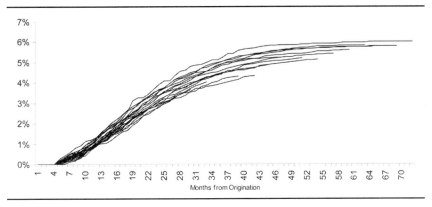

Source: Barclays Capital.

very differently under different economic situations. Changes in underwriting and servicing standards can also result in a change in the performance of the collateral. In Exhibit 11.17 we show a generic vintage charge-off analysis which helps us to identify the impact of a changing economic environment and different origination standards on charge-offs. We have assumed a 6-month charge-off policy.

The various lines in Exhibit 11.17 represent charge-offs according to the month from origination. Each line represents loans that were originated in a certain quarter, so the shorter the line, the more recently the loans were originated. For example, for all loans that were originated in January 2001, there would be 18 months of charge-off data available by the end of 2002 (loans are charged-off after being delinquent for six months and therefore 24 – 6 = 18). For loans originated in January 2002, there would be only six months of charge-off data available, and the line in would be shorter.

The exhibit shows that loans originated more recently tend to have lower charge-offs, which reflects positively on the originator's strategy.

CONCLUSION

There has been solid growth in European auto and consumer loan securitisations traditionally, both in terms of absolute size and in number of issues. Many issuers have come to market with a series of issues, giving them repeat issuer status. This has helped provide liquidity to the asset class while more investors devote time and resources to understanding the asset class and the various issuers. We feel this trend will continue in the future with the vast majority of transactions coming from established programmes.

The securitisation environment in Europe bodes well for auto securitisations which should attract banks and specialist lenders looking for alternative sources of funding and effective ways to manage their balance sheets. Transaction structures continue to improve and we may see some of the largest originators of auto and consumer loan receivables to move from the amortising structure to a bullet-type structure in the future, which should further add interest and liquidity to the asset class.

CHAPTER 12

European Public Sector Securitisations

Christopher Flanagan
Managing Director
JPMorgan

Edward Reardon
Vice President
JPMorgan

Doreen Tan*
Associate
JPMorgan

In this chapter we provide an overview of one of the fastest growing sectors in the European structured finance market: public sector securitisation. We examine the evolution of the market since 1999, including the objectives of public sector securitisations and the potential benefits to sovereign issuers, but also highlight ongoing changes in the accounting treatment of these deals. We conclude with a review of the structure, servicing, and relative value of public sector securitisations for asset-backed investors.

WHAT IS A PUBLIC SECTOR SECURITISATION?

A public sector securitisation is the sale of government-owned assets to the capital markets in the form of highly rated asset-backed bonds. Like

---

* Doreen Tan was employed by JPMorgan when she coauthored this chapter.

private sector securitisations completed by banks or corporations, these assets are transferred to a bankruptcy-remote special purpose vehicle (SPV), which in turn issues these bonds. The bonds are "asset-backed" in that the interest and principal repayment typically relies solely on the cash flows of the underlying assets—not the paying ability of the government or government agency that has sold them.[1] The majority of public sector securitisation bonds receive a AAA rating through some form of "credit enhancement" such as overcollateralisation (issuing less bonds than assets available in the SPV) or a senior/subordinate class structure (prioritising cash flows to a senior AAA class of bonds). As in private sector securitisations, the government agency selling the assets may continue to receive a fee for "servicing" the assets (e.g., making timely payment collections and managing the sale of real estate portfolios).

Throughout Europe, the use of securitisation as an alternative source of funding for corporates, banks, and sovereigns is expanding rapidly. In particular, issuance of public sector securitisations has grown since 1999 (see Exhibit 12.1) and was one of the largest sources of euro-

EXHIBIT 12.1   Public Sector Securitisation Issuance

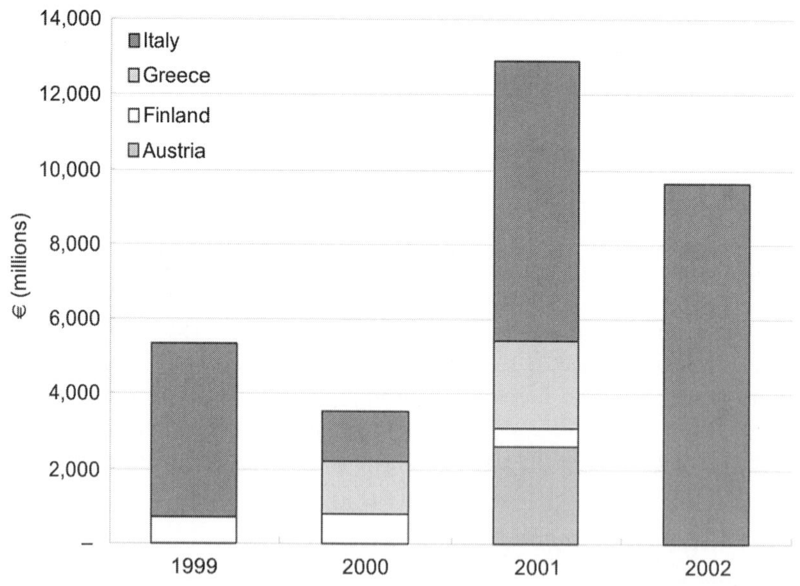

Source: JPMorgan Securities.

---

[1] Public sector securitisations that include a guarantee from a public sector entity are an exception to this rule.

denominated ABS issuance in 2002. European governments continue to hold diverse assets on their balance sheets—ranging from employee-occupied real estate to delinquent social security and tax receivables. In the coming years, we expect that governments will use securitisation as a financing tool that frequently offers both cheap funding and "off-balance sheet" accounting treatment—thus enabling governments to reduce their overall debt burden if cash proceeds are used to pay down outstanding public debt.

MARKET OVERVIEW

While *residential mortgage-backed securities* (RMBS) remain the cornerstone of the European asset-backed market, public sector securitisations represent a rapidly developing sector that accounts for more than €30 billion in asset-backed supply since 1999. European governments have used securitisation, often in creative ways, to help meet liquidity objectives and to diversify their sources of funding.

To date, the Republic of Italy (Aa2/AA/AA) has been the most active and innovative European sovereign entity in the securitisation market, with over €20 billion priced via seven separate transactions. Italian government agencies have securitised asset types ranging from nonperforming social security payments to property related assets. Other governments that have also completed public sector securitisations include Greece, Austria, and Finland.

Following the Italian government's implementation of a defined legal framework for securitisation in April 1999, the Italian Treasury also sponsored specific legislation to monetise government assets using securitisation. The Italian Treasury has securitised a diverse mix of both performing and nonperforming assets (see Exhibit 12.2).

The Hellenic Republic of Greece has been the other consistent government issuer of public sector securitisations, but total Greek supply is still a fraction of that of Italian government agencies. Greek securitisations are structurally different to those of Italy in that credit enhancement includes an explicit government guarantee, whereas Italian public sector securitisations use "internal" credit enhancement (e.g., overcollateralisation, and senior/sub classes). Because of the guarantee, the highest rating Greek transactions have achieved is the long-term rating of the Hellenic Republic A1/A/A+ (Moody's/S&P/Fitch). Rating changes of the Hellenic Republic also affect those of the bonds.

EXHIBIT 12.2 Breakdown of Italian Treasury Sponsored Securitisations, December 2002

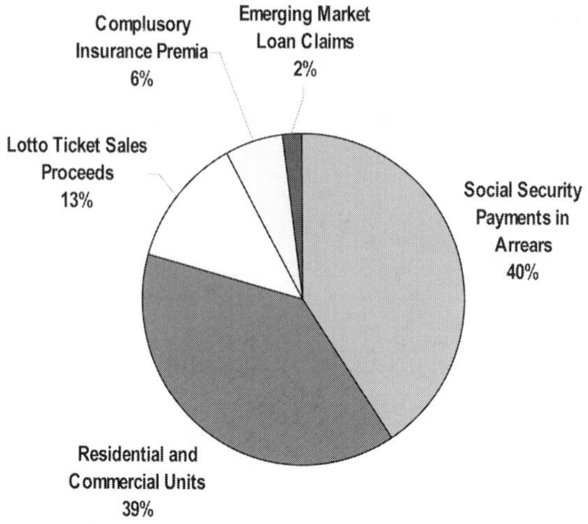

Pie chart with segments:
- Compulsory Insurance Premia 6%
- Emerging Market Loan Claims 2%
- Lotto Ticket Sales Proceeds 13%
- Social Security Payments in Arrears 40%
- Residential and Commercial Units 39%

Source: JPMorgan Securities.

PUBLIC SECTOR SECURITISATION OBJECTIVES

To date, the bulk of public sector securitisations has been driven by European governments' commitment to comply with various debt reduction targets outlined in the Maastricht Treaty and in the Stability and Growth Pact. The Maastricht Treaty outlined a group of convergence criteria for entry into the European Monetary Union, or EMU designed to align the economic growth and fiscal policy of those countries entering into EMU. They include:

- *Interest rate target:* A long-term interest rate no greater than 2% above the long-term average of the three countries with the lowest inflation.
- *Inflation target:* No greater than 1.5% above the average of the three lowest inflation members.
- *Budget deficit:* No greater than 3% of GDP (i.e., deficit ratio).
- *National debt:* No greater than 60% of GDP (i.e., debt ratio).
- *Stable currency regime:* As defined by the ERM (Exchange Rate Mechanism).

Today, Eurozone countries establish individual public finance targets, which aim to achieve a balanced budget and reduce country debt ratios in the medium- to long-term. In addition to their own stability programmes, Eurozone countries must still comply with the Growth and Stability Pact.

BENEFITS OF PUBLIC SECTOR SECURITISATIONS

Public sector securitisations are designed to achieve a number of benefits for governments. Recent clarifications of the accounting treatment of these securitisations (discussed below) have actually called into question whether these benefits hold over the long-term.

- The proceeds of securitisation can improve financial flexibility (liquidity) and reduce indebtedness. Proceeds may enhance a government's ability to meet debt targets and/or commitments.
- The securitisation of state-owned assets improves the deficit-to-GDP ratio, since proceeds are accounted for as government budgetary revenues.
- Securitisation transactions may provide yield curve diversification to existing government debt. Large and liquid benchmark asset-backed transactions also help Italy enhance and maintain its profile in international capital markets.
- By transferring public administration assets to private contracts and specialised servicers, governments can ideally improve returns on these assets by applying private sector scrutiny and technology. For nonperforming assets, securitisation may help governments avoid large delinquent portfolios in the future.
- Securitisation may enable governments to monetise otherwise illiquid assets. A government can sell assets with predictable cash flows that may be difficult to monetise through privatisation or other means.

RECENT DEVELOPMENTS: ACCOUNTING TREATMENT AND "FISCAL FLEXIBILITY"

Since their inception, European governments have used public sector securitisations to improve both debt and deficit ratios and move closer to debt and fiscal deficit targets. Securitisations may help improve these ratios by recognising cash proceeds as budgetary revenue (improving the deficit ratio) or reducing outstanding government debt (improving the debt ratio). In 2002, Eurostat (the official EU statistical body) and Standard & Poor's (S&P) reviewed public sector securitisations to ensure that they comply with EU criteria for lowering budget deficits and accurately reflect the underlying fiscal health of governments using securitisation.

Eurostat Ruling

In 2002, Eurostat released decisions on which types of public sector securitisations qualify for "off-balance sheet" treatment for the purpose of debt and deficit calculation. Eurostat's rulings required certain government securitisations to be reclassified as "on balance sheet," removing the benefits described above for some public sector securitisations. However, Eurostat's decisions also brought new clarity to the appropriate accounting treatment of these deals, which we believe is positive for the sector. The Eurostat rules are summarised as follows:

- Securitisation of *future cash flows* where the SPV cannot control the generation of these cash flows will be treated as government borrowing.
- Transactions using *government guarantees* to the SPV do not qualify as adequate risk transfer, and therefore, the transaction between the SPV and the government will be recorded as an on-balance sheet borrowing.
- A *deferred purchase price greater than 15%* of the market value of assets will be considered an insufficient transfer of risk, and the transaction will be treated as on-balance sheet government borrowing (and not as the sale of an asset).
- For a transaction between the government and an SPV to be classified as a sale of an asset, the value of the transaction must be recorded as cash received at the time of the securitisation. Any future payments are recognised only when realised as cash.

Given Eurostat decisions, we have seen certain structural changes to securitisations going forward. For example, there has been an increase in supply of lower-rated tranches with longer tenors, since rating agencies require mezzanine tranches in lieu of the significant overcollateralisation available in previous deals (i.e., the 15% rule). We also anticipate increased supply of higher quality assets. Since overcollateralisation can no longer be used as the primary form of credit enhancement (i.e., the 15% rule), governments may seek to securitise higher quality assets that do not require a high amount of credit enhancement in the form of expensive mezzanine tranches.

Standard & Poor's

S&P believes that securitisations do not materially improve "fiscal flexibility" of a public sector entity. S&P describes "fiscal flexibility" as the ability of a public sector issuer to smooth debt-service payments in reaction to economic shocks.[2] S&P believes that the use of securitisation proceeds to repay debt is initially positive for fiscal flexibility in that debt payments are reduced. However, the agency cautions that securitisations could increase default likelihood for a public sector entity if large amounts of government assets are securitised, since these assets are no longer available to pay unsecured debt. However, S&P currently does emphasise that public sector securitisations have not been large enough to have any significant impact on the creditworthiness of public entities. S&P specifically states that funding public expenditure via one-off securitisations is likely to have a negative impact on fiscal flexibility, since the public expenditures are likely to be recurring (in the absence of structural reform) while debt service is not reduced if debt is not repaid. In terms of accounting treatment, S&P classifies any securitisation revenues "below the line"—or as financing items rather than budgetary revenue.

STRUCTURE

The collateral of public sector securitisations has included real estate, delinquent social security receivables, lottery receivables, and other diverse assets. Because the underlying cash flows of these assets are very different, bond structures tend to be unique. Deal-specific structures are necessary for the bonds' principal and interest repayment to match the cashflows of the underlying assets. A typical public sector securitisation has large AAA rated tranches (i.e., up to €1.5 billion), with the high rating achieved either through overcollateralisation or subordinate tranches.[3] Nearly all public sector securitisations have been floating rate bonds and typically feature a bullet repayment profile. Because deal structure and collateral performance (e.g., credit, prepayments) varies, public sector securitisations should be analysed on a case-by-case basis, with a particular focus on the collateral and servicing aspects of the transaction. Exhibit 12.3 graphically depicts a high level perspective of a public sector securitisation.

---

[2] See Moritz Kraemer, Marie Cavanaugh, Alexandra Dimitrijevic, and Beatriz Mariro, *Accounting for Innovation: Treatment of Off-Balance Sheet Public Sector Financing Operations*, Standard & Poor's, 23 September 2002.

[3] Greek public sector securitisations have had a single-A rating due to the government guarantee.

EXHIBIT 12.3 Public Sector Securitisation

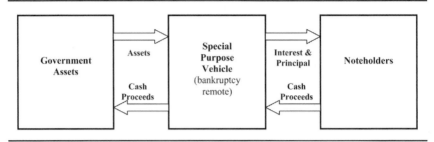

Source: JPMorgan Securities.

SERVICING

The servicing function for public sector securitisations—particularly for delinquent assets or deals without a backup servicer—is a fundamental aspect of credit analysis. Frequently, servicing is transferred from the respective government agency to highly specialised debt collection agencies (i.e., *concessionari* in the case of Italy) or redefined according to a specific business plan or agreement. In real estate-backed transactions, for example, the process of selling properties (both commercial and residential) is governed by a detailed business plan. Under this arrangement, the government agencies must market properties and file them for sale according to a specified time schedule. Sales performance and remuneration of these agencies is measured versus this business plan.

RELATIVE VALUE

Government-sponsored securitisations offer investors an opportunity to diversify their portfolios into well-structured, large, liquid benchmark transactions. Specifically, these transactions allow investors to diversify away from traditional European consumer credit ABS or Italian government debt. In some cases, there may be a spread pickup over government paper as well: Italian public sector securitisations' AAA tranches have priced at 3 Month EURIBOR + 7 (1 yr WAL) to 3 Month EURIBOR + 32 (3 yr WAL). Typically, investments in nontraditional ABS suffer from relative illiquidity. However, trading volumes of Italian state-sponsored securitisations have historically been higher than most other AAA rated sectors in European structured finance. We attribute this solid liquidity profile in the secondary market to the large size and broad investor distribution in these transactions. As with most AAA rated, euro-denominated floating rate ABS paper, banks and fund managers from across continental Europe and the UK are the dominant buyers of these transactions. In the future, we believe liquidity will further improve due to increased issuance and better investor understanding of the sector. Over time, we expect to see other European government securitisation programmes similar to that being pursued in Italy—with developments across the region spurred by the attractiveness of securitisation as a liquidity source and funding diversification tool.

CHAPTER 13

Italian Lease-Backed Securities

Andrew Dennis
Executive Director, Structured Finance Credit Research
UBS

Small and medium-sized enterprises (SMEs) are considered the dynamo of the Italian economy. The sharp fall in interest rates that occurred in the late 1990s corresponding with Italy's membership of (phase II of) EMU created a backdrop that has encouraged firms to borrow more aggressively. Financing leases in Italy allow companies to acquire assets and deduct the lease rental costs against tax.

While some leasing companies are part of larger financial conglomerates and banks, many are not. Leasing is, by definition, a capital hungry business and access to low-cost funding is a critical determinant of success. The passage of the Italian securitisation law (the now famous Law 130/99) was pivotal in unlocking a supply of cheap capital for the leasing industry. It created a legal framework within which leasing companies could raise capital markets funding inexpensively. Leasing and securitisation in Italy go hand in glove. Lease-backed ABS represent almost 20% of the Italian ABS market and growth in the asset class has been healthy.

In this chapter we review the following aspects of the Italian lease back securities market: structure of the Italian leasing industry, some legal issues associated with leasing, and credit drivers and transaction performance.

THE ITALIAN LEASING INDUSTRY

The Italian leasing market ranks among the "Big 3" in Europe alongside Germany, and the United Kingdom (see Exhibit 13.1). Aside from being

EXHIBIT 13.1 Italian Leasing in a European Context

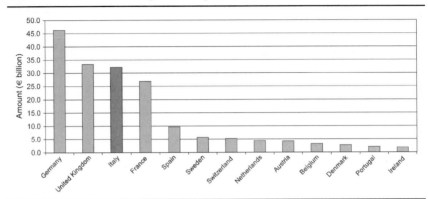

Source: LEASEUROPE 2001 Statistics

EXHIBIT 13.2 Growth in Lease Origination

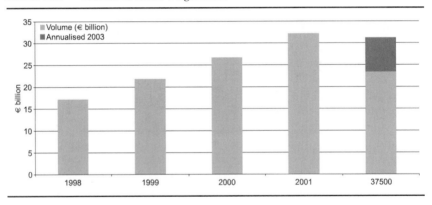

Source: Assilea.

one of Europe's highest volume markets, Italy has been growing strongly in recent years—at a compound annualised rate of over 15% (see Exhibit 13.2). The decline in Italian interest rates has boosted corporate borrowing. We believe that another critical factor that has allowed growth to accelerate has been the existence and development of the market for ABS backed by lease receivables.

While the growth in leasing is explicable and could well be healthy, it does give us cause for certain concerns. We would identify the following areas of potential risk:

■ Growth and competition could cause some relaxation in underwriting standards.

- Some diminution in profitability is likely as a result of rapid expansion and high competition.
- There could be a risk that monitoring and collection systems become stretched as portfolios grow.
- Seasoning in securitised pools may be placed under strain.
- Increasing reliance on securitisation as a source of funding could be risky if other sources of funding become more difficult to source.
- From the perspective of primary and secondary market spreads, constant new issuance in a single sector may well test capacity limits and lead to wider spreads being required by investors.

How Does Leasing Work?

The leases that back securitisation transactions in Italy are financing leases. Under a financing lease, the lessor retains title over and ownership of the leased asset and the lessee bears the operating risks of the asset.

The lessee will typically make a down payment at the inception of the lease and a series of contracted rental payments for a specified period of time. The percentage of this deposit payment varies depending on the nature of the leased asset. In Italy, anywhere between 10% and 20% is normal, with real estate contracts normally being subject to larger down payments.

At the maturity of the lease, the lessee typically has the option to purchase the leased asset outright at a marked down "residual" price. The residual is determined at the inception of the lease. In the case of automobiles or equipment, where depreciation can be rapid, it is generally no more than 5% of the initial purchase price. Real estate leases typically have higher residual values, with the market average currently standing at approximately 20% of the initial purchase price. In most cases, in Italy, the lessee has, historically, tended to pay the residual purchase price at the termination of the lease. In the event that the residual purchase option is not exercised, the leased asset is returned to the lessor, who will then sell it or re-lease it.

Although the term "lease-backed securitisation" is commonly used (in this chapter and elsewhere) the strict term should be lease receivables securitisation. The full rights and benefits under the lease agreement are not transferred. Instead, a portion of the receivable component of the lease rental is sold and securitised. This limits recourse to the underlying asset but has certain tax and operational advantages to the securitisation. It is important to point out, however, that there is no material residual risk inherent in the securitisation.

Under a financing lease, the lessee is responsible for asset maintenance and must make rental payments regardless of the asset's condition. Typically the lessor arranges insurance on the leased asset, which protects its rights in the event that the asset is destroyed and covers the lessor's third party liability. Part of the rental payment under the lease agreement is dedicated to pay the insurance premium.

In Italy, lease rental installments are subject to *value added tax* (IVA). The IVA component is collected by the lessor and then remitted to the tax authorities. In most cases, the IVA proportion of the lease rentals is not sold into securitisation vehicles so that the vehicles do not build up IVA payment liabilities.

The maturity of a lease contract will typically reflect a number of factors:

■ The nature of the leased asset—real estate leases are typically longer maturity than automobile leases whose term tends to reflect the economically useful life of the asset.
■ The purchase price of the leased asset—big ticket items tend to be leased over longer terms in order to reduce the quantum of rental payment.
■ The underwriting risk appetite of the lessor.
■ Certain fiscal considerations.

Prepayment options are typically not incorporated or permitted in lease documentation. However, by mutual agreement, prepayment can take place. Prepayment amounts reflect a calculation of the net present value of remaining payments using a penal discount rate (usually deep sub-EURIBOR).

As Certain as Death (Three Letters)?

When one sees a heavy use of leasing as a form of asset finance, tax advantage is often close by. This appears to be the case in Italy. We understand that there are a number of ways in which leasing offers companies tax advantages (although we are not giving tax advice). We outline below our current understanding of some of the tax benefits that are associated with lease financing in Italy.

■ The full amount of lease rentals is deductible as an expense for tax purposes. For real estate leases, the lease needs to have a maximum remaining maturity of eight years. For equipment leasing, the term of the lease must extend beyond the point at which half its value would have been written down for tax purposes. Different asset types are assigned different economically useful lives for tax purposes. This ability to deduct rental payments is, in our view, central to the appeal of leasing as a form of asset finance. While borrowing to finance an asset will typically permit a company to deduct interest payments, there is a component of the lease rental payment that is also capital repayment. In essence, a lessee can obtain tax deduction for both principal and interest payments.

■ A number of fiscal incentives exist to promote capital investments by businesses. Although these incentives are not directly linked to the form of financing, they do create a framework under which investment in plant and equipment is encouraged. The most important of these incentives was introduced as part of the Tremonti Law in late 2001. Under this regulation, if a company invests more than it has done on average for the preceding five years then 50% of this excess can be deducted for tax purposes.

In addition to fiscal incentives, leasing also provides companies with a low cost form of financing. Leasing rates are generally marginally cheaper than bank facility pricing and significantly lower in cost than overdrafts.

What Assets are Leased?

Three main classes of assets are leased: equipment, vehicles, and real estate. All three components have grown strongly, with real estate being the most potent (see Exhibit 13.3). The characteristics of each of these three main asset classes are different. Maturities, average ticket sizes and arrears track record will typically be different for each. Consequently, lease securitisation transactions typically break their overall collateral portfolios down into subportfolios.

EXHIBIT 13.3   Leased Assets by Type

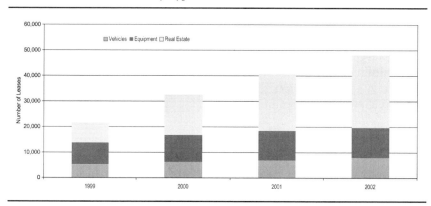

Source: Assliea—December 2002.

EXHIBIT 13.4   Lease Origination by Economic Sector (2001)

Commerce	14.0%
Metal Goods	9.9%
Agricultural & Industrial Machinery	7.0%
Transport Services	6.7%
Construction	6.7%
Textiles	5.7%
Paper and editing	4.9%
Plastic Goods	3.8%
Metals and minerals	3.8%
Electrical goods	3.5%
Other industrial products	3.3%
Food industry	2.2%
Air & Sea transport	2.0%
Public services & Hotels	1.8%
Communications services	1.7%
Chemicals	1.7%
Transportation	1.6%
Other services	19.7%
Total	100.0%

The Lessees

The leasing market in Italy tends to be focused on the SME market. Average "ticket size" for leases originated in the first half of 2002[1] was just over €96,000. It should be noted that this average does not tell the whole story of the market. Real estate leases are typically of a higher value —the average being over €1.1 million in early 2002.

The economic sectors that use leasing as a means of asset finance are diverse as Exhibit 13.4 illustrates. Equally, the geographical usage of leasing largely follows the demographic and economic pattern of Italy as a whole. Concentrations of leasing coincide with the areas of high productive economic activity in Northern Italy, particularly in Lombardy, Veneto and Piedemont.

Who is Providing the Finance?

There are almost 460 companies engaged in leasing activity in Italy. However, the top 15 companies write over two-thirds of business (see

---

[1] Based upon the top-10 leasing companies by value of leases. Source: Assilea.

Exhibit 13.5). The majority of the main leasing companies are either banks that specialise in leasing or have specific leasing subsidiaries. There are also captive leasing companies that tend to be the leasing arms of large industrial companies (such as DaimerChrysler and Ford).

Leasing subsidiaries of banks and those with assets of more than €100 million are regulated by the Banca D'Italia, which sets standards for capital adequacy, risk management and reporting, liquidity and operational management. The Banca D'Italia also conducts a supervisory role as part of its overall regulation.

Origination of leases tends to be done directly by the larger players or, in the case of leasing subsidiaries of larger banking groups, through the parents' branch networks. There is also a network of brokers and agents that assist in origination. Credit and underwriting processes tend to be somewhat idiosyncratic in Italy. In the case of larger groups and leasing subsidiaries of banks, the lessee is often known to the lessor group and may have a long-term relationship. Checks are commonly carried out through the Banca D'Italia's credit bureau and with Assilea, the leasing companies' trade association. Although strict credit scoring is not commonplace in Italy, all companies will undertake a basic risk assessment covering the financial position of the lessee, current indebtedness, projections of future cash flow and the terms of the lease will be governed by the nature of the underlying asset. In many cases, real estate valuations are carried out by in-house valuers, although there is an increasing trend towards using third party valuers. In certain instances, lessees may be required to seek external guarantees. In almost all cases, the originating leasing company will act as servicer.

SOME LEGAL ISSUES IN ITALIAN LEASE-BACKED ABS

Any analysis of securitisation, at some level, involves achieving an understanding of the legal framework that supports the deals. Since ABS transactions are designed at the outset to be robust in the face of exogenous shocks, up to and including the bankruptcy of certain parties to the transaction, an understanding of legal risk is critical. In this section, we provide a précis of our understanding of the legal issues specific to Italian lease backed ABS, based upon published reports from various sources including the rating agencies. However, this section is explicitly not a legal analysis and cannot and should not be relied upon as such. In all securitisation transactions, legal counsel provides opinions as to certain matters including enforceability and bankruptcy-remoteness. Such opinions are rarely made public (we believe the lawyers' professional

EXHIBIT 13.5 Italian Leasing—The Main Players

Rank	Company	No. Contracts	Leased Amount (€ million)	Market Share (top 10)	Average Ticket Size
1	Locat	45,351	4,532.3	21%	99,938
2	Intesa Leasing	23,218	3,053.5	14%	131,514
3	Banca Italease	20,689	2,111.1	10%	102,040
4	Fin-Eco Leasing	21,039	2,076.6	10%	98,702
5	Banca Agrileasing	15,240	1,916.8	9%	125,774
6	Sanpaolo Leasint	15,361	1,905.1	9%	124,022
7	Monte di Paschi di Siena Leasing	13,461	1,818.6	8%	135,101
8	Locafit	10,934	1,725.3	8%	157,792
9	SBS Leasing	16,154	1,355.4	6%	83,905
10	Centro Leasing	25,652	1,348.6	6%	52,573

indemnity insurance doesn't cover that), but we think it is always worthwhile asking to see them on new deals.

Insolvency Provisions

The contracts that support leases in Italy are known as *contratto atipico* and leasing itself is not specifically recognised under the Civil Code. There being no codified law that governs leasing and, as a result, certain specific issues arise for deals backed by lease receivables. The key risks we identify occur in the event that an originator/servicer of a lease portfolio falls prey to financial difficulties and enters a bankruptcy or restructuring process. There is a possibility that, in insolvency, the liquidator can reject or terminate the leasing contracts that the leasing company has entered into. If this happens, hypothetically the consequences to any securitisation that relies upon cash flows derived from those leases could be catastrophic.

In the event of insolvency and depending on its nature, a company can fall under three pieces of legislation:

- The Bankruptcy Act (Royal Decree 267/1942).
- The Banking Act (Legislative Decree 385/1993).
- Legislative Decree 270/1999 (which covers the extraordinary administration of large companies in financial difficulties).

The Bankruptcy Act covers all companies unless they are regulated otherwise (for instance, if they are banks or "qualify" as banks) and provides for two processes. Depending on their degree of financial crisis, companies can either:

- Enter a bankruptcy procedure—*fallimento*—under which a commissioner will liquidate the assets of the company in favour of the creditors. Or,
- Enter a restructuring process (*amministrativa controllata*), which provides for a controlled administration of the company that does not necessarily require the liquidation of its assets.

In essence, the Bankruptcy Act provisions relate to smaller companies (less than 200 employees) that do not fall under the Banking Act.

The Banking Act covers banks (unsurprisingly) but also subsidiaries of banks and companies that behave analogously to banks (they take deposits or conduct investment business). Similar to the Bankruptcy Act provisions, there are two possible processes depending on the severity of the financial condition of the company:

- A special winding-up procedure (*liquidazione coatta amministrativa*), which is, effectively, a liquidation of assets in favour of creditors.
- A special restructuring process whereby the bank is not necessarily liquidated. This process is known as *amministrazione straordinaria*.

For larger, nonbanking, companies, a special administrative restructuring, known as *amminstrazione straordinaria delle grandi imprese in crisi*, is provided for under Legislative Decree 270/1999. Companies can only enter this process if they qualify by way of size and are not subject to a specially regulated insolvency regime. Banks, for instance, cannot seek *amministrazione straordinaria delle grandi imprese in crisi*.

Most, though not all, leasing companies in Italy fall under the bankruptcy provisions of the Banking Act.

Leasing and Insolvency

Categorisation of Leases

Italy is a country that operates a codified system of law and, unlike the US and UK where common law plays a critical part in influencing decisions, jurisprudence tends to have lower authority. However, in cases not covered by specific legislation, jurisprudence does have authority. In 1989, the Italian Supreme Court established rules that governed the categorisation of leasing contracts based upon their substance.

There are two categorisations of leases under Italian law:

- *Leasing translativo*—or transfer leasing.
- *Leasing di godimento*—or usage leasing.

Which category a lease belongs in will depend on several factors including:

- The strike price of the lessee's purchase option compared with the market value at the maturity of the lease.
- The purpose of the parties when entering into the lease—whether there was initially an expectation by the parties that the lease would ultimately lead to a transfer of the underlying asset.
- The economically useful life of the underlying asset.
- The nature of the underlying leased asset itself.

Exhibit 13.6 gives the basic characteristics that leases exhibit that determine which category they are deemed to fall into.

EXHIBIT 13.6   Characteristics of Different Categories of Lease

Type of Lease	Defining Characteristics
Leasing translativo	■ These leases look like a sale by way of installment payments. ■ Typically the lease term is shorter than the economic useful life of the underlying asset. ■ The purchase option strike price is lower than the market value at the maturity of the lease (that is to say, the option is "in the money" and is therefore likely to be exercised).
Leasing di godimento	■ These leases look more like a rental of the underlying asset—there is less certainty that they will lead at maturity to a transfer of ownership of the asset. ■ The term of the lease is closer (or equal to) the economically useful life of the underlying leased asset. ■ The purchase option strike price is equal to or higher than the residual value of the underlying leased asset (the option expires "at the money" or "out of the money."

Bankruptcy and Leasing

We understand that a substantial majority of leases (if not the totality), which have been securitised, have fallen into the *leasing translativo* category. As such, there appears to be a risk that certain provisions of the Bankruptcy Act could be applied (Articles 72 and 73). Under Article 72, if a seller becomes bankrupt before the transfer of an asset that is to be sold, the receiver is permitted to terminate the contract. However, article 73 may negate this if the sale is one made by instalments. Therefore, the Italian legal community appears to think that, if it can be characterised as a sale by instalments, a *leasing translativo* contract may not be subject to cancellation by a receiver.

We understand that, in the substantial majority of cases, Article 73 is "invoked," thus avoiding the cancellation of the contract. However, there have been isolated cases where local courts have interpreted *leasing translativo* contracts under Article 72 and thus rejected them. As mentioned, jurisprudence, particularly set in a junior court, holds limited authority in Italy. In our view, however, it is potentially disturbing that there remains a level of doubt and ambiguity relating to the treatment of leases in a lessor bankruptcy, albeit small.

Restructuring and Leasing

As we mention above, companies have recourse to restructuring as a possible alternative to bankruptcy. Depending on the nature of the bankruptcy, the restructuring process may fall under different legislation. In the case of administration procedures under the Bankruptcy Act (*amministrativa controllata*) and the analogous provisions of the Banking Act (*amministrazione straordinaria*), the law stipulates that all contracts, irrespective of which category of contract a lease falls into, should be continued. In effect, for administration under the normal bankruptcy code and under banking regulation, leases are "safe" from the risk of rejection.

Unfortunately this does not appear to be the case for larger companies. As we discuss above, under Legislative Decree 270/1999, larger companies are entitled to go through a special form of restructuring (*amministrazione straordinaria delle grandi imprese in crisi*). Under this form of restructuring, the receiver does have the right to terminate contracts characterised as *leasing translativo* unless they are related to real estate contracts.

Is it All Bad News?

No, not in our opinion. The position, as can be seen from above, is complicated. The level of ambiguity about what might happen is a potentially disturbing factor when reviewing this asset class. Given the growth of the leasing market, the importance of securitisation as a means of fuelling this growth and the Italian authorities' proven track record of creating "securitisation friendly" legislation, it seems to us odd that more certainty has not been created by the authorities. Perhaps this will be forthcoming.

However, although the technical legal position is not entirely supportive, we would point out several factors:

- The market for securitisation has grown sharply in recent years—lead managers, transaction lawyers and investors (including investors in subordinated bonds) have gained some comfort that their position is strong. Although we do not, as a rule, subscribe to the "greater fool" theory of credit analysis, we take some comfort from these factors.
- The rating agencies particularly have spent a lot of time "getting comfortable" with these risks.
- The risks of rejection (a contract being declared void) appear to be, other than in limited circumstances, relatively remote.

The rating agencies have been at the forefront of gaining comfort on the issue of rejection risk. In a recent report, Moody's identified several reasons why it believed rejection risks could be largely discounted in practical terms:

- In a restructuring, an administrator may be reluctant to reject contracts that might pose operational complications and cause claims to be greater than those that might be achieved by selling the leased equipment.
- In the context of a securitisation, the securitisation vehicle has a claim in respect of the asset purchase price represented by the proportion of the future receivables cancelled at termination of the lease contract.
- In leasing translativo, a lessee may have a claim in respect of the difference between instalments paid up to cancellation and compensation for loss of use of the leased asset.
- In order for cancellation to represent a benefit to creditors, the liquidator would need confidence that the sale of an asset associated with a cancelled lease could take place swiftly. This may not always be easy, particularly in the case of business specific equipment.
- Many leasing companies come under the supervision of the Banca D'Italia and Moody's takes comfort that such supervision would reduce the likelihood of insolvency.
- Finally, Moody's feels that the competitive landscape of leasing in Italy coupled with high levels of profitability would mean that a competitor would be likely to regard the weakened state of a company as an opportunity for acquisition.

We find it hard to find fault with this logic. These points, in our view, mitigate against the many legal risks that are associated with lessor bankruptcy in Italy.

Beyond the Lessor—Lessee Insolvency

Many of the factors that influence the credit risks of Italian lease-backed ABS are typical of those that affect other ABS—there are common characteristics between Italian lease-backed ABS and SME collateralized loan obligations (CLOs). In particular, concentration and diversification issues play roles in the aggregate credit risk that portfolios represent. There are nevertheless certain distinctions specific to leases.

In the event of lessee insolvency, the key recourse that a leasing company has is to the leased asset. The speed at which the servicer can recover, sell or re-lease the asset will have a significant influence on its ability to substitute the cash flow lost by way of lessee default. The rights under any new lease agreement need to be assigned to the securitisation vehicle. This may be problematic if, simultaneously, the lessor becomes insolvent. The rating agencies assume low recovery rates in calculating expected losses and credit enhancement.

CREDIT DRIVERS AND TRANSACTION PERFORMANCE

The three rating agencies have established frameworks for the analysis of Italian lease-backed transactions, which, although there are modest differences in emphasis and nuance, are broadly similar. The role of the rating agencies in securitisation is threefold:

- The establishment of criteria based upon business, economic and legal factors.
- The modeling of transactions based upon these criteria and the "sizing" of credit structure and enhancements.
- The surveillance and monitoring of the ongoing performance of transactions.

The information in the hands of the rating agencies is greater in depth and scope than that available to the public. In common with many securitisation markets in Europe, information is often sketchy and hard to come by. However, we believe that the agencies' general assumptions, coupled with structural features built into transactions are conservative and offer investors significant protection against the likelihood of default or severity of loss.

In this section, we outline in brief the key factors that drive ratings and the structural enhancements built into transactions that are pertinent to Italian leases.

Underlying Asset Type

Transactions generally are made up of mixed portfolios comprising:

- Automobile (commercial and private use)
- Plant and equipment
- Commercial real estate

Each of these has different performance characteristics, particularly in light of default probability and loss severity. Recovery values in Italy have been high since recourse to the underlying leased asset is largely straightforward. Gross default rates, (i.e., where recovery action has been required), show that real estate tends to be lower than that of other assets (running, on average, at less that 20 bp over the past two years).

Equipment and vehicles tend, historically, to have comparable levels of default. Where longer-term histories are available, it is clear that historic default rates have been significantly higher than those currently being recorded. However, real estate tends to exhibit lower default frequencies than the other two asset classes. It should be noted that, in most cases, the statistics produced on transactions are net of recoveries whereas long-term historic data tends to represent gross defaults.

When sizing credit enhancement levels, the agencies "stress" default rates. They make their baseline assumptions on historic experience, whether this is general or specific to a particular originator. Stress multiples are applied when projecting cash flow. For instance, S&P assumes 5× historic defaults for an AAA scenario and 2× for a BBB scenario.

Loss severity and recovery values tend to be somewhat higher in real estate than the other asset classes. Clearly, the LTV level has an impact on this factor. One other point to note is the way that the agencies view recovery. In almost all instances they assume a liquidation of the asset rather than a repayment of the outstanding lease present value. This, they contend, most accurately reflects the recoverable value in the circumstances where the originator or servicer themselves are in financial difficulty.

Although the underlying asset type can give guidance for analysing prospective credit losses, it does not tell the full story. In many instances a single "obligor" will lease several items, often falling into different categories. The default of a single obligor, therefore, may well create defaults under a series of contracts. The agencies are increasingly focusing on obligor concentrations (in a similar way to SME CLOs).

LTV and Seasoning

Typical initial LTVs can be as much as 95% on leased assets. However, these LTVs decline as seasoning takes place. The majority of transactions we examine comprise well-seasoned portfolios of assets. The agencies look at market and originator specific recovery levels. They will then typically discount these by 20–50% depending on the ratings scenario being measured. The agencies look also at historic timing of recoveries (which can take well over two years) and stress these.

Servicing and Delinquency Management

The ability to service the securitised debt on these transactions depends critically on the quality of the originator and servicer. In the transactions we have analysed, the originators are large and experienced and all have clear underwriting policies and procedures. We believe that there is significant value in focusing on the top leasing companies. We believe that their position enables them to have much more streamlined and efficient underwriting and delinquency management than smaller companies.

Most transactions publish two measures of performance—defaults and delinquencies. Definitions of default vary (modestly) from transaction to transaction. These are transactions where payments are unpaid and overdue and where the originator is taking action (or expects to take action imminently) to make a principal recovery. The definition of delinquency, however, is more straightforward in the sense that only a single payment needs to be missed in order for a receivable to be declared delinquent. There is, however, a catch. While the substantial majority of contracts call for monthly payments, there are some where less frequent payments are required. The lower the frequency of payment, the less frequent the opportunity to "trap" problems becomes. Early warnings of problems significantly enhance the chance to find solutions. The fact that the delinquency to default ratio in all the transactions we review is high (6× to 8× is common) pays tribute to the efficiency of servicing in those transactions. We believe that a decline in this ratio (delinquencies: defaults) is a potentially early warning of future problems.

Concentration Risks and Granularity

Real estate leases are typically larger in value than other types. Therefore, while the historic loss experience and severity is typically low in percentage terms, large real estate exposures can have an effect in cash terms. We have provided graphs of the pool-by-pool (where disclosed) granularity. We note that large concentrations have a significant impact on the credit enhancement levels demanded by the agencies.

Revolving Portfolios and Excess Spread

The majority of deals are designed to reinvest cash flows in new receivables. This preserves excess spread levels but strict eligibility criteria need to be set for such transactions to operate without changing the initial characteristics of the portfolio. Some transactions also include discount purchase features that increase the effective yield on the underlying assets in order to preserve excess spread levels. Because withholding tax is deducted on bonds with less than 18 months into maturity in Italy, substantially all transactions do not have the facility to repay principal in the first 18 months of their lives. The agencies' stress analyses focus on reduced cash flow (and excess spread) when there is a lot of cash not invested in receivables. Excess cash flow, where available, usually remunerated equity. Equity is generally provided via the addition of a class of notes that is retained by the originator.

Geographical issues always play a role in Italy. Substantially all of the deals we have analysed are heavily concentrated in Northern Italy. The North is the powerhouse of the Italian economy. While this type of geographical concentration might be regarded as "good concentration," there are transactions that have significant exposure in a relative few regions. There is a risk in our opinion, if a particular region is subject to a localised economic shock.

Trigger Points, Credit Enhancement, and Protection

Transactions tend to have two forms of trigger point:

■ A level of (usually sustained) defaults or delinquencies that, if reached, traps cash and does not permit the remuneration of equity. This is the first level of an early warning and "seals" the transaction to ensure that bondholders' interests are best served.

■ A level of defaults that, if reached, causes any reinvestment of cash in new receivables to cease. These are often measured on a rolling basis but sometimes on a cumulative basis. The aim of these triggers is to protect investors if the quality of the overall portfolio is deteriorating.

Certain transactions have variations on these themes, sometimes distinguishing on a pool-by-pool basis. However, the aim of the mechanism is to protect investors over time if deterioration occurs in the quality of the portfolio.

■ Credit enhancement is provided, largely, within the capital structure and tiers of subordinated debt and "equity" in transactions. Additional enhancement comes from excess spread. Typically, leased assets generate EURIBOR spreads of between 180 and 400 bp, with the mean probably at around 250 bp. This is higher than the average funding cost of a securitisation (otherwise there would be no point doing securitisation). Discounted selling of receivables or the inclusion of a deferred purchase price component can generate additional spread. Excess spread funds a debt service reserve and additional excess spread is used to The LOMBA portfolio shows strong concentration in Northern Italy and is relatively under-represented in Central and Southern Italy. In particular, there is a strong concentration in the Lombardy region. Although Lombardy is the industrial "engine room" of Italy, we would tend to view this type of geographical concentration negatively.

CHAPTER 14

European Mezzanine Loan Securitisations

Alexander Batchvarov, Ph.D., CFA
Managing Director and Head, International Structured Credit Research
Merrill Lynch

Jenna Collins
Vice President
Merrill Lynch

William Davies
Assistant Vice President
Merrill Lynch

Mezzanine loans fill the gap between senior secured debt and equity. It is a hybrid product, which consists of lower priority debt supported by yield enhancements (options/warrants, PIKs) as compensation for higher risk than the senior leveraged loan product. In Europe mezzanine debt shares many features with senior secured debt, but is in a contractually subordinated position. Mainly used as funding tool for buy-outs, acquisitions, and organic expansions and restructuring, it benefits from a relatively strong position in the capital structure.

Mezzanine loans have long been part of loan securitisations along with high-yield and high-grade loans (and bonds) with a portfolio share as high as 20–30% of the securitised pool. Recently, mezzanine loan pools have been securitised on a standalone basis. Purely mezzanine loans in securitisation pools presents several challenges from rating agency and investor point of view related to the smaller number of exposure, definition of defaults given common practice of loan restructuring and covenant breaches, modeling PIK, warrants and their timing, longer ramp-up periods. While mezzanine loan securitisations present additional considerations and challenges, they are indeed a viable investment and diversification opportunity for ABS investors.

In this chapter we describe the basic features of mezzanine loans and their securitisation.

DEFINING EUROPEAN MEZZANINE LOAN

We apply the Standard & Poor's (S&P) working definitions to differentiate mezzanine loans from similar loan products:

- *Leveraged loan.* This is a senior, typically secured, loan priced usually around L+125 or higher. This includes secured loans to investment grade borrowers with spread range mention here.
- *Bridge-to-mezzanine loan.* A bridge loan to be refinanced by an anticipated high yield issue, which if not carried out will revert to a mezzanine loan.
- *Mezzanine loan.* A subordinated loan that is often issued in conjunction with a senior facility, is secured on a second lien basis, and is contractually or structurally subordinated to the senior loan.

Mezzanine debt can be an option for companies not having enough assets or current cash flow to qualify for senior debt, and where re-capitalisation through equity is not possible or wanted (e.g., conflicting with existing shareholders) or high yield is not a possibility due to its required large size. Basically, mezzanine debt serves to stretch out senior debt structures, especially during difficult high yield market conditions. It is used as a funding tool, especially in the cases of leveraged buy-outs/management buy-ins, acquisitions or organic expansions (corporate acquisitions, provision of development capital to meet growth opportunities), recapitalisations/restructurings (releveraging), and the like.

Mezzanine debt is also of interest as a funding option if the financial need is too small to qualify for high yield debt and if there is a preference for the information to be kept private. Mezzanine debt can be negotiated and structured individually to match exactly the financial requirements of a company. Due to this customised approach, transactions are usually nonregistered and of small size. It is normally used as support for and a part of a broader financing package.

On the borrower side, mezzanine debt is generally used as a funding tool for leveraged buy-outs/management buy-ins (LBO/MBIs), acquisitions, organic expansions and restructuring. On the investor side, the product is of interest for specialist funds, investment banks, and a number of commercial banks.

Product Characteristics

As described above, mezzanine debt provides an additional layer of financing between senior secured debt and equity. More precisely, it is a hybrid finance product incorporating equity-based options and warrants with a lower priority debt. Due to its flexible nature a mezzanine investor is thus able to benefit from the capital preservation and current-pay features of a loan and, at the same time, seek significant upside on its investment through the equity participation.

Mezzanine debt ranks behind senior debt, but ahead of high yield and equity as summarised in Exhibit 14.1. It is typically secured with the same assets as the senior secured debt, albeit on a junior basis. Covenants and the definition of default events are also very similar to the senior debt. The fact that the security will be shared with the senior lenders gives mezzanine lenders noticeable power in restructuring and insolvency proceedings (mostly under the UK regime and to a lesser extent in Germany).[1]

EXHIBIT 14.1   Priority of Different Debt Instruments in Europe

Classification	Examples
Senior secured	Loans which are supported by collateral and covenants.
Mezzanine/Junior secured loans	Mezzanine loans which usually share in the same security covenants as the senior secured loans, albeit on a junior basis.
Senior unsecured loans/bonds	Any unsecured lending. This can be loan, bonds or trade creditors.
Structurally subordinated bonds	High yield bonds which will be unsecured and in Europe are often lent to a different entity within the group structure than the above lenders.
Equity	Vendor loan notes/cumulative redeemable preference shares/ordinary shares.

Source: Fitch.

---

[1] For a detailed discussion of the insolvency and bankruptcy proceedings in different European jurisdictions, see Alexander Batchvarov, *European Bankruptcy Regimes from May 2002*, Merrill Lynch Research Report. For more detailed analysis of European mezzanine se see Fitch's report, *Mezzanine Debt—A European Definition*, July 2000.

Additionally, in most cases mezzanine debt is structurally equal to senior debt, only contractually subordinated through an "intercreditor agreement." We emphasise this feature as it clearly differentiates European mezzanine loans from US mezzanine loans and from European high yield bonds.

The mezzanine loans are usually attractive to investors because in addition to the regular coupon payments they provide investors with additional returns. Additional equity like components such as warrants, options or some convertible structures are in place to allow mezzanine investors to buy future common or preferred stock in the company and thus serve as yield enhancement in return for the risk they are taking. Such "equity kicker" gives investors a stake in the company's upside potential and makes mezzanine performance dependent on the company's ability to generate current and future cash flows. Therefore, mezzanine debt with warrants is often considered as "quasi-equity investment." From that point of view, mezzanine debt is contributing to the product continuum of the capital markets. Mezzanine investors are not seeking the relatively low returns of a loan product, and do not want to take the risk of high yield or equity investments. They are looking for the middle ground: a regular-income loan-type product with equity upside.

Warrants

Warrants are the most common form of equity components in mezzanine financing. Typically, warrants are detachable and, thus, liquid instruments. As the exercise price of an attached warrant is usually substantially below the market value of the company's stock, it will have a value at least equal to the difference between the market value of the stock and the exercise price. These warrants will typically have a 10-year term. Mezzanine lenders may also require a put option on the warrant (and on any stock purchased with the warrant) in order to secure its initial value. Equity warrants included are sufficient to provide for as high as 16–18% IRR (on a 5-year basis).

Equity-Like Components

Besides the regular coupon and the equity warrants, there is a third payment/ financing instrument, generating equity-like cash flows for the investor—PIKs. PIKs are used in mezzanine financing as a way to earn or generate income at a time when the company does not generate the cash flow necessary to pay interest on the senior debt and mezzanine debt. With PIK financing interest actually accrues and is compounded with additional interest earned on the original principal plus the compounded interest. At some point, PIK interest is converted into cash paid interest as the debt matures or is refinanced. Hence, PIK is dependent on the borrower's ability to generated sufficient future cash flow to service the debt.

PIK can be viewed as "an equity with a fixed return." Fitch goes even one step further and treats PIK as equity when rating mezzanine debt. From that point of view, PIK may raise some concerns, especially when they are used to replace equity warrants in mezzanine transactions. On one hand, it may be attractive to lock in some of the return through PIK. On the other hand, it is like taking equity risk, but eventually not getting the full equity upside.

All-in Cost to the Issuer

The all-in-cost to the issuer of mezzanine debt consists of LIBOR + %margin cash pay + %margin roll up (accrued interest, "PIK") plus warrants or additional accrued interest. It has varied within a narrow range despite its base in LIBOR.

Interest costs of mezzanine debt can be between 2% and 8% higher than those of senior debt. Warrants typically represent an amount of 1–5% of the company's outstanding stock.

Compared to traditional equity investment, mezzanine financing is less expensive. The primary expense is the equity dilution, which varies per transaction, but is less than an equity placement would require. Since mezzanine debt is a private debt instrument, it will face lower transaction costs relative to public offerings. In addition, interest is a tax-deductible expense, as opposed to dividends, which are not tax-deductible.

More complicated is the all-in cost comparison between mezzanine debt and high yield debt. Depending on the time of exit, one debt instrument may be more or less expensive than the other. In years 1 and 2 of a transaction, mezzanine is typically cheaper, converging in year 3 and thereafter becoming more expensive than high yield. Therefore, the choice of funding strategy is dependent on the exit strategy and its solution. Mezzanine may be more appropriate for "buy and build" or breakup businesses financing of an LBO transaction.

The reasons for this reversal in all-in cost are as follows:

- *Call feature and call premium.* High yield is not callable for five years or, if called, demands declining call premium thereafter set as a percentage of the bond coupon. By contrast, mezzanine debt offers much easier redemption options, imposing on the borrower moderate extra payments. A typical scheme in the past was a sliding-scale prepayment penalty of 3%, 2%, and 1% if redeeming the debt during the first, second or third year respectively. More recently somewhat lower prepayment penalties may be levied only during the first two years. Overall,

EXHIBIT 14.2   Key Differences between European and US Mezzanine Loans

		European Mezzanine Loan	US Mezzanine Loan
Characteristics	Loan-type	High-yield bond/PIK instrument
Income	Floating rate funding	Fixed rate funding
Prepayment penalty	Moderate penalty (c. 2%)	Heavy prepayment premiums
Collateral	Second ranking usually	Usually none
Ranking	Contractually subordinated	Deeply subordinated
Warrants	Yes	Yes, usually
PIK	Usually PIK	Often PIK

Source: Fitch, Merrill Lynch.

while prepayment penalties are rather deal specific they continue to play an important role in the loan structure.

■ *Target returns.* Mezzanine loans are usually targeting returns in the range of 10–13% above the cost of funds, including the equity warrants, while a single-B high yield bond has a cash coupon typically in the range of 10–20% with no equity warrants.

■ *Underwriting fees.* Underwriting fees for a mezzanine a around 3%, for high yield bonds—4–5%.

Comparison of European and U.S. Mezzanine Loans

Exhibit 14.2 compares the characteristics of European mezzanine loans to US mezzanine loans. European mezzanine is usually second lien secured loan with a term of 6 to 10 years, and typically requires interim payments of interest only, although PIK is allowed, with the principal due in a balloon payment at the end of the term.

Rating Mezzanine Loans

Mezzanine loans are rated applying the existing methodology for rating corporate loans. We illustrate that on the example of Fitch.

As indicated Fitch applies its existing loan rating methodology to mezzanine loans. In a nutshell, that requires determining the creditworthiness of the respective corporate entity and then notching up or down the rating depending on the loan's relative position in the entity's capital structure. The main focus is on (1) the quality of the collateral, (2) the position in the capital structure, and (3) the covenants in place. As described above, mezzanine loans benefit from second charge over collateral. This allows for notching up to a level consistent with the underlying insolvency regime and its treatment of secured creditors. As shown

EXHIBIT 14.3   Fitch Notching above Entity Rating for Senior Secured Loans and Mezzanine Facilities

	UK	Germany	France
Senior secured loan			
Potential	0–3	0–3	0–2
Frequency	High	Medium	Low
Mezzanine Facility			
Potential	0–2	0–2	0–1
Frequency	Low	Low	Medium

Source: Fitch.

in the Exhibit 14.3 such notching will be potentially largest in the UK and Germany, jurisdictions in which the secured creditor benefit most from the loan security. However, the frequency of notching up is low. France on the other hand will have lower notching due to the higher priority given to employee and state claims over secured creditors.

EUROPEAN MEZZANINE LOAN SECURITISATION

Mezzanine loans have long been part of loan securitisations along with high yield and high-grade loans with a portfolio share as high as 23% of the securitised pool. Recently, mezzanine loan pools have been securitised on standalone basis. Purely mezzanine loans in securitisation pools presents several challenges from rating agency and investor point of view related to the smaller number of exposure, definition of defaults given common practice of loan restructuring and covenant breaches, modeling PIK, warrants and their timing, complexities of longer ramp-up periods and related dynamic funding structure. While mezzanine loan securitisations present additional considerations and challenges, they are indeed a viable investment and diversification opportunity for ABS investors.

Mezzanine loans have been included in European CDOs on a regular basis in recent years. This has been driven to a large degree by the paucity of the European high yield bond market both in terms of volume and in terms of diversity. It was only recently that a few transactions were executed strictly on a mezzanine loan basis.

The execution of securitisations of pools consisting only of mezzanine loans faces a number of challenges in terms of deal structuring, rating and investor analysis. We highlight some of them.

Pool Composition and Granularity

Given the nature of the mezzanine loan product and market, it is realistic to expect a relatively small number of loans in a securitisation pool. A realistic range would be between 20 and 60 loans. That poses some questions particularly at the lower end of the range with regards to the higher individual loan concentration and potentially industry diversification. That requires more detailed and careful loan-by-loan analysis during the rating and investment process.

From the perspective of the rating agencies, they address the above issues by careful individual loan analysis and more severe stress scenarios regarding default frequency and loss levels.

Another aspect of the analysis is the correlation assumption of the loans in the securitisation pool. Some rating agencies assume a pair-wise correlation of 30%, which is further stressed to reflect higher individual industry or sector concentrations.

Longer Ramp-Up Period

Given that mezzanine loan market is relatively small and private as well as the need for careful selection of the loans in the securitisation pools, there is a need for a longer ramp-up period. A traditional securitisation structure with advance funding followed by a ramp-up may lead to a significant negative carry and pressure on the manager to expedite loan selection even in less favourable market conditions to the detriment of pool's credit quality, diversification and detailed due diligence. An ingenuous solution to this problem in a mezzanine loan securitisation is the dynamic funding structure. Such structure allows for successive ramp-ups as the manager raises smaller amounts of capital when necessary, and once fully invested and with advance selection of more loans raises new funds.

While this structure solves the challenges mentioned above it introduces new aspects to be analysed—the potential for less diversified pools during ramp-up, the need for tight eligibility criteria or rating agency approval of each investment, and so on.[2]

Definition of Default and Recoveries of a Mezzanine Loan

Given the private nature of the mezzanine loan market, the senior, mezzanine and equity lenders often develop a working relationship, which is rarely present on the bond market. In addition they are generally more closely involved with the borrowers and have many possibilities to work with and influence the management of the company towards a desired

---

[2] For a more detailed discussion of these issues see the Fitch report, *Dynamic Funding in Cash Arbitrage CDOs*, February 2003.

solution should problems arise. In that regard, the interests of all lenders are better realigned towards ensuring the performance of the borrower, rather than triggering a default and liquidation. Covenants are often used as early warning signals used to focus attention on the problems of the borrower and seek early restructuring rather than trigger default.

In that respect a question arises as to how to determine the default frequency of a mezzanine loan for the purposes of securitisation and how to treat restructuring for the purposes of default calculation. Given the nature of the mezzanine loan market, most borrowers are not publicly rated. They are usually rated on an individual private shadow basis for the purposes of the securitisations and their rating is reviewed on a regular basis. Rating agencies often view their shadow ratings as being more conservative than their public ones.

When rating a mezzanine loan on a shadow basis some rating agencies choose to assess the potential recovery individually, while other tend to assume a low level of recovery around 15% for the shadow-rated corporate and 30–40% for the related mezzanine loan, further adjusted to reflect the jurisdiction of the loan. The latter approach can be viewed as rather stressful especially in the light of the information regarding recoveries on European mezzanine loans, presented later in this chapter.

PIKs and Warrants

We understand that warrants are not taken into consideration when analysing mezzanine loan securitisations thus creating an additional cushion in the deal not reflected in its rating.

With regards to PIKs, they present several challenges. On one hand PIKs reduce the cash flow available for debt service in the transaction. Furthermore, some loans may have PIKs, which are triggered by breach of certain covenants, that is cash interest payments cease and interest is capitalised if certain events occur. This presents challenges from the perspective of determining what percentage of the loans have such a feature and modeling the timing of such event. While some rating agencies choose to model that, others have concluded that the effect of such event on the rating is limited so they either disregard it or address it in another way. PIKs also affect the recovery rates on a mezzanine loan depending on whether PIK interest and rolled interest are included. However, assuming overall low recoveries may address this issue altogether.

Adverse Selection Due to Prepayment

As explained earlier many mezzanine loans are expected to pay within 4–5 years, despite their original term of 7–10 years. However, this would be true for successful borrowers thus leaving lower quality borrowers in the securitisation pool over time—this is what S&P calls the "adverse successor risk."

This issue is addressed at least by some of the rating agencies for the senior tranches of the securitisation deal through the modeling assumptions—starting point being full default of the loans in the pool, over-simulated correlation and stressed recoveries.

Management

The ability of the management of the securitisation pool to source, select, supervise and get actively and timely involved in restructuring and work-outs is key to the successful performance of the securitisation transaction. This is all the more important in pools with lower granularity and low liquidity.

In this respect, the focus is on the organisational structure, track record, investment philosophy, management and investment style, personnel qualifications of the respective manager. It is another matter how the rating agencies reflect these rather qualitative factors in the rating process of a given transaction.

Role of Institutional Investors

As mentioned on several occasions the European mezzanine market has been fairly private in nature. It has been only in the last few years that more information about its workings has become gradually public. Part of the reason for that is the institutionalisation of mezzanine loans and the need for related disclosure.

The emergence of an investor base focused explicitly on larger-ticket mezzanine deals should *drive* a movement towards the use of mezzanine funding, as an alternative to high yield financing in larger buyouts. At the same time, the core base of providers of small-ticket mezzanine funding to smaller buyouts should remain stable.

Another reason is the inclusion of mezzanine loans in an increasing number of CLOs and the securitisation of pure mezzanine loan portfolios. Hence, the role of the CDO managers in the mezzanine loan market is increasing.

No Clear Trend in Prepayment Fees

European mezzanine loans often have a moderate prepayment penalty in the first two years. The available data does not point out any specific trends in terms of use or size of prepayment fees during the last few years, except maybe to say that second year prepayment fees are falling both compared to first year prepayment fees and in nominal terms. It is probably fair to generalise that loans with warrants tend to be subject to a prepayment fee more often than deals without warrants and the prepayment fee in the latter is higher. Furthermore, the higher the deal size, the more likely the deal is to have a prepayment penalty and the higher that penalty will be.

Apparently, prepayment is more flexible in mezzanine loans usually declining from 3% in year one, to 2% in year two and 1% in year three. By contrast, in the high yield market, where after a noncall period of say five years the call premium generally declines to 50% of the coupon in year 6, to one third of the coupon in year 7, to one sixth in year 8 and to zero in year 9.

Default and Recoveries

There is little conclusive data on the performance of European mezzanine loans in terms of defaults and recoveries. However, we would expect to see lower default frequency and higher level of recoveries for mezzanine loans in comparison to high yield bonds due to a number of characteristics of mezzanine loans:

- Secured nature of the mezzanine loan sharing security and covenant package with the senior loan.
- Active supervision and control of the lender over the borrowing company and ability to address company problems as they arise.
- Better work-out possibility based on the ongoing relationship between borrower and lender.

Data from the US leveraged loan market shown in Exhibit 14.4 to illustrate the significant difference in default frequency between lever-

EXHIBIT 14.4   US High Yield/Leverage Default Rates

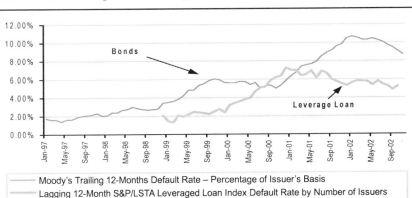

Source: Moody's, Standard & Poor's.

aged loans and high yield bonds. We emphasise, however, the differences between US leveraged loans and European leveraged and mezzanine loans Hence, the data in the exhibit is for illustrative purposes only.

Further information provided by one of the largest mezzanine loan investors in Europe—Intermediate Capital Group plc (ICG)—shows average annual default rate for the period 1990–2002 of 3.5% and recovery rate on default positions of more than 70% based on recovery of principal and exceedingly higher considering the equity value. This is against the background of an ICG portfolio under management growth from £56 million in 1990 to £700 million by mid-2002.

CHAPTER 15

Stock Securitisations

Carole Gintz
Analyst
Moody's France

Inventory securitisations present a viable alternative financing technique and an opportunity to diversify away from plain vanilla bank funding or bonds. In 2001, Moody's rated two such transactions in Europe. The first was Rosy Blue Carat S.A., which involved the securitisation of an inventory of diamonds of Rosy Blue NV, a Belgian diamantaire. The second was FCC Côte des Noirs, the second French transaction backed by an inventory of Champagne from Group Delbeck Bricout Martin (the first such transaction was the well-publicised Marne et Champagne deal which closed in 2000 and will be presented as a case study at the end of this chapter). The success of these first issues among ABS investors and corporate issuers signals a nascent receptiveness to the concept.

In this chapter, we will discuss the main features of a stock securitisation, present Moody's rating methodology on this particular asset class, and illustrate this methodology through the practical example of the "Marne et Champagne Finance ARL" transaction.

KEY FEATURES OF A STOCK SECURITISATION: BORROWING BASE AND STRUCTURE

The two key features of a stock securitisation are the borrowing base and the structure.

Borrowing Base

In inventory securitisation transactions, the funding amount (or the amount of notes to be issued) is usually directly linked to the volume and composition of the inventory, that is, the issued amount would be calculated as an authorised amount per unit weighted by the total volume of the inventory. This authorised amount per unit is detailed in a formula called the "Borrowing Base," which can take several forms: either that of a fixed amount of issuance backed by a single unit of the inventory, or a percentage of the current value of a inventory unit backed by this unit, or a combination.

For instance, for a single bottle of champagne priced at €12, there could be €8 issued in the first case (fixed amount), whereas in the second case the issued amount could be 70% of the price, that is, €8.4.

In that context, the borrowing base mechanism provides overcollateralisation between the amount of issued notes and the inventory value.

Structure and Security

Inventory securitisations are often structured as soft bullet notes to ensure ongoing financing to the seller (the proceeds on the sale of the inventory are reinvested in new assets—"revolving inventory"). The structure usually specify early amortisation events to address breach of the borrowing base, default events related to the seller, or triggers indicating a decrease in the inventory value. The noteholders being secured on physical assets (the inventory), they would have access to the inventory in order to be repaid from the proceeds of its sale (if they have not been repaid at the expected maturity).

The European transactions to date have been structured differently, but all of them used the same kind of security instrument—a pledge:

- *Secured loan structure.* The structure of the two French champagne transactions, Marne et Champagne Finance arl and FCC Côte des Noirs, consisted of a secured loan granted to the originator of the inventory. This secured loan had then been transferred to a bankruptcy-remote special purpose vehicle ("SPV") which issued the Notes. The security attached to the loan had also been transferred to the SPV. In both cases, the security consisted of a pledge *(gage avec dépossession)*, which is a very strong security under French law.
- *True sale structure.* In the case of Rosy Blue Carat, the physical inventory had been directly sold to a bankruptcy-remote SPV, which issued notes to purchase the inventory from the originator. The trustee has a pledge over the SPV's assets so that, in case of an early amortisation event, the noteholders would rank first in the allocation of cash flows generated by the sale of the inventory.

EXHIBIT 15.1 More or Less Successful Candidates for Inventory Securitisation

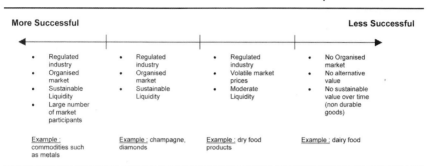

More Successful			Less Successful
• Regulated industry	• Regulated industry	• Regulated industry	• No Organised market
• Organised market	• Organised market	• Volatile market prices	• No alternative value
• Sustainable Liquidity	• Sustainable Liquidity	• Moderate Liquidity	• No sustainable value over time (non durable goods)
• Large number of market participants			
Example : commodities such as metals	Example : champagne, diamonds	Example : dry food products	Example : dairy food

Different legal environments could lead to different security mechanisms. The key element is to analyse the ability to have full access to the physical assets that constitute the inventory in order to repay the notes.

CHARACTERISTICS OF THE SECURITISED ASSETS

Recent inventory securitisations focused on luxury goods that maintain or increase in value over time. Other viable options include: assets in regulated markets with high barriers to entry and organised open markets and secondary markets; liquid inventory with high tradability; "durable" goods, and assets with historical price data. Candidates for inventory securitisation are shown in Exhibit 15.1.

RATING METHODOLOGY

Moody's approach to analysing inventory securitisation involves reviewing the items described in the following sections.

Legal Structure

Moody's analysis would focus on the following structural and legal features:

- Security instrument used to control inventory, enforceability to third parties, mechanism in case of exercise of the security. Based on the legal environments, Moody's analyses the strength of the security used to give access to the physical assets constituting the inventory.
- Early amortisation events.

Borrowing Base Mechanism

In the case of an early amortisation event, the inventory can be sold in order to repay the noteholders.[1]

▪ An analysis of the potential loss for the noteholders in case the sale price in a liquidation scenario is not sufficient to pay the amount due on the notes. Moody's applies Monte Carlo simulations to model inventory units pricing. The modeling of inventory units pricing requires a precise analysis of the historical prices of the assets constituting the inventory. It is therefore essential to have access to reliable historical data about the assets to be securitised from the company as well as from the industry. The risk remains in the possible gap between the issued amount and the inventory unit price. This risk appears to be of a different nature in the case of a fixed amount borrowing base or a price-adjustable borrowing base (percentage of inventory value).

  ▪ In the first case (fixed amount), the investor is exposed to the risk of a sharp fall in the inventory price, which would not be covered by the overcollateralisation created by the borrowing base. Moody's simulates the evolution of the value over the life of the deal, before and after an early amortisation trigger is hit, so as to be able to compare the amount due on the notes to the sale price and calculate the loss on the notes.
  ▪ In the second case (dynamic), the issued amount is adjusted based on the evolution of the price of an inventory unit so that the risk exposure is limited to the liquidation period only, as a potential gap between the two variables is covered on an ongoing basis thanks to the dynamic borrowing base mechanism.

▪ For instance, take the case of a fixed borrowing base—say €8 per unit with an initial unit price of €12. If we assume that the price falls to €8 during the period before an early amortisation event, and that the sale price per unit is then €7, this would entail a loss of €1. In the case of a dynamic borrowing base with an issued amount per unit of 70% of the unit price, the initial issued amount would be 70% × €12 = €8.4. During the period before an early amortisation event, the issued amount would be 70% × €8 = €5.6 and with a liquidation price of €7, there would be no loss on the notes.

▪ In the first case (fixed borrowing base), the structure is exposed to the risk of a long-term price decline, i.e., a deterioration in the value of the

---

[1] In case of semi-finished products, the sale may occur once the product is at a finished stage.

inventory, whereas in the case of an adjustable borrowing base, the exposure on price variation remains on a short-term basis only. In the case of a fixed borrowing base, the risk over a long-term period can be mitigated by including strong triggers to track price decline, which, if breached, would either lead to an adjustment of the borrowing base to the new price environment or result in early amortisation.

Interest Reserve/Liquidity Facility

Typically, collateral in inventory securitisation does not generate interest. The transaction must then be structured in a way to provide a source of cash flow to pay interest on the notes issued. On the secured loan type structure, the interest on the notes may be paid by the originator. However, in case of nonpayment of such interest by the originator, interest remains due on the notes. In transactions where the inventory is sold to the issuing SPV, a discount over the purchase price can be sized to cover the cost of funding on the notes.

In cases where Moody's is asked to rate the issuer's ability to pay interest in a timely manner, there will usually be either a cash reserve or a liquidity facility from a P-1 rated entity available for a specified period and amount which would cover the time needed to access the collateral and the liquidation of the inventory. In past transactions, this period has lasted up to 18 months. This period of availability is usually determined on a case-by-case basis depending on the legal environment and the liquidity of the assets constituting the inventory. In either case, according to Moody's, the total available cash should be sufficient to ensure timely payment of interest.

In the event that Moody's is not asked to rate the ability of the issuer to pay interest on time, interests and accrued interests would be paid once the proceeds of the sale are available. In that case, the borrowing base should take into account not only the potential decrease of the value of the inventory in the event of a liquidation scenario, but also the amount of interests that would have to be paid over the liquidation period.

Rating of the Notes Driven by Expected Loss

The rating of the notes is based on their expected loss over the expected average life of the transaction (Moody's rating being obtained by comparing the expected loss of notes to *Moody's Idealised Expected Loss Table* at the time horizon equal to their expected average life). The expected loss is calculated by weighting the average loss obtained through the Monte Carlo simulations mentioned above, in conjunction with a cash flow model constructed to reflect the transaction structure and payment allocation mechanics, by the probability of occurrence of such a liquidation scenario. Based on the structural features of a given transaction in which the originating entity could be more or less involved, the probability of occurrence of a liquidation scenario could be fully linked or fully delinked to the probability of default of the originating entity.

Partial Delinkage of Ratings from Credit Quality of the Sponsor

In inventory securitisation transactions, Moody's considers that the rating of the notes could reach a higher level than the intrinsic credit quality level of the original borrower thanks to the securitisation techniques and, more specifically, the security over the assets.

However, Moody's believes it might be difficult in most cases to reach the highest investment grade rating levels, that is, a Aaa rating,[2] because of a combination of structural issues, the limited liquidity of the inventory and other elements involved in a transaction. The existing transactions have achieved ratings of A2 or A3 on the most senior class of notes.

Furthermore, Moody's analyses the alternative use value of the assets involved in the securitisation. This alternative use value, if any, may limit the sales price decrease in case of a liquidation scenario. Inventory involved in securitisation transactions often consists of the core assets of the company and is fully linked to the industry in which the corporate operates. The inventory value will then be exposed to the operating volatility of a specific industry unless the assets could have a value independent from their specified use. For instance, champagne does not have an alternative use and diamonds have a very limited spectrum of activities (e.g., jewellery and electronics for rough diamonds). This is different for real estate assets as they typically generate demand for tenants from various industries or could be converted for alternative use. Consequently, properties are not comparable to physical inventories of commodities or manufactured goods.

CASE STUDY: MARNE ET CHAMPAGNE FINANCE ARL

The Marne et Champagne Finance arl transaction consists of the securitisation of a secured loan granted to three subsidiaries of the Marne et Champagne group. The secured assets included the total stock of Champagne from two categories (*Marques* and *Contre-Marques*) at each different stage of the production process (from juice in cask to finished bottles). The issued noted consist of two classes of senior notes with an A2 rating and one class of subordinated notes with a Baa2 rating. The transaction is summarised in Exhibit 15.2.

---

[2] For a discussion of Moody's approach to whole business securitisations, see Chapter 22.

EXHIBIT 15.2   Marne et Champagne Finance ARL Transaction

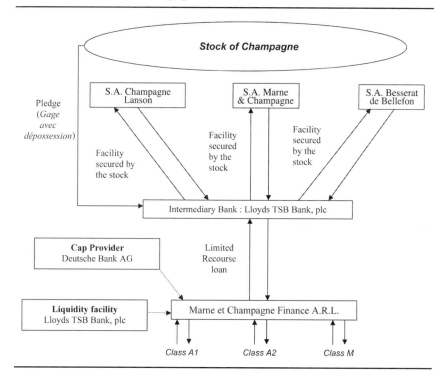

EXHIBIT 15.3   Borrowing Base Table

Stage of Production	Marque (€ per bottle equivalent)	Contre-Marque (€ per bottle equivalent)
En Cercle	6.6	4.3
Sur Lattes	7.9	5.3
Sur Pointes	8.8	5.7
Doses/Dégorgé	9.2	6.2
Habillés	10.1	6.9

The total amount of debt issued depends on the level and structure of the stock of champagne. It is calculated using the "Borrowing Base Table" with a cap at €396 million as shown in Exhibit 15.3. This exhibit will be modified if the average sale price of champagne falls below €8.99.

A Pass-Through Structure in Case of Wind-Down

In case of a wind-down events, which include nonpayment on the secured loan, insolvency of the borrower, average champagne price falling below €8.08, and breach on the borrowing base, the waterfall would be the following: payment of the fees (liquidity commitment fees, trustee, rating agencies, cash manager, paying agent…), redemption of past liquidity drawing, payment of the A1 and A2 interest (*pari passu*) before the M interest, payment of the A1 and A2 principal, and then M principal once A1 and A2 are fully redeemed.

No cash will be paid to the champagne companies before the full redemption of the notes.

Structure Analysis

If the lending bank starts the wind-down, Marne et Champagne would probably be in bankruptcy proceedings and the following would happen:

1. The company will be under the observation period for a maximum of 20 months. An administrator *(administrateur judiciaire)* will be appointed at the beginning of this observation period. During this observation period, the administrator could sell the secured stocks unless the secured debtors have given their approval.
2. At the end of the observation period, the administrator will decide to go with one of the following three solutions: continuation plan, sale of the company plan (which is only possible if the secured creditors agree with this plan), or liquidation plan.

Moody's believes that there are three scenarios that are the most likely to occur:

1. *The administrator will not choose the liquidation.* He or she will work with the lending bank to find a purchaser. This is because if he or she goes for liquidation, it will mean the end of the business and the end of all related jobs. The potential purchasers should make the same calculation as the one Moody's did, and the sale price should therefore be sufficient to repay the debt in full.
2. *The administrator chooses liquidation.* The lending bank will find different purchasers, will ask for a judicial attribution of the stock, and will sell it to the purchasers
3. *The administrator chooses liquidation.* The lending bank will ask for a judicial attribution and hire a champagne company to run and to manage the stock until the end of the manufacturing process.

Credit Enhancement Analysis

If Marne & Champagne defaults on the loan from the intermediary bank, wind-down will occur. In the following calculation, Moody's assumes that the *administrateur judiciaire* will decide that Marne & Champagne should continue its business until the whole stock has been sold (without purchasing new grapes). Therefore, the main risk are related to the champagne price, the production cost necessary to end the process of champagne production, the distribution cost, and the production timing.

Champagne prices can change. However, Moody's can assume that production cost, distribution cost and production timing are inherent to the champagne process and therefore are almost constant.

Champagne Price Evolution

Moody's modelled the evolution of the champagne price using the Black and Scholes model for stock pricing in capital markets. Exhibit 15.4 shows the distribution probability of the "Marque" champagne price on February 2004 assuming the price is described by the Black and Scholes model.

Credit Enhancement Calculation

For a given champagne price scenario Moody's proceeded as follows:

EXHIBIT 15.4

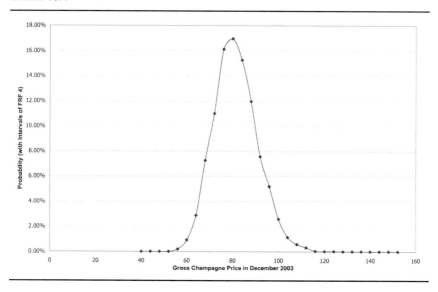

Calculation of the date of wind-down: The most likely scenario of wind-down is that a wind-down occur after four years (i.e., when Marne & Champagne will have to redeem the loan from the lending bank). However, the wind-down can occur earlier as explained in "wind-down triggers" above.

Adjustment, if need be, of the borrowing base: If the average price of champagne falls under €8.99, the borrowing base is reduced by the difference between €8.99 and the average price of champagne and the amount of notes issued at that moment is calculated from this "new" borrowing base.

Using the price distribution above on a Monte Carlo Analysis, Moody's calculated the net present value of the cash flows received by the different note holders. The comparison of this net present value and the net present value of the promised cash flow gives the expected loss related to the scenario. Finally, the total expected loss is calculated by averaging the expected losses of each scenario. The rating assigned to the different classes of notes reflects the expected loss of each of these classes.

CHAPTER 16

Rating Trade Receivables Transactions

Jean Dornhofer
Senior Vice President
Moody's U.K.

Everett Rutan
Senior Vice President
Moody's U.S.

Trade receivables constitute a large and growing portion of securitised debt. Traditionally, trade receivables transactions have been financed by *asset-backed commercial paper* (ABCP). More recently, the market has begun to show interest in financing accounts receivable transactions via term debt. For the asset-backed securities (ABS) investor, these transactions offer diversity from consumer-driven assets and exposure to transactions with shorter weighted average lives (see Exhibit 16.1).

The funding of trade receivables is a critical source of working capital to the seller of the receivables. The transactions are particularly popular in times of economic stress, based on their appeal to corporate "fallen angels"—recently downgraded companies who may no longer have access to the traditional corporate commercial paper market and unsecured bank lending. The securities are also popular among corporate treasurers who may need to diversify funding sources. Banks, pressured to increase *return on equity* (ROE) via higher margins while more efficiently using their capital base, also serve to increase the number of transactions.

EXHIBIT 16.1 Comparison of Financing Alternatives for Trade Receivable Transactions

	ABCP	ABS
Deal size (million euro)	€75–€150	€150–€200
Pricing	Less predictable	Higher
Deal tenor	5.5 years	5.5 years
Execution time	1.5 months	6 months
Credit enhancement	Aaa to A2 levels	Aaa levels
Liquidity facility	100%	6 months coupon
Costs	Low	Low to medium

The intent of this chapter is to explain the unique characteristics of trade receivables, examine Moody's methodology for sizing enhancement for credit losses, and explore other risks endemic to these transactions.

TRADE RECEIVABLES—FUNDAMENTAL SOURCES OF RISK

Trade receivable transactions are generally supported by a revolving pool of obligations generated when one business sells goods or services to another. The most distinctive risk characteristic of trade receivables transactions is their high vulnerability to the business cycle and to the fortunes of the originator of the receivables. As collections are received on old receivables, the purchaser usually can buy trade receivables that meet the eligibility criteria during a five-year revolving period. The continuous addition of new receivables can lead to significant changes in performance trends and obligor exposure.

To this end, a rating assessment of the transactions—and the level of enhancement required to achieve a particular rating—will focus not only on specific structural protections such as preset triggers, but also on asset performance, obligor concentrations, and the potential for cash flow dilution.

Among the most important characteristics to understand about the assets that underlie trade receivables transactions are the following:

- *They are noninterest bearing.* "Yield" is created by funding at a discount, and there is no spread to enhance the deal.
- *They are unsecured claims on the obligors.* Unlike an equipment lease or a consumer auto loan, there is no underlying hard asset that can be repossessed in the event of nonpayment. As unsecured obligations of business entities, 100% loss severity often results if an obligor defaults.

- *They typically include high obligor concentrations.* Obligors will generally be more concentrated by industry and large single obligor concentrations are common.
- *Assets are nonuniform.* Asset characteristics are not homogenous across transactions. Products, obligors, sales practices, payment terms, accounting, and collection policies vary greatly by industry and seller.
- *Performance varies widely.* Asset performance varies to a great degree because performance depends on variables such as the originator's relationships with its sellers, current financial condition, competitive position and strategic direction.
- *Ongoing business exposure.* The revolving nature and quick payment rates of the assets signify continued exposure to the changing fortunes of the originator.
- *Low incentive for obligors to pay on time.* The assets rarely incur finance charges and cessation of shipment is not immediate. Poor payment yields less severe consequences than defaulting on bank debt. Because timely payment is not critical, delinquencies can be high.
- *Assets turn rapidly.* Assets may turn, in many cases, within one to two months. If the dominion and direction of asset collections is not handled well in advance of a deterioration in the originator's financial condition, an investor can lose most of its collateral coverage through the commingling of this cash with that of the receivables originator.
- *Dilution risk is high.* Dilution—defined as a reduction in the amount owed for reasons other than payment or default—is a potential critical source of loss to trade receivable investors. This risk factor is heightened by the assets' pools' high turnover.
- *Cash commingling can reduce enhancement and proceeds.* Cash commingling, wherein payments received from obligors and due to the securitisation are passed through the seller's accounts can, if left unresolved, result in the loss of a significant portion of the enhancement and bond proceeds. This is a source of dilution risk.

RATING METHODOLOGY

The amount of enhancement is principally driven by asset performance, the lumpiness of obligor concentrations and the amount of dilution. Tighter eligibility criteria, especially limiting large exposures to a few obligors, and tighter performance triggers serve to reduce enhancement levels. In order to form a very approximate initial view of the possible amount of loss and dilution reserves, the aggregate of the average monthly default and dilution ratios may be multiplied by the receivables' turn days (expressed as a fraction of a month) and then multiplied by a stress factor commensurate with the desired rating level and in light of the qualitative factors discussed below. It will also be necessary to increase this initial estimate by the amount necessary for a yield reserve and, possibly, other factors.

Highly rated trade receivable transactions generally feature conservative advance rates, no commingling of cash, a true sale of and first perfected security interest or charge on receivables, frequent settling of the eligible asset balance to the outstanding debt, and an originator with several funding alternatives in the event of financial stress and significantly higher debt exposure to other creditors.

The Credit Default Risk Assessment

Both quantitative and qualitative factors are taken into account when sizing credit enhancement for credit losses. The profile of the originator portfolio performance characteristics and strength of structural protections need to be analysed in order to determine the enhancement for credit losses.

The Originator Profile Review

Our review of the originator will entail an assessment of financial condition and strategic direction, underwriting standards, and an operational review

Financial Condition and Strategic Direction The financial condition and fortunes of the seller play a prominent role in these transactions. Sellers with established market positions and with diverse markets and products will likely sustain less volatility and require lower enhancement levels. Sellers operating in inherently volatile or cyclical industries or sellers producing high tech or highly specialised goods will receive relatively higher enhancement levels. Sellers of products that demonstrate inelastic demand, such as electricity, typically have lower default rates and volatility, and hence lower enhancement levels.

To estimate future performance, it is necessary to review the whole business, including organisational structure, ownership, revenue generated, business line profitability, market share, general industry prospects, long and short term objectives and anticipated strategic changes.

■ *Insolvency: The downward spiral.* An actual or perceived imminent bankruptcy can lower obligors' willingness to pay as evidenced by higher delinquencies, slower turnover, and increased dilutions. Bankruptcy may also trigger more liberal credit underwriting policies, deteriorating collections, and higher likelihood of cash being trapped in the bankrupt originator's estate.

To mitigate the risks of such deterioration, some arrangers agree to rating triggers that stop further purchases of receivables should the seller's rating decline. Alternatively, enhancement levels may be increased significantly.

■ *The importance of funding sources other than securitisation.* In the event of originator insolvency, high reliance on securitisation for working capital financing has, in some instances, resulted in ambiguity regarding the assets' remoteness from the bankruptcy estate. Moody's therefore examines the composition of the originator's capital structure.

■ *Potential for a change in market demand or obligor mix.* The revolving nature of trade receivable transactions adds volatility to the pool's credit strength. A change in the originator's business strategy, target market, or product positioning could pressure portfolio performance. Key risk factors to review at the obligor level include the likelihood of a change in obligor mix, obligor credit quality, or obligor demand (including a study of industry competition)—and its potential to increase losses.

Underwriting Standards Superior judgement in underwriting and collection procedures will be reflected in the performance data and will result in lower enhancement levels. The seller's trade credit underwriting process is likely to be subjective and the market does not typically rely on quantitative scoring mechanisms such as credit scoring. Moody's often conducts operations review to determine the strength of the originator's underwriting procedures, however these reviews may not be necessary for granular pools financed with ABCP.

Portfolio Eligibility Criteria Review

The eligibility criteria serve to reduce exposure to riskier receivables, such as those referred to in Exhibit 16.2 and restrict exposures to obligors. Tighter eligibility criteria result in significantly lower levels of enhancement, although they may mean a lower overall advance rate against the entire receivables portfolio.

Obligor Exposure The most important eligibility criteria limit the funding of receivables from unrated or lower-rated obligors to 1% to 3% of the outstanding balance ("normal" obligor concentration limits). If that concentration limit is higher than 3% ("special" obligor concentration limits), comparatively higher loss reserves are necessary.

EXHIBIT 16.2 Risky Receivable Types

Eligibility criteria should prohibit purchases of these assets:

- Delinquent (by 30–60 days) or defaulted receivables (more than 90 days past due).
- Executory contracts—obligations in which failure to complete performance would cause a material breach.
- Unearned receivables—receivables generated before shipment or delivery of goods purchased or services performed.
- Government receivables or others for which the obligor may not be legally subject to normal collection procedures.
- Bill and hold receivables created when a good is purchased, but wherein shipment is postponed.
- Receivables related to a service sub-contracted to a third party.
- Current receivables due from obligors with significant delinquencies on other receivables ("cross-ageing").
- Receivables due from affiliates of the seller.
- Receivables subject to any dispute, offset, counterclaim or defense.
- Receivables subject to liens.

In the event that any of the above may be purchased, enhancement amounts would tend to be relatively higher because these receivable types carry a higher default and/or dilution risk.

Moody's rating of a corporate obligor speaks to its publicly rated debt, not its trade obligations. A highly rated corporation may pay its trade creditors slowly or not at all, and this may have no affect on its Moody's long-term or short-term ratings. Also, it may be possible to use another rating assessment such as a bank's internal credit score if an obligor is not rated by Moody's.

In addition to the creditworthiness of the obligor, other factors such as the degree of reliance of the obligor on the seller's business, are taken into account when ascertaining concentration limits relative to enhancement levels.

Maintaining the Net Receivables Pool Balance After applying eligibility criteria to the total receivable balance, the eligible receivables that remain are called the *net receivables pool balance*. This is equal to the total receivables balance less ineligible receivables including inter-company debt, delinquent or defaulted receivables, cross-aged receivables (nondelinquent receivables of obligors with excessive percentages of delinquent receivables), and excess concentrations.

For a trade receivables deal to be "in formula," the net receivables pool balance must be equal to or greater than the amount of securitised debt plus all required reserves. This balance must be measured frequently—at least monthly, often weekly. When receivables are found to be ineligible, the net receivables pool balance is reduced.

If a seller breaches any representations regarding receivables sold, it is obligated to repurchase the ineligible receivables. The strength of this buyback obligation is commensurate with the seller's fundamental rating.

Portfolio's Turn Days The time from the generation of the invoice to the repayment of the underlying debt is generally quick, usually 38–45 days. The accounts receivable turnover is used to determine the payment rate, which equals 30 multiplied by the accounts receivable balance over collections and expressed in units of days.

A longer repayment period provides more time for the credit worthiness of obligors to deteriorate or for other problems. Therefore portfolios with slower turnover will generally require greater enhancement than comparable portfolios with quicker turnover.

Data Review

The amount of data presented has an impact on the enhancement levels. Key variables need to be carefully reviewed in order to detect to trends and "get the story behind the numbers."

Data Sufficiency and Accuracy A review of the receivables' historical performance is key. As a general rule, at least three years of monthly performance data of the trade receivables is necessary. An absence of data in Exhibit 16.3 or the presence of a few data points leads to higher enhancement levels relative to historical default levels due to the higher degree of uncertainty.

Even in cases where data is ample and accurate, it may fail to reflect the pool's expected loss. Data from good economic times may underestimate potential loss levels during a recession.

Delinquencies: Instructive in Determining Reserves Moody's looks at the trend in roll rates (e.g., the amount "rolling" from the 31–60-day bucket to the 61–90-day bucket) to determine the likelihood that late payers will ultimately pay or end up as credit losses.

Loss Proxy—Quantitative and Qualitative Reviews Because the write-off of trade receivables is at the discretion of the seller, the best estimate of loss (the "loss proxy") is the level of severely past due (90+ days) receivables. Trans-

EXHIBIT 16.3 Data Requirements for Each Originator (Monthly, covering three years of history, minimum)

1. Sales, collections, and end-of-month receivables balance.
2. Pro forma calculation showing amount of eligible receivables obtained from total receivables pool under the terms of the securitisation.
3. Ageing amounts in 0–30, 31–60, 61–90, over 90-days past due, and write-offs.
4. Pro forma loss, dilution, and other reserve calculation for the last three years.
5. Pro forma trigger calculation under the terms of the transaction.
6. Dilution, unapplied cash, or other adjustment amounts for last three years.
7. Trade receivables turn in days.
8. Breakdown of top obligor concentrations listing ratings, payment history, and significant delinquencies or disputes.
9. Breakdown of government versus commercial receivables, foreign versus domestic receivables, and intercompany receivables.
10. In transactions with more than one originator, items 1, 3, 5, 6, and 7 above should be broken down by originator as well as provided in total.

actions with a higher loss proxy will require higher enhancement levels. A higher degree of volatility in the loss proxy, as reflected in the relationship between the standard deviation and the mean, also results in relatively higher enhancement necessary to cover a higher level of volatility.

Moody's reviews the available loss data both quantitatively and qualitatively. For example, portfolio performance is viewed in the context of strategic endeavours underway at the time, and rapid growth in receivables may mask deterioration in pool performance. Moody's also attempts to understand the circumstances that led up to the spikes in the loss proxy, and assess the probability of these circumstances reoccurring.

Seasonality Highly seasonal businesses do not easily lend themselves to efficient trade receivable securitisation. Sales, receivables, and collections may be highly concentrated in a short time period, and obligors may pay more slowly as they wait for their sales to occur. Accurate analysis of these patterns requires looking at several years of data.

Seasonality can affect the dynamic nature of the reserves in most trade receivable transactions. The rapid increase in receivables at certain times of the year requires a concomitant increase in reserves. If performance also deteriorates, reserves must be even higher, but higher enhancement levels may come too late for the seller to post additional eligible receivables. If debt is issued during the peak season of a seller's business cycle, there will be times during the revolving period when the seller is unable to generate sufficient receivables to support the level of borrowing.

For term transactions, a portion—possibly a large portion—of principal collections that would normally be invested in new receivables would be kept in an excess funding account in the absence of sufficient receivable generation. As a result, highly seasonal businesses require close monitoring with frequent (often daily) resetting of the borrowing base during the period of large sales generation and the collection of those sales.

Triggers and Remedies Review

The purpose of the trigger and remedy structure is to attenuate investor's exposure to an unexpected deterioration in the pool's performance.

Out of Formula Triggers   Moody's requires that every trade receivable transaction contain an "out of formula" trigger. A transaction is "in formula" if the outstanding debt plus required reserves is less than or equal to the amount of eligible receivables.[1] This test should apply at the time of purchase of any new receivables and on each settlement date (typically monthly), at a minimum. Being "in formula" ensures that, at least when the assets are purchased, investors will benefit from the minimum required level of enhancement. Moody's then evaluates whether the required enhancement provides adequate loss protection during the time it takes the receivables pool to pay down.

Meaningful Triggers Relative to History   Highly rated trade receivables transactions also have default, delinquency and dilution triggers set at meaningful levels relative to historic results. It is often unlikely that such performance-related triggers in trade receivables transactions are tripped, because there are some common problems with these triggers' construction:

1. Trigger levels are simply set too high (often more than five standard deviations from the mean loss proxy) relative to the historical mean and standard deviation of the loss proxy.
2. Three- or especially 12-month rolling averages smooth out the results of the trigger calculations, making them less meaningful and masking the effects of volatile performance and also the effects of escalating pool deterioration.

---

[1] Because enhancement is typically in the form of overcollateralisation, the formula refers to the asset base; if, for example, a letter of credit was also provided in enhancement, the formula would consider the amount of eligible receivables plus the available letter of credit amount.

3. The method of calculation is not responsive to the variable measured. A dilution trigger that reflects dilution in the most recent month is more effective than one that averages it over the last three months, because dilution amounts can increase very significantly very quickly.

Tighter triggers result in lower enhancement levels because they can force an early amortisation before performance deteriorates too far. Similarly, if performance-related triggers are loose compared to actual performance, enhancement levels may be set high relative to actual performance. Triggers set too close to expected performance levels might result in a too-early termination of the transaction.

Seller Related Triggers   A transaction may also have triggers related to the rating or financial condition of the originator. Triggers relating to the originator include a loss of rating level (if applicable), a change in ownership, financial covenants, a material adverse change in financial condition, payment default, cross-default and/or cross-acceleration, and bankruptcy.

Remedies   The tripping of triggers in a trade receivable transaction requires the issuer to stop purchasing receivables. Certain structural features may accelerate repayment and are therefore considered stronger. These include:

- Allowing all collections from receivables, including recoveries and, at times, those from ineligible receivables and excess concentrations, to be used to repay investors. In many deals the allocation factor for cash to senior investors is set to 100% during amortisation.
- The amortisation of enhancement "freezes" on an early amortisation and as a result, a continuously higher level of cash is allocated to the senior investor.
- Other remedies may also be applied as a result of triggers. These include higher enhancement levels, changes in servicing or control of cash flows, more frequent settlement, and the ability to waive some triggers under certain circumstances.

Determining the Amount of Loss Reserves

Moody's believes that the sizing of the loss reserves requires an analysis of the pool data from several vantages: both historical performance as well as the degree of concentration to special obligors. After determining the loss reserve levels from a purely quantitative aspect, Moody's may adjust these initial results to take into account qualitative factors, such as the originator's predilection to loosen underwriting practices in order to increase sales. In order to size the loss reserves, Moody's will need to become familiar with the terms expressed in Exhibit 16.4.

EXHIBIT 16.4 Terms Needed to Size Credit Enhancement

---

1. Concentration limits in the eligibility criteria for normal and special obligors.
2. For transactions with more than one seller: amount of seller limits.
3. Numerical amounts of key performance triggers and remedies.
4. Receivable turn days.
5. Definition of the loss proxy.
6. Pro forma calculation of all reserves and whether reserves are "fungible"—meaning, for example, the dilution reserve can potentially be drawn to cover defaults if the default reserve is insufficient.
7. For ABCP transactions: whether the program credit enhancement can be specifically allocated to support the subject pool addition.
8. For ABCP transactions: which risks, if any, in an ABCP financed transaction are being absorbed by the liquidity banks?

   ■ Cash commingling
   ■ Nondefaulted receivables found to be ineligible
   ■ Dilution
   ■ True sale

Enhancement Sizing   The appropriate enhancement for losses is a function of the mean and standard deviation of the loss proxy over the last three years; exposure amount and ratings of special obligors; the likelihood and impact of the originator's insolvency on pool performance; the potential for deterioration in the pool's risk profile over time; the strength of the triggers; the length of the receivables turn; and structural protections such as a requirement to cease purchasing new receivables or issuing ABCP.

In general, enhancement for trade receivable transactions tends to be between 15–25%. The amount of enhancement for trade receivable transactions is typically the greater of:

1. A dynamic formula that responds to changes in the pool's performance.
2. A fixed nominal percentage of outstanding eligible receivables.
3. The amount necessary to cover a number of the largest obligor concentrations.

Moody's determines the adequacy of these amounts by examining the convergence of the effects of the qualitative factors discussed above and the results from:

1. A review of the responsiveness of a dynamic calculation to changes in historical performance.

2. An examination of the repayment of the pool under stressed scenarios.
3. The results of alternative methods such as a Monte Carlo simulation or the binomial expansion method for pools with concentrations of obligors.

Dynamic Enhancement Calculation   The dynamic calculation for the default reserves often takes the form of a default ratio multiplied by a stress factor multiplied by the time over which losses can occur. For example,

$$\frac{EP \times L \times BA \times \text{multiple}}{TU}$$

where:

EP = the sum of the contractual payment terms plus the number of days a receivable is typically paid by, which will be adjusted given current trends in payment performance

L = the loss-to-liquidation ratio, which is the ratio of write-offs (typically receivables aged 91 to 120 days past due for the current month) to collections in a particular period.

BA = the outstanding balance of the seller's portfolio

TU = the receivable turn days

Moody's evaluates dynamic formulas by reviewing the historical performance of the originator's receivables. The average, median and peak of the loss proxy are compared to the amount of the dynamic calculation that would have been required at those times. The largest disadvantage of dynamic calculations is that they fail to take into account any change in the number or rating of special obligors.

Additionally, a uniform stress factor at a given target rating is not relevant, as it fails to take into account the volatility particular to the pool and the qualitative factors discussed above. The level of stress should be a function of the level of volatility of pool performance. Expected volatility may be in part determined by historical volatility and in part by the likely obligor composition in the pool.

Another potential problem is the responsiveness of the dynamic calculation to sudden changes in performance. Moody's prefers a dynamic calculation that uses a shorter period rolling average and an additional factor to cover the volatility, such as looking back to the maximum one-month default (or dilution) level reflected over the last 12 months.

Testing Adequacy of Loss Reserves   For ABCP-funded transactions, it is important to ascertain repayment even in the more stressful transactions. To determine the sufficiency of reserves, Moody's models the repayment or "wind-down" of the trade receivable pool. This analysis assumes that the "out-of-formula" trigger is tripped and reserves are precisely equal to the required levels, no new receivables are added (fully declining pool); interest on the debt continues at the contract rate; the receivables are financed until they are paid off or a loss is incurred; and loss reserves are fixed at a notional amount (reserves do not dynamically increase if losses increase). The receivable turn of the pool, the loss rate, and the dilution rate are treated as random variables and are stressed. The stress is applied to both the mean and the standard deviation of these variables. The amount of stress may be adjusted for each pool to take into account the qualitative subjective factors.

The adequacy of the average and the minimum floor reserves are reviewed separately under these circumstances. If the average reserves did not prove adequate under the stressed scenarios, reserves may increase or performance triggers tighten to limit investor exposure to performance volatility. If pool performance reflects a higher degree of volatility, and if dynamic reserves prove unresponsive, the minimum floor reserves should be adequate under highly stressed scenarios.

For term transactions, which are rated on an expected loss basis, either a Monte Carlo simulation approach is used to evaluate losses under a large number of scenarios (for randomly selected payment rate, losses, dilution, reserves and pool size) or a log normal approach is used to produce a distribution of losses. These are not mutually exclusive. The lognormal approach is simpler, faster, and less computationally complex; but the Monte Carlo approach permits modeling more complicated transactions, including large obligor defaults.

With either method, the expected loss can be compared with the expected loss tolerances for Moody's long-term debt ratings for the given tenor of the term transaction. The rating tolerances vary by term and are therefore coupled with the term of the transaction, i.e. 5-year legal final. In the case of the rated term notes or certificates, the modelled expected loss must be consistent with that associated with the expected rating.

Special Obligor Concentrations

The degree of concentration to special obligors is the second highest factor behind dilution influencing credit enhancement levels. In well-structured transactions, between 1% and 3% of the receivables pool is attributable to any single obligor and its affiliates. If a seller's receivables have no significant obligor concentrations, the risk of obligor defaults can be assessed through a statistical approach on a collective basis.

Alternatively, if a seller's portfolio includes significant exposure to particular obligors, enhancement will be a function of the size and ratings of those obligors. Higher enhancement will be required for less creditworthy special obligors, closely correlated obligors or for transactions with high obligor exposures.

Risk assessment must also look at the potential for a change in obligor concentrations as indicated by the allowable (versus actual) criteria. In each transaction, Moody's assesses the probability that the actual obligor exposures will be equal to that allowed under the special obligor concentrations in the eligibility criteria.

Slow Pay and Correlation Risk   A default or dispute by large obligor translates into large losses for the pool. In addition, depending on how closely correlated the obligors' performance is to the seller and to each other and the length of the receivable turn days, a large number of obligors may default simultaneously.

Proposed obligor concentration limits are often linked to the obligor's rating based on the assumption that the obligor's payment performance with respect to the receivable will mirror the obligor's performance on its publicly rated debt. Moody's ratings speak only to payment performance on publicly rated debt, not to payment performance on receivables. Failure to pay a trade obligation will not in itself result in Moody's downgrading the short- or long-term ratings of the obligor.

An obligor's rating is also not necessarily indicative that the obligor will pay the receivable on time, commonly referred to as "slow pay risk." Slow pay is typical in trade receivables transactions because the consequences of being delinquent on a trade receivable transaction are far less harmful than those associated with defaulting on publicly rated bonds or bank debt.

For transactions financed with ABCP, the slow paying nature of special obligors may lead to the characterisation of receivables due from these obligors to be considered a default. There are three usual mitigants to slow pay risk for transactions.

1. Limiting receivables funded from large obligors.
2. Requiring the liquidity definition of default to have a separate, longer period for larger, more creditworthy obligors.
3. Inserting a trigger based on cross ageing in which all receivables due from a special obligor with a high delinquent balances become ineligible for purchases.

The slow pay problem is not endemic to term transactions where the rating addresses the timely payment of interest (and sufficient reserves will be availed to cover the coupon on the bond) and the ultimate payment of principal.

Moody's takes correlation into account by examining the stability of the underlying industry, the level of necessary allegiance between the seller and the obligors, and the short-term nature of the obligation. High large concentrations in the same weak industry will lead to relatively higher enhancement levels because performance may reflect a higher degree of volatility as industry trends deteriorate.

Reserve Levels for Special Obligors   For large obligor concentrations, it may be necessary to model the impact of obligor default on expected loss. A Monte Carlo simulation can be expanded to consider creditworthiness of each obligor, the aggregate exposure to each obligor and its affiliates, the degree of correlation among obligors in the same industry, the degree of diversification by industry and the receivables' turnover. Another approach applies the binomial expansion method to model default risk. The business reasons for high concentration levels must be assessed as well. A review off the obligor's historical payment pattern is also relevant.

Given that different pools will require different enhancement based on the ratings and the degree of correlation among obligors, there are no rigid rules requiring a certain number of obligors be covered by credit enhancement to achieve a certain rating.

Assessing Risks Other Than Credit Default Risk

While a great deal of time and energy is concentrated on sizing enhancement for credit losses, there are other risks which can have at times an equal or even greater impact on trade receivable transactions.

Cash Commingling

A review of the cash collection process, the location, ownership and charges over all accounts, the control of the originator over the accounts, the presence of any other funds collected within these accounts, and the timing of transfer of funds to other accounts is conducted by Moody's. Ideally, all cash collections belonging to the transaction should be segregated from the originator and placed in an account in the name of the issuer.

Where cash is deposited in accounts in the name of the originator, funds may be trapped or "commingled" in insolvency. The quicker the turn of the receivables, the higher the collections that may be trapped. Because trade receivables have such a fast turn, this could be the full amount of the pool.

Moody's will require a legal opinion stating that the receivable collections will ultimately be received by the issuer notwithstanding the insolvency of the seller, and a liquidity facility will be needed to keep debt payments current until the receipt of the collections.

Certain contingent protections may be added to a structure to reduce commingling risks, including a rise in the frequency with which funds from the originator's are swept to the issuer upon a deterioration in the seller's financial condition. Transactions with a daily sweep can be expected to have comparatively lower enhancement levels.

Asset Transfers

True sale, nonconsolidation, and perfection opinions are routine for public term trade receivable transactions.

Dilution

Dilution tends to be the larger and more variable aspect of portfolio performance, and is often the reason for reserves. Dilution occurs if the amount billed is reduced for reasons other than payment or default. Typical sources of dilution include incorrect invoicing, billing/payment errors, discounts, rebates, returns, offsets, warranty claims, and disputes.

Certain receivables are more susceptible to dilution. Unearned receivables and executory contracts have a greater chance of disputes, errors in estimation costs or cancellation. Obligors of a bankrupt seller may apply to have an executory contract voided. Government receivables may become seriously diluted if the federal government sets off its obligation to pay the seller against other claims that the central government may have against the seller, such as taxes. Bill and hold receivables are more susceptible to returns and disputes as well.

Significant correlation may exist between the incident of disputes and the credit condition of the seller. The seller's quality controls may deteriorate with deterioration in financial condition. Setoffs will increase as obligors seek fast compensation for debt owed. Historical data provided during times of financial stability might not shed light on dilution in the event of deterioration in the seller's credit strength.

Setting Dilution Reserves   Monthly dilution performance can be volatile. It is fairly common for dilution to jump from very low levels in one month much higher in the next. For severe jumps, dynamic reserves, especially those based on averaging, cannot be expected to respond to this level of increases. Triggers also do not help in this instance.

Considerations in sizing the dilution reserve are the historical dilution data, industry standards and practices, and credit strength of the seller of the receivables.

A fixed, relatively high floor amount of dilution reserves coupled with a dynamic calculation that looks back to the highest dilution ratio over the last 12 months is preferred. In transactions where the impact of seller insolvency is highly unpredictable, the anticipated spike in dilution requires linking the transaction's rating with the seller's credit quality, or requiring a sizeable increase in reserves on the downgrade of the seller.

Servicing Risks

The seller typically acts as servicer and remains responsible for managing the substitution of receivables, calculating the dynamic credit enhancement, identifying eligible receivables, maintaining fraud prevention measures, collecting receivables, reporting, monitoring arrears, writing off bad debts and other daily support activities. The seller's procedures—particularly in handling billing errors—will have a significant impact on both dilution and ageing of the pool.

Servicing quality and portfolio performance may deteriorate if the seller is financially distressed. The impact of introducing a backup servicer is minimised by the fact that the receivables turn too quickly to realise the benefit of a backup servicer after the originator is insolvent.

Impact of Deterioration of Seller Credit Quality   Three scenarios are possible when a seller enters bankruptcy:

1. *Restructuring.* Many companies continue to operate and obtain revolving credit loans secured by post-filing receivables. In this case, stress analysis of the receivables supporting the rating is not based on a total interruption in servicing of the receivables, but stressed variables brought about by an insolvency.

2. *Liquidation.* Likely candidates are companies generating large negative operating margins, smaller companies, or companies entering bankruptcy for a second or third time. A review of the seller's balance sheet and the likelihood of restructuring or liquidation are key risk determinants. These companies are typically not good candidates for securitisation.

3. *Special Servicing.* A back up servicer may be introduced if the servicer's financial condition declines below a certain rating level. The quickly turning nature of the receivables mandates that switch happens significantly before an insolvency to be effective.

Carrying Costs

The rating of a trade receivable transaction also is an opinion of the timely payment of interest on the notes as well. A yield reserve is necessary in light of the noninterest bearing nature of trade receivables. The interest to support the securitised debt must be calculated as an additional discount to the purchase price of the receivables.

The yield reserve is sized in dynamically to take into account the nominal rate on the debt and a stressed payment rate of the receivables. The yield reserve is equal to the funding costs plus other transaction expenses, multiplied by a stress factor and the stressed numbers of days in the collection period/360. The discount factor should also increase during the revolving period if the average turnover rate of the receivables decreases. In ABCP transactions or term deals where the notes are floating rate without interest rate swaps, the yield reserve formula must incorporate a stress factor to address the possible increase of interest rates.

CONCLUSION

Trade receivable transactions are traditional asset classes that have historically enjoyed a wide degree of popularity. Moody's expects continued growth in both European- and United States-based receivable transactions to be financed by both term ABS and ABCP in the near future.

Moody's approach looks beyond a formulaic calculation of enhancement levels and endeavours to understand how various business factors may affect portfolio performance over the life of the transaction. While numbers-driven formulas and models are a good initial starting place, the final reserve levels will be significantly influenced by qualitative judgements concerning factors such as the originator's financial condition, business prospects, competitive arena, underwriting practices, and industry standards.

Risks other than that of obligor default such as dilution or cash commingling may significantly increase enhancement levels. Structural protections such as triggers may be introduced which serve to decrease enhancement levels.

Standard calculations for enhancement levels may not be pertinent, as often the causes of the risk and the preferred mitigants will vary with each originator.

A comprehensive explanation of the originator's particular circumstances is important to the ratings review process and in ascertaining enhancement levels.

CHAPTER 17

Moody's Approach to Analysing Consumer Loan Securitisations

Nikoletta Knapcsek
Analyst
Moody's Italia

Valentina Varola
Analyst
Moody's Italia

For the purposes of Moody's rating methodology on the securitisation of consumer loans, this category includes personal loans, auto loans and credit card borrowings. Most personal loans are unsecured and are usually fixed-rate amortising loans granted to individuals, whereas auto loans, which are designed to help finance vehicle purchases, may be secured. Credit card borrowings are funds drawn on a revolving basis, with a variable interest rate and a changing amortisation pattern.

The category of consumer loans may also include lease financing extended to small- and medium-sized companies. Leases can have either fixed or variable interest rates, and amortise following a fixed pattern until their residual value can be acquired by the debtor at an option price.[1] The final section in this chapter will focus on this particular asset class as specific characteristics apply to such receivables and need to be taken into account in the rating methodology.

---

[1] See "Let the Sun Shine: Clearing the Air of Legal Issues in Italian Lease-Backed Securitisations," *Moody's Special Report*, 17 June 2002.

Consumer loans are originated by commercial banks, specialised finance companies or captive organisations. Commercial banks usually operate through a large network of branches and benefit from a widespread client base; they use consumer loans mainly as a marketing tool. In contrast, specialised finance companies focus on consumer loan origination through a dedicated network and various partnerships. Captive entities act similarly, but within a group, where they offer financing exclusively to the group's customers. (A typical example would be that of the captive organisation of an automaker or a retailer group.)

For Moody's, the most important feature of a securitised consumer loan portfolio is its granularity, that is, its lack of substantial concentration towards a single debtor or group. The importance of a high portfolio granularity lies in the reduced impact that the possible default of a single debtor will have on the credit quality of the total portfolio.

Moody's analysis focuses on:

1. The credit quality of the securitised loan portfolio—within the wider context of the originator's ability to underwrite and to service the relevant loans.
2. The structural and legal features of the transaction—including cash flow allocation, triggers and various other protections (embedded in the structure to prevent losses on the portfolio) as well as the credit quality of the different players involved in the transaction.[2]

ANALYSING THE CREDIT QUALITY OF THE SECURITISED PORTFOLIO

The initial key focus in an analysis of the *credit quality* of a securitised portfolio is a thorough understanding of not only the originator's underwriting and servicing policy and its evolution over time, but also the economic conditions prevailing during the sample observation period. Moody's normally carries out an operational review, which entails direct contact with the originator. Analysts typically meet with individuals responsible for the origination and underwriting, servicing and recovery departments, plus IT experts and members of the senior management with a view to understanding past, present, and planned strategic moves that could have an impact on the securitisation deal.

A good understanding of the originator's past and future business, its market position, its competitive environment, its offered product

---

[2] See "French Consumer Credit Securitisation," *Moody's Special Report*, 2 September 2002.

range, and its client base as well as the broader context of its parent group or subsidiary channels, against the backdrop of the general economic environment, helps Moody's assess the potential impact the originator may have on the securitised portfolio. It is also important to review the extent to which the originator's organisation in terms of human and technical resources, including information technology, matches its philosophy and strategic goals. Indications as to the financial solidity of the originator are provided by its (estimated) rating.

The particularities of the origination and underwriting policy may affect the quality of the originator's client base. As a result, Moody's acquaints itself with the origination channels used, the methods of client evaluation (which may include scoring systems), and the details of the decision process in terms of timing and people involved.

Servicing, on both performing and problematic loans, influences the extent to which amounts due are paid on time and in full. The servicing of the contracts whose receivables have been transferred to the SPV needs to be punctual and reliable in order to ensure that relevant flows circulate smoothly through the transaction accounts, to ultimately service the debt. The proactivity of recovery procedures has an impact on the ultimate measures that are applied in the event of a loan going into default. The analysis of servicing and recovery policies includes a good understanding of past due receivables, the time lag between each step, the definition of default, and the effect of eventual judicial procedures. Moody's analyses factors such as the recovery method, the timing scheduled for each phase of the recovery activity, and the success ratio in recovering the money on difficult positions in order to form a view on the level of recovery and time to recovery which will be included in our quantitative analysis.

In the era of information technology, the accuracy and completeness of any data and any procedure depends, to a great extent, on the quality of the IT system in place. Analysis of an IT system would normally focus on backup creation, disaster recovery, and its compatibility with other systems, and transferability of the whole protocol to another entity.

The results of the analysis of the originator and the operational review are then compared with historical data provided on a comparable pool of assets of the same originator over a certain time horizon. Ideally, the historical data will correspond to the same perimeters as the selected pool and will cover a relatively long period (five to seven years, or long enough to cover an entire economic cycle). Another important point relates to consistency: Moody's will look at any material changes in the servicer's origination and recovery policies or in the definition of default applied to the portfolio of observed data throughout the analysed period, as any such change would distort the analysis. The default definition in the observed data should also be consistent with the default definition in the securitisation transaction, otherwise adjustments would be required. Finally, if the securitised portfolio is composed of various subpools, data will need to be provided for each subpool of loans when possible (e.g., used or new cars, or personal loans for various purposes).

Some data (such as those related to prepayments or delinquencies) should be in a so-called dynamic format, as opposed to the default data discussed above, which should be provided in static format. Here, "dynamic" means that percentages are defined relative to the current outstanding of a reference portfolio, instead of the level of origination for a given year. Such data extraction is similar to taking a photograph: a certain amount of delinquencies or prepayments are compared to the outstanding of the total portfolio. It is obvious that such a "photograph" may be distorted depending on the variation of the outstanding in the denominator. With growing portfolios, the ratio may be underestimated. And vice versa, declining portfolios may lead to an overestimation.

As mentioned, other kinds of data (such as those related to defaults or recoveries) are most useful when provided in a static format, that is, they follow periodic (monthly, quarterly, or yearly) generations of loans. A vintage of loans originated in a particular time period is followed throughout the following periods, and default and recovery data are extracted, in a cumulated format, as a percentage of the original amount of the portfolio in the particular vintage. An example of some static curves related to default observations over a five-year time horizon can be seen in Exhibit 17.1.

Credit card borrowings, or in general revolving credits, are an exception to the above preference. Due to their revolving nature, the default rate is calculated on the outstanding. A vintage analysis is carried out, in which the evolution of a monthly dynamic default rate by generation of accounts plays an important role. Seasoning is a key factor in estimating the default rate.

Secondly, the analysis focuses on the *characteristics of the securitised portfolio* in question. In fact, the segmentation of the loan portfolio by amount, duration, age, interest rate, geographic area and borrower type will help to assess the homogeneity of the portfolio and the main drivers of future cash flows and losses. The main drivers in the assessment of potential losses on a consumer loan portfolio can be as follows:[3]

■ Year of origination (e.g., to detect temporary looser underwriting criteria or expansion policies, or assess the impact of economic downturns).

---

[3] See "Consumer Finance ABS: Moody's Approach With a Focus on The Italian Market," *Moody's Special Report*, 5 October 2001.

EXHIBIT 17.1 An Example of Static Pool Analysis

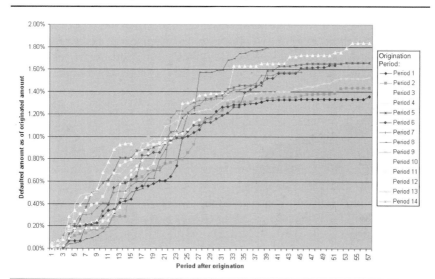

■ Seasoning: defaults usually occur in the early years of the life of the loan when the debtor's equity in the asset is low.

■ Amortisation pattern (for example, balloon loans tend to be riskier).

■ Geographical concentration.

■ Concentration per obligor or type of obligor.

■ Secured/unsecured.

■ Purpose of the loans: used cars / new cars in the case of auto loans.

■ Means of payment: direct debit, postal payments, and the like.

■ Origination channel.

Thirdly, Moody's also examines the *regulatory framework* of the region in which the originator is located as this may have an impact on the credit strength of the pool. The framework may exert various types of influence that may affect the flows coming from the securitised portfolio.

STRUCTURAL AND LEGAL FEATURES OF CONSUMER LOAN TRANSACTIONS

With regard to the key structural features of consumer loan deals for the sizing of credit enhancement, Moody's will look at:

- The existing excess spread in the transaction (i.e., the amount by which the yield on the consumer loans pool exceeds the financing and servicing costs of the structure).
- The eligibility criteria for loan additions (when a transaction features a revolving period during which new loans can be added).
- The various triggers (e.g., excess spread-trapping, early amortisation triggers) and their impact.
- The cash flow allocation mechanisms between the different tranches (pro rata, sequential, or other amortization).

The credit support can take several forms, including: cash reserve, subordinated tranches, guarantee, or excess spread. Moody's examines issues such as changes in the support over time and the circumstances under which the enhancement may be unavailable to protect investors.

The sizing of the credit enhancement depends on several factors. These include (1) the level of excess spread available in the deal; (2) the tightness of the structure (e.g., eligibility criteria, triggers, waterfalls, hedging, etc.); and (3) the difference between the expected loss on each class of notes as modelled and the level of expected loss acceptable for the required rating.

Excess spread plays a crucial role in consumer loan-backed deals as the securitised assets usually generate a significant spread that can benefit the transaction. Usually, excess spread may be sufficient to cover ongoing losses on the portfolio. When excess spread is completely depleted in a given period (which is translated into the net excess spread or net margin ratio falling below zero), then other sources of credit support can be used to offset additional defaults. In the consumer finance business, excess spread typically ranges from 3–7% per year, and even more for subprime portfolios.

However, excess spread can not typically be considered as credit support for its totality as in most transactions, any residual spread after provisioning for defaulted loans (and sometimes delinquent loans too) is given back to the seller. This "use it or lose it" mechanism makes the reliance on excess spread more difficult to assess. Typically, the excess spread will have more value as credit enhancement in the deal when the spread is trapped early, hence when the default definition is tight or when the deal includes a provisioning for delinquent loans. Specific triggers linked to delinquencies or loss levels can also be included to trap this residual spread and keep it in the transaction when the performance of the assets starts to deteriorate. There are several ways to ensure cash-trapping in the structure of a consumer loan-backed securitisation.

A special, even if not unique, feature of consumer loan securitisation is the *revolving nature* of the structure of most transactions. A revolving period means the addition of new loans in the securitised pool to replenish the loans that are amortised or prepaid. During the revolving period, principal collections (and potentially a part of excess spread) are used to purchase new loans, and investors are paid only interest.

Moody's believes that a long revolving period may have a negative impact on the credit quality of the portfolio, unless protective measures are applied right at the beginning of the transaction. The main weaknesses linked to revolving periods include the risk of adding loans with a higher risk profile due to changes in the underwriting policy of the seller over time, and the resulting possible change of the initial characteristics of the securitised pool. Protective measures may include the use of *triggers and eligibility criteria* to limit the negative impact the addition of new loans may have on the overall quality of the portfolio. The eligibility criteria for the revolving period may include the following:

- Minimum coupon per loan/for the pool
- Maximum maturity
- Minimum of x installments paid/seasonality
- Not delinquent, defaulted, previously renegotiated
- Limits for product mix (e.g., used/new cars, cars/trucks)
- Limits for borrower/geographic concentration

In fact, loan addition criteria help limit the change in the composition of the portfolio, whereas triggers would typically lead to an early amortisation of the deal to limit further deterioration if the performance of the assets deteriorates below a certain level. As eligibility criteria and triggers limit rather than prevent the asset deterioration during the revolving period, Moody's also uses some stress assumptions for the data to take into account the possible deterioration of the portfolio's credit quality during that period.

In addition to the structural features, other issues have to be examined when analysing consumer loan-backed deals. These additional matters include legal issues (such as the bankruptcy remoteness of the issuer, the true sale of the securitised receivables, and other country-specific legal problems), tax issues, commingling risk, interest rate risk and its hedging in place, and liquidity risk.

Apart from the issuer, the other parties in the transaction could include the settlement bank, the servicer and/or the back-up servicer, a guarantor, the swap counterparty, or a liquidity provider. Moody's will assess these parties' ability to fulfil their commitments in the transaction as well as the protection mechanisms in place in the event of a decline in their credit quality and/or their ability to perform. The ratings of such counterparties will have to be consistent with the required ratings of the issued notes.

A STATISTICAL APPROACH TOWARDS CREDIT ENHANCEMENT

The methodology used by Moody's is essentially statistical: The rating agency will focus on (1) the cumulative average loss that can be expected on the securitised pool over the life of the transaction; (2) the shape of the loss distribution; and (3) the volatility associated with this expected loss.

Typically, a *lognormal approach* is used for granular portfolios.[4] An observation of historical data on consumer finance portfolios has shown that the cumulative losses on various loan generations were typically distributed along a lognormal curve. An example of a lognormal distribution can be seen in Exhibit 17.2.

EXHIBIT 17.2   Probability Distribution

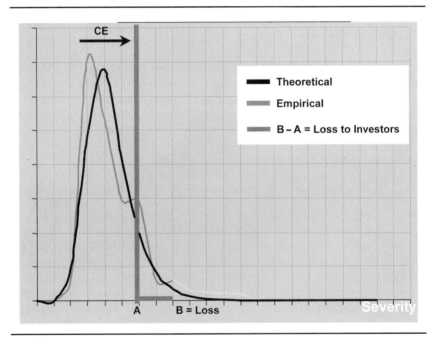

---

[4] See "The Lognormal Method Applied to ABS Analysis," *Moody's Special Report*, 27 July 2000.

Moody's will derive both the mean and the standard deviation of the cumulative default rate from the historical data provided by the seller and analysed as described above. These default parameters will be adjusted by any trend observed in the data (e.g., continuous deterioration of the default rate in recent years). A further qualitative adjustment will be made if the analyst can see reasons why the expected future performance may differ from the portfolio performance observed in the past (e.g., position within the economic cycle). The final default data, together with a measure of its volatility, will determine the whole spectrum of possible default scenarios according to the lognormal curve; hence each scenario will be entered as input in a cash flow model constructed to reflect the transaction structure and payment allocation mechanisms. For each scenario of cumulative default rate, the loss on each class of notes is calculated by comparing the initial outstanding of the class of notes with the present value of the cash flows received by such class of notes over the life of the transaction. The present value discount rate corresponds with the coupon rate of the class of notes in question. The last step is the calculation of the expected loss on the notes by weighting the result of each scenario by the probability of occurrence of such scenario (given by the lognormal distribution) and comparing it with Moody's table of idealised loss rates at the horizon corresponding to the average life of the notes.

The level of volatility of defaults around the mean has a large impact on the amount of credit enhancement. The same expected loss with a smaller volatility (i.e., a distribution curve with a small rather than fat right tail) leads to a higher rating on the notes. It must be added that the volatility of losses is difficult to assess without long-term historical data.

Other key assumptions used in the cash flow model include the *timing of default*, the *recovery rate, delinquencies,* the *prepayment rate,* and the *interest rate on the loans.*

The timing of default is typically derived from a historical observation of the originator's loss curves. In many countries, losses are concentrated in the early years of a loan, but it is not unusual to see defaults starting in later years, or sometimes evenly distributed between origination and maturity. Moody's will test the impact of various loss curves in its models.

Recovery, prepayment and delinquency assumptions are usually crystallised and one value is used in all the default scenarios carried out, but various sensitivity simulations are run using several recovery, prepayment, and delinquency rates. Delinquency rates will be modellised as they tend to negatively affect the excess spread on the transaction. It is also possible to incorporate a recovery curve in the analysis of some highly concentrated portfolios (in one region, one economic sector, etc.), where recovery values are inversely proportional to the default rates used in each single scenario. This type of analysis can have an important impact on highly rated notes.

The lognormal approach, however, works best for granular portfolios that consist of homogeneous and relatively small assets. It is possible, although not frequent, for a consumer loan portfolio to contain large exposures or to consist of several sub-portfolios that have different characteristics (e.g., Italian leases). In such cases, we might use various methodologies such as the BET (binomial expansion technique—typically used for the analysis of collateralised debt obligations) on the "chunky" part of the portfolio, or Monte Carlo simulation techniques which work very well on small- to medium-sized portfolios. Other innovative approaches are also used occasionally, for example the Fourier transform method,[5] which generates probability distributions for portfolios that combine a large number of small-sized assets with a small number of large assets.

LEASE-BACKED TRANSACTIONS: A PECULIAR, AND POPULAR, ASSET CLASS—FOCUS ON ITALY

While lease-backed deals have been structured and marketed all over Europe, the largest volumes of issuance can be found in the Italian market. In fact, as can be seen in Exhibit 17.3, for the years 2000, 2001, and 2002, leasing deals have been the success story of the Italian market. This trend is set to continue, driven both by repeat issuers and by "newcomer" leasing companies—both top- and second-tier—attracted by this source of funding. As a result, this section will focus on the Italian lease-backed market.

The reason for paying particular attention to this specific asset class derives from the peculiarity of such deals, mainly in relation to certain legal risks introduced by the potential bankruptcy/restructuring of the originator.

The Leasing Contract

A leasing contract is an agreement entered into by two parties: the owner of the asset or "lessor" (and originating company) and the user of the asset itself or "lessee" (the debtor). According to the terms of this contract, the former undertakes to make available to the latter a determined good (built or acquired under the specifications of the lessee) and

---

[5] See "The Fourier Transform Method—Overview," *Moody's Special Report*, 15 January 2003.

EXHIBIT 17.3   Lease-Backed Deals in the Italian Market

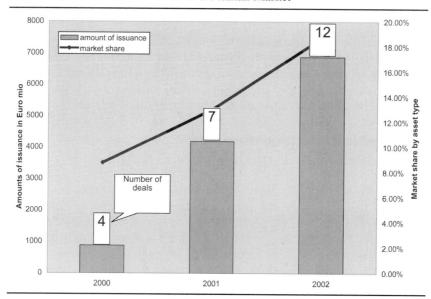

the latter agrees to make periodic payments for this service. The contract usually incorporates an option (in favour of the lessee) by which the lessee will have the right to acquire the property of the asset at the lease maturity by paying a predetermined residual price.

Leases can be classified either as operating or financial leases: the former typology can be assimilated to a rental agreement. An operating lease is usually short-term, and the good's maintenance costs are usually sustained by the lessor. On the other hand, a financial lease will usually span over a great part of the economic life of the good itself, and practically all the risks linked to the ownership of the asset will be on the lessee.

The financial lease represents an alternative source of financing for the debtor, in addition to traditional bank debt. Arguably, the appealing trait of a leasing contract is the fiscal benefit that the debtor may reap linked to the deductibility of the leasing-related payments.

Because of its characteristics, a leasing contract may be assimilated to a guaranteed loan: if the lessee stops making the relevant payments (as agreed in the contracts), the lessor may eventually repossess the asset and either sell or re-lease it. In fact the full ownership of the asset itself will be passed on to the lessee only at the end of the contract upon payment of the option price.

In the Italian market, the *Corte di Cassazione* (Italian Supreme Court) has classified the leasing contract into two main categories:

- *leasing di godimento*
- *leasing traslativo*

The criteria used to distinguish these two categories relate primarily to (1) the actual size of the residual value, (2) the intention of the two parties at the inception of the contract, and (3) the nature and average life of the financed good.[6] So far, *leasing traslativo* contracts have formed the whole of securitised lease portfolios in the Italian market.

Characteristics of Italian Lease-Backed Deals

The main characteristics of the Italian lease securitisations include:

- *A mixed portfolio.* Securitised lease portfolios in Italy are usually made up of *three subpools*: the auto pool (auto vehicles, trucks), the equipment pool (machinery), and the real estate pool. Clearly the composition will vary according to the nature of the business transacted by the originator. Recent transactions show an increasing portion of real estate leases in the portfolio; this mirrors the trend recently recorded in the Italian leasing market with real estate leases growing at a significant pace. A few single-asset type deals (e.g., Italease S.p.A. Series 2002-1(ITA 4)) or double-asset type deals (Landes S.r.e., Itaca No. 1) have also been analysed and rated.
- *Some residual value.* In several cases, the residual value component (i.e., the option price the debtor pays in order to secure full ownership of the asset) has also been included in the securitised portfolio. This inclusion gives rise to additional "issues," which need to be taken into account in our analysis.
- *Long revolving periods.* Due to Italian tax regulations, no principal will be paid on the asset-backed notes during the first 18 months of the deal. During this period, the originator is generally granted the faculty to transfer additional portfolios, which the issuer will buy with the flows coming from the amortisation of initial portfolio loans. Frequently, such revolving period extends further than 18 months, some times as long as five years. Clearly a long revolving period will have a greater impact on the transaction, as new purchases will tend to alter the initial portfolio profile. This highlights the importance of tight eligibility criteria and triggers (based on factors such as default, delinquencies and PDLs), at either the pool or sub-pool level. Triggers at the sub-pool level will, for example, inhibit the originator from buying any additional assets from a sub-pool that is performing poorly.

---

[6] See "Let the Sun Shine: Cleaning the Air of Legal Issues in Italian Lease-Backed Securitisations," *Moody's Special Report*, 17 June 2002.

■ *From large to smaller originators.* So far, lease originators have typically been the operating leasing subsidiary of a large national financial group. Moody's usually derives a relatively high level of comfort from the leasing company's being part of a national banking group, if the latter owns a substantial part of the lessor's share capital. In fact it can be reasonably anticipated that, in case of a financial distress situation of the originator, financial support from the parent group would be forthcoming. With smaller leasing companies approaching the securitisation market, it is expected that different shareholding structures will be analysed. The presence of smaller (or less creditworthy) originators increases the legal risk inherent to Italian lease-backed transactions, and raises additional issues such as the need for the presence of a backup servicer.

Legal Risks and Modeling Impact

Legal risks of Italian lease-backed deals originate from the "unpredictable" consequences that the bankruptcy or restructuring of the originating company may have on the securitisation structure in Italy.

Rejection Risk

Rejection risk relates to the possibility that the receiver(s) of a financial distressed leasing company may decide to *liquidate* the company and terminate the performing contracts. The termination of the contracts would necessarily interrupt the cash flows coming into the structure.

The prevailing view in the market (and confirmed by legal opinions) is that this risk is extremely low. Indeed, we note the following:

■ Securitised leases, in all lease-backed deals launched in Italy so far, may be assimilated to the *leasing traslativo* category, which relates to sale with reserve of title. This should mean that, in the case of originator bankruptcy, Article 73 of the Bankruptcy Law would apply, hence no contract termination should occur.
■ The termination of the performing contracts would also give rise to the following additional considerations:

　■ From a strictly economic point of view, the mass termination of the contracts could expose the receiver to claims for damages on the part of the lessees, in particular those for which the repossessed goods were key in their operating activity.
　■ Additionally, the disposal of all the repossessed goods would likely not be achieved in a very profitable manner (distressed sale).

However, it is difficult to fully exclude this risk in the credit analysis given the following:

- Current Italian law does not regulate the leasing contract in an explicit way, the leasing contract still being classified as a *contratto atipico*.
- The choice—whether or not to reject the performing contracts— depends on an individual (the receiver/curatore), whose remuneration is a function of the total recoveries achieved at the end of the bankruptcy procedure.
- Existing case law shows that a few receivers have indeed decided to interrupt all lease contracts upon the liquidation of the originator. Although such case laws are neither recent nor transparent (very limited information available), the rejection risk will be given some consideration in our analysis.

Moody's will typically use the public rating or obtain an estimated rating on the leasing company, which will be used as proxy for the probability of *bankruptcy* of the originator over the life of the transaction. This probability of bankruptcy will be adjusted (e.g., looking at the size of the company or its penetration within—and share of—its local market) to derive the probability of *liquidation* of the company. A certain small probability (and high severity) will be associated with the rejection risk in case of liquidation of the leasing company. This analysis also includes assumptions regarding the correlation between the performance of the lease portfolio and the bankruptcy risk of the company. Such correlation will be more important when the securitised portfolio represents a significant portion of the company's overall portfolio.

Additional Loss

The bankruptcy of the originator could also result in (1) the loss of the recoveries on defaulted assets as well as (2) the loss of the residual value flows (should this latter be securitised). These flows might indeed be classified as future receivables, hence their transfer to the SPV could be jeopardised by the bankruptcy of the originator under current Italian law (which does not clearly recognise the sale of future receivables). Moody's takes such risk into account, and gives no credit to the relevant flows in the originator's bankruptcy scenarios (with the exception of any spontaneous repayments on the part of the lessee, which would still be valid).

CHAPTER 18

Nonperforming Loan Securitisation and Moody's Rating Methodology

Antonio Serpico
Associate Analyst
Moody's Investors Service

Alex Cataldo
AVP-Analyst
Moody's Investors Service

Hernan Quipildor
AVP-Analyst
Moody's Investors Service

Securitisation transactions backed by *nonperforming loans* (NPLs) have unique credit risk profiles, largely as a result of the cash flows being purely derived from expected net recovery on this "distressed" debt. Moody's "recreation" of these cash flows is based on an analysis of (1) borrower and asset details; (2) any available security package; and (3) the competence of the servicer. The numerous variables and structural features characterising each particular deal make the analysis of NPL transactions a complex and multidimensional task.

Moody's NPL rating methodology requires a high degree of flexibility given that the risks in every deal can not be easily captured within a single formula or model. As a result, this chapter outlines the most common structures and provides insight into how Moody's has analysed these transactions.

Although this chapter focuses on Italian NPL securitisation, which represents one of the largest NPL markets outside the United States and Japan, Moody's considers that the structural and methodological features developed in Italian deals may be "exported" and applied to other markets. In this chapter we will investigate and outline a number of these features to best fit the needs of international investors and issuers.

NPL DEFINED

The broadest definition of a nonperforming loan (NPL) is any debt obligation for which the original contract repayment plan has not been honoured. Such debt obligations may include delinquent loans (at various levels of severity), defaulted loans and even reperforming (or restructured) loans. The term "NPL" has over the years become a synonym for "bad loan" or severely delinquent or defaulted debt. However, the key factor behind NPLs is not the definition of the term but the expected net recovery on this "distressed" debt and the timing of this recovery.[1]

Italian NPLs are debt obligations typically classified as defaulted assets according to the Bank of Italy's definition of *sofferenza*.[2]

In line with the focus on the expected net recovery and timing in NPL transactions, NPLs can be classified into two main categories: secured and unsecured.

Secured NPLs are collateralised by an asset or have a sound security package. In brief, debt obligations, such as mortgage loans, which are secured by a high-ranking economic lien with a voluntary or judicial mortgage. Typically, the mortgage is on a real estate asset, although other types of security may provide similar security on the claim. However, in order to qualify as a sound security package for NPL securitisation purposes, information on the security for each claim must be readily available, tangible and irrevocable. The recovery amount and timing will primarily depend on:

---

[1] See *Moody's Special Report*, "Credit Risks of Reperforming and Nonperforming Residential Mortgage Loans Transactions: Unique Risks Can't Be Captured in Formulas," October 2000.

[2] This definition is not attached to a specific timing or delinquency stage and depends on the severity of insolvency (although not necessarily judicially verified) or any analogous situations. Thus, as the definition allows a high degree of discretionary power, no specific fixed timing can be applied. However, on average, this generally occurs after 6–12 consecutive delinquent monthly installments.

1. The net value of the claim at foreclosure sale (which depends on variables such as market property price volatility).
2. A blend of servicing capacity to efficiently take the claim through the relevant legal procedure.
3. The ability to optimise any possible out-of-court settlement with debtors.

For *unsecured NPLs* there is no collateral available or a good quality security package. In brief, these are debt obligations, such as consumer loans, current accounts, or liquidity facilities, which do not possess a high-ranking economic lien with a voluntary or judicial mortgage. Although the claim may be secured by a low lien or have additional guarantees, there is no information to quantify whether the guarantee is readily available, tangible, and irrevocable. In these cases, both the timing and amount to recover, if any, will largely depend on the servicer's efficiency and capabilities.

It is worth mentioning that a "subperforming loan" is defined, according to Italian banking rules, as *incaglio*, which is a delinquent debt obligation in which the distress of the borrower is considered to be temporary and could be potentially resolved in a "reasonable" time frame. Some Italian NPL transactions include portions of *incaglio* loans. While fundamentally the *incaglio* can be classified as secured or unsecured as noted above for NPLs, there is some probability that these loans may return to performing or reperforming status.

MARKET OVERVIEW

According to a Bank of Italy study,[3] NPL recovery activity in the Italian banking system is characterised by the following features:

- In terms of NPL recovery methods, Italian banks prefer out-of-court settlements with debtors (41%) versus bankruptcy proceedings (21%) and foreclosure proceedings (10%).
- Amounts recovered range from 68% from out-of-court settlements to 27% from bankruptcy proceedings. However, recovered amounts are higher in cases where a real estate property secures the NPL (70% and 50%, respectively).
- Time to recover is long throughout Italy, ranging from 7.5 years for bankruptcy proceedings to 2 years for out-of-court settlements.[4]

---

[3] Bank of Italy, *Statistical Bulletin 2001*.

[4] For a detailed description of recovery timing for Italian regions, please refer to the Appendix to this chapter.

The average annual cost for banks' recovery activity is around 1.2% of the amount declared in *sofferenza* and represents 2.3% of the banks' operational costs.

Recent years have witnessed rapid growth in the use of NPL securitisation on the Italian market and the related technology involved.

Funding, balance sheet cleaning and servicing activity reorganisation have been the main rationales behind NPL securitisation.

Italy experienced its first NPL securitisation in August 1997, originated by Banca San Paolo di Torino [International credit recovery (ICR) 1 – Portfolio gross book value (GBV)[5] of €500 million]. However, the boom did not take place for another couple of years when the Italian securitisation law was enacted in 1999. The surge in popularity was largely the result of the fiscal incentive stated directly in the Italian securitisation law 130/99, allowing Italian banks to amortise NPL-related losses over a period of five years, thereby considerably smoothing the negative impact on financial results for the year in which a securitisation took place. Indeed, the first transaction under Law 130/99 securitised secured and unsecured nonperforming claims by Banca di Roma (Trevi Finance S.p.A.).

Between the enactment of this law in 1999 and April 2003, a total of approximately €31 billion (in GBV) of NPL portfolios were securitised through 34 transactions, making Italy one of the world's largest reference markets for this asset class. Exhibit 18.1 depicts the pace of issu-

EXHIBIT 18.1   NPL-Rated Notes in Italy

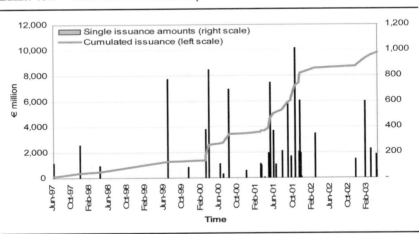

---

[5] The GBV represents the notional amount of a portfolio according to the originator balance sheet (excluding any loss provision).

ance until April 2003. However, the Italian NPL securitisation market has expectedly slowed down from 2002 onwards following the boom experienced in 2000 and 2001 (with 7 and 16 transactions, respectively). This is due in large part to the fact that the tax and accounting benefit related to NPL securitisations expired in May 2001. Nonetheless, issuances will continue to occur, albeit at a reduced pace.[6]

KEY STRUCTURES USED IN NPL TRANSACTIONS

Broadly speaking, Italian NPL transaction structures can be classified into three main types:

1. Standard structure with pure liquidity line
2. Mixed structure with an advance facility
3. Mixed structure with collateral

In addition, other potential structures are likely to appear on the market, such as synthetic NPLs.

Standard Structure

In a standard NPL securitisation structure, the risk for investors is directly linked to the expected collections and timing on the NPL portfolio.

The rating of the bonds issued by a special purpose vehicle (SPV) is based solely on the estimated cash flow coming from the securitised portfolio. No external guarantees are provided to support potential inflow shortfalls (see Exhibit 18.2). A liquidity line is provided solely to pay interest on the notes for a limited time in case of a severe cash flow shortfall. Similarly to traditional pure liquidity lines in other securitisations, it is structured so that no credit enhancement is provided to the transaction.

Mixed Structure with Advance Facility

An *advance facility* (AF, which is typically referred as the servicer *advance facility, liquidity advance facility,* or *limited recourse facility* in most transactions) is a form of credit facility made available by servicers in the case of collection shortfall (see Exhibit 18.3). With this type of structure, the risk taken by investors is linked to both the NPL portfolio inflows and the AF provider's capability to provide credit support.

---

[6] See *Moody's Special Report,* "Moody's Approach to Monitoring Italian Non-Performing Loan Transactions," December 2002.

EXHIBIT 18.2 Standard Structure

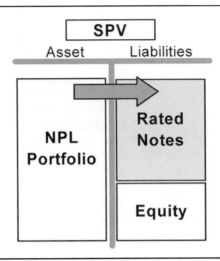

EXHIBIT 18.3 Mixed Structure with AF

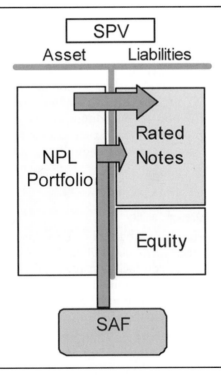

Indeed, whenever collections from a portfolio fall below a certain level, known as the *AF threshold*, the SPV is allowed to draw the shortfall amount out of the available AF. An AF threshold is defined in the terms and conditions of the issued notes and is calculated on the basis of certain recovery assumptions made before launching a transaction. The key aspect that differentiates this instrument from a mere liquidity line is where the repayment of used AF is made on the transaction's priority of payment. The interest and principal repayment of the AF drawing is made in a more or less subordinated fashion and, clearly, the more subordinated it is, the higher the credit benefit provided by this mechanism.

The rating of the issued bonds is based on both the cash flow coming from the portfolio and the AF. The impact of the AF on the notes' rating depends on (1) the rating of the AF provider (and/or the backup AF provider), (2) the eventual rating trigger mechanics; and (3) the amount and drawing conditions of the available AF. On average, the AF amount has been around 40% of the rated notes issued, ranging from 9.6% (in the case of the Ulisse 3 S.p.A. transaction) to 59% (Perseo Finance S.r.l.).

The presence of an AF is a positive element in a transaction, given that it reduces certain volatility associated with the repayment of principal to note holders in the transaction, thus easing the potential impact of negative carry associated with slower amortisation profiles.

However, the presence of an AF entails two main risk factors:

1. The AF provider's ability to honour its obligations under AF agreements. As a result, the transaction is directly exposed to the credit profile of the AF provider.
2. The possibility of the AF provider choosing not to renew the AF. (It is usually a 364-day renewable facility.)

Many structures have typically sought to reduce the direct exposure explained in the first point above, by either:

- Introducing backup AF providers, which will guarantee the same or similar obligations as the AF provider, thus reducing the exposure to the rating of the AF provider according to a jointly supported obligation approach.[7]
- Guaranteeing their obligations with collateral, either at the closing of the transaction or after certain rating triggers have been breached. This latter method forces the AF provider to collateralise its obligation, within a short time frame, should its rating fall below a certain level.

---

[7] See *Moody's Special Report*, "Moody's Approach to Jointly Supported Obligations," November 1997.

EXHIBIT 18.4   Example of SAF

Period	SAF Threshold	Actual Recoveries	Cumulative Actual Recoveries	Drawing	Re-imbursement	Cumulative Drawing
1	50	52	52	0	0	0
2	100	46	98	2	0	2
3	150	40	138	10	0	12
4	200	60	198	0	2	10

Note: Available commitment is the SAF amount still available to the SPV for drawing. The first drawing is required in period 2 (as the cumulative actual recoveries have fallen below the SAF threshold) and thus the available commitment is decreased. The cumulative actual recoveries are 12 units below the SAF threshold in period 3. However, 2 units were already used in the previous period; hence only 10 units are drawn by the issuer.

The gap between the SAF threshold and the cumulative actual recoveries is equal to 2 units in period 4, but 12 units were already used during the previous periods. This means that the SPV assets consist of 198 units (from collections) plus 12 units (from SAF), totalling 210 units, which is well above the SAF threshold. In this case, the issuer starts to reimburse those amounts previously drawn from the SAF.

[a] SAF threshold is the cumulative recovery scenario below which an SAF drawing is required.
[b] Reimbursement is the reimbursement of previously drawn amounts made by the SPV.

The credit profile of the collateral (typically cash or bonds, similar to that presented in mixed structure with collateral discussed next) and the timing and availability of the collateral will both be used to analyse the reduction of the exposure to the rating of the AF provider.

The second point above is usually mitigated by the fact that AF agreements usually provide that a substitute AF provider is to be found, within a short time frame, if the AF provider opts against renewing the AF term.

Should an AF provider fail to appoint a successor, it will be bound to pay an amount equivalent to the AF undrawn amount at that time. Exhibit 18.4 provides an example of an AF mechanism.

Mixed Structure with Collateral

In the mixed structure with collateral, the risk to investors is linked to the collections from the NPL portfolio and to the quality and availability of additional collateral (bonds, mainly Italian Treasury floating or fixed rate notes), which may be used in case of notes-related shortfall

EXHIBIT 18.5   Mixed Structure with Collateral

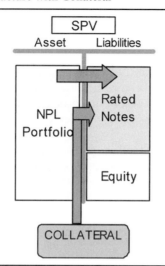

(see Exhibit 18.5). In several deals, this collateral was made available through a limited recourse loan structure. The rating on the notes depends on the credit analysis of the portfolio, as well as on the credit and market risk of the collateral (i.e., amount, rating, liquidity and market value) and the mechanics for its utilisation.

In addition, Moody's monitors the over-collateralisation ratio between the collateral and the rated notes, in order to ensure that this ratio does not fall below a certain threshold.

Usually, there are no rating triggers on the collateral and therefore any change of its rating might affect the rating of the issued notes. For instance, in May 2002, five Italian NPL transactions were upgraded following the upgrade of the Republic of Italy's rating.

Other Possible NPL Transaction Structures

Other types of NPL securitisation deal structures have included mixing portfolios of nonperforming loans with performing assets in order to provide certain cash flow stability, reach critical mass and reduce separate transaction costs.

One future structure for NPL transactions might be a synthetic one. In such a case, the risk of collections failing to meet certain predefined targets could "synthetically" be transferred to investors utilising a credit derivative contract. At the same time, the characteristics of the liability structure of the transaction could be adapted in order to better meet investors' appetites.

MOODY'S RATING METHODOLOGY

In terms of the portfolio's assets, the factors affecting the rating are the following:

- The characteristics of the NPL portfolio (e.g., secured versus unsecured NPLs; geographical breakdown; property type/location/valuation; legal status in foreclosure or insolvency procedures).
- The portfolio servicer's strategy and efficiency (e.g., servicer experience, resources).
- Any extra support availability (AF or collateral availability).

In terms of the liabilities:

- The payment priority on different notes (e.g., principal/ interest subordination) and any other structural features (e.g., liquidity, cash reserve, triggers, hedging).
- The servicer fees and running transaction costs (if not cash reserved).

The general modeling process is described in Exhibit 18.6.

In modeling asset flows, Moody's employs an approach that depends on the nature of the assets (i.e., whether they are secured or unsecured).

Cash Flow Analysis for Secured NPLs

For secured NPLs, Moody's methodology is based on a loan-by-loan analysis and uses two main assumptions: (1) the timing of collections and (2) the collected amounts.

Our assumptions concerning collection timing stem from the analysis of several factors, including:

- Type and stage of legal procedures (insolvency or foreclosure).
- Location of the court concerned.
- Servicer's estimated recovery timing (if available).
- Servicer's ability and experience to potentially minimise timing through a blend of legal and extrajudicial settlements.

EXHIBIT 18.6 Modeling Process

Moody's computes the recovery assumptions as the minimum of:

- Updated loan/claim amount (updated GBV which includes outstanding principal, accrued, and legal interest and other fees).
- Mortgage value (this is the maximum amount that the lender may claim on the real estate security and it usually ranges between 1.5 to 3 times the claim amount at origination).
- Updated forced sale value of the assets at time of recovery (please see below for "forced sale value" computation).

On top of that, Moody's evaluates the servicer's strategy, ability, and experience to potentially maximise value through a blend of legal and extrajudicial settlements.

Understanding the servicer's NPL strategy is a key factor in assessing the expected amount collected on a pool. Typically, servicers use two main recovery strategies:

1. *Traditional legal proceedings.* This is the standard option which allows the servicer to sue the debtor and to sell the property through auction[8]. Recovery amounts may be higher using this method but the timing to recoveries is slower and the costs associated with them higher. This strategy is typically used when the relationship with debtors is definitively jeopardised (i.e., a debtor is bankrupt).
2. *Extrajudicial Settlements or Discounted Payoffs (DPOs).* These are typically used when the actual debtor shows some willingness to settle the debt obligation avoiding traditional legal proceedings. Recovery amounts tend to be lower, but the timing to recoveries quicker. Thus, on a net present value basis, the net recovery amounts should be higher than those expected to be obtained though traditional legal proceedings. However, the ability to obtain maximum value DPOs depends significantly on the servicer's skill and experience and the security package.

With respect to the portion of the pool serviced through traditional legal proceedings, Moody's applies the following analysis.

Moody's looks at both the legal stage of a claim at the time of the transaction and the location of the court in which proceedings have been initiated. Based on both the typical timing between the various legal steps (from the beginning of the legal process to cash distribution) and the different timing associated with different Italian courts[9] to

---

[8] For a description of the several steps of traditional legal proceedings, refer to the Appendix to this chapter.

which the claims relate, an estimated recovery time will be calculated for each position in the portfolio.

For example, if a loan has just been declared in default and the relevant asset is located in Milan, collection timing would be determined by taking into account the time lag that is typically necessary for a court located in Milan to distribute cash collections after the security has been enforced following a declaration of default.

As for the determination of the amount to be collected through traditional legal proceedings, the analysis takes for each loan the minimum of:

■ The mortgage value (this is the maximum amount that the lender may claim on the real estate asset according to the lending agreement).
■ The amount of the loan/claim at the time of expected collection (including accrued legal interests).
■ The forced sale value (net of expenses) at the expected collection time. The forced sale value is derived from the asset market value (if available) and from property market trend expectations (in connection with asset type—residential, commercial, and industrial—and asset location).

The calculation of the first two values is relatively straightforward given that both are somehow known. However, the actual forced sale value of the property represents the true assumption, and its calculation may be divided into two steps: (1) a current assessment of the property value as of closing date of the transaction and (2) the expected evolution of the property value until the expected moment of the forced sale.

Since Moody's does not perform onsite valuations on every position in the portfolio, the current assessment of the price (the first point above) is determined by taking the lower of:

1. An updated independent third-party valuation.
2. A CTU.[10]
3. The estimated today's market value of the property, which is obtained by extrapolating the original valuation of the property. This is typically

---

[9] Moody's utilises its own assumptions on a court by court basis. For a general snapshot it should be noted that, according to the Bollettino di Vigilanza of the Bank of Italy (December 2001), Italian foreclosure proceedings for real estate have different timings depending on property location. Specifically, these are on average: 5.8 years for the northwest, 5.3 years for the northeast, 6.6 years for central Italy, 7.1 years for the south and islands.

[10] CTU stands for *Consulente Tecnico d'Ufficio* and is the official valuation utilised to set up the base price for a first auction in a foreclosure process.

done by multiplying the property original value by the average historical price growth rate of similar types of property (residential, commercial, etc.) located in the same province.[11]

An additional haircut of 20–40% may be taken on the above values, to consider the forced sale nature of the assets. This is mainly due to the common practice of reducing the property base sale price by 20% if the preceding auction was deserted.

In order to project the property current value into the future, Moody's derives some property price volatility assumptions from historical data.

These volatility assumptions are then applied to the current property price assessment according to the following formula:

$$\Delta p = \Delta p_0 + \lambda \sigma \Phi(t)$$

where

Δp_0 = the base case real estate price variation and is calculated with the following formula

$$p(t-1) \times \% \text{Growth}(t)$$

$p(t-1)$ = Property price at year $t-1$

$\Phi(t)$ = a function of volatility trough time, which is equal to square root of t minus the square ot $t-1$

$\lambda\sigma$ = a factor that takes account of the volatility of future prices

λ = an amplifying factor that follows a normal distribution $N(0,1)$

σ = the estimated volatility

$\% \text{Growth}(t)$ = what Moody's considers to be its base case assumption for the future evolution of Real Estate prices in Italy

The estimated volatility, σ, ranges from 2–10% and varies with both the geographically location of the underlying property and the asset type (residential, commercial, industrial, and so on). Hence, the initial property price increases or decreases through time until the expected resolution date explained earlier. Each of these scenarios of property price volatility is normally distributed.

---

[11] Moody's obtained data on real estate price historical cycles trough the Tamborino database publication.

EXHIBIT 18.7 Values Used for %Growth(t) Used in the Illustration

Year	%Growth(t)
1	0.0%
2	1.5%
3	3.0%
4	4.6%
5	6.1%
6	0.8%
7	−2.2%
8	−3.2%
9	−1.7%
10	−0.2%
11	1.2%
12	2.8%
13	4.3%

%Growth(t) depends on the asset type (residential, commercial, or industrial) and on the geographical location (i.e., northern province, central province, etc.). This function has been created as an extrapolation of the recent cycles of the Italian real estate market.

Using an estimated volatility (σ) of 4% and a %Growth(t) showed in Exhibit 18.7, Exhibit 18.8 displays an example of how the initial property price (100%) of a residential property located in the south of Italy increases or decreases through time. Each curve represents property price variations through the expected resolution time (13 years). Exhibit 18.7's legend shows the cumulative probability of each property price curve. For example, the probability of being below the property price curve scenario corresponding to six standard deviations away from the mean case is approximately 0.0000003% and the probability of being below the property price curve scenario corresponding to the mean case is exactly 50%. The scenario corresponding to a cumulative probability of 50% is, in fact, the mean scenario.

Multiple collection scenarios are obtained and distributed through the priority of payments of the transaction. The loss on the notes, if any, and the average life are calculated for each scenario. Subsequently, the probability of each scenario is multiplied by the loss and average life of each tranche to obtain the expected loss and expected average life of each tranche of the issued notes. From this, Moody's determines a rating thanks to its idealised loss table.

EXHIBIT 18.8 Property Price Variations

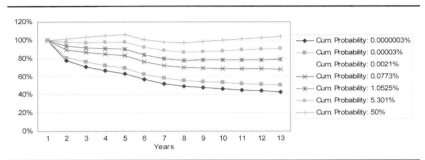

With respect to the portion of the pool serviced through DPOs, Moody's applies the following analysis. The effect of DPOs is the mere redistribution of cash flows during the first three to four years of a transaction life, thereby providing a benefit in terms of time value of money. Some limited credit to DPOs may be given depending on the servicer's track record. For instance, 5% of total final expected cash flows may be redistributed during the first three years of a deal's life to account for DPOs.

Cash Flow Analysis for Unsecured NPLs

To model the recovery cash flow profile of assets where a high-ranking economic lien on real estate collateral is not part of the security package, Moody's uses a static pool analysis (i.e., historical vintage data analysis). In most cases, Moody's has received this data for periods covering 10 to 15 years and representing amounts recovered through time as a percentage of certain predefined value (gross book value, net book value, or principal outstanding) as of default date, on an annual basis.

Understanding how these recoveries are calculated and presented may not be a simple task. For instance, in the event that recoveries represent a certain percentage of an NBV defaulted amount for several years in the past, we need to account for the fact that the NBV itself changes through time (given that it includes provisions for loss which are periodically updated). Then, if five years ago, the NBV of a defaulted asset was €100 and is now €50, this may not mean that we have already recovered €50 or that we now provision €50 for loss.

The timing and amount of average (mean) collections (gross recoveries) are established through a thorough understanding of historical data which must be representative of the securitised portfolio. Finally, an assumption of the collections' volatility around the mean assumed path is also derived from the data. Given that the data somehow represents the securitised portfolio track record, the rationale behind the approach is to assume a mean recovery experience for each of the newer vintages looking at the experience of the older ones.

The underlying concept behind this methodology is that, all else being equal, the more seasoned the vintage, the less cash flows are "still to come." In contrast, the younger the vintage, the more cash flows are ahead. Clearly, in terms of volatility of the recovery paths, the latter may be encountering higher volatility than the former, mainly due to recoveries being a more distant "future projection" as explained in the more detail in the example below.

After Moody's has assumed a cumulated long-term mean recovery amount to each vintage, a cash flow analysis is performed, testing the liability structure of the transaction, accounting for the particularities of each transaction structure, under recovery scenarios that are several "standard deviations away" from the mean. In this way, Moody's analysis covers any scenario with a nonnegligible probability of occurrence. To calculate these probabilities Moody's uses a standard normal probability distribution with historical mean and standard deviation.

Other Qualitative Issues Accounted for in the Modeling

As in every transaction, Moody's must adapt its modeling to take into consideration the particularities of the transaction. For example:

- Asset diversification: Highly diversified portfolios usually have less volatile collection profiles. Herfindarl index, geographical diversity, and asset-type diversity are good indicators of diversification.
- With regard to static pool analysis for unsecured portfolios, a good understanding of data definition is required (data presentation is not standardised).
- Results and assumptions are benchmarked with previously rated transactions for consistency purposes.
- Concentration analysis is performed, where the top positions (top 1/top 5/top 10/top 20) per recovery cash flows are singled out, to test the rating sensitivity to the success of these positions.
- Other important particularities which may impact the transaction's cash flows are accounted for. For example, agricultural credits, subsidised loans, loans to public entities, buildings under construction, pollution or environmental issues, reperforming mortgages, volcanic/seismic activity, organised crime, and particular asset exposure such as hotels or hospitals.
- Overall information quality.
- The servicer's current and future capacity to service the portfolio.

THE SERVICER

Since the performance of an NPL deal is largely based on the ability to actively resolve defaulted loans, servicers play a crucial role in such transactions. Almost all cash flows pertaining to an NPL securitisation stem from active servicing or are a direct result of actions taken by a servicer. This is significantly different from the case of performing asset securitisations, where most debtors make regular payments to their servicer pursuant to their loan agreements.

Servicers can essentially be broken down into two different classes: (1) a primary servicer and (2) a special servicer. Typically, a *primary servicer* was also the originating bank of the debt obligations and has become the servicer of the securitised NPL portfolio. A *special servicer* is a servicing company specialising in the resolution of distressed loans. The special servicer may or may not be part of the originating banking group.

In recent years, there has been an increasing trend towards more special servicers in the Italian market. There are currently five special servicers which manage Italian NPL public securitisations of over €200 million, namely: MPS Banca Gestione Crediti S.p.A. (Ulisse deals), SIB (ICR deals), IntesaBci Gestione Crediti S.p.A. (Intesa Sec. NPL), S.G.C. S.p.A. (Ares transactions), and Italfondiario S.p.A. (Palazzo). There is also an Italian Special Servicer Association.

A servicer's strategy is mirrored in its NPL managing procedures and IT system. It is essential for a servicer to have accurate updated information regarding securitised loans (e.g., the exact amount recovered by all its branches on a daily basis, all the information related to each loan) and to manage all the information by means of an efficient IT system.

Operational Review

In any NPL transaction (as well as in a performing deal), Moody's meets with the servicer. This meeting aims at both understanding its experience, capability and organisational structure and evaluating how effective the servicer is at either preventing defaults or maximising the recoveries to a transaction when defaults take place. The servicer's IT systems and reporting capacity are evaluated as well.

Furthermore, on every NPL transaction where good-quality real estate collateral is the cash flow driver, Moody's performs site visits on several selected assets in the portfolio in an attempt to cover the main asset types and locations, as well as the largest concentrations. During these site visits, usually performed together with the servicer's team, asset valuation, business plans and strategy for each selected asset are discussed.

Ultimately, some servicers may put in place a separate legal unit, usually known as a *real estate-owned company* (REO or REOCO) or *real estate unit*), aiming at shortening the loan resolution process. This unit, which is run by the servicer, may bid at auctions. Typical considerations to utilise this mechanism relate to the servicer's expected open market values, expected recovery values and expected timing. The unit will sell the property on the open market and repay the debt with the proceeds of the sale. Moody's views this procedure favourably as it enlarges the base of potential buyers when compared with an auction, given that numerous individuals may visit the property and obtain mortgage finance for the acquisition. Therefore, it will potentially help to increase collections, given that a distressed sale is replaced by an open market sale.

SOME INTERNATIONAL INSIGHTS

Due to the lack of a scheduled amortisation plan, NPL portfolio cash flows may prove to be more volatile than those related to other types of assets (such as RMBS). As a consequence, the level of protection usually transferred to investors through credit enhancement is high if compared to other asset classes. Enhancement (i.e., overcollateralisation) is typically calculated as the difference between 100% and the ratio between the total amount of rated notes and the portfolio GBV.

The Italian market has witnessed various Aaa credit enhancement levels based on GBV, ranging from 47% (e.g., Argo Finance) to 94% (e.g., Ulisse 2), depending upon portfolio characteristics (secured vs. unsecured, geographical distribution, etc.) and external support, if any. Exhibit 18.9 provides a summary of the NPL transactions rated by Moody's on the Italian market.

The overcollateralisation level for rated NPL-backed notes may vary according to the specifics of the transaction. In Japanese securitisations, for instance, this ratio ranges from 50–60%. These values are lower than the Italian levels for several reasons:

1. The method used to compute the ratio is different: Japanese transactions use the future cash flow (prospective cash collection amount) estimated by Moody's rather than its GBV. This is because the future cash flow is typically much lower than GBV (i.e., 10–20% of GBV) due to a drastic decline of land price, thereby explaining the above-mentioned difference. Recently Moody's rated some Japanese NPL deals (e.g., RCC Trust—II, RCC Trust—III and J—CORE NPL1 K.K.), where the ratio of Aaa rated notes on future cash flow ranged from 45–50%.

EXHIBIT 18.9 Italian NPL Transactions Rated By Moody's

Deal Name	Closing date	Rated notes	Rated notes in % of GBV	Special Servicer	REO
Antenore Finance SpA	10-Oct-01	170.0	21%	No	No
Ares Finance S.r.l.	18-Sep-01	580.0	38%	Yes	Yes
Ares Finance 2 S.A.	6-Dec-01	405.0	33%	Yes	Yes
Argo Finance One S.r.l.	23-Mar-01	110.0	27%	No	No
Creso 1 S.r.l.	1-Mar-00	20.0	18%	No	No
Island Finance (ICR 4) S.p.A.	31-Dec-99	380.0	27%	Yes	No
International Credit Recovery (ICR 5) S.r.l.	30-May-00	694.4	48%	Yes	Yes
International Credit Recovery (ICR 6) S.r.l.	1-Dec-00	1017.0	44%	Yes	Yes
IntesaBci Sec. NPL S.p.A.	15-Jun-01	366.0	41%	Yes	No
Island Finance 2 (ICR 7) S.r.l.	15-Mar-02	345.0	29%	Yes	Yes
Minerva S.r.l.	21-Dec-00	60.0	28%	No	No
Palazzo Finance Tre S.r.l.	26-Nov-02	600.0	37%	Yes	No
Perseo Finance S.r.l.	3-Dec-99	85.0	21%	No	No
Quadrifoglio S.r.L.Series 2001	20-Apr-01	7.2	13%	No	No
Theano Finance Spa	10-Dec-01	205.0	10%	No	No
Tiepolo Finance S.r.l.	5-Jul-01	105.0	35%	No	No
Tiepolo Finance 2 S.r.l.	23-Apr-03	185.0	23%	No	No
Trevi Finance SpA	21-Jul-99	775.0	29%	No	No
Trevi Finance N.2 S.p.A.	20-Apr-00	850.0	35%	No	No
Trevi Finance N.3 S.r.l.	25-May-01	750.0	27%	No	No
Ulisse S.p.A.	15-May-01	194.0	36%	Yes	No
Ulisse 2 S.p.A.	15-Aug-01	210.0	23%	Yes	No
Ulisse 3 S.p.A.	10-Oct-01	140.0	37%	Yes	No
Ulisse 4 S.r.l.	20-Dec-01	9.0	9%	Yes	No
Vindex S.r.l.	24-Apr-03	59.0	29%	Yes	Yes

2. Japanese transactions have different recovery timings and structural characteristics. The Ministry of Justice and Japanese courts have recently announced that the average period from foreclosure filing to cash distribution is steadily falling towards approximately one year, whereas the Italian average is a 7-year period. With respect to structural differences, Japan applies the fast pay structure, which aligns the interest of bondholder with that of the equity holder with provision for principal repayment subject to the availability of excess cash flow. An advance facility is usually made available by the servicer, with the purpose of paying real estate properties' foreclosure and maintenance costs rather than note-related shortfalls. In that sense, the Japanese NPL structure is similar to the "standard structure" described earlier in this chapter where we covered key structures used in NPL Transactions.

Recently, Japanese banks have been eager to cut NPLs from their balance sheet. As a result NPL but also SPL (subperforming loan) securitisations are emerging.

In the United States., NPL deals generally contain a specific mix of different types of loans, including nonperforming, reperforming, and even performing loans. Overall, Moody's Aaa credit support on a NPL securitisation will vary, ranging from 18% of original pool balance (GBV) on a good subprime pool to as high as 50% on a weak high-LTV loan pool, excluding any benefit for spread or other deal-specific features.

APPENDIX: THE TRADITIONAL PROCEDURE AND TIMING TO ENFORCE A MORTGAGE LOAN.

1. *Injunction to pay.* To start the procedure, the lender needs a Writ of Enforcement (*titolo esecutivo*) from a court bailiff and has to notify the debtor with an order to pay the amount due within 10 days from the notification (*precetto*). The enforcement procedure can start after that period has elapsed, but within 90 days from the injunction to pay (*precetto* notification).

2. *Deed of Attachment and sale petition.* Following the above notification, the lender is also required to notify the debtor of a deed of attachment (*atto di pignoramento*). Within 10 days from the date of the notification of the deed of attachment, the lender is required to file a sale petition or an assignment petition: the former requests the court to arrange for the sale of the property, whereas the latter requests the court to sell the property to the mortgagee in satisfaction of its claims up the market price of the property.

3. *Mortgage documentation.* After the sale/assignment petition is notified, the lender is required to file a documentation relating the mortgaged property with the court. The judge typically fixes a term of 120 days for the above documentation filing.

4. *Hearing.* Provided that the property documentation has been deposited with the court, the judge sets a hearing in order to hear all the parties involved in the enforcement procedure. If there is no opposition to the forced sale, the judge authorises the sale of the property. It is to note that an opposition may substantially delay an enforcement procedure (two to three years depending on court location and issued raised with the opposition).

5. *Appointment of the CTU (*Consulente Tecnico d'Ufficio*).* After two to three months from the hearing authorising the sale of the property, the judge typically appoints a technical consultant (CTU) in order to estimate the value of the property and to fix the base sale price of the auction. The CTU is usually requested to produce his report within three months time or, in the case of complex valuations, within six to seven months time. At the same time the judge sets a new hearing for the report discussion. After the report has been discussed, the parties often ask a further term to examine the (typically six months).

6. *Sale order.* Once the evaluation procedure has come to an end, the judge decides whether the sale is to be carried out by auction (majority of cases) or by a private sale.

   With a sale order, the judge fixes both the base sale price and the minimum amount of the bids.

7. *The Auction.* The auction takes place in the public hearing room of the relevant court under the judge supervision. Only those who have deposited a bond may be admitted (for avoidance of doubt the debtor cannot participate to the auction).

8. *Deserted auction.* Ten days after a deserted auction sale, the judge sets a new hearing, where he has three options:

   (i) Decide on the assignment petition which creditors may file before the court. An assignment petition must contain the offer to buy the property at a price equal or exceeding the base price.
   (ii) Order the judicial administration of the mortgaged property until a new auction is set.
   (iii) Order a new auction sale.

It is important to highlight that when the judge decides to set a new auction sale he or she is also allowed to reduce up to 20% the base sale price fixed in the preceding auction.

9. *Adjudication.* Provided that, in the 10 days following the latest auction, no bids are made for a price 1/6 higher than the adjudication price, the property is adjudicated to the highest bidder.

10. *Payment of sale price and proceeds distributions.* Within 30 days from the payment of the purchase price, the judge draws up a plan for the proceeds distributions among creditors.

Whole Business Securitisation

Whole Business Securitisation

Anant Ramgarhia
Associate Director
ABN AMRO

Miray Muminoglu
Vice President
JP Morgan

Oleg Pankratov
Executive Director
ABN AMRO

In simple terms, a *whole business securitisation* (WBS) can be viewed as repackaging of the credit risk associated with a highly levered long-term financing of an operating company into different tranches of both investment grade and subinvestment grade debt. Debt is serviced, usually on an ongoing basis, primarily out of the future cash flows generated by the business of the operating company or, in case of a financial distress, out of liquidation proceeds of the company's assets like real estate and inventory.

A quick comparison with standard securitisation structures suggests that WBS is considerably more holistic in approach—a standard securitisation isolates and ring-fences only specific cash-generating assets (e.g., credit cards, auto loans, receivables, noncore real estate, etc.). Cash flow from only the isolated assets can be used to service the securitised debt. WBS on the other hand is, in principle, "operating assets securitisation;" that is, all assets of the business critical to generating cash flow are involved—this includes inventory, real estate, plant and machinery, brand names and trademarks, and so on. Security over substantially all of the operating assets is usually granted by means of a fixed and floating charge, though, as discussed later, security may also be granted in other forms, depending upon the legal jurisdiction in question.

If looked at from a slightly different perspective, WBS can be considered to be the product of a financial cross between pure secured corporate debt issuance on one hand and the more traditional and commoditised asset-backed securities (e.g., mortgage-backed securities) on the other. Transactions carry a reasonable amount of pure corporate and management risk, to the extent that servicing of the debt is dependent upon the performance of the business as a whole. This is in sharp contrast with traditional securitisation structures that completely isolate the performance risk of the securitised assets from other associated business risks. On the other hand, just like traditional securitisation structures, WBS structures also include features like liquidity facilities and prefunded reserves.

Its inherent hybrid characteristics make "whole business" an esoteric asset class within the world of asset-backed securitisation.

GROWTH AND MARKET DEVELOPMENT

WBS emerged in the UK in the mid-1990s with the securitisation of future cash flows of a nursing home. Initially concentrated to a handful of transactions, average WBS transaction size has leap-frogged from just over £200 million in the mid-1990s to over £1 billion in the early years of the new millennium. As shown in Exhibit 19.1, alongside the average transaction size, the number of issuances as well as the nature of businesses fruitfully exploiting WBS as an effective refinancing tool has also increased manifold.

Majority of the growth in the WBS market has been triggered by the fact that a WBS structure can support significantly higher level of leverage than conventional unsecured corporate debt issuance. This has been made possible due to WBS structures allowing considerably longer debt tenors, typically between 20 to 30 years, as against conventional leveraged financing tenors between 7 to 10 years. The mechanics of the structure, together with a good degree of credit enhancement and a tight covenant package governing the operation of the business, act as mitigants to risks normally perceived in a conventional financing plan and therefore provide adequate comfort for higher levels of leverage supported by WBS. A comparatively lower cost of funds, thanks to a rating upgrade over the underlying corporate rating of potentially one to four notches, is an added advantage.[1]

---

[1] Standard & Poor's, "Principles for Analyzing Structured Finance/Corporate Hybrid Transactions," July 2, 2001.

EXHIBIT 19.1 WBS Market Evolution

Year	No. of WBS Issuances	Total Issuance Volume (£ million)	Average Issuance Size (£ million)	Range of Businesses Using WBS
1997	2	421	211	Nursing homes, motorway operators
1998	4	1,028	257	Pubs, hotels, motorway operators
1999	8	2,222	278	Nursing homes, pubs, theme parks, airports, ferry operators
2000	6	2,184	364	Pubs, theatres, healthcare
2001	9	4,698	522	Food manufacturing, water utilities, pubs, port authorities, healthcare, office telephone systems, ferry operators
2002	7	7,004	1,001	Pubs, television rentals, ferry operators, healthcare, water utilities, forestry lands
2003[a]	5	3,050	610	Funeral services, healthcare, care homes, water utilities, London Underground

[a] Year-to-date September 2003
Source: Analysis of publicly available information by the authors.

Higher debt quantum and lower cost of funds have led financial sponsors over the past few years to aggressively use WBS as an effective tool for acquisition financing (or refinancing) in the context of leveraged buyouts.

BASIC WBS STRUCTURE

The basic underlying legal structure of a WBS is based on the UK-secured loan framework rather than a true sale of assets (see Exhibit 19.2).

A special purpose vehicle (SPV) is set up to issue the securitised debt. With the proceeds of the issuance, the SPV makes a secured loan to the ring-fenced operating company or companies (the "borrower"). The loan is

EXHIBIT 19.2   The UK-Secured Loan Framework for WBS

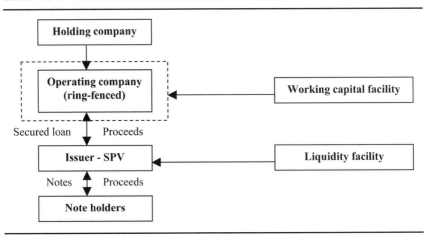

secured by a fixed and floating charge over substantially all the operating assets of the borrower. The borrower repays the loan periodically out of the cash flows generated from its business. Liquidity facility is usually established to fund temporary cash flow shortfalls at the SPV level, while working capital facility is usually established at the borrower level to fund the interyear fluctuations of the working capital of the seasonal businesses.

An in-depth analysis of the above structure reveals that the UK-secured loan legal framework, inherent in the Insolvency Act of 1986, forms the backbone of WBS transactions. Key to the secured loan framework is the ability to grant fixed and floating charge over substantially all the operating assets of the borrower. The charge is usually held by a security trustee who acts on behalf of and in the best interests of the note holders. The charge conveys upon the security trustee the right to appoint an administrative receiver in the event of default under the WBS debt. The administrative receiver can then assume responsibility for managing the business and, acting for the note holders, can ensure that note holders are repaid in full.

The recent changes to the Insolvency Act of 1986, including restrictions on the creditors' right to appoint an administrative receiver, do not affect the WBS capital market transactions larger than £50 million.

ALTERNATIVE WBS STRUCTURES

Secured creditors enjoy an advantageous preferential position upon the insolvency of a company only in a limited number of legal jurisdictions (e.g., New Zealand and Australia) besides the UK. In most of the Continental European countries as also in the United States, the fate of the creditors in general is decided by the court. The court, in turn, may appoint an insolvency administrator to ensure that the interests of all creditors (not only the secured creditors) of the insolvent company is protected. In such jurisdictions, due to the nature of the insolvency regime, issuing corporates are generally not able to grant a floating charge over substantially all of their operating assets. This lack of ability to grant security to potential note holders by means of a floating charge and lack of ability to control insolvency proceedings via appointment of an administrative receiver potentially restricts the applicability of WBS in such jurisdictions.

However, in the recent past, issuers have got around this legal bottleneck by developing more customised WBS structures. These alternative structures ensure business continuity in the face of a potential event of default, such that cash flows continue to be generated and the WBS debt continues to be serviced. A prime example of such an alternative structure is Tenovis Finance Limited,[2] a path-breaking €300 million WBS which came to the market in 2001 (see Exhibit 19.3). The transaction was the first secured loan structure in Germany, and the WBS debt is secured by receipts under lease and service outsourcing contracts for

EXHIBIT 19.3   Tenovis Finance Limited: Simplified WBS Transaction Structure[a]

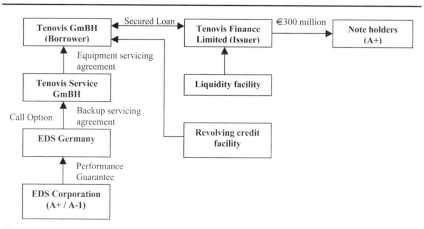

[a] The detailed transaction structure can be found on page 3 of Moody's pre-sale report, "Tenovis Finance Limited" (October 15, 2001), and page 2 of Standard and Poor's new issue report, "Tenovis Finance Limited" (October 15, 2001).

---

[2] Tenovis is a leading office telephone systems provider in Germany. Detailed pre-sale reports for this transaction can be found on www.standardandpoors.com and www.moodys.com

private automated branch exchange systems (PABX) to over 40,000 German corporates. Equipment is rented by customers under five- to ten-year contracts, under which Tenovis also continues to provide maintenance on the equipment. Early termination clauses in the lease contracts provide that customers have to pay up to 95% of the present value of future lease payments in the case of an early termination.

The structure was designed to ring-fence the operations of Tenovis akin to the popular UK WBS structure. Effective bankruptcy remoteness was achieved, despite Tenovis performance risk and limited value of the underlying collateral, by appointing a rated backup servicer (EDS Germany) at the very outset of the transaction. Under the backup servicing agreement, upon the occurrence of certain trigger events, the backup servicer would assume all obligations and rights under the equipment servicing agreements and effectively replace Tenovis. This ensures business continuity and cash flow generation by means of availability of a fully functional maintenance operation upon the insolvency of Tenovis. Additionally, since the back-up servicer may also need the employees and technological know-how of Tenovis to continue performing the servicing and maintenance obligations under the original contracts, it also has a call option to acquire all shares in or assets of Tenovis at a fair market value.

It is important to note here that under the German Insolvency Code, the court appoints an insolvency administrator to monitor the interests of all the creditors. However, the structure derives comfort from the fact that it may not be unreasonable to believe that the administrator, acting in the best interests of the creditors, would actually allow EDS to carry on the business in a post-Tenovis insolvency scenario. Given that there is very little tangible collateral with a substantial postinsolvency sale value in the business, business continuity is likely to be the most economically viable route to generate cash and pay off the creditors.

Besides structures customised for particular legal jurisdictions, Moody's has published a more generic (US-oriented) WBS structure which in turn can be tailor-made for specific legal regimes (see Exhibit 19.4).[3] Moody's generic structure captures the essential ideas underlying most WBS structures.

In the generic structure shown in Exhibit 19.4, the operating company transfers its operating assets to a holding SPV in return for its equity, equity (H). Equity (H) is then transferred to another newly-formed SPV, the issuer SPV, in return for its equity, equity (I). The operating company, therefore, finally ends up holding equity in the Issuer SPV, that is, equity (I). The issuer SPV sells notes to note holders,

---

[3] *Moody's Special Report*, "Moody's Approach to Rating Operating Company Securitizations," February 8, 2002.

EXHIBIT 19.4   Moody's Generic WBS Structure

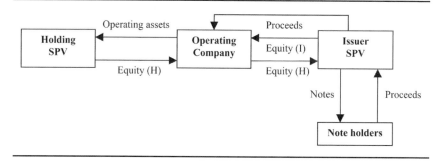

backed by its holding of equity (H). The proceeds are then passed on to the operating company in the form of a one-time dividend. At closing, the operating company enters into agreements with the holding SPV and the issuer SPV to service the assets in the holding SPV. A backup servicer may also be appointed to service the operating assets in the holding SPV, should the operating company become insolvent.

In summary, though different WBS structures allow security over the operating assets to be passed on to the note holders in different ways, the underlying theme centres around the ability to carry on the business as a going concern in a postinsolvency scenario.

BUSINESS CHARACTERISTICS FAVOURABLE FOR WBS

Not all businesses are prime WBS candidates. Given the relatively long tenor of WBS debt and also its usual sequential pay-down profile, it is important that a business issuing WBS debt demonstrates a reasonable degree of stability in generating cash flows over the years in order to be in a position to comfortably meet its debt service obligations. Standard and Poor's places great emphasis on cash flow predictability and asset diversity in evaluating WBS transactions.[4] Besides a stable and predictable cash flow stream, businesses that generate cash flows from a number of well-diversified discrete assets are usually considered to be prime candidates for WBS. Ideally, the higher the cash flow predictability and the asset diversity, the better a business is suited for a potential WBS.

In general, businesses, which exhibit the following characteristics, are ideal candidates for WBS:

---

[4] Standard and Poor's, "Principles for Analyzing Structured Finance/Corporate Hybrid Transactions."

Immunity from economic cycles. Building over and above the cash flow predictability argument, it is equally essential the businesses which lend themselves to WBS have an ability to generate cash evenly over the entire course of an economic cycle. An impairment of cash generation ability during economic recessions can severely impact the ability of a business to meet debt service coverage during such periods and therefore potentially lead to a default situation under the WBS structure. It is for this reason that businesses with "utility-like" cash flows are best suited for WBS—utilities, by definition, are essential services and continue to remain in demand, not withstanding the general overall economic situation.

Earnings with a high cash component. Often, businesses that report consistent earnings year after year may not be the ones that actually have a stable cash generation profile. This may happen due to a variety of reasons, such as, sporadic and lumpy capex profile, cash tied up in working capital, and so on. Given that WBS debt usually has a sequential pay-down profile, it is important that not only the cash from operations, but also the other cash items (including capital expenditure, tax and changes in working capital) be reasonably stable and predictable for the business to churn out reasonable amounts of cash year after year. Therefore, it is essential that the overall business model be reasonably cash generative.

Fortified market position. A fortified market position is created not only by an existing strong market share situation, but also by the fact that the market be reasonably well-guarded by barriers to entry. This is in line with the argument around business continuity and stable cash flow generation which is central to all WBS transactions.

Regulatory environment. The regulatory environment (or the lack of it) in which the business operates can be both a pro and a con from the WBS perspective. Clearly, in the case of WBS in the UK water utility sector, regulation is a plus in so far as it obviates the pressure of competition and provides substantial comfort around the financial viability and continuity of the business being securitised. However, viewed from a different perspective, regulation can also be a cause for concern in as much as the government takes a view on privatisation of certain businesses and allows greater competition to infiltrate previously protected grounds as a means of allowing the end-consumer to make the final choice.

Value realisation strategies upon a potential insolvency. This follows directly from Standard & Poor's argument about asset diversity being important for WBS transactions. A good example to note here is WBS in the UK pub sector. Pubs in the UK clearly represent a portfolio of well-diversified and discrete cash generating assets. In the potential event of an insolvency of the borrower under the WBS, an administrative receiver has multiple strategies to realise value out of the estate, that is, it may choose to carry on the business of the entire portfolio as a going concern, or he may choose to sell a certain portion of the portfolio and continue managing the rest; or it may choose to sell the entire portfolio. WBS structures with such multiple value realisation strategies provide great comfort to note holders.

Actively managed property portfolio with an alternative use value. In most cases, the property portfolio of the business constitutes the underlying collateral for a WBS. Most WBS offering circulars carry a valuation report from a firm of certified property valuation professionals expressing opinion on the value (usually existing use value, discussed in greater detail in the next section) of the underlying property portfolio. All else being the same, for a given level of LTV (Loan-to-Value) ratio, the higher the property valuation, the higher is the debt quantum supported by the WBS. Therefore, it is absolutely essential that the property portfolio is well-maintained and actively managed. Alternative use value for the properties is necessary so as to be able to delink the WBS structure from the business of the borrower. A high alternative use value provides disposal proceeds in a fire-sale situation to meet debt service obligations.

Besides the above, rating agencies and investors also attach considerable importance to the tenure (i.e., freehold, long-leasehold or short-leasehold) of the underlying properties. This is discussed at length in the next section.

RATING AGENCY APPROACH TO SIZING WBS

Expressing the WBS debt quantum as a multiple of earnings before interest, taxes, depreciation, and amortisation (EBITDA) is common among the financial sponsors, arrangers, investors, and rating agencies. Exhibit 19.5 sets out WBS EBITDA multiples achieved on certain businesses in the past.

EXHIBIT 19.5   Select WBS EBITDA Multiples

Industry	EBITDA Multiple Range
Pubs	5.8×–10.0×
Healthcare	5.7×–7.3×
Ferry Operators, Port Authorities	5.5×–8.7×
Theatres, Theme Parks	6.1×–6.6×
Motorway Operators	9.0×–11.9×

Source: Analysis of publicly available information by the authors.

As an EBITDA multiple is such a popular metric, it is a common misconception that WBS sizing is based on assigning an EBITDA multiple attributable to a specific business. In fact, the rating agencies approach is much more complex and, in addition to general credit and structure analysis, typically includes the following:

■ Cash flow analysis and modeling
■ Analysis of real estate valuation and LTV ratio
■ Minimum equity level analysis

Cash Flow Considerations

Rating agencies' cash flow analysis establishes the ability of the securitised business to generate adequate cash, even during periods of economic stress, to comfortably service the WBS debt. It is important that the cash flow tests are designed so as to be able to determine the ability of the business to generate cash continually year after year—this is because most WBS transactions have amortising debt pay-down profiles.

Cash flow stresses used by the rating agencies are designed to identify key drivers of business' cash flow and examine a variety of scenarios (or even use Monte Carlo simulations) to determine how these drivers may potentially behave over the life of the transaction. These cash flow stresses can be broadly classified as margin squeeze stress and recessionary stress.

Margin Squeeze Stress

Margin squeeze stresses usually concentrate on implicitly stressing the underlying EBITDA by stressing the overall or specific elements of revenue and cost items. These stresses usually tend to affect the entire remaining term of the securitisation from the moment they first hit the transaction cash flows, rather than being concentrated over predefined time pockets. The severity of the stress may vary with the different rating levels being sought on different tranches of the WBS debt.

A good example of a margin squeeze stress is the one used by Fitch Ratings in a 2002 UK healthcare WBS.[5] Taking a view that the UK healthcare sector had in general witnessed an increase in staff costs over the years, Fitch used this cost item to simulate a margin squeeze on the cash flows of the hospital group being securitised. At the A rating level, it was assumed that all staff costs increased by 1.10% per annum for the entire life of the transaction. Revenue and other costs were held constant. This had the effect of gradually reducing the EBITDA margin from 21% at the outset of the transaction to 7% at the deal end. Margin stress at the BBB rating level again involved keeping revenue and non-staff costs constant, and applying a 1.00% per annum increase in staff costs. This gradually reduced the EBITDA margin to 8.5% at the deal end.

Similar stresses have also been actively used by the rating agencies in the context of WBS within the UK pub sector, the key stress variable being a gradual decline in beer margins over the term of the securitisation.

Recessionary Stress

Recessionary stresses are engineered to test the robustness and resilience of the WBS structure in periods of economic difficulties. Unlike margin squeeze stresses that are more gradual from a timing perspective, recessionary stresses are more in the nature of "financial shocks" and directly impact the EBITDA of the business. These stresses usually last over a pre-defined number of stress periods, where each period in turn may have a pre-defined number of stress years. It is common to see three recessionary stress periods, each period lasting for three years, over a 25-year WBS structure. A good example of the recessionary stress used by the agencies is the cash flow analysis performed by Fitch in the case of THPA Finance Limited, a WBS of port operation business in the UK.[6] In this transaction, on an average, EBITDA was reduced by 40% at the A stress level, 25% at the BBB stress level, and 10% at the BB stress level for the term of the transaction. Credit for inflation was given only at the BB level.

Real Estate/Valuation Considerations

The rating agencies attach considerable importance to a detailed property analysis and the valuation of the underlying portfolio in sizing and rating WBS debt. Besides the valuation of the property portfolio as a whole, the agencies often tend to split up the portfolio by the tenure of the underlying properties, that is, freehold, long leasehold, and short leasehold. Leasehold properties with remaining lease terms in excess of

---

[5] Fitch Ratings Pre-Sale Report, "UK Hospitals No. 1 S.A.," June 20, 2002.
[6] Fitch Ratings Pre-Sale Report, "THPA Finance Limited," March 20, 2001.

the proposed tenor of the WBS are usually considered to be long lease-holds; other leasehold properties are usually considered to be short-leaseholds. In most cases rating agencies conservatively assume for modeling purposes that the cash flows associated with short leasehold properties only continue until the expiry of the lease.

Moving on to the valuation of the entire property portfolio, it is important in the first place as it indicates the levels of LTV up to which the rating agencies are comfortable in rating the different tranches of WBS debt.[7] Historically, however, WBS LTV levels have varied considerably even within similar businesses. For example, in the case of WBS in the UK pubs sector, LTV levels have ranged from around 63%[8] on some of the more recent transactions to 85%[9] on some of the more previous transactions. Therefore, LTV may not necessarily be the best yardstick for comparing transactions across the WBS spectrum. This is due to the obvious differences between a pure property-based structured financing and a WBS, which actually involves much more than only a securitisation of cash flows from the underlying properties.

Minimum Equity Considerations

The amount of equity in the capital structure of the business is an indication of the financial sponsor's commitment to the business. The rating agencies look upon this component as incentive for the financial sponsor/management to keep the business healthy and profitable, something that is of critical importance in WBS to be able to meet debt service obligations in the first place. Though there are no set benchmarks, depending upon the business being securitised, the agencies may require a certain minimum level of equity to be left in the business.[10] The purchase price paid by the financial sponsor, less the minimum equity component, may potentially act as a cap on the WBS debt quantum.

---

[7] Property valuations for WBS transactions are mostly carried out on an *existing use value* basis. This implies valuation of the properties fully equipped as operational entities and having regard to their trading potential, that is, valuation of the properties as a collective whole necessary to keep the business going, rather than an arithmetical summation of standalone valuations of individual properties. The relevance of such a valuation methodology for WBS is quite intuitive, given that WBS relies upon business continuity rather than a liquidation and disposal of assets to ultimately repay the note holders.

[8] Spirit Funding Limited, April 2002.

[9] Punch Taverns Finance Plc, March 1998.

[10] For some WBS transactions in the regulated UK water sector, the agencies have often not attached much importance to the equity component of the business and have allowed leverage levels up to 93% of the Regulated Asset Base (RAB) of the business. For further details, see Standard & Poor's Pre-Sale Report, "Dwr Cymru Financing Limited," April 2, 2001.

KEY FINANCIAL AND OPERATING COVENANTS GOVERNING WBS

Though a WBS allows raising long-term financing at a relatively competitive cost of funds, the underlying legal structure clearly defines certain covenants around cash take-out and business operations in order to protect the interests of the note holders. Some of the significant material covenants governing WBS are discussed below.

Debt Service Coverage Ratios

Covenants typically include quarterly coverage ratios tests. Typical examples are debt service coverage ratio (DSCR) defined as EBITDA divided by debt service (being the sum of net interest and mandatory principal repayments) and free cash flow debt service coverage ratio (FCDSCR) defined as free cash flow[11] divided by debt service. The issuer is usually required to maintain a DSCR at a minimum of 1.25×–1.30× and FCDSCR at a minimum of 1.1×–1.2×, each on a rolling four-quarter basis. Failure to comply with any of the coverage ratio tests, if not cured, can lead to a default.

Note that definitions of the ratios vary and, hence, ratios reported for two different WBS transactions may not be directly comparable.

Net Worth

Net worth covenant is common for the UK pubs transactions and requires the issuer to maintain a certain minimum net worth.

Restricted Payment Conditions

Restricted payment conditions govern the distribution of post-debt service excess cash (e.g., dividend distributions) in the context of WBS. The restricted payment conditions vary from deal to deal and may include requirements to pay down a certain amount of debt, leave certain amount of cash in the business, keep certain accounts funded, and the like. Generally, at least all of the following conditions need to be satisfied in order to be able to take excess cash out of the WBS structure:

- DSCR should be above a predefined floor level (e.g., 1.70×).
- FCDSCR should be above a predefined floor level (e.g., 1.30×).
- No amounts should be outstanding under the liquidity facility.

There may be a requirement to keep the ratios at their floor levels after making the restricted payments.

---

[11] Free cash flow is usually defined as the cash available to meet debt service obligations, that is, EBITDA – Maintenance capex – Taxes (if any)

Capex

Requirements with respect to capital expenditure are driven by the conflicting concerns about spending too little to properly maintain the business or spending too much and therefore straining the financial and management resources of the business. Usually, covenants define a required maintenance capex level for the business. Of this, a certain portion is the bare minimum maintenance capex that the business must spend in any given year—the balance can be deposited into a reserve account and can be used in future periods which have greater maintenance capex requirements.

Besides maintenance capex, covenants may also allow for development capex to be spent for further enhancement and development of the property portfolio. The amount of such capex is governed by both the type of the proposed development (expansionary versus "greenfield") and also the overall performance of the business.

Acquisitions

WBS structures usually allow existing businesses to make further acquisitions in the same business area, albeit upon the satisfaction of certain conditions. Such conditions vary from transaction to transaction. Illustrative examples of such conditions include the acquired business to have a positive EBITDA, satisfaction of certain EBITDA DSCR and FCF DSCR tests, capping the total value of acquisitions in terms of a certain percentage of the capex spent over a defined historical time period, acquisitions to be made on an arms length basis and so on. Sometimes, in order to ensure that businesses are being acquired at fair values, profitability of the proposed acquisitions, together with the profitability of all acquisitions made till that point in time, is compared with the profitability of the entire portfolio—the objective of the test is to ensure that the former is at least equal to the latter.

Acquisitions may be funded out of equity, proceeds from the disposal of properties, excess cash[12] or even a further issuance.[13]

Disposals

Covenants under WBS do not prevent asset disposals. Disposals, however, are usually subject to the satisfaction of certain conditions or subject to rating agency review and approval. Disposal conditions may cap the absolute amount of the total disposals that can be made in any given fiscal year or cap the disposals to a certain maximum percentage of the

---

[12] Subject to the satisfaction of the restricted payment conditions.
[13] Popularly called "tap issuance."

profitability of the entire portfolio. Additionally, there may be restrictions on the types of properties that can be disposed of—it is obvious that the rating agencies would usually place restrictions on the disposal of certain revenue-critical properties.

The disposal proceeds are usually kept separately in a specified account and could be used either for making permitted acquisitions or prepaying the WBS debt (subject to certain DSCR tests being fulfilled).

Change of Control/IPO

Change of control/IPO is generally not an issue with investors buying a wrapped tranche of WBS debt.[14] However, investors holding an unwrapped junior tranche usually have a preference for debt prepayment in the event of an IPO. Given the ongoing nature of the businesses suitable to WBS, it is unusual to see "change of control" covenants in the WBS structures.

Issuance of Further/New Debt

WBS allows the flexibility to issue additional term facilities at all levels in the capital structure. Such issuance however needs to be backed by a permanent improvement in EBITDA performance and asset valuation or can also be made to accommodate permitted acquisitions. A further issuance usually needs to meet a certain minimum issuance amount and be such that the ratings of the existing notes are not adversely affected as a result of the further issuance.

Prepayment

The floating-rate tranches of WBS debt are generally not subject to any prepayment penalties. Investors may, however, sometimes require a 2- to 3-year no-call period. Fixed-rate tranches usually attract a prepayment fee over and above the par value of the securities ("make whole premium").

OTHER FEATURES OF WBS STRUCTURES

Credit enhancement for WBS structures can be internal as well as external to the structure. A common form of internal credit enhancement is the creation of cash reserves. The cash reserves can be kept for different specific purposes (e.g., payment of debt service) and can be drawn upon to meet certain obligations in periods of unforeseen financial contingen-

---

[14] A wrapped tranche is a rated tranche on which principal and interest payments have been guaranteed by a AAA rated monoline bond insurer (e.g., AMBAC or MBIA).

cies. The reserves can be created at the very outset of the transaction by setting aside a predetermined amount of the proceeds in a separate account. Alternatively, the reserves can be gradually built up to a predetermined level over a period of time by using post-debt service excess cash.[15] It is often required that no restricted payments can be made until such time that the cash reserves have been funded to the desired level.

External credit enhancement is usually provided by means of a liquidity facility. The liquidity facility is made available at the issuer level to fund temporary cash flow shortfalls for meeting debt service obligations and is usually structured as a rolling 364-day facility. The size of such a facility depends upon the individual characteristics of each transaction. It is common to see liquidity facilities covering 12 months to 24 months of debt service obligations.

Additionally, a working capital facility is made available, albeit at the borrower level, to fund the seasonal fluctuations in cash flow requirements of the borrower. The facility is usually sized based on a thorough analysis of the difference between the peaks and troughs of cash flow in any given 12-month period.

It is important to note that the liquidity facility always and the working capital facility almost always rank senior to the note holders in the payments waterfall. Failure to timely replenish any amounts drawn under such facilities may lead to a default situation under WBS covenants.

INTEREST RATE HEDGING CONSIDERATIONS

Since businesses using WBS as a refinancing tool usually have a relatively stable cash flow profile which does not necessarily vary with the level of interest rates in the economy, it is important to hedge the interest rate exposure of any floating-rate notes issued under the WBS structure. This can be achieved by entering into a plain vanilla fixed-to-floating interest rate swap with a suitable counterparty or by using a suitable interest rate cap. An interest rate cap will have termination gains in the event of a prepayment of WBS debt—however, it will involve an upfront fee to the cap provider. The fee can be funded by a sale of an interest rate floor. Termination of the floor may incur costs. A plain vanilla swap may also have termination costs (or gains) in the case of prepayment of the principal outstanding under the notes.

The dual concerns around prepayment risk and the payment of swap termination costs in the potential event of a prepayment may be overcome by using an innovative swap product like the "Flexi-Swap"

---

[15] Subject to the satisfaction of the restricted payment conditions.

EXHIBIT 19.6   The Flexi-Swap Structure

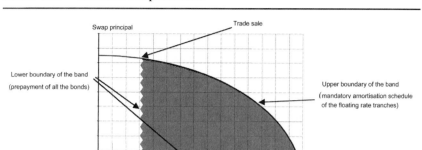

(see Exhibit 19.6). As the name suggests, the Flexi-Swap allows the borrower to reduce the notional outstanding under the swap or terminate it completely within predetermined boundaries at no cost. A swap break cost would, however, have to be incurred if the swap principal is reduced below the lower boundary. The boundaries are usually determined according to the company's needs.

The WBS swap documentation should comply with rating agency criteria—additionally, the swap should survive the bankruptcy of the borrower and only default in the event of a nonpayment.

WBS SPREAD LEVELS

Unlike traditional securitisation structures involving standard asset classes like credit cards, residential mortgages, auto loans, a WBS carries much more corporate-specific risk rather than pure asset-specific risk only. Therefore, even for similar WBS transactions, spread levels may vary from transaction to transaction, depending upon the perceived risk of the underlying corporate. For example, WBS structures that involve a utility are likely to attract tighter spreads. In general, it may be fair to say that WBS spread levels tend to be below unsecured corporate spread levels, the difference being attributable to the credit notching due to the robustness of the underlying WBS structure.

Following are some indicative spread level ranges at the time of this writing on typical 25-year WBS transactions in the UK, for different tranches of rated debt:

A rated tranche (average life ~ 10 years):   90–125 basis points
BBB rated tranche (average life ~ 20–25 years):   175–275 basis points
BB rated tranche (economic life[16] ~ 5–10 years):   500–600 basis points

Whilst these spreads may seem well in excess of plain vanilla corporate spreads with the same ratings, from a weighted average cost of funds perspective, taking into account that most transactions have more than half of their capital structure in A rated bonds, the WBS spread levels represent significant cost savings for the borrowing entity compared to the overall costs of leveraged funding.

WBS CASE STUDY: RHM FINANCE LIMITED[17]

Rank Hovis McDougall (RHM) is one of the leading food manufacturing companies in the UK with popular brands such as "Mr. Kipling," "Hovis," and "Bisto." In August 2000, Doughty Hanson, a financial sponsor, in the largest leveraged buy out in Europe till that time, purchased RHM from Tomkins Plc. The acquisition facilities were refinanced through a £650 million WBS. WBS refinancing technique was used only for "RHM Foodbrands+," a mature and stable business with an exceptional brand portfolio, a strong and well-invested asset base, market leadership positions, predictable cash generation, and sustainable barriers to entry. The more growth-oriented and entrepreneurial "RHM Food Solutions" was refinanced through a bank loan. The capital structure of the WBS was rated by Moody's Investor's Service and had the following profile:[18]

Debt Class	Size (£ million)	Rating	Yield	Legal Final Maturity
Class A1	50	Baa2 (BBB)	6 month LIBOR + 135 basis points	2004
Class A2	200	Baa2 (BBB)	6 month LIBOR + 300 basis points	2013
Class A3	240	Baa2 (BBB)	8.80%	2019
Class B1	135	Ba3 (BB-)	11.50%	2022
Class B2	25	Ba3 (BB-)	6 month LIBOR + 575 basis points	2022

Payment frequency for all classes of debt is semiannual in the above capital structure. No dividend payments are allowed as long as any

---

[16] By the end of the economic life period, the notes have to be either repaid in full or refinanced. Otherwise, they may attract interest rate step-up provisions.
[17] Sole Arranger: J.P. Morgan Securities Limited. Launched in February 2001.
[18] Source: RHM Finance Limited Offering Circular

amount under the A1 notes (average life 1.3 years) is outstanding. The A2 notes (average life 6.5 years) are prepayable at 100% any time after the end of year 2. The A3 notes (average life 14.0 years) are prepayable subject to a make whole premium calculated on the basis of Gilts + 50 basis points. The B1 notes (expected average life 6.9 years) are prepayable at the end of year 3, with semiannual step-down prepayment prices of 106%, 105%, 104%, 103%, 102%, and 101%. The B1 notes also have a coupon step-up feature in year 10. The B2 notes (expected average life 6.9 years) are prepayable at the end of year 2 and also have a coupon step-up feature in year 10.

Real estate valuation was provided by DTZ (£450 million) while the brand portfolio was valued by Interbrand (£420 million). RHM Finance Limited was the first WBS of a manufacturing company in the UK. The transaction was awarded "Corporate Securitisation of the Year, 2001" by the *International Financing Review* (IFR) magazine.

SUMMARY

WBS is an ideal financing technique for businesses with stable and predictable cash flows and a well-invested property portfolio. High leverage, longer amortisation profile, and a competitive cost of funds makes it an attractive financial tool for financial sponsors. Though initially a UK-focused product, the applicability of WBS has steadily increased over the years, with newer jurisdictions coming into the fold of WBS with the development of more customised legal structures.

CHAPTER 20

Principles for Analysing Corporate Securitisations

Elena Folkerts-Landau
Director
Standard & Poor's

Pascal Bernous
Associate Director
Standard & Poor's

Adele Archer
Director
Standard & Poor's

Anthony Flintoff
Director
Standard & Poor's

Apea Koranteng
Managing Director
Standard & Poor's

In this chapter we detail Standard & Poor's principles underlying its approach to rating transactions carrying risk that is a hybrid between corporate risk and the risk associated with standard securitisations backed by financial assets or diversified pools of corporate exposures, as in collateralised debt obligation (CDO) transactions. These hybrid transactions are generally known as *corporate securitisations* and in some cases as *whole business securitisations*.

CHIEF FINANCIAL BENEFITS

Corporate securitisations offer corporate borrowers a number of financial benefits relative to standard secured financing. The benefits arise from the transaction structure's enhanced financial capacity to service debt, which in turn is due to features borrowed from asset securitisation techniques.

Corporate securitisations tend to support greater financial leverage due to their enhanced debt servicing capacity; they often entail a lower average cost of debt due to higher credit ratings; and they may incur less refinancing risk due to longer terms to maturity.

Noteholders benefit from covenants, controls, and credit supports embedded in the transaction structure. Credit supports such as cash reserves and dedicated liquidity facilities can provide cash resources to meet timely debt repayment in circumstances when operating cash flows experience a temporary shortfall. Covenants and controls provide periodic signals of the operator's financial performance and the potential vulnerability of the debt to financial distress. Signals can include the fundamental message about payment capacity embedded in an amortising, rather than a bullet, debt structure, threshold benchmarks that can trigger early amortisation or remedial action, and financial reports.

CLASSIFICATION

Corporate securitisations fall within the spectrum bounded by corporate risk on the one end and commoditised asset-backed securities (ABS) on the other end. Corporate securitisations embrace a breadth of operating assets, including for-profit and nonprofit entities, as well as discrete assets such as inventories, whole businesses, and parts of a business. Since each transaction falls on a unique point within the spectrum, there is no standard blueprint for rating corporate securitisations. The assets tend to be unsuited to actuarial analysis.

Individual corporate securitisations, unlike standard ABS transactions, are structured on a made-to-measure basis. Their hybrid collateral includes a unique set of operating assets in ongoing use, and in this respect shares many features of standard corporate ratings. Additionally, corporate securitisations are reinforced by structural elements normally utilised in asset-backed securitisations and sometimes in project finance.

The hybrid collateral underlying corporate securitisations contrasts with the collateral of structured ABS, such as mortgage-backed or credit card-backed securities, insofar as the former normally lacks an extensive performance track record and may be less amenable to statistical analysis. Furthermore, operating assets tend to be less diversified, less homogeneous, and need to be actively managed in order to generate cash flows. Therefore, their revenue-generating characteristics can often be more closely aligned with a specific operator's performance. Not least, the vulnerability of the collateral to operational risks may be substantial.[1]

RATINGS OBJECTIVE

Corporate securitisations may be identified by their specifically adapted capital, cash flow and legal structures, the likely presence of debt tranching and significant debt leverage, the availability of credit enhancement, and the application of performance criteria to determine the potential intervention of third parties and possibly their maturity. Together, these features address issues related to the unique assets being used as collateral. Ratings guidelines will address the principles of analysis of these transactions rather than provide a blueprint for meeting criteria.

Whereas Standard & Poor's criteria for traditional asset-backed structures involve solving for the level of credit enhancement that supports a given rating, with other variables fixed, this is not the case for corporate securitisations.[2] Instead, the rating of corporate securitisations entails the optimization of a number of variables, including credit enhancement, risk capital, and both average life and final maturity of the debt tranches. Standard & Poor's objective is to strike the best balance in the value-added of numerous variables, some of which are more conducive to negotiation during the structuring process than others.

Relevant Inputs Into the Ratings Analysis

The rating process is essentially a blending of corporate business risk and structured finance analysis that builds on the principles of both with the ultimate goal of maximizing noteholders' control over the cash-generating assets.

To this end, Standard & Poor's conducts an analysis on the basis of:

---

[1] See Standard & Poor's, *Operational Guidelines Underlying the Rating of Corporate Securitizations*, August 23, 2002.

[2] See Chapter 28.

- A business risk assessment.
- An assessment of management and operations.
- An alternative operator/servicer.
- The cash flow structure and modeling.
- The capital structure, including the commitment of appropriate risk capital.
- The legal and tax structure.
- Credit enhancements and other structural supports.
- The effectiveness and/or enforceability of mitigants in the form of covenants and third party activities, such as asset valuation, servicing, and audits.

Similarities to Corporate Analysis

There is considerable overlap between the information gathered and analyzed by Standard & Poor's for a corporate securitisation and a standard corporate credit rating. Critical inputs into the business profile of both include:

- The business plan.
- Management intensity.
- The competitive position in the industry.
- The economic development of the industry.
- Barriers to market entry (regulatory or commercial).
- Income diversity through product line, assets, and geographical distribution.
- Cash flow stability, in terms of the business operator's track record, the predictability of demand for core products and services, and a contractual revenue stream generated by concessions or leases.
- Counterparty risk.
- Growth prospects.
- Capital intensity (with emphasis on proven capacity).
- Technology risk.
- The capital structure.

Similarities to Structured Finance Analysis

There is somewhat less overlap between the information gathered and analyzed for a corporate securitisation and a financial asset securitisation, because the assets involved are not self-liquidating and may be highly illiquid. In addition, corporate securitisations have a far more limited capacity to lend themselves to an actuarial approach.

Nevertheless, there are some noteworthy similarities between the approaches taken by Standard & Poor's for corporate and standard structured finance transactions. A detailed cash flow model of assets and their matching to the debt liabilities is stressed and the results analyzed. Structural support in the form of a liquidity facility and/or cash reserve is common and often crucial to the ratings outcome. Both types of transactions entail debt tranching and structural subordination, although smaller transactions often entail a single tranche. Sequential repayment of debt tranches is frequently taken into consideration.

More critical in corporate securitisations than in many standard asset-backed transactions is the discipline imposed on the business operator to adhere to a specified plan and to a specified minimum level of performance. This is accomplished by means of features of the transaction structure, in particular through:

- Continuous vetting and supervision of information, accounts, as well as the legal and regulatory framework.
- Covenants, both to constrain the behavior of parties to the transaction and to provide for remedial action including early termination of the debt.
- The record of judicial enforcement in the relevant jurisdiction.
- The performance and incentives of stakeholders in the transaction, including the servicer, owners (equity holders), managers, and employees.

Link Between Corporate Business Risk and Corporate Securitisation Ratings

The first step in optimizing the key variables so as to maximize noteholders' control over the cash-generating assets is to isolate financial risks from business risks to the extent feasible. Structural features frequently employed in standard asset securitisations are introduced into the hybrid structure with the aim of compensating for a host of financial risks, including operator insolvency risk, the operator's willingness to pay, set-off risk, secondary tax issues, refinancing risk, event risk, portfolio concentration risk, and the cost of delays in implementing agreements.

THE BUILDING BLOCKS IN RATING CORPORATE SECURITISATIONS

Standard & Poor's corporate credit rating measures an obligor's ability and willingness to meet its financial commitments as they come due. Structural reduction of financial risks mitigates the risk associated with a firm's willingness to service its debt. It also results in a hybrid transac-

EXHIBIT 20.1   Building Blocks

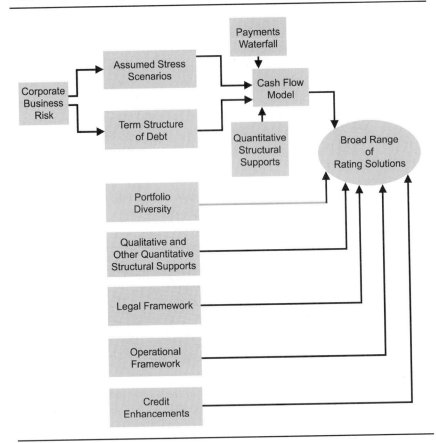

tion structure that is characterized principally by a significant level of business (i.e., operating) risk and an uncertain level of cash flow sustainability. The corporate business risk assessment serves as Standard & Poor's starting point in establishing a rating (see Exhibit 20.1).[3]

If Standard & Poor's has already provided a corporate (unsecured) credit rating for the relevant business operator, then there is potential to raise the rating for secured creditors, all other factors being equal. This is a result of the risk mitigation generated by isolating the transaction structure from financial risks, via a true sale of the collateral or a favorable secured loan structure, which effectively provides for noteholders' control over the collateral.[4]

---

[3] See Chapter 21.

To date, Standard & Poor's has been involved in rating secured corporate debt, which in theory could benefit from a rating uplift ranging in the UK between one and four notches—and averaging two notches—over the corporate (unsecured) credit rating on the issuer. Standard & Poor's may assess additional benefits to specified debt tranches in response to structural features, such as the ranking of payments under the priority of payments structure, a variety of credit enhancements, incentives aimed at optimizing the operator's financial performance, and the quantum and mix of debt and equity.

The numerous permutations of such potential benefits mean that there can be no single formula for arriving at a final rating on a corporate securitised debt tranche. Instead, a broad range of rating solutions follows.

KEY VARIABLES IN ASSIGNING RATINGS

Standard & Poor's looks at three types of variables in assigning ratings to corporate securitisations. First, there are quantitative variables, whose values tend to be fixed by circumstance or inherent business characteristics. Second, there are qualitative variables whose values likewise tend to be fixed. Third, there are qualitative variables whose values can be negotiated and eventually "tweaked" in order to optimize their value-added in respect to the rating on the transaction's notes.

Quantitative variables consist primarily of measures of cash flow relevant to the business and incentive "hooks" on the sponsor, such as cash equity and dividend restrictions. The importance of keeping the sponsor motivated to keep the transaction performing cannot be understated.[5] Inputs into a cash flow model capture the volatility and assumptions underlying projections for key income and cost variables for each relevant asset, and generate free cash flows which are assessed in terms of their minimum level of sustainability. Standard & Poor's typically looks through all relevant income and cost items in a company cash flow statement. The aim of the analysis is to unmask and assess cash flows available for debt service, given that historical cash flows may not always be the best guide to future performance. The range of line items may be narrowed, depending on the importance of any single line item to overall cash flow contribution. Cash flow variables, including EBITDA, may be adjusted to take account of accounting practices that may not be suitable to the essence of the credit analysis.

---

[4] See Standard & Poor's, *Analyzing English Secured Loans*, September 11, 1997.
[5] Standard & Poor's, *Corporate Securitizations: The Role of Risk Capital in Aligning Stakeholder Interests*, September 18, 2003.

As the cash flow data does not normally lend itself to an actuarial analysis because of its limited history and concentration in one industry, Standard & Poor's undertakes a range of stress flow analyses. Monte Carlo simulations can be a useful tool in some cases, but may be inappropriate when insufficient historical data is available to develop the requisite assumptions fully. The stress tests to be applied are determined on the basis of a detailed analysis of the business risk inherent in the transaction, the vulnerability of cash flows to specific variables over time, and the likely quality of the cash flow generated.

Among the qualitative variables, whose values are largely fixed before the rating process has commenced, are the business-risk assessment, the extent of portfolio diversity in the collateral stock, the legal framework, and the degree to which continuous supervision of operator performance is feasible over the life of the debt.

With respect to the business risk, Standard & Poor's assesses the degree and scope of operating risk *and* residual financial risk inherent in the proposed transaction structure, as well as any other relevant aspects of business risk. Key elements in the legal structure are the nature of the security that is proposed, the jurisdiction in which the legal provisions and covenants in the transaction documents would be enforced, and tax issues which could create unforeseen liabilities. The nature of the security on the collateral stock relates to the degree to which a true sale away from the operating sponsor, or equivalent true control over the relevant cash-generating assets, is achieved. In addition, Standard & Poor's looks favorably upon a high degree of delinkage of any proprietary expertise of the business operator from the assets' cash-generating capacity. This is frequently effected through a committed and competent servicer, or backup servicer. Alternatively, where a committed back-up does not exist initially, the analysis focuses on the ability, cost, and timing implications of sourcing alternative operators or servicers as needed.

Covenants can serve a number of functions, including preserving repayment capacity; protecting the integrity of the assets and business position; aligning stakeholder's incentives with those of noteholders; providing signals and triggers to ensure the steady flow of information, introduce early warning signals of credit deterioration, and place the bond trustee in a position of influence should deterioration occur; and purposes that are standard in ABS transactions.

The ratings process also focuses on the set of variables in respect of which there is scope to improve the risk profile of the securitized debt. Many are structural supports, such as covenants aimed at disciplining the operator or triggering early termination of the debt and/or of the secured loan to allow enforcement of the underlying security when negative signals occur about the business' future cash-generating prospects.

Other negotiable variables include the choice of collateral, which may affect the diversification of the asset portfolio, the final maturity of the debt, the average life and their respective ranking within the payment waterfall of individual debt tranches, and the degree of debt leverage. Indeed, the scope for leverage and, ultimately, the amount of total debt that can be raised in a corporate securitisation are positively influenced by the size of the cash equity contribution (throughout the life of the rated debt), dividend restrictions, provisions for cash reserves, credible internal controls and reporting, and the senior/subordination structure.

Subordinated debt can take the form of traditional securitised debt tranches as well as unrated debt and preferred stock that demonstrate equity-like characteristics. In rating securitisations of nonprofit operators, which typically have little or no equity capital, Standard & Poor's will assess the level and willingness of governmental and regulatory bodies to provide support. For example, the support and oversight provided in the Dwr Cymru (Financing) Ltd. water transaction to a not-for-profit group — Dwr Cymru Cyfyngedig (Welsh Water) — by the Welsh Assembly and the Office of Water Regulation were important offsets for the lack shareholders and for the possibly limited incentives on management to earn a return on equity capital.

Taken together, the quantitative and qualitative variables produce a range of potential rating outcomes. Standard & Poor's assesses alternative values of the variables (to the extent that there is scope for their negotiation or "tweaking") according to their relevance and capacity to achieve ratings objectives.

DISTINGUISHING CHARACTERISTICS OF CORPORATE SECURITISATION RATINGS

The rating of corporate securitisations has tracked the evolution of this type of financing tool. Guidelines will develop into market standards as experience is gained.

Volatility

On average, ratings assigned in corporate securitisations are expected to be less variable than corporate ratings and more variable than the ratings on standard ABS. Potential ratings volatility arises because of the likelihood of cash flow volatility within the transaction structure, in reflection of the inherent and unhedgeable business risk. Like corporate ratings, corporate securitisation ratings are far more sensitive to the inherent business risk than are standard ABS ratings.

Ratings volatility is partially stemmed, however, by the application of structural supports. In corporate securitisations to date, the business risk has tended to be moderate, representing largely mature, stable businesses, and is characterised by Standard & Poor's as "average" or slightly "below average." Furthermore, the frequent lack of an historical record for the business operators' performance in these transactions exacerbates the level of uncertainty about the future.

Boundaries

The upper boundary of corporate securitisation ratings, in principle, is the rating level that applies to classical, highly leveraged, highly rated, and commoditised asset-backed securitisations. Debt can be rated up to AAA if sized on the basis of liquidation value in a transparent market, as in CMBS transactions, or if an external financial guarantee provided by a AAA rated monoline insurer wraps the debt. As a practical rule, however, the highest corporate securitisation rating achieved to date has been AA on an unwrapped basis; a senior tranche A rating is far more common. Standard & Poor's has not as yet rated a corporate securitisation with underlying business risk assessments weaker than slightly "below average."

Operating sponsors whose business risk corresponds to a rating below BB are unlikely to benefit from a corporate securitisation. This is so because their future cash flows are, by definition of the rating, so uncertain that in the opinion of Standard & Poor's they cannot justify stretching the maturity of the debt or supporting a larger debt amount than in a standard corporate risk transaction. Likewise, certain kinds of businesses are unlikely to benefit from securitisation. These include businesses that are capital intensive, are reliant on unique management skills, or are rapidly evolving (owing to a high degree of technology risk).

In contrast, there are four types of business operations that are particularly well suited to corporate securitisations. These are:

■ Transactions involving a portfolio of fixed assets, such as public houses (pubs), not-for-profit housing, and private hospitals, which involve cash flows generated from contracted or regulated rental payments, purchase contracts, or payment streams from governments and other highly rated offtakers, or other business revenues where demand is highly predictable and there are effective barriers to entry.

■ Transactions involving discrete assets, which generate predictable cash flows from revenues in a small number of businesses, such as regulated water companies and timber business on forestland. The presence of supportive regulation, stable demand patterns, and monopolistic busi-

EXHIBIT 20.2 Cash Flow Quality Grid

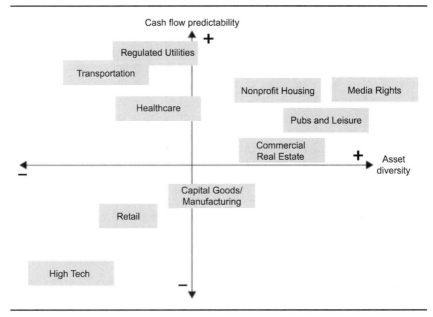

ness positions in sectors such as water utilities and transportation make these types of assets especially well suited.

■ Market value transactions, such as the March 2000[6] transaction and the May 2003[7] CP transaction, which involve cash flow generated from the liquidation or turnover of inventories.

■ Transactions secured by tangible or intangible assets (for example, film, publishing, and sponsorship rights).

The types of companies, asset classes, and industries lending themselves to corporate securitisations are summarized in Exhibit 20.2.[8]

POTENTIAL EFFECT ON CORPORATE CREDIT RATING

Standard & Poor's will review the effect of a corporate securitisation on the credit profile of a firm in much the same way as off-balance-sheet

---

[6] Marne et Champagne Finance a.r.l.

[7] Arth Capital Corp.

[8] See Standard & Poor's, *Facing Up to the Rating Challenges of Whole Company Securitizations*, December 15, 2000.

financing, project financing, or real estate sale leasebacks. For instance, debt contracted in the context of a securitisation of financial assets, such as a receivables program, is added back to the balance sheet with attendant assets for the purpose of ratio calculations. This permits a better comparison with firms that have chosen other avenues of financing, since guidelines on credit measures assume that comparisons between companies are not flawed by diverse flexibility levels and balance-sheet structures.

In the case of a corporate securitisation, which involves the securitisation of operating assets, Standard & Poor's will consider the strategic and economic importance to the rest of the company in order to determine whether or not to consolidate the debt. In any event, both the corporate credit rating and the unsecured debt rating can be affected, and in different ways. In addition, Standard & Poor's integrates the implications of the securitisation into its understanding of the company's financial policy, notably in respect of any reinvestment of the issuance proceeds, potentially in riskier assets.

If Standard & Poor's assessment is that a firm would not support the securitised assets in the event of financial stress, the firm's credit profile is reviewed accordingly. The effect of a corporate securitisation on a firm's business profile would be negative to neutral, depending on the quality of the assets securitised and the attendant cash flow. However, the potentially negative effect could be somewhat offset by the positive effect of the firm's finances, if such a transaction results in debt reduction or improved financial flexibility.

Conversely, Standard & Poor's could deem that the assets being securitised are key to a firm's strategy, and that the firm would support them both financially and/or operationally in case of stress. In this instance, it would be difficult to decouple the securitised assets from the firm. The impact of such a transaction on a firm's credit profile may be negative, as debt leverage would likely increase while the business profile would remain unchanged.

CHAPTER 21

Balancing Cash Flow Predictability and Debt Capacity in Corporate Securitisations

Blaise Ganguin
Managing Director
Standard & Poor's

Apea Koranteng
Managing Director
Standard & Poor's

Michael Wilkins
Managing Director
Standard & Poor's

Adele Archer
Director
Standard & Poor's

Corporate securitisations can serve as a tool for operating companies (as distinct from financial companies) to diversify funding, generate higher returns on equity, maximize leverage, or reduce their weighted-average cost of funding. While used primarily in connection with the financing of acquisitions, corporate securitisation techniques can also be applied to refinancings and recapitalizations.

The use of securitisation technology in business financings has grown in recent years, mostly in the United Kingdom but also in continental Europe, Australia, and North America. Transactions have grown to capture a more complex variety of assets as well, evolving from receivables to include substantial parts of a company's business, or even its entire operations. Such corporate securitisations have emerged over the past few years as a hybrid form of leveraged finance, inasmuch as they apply a mix of financing techniques derived from conventional project finance, securitisation, and leveraged finance.

The concern at the heart of all securitisations is whether cash flows generated by the underlying assets will be sufficient to service debt payments on the securities issued. All else being equal, the more sustainable and predictable the underlying cash flows, the lower the transaction's overall risk of default over time. Structural features such as cash reserves, liquidity facilities, and bankruptcy remoteness may mitigate the risk of short-term cash flow interruptions. However, a full hedge against the business risks associated with the company (or originator) generating the cash flow is most likely unfeasible.

To address this risk, Standard & Poor's identifies, analyzes, and quantifies the characteristics underpinning a company's business operations to establish the key variables affecting the predictability of the cash flows required to meet a given ratings objective. In addition, within any given business sector, the maturity of the securities issued must also be selected to correspond to the future sustainability of the business in question. The degree of predictability of key cash flow variables captured in Standard & Poor's business risk assessment also affects the proportion of senior to subordinated debt in a structure, the rating levels of individual debt tranches, the leverage a transaction can absorb, and the level of structural credit enhancements needed. Finally, Standard & Poor's develops stress scenarios in line with its business risk assessment and integrates them into a cash flow model to test the adequacy of cash available for debt service.

IMPLICATIONS OF BUSINESS CHARACTERISTICS FOR CASH FLOW PREDICTABILITY

A number of characteristics determine the predictability and sustainability of a business's cash flow. Among these are:

- Barriers to entry

- The maturity of the sector
- Obsolescence and substitution risks
- The ability to identify cash flow generating assets
- Asset concentration risk
- Management discretion
- Reputation risk

Barriers to Entry

Barriers to entry reduce exposure to competitive threats by limiting access to new entrants, and thereby render the operator's cash flows more predictable. Barriers to entry can take many forms, such as regulation, situational monopoly, economies of scale, and branding, among others.

The business risk of most corporate securitisations rated by Standard & Poor's is marked by some barriers to entry. This is the case with transactions involving ports, airports, hospitals, water distribution, as well as movie theaters, crematoriums and burial grounds, and even auto racing.

By contrast, businesses whose main assets are brands or intellectual property, such as in the sports rights business, may have difficulty securing long-term financing through securitisation; while demand for the underlying business, such as football, may remain strong within a culture, the barriers to entry for a particular organization operating in that sector may not be as compelling.

Sector Maturity

Mature business sectors tend to display relatively predictable cash flows as a result of having achieved a better balance between supply and demand. These sectors may also have benefited from consolidation, thereby reducing competitive threats and potentially resulting in somewhat more stable cash flows. The U.K. pub business is illustrative of a mature sector. Pubs are experiencing gradual, yet fairly predictable, declining volumes of beer sales, which are somewhat offset by rising beer prices and other sales. Similarly, the water sector benefits from steady usage and demand patterns characteristic of a mature sector, as do most utilities and infrastructure providers.

Obsolescence and Substitution Risks

Businesses subject to a high degree of technological risks may require significant investment in order to maintain their competitive position or market share over time. Moreover, capital spending under these circumstances is difficult to predict. Standard & Poor's has reviewed corporate securitisation proposals in the mature subsectors of the telecommunications industry, which typically benefit from high barriers to entry, but are also subject to obsolescence risk. While a lack of long-term sector visibility dramatically constrains cash flow predictability, Standard & Poor's considers that the more mature subsectors in the telecommunications industry, such as the cable subsector, can present viable opportunities for corporate securitisation, albeit with shorter debt maturities and lower ratings to account for the higher risk. In contrast, the underlying real-estate asset base (and attendant alternative-use value) of the Telereal Securitisation PLC transaction (closed December 12, 2001), which securitized British Telecommunications PLC's (A-/Stable/A-2) fixed-line assets, was key to getting Standard & Poor's comfortable with the industry obsolescence risk and the transaction's long-term maturity (more than 30 years).

Identifiable Cash-Flow-Generating Assets

Most corporate securitisations involve businesses supported by clearly identifiable assets, scopes of business activity, and cash flow drivers. The reason why is fairly straightforward: The variables driving cash flow can be more easily isolated for businesses whose assets and business scope are well identified; this, in turn, increases the confidence level at which the cash flows can be predicted. By contrast, fungible or portable assets are more difficult to secure as collateral and to ring-fence within a legal framework. Also, taking security over intangibles and maintaining value in a default scenario can be a challenge, given the higher reliance on management quality and contractual arrangements.

Concentration Risk

Asset concentration within a portfolio generally raises the level of business risk, due to the greater impact a single loss can have on cash flow generation. In some sectors, talent retention, for example, in advertising or "bust" risk in the movie, music, or book businesses constitute key risks. The occurrence of negative events, such as a string of bad films or the loss of a creative talent, could have a dramatically negative effect on cash flows. In private acute-care hospital transactions, the top-tier players generally do not own more than 50 hospitals, resulting in concentration risk. Therefore, Standard & Poor's stress analysis is intended to test the effect on cash flows of the loss of one or several hospitals for a period of time; also, any reliance within the cash flows on a few hospitals, on specific types of procedures, or on particular consultants referring patients are examined and could also be stressed.

Management Discretion

Most corporate securitisations rated by Standard & Poor's involve businesses whose cash-flow-generating capacity resides primarily in the assets themselves. These businesses tend not to require critical decision making on the part of management to generate sufficient cash flow. They also tend not to rely on any single individual or small group. Stakeholders' skills, talent, and personality should be replaceable rather than indispensable. Cash flow predictability requires that, in the event of the business operator's insolvency, skilled management can readily be found and quickly put in charge of operations.

Reputation Risk

In the service sector, businesses' key assets are often brands or franchises rather than tangible "brick and mortar" assets. Changes in the reputation of a brand or franchise can make or break many businesses: a sudden loss of confidence on the part of clients can compromise the value of a business in a very short time. This can be seen in the hospital and home-care sectors, where malpractice claims or the delivery of poor patient services can result in the loss of consumer confidence or the cancellation of contracts by private insurers or local authorities, which fund the bulk of hospital cash flows.

Reputation risk is not limited to the service sector, however. In the consumer products sector, serious safety or hygiene problems related to a branded product can result in significant loss of cash flow. Nevertheless, some brands are so solidly entrenched in consumers' minds that it is difficult to imagine a total meltdown, even following serious crises. Both the Coca-Cola Co. (A+/Stable/A-1) and McDonald's Corp. (A/Negative/A-1), for instance, have survived temporary hygiene problems at various times in their respective histories, none of which have threatened the existence of the firms. Given the varying strength and importance of brands to any business, Standard & Poor's reviews the reputation risk associated with each business on a case-by-case basis.

DETERMINING THE TRANSACTION'S TIME HORIZON

To ensure an adequate level of cash flow predictability, Standard & Poor's looks to a correspondence between the term-to-maturity of the debt securities and the timeframe during which a predictable and sustainable business outlook can be formed. While a near-term analytical outlook on a sector and business operator should bear a high degree of confidence, certainty declines over time. An important element in any transaction is therefore to "slice" time to reflect diminishing levels of predictability. Generally, Standard & Poor's expects the average life of the issued securities to be shorter than the point in time when business visibility becomes poor and forecasting loses its purpose.

In the case of a European classified telephone directory business, for example, the thresholds for assessing cash flow predictability are approximately as follows:

- In the first five years, cash flows should be fairly predictable, as the visibility on the sector and the business should be adequate.
- Looking five to 10 years ahead, the visibility of the business will become murkier. Standard & Poor's will most likely assume some deterioration of the business, but may not question the fundamental business model.
- Beyond 10 years ahead, Standard & Poor's will start questioning the assumptions underlying the business risk. For example, could classified directories, today the best advertising means for small and midsize businesses, be substituted by a new, unforeseen business model? Would a prolonged economic downturn cause unforeseen erosion in profitability? Could a new entrant shake up the market equilibrium, causing a price war?

In the above illustration, Standard & Poor's would expect at least half of the principal amount of a corporate securitisation to be repaid during the period of high cash flow visibility. Depending on the specific competitive position of the business being securitized and the structure and covenant package, the average transaction life may be closer to either five years or 10 years, but is unlikely to be much shorter or longer for purposes of meeting a ratings objective.

Standard & Poor's level of comfort with the legal final maturity of a transaction will not only depend on the average transaction life, but also on the amortization profile of the transaction. If the amortization is front-ended, Standard & Poor's may accept a longer final maturity, provided that the business outlook shows potential for a long cash flow tail. Even in businesses facing the risk of increased competition or of a loss of regulatory protection over time, a minimum level of long-term demand may ensure a stable, yet much reduced source of cash flow even in a very unfavorable scenario.

IMPACT OF THE BUSINESS RISK ASSESSMENT ON SENIOR-SUBORDINATION AND DEBT LEVERAGE

Standard & Poor's is often asked to indicate whether a proposed debt quantum, expressed as a multiple of earnings before interest, taxes, depreciation, and amortization (EBITDA), could serve as a basis for assigning ratings to a corporate securitisation. While many market participants, particularly in acquisition finance, approach financing proposals in these terms, Standard & Poor's analysis focuses first and foremost on debt service coverage. Debt is an output, not an input, inasmuch as the amount of debt must be serviceable by the cash flow generated by the business with a level of confidence that corresponds to a given rating. For this reason, Standard & Poor's requires that financing proposals be supported by an interactive cash flow model, the purpose of which is to test the ability of the expected cash flow to service the debt under a series of stress scenarios. The choice of stresses will reflect possible business conditions over the term of the transaction.

Standard & Poor's business risk assessment, expressed in qualitative terms ("above average," "average," and "below average," from the least to the most risky), is a useful starting point to set stresses on cash flow drivers in relation to the target rating on a specific debt tranche. In general terms, and with all other structural and legal elements being equal, the narrower the gap between the target rating and the business risk assessment, the more benign the cash flow stresses will be; the wider the gap, the more severe the stresses. While this approach provides practical guidance to setting stresses for a target rating, it should be interpreted with caution. For instance, stresses could very well be the same for debt tranches with different target ratings during the first few years while business "visibility" remains good, but would evolve differently over time.

For cash flow modeling purposes, "base-case" assumptions should reflect a continuation of the past, with somewhat conservative stresses. In a typical base-case scenario, revenues and margins would contract over time, and little or no benefit would be given to assumptions of new investments in the business or expectations for cash flow growth. Moreover, because accurate forecasting becomes more difficult as the time horizon lengthens, stresses for all debt tranches become increasingly harsh over time. A harsh stress scenario would entail more severe revenue and margin contractions and a significant increase in capital expenditures, whereas more benign stresses would likely give some benefit to management initiatives.

Going back to the example of classified telephone directories, assume that Standard & Poor's concludes that the business risk of a specific firm is "average." As such, stresses for a BBB debt tranche would be close to a base-case scenario; in other words, a continuation of past performance under somewhat conservative assumptions. In contrast, stresses for a A debt tranche would be much harsher, reflecting the gap between the business-risk assessment and the targeted debt rating. Again, such stresses would most likely entail more stringent revenue and margin contractions, as well as a significant increase in capital spending.

Irrespective of the target debt rating considered, stressed cash flows should always meet debt service needs.

Tranching debt into senior, mezzanine, and junior instruments, and sizing the equity contribution is akin to "peeling off" cash flows by layers of predictability. The least predictable sources of cash flow represent the highest risk (and potentially the highest rewards), and hence should be financed with equity or with a combination of lower-rated debt and equity. In the context of a corporate securitisation, cash flows to be generated from future investments are highly uncertain, as are cash flows generated by marginal assets; as a result, both may be too risky to be financed with debt. Conversely, cash flows generated by a company's core assets normally enjoy a much greater degree of predictability and thus may be steered into senior debt tranches.

EXPRESSING BUSINESS RISK IN TERMS OF VARIABLES IN THE CASH FLOW MODEL

There are four groups of cash flow drivers that affect debt service coverage: revenues, costs, other cash items, and debt. For each transaction it rates, Standard & Poor's expresses key dimensions of business risk by developing stress scenarios for these four variables at specified ratings levels. Given the often long-term nature of corporate securitisations, Standard & Poor's considers that a transaction's ability to service debt depends on available cash flow after required investments, taxes, and other priority payments, rather than purely on EBITDA.

Revenues

Standard & Poor's identifies key revenue drivers, and stresses these to correspond to the level of certainty implied by the targeted rating. In addition, to reflect the mature business sectors from which corporate securitisations tend to originate, the assumptions applied by Standard & Poor's in cash flow models tend to assume declining revenues over the course of the transaction. Moreover, for senior debt tranches little, if any, benefit is given to revenues from new investments, as they are less likely to generate revenue than existing assets. No benefit is usually given to inflation unless the regulatory regime supports it, as is generally the case for water utilities.

Demographics and other forces can also come into play. For example, hospitals in the UK have strong growth prospects due to increasing public expectations of health care services and an aging population. While these strengths can help mitigate a downside scenario, little growth would be assumed in a base-case scenario.

Standard & Poor's stress analysis also assumes a number of recessions throughout the course of the transaction, with the first one typically coming in the early part of the transaction term, in order to test liquidity. These recessions are typically projected to last five years, with the assumption that revenues would return to prerecession levels at the end of each downturn. These assumptions are more favorable when factors reducing revenue uncertainty are present, such as long-term contracts referencing volumes and/or pricing.

Costs

Standard & Poor's is wary of modeling assumptions that entail increasing profit margins over time, unless management can point to a tangible track record of cost cutting and margin improvements. In general, businesses with low operating costs and capital intensity, such as tenanted pubs, generate higher and generally more stable cash flows more suitable to supporting greater financial leverage. In contrast, sectors where operating costs include a significant labor component, such as hospitals, can experience wage inflation in excess of revenue growth and should be stressed accordingly.

Standard & Poor's gives credit to factors mitigating uncertainty about costs, such as hedges. Standard practice requires foreign-exchange and interest-rate risk be hedged with highly rated counterparties, and any remaining unhedged risk to be stressed in the cash flow modeling. The assumptions of declining revenues on the one hand, and increasing costs on the other, imply squeezed margins over time. It is therefore not unusual for the cash flow model to generate operating margins (expressed in EBITDA as a percentage of sales) that decline into single digits towards the end of the term, particularly for the more senior debt tranches.

Other Cash Items

Cash and noncash items defined in the cash flow models include, among other variables discussed below.

Capital Spending

Standard & Poor's differentiates between essential investments required to run and maintain the business as is, and discretionary investments aimed at growing the business—the latter often being akin to an equity risk that can be borne only when all other expenses have been paid. It can be difficult to define maintenance spending, on the one hand, including defensive refurbishments necessary to maintain the existing level of revenues, and on the other hand, capital spending used to grow the business. Increasingly, both minimum and maximum investment levels are modeled to discourage both under- and overspending. In regulated businesses, such as water utilities, maintenance capital spending is mandatory, and Standard & Poor's focuses its analysis on premaintenance and postmaintenance ratios. Historical data on capital expenditures (capex) may be of limited use to size future requirements if spending is "lumpy" in nature, or has been too low due to neglect or too high due to a recent period of "catch-up" spending. The use of independent experts on a periodic basis can be useful to ensure that the necessary level of future "maintenance" capex is objectively identified and/ or resized if necessary over the life of the transaction.

Working Capital Changes

Most corporate securitisations rated by Standard & Poor's have not involved significant amounts of working capital, outside of mark-to-market, inventory- or receivables-based transactions. Modeling assumptions about significant changes in working capital would aim at reflecting either significant growth or decline in the underlying business, a fairly unlikely scenario. Working capital assumptions would most likely be combined with other assumptions about rotation ratios to assess their impact on liquidity.

Payments on Contingent Liabilities or Deferred Items

Payments on contingent liabilities or deferred items include, among others, obligations under pension liabilities, rents, legal settlements, and guarantees. In general, and because of their contingent nature, these liabilities are difficult to size with any significant confidence. Standard & Poor's analysis assesses the risk that cash flows being relied upon to service debt could be subject to unexpected shocks and uncertainty during the life of the transaction, due to, for example, unfunded pension liabilities.

Debt and Other Financial Obligations

Subject to assessments of business value and required equity contributions, a company's aggregate debt may be only as high as can be serviced from stressed cash flows, after taking into account additional commitments and obligations which need to be serviced in the normal course of business or which otherwise have a likelihood of arising (e.g., postretirement obligations and medical benefits, and environmental liabilities). Some commitments may simply pose liquidity concerns, rather than act as a credit drain on the cash flows. In such cases, available liquidity structured into the transaction can mitigate the potential risk.

SUMMARY

The increasing number of corporate securitisations being rated by Standard & Poor's indicates just how much operating companies are realizing the benefits this form of financing can bring. The growth witnessed in the market is not restricted to issuance volumes, but also asset types, jurisdictions, and purpose.

CHAPTER 22

Credit Analysis of Whole Business Securitisations

Benedicte Pfister
General Manager
Moody's Italy

While a standard securitisation structure isolates certain specific assets (e.g., mortgages, consumer/corporate loans, etc.) from a company and uses the precontracted cash flows derived from those assets to service the debt, a whole business securitisation relies on future—usually less predictable—cash flows derived from the entire business of an operating company. Whole business securitisations emerged in the mid-1990s in the United Kingdom with the securitisation of cash flows generated by a nursing homes company. Several transactions followed, involving assets as diverse as hotels, pubs, theme parks, and airports.

Structurally, whole business securitisations lie midway between standard securitisations and secured corporate debt. Similar to secured corporate debt, the debt issued in a whole business securitisation is a direct or indirect liability of the operating company. Ownership of the assets remains with the operating company, and bondholders are only granted a charge over those assets. As these assets usually require active management, the repayment of the secured debt will depend on the quality of the company's management. Bondholders are thus exposed to operating or servicing risks consistent with the intrinsic rating of that company. However, similar to a standard securitisation, the assets that secure the new debt are intended to be isolated from the effects of an

373

insolvency of the operating company. This is achieved by the creditors' ability in the UK, up until now, to replace the insolvent (or underperforming) operating company by a third party who will then manage the assets solely for the benefit of the creditors.[1]

While an insolvency of the operating company would most likely trigger a default on the company's corporate debt, the securitised debt should remain unaffected thanks to some form of external liquidity provided and the predefined replacement mechanism. This predefined replacement mechanism also provides more certainty that the securitised assets will continue to be managed as an ongoing concern after the insolvency of the operating company. Moody's believes that the value of assets which continue to be operated is likely to be higher than the value of assets in a bankruptcy liquidation. It follows that both the probability of default and the recovery assumptions after a default may be more favourable for securitised debt than for straight corporate debt. The final rating on the securitisation debt may thus differ from the intrinsic rating of the operating company.

The present chapter will focus on Moody's methodology to analyse the credit risk of whole business securitisations with a bias towards UK transactions.

WHOLE BUSINESS SECURITISATIONS RATING AND CORPORATE RATING

The ability in an insolvency scenario to replace the borrower and continue to operate the assets without incurring a default on the securitised debt may allow the rating on that debt to differ from the intrinsic rating of the borrower. The extent by which the final securitised debt rating can exceed the borrower's corporate rating is, however, very dependent upon the structure in place and the assets and industry concerned. The securitisation structure will attempt to minimise the risk of bankruptcy, preserve the value of the assets, organise external financial or operating assistance in case of underperformance, and trigger a change of control in case of prolonged underperformance or insolvency. However, the benefits of these structural features on the securitised debt rating will largely depend on the likelihood that the assets and industry remain valuable enough to attract a substitute manager after an insolvency of the borrower.

---

[1] As of August 2003. The Enterprise Act 2002 led to changes to the insolvency rules in the UK, but envisages a capital market exemption which is expected to apply to whole business securitisations.

Long-Term Commodity Assets and Ease of Replacing the Borrower

The secured loan structure relies upon the appointment of an administrative receiver in case of default or insolvency of the borrower. That receiver will be expected to actively manage the assets of the borrower on a day-to-day basis until the loan is fully repaid or the portfolio liquidated. Consequently, the structure relies upon the critical assumption that another operating company or third-party servicer can be found, which is willing to take over and run the assets at the time of default. This in turn assumes that, despite the insolvency of the borrower, its assets and the industry in which it operates will be viable and attractive during the life of the transaction, which might extend to twenty years or more. The long-term sustainability of the borrower's assets as cash flow generator within its industry is thus fundamental in rating whole business securitisations.

The long-term sustainability of the borrower's assets within a specific industry will depend on the intrinsic quality of the assets as well as their diversity. Indeed, Moody's recognises the benefits provided by a diversity of assets within a pool over the loss severity assumptions in a default scenario or in recessions. Both the stability of the industry, and the quality and diversity of a company's assets are also aspects highly valued by Moody's corporate analysis. However, their positive impact will be leveraged in a securitisation thanks to structural features that allow the assets to be managed as a going concern even after the insolvency of the borrower. The cash flows generated through continued operation of the assets would be expected to allow full repayment of the securitised debt.

A few transactions rated by Moody's may serve as an illustration of the above (see Exhibit 22.1).

Tenanted pub securitisations provide a good example to highlight the ease of finding a "substitute manager," thus allowing continued operation of the assets. Despite certain declining trends, the long-term sustainability of the UK pub industry in general is well accepted. Pub securitisations rated by Moody's consisted of assets of various quality, leading to differ-

EXHIBIT 22.1   Commodity Assets, or Ease of Finding a Substitute Borrower

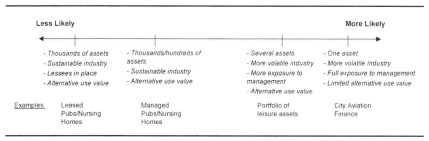

ent assumptions in terms of the long-term sustainability of the assets and cash flows. The two Punch deals, for example, were secured by well-located high quality pubs. It is reasonable to assume that a substantial number of these pubs will continue to operate as pubs during the whole life of the transaction. Avebury and Alehouse were not comprised of top quality assets, and Moody's assumed a higher number of closures during the life of the respective transactions. However, those portfolios did also benefit from a considerable diversity, both geographically and in terms of type of pubs, which Moody's assumed would protect the cash flows in case of industry recession. An additional advantage in pub securitisations comes from the structure of the industry. Most of the securitised pub portfolios consisted of leased pubs under a "tie," which are pubs owned by the pub company but leased to long-term lessees.

The lessee operates the pub, and only interacts with the landlord to pay the rent and purchase beer from him. The role of the landlord is thus limited to collecting the rent and earning a margin on the beer he purchases from brewers and sells to lessees. This means that in the case of a default or bankruptcy of the pub company, the pubs will still be operated by the lessees, and cash flows will still be generated (although probably at a lower level if we assume some correlation between the pub company default and the general performance of the pub industry). While management adds value, the structure contemplates that their function can be readily assumed by an available third party. Indeed, it would be relatively easy to replace the pub company by a receiver whose role is limited to the collection of rents and beer margin. Even in portfolios comprising managed pubs and not just leased pubs, as in the Punch Funding II transaction, one could assume that a large proportion of the managed pubs (as the name indicates, directly managed by the pub company) could be converted into leased pubs if necessary.

Similarly, with nursing homes, the aging trend in the UK—and the social importance of those homes—suggests that nursing homes in general will remain valuable assets throughout the next two or three decades despite the currently prevailing pressure on UK operators' cost base. Sufficient quality, adequate market selection and diversity of nursing home portfolios can provide comfort regarding the long-term sustainability of cash flows generated by such assets.

At the other end of the spectrum lie single asset, single operators deals, such as the City Aviation Finance transaction, involving the securitisation of the revenues generated by the London City Airport. At the time of the rating, the transaction benefited both from good prospects in the air travel industry and a successful high quality asset. In addition, the sector is partially protected from new competition by high barriers to entry linked to the capital-intensive nature of the airport business and the currently highly restrictive UK planning permission policy. However, the transaction depends on one single asset in a market that is already quite competitive. In theory, a potential bankruptcy of the airport might be the result of mismanagement or the outcome of an unattractive concept. In the latter case, it is unlikely that a replacement company would be found to take over the business after an insolvency. In addition, the alternative use value of the airport, even considering the land, is limited. In summary, in a "hypothetical" bankruptcy scenario, there is less certainty to find a substitute borrower, and the liquidation value of the assets might be of limited value. Consequently, the rating reached on the City Aviation Finance transaction does not differ much from the intrinsic rating of the borrower.

Maintaining Value and Maximising Recovery

The intrinsic value of the borrower's business, the related purchase price of the assets, and the overall ability to find a substitute borrower or replacement servicer, will be greater if the borrower is not bankrupt and liquidated in a distressed situation. Thus, it will be in the interest of bondholders to recognise early signs of severe problems and act accordingly in order to prevent a bankruptcy from occurring. This is usually achieved by the way of financial covenants which, if not complied with by the borrower, lead to a default under the secured loan agreement, the enforcement of the security and the appointment of a receiver. Meanwhile, the liquidity facility will ensure that no default occurs under the rated bonds. The receiver will act in the sole interest of the creditors. Provided the assets are still valuable, the receiver would be expected to continue generating sufficient cash flows to service the securitised debt, or to sell the assets. Before loosing control of its assets, the borrower usually benefits from a grace period during which he has the option to remedy the breach. Long-term remedies such as new equity or defeasance (as opposed to a temporary injection of cash to cure the breach) tend to be more powerful protections for investors.

One of the most efficient and often used financial covenants is based on a minimum *debt service coverage ratio test* (DSCR), defined as adjusted EBITDA over debt service. The EBITDA figure is adjusted for noncash items and exceptional items which could cloud the real operating result.[2] The level of this DSCR is generally sized well above 1.0× to incorporate any essential capital expenditure ("capex") and tax, so that a flag is raised before the borrower is no longer able to generate sufficient cash flows to pay capex, tax and debt service. In this respect, this DSCR reflects Moody's focus on the free cash flow coverage of the transaction. This test is usually calculated both for the last quarter and on a rolling 4-quarter basis (potentially backward and forward) to spot problems as

---

[2] See Moody's *Special Report*, "Putting EBITDA In Perspective," May 2000.

early as possible as well as highlight longer-term trends. The test will be adjusted for any particular seasonality specific to the borrower's business.

A higher DSCR covenant could be used as an early signal of a potential problem. In the Punch Funding II transaction for example, a property adviser will be appointed if the DSCR falls below 1.35× (while the default trigger is set at 1.25×). This property adviser will work with the borrower's management in an attempt to improve the performance of the assets. The adviser will also control the use of the reserve fund and any capex requirement. Finally, it will advise on the long-term nature of any remedy proposed by the borrower after a default.

Typically, the tax burden of the borrower will increase with time as the debt amortises and less interest becomes deductible. This increased cash outflow will also need to be factored into the level of the DSCR test. To mitigate this risk, tax shields are put in place. The Punch Funding II transaction offers a good example of an efficient tax shield: Equity-like capital is provided through a deeply subordinated loan from a Punch party outside the securitisation group. In case of poor performance of the securitised assets, no payment of interest or principal will be made under the subordinated loan. However, interest under that loan, even if unpaid, will still be fully deductible at the borrower level. This mechanism allows the borrower to limit his tax burden in a recession scenario.

Preserving the Assets, Limiting Corporate Volatility and Event Risk

When analysing the probability that the borrower or its successor will generate sufficient cash flows to repay the debt at or before maturity, Moody's relies upon a specific business, specific assets and specific cash flows to be present in the deal. Accordingly, some safeguards need to be incorporated into the structure to avoid too great a variance in the business, assets and cash flows of the borrower during the life of the transaction. This may include some *minimum maintenance capex* that the borrower needs to spend on the assets in order to preserve their quality. The structure may also envisage some *limitations in terms of permitted disposals*, in particular on key assets. Minimum transfer prices on these assets will assist in ensuring that the disposal proceeds as an EBITDA multiple will be at least equal to the securitisation debt to EBITDA multiple. Sale proceeds from the disposal of key assets will be used first and foremost to redeem debt or invest in new assets. It may be appropriate, however, to restrict new investments if the borrower's business is already underperforming.

Usual covenants also include *restrictions in terms of business activities* that the borrower can get involved in through investments or acquisitions. In Punch Funding II for example, Punch's management is permitted to use free cash flows post debt service to purchase restaurants. However the number of restaurants in the portfolio is limited to a maximum of 2%, as debt repayment is expected to come from pub cash flows and no track record is available regarding the management's ability to run restaurants instead of pubs.

More generally, Moody's values structures that are designed to use the cash generated by the business mainly to preserve or improve the existing assets, purchase similar assets and repay debt. Only if the borrower generates sufficient cash flows would those cash flows be used to invest in new—potentially risky—areas or distributed as dividends to shareholders. This is usually achieved by *restricting the use of free cash flows* (i.e. post capex and tax) if the debt service coverage ratio (usually defined as EBITDA less capex less tax, divided by debt service) is below a certain level. Some transactions consider various levels of outside payments restrictions, depending upon a given combination of debt pre/re-payments and corresponding DSCR levels.

The limitations identified in Exhibit 22.2 will help both mitigate the operating volatility of the borrower's business and signal to investors any excessive volatility. This in itself should theoretically limit the event risk incorporated in the corporate rating of the borrower. Restrictions in terms of *permitted indebtedness* will also help in that respect. Moody's

EXHIBIT 22.2   Selective List of Relevant Loan Covenants

Covenant	Basis	Comment
Financial covenant	Cash flow coverage test	Leads to outside payment restrictions (e.g., dividend distributions)
		Leads to appointment of a property adviser
		Leads to default/enforcement of the security
		Remedy to default needs to be a long-term remedy (e.g., new equity, defeasance)
Business covenant	Limits	Permitted disposals
		Permitted indebtedness
		Permitted business activities
		Permitted merger and acquisitions
		Minimum maintenance capex
		Negative pledge
		Change of control
		Amendments to main contracts

will particularly look at the limitation of any additional secured indebtedness and unsecured *pari passu* or senior indebtedness that could give new creditors the right to accelerate the new debt or file for bankruptcy. In addition, as long as there are any amounts outstanding under the secured loan, the borrower will covenant not to take any steps towards initiating bankruptcy proceedings.

However, many businesses also need to retain a certain level of *operational flexibility* to remain viable, and a balance needs to be found between preventing fundamental changes of the borrower's current strategy and operations, and allowing the borrower to manage his business efficiently. The economic circumstances of a company may change, requiring the company to alter its method of operating its business in order to survive. Therefore, Moody's will carefully examine the limitations on the operational flexibility of the borrower. The preservation of the borrower's operating flexibility stresses the importance of meaningful performance triggers, as well as the value of the ongoing monitoring process and the necessity of receiving appropriate information from the borrower. At the same time, it may limit the industries that whole business securitisations are suitable for.

Equity Component

The amount of economic equity in the business is valued both in straight corporate debt and in whole business securitisations, as it provides both a cushion to absorb losses and a qualitative comfort that the owners and managers have a strong incentive to manage their business efficiently.

Amortisation and Tranching

Similarly to a standard securitisation, the large majority of whole business securitisations use the cash flows generated by the assets during the life of the transaction to amortise the debt. Amortisation is an important factor in securitisations, as it reduces investors' exposure to the assets and the borrower over time, thus enhancing the recovery assumptions in a default or insolvency scenario. Accordingly, Moody's will particularly value front-loaded amortisation profiles, which will maximise the amount of amortisation generated in the early years of a transaction when the certainty of the cash flows is higher. However, too much amortisation resulting in a heavy debt service burden in the early years may also increase the probability of default of the borrower under the loan. Moody's will incorporate these factors in its analysis of the impact of the amortisation profile over the overall credit strength of the transaction.

Senior/subordinated structures used in securitisations will particularly benefit from the amortisation of the borrower loan. As opposed to a corporate debt structure where the senior and subordinated debt are expected to have a similar default probability (consistent with the corporate rating) and different recovery rates, a securitisation structure may change both the probability of default and the severity assumptions of the senior and subordinated debt. For example, at the time of a default or insolvency of the borrower, the senior debt may already be fully amortised, and no default under that debt will occur. If it is not fully amortised yet, the cash flows expected to be generated through the continuing operation of the assets by the substitute borrower might be sufficient anyway to fully pay down the senior debt (and the liquidity facility will have prevented any interruption of debt service).

An example of the benefit of both amortisation and tranching is outlined in Exhibit 22.3.

Although amortisation is also factored in a corporate analysis, *less value* is attributed to it as the fundamental rating focuses more on the likelihood of default (which varies from company to company) and less on the expected recovery (assumed to be more generic for a particular type of rating: i.e. senior/subordinated or secured/unsecured).

EXHIBIT 22.3   Benefit of Amortisation and Tranching

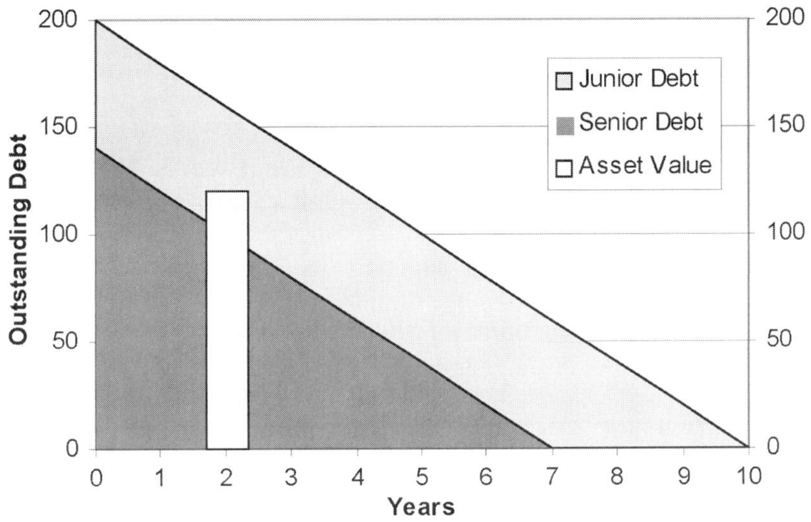

Assumptions:

- Insolvency of the borrower: year 2
- Value of the assets an ongoing operation: 120
- Senior Bonds outstanding: 100 → no default
- Junior Bonds outstanding: 60 → default, 20 recovered

Alternative Use Value

Whole business securitisations may deserve different ratings depending on the credit enhancement structures and the assets and industry considered. Assuming an underlying corporate rating in the "Ba" category, a securitisation may, for example, achieve a standalone rating in the "Baa" category untranched, and a "A" rating after tranching. There is, however, a limit to the number of notches that a securitisation structure can add to the borrower's corporate rating, even after tranching. This is due to the fact that a tranche needs to have a minimum size to be marketable. This limit stems from the fact that the cash flows are still dependent on the operating volatility of a specific industry, unless the assets themselves have a value independent of their specified use in that industry. Some nursing homes or pubs may, for example, be converted into residential properties or general retail use, and Moody's will look at the realisation value of these residential properties after deducting any conversion costs. This concept of "alternative use value" allows a *full* delinkage between the securitised debt and the borrower's business or industry. As such, it is a very powerful tool to enable higher debt ratings independently from the borrower's underlying rating. Based on this concept, Moody's was comfortable in assigning a rating as high as "Aa2" to the senior tranche of the Hotel Securitisation No. 1 transaction, and was able to reach a tranched "A2" rating on Madame Tussauds.

Conclusion

A corporate debt rating and a securitisation rating will be based on the same underlying assets and business. However, a securitisation will benefit from structural features aimed at limiting the corporate volatility of the borrower, preserving the assets, and organising assistance in case of poor performance. More importantly, the ability in an insolvency scenario to replace the borrower (or any other parties) and maintain the operations of the assets as an on-going business without any interruption of debt service, will change both the probability of default and the severity assumptions for the securitised debt. The final expected loss on the debt will be further enhanced by traditional securitisation techniques such as amortisation, tranching or hedging. Exhibit 22.4 summarizes the main structural features that benefit whole business securitisations.

Whole business securitisations are best applied to companies within stable or essential industries benefiting from high barriers to entry and limited existing competition, which generate predictable cash flows from a portfolio of diverse long-term sustainable assets with substantial alternative use value.

EXHIBIT 22.4   Structural Features in Whole Business Securitisations

■ Organised bankruptcy process	■ Covenants/triggers
■ Liquidity facility/Reserve fund	■ Property adviser
■ Commodity asset	■ Lock box
■ Fully amortising debt	■ Hedging

Moody's ratings on whole business securitisations reflect the operating nature of these transactions and the potential volatility associated with them.

RATING METHODOLOGY THROUGH THE EXAMPLE OF PUNCH FUNDING II

The Punch Group was formed in December 1997 to purchase from Bass PLC, the UK brewery company, a portfolio of 1,428 leased pubs. The company subsequently purchased Inn Business (a portfolio of 700 smaller pubs) in July 1999, and the Allied Domecq retail estate (1,515 leased pubs, 1,909 managed pubs, and a 50% stake in an off-licence chain called First Quench) in October 1999. After a few disposals, the Punch Group became the largest pub landlord in the UK with approximately 5,100 pubs. The Punch Funding II transaction represented the securitisation of the majority of the portfolio acquired from Allied Domecq in 1999 and was the first securitisation including a mix of both leased and managed pubs.

The above section shows that in many respects, the Punch Funding II transaction is a good candidate for a whole business securitisation. Indeed, (1) the notes are secured by a large portfolio of comodity-like valuable assets within a long-term sustainable industry; (2) the assets are located in the UK, which benefits from a creditor-friendly legal environment; (3) a set of strong covenants are in place to maintain the long-term value of the assets, provide external support or change of control upon certain performance triggers, and limit cash outflows in case of underperformance; (4) the assets have substantial alternative use value; (5) the transaction benefits from the usual securitisation features such as liquidity, hedging, amortisation.

Moody's used several complementary approaches to analyse the credit risk in this transaction:

1. An indicative rating was assigned to the Punch Group by Moody's fundamental analysts.

2. A traditional property analysis was performed as a preliminary tool for assessing the level of debt proceeds that could reasonably be raised against the assets. Indeed, many whole business securitisations such as the Punch Funding II deal have been applied successfully to property-related assets. The two primary components of Moody's property analysis are the *loan to value* ratio (LTV) and the *debt service coverage ratio* (DSCR).

▪ With respect to the LTV ratio, Moody's CMBS team uses *indicative target LTV levels* (based on Moody's value) for single large loans[3] in the U.S. by rating categories as illustrated Exhibit 22.5.

For the Punch Funding transaction, the above levels were adjusted to reflect (1) the large number of assets (hence diversity) within the pool; (2) the creditor-friendly legal environment in the UK; (3) the cash flow volatility within the leased and managed pub industry compared to the real estate sector. These adjustments combined with the expected rapid deleveraging of the transaction post closing through the sale of the First Quench business allowed the transaction to reach higher LTV levels on the notes.

▪ With respect to DSCR levels, Moody's used the net cash flow (i.e., EBITDA adjusted for tax payable and maintenance capex—this last item was material for the managed assets) over a normalised debt service based on the average cost of capital (as the transaction was fully hedged) and a standard mortgage-based amortisation profile over 25 to 30 years (corresponding to Moody's then opinion of the useful life of the Punch Funding II assets).

This preliminary *static analysis* was used to compare the leverage and cash flow debt cover achieved for various rating levels in this transaction with similar figures observed in previous pub transac-

EXHIBIT 22.5   Example of Moody's Target LTV Levels for Large Loans

Rating Level	Target LTVs (%)
Aaa	40
Aa2	48
A2	56
Baa2	64
Baa3	67

[3] See: *Moody's Special Comment*, "CMBS: Moody's Approach to Rating Large Loan/Single Borrower Transactions," July 2000.

tions. Comparisons between pub transactions is facilitated by the fact that valuations on the pub industry are often provided by the same group of valuers. The high quality of the assets included in the Punch Funding II transaction was an important factor in this analysis. In analysing the managed estate, we looked at both the current performance of the portfolio and the hypothetical performance of such a portfolio should it be converted into a tenanted estate. Moody's believes that this scenario, which provides for a lower average profitability offset by a lower performance volatility, represents a meaningful worst case scenario.

3. A *Monte Carlo* simulation incorporating a detailed cash flow model of the transaction and underpinned by assumed distributions driving the performance of the pubs was the principal tool used in estimating expected losses on each class of notes. The parameters of the input distributions (i.e., revenue, cost and capex elements) were set by a conservative analysis of the historic performance and future projections for the pub industry. Moody's also took into account the economies of scale expected from the integration of the Vanguard and Managed business to the Punch/Inn estate (overhead costs reduction, improved beer supply terms, improved flow monitoring).

Moody's mean assumptions for the key income and cost elements and resulting mean EBITDA figures for the Vanguard and Managed portfolios are outlined in Exhibit 22.6.

Based on both historical figures and industry studies, some *volatilities* were assumed around the mean point for all the major variables. In addition, *different scenarios* were tested to estimate the impact of key assumptions, such as:

■ Gradually declining number of pubs in the portfolio, due to reduced alcohol consumption in the UK.
■ A sudden and significant closure rate of existing pubs due to an unforeseen fundamental problem in the industry.
■ A default and replacement of the servicer, resulting in a 1-year drop in beer volumes (followed by a partial recovery) and a temporary fall in the collection rate.
■ Recessions, occurring with a 10% probability per annum, lasting 2 to 3 years and resulting in a decline in rents and beer margins in the Vanguard portfolio as well as a decrease in overall margins in the managed estate (followed by a partial recovery). Moody's noted that during the last recession in the UK, the pub industry experienced a large drop in pub portfolios valuations, but cash flows remained relatively stable.

EXHIBIT 22.6 Mean Assumptions for the Vanguard and Managed Portfolios, 2000

Assumptions	Vanguard	Managed	Comments/Input Distribution
Inflation	1.25%	1.25%	Driving beer price and margin, rent per pub, other income, repair & maintenance, capex
Rent per pub	24,300		Growing with inflation
Beer Volumes per pub	228 barrels	386 barrels	In the range of −5% to +1% p.a., and declining by 1.7% p.a. on average
Beer Margin per barrel	Confidential		Growing with inflation
Operating Costs (% revenues)		40%	
Central Cost per pub	£6,000	£35,000	For the managed estate, declining to £28,000 over a few years
Maintenance Capex	£1,000,000	£18,000,000	
Resulting mean EBITDA			
EBITDA Y2000	£74,000,000	£92,000,000	Total of £166,000,000
EBITDA Y2001	£82,000,000	£100,000,000	Total of £182,000,000
EBITDA Y2005	£85,000,000	£105,000,000	Total of £190,000,000
EBITDA Y2010	£86,000,000	£110,000,000	Total of £196,000,000

EXHIBIT 22.7 EBITDA Distribution—50,000 Runs

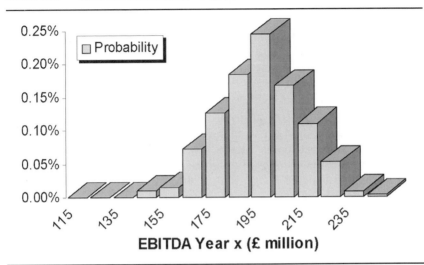

- Market value decline of pub portfolios despite current valuations.

Some *structural features* were also incorporated in the model such as the existing liquidity facility or the DSCR test which, if not met for a defined period of time, does trigger the enforcement of the security and the subsequent disposal of the portfolio. The value of the portfolio at this time would be the highest of (1) the discounted value of future cash-flows and (2) an assumed alternative use value. DTZ Debenham Thorpe reviewed a sample of 150 pubs in order to provide an assessment of possible alternative use values of these individual assets. The average alternative use value for the leased pubs represented approximately 58% of their respective pub values, while the average alternative use value for the managed pubs represented approximately 35% of their respective pub values.

Moody's typically run several thousand scenarios, each scenario varying each of the main revenue, cost and capex elements within the assumed distribution. The model displays the projected EBITDA and net cash flow distributions for the life of the transaction, resulting from the several thousand scenarios run. The distribution of the Punch Funding II EBITDA for a specific year resulting from 50,000 runs is shown in Exhibit 22.7.

The resulting mean portfolio EBITDA figure from approximately 40,000 runs was £181 million for year 2001, £185 million for year 2005, and £188 million for year 2010. Those figures differ from the figures mentioned in the above table due to the unsymmetrical shape of the distributions assumed for each main variable. As an indication of the level of stress included in the model, the minimum EBITDA figure for year 2010 was around £105 million

The cash flow output on the asset side is then used as input on the liability side. The model calculates the resulting average *expected loss*, probability of default and average maturity for each class of bonds, which is then mapped to a Moody's rating.

Moody's assessment on the Punch Funding II transaction was based on the prevailing regulatory framework of the UK pub industry and the Punch group's competitive position in this market. Continued success, however, will depend on the fundamentals of the beer and pub industry, its European-wide regulation, as well as the risk profile, strategy, and management of Punch's operating business. All these are characteristics of traditional corporate debt issuance. Investors should be aware that the ratings on a whole business securitisation such as the Punch Funding II transaction are sensitive to any such changes despite the benefit of some structural features particular to asset-backed securitisation.

CHAPTER 23

Securitisation of UK Pubs

Andrew Dennis
Executive Director, Structured Finance Credit Research
UBS

There are approximately 61,000 pubs in the UK—one for every 1,000 man, woman, and child. There are more pubs than there are places of worship and pub attendance certainly outstrips church attendance. The pub industry estimates that approximately 74% of adults in the UK go to pubs regularly and that nearly 30% will eat a meal in a pub at least once a month. The bar and pub industry is estimated to employ approximately 429,000 people as well as 80,000 independent licensees. Alcohol on-sales (not consumed in the home) in 2001 were approximately £26 billion. The industry, therefore, can be considered as one of Britain's largest.

The pub industry has undergone significant change in the past decade. This has been most apparent in the ownership of pubs. A combination of regulation and a change in the commercial focus of a number of the large brewery companies has led to a significant shedding of retail estate. In 1991, brewers owned 29,500 licensed premises. At the end of 2001, they owned only 10,100. Over the same period, the number of pubs owned by pub companies (pubcos) has risen from 12,700 to 31,600.

The nature of the pub business, broadly speaking, is one of stability. There has been a modest decline in the consumption of beer, the staple of the pub, but pubs have largely offset this by broadening their product offering. Pubs are cash generating assets whose capacity to deliver cash flow is, to some extent, insulated from economic cycles. This is particularly true of "local" pubs—which tend to attract customers by virtue of their convenient location rather than a particular differentiating consumer proposition. These businesses require relatively modest capital expenditure to maintain their cash generative characteristics. Therefore, as well as being cash generative on an operating basis, pubs can also generate stable free cash flow.

Enterprises that exhibit such characteristics can support more debt than less stable or cash generative businesses. Adding to this, a strong framework of security for creditors and rigid covenant controls, substantial debt leverage can be achieved. These factors have permitted pub companies to finance their purchases of pubs with a large quantum of debt. This debt has been raised or refinanced in the bond markets and there have been over £5.4 billion of pub securitisation bonds. Pub securitisation, therefore, is a significant subsector in the sterling market.

In this chapter we provide an overview of the secuitisation of pubs in the UK.

THE UK PUB INDUSTRY

For many years, pub ownership was a vital part of the vertical integration strategy of the major UK brewers. Owning pubs allowed the brewers to create "tied" houses—where only the range of beers offered by a single brewer could be sold. Many brewers saw control of the distribution network (pubs) as vital to their ability to capture the full margin on their product. In 1967, brewers owned more than two-thirds of all fully licensed premises in the UK.

For many years, during the 1960s, 1970s, and 1980s, repeated assaults were made on this effective monopoly position. Principally, their opponents charged the brewers with anticompetitive behaviour that damaged the private landlord and, ultimately, the consumer. In 1989, the Monopolies and Mergers Commission (the forerunner of the Competition Commission) published a report on the supply of beer, which focused on the potentially anticompetitive nature of the tied estate structure. The report concluded that the then prevailing industry structure was, indeed, anticompetitive and in a Statutory Instrument enacted in 1989 (known as the *Beer Orders*), a number of measures were promulgated that would change the face of the industry. The Beer Orders called "last orders" for the brewers' vertical integration strategy. Most fiercely targeted were the "national brewers"—those that owned more than 2,000 pubs at the time of enactment. The key terms of the Beer Orders were as follows:

■ Tenants and lessees were free from tie-in terms of buying nonbeer drinks and low alcohol beers.

■ Tenants and lessees could buy in a "guest beer"—they could buy in a cask beer and a bottled beer.
■ Most importantly for the future development of the industry, brewers were only able to tie a certain number of pubs. This forced them to sell approximately 11,000 of the 60,000 pubs in the UK.

The Director General of Fair Trading (DGFT) reviewed the effect of the Beer Orders in 2000 and found that the 1989 Beer Orders had achieved what had been intended. In particular, the rise of the independent pub companies had created a far more competitive market for beer (and other liquor and soft drinks) in the UK. Earlier in 2002, the government announced that they intend to revoke the Beer Orders.

With regulation having altered their beer distribution strategy, it is interesting to note that many of the major UK brewers have undergone radical changes in focus. Some have removed themselves altogether from the brewing and pub ownership business. The dominant force in the pub industry today is not the brewers but the independent pub companies. Within this group, a leading pack of pub companies has developed and have moved rapidly to consolidate the industry. Beyond the largest companies, the market remains highly fragmented.

Pub Ownership

Pubs break down into three categories:

■ *Managed*. These are pubs that are operated by their owner (brewer or pubco) and where the operation is undertaken by a staff employed by the owner. The owner derives its income directly from the sales of the pub and, as a consequence, managed pubs are subject to a high degree of operational gearing. Equally, the owner is responsible for all capital expenditure in the pub. Managed houses tend to exhibit higher barrelage and, in consequence, have greater turnover than tenanted pubs.
■ *Tenanted/Leased*. A pub is leased by the owner to a pub landlord. The landlord will pay lease rental payments to the owner and is usually tied to purchasing beer and (often) other products from the owner. In most instances, a tenanted pub will also be the primary residence of the landlord. Tenancies are, technically, different from leases in so far as they cannot be assigned or transferred. We use the terms interchangeably however since the economic effect is similar.
■ *Free Houses*. These are pubs where the licensee is the owner. They tend typically to be low turnover outlets and do not benefit from the bulk purchasing power that is common in the brewery or pubco owned sec-

tors. Free houses have progressively been seen as potential purchases for pubco chains.

Industry Trends

What does this industry structure imply? We would suggest several trends:

- *Brewing company divestitures.* Much of the wholesale estate divestiture by major brewers has already taken place. There may be further shedding of estate from companies such as Scottish & Newcastle (that runs approximately 1,500 tied pubs) and Greene King (600 pubs).
- *Large block acquisitions.* There has been a certain amount of trading of portfolios between larger pubcos. We anticipate that this will continue, albeit at a less febrile rate, as each pubco modifies its portfolio to satisfy its individual strategy. We make a point repeatedly in this chapter about the importance of scale to pubcos. This, we would contend, is a key theme in this sector.
- *Small block acquisitions.* There are over 30 companies that have between 30 and 60 pubs. It is, in our opinion, inevitable that many of these pubs will migrate into the hands of the larger pubcos.
- *Small acquisitions and disposals.* Most of the main pubcos trim their portfolios, making piecemeal acquisitions and disposals. Furthermore, approximately 18,000 pubs in the UK operate as "free houses"—businesses that are owned and operated as small businesses by their licensee. Over time there may be a migration towards selling these businesses to pubcos.

We would expect each of the main pubcos to grow their portfolios. The larger the portfolio of pubs, the more advantageous the supply agreements that can be negotiated with drinks suppliers. Other central cost economies of scale can also be achieved.

The prime movers of investment in pubcos are private equity firms. These range from Nomura, which originally bought pubs from Bass, to Alchemy partners. The industry has attracted financial buyers for several reasons:

- The initial impact of the Beer Orders was to create forced sellers among the major brewers.
- The ability to extract value by converting managed to tenanted estate.
- The availability, through the application of securitisation technology, to finance a significant proportion of acquisition with debt.

- A belief that focused management can exploit superior returns from an estate.
- The ability to create significant economies of scale from the amalgamation of smaller portfolios and, by doing this, to improve purchasing discounts with brewers.
- The belief that, once "critical mass" is achieved, the business can be floated (or otherwise disposed of) at a higher value than that which it was acquired at.

Some companies are in different points in this cycle.

Regulatory Structure

Licensing Regime

The retail sale of alcohol in the UK (and some other activities in pubs) is strongly regulated and operates under a regime laid down in the Licensing Act of 1968. Licensing covers pubs, restaurants, off-licenses, supermarkets and all other places where alcohol is sold on a retail basis. Pubs require a full on-licence to sell alcohol for consumption in the pub. The licence is almost always granted to the retailer rather than the owner of the pub. The licensee must satisfy the licensing authorities (these are usually local magistrates) that, among other things, he is a fit and proper person to be granted a licence.

The other form of license that may be granted permits sales of alcohol ("intoxicating liquor") for consumption off the premises—these are known as off-licenses. These are granted to supermarkets, off-licenses (hence the name), wine merchants, and, in certain instances, pubs.

A pub, in addition to its primary license, may also need other licenses to operate:

- Gaming permits are required if the publican wishes to operate a gaming machine, known as an *amusement with prizes* (AWP),
- A "supper hours" allows a publican to extend his sale of alcohol by one hour if the alcohol is served "incidental to a substantial meal,"
- An entertainment license to enable dancing or "organised" singing (rather than impromptu renditions of popular ditties by customers) such as karaoke or disco evenings,
- License extensions—a licensing authority may grant a late extension periodically (for instance on New Year's Eve).

On-licences are renewed every three years. They may be revoked at any time for serious breaches such as serving underage patrons.

The development and construction of new pubs or renovations of existing pubs are subject to applicable planning, land use, and environmental regulations. Changes to trading area or access also require the consent of the licensing authorities.

The government has indicated that it will transfer responsibility for licensing from the magistrates' courts to local authorities. This may, if implemented, mean a lengthier, more expensive licensing process.

A significant part of the thrust of the licensing regime governs opening hours. The current opening hours in England and Wales (Scotland has taken a more "enlightened" view for some years) are a legacy of World War I. The government became concerned that the production of munitions was being disrupted by the liberal availability of alcohol. They sought to moderate and regulate consumption by the imposition of opening hour limitations. These opening hours have seen only modest changes since that time despite significant lobbying by the brewing and hospitality industry. Periodically, "liberalisation" has found its way into election manifestos. Even if drinking deregulation is a vote-winning manifesto promise, it is easily pushed down the list of legislative priorities once governments reach power.

The Labour Party followed the trend in including licensing reform in their most recent manifesto. Although it was passed over for consideration in the last parliamentary session, it does appear that it will get some legislative consideration in the forthcoming parliamentary session.

The Queen's Speech in November 2002 flagged impending change in licensing laws. The speech promised that the government would "bring forward legislation to streamline the licensing system for premises selling alcohol. This will abolish fixed opening hours and introduce a range of conditions to reduce antisocial behaviour."

It looks as though the key aim of any legislation is to help eliminate or alleviate the problem of a uniform "chucking out time." In many towns and city centres, the 11 P.M. pub closing time is followed by large numbers of inebriates being cast into the streets simultaneously. This inevitably gives rise to antisocial behaviour. The government seems to want to give more flexibility to license-granting authorities to stagger (no pun intended) closing times. It also looks as though more power will be given to local residents to have the licenses of more unruly pubs suspended if they cause a nuisance.

The Queen's Speech put the issue on the agenda, but we will have to wait and see what the draft legislation actually says.

It would appear that these measures are targeted at town-centre pubs. Pubs with town-centre level turnover will be able to employ the additional staff needed to "man the pumps" at unsociable hours. As we discuss in this chapter, the bulk of the securitised universe tends to be local pubs. It is, in our view, less likely that such pubs will be tempted towards significantly extended opening hours given the higher costs that this may entail. It is likely that there will be honeymoon period, where licensees experiment with later opening to see if it leads to higher sales without pushing staff costs up excessively. If higher pub income can be obtained, this is beneficial for the sector. If not, pubs are likely to revert to more traditional hours. Outside the town centre, there may be sufficient demand to support one or two pubs in each locale that have late opening. The rest will probably end up offering the same hours (with perhaps a modest extension on certain evenings).

Competition Regulation

Pubcos, broadly speaking, owe their existence to competition regulation and its impact on the major brewers. Given the concentration of pub estates with a relatively few companies, there could, conceivably, emerge a risk that the current industry structure is seen as anticompetitive by regulators. However, the attention of the competition authorities, both domestically and within the European Union has been on access to distribution channels by brewers rather than on the tied relationship between the pubco and its tenants. As long as the landlord's tie with the pubco enables him to sell the product of a number of brewers, even if this is done through a distribution channel tied to the pubco, there seems little regulatory risk.

The industry does not currently feel under threat from the competition authorities. However, we believe it will be interesting to see how the authorities deal with the potential buyout of Unique by Enterprise Inns (who hold an option over the equity of Unique they do not already own). One area where competition problems may arise is where a pubco has a dominant (or at least anticompetitive) position in a specific area. This may lead to material trading of estate.

Smoking Regulation and Legislation

The government is developing policies on smoking in public places. This may lead to restrictions on smoking, which could have a negative affect on pub usage. At this time, there is an informal agreement between the hospitality industry (represented by industry pressure groups and lobbyists) and the government that revolves around the provision of smoke-free zones and general smoke abatement. Under the agreement, by the end of this year, 35% of pubs should either have nonsmoking areas or have ventilation that mitigates the smoke in the atmosphere.

It would appear that the industry is taking the stance that it needs to clean up or be cleaned up. The consequences of draconian measures on smoking could be dire. To combat this threat, it is taking strides to ensure that pubs are healthier and more pleasant (at least from an atmospheric point of view). This programme will inevitably increase the capital expenditure burden of the industry, at least in the near term.

WHY SECURITISE?

We believe that the success and prevalence of whole business securitisation in the UK rests on two factors:

- The existence of a legal framework that places secured creditors in a strongly controlling position in the event of insolvency. In particular, beneficiaries of a floating charge can, in the case of insolvency, appoint an administrative receiver and frustrate the appointment of an administrator. This gives creditors a high degree of control over asset disposal and management in the event that an enterprise begins to fail.
- The existence, in the UK, of a vibrant long-dated bond market is key. The rating agencies, and indeed any credit analyst, wish to see full amortisation of debt and absolutely minimal refinancing risk. The ability to finance assets over long periods allows for relatively higher leverage to be achieved. As well as strong institutional demand for long-dated fixed rate paper, with a variety of ratings, there is demand from funded investors (banks, etc.) for longer-dated floating rate paper. The historically low interest rate environment in the UK is another attractive feature in terms of maximising leverage potential.

Notwithstanding these conditions, it is not every business that can be securitised. The risk characteristics of the pub business are such that, with adequate covenant and other controls, an income stream to service debt can be relied upon with "investment grade" levels of confidence. The constraints applied through whole business securitisations allow for debt multiples to be high.

Virtually all the main pubcos are (or were at one stage) MBO/LBO transactions. Typically, such transactions are heavily debt financed and the main routes for seeking such financing tend to be:

- Leveraged bank finance
- High yield bonds
- Mezzanine funding
- Most often a combination of the above

However, these traditional approaches can have two distinct disadvantages compared with whole business securitisation:

- They can be more expensive in cost terms.
- They may not be able to deliver an equivalent level of leverage.

In a leveraged acquisition, the quantum of leverage can have a significant influence on equity returns. It is idiomatic that the higher the leverage, the higher the potential equity returns can be. All generalisations are wrong, and this is no exception. Sponsors and management will be cautious of high leverage if:

- It pushes the cost of capital on a transaction beyond supportable limits.
- The providers of capital place burdensome controls on business operation that reduces the scope of management to generate returns.

Certainly current securitisation pricing does not push costs to prohibitive levels. Equally, the constraints placed on management in pub securitisation appear, in our view, to balance the interests of creditors with the ambition of management.

The cost and flexibility of the debt financing, while critically important, is not the end of the story for pub securitisation. Leverage levels are built around stressed projections of future cash flow. Management projections are based on what value they believe they can add to the management of the business. Adding value will increase the price at which the business can be sold or floated. Here there is a co-alignment of interests between management and creditors. This is the "carrot" part of the relationship. The "stick" part is characterised by the security interest that creditors have over the business and the threat to the existing owners' equity.

There is liquidity in the pub estate market. Blocks of pubs have routinely changed hands in since 1999 and we would expect this trend to continue. We believe that there will be periodic trading—with the larger companies acting as consolidators. Scale, we would argue, is among the most critical factors in achieving success as a pubco. Those pubcos that have securitised have tended to use existing transactions as vehicles for future acquisitions. Each time an acquisition arises, it is funded (or refinanced at least) through the extant security structure. For relatively minor acquisitions, this can be done without significant restructuring. For larger transactions, as was recently the case with Unique and Pubmaster, more fundamental restructuring can take place. This is a trend we would expect to continue. The reason that securitisation vehicles are reused is, in our view, twofold:

EXHIBIT 23.1   Pubcos—More or Less All Securitised

Group	Owned	Securitised	Difference
Punch	4,300	4,038	262
Unique	4,200	4,074	126
Pubmaster	3,123	3,123	—
Spirit	1,060	1,032	28
Innspired	1,021	1,021	—
Wellington	840	835	5
Avebury	800	646	154

Source: BBPA/Company reports

- The costs of collapsing transactions with fixed rate tranches tends to be prohibitive, given that they generally contain Spens prepayment clauses.
- The costs of establishing a new structure can be high.

It is also instructive to look at the major groups to see how many pubs are in securitisation groups and how many are held in other parts of the respective groups. Judging from the data in Exhibit 23.1, it would appear that there is only limited scope for new issuance out of existing unsecuritised portfolios.

Changes in Law

The Enterprise Act of 2002 is now on the statute book. This act is a wide ranging piece of legislation that, among other things, will streamline the insolvency process in the UK. One of the underlying tenets of the legislation is to move insolvency towards a process that encourages restructuring rather than liquidation. Under the previous legislation, the 1986 Insolvency Act, holders of a floating charge of all (or substantially all) the assets of a company could, in an insolvency, appoint an administrative receiver to liquidate assets to repay their debts. Specifically, floating charge holders could frustrate the appointment of an administrator, thus placing them in a strong position. The government saw this right as unfairly favouring bank creditors and contrary to their objective of promoting an enterprise culture.

This could, conceivably, have posed a problem to whole business securitisation, which relies heavily on the safeguards afforded floating chargeholders under current UK insolvency regulations. However, the government, in drafting the legislation, looks to have taken advice from the City of London. Specific safe harbours have been incorporated into the legislation for capital markets transactions. Additionally, insolvency lawyers think it is highly improbable that a change in the law would have a detrimental effect on existing securitisation transactions. It looks, therefore, as thought the whole business securitisation technology remains firmly in place.

VALUE DRIVERS—THE KEY TO CREDIT ANALYSIS

Pubs, individually, are relatively simple businesses, but measuring their characteristics en masse *can be more complex*. In this section, we discuss what we consider are the key value/risk drivers of a pub portfolio.

Tenanted and Managed

Earlier in this chapter we outlined the different pub types. From the perspective of their business and financial profiles, the different types of pubs have different characteristics.

Managed Pubs

Managed pubs are typically larger than tenanted pubs in terms of floorspace, traffic, and barrelage. Because they are managed by a salaried staff and controlled directly by their owner, managed pubs will typically have a higher fixed cost base than tenanted or leased pubs. Higher turnover is achieved in several ways:

- *Location.* Managed portfolios tend to exhibit higher concentrations in city centres, close to railway stations, near football grounds, and other areas with high consumer traffic. Equally, because of its higher fixed cost base, managed pubs need to attract customers throughout the serving day. This is often achieved by offering comprehensive food and restaurant services for lunchtime consumers (shoppers, workers, etc.), discounted drink prices ("happy hours," etc.) to attract afternoon and early evening drinkers, and entertainment in the evenings to attract evening drinkers.
- *Branding and "theming."* Offering a branded or themed product offering will also often improve sales. Theming can take the form of sports bars, real ale pubs, young people's venues, food-led venues, Irish pubs, etc. A number of identifiable "brands" have also developed such as O'Neils, All Bar One, J.D. Wetherspoons, Firkin Pubs, Pitcher and Piano bars, and Big Steak Pubs. These pubs will often be decorated in a similar fashion to appeal to a specific segment of consumers (age, gender, interest, etc.).

With a higher fixed cost base at the outlet and central levels, managed pubs tend to be more operationally geared. Incremental increases in revenue above the fixed cost base have a more direct impact on income direct to the owners. Central management by the owner is also a factor. A managed portfolio will benefit from discounts in buying beer and other products.

From the perspective of a securitisation, however, managed portfolios have some negative features that should be borne in mind.

- Because of their typically high traffic locations, managed pubs are often in direct competition with neighbouring pubs. This obviates the need to refresh their product offering regularly to ensure that they continue to attract the volume of customers they require. This leads to higher levels of capital expenditure (both routine maintenance capex and major overhaul capex). Failure to invest in a managed estate can have a significantly negative effect on revenues, as sales can easily be lost to competitors.
- Unlike tenanted/leased pubs, managed estates do not generate a contractual income stream to their owners.
- Margins tend to be lower (18–25%) in managed pubs.
- There are higher staff risks in managed pubs. Since the owner is the proprietor, he will need to acquire and retain management and offer a sufficient incentive package to ensure that the pub operates at an optimal level.
- The owner bears all, or substantially all, the business risks associated with the operation.

Tenanted/Leased Pubs

In order to produce adequate returns, a managed pub needs to be large enough to comfortably cover its relatively higher fixed cost base. Tenanted pubs are, in contrast, typically smaller than managed pubs in size and turnover. They tend to be in less prominent or busy locations. The quality of the pub may appear to be lower since they are often faced with less competition for custom. A tenanted pub is most often typified by being a "local," although a number of the major tenanted portfolios do have "destination" pubs within them. Rather than offering a branded or themed experience, a tenanted pub will most often have a loyal local following.

The tenant is responsible for running a business that represents both his livelihood and, frequently, his home. The tenant will also often have significant capital tied up in the pub. Most commonly, this capital represents his or her "core life capital"—not borrowed money. We view this proprietary interest as central in making a risk assessment of the sector.

The principal source of revenue from such pubs tends to be the rental stream received by the owner and this is typically secure. Clearly the terms of the lease are important. Some lease terms allow for upward only (and sometimes index-linked) rent reviews and many leases are fully repairing and insuring. Other operating costs are for the account of the landlord. These features reduce the fixed cost component and, by consequence, the operational gearing of the concern.

Another positive feature of tenanted pubs is that they typically operate at higher margins than managed (40%+ margins are typical). However, this has to be viewed alongside the lower barrelage commonly exhibited by tenanted pubs. Virtually all the pubco-owned pubs require their licensees to purchase beer and other products through a tied arrangement. This allows the pubco to make bulk purchases from brewers and other suppliers and to command a (regularly significant) discount on such purchases. The benefits of such discounts are for the account of the pubco and, in securitisation transactions, is used for debt service.

A major trend among pubcos is to substitute beer-related revenues with higher rents. Rent is, by nature, a more secure income flow. Pubcos are implementing new lease arrangements that pass more discounts onto tenants, particularly if they meet or exceed sales targets. In return, the tenant pays higher rental.

If the tenant mismanages the enterprise and his barrelage/income falls below the critical break-even levels, the rental flow can come under threat. Current experience of collection rates in the industry is positive, with collection rates well over 99% on average. Rental defaults can be remedied by eviction and re-letting the pub, however such mismanagement could present a threat, if it becomes sufficiently widespread in a portfolio.

Most of the major pubcos actively seek to find potential tenants but there is a risk that there is a shortage of suitable tenants. The major pubcos dedicate resources to training and landlord development. We believe that this is key since, for many tenants, running a pub may be their first experience of owning and managing their own business.

Conversions

The trend within pubcos, broadly speaking, has been to convert many suitable managed pubs to tenanted pubs. This process has an element of risk in our opinion. If a pub manager knows that his pub is likely to be converted, and this would lead to him losing his livelihood, there are risks that a pub can become quickly run down. Long-term tenancy agreements are somewhat like residential mortgages—many of the risks become evident in the early years. Just as in a mortgage securitisation, where seasoning is a factor in determining risk levels, so it is in pub securitisation.

In this chapter we have focused on transactions for leased estates only.

Estate Valuations

The service of the securitised debt comes from revenues derived from the estate (rental income, beer-related income, AWP income, etc.). To the extent that each transaction is analysed on a going concern basis, it is these revenues that need to be monitored, forecast and stressed.

However, should the business not perform as expected, it is critical for bondholders that there is sufficient asset value in the property portfolio to cover the amount of outstanding debt at the time a problem occurs.

For most of the chartered surveyors that provide valuations, a significant part of their estimate of value is derived from where another pubco might purchase an estate. Given that securitisation is the most frequently used form of financing purchases, there seems to be a degree of circularity in the valuation technique.

In our modelling, we assume that, under stress, property valuations (as expressed as multiples of EBITDA) decline.

In the event of a systematic deterioration in profitability, valuations may well come under significant pressure.

Scale

A theme we repeat throughout this chapter is the value of scale. Scale is important, in our opinion, for two reasons:

- Leverage with brewers and other suppliers,
- Reduction of central cost overheads.

Both these factors are drivers towards industry consolidation and are persistently quoted by management of pubcos. While we would concur, in general, with this view, we also see risks. As Exhibit 23.2 shows, there is a direct correlation between profitability (measured by EBITDA/pub) and size. It should be borne in mind that the Punch transactions (Taverns and Funding) are served by a central supply and procurement function—thus capitalising on the purchasing power of the group as a whole.

It is common for pubcos to enter into supply contracts with brewers and other suppliers. If the estate finds it challenging to absorb and retail the supply, costs and penalties could accrue to pubcos.

Equally, while central cost reduction can benefit creditors, risks could also arise from running a central management that is too small. This risk, in our view, comes potentially to the fore during an integration process.

EXHIBIT 23.2 Scale—Critical to Profitability

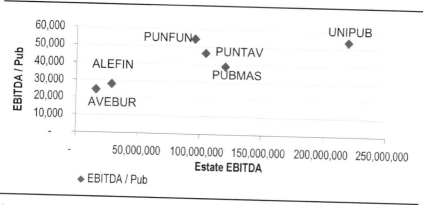

Source: Company reports.

Management

As in any business, the quality of management is key. Management needs to be highly proactive in leased estates. The role of management can be defined simply: to increase returns from the pub estate. In a business that relies significantly upon the enterprise of its tenants, management has relatively limited tools available to do this. Critical to effective management is the availability of information on performance of the estate and individual businesses within it. All the companies we review have a regional management system combined with computerised ordering systems. We would identify several factors where management can add value and reduce risk.

■ *Churn.* Within all portfolios, there are pubs that underperform. It is incumbent upon management to be able to identify which assets are not performing. Pubs may fail to perform for numerous reasons ranging from having a poor tenant to being in a disadvantaged location. Where no immediate remedy can be found, management needs to be able to dispose of the property and, where necessary, replace it with a property capable of generating better returns. Knowing what to buy is probably as important as knowing what to sell. Close attention should be paid to performance of an estate as its nature changes. We have not identified any particular estate that seems to underperform meaningfully in this respect.

■ *Portfolio investment.* A leased pub is, largely speaking, the tenant's business. It is the tenant that will operate the pub and try and boost income as best he or she can. However, defensive and development capex by the pubco is an important means of enhancing and preserving yield. Development capex will often take place prior to granting a lease. This will most commonly be spent on renovating or refurbishing a run-down pub, putting in food services, adding a play area in the garden, etc. Defensive capex tends to be dedicated to material repairs and is often done jointly with a tenant. Other items of capex that can enhance returns include the installation of beer metering systems that prevent buying-out.

- *Policing*. Ensuring that buying out (the practice of buying out of tie) is minimised is key. Pubcos monitor closely the performance of each pub versus budgeted sales levels. Any significant deviation is investigated. Increasingly, pubcos are installing metered pump systems that measure barrelage and reduce fraud. Equally, market kegs and barrels allow for buying out to be identified with a cursory inspection.
- *Creating incentives*. All of the companies have introduced tenancy and lease arrangements that incorporate economic incentives for landlords to sell more products. Achievement of targets is rewarded with increased discounts. Equally, pubcos provide landlords with the ability to source a broad range of nontied products through central ordering systems.
- *Recruitment, training, and support*. Running a pub is a challenging job. Pubcos are keen to recruit good tenants and there is good anecdotal evidence that initial training of tenants provides for improved returns.

Income Mix

Income mix is an important determinant of risk in our view. Rental flows are, in our opinion, significantly more stable and predictable than beer-related income. Beer income tends to be more volatile. Rental income, in contrast, is contractual in nature and, from the landlord's perspective, is high on the priority of payments. Virtually all the pubcos are implementing plans to boost the rental component of cash flow. Other income, such as that from AWPs, is important but tends to be less material.

There is some considerable variation between the different transactions in respect of income mix as can be seen in Exhibit 23.3.

Geographic Location and Concentration

Geographic diversity, as in any business, should be regarded as a risk reduction feature in our view. Reliance on a single region or market logically imposes risk, which can be mitigated by diversification. The larger estates are well diversified, with UNIPUB being the best (Unique does not provide specific regional breakdown—but the map they provide

EXHIBIT 23.3   Income Mix—Deal by Deal

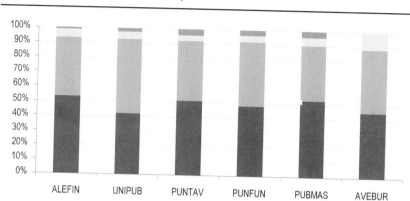

Source: Company reports/Rating Agencies.

does indicate a very diverse portfolio). ALEFIN, in our view, is the most heavily concentrated portfolio, with a large exposure to the South West.

Geographical diversity is not always a positive in our view. A widely diversified portfolio may place pressure on management or increase central costs. We would identify AVEBUR as potentially falling prey to this risk.

Lease Terms and Expiry Schedule

The terms of the leases, which underpin securitisations is a key factor. Many of the pubcos, by virtue of their acquisition strategies, have inherited legacy arrangements. Most pubcos seek to replace these arrangements with their own product offering. As we mention elsewhere in this chapter, a common feature of such "new leases" is that they tend to be at higher rental levels and offer tenants higher discounts on beer. The substantial majority of lease agreements underpinning lease portfolios are fully tenant repairing and insuring. Again, the vast majority of the leases have either upward only RPI or peer-compared, rent review provisions.

When pubs are waiting for a new, long-term tenant, pubcos tend to grant short-term tenancies known as *tenancies at will* (TAWs). TAWs tend to be cancellable at short notice and place the burden of repairs and insurance on the owners. Such arrangements are necessary as estates undergo transition and new leases are put in place. However, should large numbers of TAWs persist, we would identify this as a risk.

Acquisitions and Disposals

As we have already discussed, trading the portfolio is a crucial tool for portfolio yield enhancement. Securitisation structures need to balance this need for flexibility with the requirement to protect bond-holders. Each of the transactions we review sets a framework for acquisitions and disposals. Each deal differs, but the transactions follow a similar path:

- The total value of disposals and acquisitions tends to be controlled.
- Funds raised from disposals need to be applied to acquisitions or, if unused for a specified period, applied to debt reduction.
- Free cash flow or surplus cash can only be used for acquisitions if certain conditions (DSCR hurdles commonly) are met.
- Transactions should allow only the disposal of assets that are clearly performing below average within the portfolio.
- Equally, acquired assets should meet or exceed minimum return conditions.

Most transactions carry a general carve-out for transactions that receive rating agency approval—allowing them do to almost anything that does not lead to a downgrade.

Larger block acquisitions tend to lead to tap issuance from transactions. In these cases, rating agency approval is necessary.

Capital Expenditure and Controls

Just as portfolio churn is a vital key in risk reduction and return enhancement, so is capex. We would argue that some level of defensive capex is vital in order to preserve the yield generation capability of a portfolio. Each transaction has a framework that retains the balance between ensuring that defensive capex is sufficient to preserve portfolio yields and "gold plating."

Restricted Payments

Investors in pub securitisation transactions look to the assets of and cash flows deriving to the securitisation group. It is critical to restrict any haemorrhage of cash that might prejudice the credit position of credit investors. Equally, the equity (private or public) in a pubco does not want to see excess cash build up trapped in a securitisation. Those entities with listed equity, such as Punch, will typically need to demonstrate to equity investors that they can pay dividends. Each of the transactions we have analysed incorporate strict dividend restrictions. We have outlined these in our transaction review section. In most cases they do not permit dividends (or analogous payments) outside the securitisation group, unless debt has reduced by prespecified levels and coverage ratios are above specified hurdles. The formula is often graduated.

Financial and Other Covenants

Financial covenants play an important role in pub transactions. They provide an "early warning" system that should give an alert on potential deterioration of creditworthiness. All the transactions contain a DSCR test, measured either quarter by quarter or on an annual trailing basis. Based on our review, none of the issuers "play games" with the numerator part of the equation. However, we would alert investors (we detail in our transaction reviews) that some differences exist in the construction of the denominator. Rather than dividing by the scheduled *principal and interest payments, some transactions look at the* actual *payments. While prepayment is not fundamentally a problem—indeed it is on balance credit positive—the effect may be to create a DSCR that is more like an interest cover ratio. This, in our view, may reduce the covenant's value as an early warning system.*

Transactions also carry net worth tests. In our view, these are of limited value.

The Role of the Rating Agencies

The rating agencies' role in these transactions extends beyond their normal role. As well as providing original ratings and supervision/surveillance they can play a more active function. These transactions all operate within a complex framework of covenants, dividend restrictions, acquisition and disposal restrictions, and so forth. In many transactions, these restrictions can be overridden if the rating agencies provide affirmation that no negative rating action would derive from breaching these restrictions. Securitisation transactions have had this type of provision in them for some time, but this sector appears to rely upon the rating agencies heavily.

In our view, this is a modest credit positive. The rating agencies have far more depth of understanding than do, for instance, security trustees. They are privy to a significant amount of nonpublic information. Although the agencies themselves are probably not entirely comfortable with playing such a pivotal role, we believe investors can take comfort from their position.

The Presence of Monoline Insurers

Certain pubcos have engaged monoline insurers (AMBAC and MBIA specifically) to provide guarantee wraps to certain tranches of their deals. We would make a number of observations:

- Monoline guarantees can significantly reduce execution risks.
- It is possible that there is some arbitrage available to pubcos. The cost of AAA bonds plus the cost of the guarantee may be lower than the cost of selling single-A senior bonds.
- Although the monolines tend to rank pari passu with senior bondholders in right of payment, they often have more control in the event of a default.

The monolines, like the rating agencies, work on these transactions from their genesis. They are privy to significant amounts of information that bondholders never see and they can have significant input into the setting of terms and covenants. Where bondholders have a certain degree of liquidity, the monoline insurers are exposed for the whole life of the bonds they are insuring. They often, therefore, get more performance information than public bondholders (or analysts). We believe that investors can take a degree of comfort from the presence of monolines in a transaction, even if they own bonds that do not benefit from a guarantee.

Liquidity Facilities and Reserves

Liquidity facilities and reserves are important components of transaction structures. We detail in our transaction reviews the details of how liquidity is applied. We think that there are several factors that investors should bear in mind:

- Liquidity facilities often have a "super senior" status in right of payment.
- The amounts that can be applied to different tranches vary from deal to deal.

SUMMARY

The pub industry has undergone significant change in terms of its ownership structure, with pubcos now the dominant players in the market. Estates of pubs, especially leased and tenanted pubs, generate significant free cash flow and are subject to relatively low levels of volatility. Combined with a highly creditor-friendly securitisation and insolvency regime in the United Kingdom, this has led to a significant growth in securitisation of pub estates. Securitisation offers pubcos and their owners the opportunity to gear up acquisitions significantly beyond the levels available using more conventional financing techniques. Equally, investors in the United Kingdom have become increasingly comfortable with the issues surrounding pub securitisation and the performance of the transactions executed until now. Whole business securitisation has developed rapidly in the United Kingdom, sometimes with mixed results. However, there can be little doubt that this technology as applied to pubs has been highly successful for all participants.

Mortgage-Backed Securities

European Residential Mortgage-Backed Securities

Phil Adams, Ph.D.
Director
Barclays Capital

Residential mortgages were the first asset class to be securitised in Europe. Although the introduction of new asset classes has reduced the dominance of *residential mortgage-backed securities* (RMBS), it remains the largest sector today, typically accounting for approximately 35–40% of new issuance. European RMBS have been popular with investors, not least because their performance has been very good. Since the beginning of this market there has never been a default on a European RMBS transaction, very few transactions have been downgraded and none of these downgrades have occurred as a result of a deterioration in the performance of the collateral. These downgrades have all been as a result of the downgrade of third parties supporting the transaction. European ABS are now much less reliant on third-party support, so the level of downgrades experienced between 1991 and 1994 should be less likely to happen again if similar circumstances arose.

The European RMBS market was started in the United Kingdom in 1987 by the centralised lenders that had been set up following the deregulation of the mortgage market in the mid-1980s. The United Kingdom was followed by Spain, which saw its first RMBS issue in 1991. The recession in the early 1990s caused several RMBS issuers in the United Kingdom to withdraw from the market and there was little or no issuance in the United Kingdom or Spain for a few years. The market started to expand again in the mid-1990s (see Exhibit 24.1) and

EXHIBIT 24.1   Issuance Volumes of European RMBS

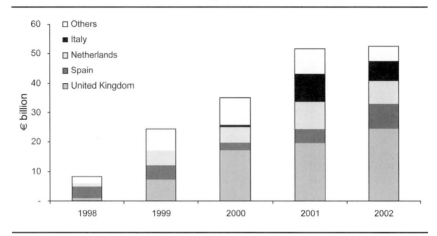

Source: Barclays Capital.

it was around this time that RMBS started to be issued in other European countries. This growth has generally relied on changes to the legal framework within each country and has been driven by a number of factors. For a number of lenders, securitisation provides their primary source of funding. Banks have found that deposits have been switched to other investments and that there has been a need to access new investors as their traditional investors have sought to diversify across other euro assets.

Although we may refer to the European RMBS market as if it is a single entity, in practice it is a collection of diverse markets, with each individual country's issuance reflecting its unique cultural and legal environment. However, there are also considerable similarities between the basic characteristics of European mortgages, and RMBS structures largely follow just a few standard models.

INDUSTRY OVERVIEW

The economy drives the mortgage markets, but governments also play a role. In many countries it has been long-term government policy to promote home ownership, usually through the tax system, and particularly targeting low income households. These schemes have generally been successful but the level of home ownership still varies considerably across Europe (see Exhibit 24.2).

EXHIBIT 24.2   Home Ownership Rates in Europe

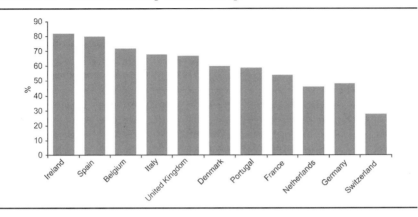

Source: European Mortgage Federation.

EXHIBIT 24.3   Outstanding Mortgage Debt

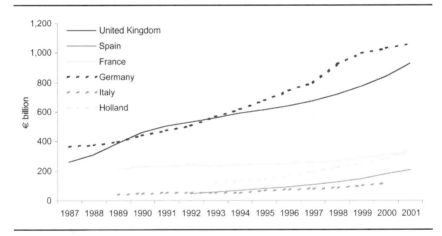

Source: European Mortgage Federation, Bank of England, Bank of Spain, Bundesbank, Datamonitor.

The economic environment has been favourable for the mortgage markets since the recession in the early 1990s in most European countries. Economic growth has been robust, which has brought with it an extended period of real earnings increases and a reduction in unemployment rates. In addition, inflation has been reduced in many countries, allowing interest rates to fall to historically low levels. Against this background, it is not surprising that the mortgage markets have been growing strongly (see Exhibit 24.3).

Strong economic growth with falling unemployment and high consumer confidence has fuelled the demand for housing. Strong real wage growth and falling interest rates improved the affordability of mortgages, and as a result house prices have risen substantially in many countries (although Germany is a notable exception).

This period of strong house price appreciation has followed a period of lacklustre growth or even declines in the early 1990s. The UK housing market was affected particularly severely. Legislative changes in the mid-1980s opened up the UK mortgage market to bank insurance companies and other lenders. Centralised lenders and some foreign lenders entered the UK market and the competition that ensued led to the development of innovative mortgage products, such as self-certified mortgages, 100% loan-to-value loans, and a range of new repayment methods. In addition to the new products, the competitive environment and the favourable economic background caused many lenders to relax their lending criteria. This contributed to the high number of defaults when house prices started to decline in 1989.

During the recession that followed, some lenders withdrew from the market, and those that remained were forced to review their underwriting criteria. As a result, the industry became more risk averse. The recession also left a large number of potential borrowers with adverse credit histories who were then unable to borrow from traditional lenders. This set the stage for the emergence of the nonconforming mortgage sector as the housing market improved. These niche lenders took a risk-based pricing approach to mortgage lending and specifically targeted clients who were unable to borrow from mainstream lenders. These lenders have become significant issuers of mortgage-backed securities.

In addition to the emergence of the nonconforming sector, the United Kingdom has also seen the development of an active "buy-to-let" market, flexible mortgages, and a reverse mortgage market, all of which have been used as collateral for MBS transactions.

Types of Mortgages

There is a considerable variety of mortgages on offer to European consumers, many tailored to the particular circumstances or borrower preferences of a particular country. However, for an investor in an RMBS transaction, these various characteristics can be divided into two largely separate categories: factors affecting the credit quality of the mortgage and those influencing the borrower's payment profile. To a certain extent, the required payment profile on a loan can affect its credit quality so this artificial categorisation is not perfect but it is useful for this discussion. We discuss the factors affecting credit quality later, and the remainder of this section concentrates on the cash flow properties of mortgages.

Interest Rates

The type of interest rate charged on mortgage loans varies between countries. UK mortgages have traditionally charged a variable rate of interest, which has been adjusted at the discretion of the lending institution. However, interest rates that are tied to a particular benchmark interest rate (such as LIBOR or the Bank of England Repo Rate) have become more popular. In Spain, for example, variable rate mortgages must be tied to one of a number of benchmark rates specified by the regulator.

In many other European markets interest rates are normally fixed for a specified number of years agreed at the start of the mortgage. At the end of this period, the borrower may choose to refix the interest rate for a further period at the rates on offer at the time.

Increasing competition has encouraged lenders to offer special incentives to attract new customers. These usually take the form of an initial discounted or a fixed rate period, which will give the borrower lower payments or certainty over the size of the payments in the first few years of the loan.

Repayment Profile

The repayment profile of a mortgage can take one of two basic forms: (1) a capital repayment loan, where the borrower makes regular payments consisting of the interest due and a portion of the capital outstanding so the loan is repaid in full at maturity; or (2) an interest-only loan, where the capital must be paid in full on the maturity date of the mortgage. Repayment mortgages are often constant payment amortising loans but in certain markets linear amortisation is the norm.

Prepayments

A borrower has the right to repay a mortgage loan (in part or in full) at any time. This can be for a number of reasons, but as interest rates have declined and competition has intensified, reducing margins on mortgage products, the number of borrowers refinancing their mortgages with other lenders has increased. This has been helped in part by the house price increases in many countries.

The borrower may have to pay an early redemption fee. In some markets the rates are tightly regulated but they tend to vary among lenders and mortgage products. These charges can sometimes be high, especially for mortgages with long fixed rate periods where the prepayment penalty can often largely negate any benefit of refinancing as interest rates decline.

Flexible and Offset Account Mortgages

Flexible mortgages are an increasingly popular innovation. They allow the borrower to make prepayments on a loan at any time without penalty. With most flexible products, the borrower will then be allowed to redraw these prepayments at a later date, either as cash or by taking a payment holiday, provided the original paydown schedule is not exceeded. Offset account mortgages offer the borrower more flexibility by only charging interest on the difference between the outstanding balance of the mortgage and the credit balance on the associated bank account.

COLLATERAL CHARACTERISTICS

RMBS transactions consist of a number of classes of notes that rely on the cash flows generated by an underlying pool of mortgages. The credit assessment of an RMBS transaction can be broken down into two distinct parts: the credit assessment of the collateral and the assessment of the protection provided by the transaction structure. In this section we discuss the key factors to consider when assessing the collateral supporting an RMBS transaction and how these factors can influence performance. Most of these considerations apply to any mortgage irrespective of its origin, although differences between countries make direct comparisons difficult. For example, the tax system in the Netherlands encourages borrowers to take a large mortgage loan, so loan-to-value ratios tend to be significantly higher than in other countries.

Affordability

The key to assessing the probability of borrower default lies in assessing their ability and willingness to pay. Affordability is usually measured either as an income multiple for the loan or the ratio of the borrower's monthly debt obligations to their monthly net income. The higher the level of borrower income is relative to debt obligations, the better the ability of the borrower to absorb any financial shocks.

Loan-to-Value Ratio

The *loan-to-value ratio* (LTV) gives a measure of the equity a borrower has invested in a property. A large equity stake provides an important motivation to avoid defaulting on a loan. The ability to save a large deposit may indicate a higher level of financial discipline by the borrower, which should also indicate a lower likelihood of default.

The LTV ratio also has an important impact on the extent of any losses sustained in the event that a loan goes into default. A lower LTV loan can absorb a greater decline in the value of a property before losses are realised in the collateral pool. Lenders will often have recourse to other assets belonging to the borrower, in addition to the secured property to cover any losses in the event of default, although this is usually ignored in any credit assessment.

When comparing LTVs across countries, it is important to consider the basis for the valuation. Most valuations will be an assessment of the estimated market value of the property provided there is a willing buyer. Valuations that are based on a forced sale assumption (as in the Netherlands) will be lower and therefore the reported LTVs will be correspondingly higher.

Mortgage Type

The type of mortgage can also influence the credit quality of the loan. In summary, mortgage products that exaggerate payment shocks are likely to experience increased levels of defaults, whereas those that provide a degree of stability or payment shock protection are likely to see fewer defaults.

In countries where mortgage interest rates are predominantly variable, an increase in interest rates will immediately feed through to the payments required from mortgage borrowers, so a rapid increase in rates would cause a significant payment shock for borrowers. In countries where mortgages are mostly fixed rate, the rates are not normally fixed for the entire life of the loan but have periodic reset dates. Therefore, short-term changes in interest rates will be less of a concern but payments may change significantly on the interest rate reset date.

Mortgages that offer an initial teaser rate present a payment shock at the end of the discount period that may cause problems for the borrower, so these loans are often penalised in rating agency analysis. Similarly, a loan that charges a fixed rate of interest for an initial period could also create a payment shock when the rate becomes variable but, to a certain extent, this is mitigated by the stability of payments during the early years, protecting the borrower from rate rises when the risk of default is highest.

Interest-only mortgages, where the full balance of the loan has to be repaid at maturity, present a potentially significant payment shock to the borrower. These loans may be linked to a savings or investment product designed to help repay the loan on maturity. Loans without a repayment mechanism rely on the borrower's ability to repay or refinance the loan at the time. These loans are usually penalised in rating agency analysis of the collateral.

Flexible mortgages and current account mortgages have the advantages for the borrower of being able to prepay without penalty and then, at a later date, recover some of these prepayments either through a capital redraw or through a payment holiday. For credit assessment, they are usually treated as a standard interest-only or repayment mortgage.

Buy-to-let mortgages are another type of mortgage product, which started to become popular in the United Kingdom during the late 1990s. It is generally assumed that default probabilities will be higher for a buy-to-let mortgage than one for the borrower's primary residence. However, in the event of default, the lender will have the ability to appoint a receiver of rent to collect rental payments directly from the tenant, and there is a less time-consuming process for gaining vacant possession of the property. These factors should serve to reduce the loss severity.

Seasoning

Standard & Poor's analysis of historical data for UK mortgages indicates that a borrower is most likely to default in the first five years of a loan. So a mortgage that has been outstanding for some time and is up to date with its payments should represent a lower risk than a new loan. As earnings and wages tend to rise over the long term, the borrower's ability and incentive to maintain the mortgage payments should increase over time.

Many securitisations by regular issuers of MBS will have a relatively low average seasoning on their collateral pool at launch. Loans that have been originated relatively recently will have had little opportunity to fall behind with their payments so this pool is likely to have low arrears. Experience suggests that arrears tend to increase over the first two years and then stabilise as the collections process and, if necessary, repossessions take effect. Therefore, when comparing the arrears within collateral pools, it is important to also consider the age of the loans in the portfolios.

Loan Purpose

Loans used to purchase or refinance the purchase of the borrower's primary residence are expected to be less likely to default than loans for second homes or investment properties. It is assumed that a borrower with financial problems is most likely to ensure the family home is secure before paying other debts. Remortgages that involve the withdrawal of equity are often used for debt consolidation or to finance spending above the level of available savings. The rating agencies consider loans that release accumulated equity in a property to be higher risk than purchase or simple refinancing loans, and penalise them accordingly.

Borrower Profile

European RMBS are generally supported by mortgages to borrowers with stable earnings and good credit records. Self-employed borrowers are generally considered to present a higher risk of default than those that are paid a salary, although this depends to a large extent on the nature and size of the business.

In the United Kingdom, the specialist nonconforming lenders have built a business from lending to borrowers that would be turned down by mainstream lenders. They will consider lending to borrowers who have had previous credit problems, mortgage arrears, county court judgements against them for not paying debts, or even those who have been declared bankrupt in the past. In addition, they are willing to extend self-certified loans to people who find it difficult to provide sufficient proof of their earnings for the mainstream lenders. These borrowers can have a considerably higher risk of default, depending on the individual. The interest rate these borrowers will be charged will depend on the lender's assessment of this default risk.

Geographic Distribution

European RMBS transactions contain mortgages originated in a single country, so investors wishing to build a diversified European RMBS portfolio will have to invest in a selection of transactions. However, even within a single country property prices can behave differently between regions. So geographic diversity, or at least the absence of a significant regional concentration, is an important characteristic, as it will help mitigate the impact on the transaction of a housing downturn in any one region of the country.

Property Values

Expensive properties tend to experience proportionally greater declines in value in a deteriorating market than homes with an average market price. This greater volatility is due to the limited number of potential purchasers for these properties, causing a lack of liquidity in this market, and less precise pricing information due to the lack of comparable benchmark homes. Very low value properties also tend to realise lower recoveries than average.

Arrears

Arrears on a mortgage loan indicate that the borrower is likely to be suffering some degree of financial stress and, as such, these loans have a higher risk of going into default. The rating agencies usually take the pessimistic assumption that any loan more than 90 days behind with its payments is going to default, and increase the default probability assumptions significantly for loans with less serious arrears. When using arrears as an indicator of the quality of a mortgage pool, it is important to take the seasoning of the pool into account. Arrears levels generally start to stabilise when the average seasoning reaches two to three years. Earlier than this the arrears are likely to be below their long-run sustainable level.

Loss Severities

The severity of losses experienced on enforcement of a loan will depend on the proceeds of the property sale, foreclosure costs, carry costs, the LTV of the loan, and the priority of the charge on the property. In some cases it is possible to recover a proportion of any remaining debt from the borrower after the security has been realised, which would serve to reduce the loss severity. But this cannot be relied on, and so is normally ignored in any credit assessment.

Foreclosure and Carry Costs

The final components of the loss severity are the foreclosure costs and the loss of interest during the foreclosure process. The time it will take to repossess and sell a property will depend largely on the legal process in the relevant country. For example, the time from when the borrower stops paying until sale will typically take 12 months in the Netherlands and the United Kingdom, but this process can take several years in Italy. During this period, the transaction will not be receiving interest on the loan, causing a stress on the revenue generated by the collateral pool.

RATING AGENCY ANALYSIS

The rating agencies make an assessment of the overall robustness of the collateral and the transaction structure by applying certain assumptions about how loans will behave in an economic downturn rather than simply looking at the current situation. These assumptions are more pessimistic the higher the rating being considered. As a result, the ratings on RMBS transactions (and other ABS) are resilient to deterioration in the economic outlook.

Each rating agency has its own methodology for assessing the robustness of an RMBS transaction; the details vary from country to country and will be adjusted from time to time but the principles are similar in each case. This section provides an illustration of the rating process based primarily on Fitch's criteria for assessing UK RMBS transactions described in their publication, *UK Residential Mortgage Default Model II*, 13 October 2000.

Default Probability

The first step in the Fitch rating process is to estimate the probability of default for each loan in the collateral pool. This will take into account all the factors discussed in the previous section.

Loan Affordability and LTV

Fitch uses the combination of the LTV and the affordability measure for a loan in order to arrive at a base case default probability for any particular borrower in a particular rating test. In the United Kingdom, the income multiple has traditionally been used as the measure of loan affordability, and Fitch places loans in one of five classifications based on this measure (Exhibit 24.4).

The base case default probability will then depend on the rating being considered and the LTV of the loan. Exhibit 24.5 shows the Fitch default probability assumptions for loans where the income multiple is between 2.75 and 3.00 for various ratings tests.

EXHIBIT 24.4   Fitch Income Multiple Classifications

Income Multiple	From	To
Class 1	0.00	1.99
Class 2	2.00	2.49
Class 3	2.50	2.74
Class 4	2.75	3.00
Class 5	3.01	

Source: Fitch, *UK Residential Mortgage Default Model II*, October 2000.

EXHIBIT 24.5   Fitch Default Probability Assumption for Class 4 Loans

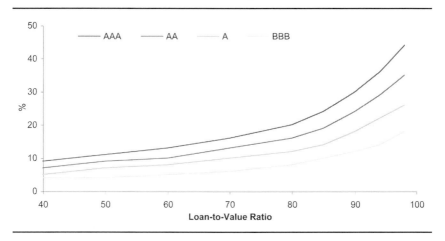

Source: Fitch, *UK Residential Mortgage Default Model II*, October 2000.

Other Factors

The initial default probability assumption is then adjusted (usually increased) to take into account any other important features of the loan. These factors include:

- *Mortgage type.* Interest-only mortgages that are not linked to a repayment vehicle will have the base case default probability increased by a factor up to 1.33, depending on the time to maturity of the loan.
- *Equity withdrawal.* Loans taken out to refinance an existing mortgage will not be penalised unless the borrower uses the opportunity to withdraw equity from the property when the default probability will be increased by 1.10–1.25×.
- *Second homes.* The assumption is that a borrower in financial difficulties will be more likely to default on a second home than the primary residence (1.10–1.25×).
- *Buy-to-let properties.* These loans are assumed to have a higher probability of default as for a second home but the loss severity may be reduced due to an easier repossession process and the ability to appoint a receiver of rent.
- *Borrower profile.* A number of special factors may arise with nonconforming borrowers. These range from people with court judgements against them for failing to repay a debt or even a previous bankruptcy (1.25–2.50×) to borrowers who cannot provide sufficient proof of income (1.25–1.75×).
- *Servicer quality.* There is qualitative judgement based on the quality of the underwriting and servicing processes and systems. This can increase or decrease the final default probability assumption.

Property Value Declines

Fitch has carried out an analysis of property price movements by region in the United Kingdom and has used the results to assess the amounts by which property prices might be expected to fall in a time of stress. These assessments become progressively more pessimistic for higher ratings categories, as illustrated in Exhibit 24.6. Fitch has similar tables for other countries.

Fitch will increase the market value decline assumptions for very high or very low value properties or if there are significant regional concentrations in the collateral.

Loss Severities

The expected loss severity for each loan can then be calculated by taking into account the LTV of the loan, market value decline on the property, foreclosure and selling costs, and the cost of carry during this process.

EXHIBIT 24.6   Fitch Regional UK Market Value Decline Assumptions (%)

Region	AAA	AA	A	BBB	BB	B
London	48	44	39	35	30	27
Outer Metro	43	39	35	31	27	24
Southeast	42	38	34	30	25	23
N. Ireland	42	38	35	32	29	26
East Anglia	41	36	32	27	22	20
W Midlands	38	34	30	26	22	20
Southwest	37	33	29	25	22	19
E Midlands	37	33	28	25	21	19
Northwest	37	32	28	24	20	18
Yorks./Hum.	30	26	22	17	11	10
North	29	25	22	18	14	12
Wales	27	24	20	18	15	13
Scotland	27	23	19	15	11	10

Source: Fitch, *UK Residential Mortgage Default Model II*, October 2000.

The default probability and expected loss estimate allow Fitch to calculate an expected loss on the entire transaction for each rating assessment.

Ratings Assessment

The final ratings assessment of the RMBS notes will reflect the ratings scenario under which the notes will continue to receive all amounts due. This assessment will also take into account the potential variations in the timing of the losses and uncertainty in the prepayment rate on the mortgages.

RMBS TRANSACTION STRUCTURES

The challenge facing the designers of RMBS transactions is to provide a structure that will provide an attractive investment while being able to handle the uncertain nature of the cash flows generated by the underlying mortgages. A transaction will usually be structured into several classes of notes with different expected maturities and different risk profiles to appeal to a variety of investors.

EXHIBIT 24.7   A Generic Cash Flow Waterfall

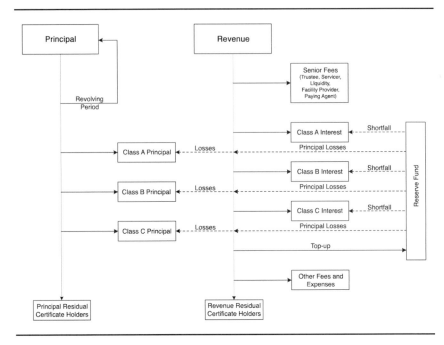

Credit Protection

European RMBS transactions contain a combination of various features designed to protect investors from the impact of defaults on mortgages in the underlying collateral pool, including excess spread, reserve fund, and subordination of any lower priority notes.

Cash Flow Allocation

The heart of the credit protection in a RMBS transaction is governed by rules that determine how the cash flow in the transaction is allocated. Exhibit 24.7 illustrates a generic cash flow allocation scheme (the cash flow waterfall).

Principal and interest are separated and the principal component may be used to redeem notes, to purchase additional collateral or returned to the mortgage originator depending on the type of structure involved. The nonprincipal amount, or revenue component, is used to pay any necessary fees and expenses for the transaction, the interest on the notes, and to cover losses.

Excess Spread

It is normal in European RMBS transactions for the entire revenue component of the receipts from borrowers to flow through the cash flow waterfall. The average interest rate charged on the mortgages will exceed the weighted average rate payable on the notes plus fees and expenses, so there will be excess cash flowing through the waterfall (excess spread). Excess spread will be used first to cover any losses that have been incurred, second to top up the reserve fund to its required balance (if necessary), and finally any remaining amounts are paid back to the originator of the mortgages as its profit.

Principal Deficiency Ledgers

In European RMBS transactions, bonds are not generally written down when losses are incurred in the collateral pool. Instead, the losses are recorded in a principal deficiency ledger, which records the extent to which the balance outstanding on the notes exceeds the remaining assets. Usually, both excess spread and the reserve fund can be used to cover losses and so pay down the principal deficiency ledger. This mechanism is beneficial to holders of the lower-rated notes because the notes do not get written off immediately and any future excess spread will be used to cover the loss.

Reserve Fund

The reserve fund consists of a cash amount that the issuer places on deposit at launch, which is available to cover any shortfalls in income and any principal losses during the life of a transaction. If the reserve fund is used, future excess spread will be retained until it is replenished up to its required balance. The required balance is usually a fixed monetary amount, but some transactions allow the reserve fund to amortise or even require it to increase depending on collateral performance.

Subordination

The cash flow waterfall encapsulates the subordination of the junior classes of notes. As all cash received is used to pay items on the senior notes first, this will inevitably mean that any loss that cannot be covered through trapping excess spread or from the reserve fund will result in a shortfall in the funds available to redeem the most junior class of notes.

Insurance

Many lenders require borrowers taking out high LTV loans to pay for *mortgage indemnity guarantee* (MIG) to cover the high LTV portion of the loan. If the borrower were to subsequently default, the lender would be able to claim for any additional loss incurred as a result of lending above the standard LTV. This has the advantage for the lender, and consequently the investor, that the loss severity will be reduced. However, it would introduce an element of sensitivity to the financial health of the insurer into the transaction. The conditions and cover provided by MIG insurance vary, but it is usual for the claim to be settled after repossession and sale of the property. This process may take considerable time during which the transaction will need to cover the carry cost for the loan.

Liquidity Facility

Many transactions include a liquidity facility. Although it does not provide protection against losses on the underlying collateral, it is available to cover temporary shortfalls in revenue receipts.

Pass-Through Transactions

Traditionally, European RMBS transactions have been structured as pass-through notes, where the principal received from borrowers is used to repay noteholders. This has the advantage of keeping the outstanding balance of the collateral and the notes in balance, but the disadvantage for noteholders is that the timing of their cash flows is uncertain.

Redemption

In a pass-through transaction, the notes will normally be split into a number of classes that will be redeemed in order of priority. The actual speed at which the notes are redeemed will depend on the underlying repayment schedule of the mortgages in the pool and the rate at which the borrowers prepay their mortgages (see Exhibit 24.8 for a generic example).

Transactions may include a substitution period during which the issuer is allowed to use principal receipts to purchase additional mortgages. This, in effect, allows the issuer to prevent the collateral pool (and therefore the notes) paying down, giving noteholders certainty of cash flows during this period. However, at the end of the substitution period, principal payments will be used to redeem notes in the normal manner.

One consequence of the sequential paydown of the notes is that, as the highest rated notes are paid down first, the average cost of the notes increases during the life of the transaction. This will reduce the excess spread and therefore the cash flowing back to the originator. The erosion of excess spread can be reduced by allowing the notes to redeem on a pro rata basis. This will only be allowed after some performance triggers have been met, which usually include the credit enhancement on the senior notes reaching a certain minimum level, the reserve fund being fully funded, and the arrears being below a specified level (see

EXHIBIT 24.8 Example Paydown Profile for a Pass-Through MBS Transaction (15% CPR)

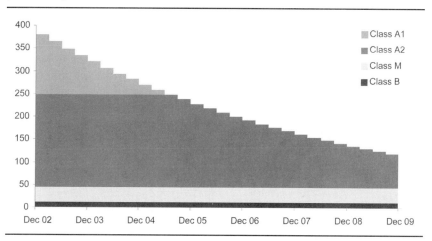

Source: Barclays Capital.

EXHIBIT 24.9 Example Paydown Profile with Switch to Pro Rata Redemptions

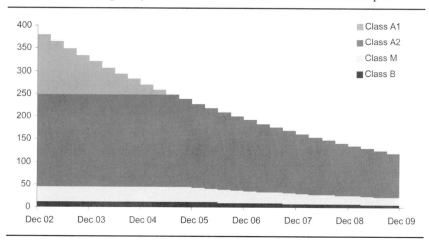

Source: Barclays Capital.

Exhibit 24.9). These transactions normally revert to sequential redemption when the collateral pool reaches a certain minimum size.

The effect of a switch from sequential to pro rata redemption will stop the gradual erosion of excess spread but this will be accompanied by a reduction in the rate of improvement in credit enhancement.

Legal Maturity

The legal final maturity of the notes in a pass-through transaction is normally set to be two years after the maturity date of the longest-dated mortgage. This should allow time for the administrator to repossess and sell the property even if the borrower defaulted on the last mortgage payment. In a few transactions, the fastest paying class of notes may have a shorter legal final maturity if there is a sufficient quantity of mortgages in the pool maturing early enough to guarantee payment by this date, but this is unusual.

Optional Redemption

In a pass-through transaction the issuer normally has the option to call the notes under three specified circumstances:

- The imposition of withholding tax on noteholder interest payments.
- The aggregate balance of the mortgage pool falling below a certain percentage (usually 10%) of the initial amount outstanding (a cleanup call).
- On a specified date, usually five or seven years after launch.

When the issuer has the option to call the notes on a specified date, the interest margin on the notes will usually increase. This gives the originator an additional economic incentive to arrange for the notes to be called. However, in certain jurisdictions this type of call may prevent the off-balance sheet treatment of the securitised loans, so this step-and-call feature is not found in all transactions.

Prepayments

Prepayments are the most important factor in determining the redemption profile of the notes in a pass-through transaction. The prepayment rate is usually measured as an annualised *conditional prepayment rate* (CPR), which is defined as the proportion of the outstanding balance of the mortgages that is paid down ahead of schedule during the period. Exhibit 24.10 illustrates the paydown profile for the same example transaction as in Exhibit 24.9, but with an increased prepayment rate of 35% CPR.

The factors driving prepayments will include the path of interest rates, the economic and competitive environment, the type of mortgage, and borrower profile, so they are difficult to predict. Most European RMBS are floating-rate notes and so prepayments will have a limited impact on investors, and with many mortgages being variable rate or having large prepayment penalties, falling interest rates do not necessarily give the borrower the opportunity to refinance at a more competitive

EXHIBIT 24.10   Example Paydown Profile at High Prepayment Speeds (35% CPR)

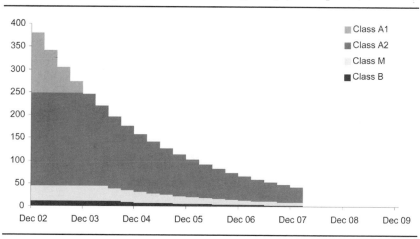

Source: Barclays Capital.

rate. This is in contrast to the United States where both the RMBS and the underlying mortgages are mostly fixed rate. Although European RMBS do not suffer the same degree of negative convexity as their US counterparts, European RMBS are unlikely to trade at a significant premium due to prepayment (and therefore average life) uncertainty.

Credit Enhancement

The credit enhancement for a particular class of notes is the sum of all the credit support provided by the subordinated notes (if any), the reserve fund, and the protection provided by the excess spread. As the collateral is paid down and the notes redeemed, the credit enhancement for all classes of notes will improve. This steady improvement is the main reason behind the ratings upgrades in European RMBS.

Exhibit 24.11 illustrates how the credit enhancement (excluding excess spread) improves during the life of a pass-through transaction. The exhibit corresponds to the generic paydown profile shown in Exhibit 24.9, and illustrates the reduced rate of improvement in credit enhancement once the notes are paying down on a pro rata basis.

Flexible Mortgages

Flexible and offset account mortgages present a significant challenge to pass-through transaction structures. This arises because the borrowers' requests to redraw previous prepayments could in aggregate exceed the principal receipts. The experiences of Australian mortgage lenders, which

EXHIBIT 24.11   Example Credit Enhancement Growth (% of subordination)

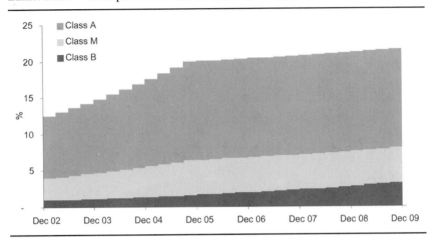

Source: Barclays Capital.

have considerable experience in originating this type of collateral, suggest this is unlikely to happen. However, the possibility is covered in RMBS transactions by a borrowing facility (redraw facility), which is available to meet the excess redraw requests if the need arises. If this facility had to be exercised, subsequent principal receipts would be used to repay the redraw facility provider before resuming note redemptions.

Reverse Mortgages

Reverse mortgages are designed to allow older customers to borrow some of the accumulated equity in their homes. The borrowers do not make any interest payments on these loans. The return for the mortgage lenders is taken from the sale proceeds when the borrower moves, enters long-term residential care or dies.

There are two main types of reverse mortgage. The shared appreciation mortgage is structured so the mortgage lender receives back the original loan amount and a proportion of the increase in property value. This has certain advantages but does mean that the proceeds are entirely dependent on house prices. The Millshaw SAMS No.1 transaction is backed by this type of mortgage collateral. The notes do not pay interest but pass these cash flows directly on to investors.

The second type of reverse mortgage, securitised in *equity release funding* (ERF) transactions, accrue interest at a rate set out in the mortgage agreement. The notes in these transactions pay interest, but in the early stages of the transaction these payments are met by borrowing from a large liquidity facility. When the property is eventually sold, there is a risk that the proceeds will not fully cover the debt plus accrued interest. In the ERF transactions, this risk is covered by an insurance policy with Norwich Union, the mortgage originator.

Reverse mortgages differ from standard RMBS transactions by their increased dependence on house-price movements and sensitivity to borrowers' life expectancy and health.

The VPTN Type Structure

The variable pay term note (VPTN) structure was first introduced in automobile transactions in the United States. It was created to mitigate two features of the pass-through structure: the long legal maturity of the notes even if they have a short average life, and the uncertainty in the redemption profile.

Redemption Profile

In the VPTN type structure, an additional class of notes (Class A1R) is issued to a note purchaser. The notes are issued partly paid and the purchaser is obliged to pay the remaining value of the notes on a specified future date. The notes are designed to mirror an existing class of notes. This allows the issuer to use the proceeds from the sale of these notes to redeem the existing outstanding class on the next interest payment date (see Exhibit 24.12). The original notes can then have a short legal maturity, as the redemption depends on the note purchaser and not the collateral.

EXHIBIT 24.12 Note Redemptions in a VPTN Type Structure (RMS 11 Estimate at Launch)

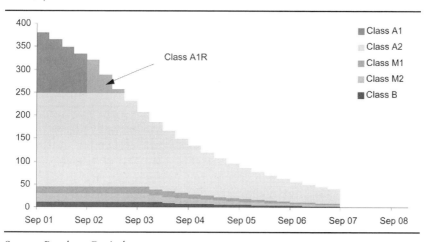

Source: Barclays Capital.

The new note then effectively replaces the old note that has been redeemed, and it will be repaid as in a standard pass-through structure illustrated in Exhibit 24.9.

The combination of this redemption profile with a substitution period and/or a cash accumulation account would allow the creation of bullet securities, although at the time of writing this has not been done for a European issuer. This is not the only way to create notes that expect to have a bullet redemption profile. In the Delphinus 2002-II transaction, the substitution period extended up to the step-and-call date, so the notes are likely to be redeemed on that date. However, if for any reason the issuer is not able or willing to call the notes, they will redeem as in a standard pass-through transaction, and so the legal maturity is dependent on the term of the underlying mortgages.

Master Trust Structures

The master trust represents an alternative method for creating bullet securities from mortgage collateral. This method has the advantage of not relying on any third party for the redemption of the notes on the maturity date. However, in order to be efficient, these master trusts need to be large, and the requirement for a seller's interest in the trust means that it is not possible to fully fund the mortgage operation through this type of securitisation. This makes them most suited to the large prime issuers that have access to alternative sources of funding.

The master trust structure was first introduced in the United States in 1988 for credit card securitisations. This allowed the creation of a series of securitisations by multiple issuers using the same collateral as security. The abolition of MIRAS (tax relief on mortgage interest payments) in the United Kingdom in April 2000 paved the way for the creation of master trust structures based on UK mortgage collateral. To date, five such mortgage master trusts have been created, all by large UK mortgage lenders, and the transactions originated from these programmes account for a significant proportion of European RMBS production.

Structure

The structure of a mortgage master trust is essentially identical to a credit card master trust except that credit card receivables are replaced with mortgage collateral (see Exhibit 24.13). The originator sells an equitable interest in a specified group of mortgages to the master trust. This can then be used as collateral for a number of securitisations. Over time, additional mortgages may be added to the trust, subject to various constraints to protect the quality of the collateral. The same pool of mortgages will support all the series of notes issued by all issuers, with

EXHIBIT 24.13   Master Trust Amortisation Structure

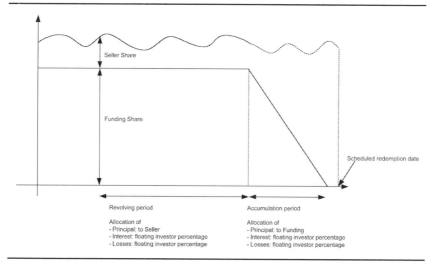

Source: Barclays Capital.

no particular series having rights to specific mortgages within the pool. The master trust may be used to support a new securitisation providing the trust is either large enough to support both, or sufficient additional mortgage collateral is transferred to the trust. In this case, both the existing and the new transaction would be supported by the original and new pool of mortgages.

Mortgage master trusts require the seller to maintain a certain minimum interest in the collateral pool held by the master trust. In credit card transactions this is used to absorb the monthly fluctuations in the balance outstanding on the credit cards and ensure there is always sufficient collateral to support the notes. In RMBS transactions, the minimum seller's interest tends to be smaller as the mortgages have a more stable repayment profile, and this is primarily available to cover setoff risk in the event of originator insolvency. In existing transactions it is the minimum trust size rather than the minimum seller's share that has been the key constraint.

Principal Cash Flows Within a Master Trust

The trust will tend to reduce in size as principal payments are received on the mortgages, and this principal can be used in one of three ways. Outside an accumulation period and when there are no amortising notes being redeemed, the principal receipts will be paid to the seller. In an accumulation period for a bullet or scheduled payment, all principal receipts on the entire trust will be collected in the cash accumulation account until the balance is sufficient to meet the required payment. While the junior pass-through notes are redeeming, principal receipts are allocated between the issuer and the seller according to their relative shares in the trust, and issuer's principal receipts are used to redeem the notes.

Redemption Profile

The master trust structure gives originators a high degree of flexibility over the redemption profiles of the notes they can create. The emphasis has understandably been on creating bullet securities in order to attract investors who would prefer to invest in securities with traditional bullet redemption profiles and short legal maturities. There have also been notes with a scheduled redemption profile issued from master trust structures and, in practice, the redemption profiles that can be created will only be limited by the size of the trust, the length of the required accumulation period, and any other note redemptions that are due from the same trust.

The ability to create bullet securities from mortgage collateral is limited by the fact that mortgages are long-term agreements with an uncertain repayment profile (and principal payments are usually small proportion of the regular payment) so the subordinate notes in the master trust transactions have been structured as pass-through notes. The senior notes generally account for more than 90% of the aggregate nominal value of the series. So, when the senior notes have been redeemed, the issuer will be able to call the subordinate notes, and therefore these are also expected to be bullet securities.

Prepayments

The master trust structures we have seen in the United Kingdom so far have been designed to remove, to a large extent, the sensitivity of the senior notes to prepayments on the mortgage collateral. In most cases this is achieved by creating bullet or scheduled amortisation notes, however this is not always the case. For example, the notes secured on the Granite Financing Master Trust, issued by Northern Rock plc, are amortising rather than having scheduled redemption profiles, but the sensitivity of these notes to prepayments is limited by a predetermined maximum amortisation schedule. As mentioned above, the redemption profiles of the subordinated pass-through notes in master trust structures may be dependent on the prepayment rate, but normally the cleanup call allows the issuer to call the notes before they start amortising.

The master trusts have been recording prepayment rates that are higher than on more traditional RMBS transactions. This is because the seller is required to repurchase any mortgage where the borrower wishes to switch product type or where the borrower has been granted a further advance. So these loans have been considered as prepayments in these transactions, even though they would not have been in a traditional MBS transaction. Faster prepayments will help shorten the amortisation periods for scheduled note redemptions and the minimum trust size requirement will protect investors against the erosion of the collateral.

Optional Redemptions

The optional redemption features of the master trust transactions are essentially the same as those for a pass-through transaction. The issuer typically has the option to call the notes for any of the following circumstances:

- Withholding tax being imposed on noteholder interest payments.
- The aggregate balance of the notes within a single series falling to a certain percentage (usually 10%) or less of their initial aggregate size outstanding.
- On or after a specified date.

The interest margin on the notes will usually increase on the date the issuer has the option to call the notes. This gives the originator an additional economic incentive to arrange for the notes to be called.

Performance Triggers

There are a number of performance triggers within the master trust transactions that serve to protect the senior noteholders against certain events. These events can be divided into two categories: asset performance related and nonasset related.

An asset performance trigger event would occur if a principal deficiency is recorded in the Class A Principal Deficiency Ledger. This means that the total balance of realised losses that have not been covered by either the reserve fund or with excess spread exceed the aggregate outstanding amount of the subordinate notes. If this occurs, all receipts on the mortgages will be allocated to the issuers and the seller on a pro rata basis. The notes will start to redeem early with all the Class A notes being redeemed on a pro rata basis. When all the Class A notes have been redeemed in full, the Class B notes would be redeemed, and so on for all other classes of notes until all the notes are redeemed or the trust no longer has any assets.

There are also circumstances where the principal due to Class C noteholders and, if applicable, Class B noteholders may be deferred. These conditions include:

- A principal deficiency being recorded on the Class C or Class B principal deficiency ledger.
- The reserve fund being used to cover a principal deficiency and not being replenished.
- Arrears in excess of three monthly payments are greater than 5% of the mortgage pool.
- Breach of certain minimum trust size triggers.

The nonasset trigger events relate primarily to the financial health of the originator and servicer, the maintenance of the minimum seller's share, and the minimum trust size. If a nonasset trigger event occurs, all principal payments from the trust (including the seller's share) will be used to redeem the notes. However, in this case the Class A notes will redeem in order of legal final maturity date. When the Class A notes have been redeemed in full, the Class B, Class C, and Class D notes will be redeemed in turn.

Credit Enhancement

The credit enhancement in the master trust transaction is the sum of all the credit support provided by the subordinated notes (if any), the reserve fund, and excess spread.

The calculation of credit enhancement for notes in a master trust transaction seems more complicated than in a traditional pass-through transaction because subordinated notes from an earlier series are expected to be redeemed before the senior notes of later series. However, if the mortgages were to perform poorly, the trigger events ensure that all outstanding junior notes would only be repaid after all the senior notes. So the credit enhancement can be calculated as the aggregate balance of subordinate notes as a proportion of the total notes outstanding.

The notes are expected to redeem a whole series at a time, so the proportions of senior to junior notes will stay approximately the same and there is unlikely to be any upwards ratings drift due to notes being redeemed.

Excess Spread

Excess spread is available to build up the reserve fund to its required level and cover any principal deficiencies. For example, in the Holmes Financing transactions there is a mechanism whereby, if the yield on the mortgages falls below a certain specified level, excess spread will be trapped in a second reserve fund to provide additional credit enhancement as compensation for the reduction in excess spread.

Reserve Fund

To date, the main reserve funds in master trust transactions have been standard fixed cash amounts that are available to the issuer to cover any shortfalls in income or principal losses during the life of the transaction. The reserve funds are built up to their required levels through trapped excess spread.

The Ratings Process

The integrated nature of a master trust transaction means that when a new securitisation is issued that is secured on the same master trust, the rating agencies will have to ensure that the addition of the new transaction still allows all the existing notes from earlier transactions to meet their required payments and does not adversely affect the ratings of any existing notes. In effect, the agencies have to rerun the ratings process for all existing classes of notes every time a new transaction is issued.

Advantages of a Master Trust

A master trust allows an RMBS issuer to establish a sizeable securitisation programme, even with many series of notes secured through multiple SPVs, at a dramatically lower cost than through traditional separate securitisations. The ability to issue notes with a variety of maturities and redemption profiles allows the issuer to expand the available investor base and to tap into specific demand in the market. However, this process does rely on economies of scale and so is probably not the ideal form of securitisation for a smaller lender. Also, the requirement to maintain a minimum seller's share in the trust would make this type of structure less suitable than others for lenders wishing to securitise 100% of their balance sheet.

This type of structure has a number of advantages for investors. The large size of the collateral pool means these transactions have a much greater diversity of assets than a standalone transaction. In a traditional transaction, the diversity declines during its life as mortgages are redeemed, but while the master trusts are increasing in size, so too is the diversity of the collateral. In addition, investors with an interest in several notes secured on the same trust need only track the performance of the underlying master trust rather than each collateral pool separately. The large size of these transactions also leads to better secondary market liquidity for the notes but, most importantly, these structures give investors who require bullet securities and/or short legal life investments the opportunity to invest in RMBS.

COLLATERAL PERFORMANCE

The ultimate aim of any performance analysis is to help form a judgement of the probability that investors in a transaction might not receive the payments they expect at the time they expect them. The differences between the master trust and the pass-through type transactions mean that it is worth considering them separately. It is also useful to look at the performance of the UK nonconforming transactions. The lower quality of borrower in these transactions leads to higher arrears and losses, and the large number of this type of transaction enable us to make some generalisations about the performance of this type of mortgage.

Master Trust Transactions

The master trust transactions are all supported by mortgages to high credit quality (prime) borrowers. These borrowers show very good credit performance and so arrears in these transactions are low and losses are generally negligible. Below the performance of the Holmes Financing Master Trust is used in the illustration. This transaction contains mortgages originated by Abbey National, one of the largest mortgage lenders in the United Kingdom.

Trust Size

Between September 2000 and November 2002, the Holmes Financing trust grew substantially, and there are certain occasions where the changes in the statistics are largely due the inclusion of new collateral. On three occasions during this period, the trust gained a significant quantity of additional mortgages (see Exhibit 24.14).

Arrears

Arrears rates provide an early indication of potential future losses and so are the single most closely followed performance statistic for RMBS transactions. Whether arrears actually result in losses will depend on the property value in relation to the size of the loan, and whether these borrowers are able to recover, or at least make sufficient mortgage payments to allow the lender not to foreclose on the loan.

The level of arrears in a relatively young pool of mortgages is likely to be low initially, particularly if there are restrictions on the selection of arrears loans in the representations and warranties for the RMBS transaction. The level of arrears would then be expected to increase as the loans season. This effect has been observed for the Holmes Financing Master Trust during this period (see Exhibit 24.15), although the general rising trend has been interrupted by the occasional addition of

EXHIBIT 24.14 Holmes Financing Trust Size (£ billion)

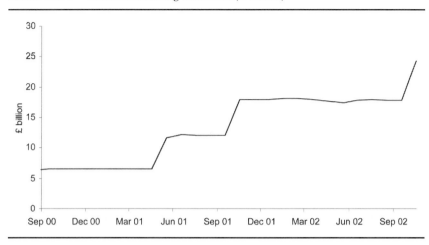

Source: Investor Reports.

EXHIBIT 24.15 Loans More Than Three Months Behind with Payments (% by balance)

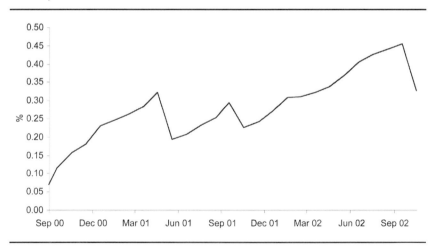

Source: Investor Reports.

new, less seasoned mortgages with lower arrears. This rising trend can be expected to slow as the arrears mortgages that are either recovering or progress through to foreclosure begin to balance the number of new mortgages falling behind with their payments.

EXHIBIT 24.16   Charge-off Rates in Holmes Financing Transaction

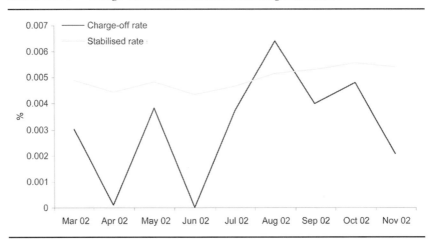

Source: Barclays Capital, Investor Reports.

Losses

Losses in master trust mortgage transactions can be recorded as an annualised charge-off rate in a similar manner to the standard method in credit card transactions. However, losses on prime mortgages are generally very small and intermittent so this measure will tend to be relatively volatile. The results for the Holmes Financing transaction provide a good illustration of this point (see Exhibit 24.16).

Using cumulative loss figures to arrive at an estimate of the average loss rate on a transaction over its life also presents difficulties when the trust is changing size significantly. However, taking the ratio of cumulative realised losses to cumulative mortgage redemptions gives an estimate of the stabilised long-run average loss rate on the collateral.

Excess Spread

If any losses are realised on loans in the collateral pool, they will be covered by trapping any excess cash flowing through the cash flow waterfall, so the size of excess spread relative to the losses being incurred is an important indication of the transaction's financial health. In the Holmes Financing master trust, excess spread is measured on a quarterly basis. Exhibit 24.17 shows it that has been averaging around 60 bps per year, massively exceeding the 0.5 bp loss rate.

EXHIBIT 24.17 Excess Spread in Holmes Financing Transaction (% pa.)

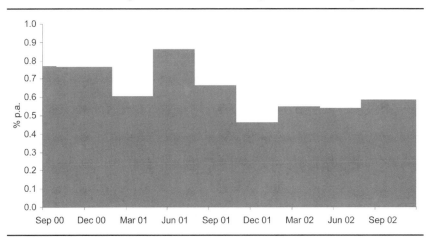

Source: Investor Reports.

Prepayments

The master trust transactions are largely insensitive to prepayment rates. The only requirement is that the principal receipts in the trust are sufficient for it to accumulate the bullet payments to meet the scheduled redemption dates. The principal payment rate, measured as the proportion of collateral redeemed or repurchased, has been running at an average rate of 4% per month.

Exhibit 24.18 shows the principal payment rate is somewhat erratic on a monthly basis but has generally been increasing. However, with a collateral pool of £24 billion and principal collections running at their average rate of 4%, it would take less than one month to accumulate the principal required to redeem the largest outstanding note.

Pass-Through Transactions

The performance analysis of pass-through transactions will be similar in many respects to that described above. However, as the collateral pays down, the credit enhancement in the transaction will improve and therefore these transactions become more financially robust as they age.

In the remainder of this section we discuss the performance of the UK nonconforming mortgage sector. Many of these transactions are backed by collateral that has been originated within a relatively short period of time. These transactions do not have a revolving period, which allows us

EXHIBIT 24.18   Monthly Principal Payment Rate (% of collateral by balance)

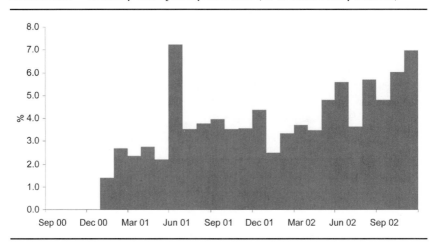

Source: Barclays Capital, Investor Reports.

to track the performance of a fixed set of mortgages over time, giving some additional insight into the behaviour of this type of borrower.

The average seasoning of the loans in collateral pools can vary considerably between different transactions and so a direct comparison may be misleading. For this reason the analysis presented here tracks the performance of the collateral against the estimated average seasoning of the collateral.

In this analysis (see Exhibits 24.19, 24.20, and 24.21), the solid lines indicate the average level of arrears, losses, and prepayments for collateral pools of any given age; the two dashed lines indicate one standard deviation either side of the average. The majority of collateral pools have an estimated average seasoning of 42 months or less and the number of transactions decreases as we look at seasoning beyond this. As the number of transactions decreases, the average will become less smooth. The exhibits only display the average provided it is based on at least four transactions.

Arrears

Exhibit 24.19 shows the average proportion of the collateral that are more than three months behind with their payments, measured against the average age of the mortgages in the pool. As expected, arrears tend to increase during the early stages of a transaction and then stabilise after approximately two years, typically in the 12–14% range. However, there has been considerable variation between issuers.

EXHIBIT 24.19   UK Nonconforming MBS with Arrears Over Three Months (% by balance)

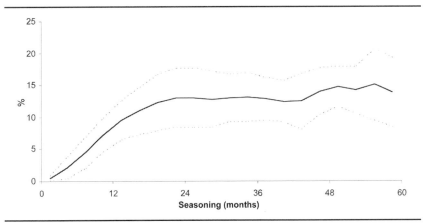

Source: Barclays Capital.

EXHIBIT 24.20   Cumulative Marginal Loss Rates (% of total redemptions by value)

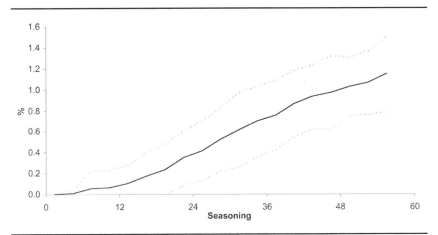

Source: Barclays Capital.

Losses

Similar analysis of the losses within the collateral pools supporting the MBS transactions gives the loss profile shown in Exhibit 24.20. The marginal loss rates used in this analysis are calculated as the total cumulative loss on the transaction as a proportion of the collateral that has been

EXHIBIT 24.21   Prepayment Rates on UK Nonconforming MBS

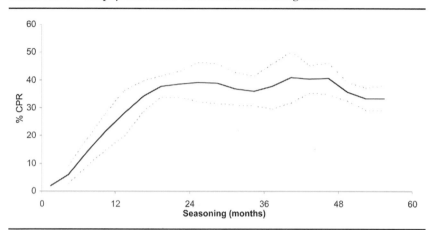

Source: Barclays Capital.

redeemed since launch. (This is essentially the same calculation as the stabilised loss rate for master trust transactions.) This produces a higher figure than the traditional calculation, which compares total losses against the original collateral size, but its advantage is that it should settle down to a more stable value more quickly. While this is evident in this analysis for individual transactions, the average loss rate shows a rising path as a result of the older transactions generally having higher stabilised loss rates than the more recent transactions.

Prepayments

Prepayments have been more consistent across different MBS transactions than either arrears or losses (see Exhibit 24.21). Traditionally, UK nonconforming MBS transactions have been priced using the assumption that the prepayment speed would be at a CPR of 25%. Exhibit 24.21 shows that prepayments have generally started at a much slower rate but then have accelerated up to a CPR of 35% by the time the mortgages are approximately 18 months old. As a result, a 25% CPR assumption is likely to underestimate the average life of a fast-pay security but probably overestimate the average life of a longer-life security.

CONCLUSION

The European RMBS market has grown significantly since its beginnings in the United Kingdom in the 1980s. Although this chapter has concentrated to a large extent on the UK RMBS market because of the additional variety of mortgage types and transaction structures seen in this market, there are well-established RMBS markets in most major European countries.

The performance of this asset class has been very strong. As of early 2003, there have been no defaults, very few downgrades, and a good number of upgrades. This safe-haven status and the increasing variety and liquidity of the transactions should continue to attract investors to this sector.

CHAPTER 25

Italian Residential Mortgage-Backed Securities

Andrew Dennis
Executive Director, Structured Finance Credit Research
UBS

I taly, perhaps more than any other participant, has benefited from its membership of Economic Monetary Union (EMU). The Italian economy between the 1970s and mid-1990s could be characterised as volatile. EMU membership has brought with it a significant degree of economic reform, improved stability and, importantly for the mortgage market, significant declines in interest rates. Mortgage borrowing has grown steadily over recent years as Italians capitalise on improved stability and lower interest rates. At the same time, Italian lawmakers have been at the vanguard of developing legislation that permits securitisation to take place efficiently. In particular the Securitisation Law (130/99) provides a clear platform for securitisation to take place.

A rise in mortgage borrowing has forced a response from the Italian banking industry. Italian banks themselves have been undergoing a phase of rapid consolidation with capital pressures never far from the surface. The coincidence of securitisation legislation with a rise in mortgage demand has led, therefore, to a sharp growth in Italian RMBS issuance.

In this chapter we examine some of the key legal and technical features that characterise the market. Like all jurisdictions, Italy has local nuances that dictate a localised approach to securitisation. We examine these and the impact they have on the structure of transactions.

MORTGAGE PRODUCTS

Compared with a market such as the UK, the range of mortgage products in Italy remains restricted. Traditionally, variable rate, annuity style products has been the standard. These mortgages are referenced to a range of floating indices including EURIBOR, the ABI (*Associazione Bancaria Italiana*) prime rate, TAS (the official discount rate—*Tasso di Sconto*) and other bond-related indices.

As long-term interest rates in Italy have declined during the convergence process, fixed rate mortgages have become increasingly popular. The appeal of fixed rate loans to borrowers is that they reduce uncertainty. However, in a falling rate environment, borrowers often are fearful of being stranded with a high cost fixed liability with prepayment penalties in the event that they wish to refinance.

Approximately 20% of the mortgages in a sample of securitisations that we have analysed are described as "modular." These are typically products with some form of interest rate change embedded, either optional or automatic. For instance, a popular structure is a floating rate mortgage where the lender has the right to switch to a fixed rate at a specific point in time.

The market is undergoing change. Innovation only comes in a climate of competition and the fact that we are seeing more innovation would indicate that competition is mounting. Mortgages are only now becoming, as they are in many other countries, a consumer finance commodity in Italy.

Notwithstanding the various interest rate structures that are embedded in the underlying mortgage, these are stripped out through swaps and other hedging products when the mortgages are purchased ahead of securitisation. Because of embedded value (high coupon mortgages), it is sometimes the case that a special purpose vehicle (SPV) issuers will buy mortgages at a premium to par. This premium is then, effectively, defeased through the swap mechanism.

Italian mortgages have a maturity range of 5–20 years—although 15–20 years is most typical. Mortgages tend to amortise on an annuity basis, although increasingly originators are developing more "sculpted" products to appeal to specific audiences. These include accreting structures (low initial repayments). Until now, however, a meaningful market for interest-only loans has not developed.

Between 5% and 10% of all residential mortgage loans are subsidised loans (*agevolato*), which are made to fund developments that are sold or rented to disadvantaged individuals and families. Certain subsidised mortgages can benefit from a government (central or regional) guarantee.

There also exist so called "fractionated" loans. These are mortgages that are raised to build multifamily dwellings, which are subsequently split among several obligors, with security then granted on their individual properties.

MORTGAGE LEGISLATION

There are two different classes of mortgage loans in Italy; *mutui fondiari* and *mutui ipotecari*. *Mutui fondiari* loans are made for the purchase or construction of property, and are secured by that property. *Ipotecari* are more general loans that are secured by property. Approximately 90% of residential mortgage loans in Italy are in the form of *mutui fondiari*, whereas *mutui ipotecari* are more typically used in commercial transactions.

The significance of the different types of mortgage is twofold. *Mutui fondiari* loans are subject to an LTV cap of 80%. This limit can only be exceeded in the event that a third party guarantor, who will often pledge income, can be provided. Secondly, the foreclosure process for *mutui fondiari* loans is, in most circumstances, more straightforward. Both these factors are, although incidentally, securitisation friendly.

THE USURY LAW

Italian consumers benefit from a piece of consumer protection legislation called the Usury Law (Law 108/96). This law places an upper limit on the interest rate chargeable on a wide variety of consumer loans, including mortgages. In effect, banks are not permitted to charge more than 50% above the average loan rate for the preceding quarter. Banca D'Italia publishes the relevant data regularly. Any interest charged above such a threshold is effectively illegal and borrowers can claim back any such interest from lenders.

Almost by definition, variable rate mortgages are unlikely to be affected by this legislation, except in volatile interest rate environments. Fixed rate loans, however, do fall prey to this law.

In securitisation transactions, the originators indemnify the issuer vehicles against the Usury Law risks. This, on the one hand, is a risk mitigator for securitisations, but it does add a modicum of recourse to the originator.

In addition to the usury legislation, lenders are compelled to abide by rules that govern full disclosure of all terms, conditions and costs relating to mortgage loans.

UNDERWRITING PROCESS

Italian banks have grown the number of branches. Many of the underwriting decisions are made at branch level, although following policies set centrally. The average loan size is, by most standards in developed European countries, small. The average loan size is just over €52,000.

Italian lenders are beginning to move towards a credit scoring methodology. Today, they have access to a database, operated by Banca D'Italia, known as *Centrale dei Rischi*. Italian banks contribute information about individual borrowers, their exposures and any arrears that may be registered to their names. Lenders will also look for evidence of income from the borrowers and disclosure of other liabilities. Credit reviews can take between three and four weeks to complete—taking out a mortgage in Italy is not a quick process.

Although the more fragmented origination methodology contrasts starkly with that seen in many other countries, most obviously the UK and US, its outputs are often more conservative than other mortgage markets. In a sample of securitisation transactions we analysed, the weighted average LTVs was approximately 53%. This compares with 70–80% in the UK Prime RMBS market. Lending is typically done on a 30–40% debt service to post-tax income basis.

There is significant variability of methodology in property valuation and much inconsistency between institutions. In many cases, third-party surveyors, who will base their assessment of open market value on precedent transactions, undertake valuations. Open market values can often be misleading for the purposes of mortgage advances, where "distress sale" prices reflect realisable value more accurately. For small loans, valuations are often not required by lenders. In the case of larger loans, in-house valuers often confirm third-party valuations. Lenders require buildings insurance.

In our view, the idiosyncratic origination practices of Italian banks will become increasingly standardised. All three rating agencies note that inconsistencies in origination practice are a risk factor in their assessment of Italian RMBS. Ultimately, the originators "pay" through the amount of credit enhancement that needs to be provided to execute securitisation. This is especially apparent when contrasted with the relatively lower (compared to other European countries) LTVs.

LOAN SECURITY—LEGAL VERSUS ECONOMIC

Loans are secured by an *ipoteca*, a mortgage charge, over a property. These are registered, in the presence of a notary, with the local land registry. The actual amount of the *ipoteca* will often exceed the face amount of the loan by a factor of two to four times. This allows for the recovery of unpaid interest and enforcement costs in the event of a default by the borrower. *Ipoteca* have a 20-year term, unless extended or renewed, which explains the absence of any material lending capacity beyond 20 years.

In some cases, there may be existing mortgages outstanding at the land registry. In such instances, borrowers will undertake a check to see if the existing lien places their loan in a subordinate position. Very often, however, the existing lien will have been fully discharged, although it may remain on record as a matter of legal technicality. In such instances, the mortgage is termed as being *ipoteca di primo grado in senso economico* or having an economic first charge.

The majority of securitisation transactions comprise mortgages with either legal or economic first charges. Where there are mortgages that do not benefit from a first charge, the rating agencies impose "penalties" in sizing credit enhancement. For instance, Standard & Poor's assume that default frequencies on loans with second charge mortgages are 1.5× those with first charge liens.

SERVICING

Servicing and management of mortgage loans are other areas where there are differences between lenders. There have been some moves towards the establishment of specialised servicing companies. Thus far, however, their efforts have been largely concentrated on the nonperforming and unsecured consumer credit segments of the market. We would identify three key areas where, in Italy, servicing varies between institutions and transactions.

- *The percentage of collections made by direct debit (*Rimmessa Interbancaria Diretta—*RID).* In most securitisation transactions this is generally above 90% and in most cases approaches 100%.
- *The periodicity of payments.* Mortgages are paid on either a monthly, quarterly or semiannual basis. For the purposes of asset management, "event trapping" is important. Borrowers that find themselves in difficulties will be identified more quickly in a monthly paid loan than, say, in a loan that is paid twice a year. Italy is no different from other countries: The quicker problems are identified, the higher the probability of an acceptable recovery. The rating agencies penalise transactions with a high percentage of quarterly and semiannual payments.

■ *Arrears management.* The Banca D'Italia lays down guidelines and rules for when a loan can be categorised as delinquent or in default. However, individual originators/servicers have latitude, within this framework, to manage arrears proactively. As mentioned above, identification of arrears can only take place at the point where a payment is due. Much of the initial management is conducted at branch level, where managers will look to see if obligors have sufficient cleared funds available to meet their payment obligations ahead of such obligations falling due. When and if a payment is missed, there is some variability as to when a loan is classified as in default (*"in sofferenza"*). It is common practice to attempt to secure payment through informal means (sending reminders, making personal contact, etc.) before a formal process is started. Again, evidence suggests that loss rates are much lower where intervention takes place early.

FORECLOSURE AND RECOVERY

The Italian legal framework for foreclosure and recovery is cumbersome, slow, and tends to favour the borrower rather than the lender (see Exhibit 25.1). Recoveries can take up to seven years and the formal enforcement process is often paralleled with an informal approach where lenders attempt to settle out-of-court.

Once a mortgage is declared to be *sofferenze* (borrower insolvency or similar status), the lender may commence foreclosure proceedings by seeking a court order in the form of a writ of enforcement (*titolo esecutivo*) from the court in whose jurisdiction the mortgaged property is located. The *titolo esecutivo* provides the legal basis of the enforcement process.

The court injunction (for "judicial" mortgages or *ipoteche giudiziarie* registered with the local land registry) must be served on the debtor, issued by the court in whose jurisdiction the mortgaged property is located.

Where the mortgage loan documented under a public deed ("voluntary" mortgage or *ipoteche volontarie*), the mortgage lender can serve the mortgage loan agreement, stamped by a notary with an order for execution (*formula esecutiva*) directly on the debtor. An *atto di precetto* is notified to the debtor, together with either the *titolo esecutivo* or the loan agreement.

Within 10–90 days from the date on which notice of the *atto di precetto* has been issued, the lender may request attachment to the mortgaged property (*pignoramento immobiliare*) through a court order, which must then be filed with the local land registry. The court may, if the lender requires, appoint a custodian to manage the mortgaged property. If the mortgage lender does not make such a request, the debtor automatically becomes the custodian.

EXHIBIT 25.1   Enforcement Procedures—Long—Even in the Best Cases

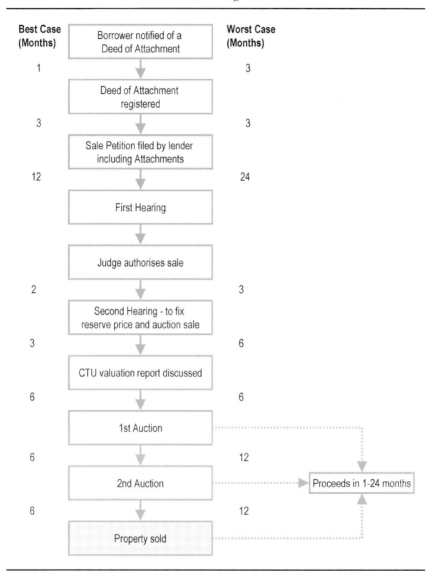

Source: Fitch/UBS Warburg.

The lender must search the land registry to ascertain the identity of the current owner of the property, and must then serve a notice of the request for attachment on the current owner, even if no transfer of the property from the original borrower or mortgagor to a third-party purchaser has been previously notified to the lender.

At this stage, the lender may also request attachment to a borrower's other assets (*pignoramento mobiliare*), which must be registered with the land registry.

Within 10–90 days after serving the attachment order(s), the mortgage lender may request the court to sell the mortgaged property. The court may delay its decision to hear any challenge by the debtor. Technical delays may also be caused by the need to append to the mortgage lender's request for attachment copies of the relevant mortgage and *cadastrial* certificates, which usually take some time to obtain. However, Law No 302/98 should reduce the duration of proceedings as it allows the lender to substitute such *cadastrial* certificates with certificates obtained from public notaries, and by allowing public notaries to conduct various activities, which were before exclusively within the powers of the courts.

The first hearing typically occurs between one and two years following the notification of the borrower. If the borrower files an opposition to the deed of attachment, the first hearing is postponed while the court opines on the objection. It is only once the court has overturned all objections that the foreclosure can resume. If there are no objections at the time of the first hearing, the court will typically decide to proceed with the auction (*vendita con incanto*) of the mortgaged property. It will usually appoint a technical consultant (*Consulente Tecnico d'Ufficio*, or CTU) prior to ordering the sale by auction. The court determines on the basis of the expert's appraisal the minimum bid price, and may also refer to official price lists. However, delays may occur should either party request a supplemental valuation.

If an auction fails to result in the sale of the property, the court will arrange a new auction with a lower minimum bid price. It lies within the discretion of the court to decide whether—and to what extent—the bid price should be reduced, although the maximum permitted reduction is 1/5 of the minimum bid price of the previous auction. In practice, courts tend to apply the legal maximum. The timing of any successive auction depends on the workings of the court, and its timeliness in approving a new reserve price and auction date (usually between 6–24 months). In the event that no offers are made during any auction, the mortgage lender may apply for a direct assignment of the property. In practice, however, the courts tend to hold auctions until the mortgaged property is sold.

The sale proceeds, after deduction of the expenses of the foreclosure proceedings, INVIM (a tax payable by the debtor in respect of any increase in the value of the mortgaged property during the time it was owned by him until year-end 1992, which will be abolished with effect from 1 January 2002), and any expenses for the deregistration of the mortgage, will be applied towards the lenders in priority to the claims of any other creditors (except for any property-related taxes).

Pursuant to Article 2855 of the Italian Civil Code, the senior claims of the lender in respect of unpaid interest may be satisfied in an amount equal to the aggregate of: (1) the interest accrued at the contractual rate of the year when foreclosure proceedings commenced, and the two preceding years; and (2) the interest accrued at the legal rate (currently 2.5%) until the property is sold. Any amount recovered in excess of this is applicable towards any third-party claims of any creditor participating in the foreclosure process. The lender is entitled to participate in the distribution of any such excess as an unsecured creditor. The balance, if any, will then be paid to the debtor.

THE ITALIAN RMBS MARKET

The Italian RMBS market has, since 1998, seen significant growth (see Exhibit 25.2). In our view, there remains significant room for further growth, since many of the major banks have yet to embark on a securitisation programme. We believe that the structural pressures on the Italian banking market are such that we will see significantly greater issuance going forward.

EXHIBIT 25.2 Growth of the Italian RMBS Market

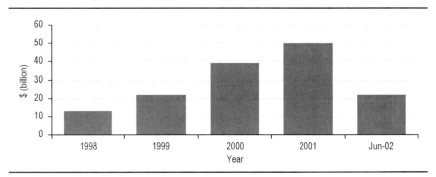

Source: Bondware.

As we describe below, we believe that the credit risk associated with Italian RMBS is relatively low. We believe that the sector is, to an extent, penalised by the rating agencies for having idiosyncratic origination and servicing processes. As a consequence, credit enhancement levels are higher than in other European RMBS markets. This in spite of:

- Lower general LTV levels
- Higher levels of excess spread

However, the potential for growth in supply is likely to cap spread performance.

Structural Considerations—Legal

Prior to Law 130/99, Italian originators had to use structures through which the originator assigned the relevant assets either to an Italian company formed specifically as a factoring company (under Law 52/91, the Factoring Law) or to a bank incorporated within the EU.

The economic benefit of the assets was then transferred to the ultimate issuer of the asset-backed notes, incorporated in a jurisdiction other than Italy. The basic rationale behind this rather cumbersome and expensive set-up was essentially twofold:

- Firstly, Italian companies were restricted from issuing debt instruments in excess of the amount of their share capital.
- Secondly, any interest payments made by an Italian company to investors outside Italy were liable to withholding tax. Since the enactment of Law 130/99, however, the structural format of Italian transactions has become more straightforward and fairly standard, applying the typical structural and legal technologies used in other true sale transactions (i.e., domestic bankruptcy-remote issuer SPV, whose shares are held on trust for charitable purposes).

Legal Structure and Special Considerations

A number of specific legal factors are pertinent to the Italian RMBS market. These are discussed in the following sections.

Italy's Securitisation Law

Law 130/99 applies to transactions involving the true sale (by way of nongratuitous assignment) of receivables to a purchasing company (being usually the issuer, too), with the purchasing company established in accordance with Article 3 of Law 130/99. Law 130/99 does not exclude any asset classes in principal, whether performing or nonperforming, provided that—in the case of pooled receivables—they are distinguishable by a common feature (*individuabili in blocco*). This is typically taken to mean a requirement for homogeneity among securitised receivables.

Purchaser versus Issuer

Pursuant to Article 1 and 2 of Law 130/99, the purchasing company may be—but does not have to be—the ultimate issuer of the notes. As Article 3 provides for the segregation of the pool from the assets of "the company"—which Article 1 defines as the purchaser—it is not clear whether this protection would also apply to the issuer, where the issuer is not the purchaser. However, with issuer SPVs all Italian RMBS transactions to date being both the purchaser and issuer, this is in effect more of a theoretical, rather than a practical issue. In any case, where the purchaser and the issuer are separate legal entities, forming both entities as fully bankruptcy remote vehicles effectively mitigates the risks associated to such a setup.

The corporate purpose of the purchasing company or of the issuer, if different from the purchasing company, must be restricted to undertake one or more securitisation transactions. This raises a question as to what extent the purchasing company may purchase other assets or enter into different transactions that may be required for hedging, liquidity or credit enhancement purposes. In the absence of any requirements as to the corporate form of the purchasing company and the issuer, it is possible for them to be incorporated as a stock company (*Società per Azioni* or SpA), limited partnership (*Società in Accomandita per Azioni* or SApA) or as a limited liability company (*Società a Responsabilità Limitata* or Srl). Transactions to date have been centred on stock or limited liability SPV companies.

While Law 130/99 contemplates the possibility of using Italian investment funds as purchasing companies, as has for instance been done in France and Spain, all Italian securitisation transactions completed to date under Law 130/99 have used SPVs. Structuring a transaction where an Italian investment fund is the assignee of the receivables may be more costly and time consuming, but may represent a tool for the mutualisation of different portfolios.

Bankruptcy Remoteness

Article 3 of Law 130/99 provides that the securitised assets are segregated for all purposes from all other assets of the purchasing company (whether or not the purchasing company is also the issuer). On an insolvency or winding-up of the purchasing company, the assets are only available to the holders of the notes and senior creditors, such as the hedging and liquidity provider. The assets relating to a particular transaction are not available to the holders of notes issued to finance any other securitisation transaction or to general creditors of the purchasing company. This provision substantially strengthens the bankruptcy-remoteness of transactions and is particularly valuable where the purchasing company is a multiportfolio issuer. Transactions will typically also create security in favour of the note holders on assets of the purchasing company or the issuer, which do not constitute receivables or proceeds from the receivables.

To strengthen the bankruptcy remoteness of the securitised assets, the Governor of the Bank of Italy issued guidelines on 23 August 2000, which require the purchasing company and the issuer to take steps to ensure that the assets of different transactions are not comingled and to account for each transaction separately. In particular, the Bank of Italy must now be regularly updated on each transaction by being given the same information supplied to the investors during the life of the notes.

Assignment of Assets

Article 58 governs the assignment of the receivables under Law 130/99, Paragraphs 2, 3, and 4, of the Consolidated Banking Act (Law 385/93). Article 58 provides for the perfection of security over the underlying homogeneous pool of receivables subject to giving public notification in the *Gazzetta Ufficiale della Repubblica Italiana*, which avoids the need for notification to be served on each assigned debtor under Article 2160 of the Civil Code. As of the publication date, the assignment becomes not only enforceable against the originator, assigned debtors and any third-party creditors, but also against any liquidator or other bankruptcy official of an assigned debtor, as well as any prior assignees of the assets who have not perfected their claim. Law 130/99 extended the transfer methodology under Article 58 to SPVs set up in accordance with the new law, and specifically provides for the segregation of the assets of a Law 130/99 company in favour of the note holders and other senior parties to the SPV. Any guarantees or security interests linked to the assigned assets is transferred automatically, and is perfected with the same priority in favour of the purchasing company, without the need for any formality or registration. This provision under Law 130/99 is particularly important within the context of RMBS transactions as it removes the need to register the assignment on the mortgage entry at the land registry to vest the benefit of the mortgage in the assignee.

Ring-Fencing of Assets

Law 130/99 provides that SPVs may engage in multiple transactions, with the provision that asset must be fully ring-fenced (Article 3). In a winding-up scenario, the segregated assets and associated cash flows are consequently only available to the respective note holders, and cannot be claimed by any general creditor(s) to the issuer.

Setoff Risk

Under the general principles of Italian law, borrowers are entitled to exercise set-off rights in respect of amounts due under any mortgage loan against amounts payable by the originator. Under the terms of the corresponding warranty and indemnity agreements, however, originators have agreed to indemnify issuers against any reductions in the amounts received as a result of borrowers exercising their setoff right.

Claw Back Risk

Claw-backs are still possible under certain scenarios (Article 67 of Royal Decree No 267/42 [Bankruptcy Law]), but only within three months of the originator's admission to compulsory liquidation under the Consolidated Banking Act, or within six months of the originator's admission to compulsory liquidation. As a result, originators are required to certify their solvency as of the time of the transaction date under the warranty and indemnity agreement.

Usury Law

Claims under the Usury Law (Law 108/96) may affect both payments which have been received, or which are to be received, by the issuer under the mortgage loans. Originators do, however, undertake in the corresponding warranty and indemnity agreements to indemnify issuers against any losses, costs, claims, damages, or expenses incurred in connection with any such interest accrual prior to the execution date.

Compounding of Interest (Anatocismo)

Pursuant to Article 1283 of the Italian Civil Code, interest may be capitalised on claims after a period of more than six months, or from the date when legal proceedings are commenced. Article 1283 allows for the derogation from this provision in the event that there are recognised customary practices to the contrary. Banks have traditionally capitalised accrued interest on a 3-month basis on the grounds that such practice could be characterised as a customary practice (*uso normativo*).

However, a number of recent judgements from Italian courts (including the judgement from the Court of Cassation No. 2374/99) have held that such practices are not customary practices (*uso normativo*). Consequently, if borrowers were to challenge this practice, and such interpretation of the Italian Civil Code were to be upheld before other courts, there could be a negative effect on the returns generated from the underlying mortgage loans.

Originators have therefore undertaken in the corresponding Warranty and indemnity agreements to indemnify issuers against any losses, costs, and expenses that could arise in connection with any challenge to this practice. Also, it should be noted that Article 25 of the Legislative Decree No 342 of 4 August 1999 (Law 342/99), enacted under a delegation granted pursuant to Law No 142 of 19 February 1992 (*Legge Delega*), has considered the capitalisation of accrued interest pre-October 1999 to be valid.

The practice is also still possible post-October 1999 (when Law 342/99 came into force) subject to the terms established by a resolution of the Inter-ministerial Committee of Credit and Saving (CICR) issued on 22 February 2000. Law No. 342 has, however, also been challenged before the Italian Constitutional Court on the grounds that it falls outside the scope of the legislative powers delegated under the *Legge Delega*.

Tax Regime Applicable to the Issuer SPV

The tax regime applicable to the issuer is still unclear and subject to debate. Law 130/99 does not provide for any clarification and the only official guideline, which was released by the Bank of Italy in March 2000, relates to the accounting treatment of pools purchased by the issuer or the purchasing company. The normal tax position would be that, being an Italian corporate entity, the issuer would be subject to Italian corporation tax, with annual profit typically represented by the fees received or retained by the issuer in connection with the management of the pool, being subject to taxation.

However, under the Bank of Italy guidelines, the assets and liabilities, as well as any other values attributed directly to the pool, are treated as off-balance sheet assets and liabilities. As a consequence, income deriving from interest, capital gains and other revenues accrued by the issuer or the purchasing company are excluded from the calculation for income tax purposes. This view has received strong support from the Association of Italian Stock Companies (*Assonime*). Ultimate clarification on this issue is still awaited from the Italian tax authorities.

Tax Regime Applicable to the Issued Notes

Law 130/99 also provides for the withholding tax exemption of interest payments made on the notes issued by Italy-domiciled SPVs for investors resident outside Italy, subject to qualifying double taxation treaties with Italy (12.5% otherwise).

Listings

Since February 2000, it has become possible to list asset-backed securities on the Euromot section of the Italian Stock Exchange. To date, however, all notes issued under Law 130/99 have been listed on the Luxembourg Stock Exchange.

Financing Structures

Italian RMBS transactions are structured almost exclusively as floating-rate sequential pass-through bonds to attract the broadest investor audience. Many transactions also include either stepup or cleanup calls. A particular characteristic of Italian securitisations is, however, that they always apply an initial 18-month period during which no payment are made under the notes. This, in turn, reflects the fact that under Italian legislation, any payments made during this period would be subject to 20% taxation.

Italian RMBS typically include a super senior, soft bullet tranche with a weighted average life (WAL) of >18 months (otherwise subject to 27% taxation, except for government-sponsored transactions), with any pool cash flows being either deposited into a GIC account, or reinvested into eligible investments. Alternatively, some deals use an ≥18-month revolving period (i.e., cash flows derived from the pool is re-applied towards the purchase of new assets meeting the general pool criteria). (See Exhibits 25.3 and 25.4.)

EXHIBIT 25.3   The Soft Bullet Structure

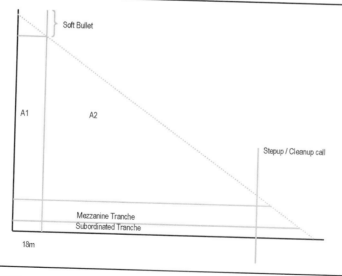

Source: UBS.

EXHIBIT 25.4   The Revolving Structure

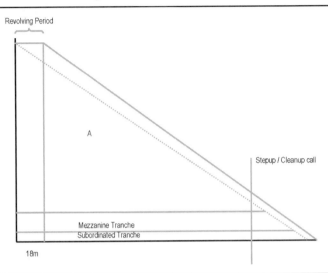

Source: UBS.

Prepayment Profiles

Italian RMBS transactions have consistently achieved prepayment rates (as measured by Constant Prepayment Rates—CPR) of 3–5% annually. There is some evidence of interest rate sensitivity, but the link, in our view, is modest. The level of CPR in the Italian market is significantly lower than that experienced in other European RMBS markets. Both the Dutch and Irish markets show rates around 7–15% CPR and the UK market shows rates of 16–20%. Several factors, we believe, are at play in Italy that make prepayment rates low:

- The relatively short scheduled maturity—10–15 years—makes prepayment more burdensome.
- The high proportion of floating rate mortgages makes prepayment less beneficial.
- Prepayments are often subject to penalties.
- Consumer loyalty, combined with inefficient competition, is a behaviour pattern that militates against high prepayment rates.

Credit Analysis and Credit Enhancement

The three agencies conduct broadly similar analysis to derive the levels of credit enhancement required to issue AAA rated RMBS in Italy. The analysis consists, broadly speaking, of four areas:

- An assessment, qualitative and quantitative, of the origination and servicing capabilities and limitations of the relevant originator/servicer.
- A thorough analysis of the legal structure of the securitisation.
- An analysis of the parties interfacing financially with the SPV issuer, particularly focusing on where there are payment risks. This analysis will focus on counter parties such as swap providers, liquidity providers, and cash managers. An analysis of how the transaction behaves in the event of a failure of one or all such parties is conducted.
- A loan-by-loan analysis of the assets underpinning the securitisation.

Both Standard & Poor's and Fitch publish their quantitative criteria clearly, but we see no compelling evidence that Moody's apply a materially different approach.

As with all ABS transactions, credit enhancement required, and hence the ratings, is a function of expected loss combined with robustness of modelled cash flow. Expected loss is the product of default or foreclosure frequency and loss severity. In the table below, we outline the key factors that the agencies look at in their quantitative analysis. The figures quoted in Exhibit 25.5 represent a blend of S&P and Fitch's published levels for AAA ratings.

Probably the most important factor from those listed above is LTV. Historic evidence shows (in most countries) that higher LTV mortgages have both a higher chance of default and a lower recovery rate.

Once a probability of foreclosure is calculated, a loss severity model is applied. The loss severity is a function of several factors:

- Market value declines—region specific and larger for large loans
- Foreclosure costs
- Priority of claim

The market value declines applied by S&P are outlined in Exhibit 25.6. The foreclosure cost assumptions made by Fitch are outlined in Exhibit 25.7.

In the cash flow analysis that the agencies undertake, they model a recession period, lasting up to three years, commencing early in the life of the transaction. Particularly important in Italy are timing risks. As we describe above, the period between default and recovery can be protracted. It is critical that the transaction has access to sufficient liquidity to ensure that debt is serviced on a timely basis according to each tranche's rating. The agencies will also stress test the yield on trapped cash.

As is the case with all ABS transactions, the AAA element is expected to "survive" significantly higher levels of stress than lower rated classes. Equally, the assumed stress levels are significantly higher in almost every respect than any that have actually been experienced.

EXHIBIT 25.5 Credit Analysis Process

Factor	Significance
Performing	Agencies will look at the percentage of the loans in the pool, which are, at the time of issue, in arrears. They will look at the nature and severity of these arrears and, where necessary, incorporate their foreclosure costs and timings into their analysis.
Commercial versus residential use	Commercial loans tend to demonstrate a higher foreclosure frequency than residential loans. Commercial loans in a portfolio will increase assumptions about foreclosure probability (for those loans) of between 50–100%.
First or second home	Defaults are less likely in the primary dwelling than in a second home. Second homes are therefore deemed to be up to 30% more likely to enter foreclosure.
Junior charges	Where the loan does not benefit from a first economic lien it is thought likely to be up to 50% more likely to default.
LTV ratios	Depending on the LTV ratio of the loan, the default frequency is adjusted. A loan with a <50% LTV will have a foreclosure probability 80% of base case; an 80% mortgage will have double the likelihood of entering foreclosure.
Large loans	Larger loans (>€150,000) are 20% more likely to enter foreclosure than base case.
Originator servicer adjustments	The agencies' assessment of the originator and servicer will affect the foreclosure probability. A thorough review of systems and processes us undertaken.
Collection frequency	Monthly collections are preferred. Less frequent collections are penalised.
Seasoning	The longer a mortgage is outstanding, generally speaking, the less likely it is to be defaulted upon. The agencies give benefit for loans with long seasoning and penalise relatively new ones.
Modular loans	Loans where the lender can alter the interest rates are assumed to be more problematic than normal loan structures since they can expose borrowers to sudden payment stresses.
Geographic location/concentrations	The agencies will tend to penalise portfolios that are heavily exposed to the south of Italy and the islands as a result of the more volatile economic conditions that prevail in these regions. North and central regional concentrations are not penalised unless there are excessive weightings in a single city.

Source: S&P/Fitch.

EXHIBIT 25.6 S&P Market Value Decline Matrix

Rating	Assumed MVD
AAA	35%
AA	30%
A	26%
BBB	22%
BB	20%

Source: S&P.

EXHIBIT 25.7 Foreclosure Cost Assumptions at Different Rating Levels

Rating	Increase to Recovery Costs
Base Case	7–10% of loan amount
AAA	10.0%
A	9.2%
BBB	8.8%

Source: Fitch.

Credit Enhancement

Credit enhancement can come through cash reserves or via distributed junior tranches. This is illustrated in Exhibits 25.8 and 25.9.

Excess Spread

As in other European RMBS markets, excess spread represents the first layer of loss absorption for bondholders, being the residual amount received from borrowers after payment of senior fees and expenses, note holder interest, and any realised losses.

As such, excess spread is the most sensitive indicator of a transaction's underlying performance, reflecting changes in competitive pressures among mortgage lenders, pool defaults and losses, and prepayment speeds.

Excess spread in Italian RMBS transactions is materially higher than for other European jurisdictions, typically amounting to 75–100 bps on the back of portfolio spreads of roughly 125–175 bps. This compares to excess spread levels of usually around 45–75 bps in Dutch RMBS, 50–75 bps in UK prime RMBS, or 175–275 bps in UK sub-prime RMBS.

EXHIBIT 25.8   Prefunded Reserve Building Up

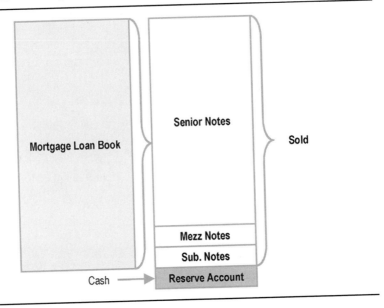

Source: UBS.

EXHIBIT 25.9   Junior Tranche Retained, with Reserves Building Over Time

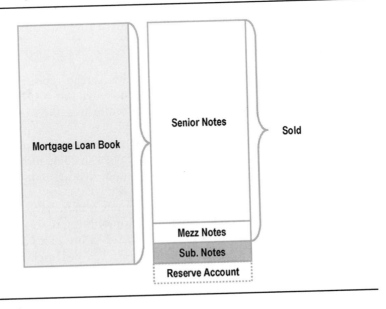

Source: UBS.

Reserve Fund

A second layer of structural support may be provided through a reserve account, which may be unfunded (if junior tranche is retained by the originator), or fully/partially funded by the originator as of the issuance date. Usually sized at between 1–3%, the ultimate funding of reserve accounts in Italian RMBS transactions tends to be twice the level typically seen in UK and Dutch prime RMBS, but is fairly similar to UK subprime RMBS (1.5–2.5%). Where reserve accounts have initially been unfunded or partially funded, excess spread is trapped until the required amount is met (usually within no more than three years).

In the event that the reserve fund is required to cover any shortfalls, subsequent excess spread will be used to replenish the reserve fund back to this level. The reserve fund may incorporate a contingency fund amount, which is usually only available to cover any costs incurred in the event that the substitute servicer steps in. The use of the contingency fund for any other purpose typically requires approval by the rating agencies.

Credit enhancement provided through subordination typically comes in at between 7–10% for Italian RMBS transactions, although this may vary quite dramatically in individual cases, dependent on the specific characteristics of the underlying mortgage pool. Ultimately, this provides for a credit enhancement—excluding excess spread—of usually between 12–15%. These levels are again significantly higher than requirements for benchmark European RMBS issues (about 9–10%), but are similar to UK subprime RMBS deals (13–15%).

CHAPTER 26

European Commercial Mortgage-Backed Securities

Phil Adams, Ph.D.
Director
Barclays Capital

Commercial mortgage-backed securities (CMBS) represent an important and growing sector of the European securitisation market. However, in many cases there are significant differences between transactions, even those backed by collateral from the same originator, and it is these differences, in both collateral types and structural features, that make European CMBS such an interesting asset class. This chapter focuses on some of the more important aspects that investors should consider when analysing the collateral supporting these transactions and briefly looks at the key features of the common transaction structures.

CATEGORISATION OF SECURITSATION TRANSACTIONS

There is a wide variety of European securitisation transactions that are backed by one form or another of commercial property. This variety stems from the range of types of commercial property that may be included in the collateral pool, the type of borrower or borrowers, and the level of exposure to any underlying industries or sectors. As a result, it is not always clear where this sector begins or ends, and although it may be tempting to invent new subclassifications for the various fragments of the sector, this is not necessarily particularly helpful for investors or the market in general. To complicate matters further, a number

471

of different structure types are used to create these securities and they are sometimes used as a means of categorising transactions.

Whatever the structure, however, it is the performance of an underlying ring-fenced pool of commercial property backed loans (and therefore the commercial property itself) that will primarily determine the performance of the securitisations, and we believe that it is probably more appropriate, from an investor's perspective, to group transactions according to the type of credit analysis that is most useful for comparing these securities.

Securitised commercial property exposure can be largely broken down into three categories, as described below:

- Large multiborrower deals, where numerous commercial property loans, originated to numerous borrowers and secured on a variety of properties are grouped together into one transaction, in a similar way to a traditional residential mortgage deal. Such a deal may be either a traditional true sale transaction or a synthetic credit-linked structure.
- The securitisation of either a single or limited number of loans secured by a similar number of properties.
- A commercial property based whole business securitisation, where a portfolio of properties generates the principal revenues in support of the business. Deals such as pub or healthcare transactions typically fall into this category. Such deals can range from a single asset to the highly diversified portfolio (by number if not by industry exposure).

While there are other forms of corporate property securitisation transactions (such as sale and lease-back transactions) and there may be some blurring of the distinctions between these categories, the majority of exposures reliant on the performance of the underlying real estate fall largely within the categories identified above.

Large Multiborrower Transactions

The multiborrower securitisations are typically made up of commercial mortgage loans originated by a bank. The ability of the underlying borrowers to service the loan will usually—but not always—be dependent on the ability of the underlying real estate to generate sufficient cash flow. This may be directly linked to the servicing of a lease obligation, for example a tenant of an office building, or may have greater operational dependency as in the case of a loan to a hotel. Importantly, each loan will have undergone separate credit assessment and there will be distinct loan-to-value measurements for each loan facility. The credit assessment for this type of CMBS is usually built around a simulation of the performance of a pool of such loans because statistical techniques become more appropriate the greater the diversification of the borrowers, property types, and regional and industrial dependencies.

Single or Limited Asset Securitisations

For securitisations backed by a limited number of properties, the statistical techniques that can be used in large portfolio transactions become less appropriate, and it is important to undertake more detailed due diligence of the real estate asset or assets and the property company's management.

Property-Based Whole-Business Securitisations

Almost all of the whole-business securitisations derive a significant proportion of their revenues from real estate assets owned or leased by the operating company. As a result, these could be classified as CMBS transactions. However, any credit analysis will need to address not only the operational performance of the company's assets but also the industry in which it operates. The key concern here is the potentially high correlation of overall performance with industry factors and the very high operational gearing of the underlying tenants. As this category extends beyond the CMBS sector, even occasionally without property backing, these transactions are often treated as a separate asset class.

COLLATERAL CHARACTERISTICS

Different techniques are necessary when analysing a large multiborrower CMBS transaction compared to one secured over a single or limited number of assets. This is reflected in the following sections, which briefly describe some of the more important factors in these analyses. In practice, a transaction may include a large number of loans, but with significant exposure to a few valuable properties, in which case a combination of techniques will be most appropriate.

Credit Assessment of a Multiborrower Transaction

Where a transaction includes a large number of loans, a property-by-property analysis is unlikely to be justifiable (or even possible) so a higher-level approach will need to be adopted. We believe investors should consider a number of key features in a multiborrower deal:

- Weighted average loan-to-value ratio (LTV).
- Underlying portfolio weighted average debt service cover ratio (DSCR).
- Underlying profile of occupational lease expiry over the term of the transaction.

- Average tenant quality (if known/available).
- Weighted average loan seasoning.
- Industry and geographic concentrations.
- Significant single loan or property exposures.
- The quality and ability of the loan origination and servicing process.

Many of these factors, which we discuss in more detail below, also apply to single property analysis.

LTV Ratio

The weighted average LTV ratio provides an overview of the average loan size against the value of the property providing security for the loan on a weighted basis. This provides the investor with a good overall view of the average level of equity the underlying borrowers have in the properties, and as such how far the sale price would have to fall if a borrower defaulted and the property was subsequently enforced before a loss would be incurred.

Although extremely useful, potential limitations should be considered. First, there is the timing and method of the valuations. If the values were obtained at origination, they may be several years old. This raises the question of whether anyone really knows what the value would be in the current market. Also, did the valuers actually visit the properties or were the valuations produced as a "desktop" exercise, which might limit their accuracy?

The profile of the LTVs of individual loans in the portfolio should also be considered. For example, two portfolios, each with a weighted average LTV of 70% may have different profiles. One may have loans evenly spread around the 70% mark, whereas the other may be "barbelled," with a high number of very low LTV loans compensating for a high number of very high LTV loans. In most circumstances, if defaults were to occur, the loss severity would be higher for the barbelled portfolio.

It is often widely commented that LTV is not an indicator of default probability. However, we would argue that a borrower with a 50% equity stake at risk from a potential forced sale of a property would have a greater incentive to maintain debt service payments than if the same borrower had an equity stake of, say, 20%, and so although it may not be the most important influence, the LTV of a loan could be expected to have some influence on the default rate.

Debt Service Cover Ratio

The weighted average debt service cover ratio (DSCR) is an important element in the analysis of commercial property-backed loans. It indicates the level of income received by the borrowers from the properties (be it rental receipts or operating profits) compared with the amount of principal and interest due under the loans. This provides an indication of the amount of deterioration in cash flow the borrowers are able to withstand before they are likely to default on their loans. Just as with LTV, investors should consider the profile of DSCR levels, and whether the weighted average is broadly representative of the portfolio, or distorted by very good and very bad DSCR levels.

A low DSCR does not, by itself, imply that the probability of default is necessarily high. It will depend very much on the nature of the underlying loan, the property, and the cash flow derived from it. A property with very stable rents, let to high quality tenants on long leases should be much more able to support high leverage and a consequent low DSCR than a property with volatile cash flows. As such, it is important to consider the nature of the portfolio when reviewing DSCR levels.

Investors should also determine the basis on which the DSCR level has been calculated. For example, does it include principal payments? Where the borrower pays principal from year two, has this been factored in or has the level been calculated using interest payments only? Also, what interest rate has been factored into the calculation: the current floating rate or a more sustainable longer-term interest rate?

Lease Expiry Profile

Where the majority of properties are tenanted via occupational leases, as is common in CMBS deals, it is useful to consider the profile of the expiry of those leases within the term of the transaction. Indeed, where investors rely on a refinance of certain loans in order to repay the principal, the lease profile after the loan maturity may also be important.

Where a significant proportion of the leases expire within the term of the loan, investors will rely on the quality of the property and the ability of the property manager (who may also be the borrower) to relet the underlying properties in a timely manner, at a level sufficient to service the loan. This will tend to increase the investors' exposure to the property fundamentals, while reducing the importance of the quality of the tenants.

Average Tenant Quality

In many instances, and especially in the United Kingdom, the majority of the underlying properties are occupied by a diverse range of tenants on long-term leases (15–25 years) who share the responsibility for maintenance, repair and insurance. In this case, portfolio analysis can sometimes become as much a consideration of the nature and strength of the tenants as a review of the property itself. This is particularly true where the securitisation is significantly shorter in term than the majority of the occupational leases.

However, where the portfolio contains a significant number of multi-tenanted properties, it is likely that only a few will be credit rated; many could be small regional tenants with neither the need for nor the means of obtaining a credit rating. This will increase the importance of any checks and controls in the origination and underwriting processes.

Seasoning

Loan seasoning is the time since the loan was first originated. Where a loan has existed for a considerable period, comfort can be taken from the fact that the borrower has proved to have a good payment history, and may also have made inroads into loan amortisation.

When loans have been originated against the background of a long-standing relationship between the originating bank and the borrower or borrower sponsors, it may be relevant to consider the length of that relationship. However, when other loans are already in place investors should also consider whether any decisions made in the interests of the originator's overall exposure to the borrower could negatively impact the securitised loan in the event of default.

Industry, Geographic, and Other Concentrations

Where credit exposure is spread across geographic and industry sectors, the risk associated with localised events or problems in any individual sector will be much reduced. Where concentrations do exist, it is important to understand the underlying factors that will affect the performance of those loans.

Taking concentration risks one step further, it is not uncommon for a portfolio to have a single loan that accounts for 10% or more of the overall portfolio. Where this is the case, investors should consider the credit fundamentals of this exposure separately in a manner similar to that used for a single-property transaction.

Origination and Servicing

Investors should review the lender's origination process, the lending criteria for the loans and any warranties for that specific transaction. This review should consider the extent of the origination process, where the lender obtains its business and what resources are available to perform it. Any procedures for assessing the creditworthiness of the borrower will be important, particularly for the smaller borrowers, as well as the valuation process.

Similar considerations apply to the servicing capability. A good servicing operation can limit the instance of loans becoming delinquent and also maximise recoveries should loans default.

Credit Assessment of a Single-Property Transaction

The previous discussion has centred on some of the key credit areas for investors analysing multiborrower CMBS transactions. While much of this also applies to single-property transactions, the analysis necessary for these transactions differs significantly in its detail. Listed below are some of the key additional areas we believe investors should consider when analysing a single-asset deal:

- Cash flow stability and loan leverage
- Property valuation
- Property marketability
- Capital expenditure requirements
- Environmental and planning issues
- Loan structure

These areas are property specific and so an investor will require much more detailed information than would be the case for all but the largest exposures in a multiborrower transaction.

Cash Flow Stability and Loan Leverage

Perhaps the most important aspect of commercial property analysis is the nature and stability of the underlying cash flows. These are usually derived from a large number of tenants occupying a single commercial property. The stability and sustainability of these cash flows are used in part to produce a valuation, and they also determine whether the leverage applied to the property is in itself sustainable.

The review of the cash flows is likely to comprise the following components:

- A review of the tenants and their susceptibility to an economic downturn.
- The nature of the underlying leases, the expiry profile of the leases, and the level of borrower responsibility for items such as capital expenditure and insurance.
- A comparison of the rental level with that in comparable properties in order to assess the sustainability of the rental income.

Having gained an insight into the nature of the cash flow, an investor can then compare it to the anticipated DSCR level to ensure the leverage is appropriate when taking into account the likely volatility and sustainability of the rental income.

Property Valuation

The launch valuation is a useful guide to the refinance value of the property and also as a starting point for estimating the value in a forced sale situation. However, remember that the valuation for a commercial property is directly linked to the amount of income it can generate. As most commercial properties are owned by special purpose companies, with the income from the property used to finance the debt, any difficulty in maintaining the mortgage payments is likely to be a direct result of a reduction in the cash flows from the property. This will reduce the property's value in a forced sale situation.

Property Marketability and Longevity

The key to evaluating the likely future desirability of a property will be the nature of the physical building itself. However, any analysis needs to look at more than just the property. It needs to encompass the surrounding area or sub-market, transportation links, parking facilities, additional infrastructure and the like. An analysis to determine likely future demand for a property should encompass all elements that affect desirability, including possibly the most important factor—competition.

It is important to consider the extent to which new or redeveloped properties may enter the market in the foreseeable future, increasing the level of competition. This will be particularly important when the term of the transaction exceeds a significant level of lease expiries, as this places increased reliance on successfully reletting.

Capital Expenditure Requirements

Different properties require different levels of capital expenditure (capex), depending on a number of factors, including age, construction, and usage. Capex can be broken down into two types—that required for the continual maintenance of the building (maintenance capex) and that required to upgrade or refurbish a building (development capex). Investors should establish who is responsible for each of the above. In the United Kingdom, maintenance capex is usually the tenants' responsibility, but investors should not assume the borrower is immune from capex spend.

On occasion, a borrower is likely to be required to fund general refurbishment to maintain the standard of the property. There may also need to be considerable amounts spent after a major tenant has vacated a property in order to attract a new tenant to that space. Investors should check that a prudent level of capex spend has been factored into the future property cash flow assumptions. In fact, many transactions require a minimum amount to be either spent or reserved for capex each year.

Environmental and Planning Issues

Ideally, the valuation should also identify any environmental or planning issues associated with the building. Environmental issues primarily relate to the land on which the property has been built. Where this is deemed contaminated, the cost of decontamination may well fall with the borrower. Planning issues may also require additional spend during the life of a transaction.

Loan Structure

Loan structure is more than just leverage (an area previously discussed). It includes such elements as the loan amortisation schedule and any performance triggers such as minimum debt service cover ratios. These should also be considered in any credit analysis.

Amortisation is the first consideration. There is a significant difference between a deal that amortises in full over the term of the loan and one that only partly amortises and therefore relies on a refinancing of the property to repay the bonds at maturity. A property is not guaranteed to increase in value over the life of a transaction.

A valuable structural protection for investors is often provided by the use of a DSCR threshold mechanism. Once the ratio reaches a predetermined minimum level, usually some way above what would be needed to meet all the debt service obligations, all free cash will be retained in the structure, for the benefit of the bondholders.

Summary of Collateral Characteristics

Investing in CMBS, whether they are single-asset or multiborrower transactions, requires an appreciation of the nature of the underlying properties and the inherent sensitivities of the cash flows they generate. The type and extent of analysis undertaken should be tailored to reflect the characteristics of the collateral pool and also whether the proposed investment is at a senior or junior level in the capital structure.

In particular, many investors take comfort from a well-diversified multiborrower portfolio and seek to limit the concentration of risks associated with a single-asset transaction. While this approach is understandable and relevant to senior bondholders, this diversification is not necessarily beneficial to junior noteholders who are then exposed to potential losses across the entire portfolio.

CMBS TRANSACTION STRUCTURES

A number of different transaction structures are used in CMBS securitisations. The most appropriate one for any particular case will depend on the nature of the security over the real estate assets, the type of borrower, the number of jurisdictions involved, and any tax implications for the owner of the properties.

Pooled Commercial Mortgage Transactions

There are two basic forms of pooled commercial mortgage transactions: the true sale and the synthetic structures. The true sale mechanism, as its name suggests, involves the sale of assets from the originator's balance sheet to an SPV, which are then used as security for the issue of notes to investors. Synthetic structures, by contrast, involve the creation of a credit derivative linked to the performance of a pool of loans. The loans themselves remain on the balance sheet of the originator but the credit risks associated with these loans are transferred through the credit derivative to investors. Synthetic structures can simplify the issuance process and avoid many of the complexities (and costs) associated with the sale of assets in many jurisdictions.

True Sale Transactions

A typical UK commercial mortgage loan securitisation involves the equitable assignment of a pool of mortgages by the originator of the loans (usually a bank). The loans and all ancillary rights are held in trust for both the originator, who retains the legal title to the properties, and the special purpose vehicle company (SPV). Importantly, a power of attorney is also granted by the originator to the trustee to enforce the loans in the name of the originator and, if necessary, to transfer the originator's legal title to the SPV. This legal structure achieves ring-fencing of the assets such that even in the event of the insolvency of the originator, the cash flows derived from the underlying loans will be available to service the debt issue. This process avoids incurring stamp duty. Monument Securitisation No. 1 PLC, comprised by loans originated by Anglo Irish Bank Corporation plc, is an example of this type of structure and is illustrated in Exhibit 26.1.

Synthetic Structures

Synthetic structures can significantly simplify the structuring and issuance process. This advantage is particularly marked when dealing with a portfolio of loans spread across multiple jurisdictions. The difficulties involved in designing a structure for a true sale transaction to cope with different insolvency regimes, unharmonised tax regimes, and vastly dif-

EXHIBIT 26.1   Loan Assignment Structure

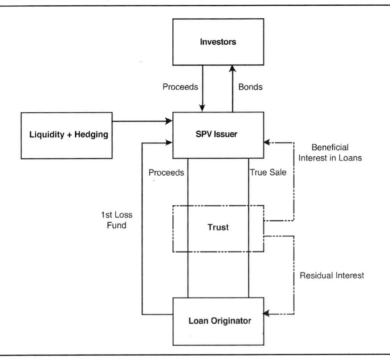

Source: Barclays Capital.

ferent property and foreclosure laws make synthetic structures far more suited to this type of transaction.

In many ways, the synthetic structure is much simpler than one involving an assignment of underlying loans. In these structures, the proceeds of the issue are not used to purchase the reference portfolio of commercial mortgages but instead to purchase other collateral, which might include one or more of the following: Pfandbriefe, notes from the originator, or other securities. This collateral is then used to collateralise the issuer's debt obligations. An example structure for a synthetic transaction is shown in Exhibit 26.2.

Under a guarantee agreement, the originator is able to recover an amount equal to the net realised losses on the reference pool of loans, including the costs incurred in the foreclosure and recovery process, in return for a periodic payment of a guarantee fee. This fee is calculated to make up any shortfall between the interest received on the credit-linked note collateral pool and the expenses and interest costs of the issuing SPV. Realised losses are applied in reverse sequential order to the notes, by can-

EXHIBIT 26.2   Typical Synthetic Structure with a Credit Default Swap

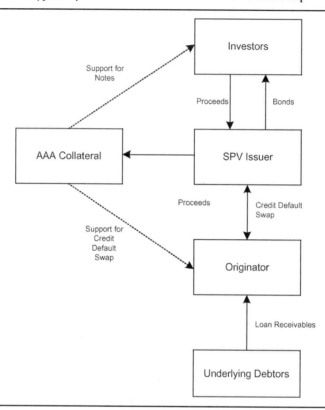

Source: Barclays Capital.

celling a portion of the most junior class outstanding to cover the loss, while amounts equal to the loan redemptions are paid through sequentially.

Double credit risk is a particular feature of such synthetic transaction structures. Not only are investors exposed to the performance of the reference pool of commercial mortgages, but also to the performance of the collateral the issuer is holding. If this includes notes issued by the originator itself then this will also include exposure to the credit rating of the originator.

Secured Loan Structures

A true sale structure, while appropriate for the securitisation of closed-end loans, is likely to have unfortunate tax implications where a property owner wishes to retain overall economic benefit of the asset. This can be overcome through a secured loan structure.

EXHIBIT 26.3 Secured Loan Securitisation Structure

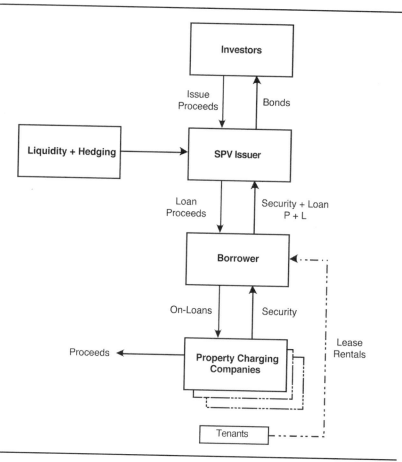

Source: Barclays Capital.

Under this structure, ownership of the assets remains with the borrower, but bondholders have the benefit of a charge over the assets. A bankruptcy remote SPV raises the debt and on-lends the proceeds to a borrower company under a lending arrangement, usually termed the "issuer-borrower" loan. The borrower may then on-lend to one or more property owning companies. A comprehensive security package will include security over all the issuer's assets, first priority fixed charges over the properties charged by the borrower or by the other property companies, and assignment of rental income received from the charged properties in addition to security over other assets such as bank accounts. A typical secured loan structure is illustrated in Exhibit 26.3.

In standard CMBS transactions of this type, rents will be received into a fixed-charge account. This is in contrast to most whole business securitisations in which it is more practical to pass operating income through floating charge accounts.

Under the secured loan structure, the trustee might find it necessary under certain circumstances to enforce the fixed and floating charges. Such circumstances could include unremedied events of default under the issuer-borrower loan, or if third-party creditors were to attempt to put the company into administration. In this case, the trustee would seek to have an administrative receiver appointed on behalf of the secured creditors. However, the process could disrupt the receipt and payment of cash flows. The ratings of the notes are based on timely payment of interest (and sometimes principal) so the transaction will include some form of liquidity support, which is typically sized to enable the issuer to cover one year's debt service.

Sale and Leaseback Structures

The sale and leaseback concept enables a company to retain the operating benefit of the properties while divesting of ownership. The typical structures avoid the adverse tax consequences of a normal sale and can, in comes cases, gain certain tax advantages.

In a securitisation structure, a bankruptcy-remote SPV uses the proceeds of the debt issue to acquire the properties. It then leases them back to the seller for a term that will equal or exceed the tenor of the debt issue. Lease payments will service the debt in one of various ways: The debt may be fully amortised over the term (although this gives rise to a significant tax mismatch); the debt may be partially amortised, which requires refinancing or a sale of the property to ensure repayment of the debt at maturity; or the issue size may be increased to fund the purchase of a zero coupon bond to repay the principal at maturity. A typical structure is illustrated in Exhibit 26.4.

CONCLUSION

The European CMBS market presents investors with a wide variety of investment opportunities ranging from short-dated floating rate notes to long-dated, fixed rate issues across a rating spectrum from AAA to BB, and so it should appeal to a wide section of the investor community. It is, however, a relatively complex asset class. There are many underlying asset types, which can be spread across more than one country, and there are a number of possible transaction structures. As a result, it is not always easy to compare one transaction against another.

EXHIBIT 26.4   Simplified Sale-and-Lease-Back Structure

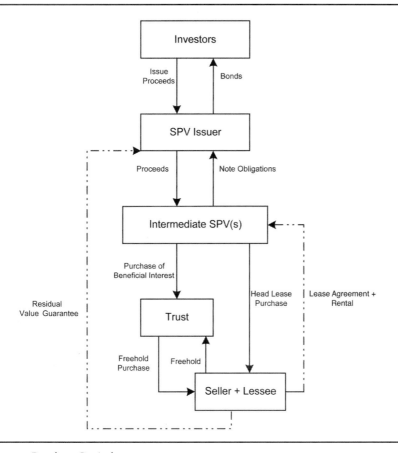

Source: Barclays Capital.

Given the variety and potential volatility of the some of the underlying collateral, different analysis techniques are more appropriate for assessing the various transactions. This is clearly illustrated by the difference between a highly diversified multiborrower pool and a transaction supported by a single prestige property. However, in practice the distinctions are likely to be less clear-cut and a combination of techniques may be more appropriate. Certain key factors underlie all the analysis and these include an assessment of the leverage and cash flow coverage of the debt; the property value; the structure of the loan; any mechanisms designed to protect investors; and an understanding of the sensitivities of the tenants who are ultimately the source of the cash flow within the transaction.

CHAPTER 27

Rating Approach to European CMBS

Benedicte Pfister
General Manager
Moody's Italy

While Moody's general approach to commercial mortgage-backed securities (CMBS) is similar across jurisdictions, certain adjustments are required to accurately reflect the specificities of each market, either in terms of commercial property particulars, lending practice or legal framework. In the United Kingdom, for example, most leases tend to be long-term, "fully repairing and insuring" (FRI) leases, with lenders benefiting from the creditor-friendly legal system. In Italy, France, and Spain, on the other hand, shorter-term leases are more common, and the foreclosure process takes substantially longer.

Due to the fact that commercial mortgages tend to be heterogeneous and relevant historical information is limited, much of Moody's analysis is based on a fundamental assessment of the underlying properties securing the mortgages.

In addition to observing transactions from a number of different countries, the European market has also witnessed a wide variety of transaction structures and portfolio characteristics during its relatively short existence. Moody's attempts to reflect this variety by using different rating methodologies. For well-diversified portfolios of similar assets within a single country, Moody's will tend to use an approach originally developed for US conduit transactions. As such, this model is commonly known as the *conduit approach* and has been modified to reflect the unique qualities of the respective European markets. Transactions secured by one asset or a relatively small number of assets require a slightly different form of analysis, which, for the purposes of this chapter, will be referred to as the *large loan approach*. For a portfolio of homogeneous FRI long-term credit tenant leases, where the risk of default is best represented by the rating of the tenant, it may be more appropriate to use a binomial expansion type model called the *credit tenant lease methodology*. Recently, many European transactions, however, fall outside these three methodologies. For this reason, Moody's has developed a fourth approach based on a *Monte Carlo simulation*, which allows for any combination of the existing approaches, and as a result is particularly well suited to pan-European CMBS transactions, non-homogenous credit tenant lease financing or small portfolios. The above four models are often used in conjunction.

Each of the above-mentioned methodologies aims at deriving an *expected loss* on the rated bonds, which will then be mapped to a Moody's rating.

FUNDAMENTAL REAL ESTATE ANALYSIS

Unlike many other types of securitised assets, commercial mortgages are not homogeneous, and relevant industry-wide loss information, particularly in Europe, is rarely available. As a result, it is not possible to rely on a statistical analysis of historical performance data to estimate the credit risk of a pool of commercial mortgage assets. Instead, Moody's analyses the fundamental real estate credit risk of *each asset* to estimate the expected frequency and severity of losses in the mortgage pool.

The credit risk of a mortgage loan will depend primarily on the characteristics of the underlying properties securing the loan (cash flow, quality, type of property, tenants, diversity), as well as on the loan structure (leverage, amortisation profile, interest rate, reserves, cross-collateralisation, seasoning, and delinquency history). The interaction between these two factors may be reflected to a large extent in the debt-service coverage ratio (DSCR) and the loan-to-value ratio (LTV) associated with the mortgage loan. This suggests that both DSCRs and LTVs would be good proxies for the credit risk on a mortgage loan. Moody's believes that DSCR is the main driver of frequency of loss, while LTV is the key determining factor for the expected severity of loss.

The credit risk of the mortgage pool will depend on the credit risk of each loan as well as on the overall portfolio diversification and other factors, such as the *transaction structure*, *legal risk*, and *servicing quality*.

The above elements are the major inputs in Moody's rating models described later in this chapter.

Property Characteristics

The bulk of the fundamental credit analysis is carried out at the individual property level, and therefore most of the models are based on property-related data, and roll the results up to the loan level and ultimately to the overall bond level. The amount of time spent on analysing each property and loan will depend on the number of assets included in the securitisation and the importance of any specific asset.

Sustainable Cash Flow

The first step of the real estate analysis process is to estimate how much cash flow can be generated by each property on *a long-term sustainable basis*. Moody's focuses on *net cash flow* (NCF), defined as earnings before interest, corporate tax, depreciation, and amortisation (i.e., EBITDA, or net operating income), less capital expenses and other fixed charges. NCF provides an accurate picture of actual funds available to service the debt on a long-term basis.

Sustainable cash flows are meant to represent the cash-generating potential of a property looking through real estate cycles. Currently, many markets exhibit historically low vacancy rates and have experienced significant increases in rent. It is unlikely that this situation will continue over the long term, and this explains why Moody's believes it is more appropriate to adjust the numbers to reflect long-term sustainable levels.

Ideally, Moody's is able to review at least three years of historical (audited) financial statements as well as projections for the following year. This process can be altered if such information is not available; however, the resulting numbers are likely to be more conservative to reflect the lower confidence level associated with the calculations. Moody's analyses each component of NCF as outlined below.

Revenues   The starting point in deriving sustainable revenue are current in-place rents. To the extent that relevant information is available, this number may be adjusted if, inter alia:

- Current levels are significantly different from historical levels.
- Current rents exceed estimated rental values (ERV), or the market in general.
- Supply and demand in the market are not in equilibrium or are likely to move out of equilibrium in the future.
- Concessions, such as free rent, are (or are expected to be) present in the market.
- Current occupancy is not in line with Moody's estimate of sustainable occupancy.

Moody's also includes expenses reimbursed by tenants and other income in the NCF figure if information confirms that it will be sustainable on a long-term basis. As with rents, other sources of income derived from the tenants will be adjusted by a sustainable occupancy factor and will take into account the credit quality of the source of such income.

General Expenses Expenses, such as rates/taxes, insurance, operating costs, management fees and/ or overhead costs are deducted from revenue to estimate EBITDA. Expenses borne by the landlord vary significantly by property type and from one country to the next. For example, in most FRI leases found in the UK, tenants are responsible for paying rates and practically all costs associated with operating the property. Minimal costs are borne by the landlord so long as tenants are in occupancy and honouring their obligations. However, landlords would bear a portion of such costs at some point in time unless a replacement tenant immediately steps into the obligations upon expiration of, or default under, the original lease. As a result, Moody's will typically assume a minimal amount of expense even for FRI leases. The expense assumption will be greater in countries such as Germany where the landlord is responsible for paying a larger portion of expenses.

As with income, the goal is to determine a stabilised level of expenses. Therefore, Moody's will generally adjust any expenses that are temporarily below, or in some cases above, the long-term normalised level. An example of such an adjustment is one made on a property for which taxes have been reduced temporarily as part of a development incentive programme. To assume current below-market tax expenses would give an inaccurate projection of sustainable cash flows and therefore a pro forma amount would be used.

Exhibit 27.1 indicates typical ranges of expense ratios per property type in Europe. These ranges are merely a guideline and will be adjusted to reflect as closely as possible the current lease structure and prevailing market norms.

Operating leverage affects the potential cash flow volatility of an asset, and consequently, its risk profile. Indeed, as the expense ratio increases, the performance of a property will become more sensitive to any fluctuations in wages, tax rate, utility price, or other operating costs. The ratio of fixed to variable costs is also an important factor consider: as a significant portion of operating expenses are usually fixed costs, a decrease in occupancy will have a larger impact on properties with high expense ratios.

EXHIBIT 27.1   Example of Expense Ratio Varying with Property Type

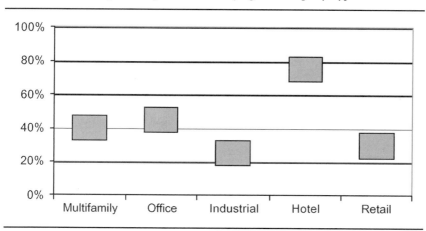

Capital Items   To the extent capital items have not been included as part of general expenses, they will be deducted from EBITDA to derive NCF. For analysis purposes, Moody's assumes capital expenditures to include replacement reserves, re-letting costs and other capital improvement costs designed to bring the property up to market standards or maintain its current competitive position. Capital expenditures designed to improve the property are excluded from the calculation, as no credit is given for income derived from development projects. Re-letting costs include brokerage commissions, void costs, free rent, as well as other costs of finding a new tenant. In addition to historical and market information, Moody's reviews valuations and structural surveys for an indication of both immediate capital requirements as well as ongoing expenses.

Moody's uses its determination of NCF to compute the relevant DSCR for each loan. DSCR is one of the key factors in Moody's assessment of the frequency of default of a given loan. NCF is also used to compute the LTV ratio.

Quality Grade

Moody's quality grade on a property reflects our assessment of the quality of that property relative to the national market for such property type, taking into account factors such as construction quality, neighbourhood, local market, competition, tenancy profile and quality of income. In other words, this grade measures the desirability of a property within a certain property type, also reflecting as a result the volatility of the property cash flows. Moody's scale ranges from 1 (best) to 5 (worst).

Property Type

Moody's views on mortgage loan credit quality are being influenced by the inherent risks of each property type securing the mortgage loan.[1] The ranking will vary from one country to the next. However, in many Western European countries, the stability of cash flows and asset values of the major property types, ranked in order from lowest to highest volatility, is as follows: multifamily, anchored retail, industrial, unanchored retail, office, and hotel. However, there are exceptions as exemplified by UK-style FRI leases for many high quality office properties reducing the average UK office related credit risk compared with other European countries.

Higher DSCRs will be required for more volatile asset classes in order to reach comparable rating levels.

Tenants

Moody's will adjust the quality grade of a property to account for the credit quality of the tenants. If a property is leased to a highly rated entity through to the maturity of a fully amortising loan, the default probability under the mortgage loan will be directly derived from the credit rating of the tenant.

Diversity

Moody's will recognise the diversity benefit of *cross-collateralisation* among properties through an appropriate adjustment of the property grade.[2] In such case, indeed, equity and excess cash flows from performing properties will be available to support weaker properties. This should, as a result, improve both the probability of default and the recovery assumptions on the loan. However, in order to achieve the maximum benefit, the release premium on cross-collateralised properties sold before the maturity of the loan will need to reflect the equity component of the released property.

Loan Structure

Certain loan features (e.g., amortisation profile, interest rate risk, seasoning, cross default/collateralisation, etc.) will have a direct impact on the risk profile of such loan and are discussed in the next sections.

---

[1] See "CMBS: Moody's Approach to Rating Loans Secured by Industrial Properties," "CMBS: Moody's Approach to Rating Loans Secured by Office Properties," "Moody's Approach to Rating Multifamily Housing Transactions," and "CMBS: Moody's Approach to Rating Assisted Living Facilities" for a specific analysis of various property types.

[2] See "CMBS: Moody's Approach to Rating Cross-Collateralised and Cross-Defaulted Loans."

Amortisation Profile

Interest-only loans and partially amortising loans are likely to have a lower probability of default during the term of the loan due to their lower debt service. However, the probability of default at maturity may be significantly higher as the likelihood of a successful refinancing will depend, inter alia, upon the marketability of the property and the interest rate environment at that time (both uncertain). Accordingly, Moody's will particularly value front-loaded amortisation profiles, which will maximise the amount of amortisation generated in the early years of a transaction when the certainty of the cash flows is higher. In addition, amortisation will reduce a lender's exposure to the assets over time, thus enhancing the recovery assumptions in a default scenario.

While US mortgage loans are typically structured to provide for a substantial balloon payment at maturity, many European CMBS transactions include fully amortising loans.

Floating Rate Loans

Floating rate loans have the additional credit risk associated with rising rates during the term.[3] However, in Europe, CMBS transactions usually benefit from some hedging arrangements intended to limit this risk. In particular, the issuer often enters into a cap agreement with a third party that mitigates the impact of increased borrower default due to the higher debt service on the loans. In some transactions, the benefit of the cap is passed on to the underlying borrowers.

Seasoning and Delinquencies

Current and historical arrears will be incorporated in the overall assessment of the quality of the loans, typically via an adjustment in the loan quality grade. Seasoning will be viewed favourably, particularly for loans which have survived a recessionnary period within their region and property type.

Other Loan Features

Existing reserves or trapping of excess cash for capital replacement, tenant improvement or leasing costs improve the risk profile of a loan. Crossing between loans will also improve the stability of cash flow and will be accounted for in a similar way as crossing between properties within a loan (see above). In such a case, the DSCR will be computed on a consolidated basis. Other features such as subparticipation or borrower's quality will be incorporated into the analysis.

---

[3] See "CMBS: Moody's Approach to Rating Floating Rate Transactions."

Implied Loan DSCR and LTV

The core of Moody's CMBS analysis is the estimate of cash flow that will be available to service the debt during the term of the loans and any refinancing if necessary. The estimate of NCF is used to derive DSCR and LTV. The various methlogies that Moody's uses for CMBS analysis rely on both DSCR and LTV but each approach places a different emphasis on the importance of each ratio.

The quality grade assigned by Moody's to a property and/or the property type will have a direct impact upon the calculation of these ratios as well as upon the credit enhancement for each loan at a given rating level.

LTV

Once a sustainable cash flow is determined, Moody's applies a stabilised yield or *capitalisation rate* to arrive at the long-term sustainable value for the asset (assuming a long-term useful life for that asset). Yields applied to each property vary depending on property type, country, location within a market, tenancy strength, construction quality, point in the property cycle, and other relevant risk factors. Yields are intended to result in stabilised values, and, as such, the yield and the resulting value may vary significantly from market rates and values at various points in the cycle.

Exhibit 27.2 reflects Moody's current views on average UK cap rates for different property types and quality grades.

A current and balloon LTV ratio will be calculated as (1) the outstanding balance of the loan, either at closing or at maturity, divided by (2) the Moody's derived value. Most models use the LTV primarily to determine the likelihood of a default at maturity (along with the DSCR) as well as the extent of a loss in the event of default, referred to as the severity of loss.

EXHIBIT 27.2   Example of UK Cap Rates by Property Type and Quality Grade

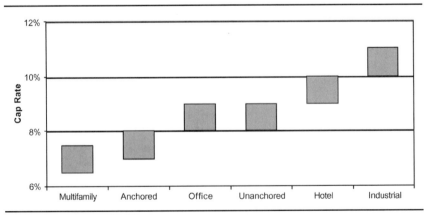

Actual and Hurdle Rate DSCR

DSCR is defined as NCF divided by the debt service payment, including both interest and principal amortisation payments. Moody's reviews two different DSCR calculations: The first calculation is based on actual in-place debt service and the second is based on an assumed "hurdle" rate. A hurdle rate can be thought of as an idealised loan rate derived by dividing a pro forma debt service payment by the loan amount. The pro forma debt service payment assumes long-term, risk-adjusted interest rates and a standard mortgage-based amortisation schedule over what Moody's considers to be the useful life of the assets. A limited balloon payment at maturity may be assumed on certain assets.

■ This *useful life* concept aims at reflecting both the physical and the economic life of the assets, and takes into consideration, inter alia, the age, quality, condition, location/submarket and property type of those assets. Because of the limited space available for new development and the restrictive planning permission policy in many European countries, European assets may exhibit longer useful lives than in the U.S. For small pools and large loans, Moody's will assess the useful life of each asset individually.

■ The cost of capital in the hurdle rate calculation will be adjusted for any rate volatility associated with unhedged floating rate debt, or with loans exposed to refinancing risk (either on the balloon date for non-fully amortising loans, or after a default and liquidation of the assets on a fixed rate loan).

Hence, the hurdle rate takes amortisation and hedging into account.

The actual DSCR provides an indication of default risk during the term of the loan, whereas the DSCR calculated using the hurdle rate is meant to be a proxy for refinancing risk, either in the event of a default during the term of the loan or at maturity. A hurdle rate derived DSCR calculated at the onset of the transaction also makes it easier to compare DSCRs for different loans as the effect of advantageous financing or interest rate movements is minimised and a common benchmark rate can be used.

To illustrate the above, let us take an interest-only loan with a notional of £100, a 10% annual coupon, a 10-year maturity, and secured over a property with a useful life of 25 years:

■ At closing, the hurdle-based or "normalised" annual debt service based on a constant payment over the life of the asset will be £11.02. This corresponds to an 11.02% hurdle rate. A DSCR calculated on this debt service amount will reflect the initial risk associated with the loan independently from its financing.

■ At maturity (i.e., year 10), the whole balance of the loan will need to be refinanced. At that time, the asset will have a remaining useful life of 15 years. Interest rates may have moved, and we may want to take a cushion against uncertainty, say 2%. Hence the normalised debt service in this refinancing scenario will have increased to £14.68. If the transaction benefits from hedging arrangements beyond the maturity of the loan, this will mitigate the uncertainty in respect of refinancing rates, and the rate cushion used in the calculation may be reduced.

■ If the loan defaults at year 5, the remaining life of the asset will be 20, and a 1% rate cushion may be sufficient. The debt service will then be £12.56.

The above "hurdle" analysis tends to penalise long-term interest-only loans (or loans with minimal amortisation) as the useful life of the asset decreases over time while the loan balance remains constant. To mitigate this effect, Moody's will also look at LTV levels at maturity, in particular for well-located assets which are likely to benefit from a significant "redevelopment option value" at the end of their useful life.

Portfolio Level Analysis

Most transactions benefit from characteristics beyond just the credit quality of individual properties or loans. The main factor is the portfolio diversification.

Portfolio Diversification

The diversity of a portfolio of assets will have an impact on the volatility of expected loss for the pool, which in turn affects the level of credit enhancement needed for rated bonds. Diversity is examined by property type, geographic location, economic sector, and loan/borrower concentration.[4] Geographic and property-type diversity work best when there is no significant loan concentration or, in the case of a single loan/multiple assets transaction, no significant property value concentration.

Moody's measures loan/borrower concentration by applying a diversity scoring system based on the *Herfindahl Index*.[5] This index effectively converts a pool of loans of uneven size into a measurement of diversity as if all loans were the same size. This diversity score may then be qualitatively adjusted for geographic and property-type concentrations.

---

[4] See "Gauging Economic Diversity in CMBS."

[5] See "CMBS 1Q 99 Review & Outlook: Smaller, But Still Solid Market for 1999 Holds Different Risks For Investors" for calculation of the Herfindahl Index and a detailed example.

$$\text{Herfindahl Index} = 1/(\text{SUM}((\text{Loan Balance/Pool Balance})^2))$$

We will also look at portfolio diversity by using a *diversity score* similar to what is used in collateralised bond obligations (CBO) analysis.[6] As further discussed in the credit tenant lease section below, this diversity score has the benefit of incorporating loan/borrower, geographic and property-type diversity in the same calculation. However, it requires the definition of correlations within various property types and geographical locations.

Properties can be widely dispersed geographically but still be situated in regions that have the same fundamental economic drivers. The strength of demand for real estate in regions with similar industry profiles will tend to be correlated. As a result, Moody's will also consider the pool's exposure to various sectors of the economy and incorporate this analysis of economic diversity into its rating assessment.

Other Adjustments

Aspects such as *legal risk*, *quality of information*, or *quality of servicer* are generally incorporated at the portfolio level through qualitative adjustments to the portfolio's overall credit enhancement.

RATING ANALYSIS OF CMBS TRANSACTIONS

Moody's has developed a number of different rating approaches and corresponding models to cope with the variety of transactions in the European property securitisation market.[7] The four main models are discussed below and summarized in Exhibit 27.3. Each rating approach is best suited for a specific type of transaction, although some have a relatively wide spectrum. Often, the models are used in conjunction, either because the transaction type falls inbetween the standard models or, more often, simply to provide support for the primary model used. In addition, other general structured finance tools may be used to test the results of the real-estate-based models. The models are designed to automatically assess the credit quality of each asset or loan. However, given the unique characteristics of CMBS assets, all of the rating approaches rely on the appropriate real estate assessment as a qualitative input.

---

[6] See "Moody's Approach to Rating Multisector CDOs."
[7] Specific reports have also been published by Moody's on our approach to rating CMBS in the U.S., Canada, and Japan.

EXHIBIT 27.3 Main Characteristics of Moody's CMBS Rating Methodologies

Models	Conduit	Large Loan	CTL	Monte Carlo
Spectrum	Wide	Narrow	Narrow	Wide
Type	Static	Static	Simulation	Simulation
Type of analysis	Real estate	Real estate	CDO	Real estate
Best use	Diversified portfolio	Small number of assets	FRI long-term credit tenant leases	Pan-European transaction
	Similar asset type	Single borrower	Homogeneous pool	Heterogenous pool
	Single country	No credit tenant lease	Medium-to-large pool	Small portfolio
Main driver	DSCR	LTV	Tenant credit rating	Loan rating estimate
Main inputs	DSCR (hurdle-based)	LTV (going-in & balloon)	Tenant rating (assigned or shadow)	DSCR (actual and hurdle-based)
	LTV (ongoing & balloon)	DSCR (hurdle-based)	Diversity score (via correlations)	LTV
	Quality grade	Quality grade	LTV	Quality grade
	Property type	Property type		Property type
	Herfindahl index			Correlations
				Tenant rating

498

Conduit Transactions[8]

The conduit approach is commonly used for reasonably well-diversified pools of assets and works best for pools containing assets of similar size and credit quality within the same country. It can, however, be adapted or combined with other models to handle "chunky" pools as well as multijurisdiction portfolios. Information is analysed on a property-by-property basis.

Drivers of Credit Enhancement at the Property/Loan Level

The model assumes that the default probability of a loan is highly dependent on the DSCR. The LTV associated with the underlying mortgage loan is the main determining factor for the expected severity of loss in the event of a default. The DSCR used in the model is the hurdle-based DSCR at the onset of the transaction, in order to compare the assets on a similar basis.

The starting point of the model is Moody's opinion with respect to the minimum credit enhancement required for a loan with a specific DSCR, quality grade, and property type in order to achieve a Aa2 rating level. This opinion is derived from a detailed analysis of long-term real estate data in the US (as relevant performance information for European markets remains limited). Hence, many adjustments were necessary to reflect country specific characteristics. For example, all else being equal, lower credit-enhancement is generally acceptable for UK transactions due to the creditor-friendly legal environment, which suggests higher recovery assumptions. The limited space available for new developments and the restricted planning permissions in the UK also reduces the risk of new construction.

Exhibit 27.4, for example, shows Moody's target Aa2 credit enhancement for a loan secured over a medium-quality property located in continental Europe, as a function of DSCR and property type. Low quality assets within risky asset types will tend to exhibit more volatile cash flow, and hence will require more credit enhancement to reach the same rating category. Credit enhancement levels will be most sensitive to variations of DSCR in the region between 1.0× and 1.3× (the steeper part of the curve). Indeed, loans with DSCR above 1.3× will have some minimum cushion to withstand temporary problems or typical cash flow volatility resulting from the economic cycle. Similarly, loans with DSCRs below 1.00× are generally assumed to have a frequency of

---

[8] A more detailed description of the conduit approach may be found in a special report entitled "CMBS: Moody's Approach to Rating U.S. Conduit Transactions." Note, however, that this report reflects a US perspective and therefore certain information may not be applicable to most European markets.

EXHIBIT 27.4   Example of Aa2 Credit Enhancement for a Grade 3 Property by
DSCR and Property Type

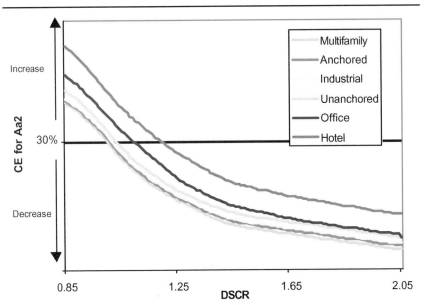

default approaching 100%, as borrowers are not expected to fund cash
flow shortfalls for an extended period of time. However, some credit is
given for a potential recovery from a sale of the assets.

Total credit enhancement for the pool at an Aa2 level is calculated
based on the sum of the credit enhancement for each loan weighted by
the loan contribution in the pool. The credit enhancement for the pool
at other rating levels is then derived from adjusting the Aa2 enhancement level by a multiple specific to each rating category.

Adjustments at the Pool Level

Moody's also assesses the portfolio diversification of the pool using the
Herfindahl Index calculation based on the number and size of the properties. Exhibit 27.5 shows Moody's typical Aa2 credit enhancement
adjustment for concentration in absolute terms. Adjustments for delinquencies, seasoning or the security package may be included at the loan
level but are typically made at the pool level. Other aspects, such as
legal risk, excess spread, interest rate risk, concentration issues (in terms
of property type or regions), quality of information or of servicer will be
incorporated at the portfolio level.

EXHIBIT 27.5   Typical Credit Enhancement Adjustment for Concentration

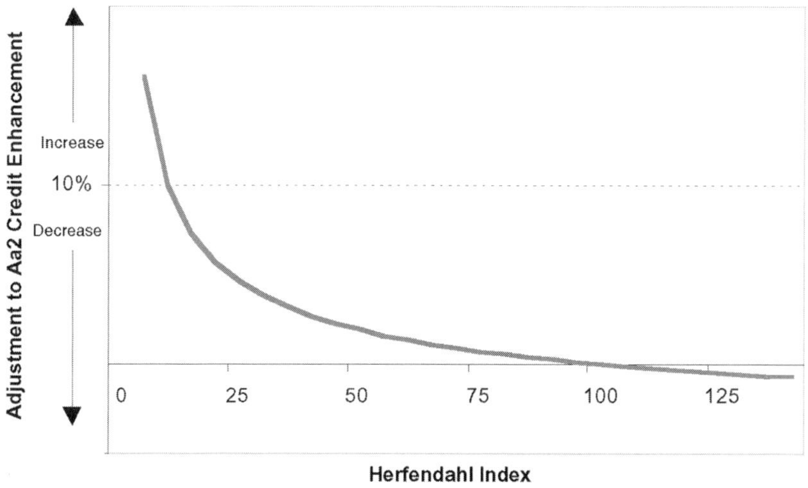

*In absolute terms

EXHIBIT 27.6   Moody's Typical LTV Range

Rating Level	Target LTVs (%)
Aaa	40–55
Aa2	48–64
A2	56–72
Baa2	64–79
Ba2	73–85

Additional Support through LTV Analysis

In order to provide support to the above analysis, Moody' will also consider the going-in and balloon LTV on each asset. In this approach, the structure's credit enhancement is quantified by the maximum loss of value on the asset the securities are able to withstand under various stress scenarios without causing an increase in the expected loss for various rating levels.

Exhibit 27.6 shows the range of target LTV levels for each loan in a pool, depending on the size and diversity of that pool. The upper band, for example, may be appropriate for a large multi-property, multi-borrower, multi-jurisdiction pool within creditor-friendly legal environments. These target LTV levels are intended to approximate the default frequency and severity of each rating category.

Moody's credit enhancement on a loan for a target rating category will be derived, *inter alia*, from the difference between the loan LTV and the target LTV for this specific loan and rating category. Total credit enhancement for the pool is then calculated based on the sum of the credit enhancement for each loan weighted by its contribution in the pool. As the pool diversity is already reflected in the LTV target at the loan level, *no further adjustment for diversity* will be necessary at the pool level.

Credit enhancement levels suggested by the above LTV analysis may be more relevant at lower rating levels, as the related probability of default increases and the recovery assumption derived from the LTV ratio becomes more important.

Limits to the Conduit Approach

The conduit approach was originally intended for pools of 50 or more loans, in a tight LTV band of aproximately 80% to 90%, as typical of early U.S. Conduit transactions. Because the amount of data collected was larger and the analysis more refined for pools with these characteristics, the conduit model is particularly appropriate for this type of pool and may be more imprecise for other pool profiles.

The conduit approach looks primarily at the quality and cash flow of each asset in the pool. Support from long-term quality tenants or recourse to a well-reputed borrower may be incorporated into the quality grade of the property. However, this grade adjustment may not fully reflect the change in the loan credit profile due to that external support. When a portfolio includes a significant portion of these loans, we will use in priority the credit tenant lease methodology or the Monte Carlo simulation.

In addition, other important asset credit characteristics are reflected through *qualitative* adjustments at the *portfolio level*, and as such, these adjustments may be imprecise.

Large Loan Transactions[9]

Large loan and single-borrower-type transactions, such as Canary Wharf Finance II plc, the Trafford Centre Finance Limited, and Morgan Stanley Mortgage Finance (Broadgate) plc, are not uncommon in Europe. Moody's analysis of such transactions focuses primarily on the credit characteristics of each asset. When the assets benefit from long-term credit tenants, the risk profile of the pool can be directly related to that of the tenants.

---

[9] A more detailed description of Moody's approach may be found in the Special Report entitled "CMBS: Moody's Approach to Rating Large Loan/Single Borrower Transactions." Note that this report reflects a US perspective. As such, the target LTVs are lower than the above UK levels and the capitalisation rates found in the Appendix would not be applicable to most European markets.

EXHIBIT 27.7   Moody's Target LTV Levels for Large UK Loans

Rating Level	Target LTVs (%)
Aaa	45
Aa2	53
A2	61
Baa2	69
Baa3	72

Otherwise, the approach for this type of transaction is *LTV driven*, focusing primarily on initial and balloon LTVs. To the extent that there is a pool of cross-collateralised properties or loans, the benefits are incorporated along with any structural features. This approach is, in many respects, comparable to that described in the LTV analysis for Conduit Transactions presented in the previous section.

The starting point is a target LTV for each rating level based on a single asset loan in a specific country. The target LTV levels assume, inter alia, (1) a Baa3 shadow rating on the loan, and (2) a 25 to 30-year mortgage-based amortisation profile (depending on the asset). The expected LTV over time based on this amortisation profile provides a good indication of the loan refinancing risk that could be supported at various maturity dates. Exhibit 27.7 shows the target LTV levels for a single UK property loan.

The indicated levels reflect the UK legal environment and would need to be adjusted downwards for assets located in Continental Europe. Indeed, the UK CMBS market benefits from both long-term leases and a creditor-friendly legal environment leading to the rapid enforcement of security over assets in a default scenario, thereby justifying a lower severity assumption. The combination of these two factors allows for higher LTV levels at each rating category.

As indicated, the above levels are for loans secured by a single asset. Moody's recognises the benefits provided by the *diversity* of assets within a single borrower pool. Hence, cross-collateralised assets in different markets could potentially gain, for example, up to 3% in proceeds at certain rating levels.[10]

Values, via cap rates, already reflect the cash flow volatility associated with each property type. Hence, the above levels do not need to be adjusted for the type of property considered in the transaction.

---

[10] See "CMBS: Moody's Approach to Rating Cross-Collateralised and Cross-Defaulted Loans."

Moody's suggested credit enhancement for a given loan and rating level will be derived, inter alia, from the difference between the loan LTV and the target LTV for that rating category.

Moody's will also incorporate the actual and hurdle rate-based DSCRs into its analysis, as described in the Conduit Transactions section above. The limitations mentioned at the end of that section also apply to the Large Loan approach.

Sale-and-Leaseback Transactions and Credit Tenant Leases[11]

Properties leased to quality tenants with strong covenants tend to exhibit low DSCRs and high LTVs. This is because the rental income from credit tenants is considered to be more stable and of higher quality than the average rental stream. Furthermore, in many markets these leases tend to be longer than average and the landlord bears next to no costs associated with operating and maintaining the property ("fully bondable lease"). Specifically, a typical credit-tenant lease (CTL) will unconditionally obligate the lessee to pay indirectly interest and principal due under the loan as well as all costs associated with occupying and maintaining the property.

Assuming no refinancing risk of the loan, the probability of default is best represented by the rating of the lessee. When a tenant is not rated, Moody's will assign an internal shadow rating on the company. Usually, the tenant's obligation under the loan is secured by a mortgage over the property. As a result, the recovery assumption on each loan will be derived from the LTV of the loan as well as from Moody's view on the volatility of the property valuation.

The credit enhancement levels generated by the aforementioned models need to be manually overridden to reflect the true risk of this type of property. Rather than having to rely on adjustments to other models, a model designed specifically for relatively homogeneous long-term credit tenant leases is used for such transactions.

Traditional CDO Approach

The model uses a binomial expansion technique, similar to that used in rating collateralised debt obligations (CDOs). This approach consists of reducing an actual pool of potentially correlated loans or bonds into a smaller idealised pool of uncorrelated and homogeneous assets that will mimic the default behaviour of the original pool.

---

[11] Readers interested in a more detailed explanation of the CTL approach are referred to "CMBS: Moody's Approach to Rating Credit Tenant Lease (CTL) Backed Transactions."

The method is based on the *diversity score* concept. In traditional CDOs, a diversity score is computed by grouping the original assets according to the industries and geographical regions that they represent. Some correlations will then be assumed between assets within the same industry and/or region. For example, empirical data suggest that in non-emerging market countries, defaults on assets in the same region and industry have a correlation of approximately 25%. A diversity score (D) will be derived from these correlations and from the respective contribution of each asset in the pool. This figure will represent the number of independent homogeneous assets in the idealised portfolio.

All assets in the idealised pool will then be assumed to have the same maturity, coupon, amortisation profile and probability of default, corresponding to the weighted average maturity, coupon, amortisation profile and probability of default of the original pool. The average default probability of the original pool will be directly derived from its *weighted average rating*.

The behaviour of this homogeneous pool of D assets can be fully described in terms of D possible scenarios: one defaults, two defaults, and so on, up to D default. Each scenario has a certain probability of occurring, which can be computed using the binomial probability density function.

Moody's assumptions about the *timing of losses* are based on our default studies, which provide a comprehensive account of bond default experience by rating category and maturity over approximately 80 years. As a pool of CTLs is much less diverse than the sample on which the default study is based, our default timing assumptions are more conservative than most actual historical loss patterns. Accordingly, Moody's default scenario calls for a majority of the losses to occur in the early years. This default pattern is further adjusted to reflect the composition of the pool, as typically, low-rated assets are likely to default more rapidly. Exhibit 27.8 shows two examples of default profile used by Moody's. In the first example, the timing of default depends on the proportion of the pool balance in each rating category. The second example assumes that half of the pool will default in the first year and the remaining portion equally over the following five years.

Finally, the cash flow output on the asset side (post recoveries) will be used as input on the liability side of the transaction, incorporating the proposed transaction structure and appropriate tranching. Excess spread (when available to the transaction) and other timing characteristics are automatically taken into account when using this rating approach. Each of the above D scenarios will lead to a different loss under the rated bonds. The final expected loss on each class of bonds would then be calculated as the sum of the loss on the bonds in each scenario, weighted by the probability of occurrence of that scenario.

EXHIBIT 27.8

End of Period	Default Profile	
	Example 1	Example 2
0	Caa	
1	B3	50%
2	B1–B2	10%
3	Ba3	10%
4	Ba1–Ba2	10%
5	Baa1–Baa3	10%
6	A1–A3	10%
7	Aaa–Aa3	

Incorporation of Real Estate Benefit

In addition to the credit of the tenant, Moody's will also look at the importance of the real estate asset for the operations of the lessee. It is possible that the lessee (or its insolvency administrator) would prefer to default on some of its unsecured debt rather than on a lease over a property that might be essential to its business. Moody's will adjust the probability of default derived from the senior unsecured rating of the company accordingly.

Recovery rates for standard corporate debt are usually measured by average postdefault market prices for debt issues. In a CTL transaction, however, investors benefit from a mortgage over the property. As such, recovery rates will be derived from the appropriate *LTV* levels reflecting a vacant possession value net of transaction costs (and any additional unsecured claim for the rent). Furthermore, LTVs will usually decrease over time as debt typically *amortises* in a credit-tenant lease financing. This differs from standard corporate debt, which is often structured as interest-only debt with some refinancing risk at maturity.

Limits of the CTL Method

The first constraint in using the CTL method comes from the limited data available on correlations within industries or geographic areas in Europe that are typically reflected in CTL portfolios. Currently, Moody's uses both extrapolations from US data and the experience of its corporate team to come up with correlation factors in its models.

The CTL approach is particularly effective when looking at a large pool of homogeneous assets. However, small pools and pools showing a wide diversity of assets (in terms of size, rating, amortisation profile, maturity, etc) are not usually good candidates. Indeed, in such a case, it is more difficult to reduce the original pool to an idealised pool of uncorrelated and homogeneous assets that will accurately mimic the default behaviour of the original pool. However, if a pool of heterogeneous assets can be split into a limited number of homogeneous subpools, it will be possible to use the CTL approach at the subpool level to infer an expected loss at the pool level.[12]

Finally, this method would not be appropriate for pools of short-term credit-tenant leases, which do not allow for the full amortisation of the securitised debt. Rather, Moody's would rely on traditional real estate analysis to evaluate the probability of finding new tenants during the term of the transaction.

Monte Carlo Simulation

In response to certain limitations of other rating approaches in reflecting the specificities of the European CMBS market, Moody's has developed an approach to rating CMBS transactions based on a Monte Carlo simulation. This loan-by-loan approach starts by assigning shadow ratings to each loan in the pool based on a fundamental real estate analysis of the loan (or, in the case of a long-term credit tenant lease, directly on the rating of the tenant, if appropriate). Thereafter, the model assumes that each loan will default over time according to both the probability of default associated with its rating, and any correlation it might have with other loans in the pool.

Assigning Loan Shadow Ratings

The model works on the basis of key information including loan balance, maturity, coupon, amortisation profile, LTV, DSCR, property type, location, and loan grade. Both LTV and DSCR figures are based on Moody's assessment of the cash flow expected from the property/properties backing each loan. Cross-collateralised loans will be treated as a single loan, but reflecting the appropriate credit for the lower default probability and higher expected recovery of such a loan.[13]

Moody's will shadow rate each loan in a small portfolio, but automate the approach for larger portfolios to assist its analysis. Grids have been developed that automatically suggest shadow ratings based on DSCR and/or LTV, quality grade, and property type. Both the asset quality and the property type will reflect the potential volatility of the

---

[12] See "The Double Binomial Method and Its Applications to a Special Case of CBO Structures."

[13] See "CMBS: Moody's Approach to Rating Cross-Collateralised and Cross-Defaulted Loans."

EXHIBIT 27.9 Rating Category for Residential Assets by DSCR and Quality Grade

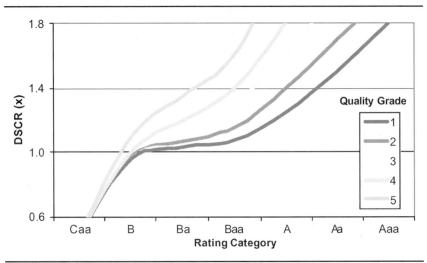

cash flow, hence the credit risk of the asset. Hotels, for example, are cyclical assets, and usually exhibit more volatile cash flows than other property types like residential assets. Hence, ceteris paribus, Moody's will require higher DSCR levels for a hotel than for a residential asset to reach the same rating category. Exhibit 27.9 indicates the range of ratings Moody's would assign on a residential asset depending on its DSCR and quality grade.

The model incorporates the actual DSCR (based on actual debt service) during the life of the loan. For nonfully amortising loans, Moody's will compute a hurdle-based DSCR based on the expected balloon payment and remaining life of the asset to reflect the *refinancing risk* at maturity. Interest-only loans, in particular, will be very sensitive to any increase in interest rates or any reduction in the useful life of the underlying assets by the maturity date, and their probability of default is likely to increase substantially at that date. As a result, loans with refinancing risk at maturity will have two different shadow ratings, one during their life and a "stressed" one at maturity.

It is also possible to integrate any specific feature of a loan likely to affect its risk profile (e.g., delinquencies, seasoning, etc.) as an adjustment to the property cash flow or quality grade, hence to the credit rating derived from the automatic assignment process.

Large loans will be reviewed individually and their shadow rating adjusted if necessary.

Modeling Defaults and Correlations

The model generates a normally distributed random number for each loan each year, by drawing three normally distributed random numbers. These three random numbers represent (1) the loan's contribution to its default (based inter alia on factors such as its DSCR, LTV, or quality grade); (2) the contribution from its property type; and (3) the contribution from its region of domicile. The latter two factors reflect the correlation between the loans. The relationship can be mathematically transcribed as:

$$Z = \omega_1 N_R + \omega_2 N_P + \omega_3 N_L$$

$$\sum_{n=1}^{3} \omega_n^2 = 1$$

where N_R, N_P, and N_L represent region, property type, and loan respectively.

The *correlation weights* ω_1, ω_2, and ω_3, are directly derived from Moody's assumptions in terms of correlation between two assets within the same property type and/or same location. Extensive studies based on Moody's default database determine the values of the weights ω_1, ω_2, and ω_3 in the U.S. corporate sector as being between 0.3162 to 0.3873 for ω_1 and ω_2, and between 0.8367 and 0.8944 for ω_3. This is equivalent to a 10% to 15% correlation coefficient for two obligors in the same geographical region but different industries (or vice versa) and a 20% to 30% correlation coefficient for two obligors in the same geographical region and the same industry. As limited data are available within the *real estate* sector in *Europe*, Moody's uses the above correlation ranges for European CMBS transactions. Real estate assets, however, have greater diversity characteristics than other single asset classes given the variety of property types and tenants. Hence, Moody's tends to consider that different property types are equivalent to different industries. Note that the correlation coefficients used in our models are likely to vary over time as more European data become available and relations between economic regions and sectors vary.

The normally distributed random number Z, that is generated for a loan in a particular year, is mapped onto a uniform random number, which is then compared to an *annual default threshold*. That threshold corresponds to the loan's respective marginal probability of default for that year. The marginal probability will be derived from Moody's idealised cumulative default probability tables.

To illustrate the above, consider a one-year loan with a Ba2 rating. The one-year marginal probability of default (equivalent to the one-year cumulative probability) for a Ba2 asset is 1.56%, as obtained from Moody's idealised cumulative default probability tables. Thus, there is a 1.56% chance that the loan will default this year; equivalently, there is a 98.44% (i.e., 100% – 1.56%) chance that it will not default this year. A random number in the interval (0,1) will be generated as described above. If we generate a number equal to or above 98.44%, then a default is recorded for the loan.

Recoveries

When a loan defaults, the recovery amount will be computed as the product of a defined recovery rate and Moody's value for the property. As loan recovery procedures and secured creditors' positions vary widely among European countries, Moody's will use different recovery rate assumptions depending on the location of the assets[14] (see Exhibit 27.10—note that our assumptions may be adjusted as new information/loss experience is processed). Truncated normal recovery rate distributions are often used to reflect uncertainty on expected recoveries. As for the mean of the distribution, the standard deviation may vary by country.

Amortising loans will benefit from higher recoveries over time, as it is more likely that any proceeds from a sale of the assets will successfully repay the remaining balance of the loan.

EXHIBIT 27.10   Example of Recovery Rates Assumptions by Country—Mean for Distributions

Country		Tier	Recovery Rate[a]
Netherlands	UK (+ Ch. Is.)	A	60%–70%
Germany	Sweden	B	55%–65%
Ireland	Switzerland		
Austria	Iceland		
Belgium	Liechtenstein		
Denmark	Luxembourg	C	45%–50%
Finland	Norway		
France	Spain		
Greece	Portugal	D	30%–35%
Italy	Eastern Europe		

[a] Secured loans—assumes 1-year delay to recovery.

---

[14] See also "Modelling Recovery Rate in European CDOs."

Expected Loss Calculation

The cash flow output on the asset side will be used as input on the liability side for the proposed securitisation, based on a target tranching. Available excess spread and timing characteristics are automatically taken into account through the pass-through structure. The main structural features are also integrated in the analysis, such as any existing reserve fund or liquidity facility. Moody's will run several thousand scenarios, each resulting, potentially, in a loss under the rated bonds. The average expected loss, probability of default and life of each class of bonds resulting from thousands of scenarios will then be mapped to a Moody's rating.

Limits to the Monte Carlo Simulation

This approach integrates the major elements of the conduit style analysis and the credit tenant lease analysis, without facing some of their limitations. All adjustments are incorporated at the loan level rather than at the portfolio level, allowing more precise quantification of their impact. This method also allows, in theory, the use of a detailed correlation matrix between assets of various property types and locations. For example, the correlation between "office" and "retail" is often seen as stronger than between "office" and "hotel," as both "office" and "retail" are less correlated to GDP than "hotels." The major limitation of this approach, however, remains today's limited data availability on correlations in the European real estate market.

CONCLUSION

Regardless of the type of model used, Moody's rating on a specific class of bonds is ultimately meant to reflect an opinion on the amount of losses attributable to credit events expected over the life of the bonds. Each of the above-mentioned methodologies aims at deriving an *expected loss* on the rated bonds, which will then be mapped to a Moody's rating. The expected loss on the bonds will itself depend on the frequency, severity, and expected timing of credit losses on the asset pool, as well as on the credit enhancement available in the transaction.

Finally, although each of the approaches described in this chapter relies on quantitative methodologies, the qualitative real estate inputs remain the major driver of Moody's analysis, be it the Aa2 credit enhancement tables in conduit transactions, the value assessment of the large loan approach, the tenants' shadow ratings and correlations in the CTL method or the automatic rating assignment process in the Monte

Carlo simulation. The qualitative inputs are usually derived from the real estate experience of members of the CMBS team and an analysis and interpretation of a wide range of data. The challenge in analysing European CMBS transactions stems from the lack of applicable and accurate information (e.g., default data, property market correlations, economic life of assets, expense ratios). Thus, to the extent that better information becomes available, Moody's will endeavour to improve its methodology as indicated in this chapter. Nonetheless, Moody's believes that with a reasonable amount of information, an understanding of the market and a consistent rating approach based on expected losses, it can accurately reflect today's credit risk of European property securitisations.

CHAPTER 28

Differentiating CMBS From Other Real Estate Securitised Financings

Elena Folkerts-Landau
Director
Standard & Poor's

Clayton Hunt
Managing Director
Standard & Poor's

Ronan Fox
Director
Standard & Poor's

Adele Archer
Director
Standard & Poor's

Ian Bell, Esq.
Senior European Legal Counsel
Standard & Poor's

As the commercial mortgage-backed securities (CMBS) market develops, CMBS technology is being adapted to securitisations in which the risk profile is determined primarily by the originator's business operations, rather than by the property's characteristics. Although the property component in a transaction's overall risk profile may be significant, it is dominated in the opinion of Standard & Poor's by the operating risks associated with a going concern.

In this chapter we examine the key differences in rating approach between standard CMBS transactions and these property intensive corporate securitisations.

In rating standard CMBS debt, Standard & Poor's analysis places emphasis on solving for the level of overcollateralization that supports a specified rating. In rating property intensive corporate securitisations, Standard & Poor's seeks to maximize the value added of a number of variables including business risk, overcollateralization, amortization schedule, final maturity, and capital structure.

For example, standard CMBS transactions typically have an expected maturity of between five and seven years, with a legal final maturity two or three years later. Property intensive corporate securitisations, in contrast, may extend over far longer periods—a 20-year legal final maturity is not unusual.

The different rating approaches are likely to affect both the capital structure and the highest credit rating that a securitised property financing can achieve.

WHEN DOES A TRANSACTION'S RISK PROFILE REFLECT PRIMARILY THE UNDERLYING REAL ESTATE?

In standard CMBS transactions, credit risk is pinned almost entirely on the underlying real estate and the sustainable revenues it can generate from diverse sources. Commercial properties backing a CMBS issuance typically boast robust diversification of sustainable income, and thus sustainable value, which substantially mitigates credit risk. Simply stated, most CMBS financings achieve AAA credit ratings because there is an asset or asset portfolio that is not restricted to a particular sector or usage, and whose value can be realized through a liquidation.

Other securitisation transactions, in contrast, while also supported by real estate assets, cannot achieve a AAA rating or indeed an investment-grade rating. These transactions have crossed the conceptual line between CMBS issuance and corporate securitisation. Unlike the risk involved in the exclusive operation of a real estate asset, such as a hotel, other factors overwhelm the risk profile of a property intensive corporate securitisation, resulting in a limit to the credit ratings that can be achieved.

WEAKEST LINK IN THE RISK PROFILE

Credit ratings assigned in securitised financings are generally capped by, or tied to, the weakest link in a transaction's risk profile. The weakest link may refer to a risk factor in the transaction structure or in the collateral supporting the transaction.

Where a concentration of risk exists in a transaction, the ratings may be constrained by the elements of concentration.

A property financing whose cash flows come from a single tenant, for example, may have its credit rating limited or linked to the credit rating on the existing tenant. These transactions are typically called "credit lease transactions." A recent example of this type of transaction is Juturna (European Loan Conduit No. 16) plc., in which rental payments due by the (BBC) on its central London headquarters building and key broadcasting facility were securitised. The transaction was rated AAA, reflecting the financial guarantee of MBIA Assurance S.A., but the underlying transaction rating was AA–. Similarly, where a property is specifically designed or designated to serve only one type of use, such as a telecommunications center, a transaction's credit ratings may be limited by the risks associated with the operator, and more broadly with the telecommunications industry.

KEY RISK CHARACTERISTICS OF CONVENTIONAL CMBS

There are two key risk characteristics of conventional CMBS debt: cash flow sustainability and risk diversification.

Cash Flow Sustainability

Three generic categories of real estate collateral are usually regarded as generating diverse and sustainable income streams, and therefore sustainable value: places of residence (housing), work (offices), and shopping (retail facilities).

By evaluating individual properties, CMBS analytical methodology focuses on whether a property's characteristics will allow it to sustain occupancy over time, and thus sustain its income and value. Factors that are assessed range from an office building's floor area, to a warehouse's floor-to-ceiling height, to the size of a shopping center's anchor store. These factors may indicate whether a property will be able to compete for tenants and income over the term of the rated debt. Testing assumptions affecting tenants' longevity, space re-letting prospects, and prospective rental levels are all core elements of determining the sustainability of cash flow.

CMBS analysis takes into account not only what is current, but also what is likely to be sustained. It tends to assume lower future cash flows and property values relative to current levels. Taking away the froth generated during periods of speculative exuberance recognizes the reality of the economic cycle and the inherent uncertainty of cash flows and property valuations.

Diversification

While sustainability of income is critical for a rating, it is risk diversification that permits credit ratings up to AAA for CMBS transactions. Multiple leases of differing tenors to various tenants from diverse industries provide credible risk diversification. Office buildings, as well as complexes such as Canary Wharf and the Broadgate Estate in London, can attract tenants from every facet of the corporate world. Shopping malls like the Trafford Centre in Manchester or Meadowhall in Sheffield have hundreds of tenants, providing strong diversification of income. These properties have been able to sustain sufficient income from a broad diversity of tenants to achieve the highest credit ratings.

Risk Concentration as the Critical Factor

Beyond conventional CMBS assets—primarily housing, office buildings, and retail malls—other types of property tend to undermine a transaction's capacity to achieve a AAA rating. Over recent years, issuers financing English pubs, hospitals and care homes, airports, seaports, buildings housing telecom assets, and the BBC's headquarters building have crossed the boundary of traditional CMBS. In these property intensive corporate securitisations, risk concentration dominates the credit risk assessment.

In assessing transactions with a substantial real estate component, Standard & Poor's determines whether there is sufficient diversity of risk to reduce the rated debt's probability of default to a level corresponding to the highest possible credit rating.

Often, property assets can be characterized as "risk diverse" even though they appear to be concentrated. For example, the credit analysis must consider whether a financing backed solely by English pubs enjoys adequate diversification of risk because multiple operators source the cash flows, or whether the concentration of risk within a single industry sector is so high that it constrains the transaction's credit ratings. Can overcollateralization compensate adequately for the risk of individual pub defaults? Answers are rarely definitive *ex ante*.

To address the risk issue from a different perspective, it is sometimes possible to assume that the assets are fungible, thereby looking past the sector concentration and focusing instead on the assets' convertibility to an alternative use, such as housing. A property's convertibility depends on many factors, including cost, planning permission, and future demand. Any assessment of asset convertibility is subject to a high level of uncertainty, which in turn undermines the likelihood of achieving the highest rating and/or can materially reduce the amount of rated debt that can be raised.

In the field of transportation infrastructure, the real estate value of an airport, for example, must be viewed in the context of its cash-generating value as an essential and quasi-monopolistic public service infrastructure asset. The value may be significant, provided the use of the infrastructure to generate cash flow will be maintained even in the event of insolvency of the operator.

The risk profile of property portfolios relating to European telecom companies has been explored in connection with sale and leaseback transactions. European property companies and opportunity funds may seek to leverage property portfolios that include office and warehouse accommodation containing local telephone exchanges that are essential to fixed-line networks, and in some cases, mobile networks.

In its approach to such transactions, Standard & Poor's weighs the business risk in the context of the property assets' projected value over the life of the rated debt. A determination is made whether a transaction backed by buildings let to a telecom operator will be analyzed as a conventional CMBS transaction, or whether the ratings will be constrained by the creditworthiness of the operator, the type of usage the building serves, or by the building's essentiality to a telephone network. For example, the ratings on Telereal Securitisation PLC, which closed in December 2001 and involved the securitisation of rental payments due on the fixed-line real estate properties of British Telecommunications plc., were constrained by the credit quality of British Telecommunications and the business and cash-generating prospects of the U.K. fixed-line market over a 30-year term.

Reducing the Link Between the Credit Rating and the Underlying Operating Risk

Standard & Poor's applies an analytical methodology that incorporates the business risk assessment into the rating of corporate securitisations.[1] The methodology can lead to a reduced link between the risk represented by the creditworthiness of a single tenant and the ratings assigned to the transaction, by inducing issuers to introduce structural

---

[1] For a full discussion on the effect of business risk assessment in corporate securitisations, see Chapter 21.

features into their transactions. These structural features may allow for debt to be rated at a higher level than the credit rating on the tenant, and may also result in a binding constraint on the amount of such debt. Debt sized on the basis of the liquidation of assets or alternative use value will no longer be available to service any remaining debt obligations of the transaction on a going concern basis, which may affect the debt rating(s) and amount achievable on lower rated tranches, if any.

Usage of properties may constrain the ratings. If the properties were specifically designed for telecom use, or if their zoning prohibits an alternative use or user, then the risk of the transaction may be concentrated in the telecom business sector. In respect of property that is essential to the fixed-line network, Standard & Poor's uses its business risk assessment to define appropriate stress assumptions for application in a cash flow model, which then aligns an amount of debt corresponding to a specified rating.

The tenant and/or sector may be vital to the national interests of a particular country. If so, liquidation of the assets to repay noteholders in a default scenario may be infeasible, and would therefore constrain the rating.

To achieve a high degree of delinkage of credit risk from property value in a telecom financing, the issuer would need to demonstrate that the real estate assets were neither essential to running the telecom network nor to the national interests of the country, and that the assets could readily be re-leased to a wide and varied set of corporate users outside the telecom sector.

The Operator's Business Risk

Whether or not a business operator's risk dominates the risk profile of a property transaction is a complex issue. Hotels are real estate assets whose financial viability is closely tied to the management skills of their operator. Sustainability of income is highly variable given the short length of leases (overnights stays) on the basis of which income is derived from tenants (guests).

An operator may be able to significantly affect occupancy. Given the high fixed costs of the business, small drops in occupancy can have a dramatic effect on free cash flow and the ability to service debt obligations. The hotel sector's variable revenue and high proportion of fixed costs corresponds to a high level of cash flow volatility, which is a weak link in the overall credit risk profile. The operator's skill may constitute another weak link. The same could be said for airports and seaports, where the incumbent operator plays a vital role in maintaining the business and defining its strategy. There are differences, however, in that such essential infrastructure assets can often withstand operator insolvency, provided demand is strong enough.

These risks notwithstanding, there are a number of reasons why transactions backed by hotels may achieve AAA ratings. Firstly, the hotel industry has relatively transparent cash flow, with a lot of information available to assess relative performance and value. Secondly, the potential to convert a hotel to an alternative use may be credible on the basis of historical evidence in many urban areas. While this may raise the level of confidence of a probabilistic outcome, the convertibility of any property asset is always highly uncertain. The future valuation of such a conversion is relative guess work, and therefore very much a secondary argument.

Thirdly, there are many skilled operators in the hotel industry, making the issue of dependence on a given operator rather mute. Finally, historical occupancy information may demonstrate a hotel's viability over time and its drawing power to ensure a relatively sustainable performance. Proper underwriting to incorporate adequate reserves for furniture, fixtures and equipment, other ongoing capital expenditures, and market level expenses for management and administrative fees can ensure that hotels will be kept up and managed to current standards.

From a real estate perspective, hospitals seem to entail more business risk than hotels, with perhaps less transparency of information to benchmark performance, convertibility, and alternative use value. Whereas hotels are a liquid asset class that actively trade hands and attract a wide variety of investors as owner/operators or third parties, hospitals are altogether different as a real estate asset class.

Few participants in the commercial property market consider hospitals to be a revenue-generating asset. The dynamics of revenue generation are particular to the health care industry. The sector concentration risk appears very high relative to other real estate assets. Convertibility to alternative use is understood to be generally limited, with demolition and redevelopment of land as the usual approach, but the costs and related planning issues remain constraints.

RISK MITIGANTS

As owners of real estate use securitisation to leverage their assets, their challenge is how best to mitigate concentration risks, regardless of property type, to achieve higher ratings.

Structural features can mitigate tenant concentration risks, such as prefunded reserves for leasing costs or tenant improvements, as well as liquidity facilities in the event of tenant defaults or lease expirations. A common feature of CMBS offerings are cash flow and valuation coverage tests, which when breached trigger either a borrower level default (giving a lender control over a property before the bonds default), or a cash sweep of rents into a lock box (which preserves the integrity of funds destined for investors before borrowers). These features may also be incorporated into a property intensive corporate securitisation to mitigate concentration risk factors.

Some transactions have sought to employ a hybrid approach, for example combining some linkage of certain tranches of an issuance to the weak link, while structuring other features to allow debt to be issued with ratings higher than the weak link, as was achieved in transactions such as Werretown Supermarkets Securitisations plc. and Eros (European Loan Conduit No. 10) FCC. This may be particularly beneficial when tenant concentration risk exists and the tenant has an investment-grade credit rating. The structural elements to separate the higher ratings from the weak link, whether business or tenant risk, must be clear and robust.

Another structural feature is the pooling of assets or loans into larger, diversified pools, in essence mitigating the risk posed by a single property transaction by making it a small part of a larger portfolio. Financing of properties within the framework of a much larger pool may allow some debt associated with those property types to achieve higher ratings than might otherwise be the case on a standalone basis.

THE LEGAL DIMENSION

The legal structure underpinning a transaction and the governing jurisdiction may also determine whether a transaction will be rated as a standard CMBS transaction or as a corporate securitisation. Key legal issues are tenancy rights, security rights, and the treatment of secured creditors in insolvency.

Tenancy rights are crucial to determining whether the noteholders can ultimately rely on either the re-letting of the real estate or its sale. If the tenant ceases to pay and cannot be made to vacate the property for reletting within a reasonable time, the corporate rating on the tenants becomes crucial.

Transactions seeking to rely on a CMBS analysis will usually need to demonstrate one of two features: either the corporate owner of the property is substantially unlikely to become bankrupt or, in the event of its bankruptcy, the noteholders can retain the benefit of the properties and the attendant rental flows.

The first scenario is likely to result from the property owning company being an insolvency remote SPE. To be treated as such by Standard & Poor's, such a company needs to be able to demonstrate a number of legal features, one of which is the provision of enforceable security over its assets. It must also be situated in a jurisdiction with appropriate rules concerning its tax treatment, its protection from substantive consolidation, and the effectiveness of limited recourse provisions in its credit agreements. The second scenario, in which noteholders are shielded from the consequences of the property owner's bankruptcy, is usually achievable where the legal system provides strong rights to secured creditors. Specifically, noteholders or their representative must have the right to obtain control of the relevant property within a clearly defined period of time.

In addition, tax matters require a thorough analysis.

BROAD APPLICATION

Over recent years, property owners have sought to leverage their assets through securitised financings, particularly in Europe. The broad variety of property types have included multifamily units, nursing homes, offices, warehouses, retail facilities, pubs, self-storage facilities, seaports, airports, and leisure parks, as well as buildings providing roadside motorway services, entertainment, and hospitality. The application of structured finance technology can mitigate some of the inherent risks, whether such transactions are classified as CMBS or corporate securitisations.

To achieve and sustain specified credit ratings, these transactions must withstand rigorous analysis and stressing of individual property cash flows and valuations. Those that have achieved AAA ratings have evidenced diversification and sustainability of income and value over the term of the rated securities, whether through current usage or an unequivocal capacity to maintain these characteristics. Where risk has been concentrated in a business sector or single usage, Standard & Poor's has applied credit ratings corresponding to an overall level of risk linked to the business risk and both structural and legal mitigants. In all cases, Standard & Poor's tailors its ratings approach to the risk characteristics of each transaction.

CHAPTER 29

The German Pfandbrief and European Covered Bonds Market

Graham "Harry" Cross
Research Partner
YieldCurve.com

There is no formal equivalent of the U.S. market in agency mortgage-backed securities within Europe. The German Pfandbriefe market, which is informally backed by the Federal government, is the nearest such product. This is complimented by the growing market in "covered bonds," which have been issued by mortgage banks across Europe. All these securities are considered to be structured finance securities, due to the nature of their asset backing. They are part of the overall market in residential mortgage-backed securities in Europe.

This chapter describes the German mortgage bonds or Pfandbriefe market, its institutions, and working practice. We also consider other aspects of the European covered bond market. The instruments themselves are essentially plain vanilla bonds, and while they can be analysed in similar ways to US agency bonds and mortgage-backed bonds, there are also key differences between them, which we highlight in this chapter. Mortgage-backed securities are described in Chapter 24.

THE PFANDBRIEF MARKET

Pfandbriefe[1] are bonds issued by German mortgage banks, which are subject to special governing legislation. These bonds are "covered" or backed

---

[1] *Pfandbrief*—the literal translation is *Letter of pledge.*

by underlying asset pools, equating to at least the same nominal amount of the issue. The assets contained within these pools must be recorded into a cover register, maintained by the mortgage bank, to ensure that these are easily identifiable. In this regard, covered bonds such as Pfandbriefe are considered highly secure. In the event of the issuing mortgage bank becoming insolvent, the creditors would receive a preferential claim over the assets in the cover pool, which is there solely to protect them.

Pfandbriefe are categorized into two types. *Öffentliche Pfandbriefe,* which are bonds fully collateralised by loans to public sector entities (also known as "public" Pfandbriefe), while *Hypotheken Pfandbriefe* (mortgage Pfandbriefe) are fully collateralised by residential and commercial mortgages, whose loan-to-value ratio must not exceed 60%. The former constitute just over 90% of the overall Pfandbrief market.

The market, with an overall volume of €1.1 trillion, has become the largest asset class on the European bond market and is ranked the sixth largest in the world. It is regulated within a stringent legal framework and is under special supervision.[2] The mortgage banks—the largest group of issuers on the Pfandbriefe market—are, in addition to be bound under the terms of the German Banking Act (KWG), by which all German banks are governed, are also subject to the provisions of the Mortgage Bank Act (HBG) as well. It is noteworthy that since the inception of the Mortgage Bank Act over 100 years ago, there has not been one case of insolvency. All of these factors have in the past assisted issuers in obtaining the highest possible ratings (AAA) for their Pfandbrief paper. This situation has in some cases, however, changed somewhat and this will be discussed in detail later.

Although the German Pfandbrief market has a history dating back well over 200 years, its recognition as an asset class by international investors has only occurred recently in the mid-1990s with the advent of the *jumbo* Pfandbrief. The name "jumbo" is derived from the large issue volume, with the size requirement of €500 million. This sector of the market, founded in the spring of 1995, and geared towards the liquidity criteria of large international investors, has managed to establish itself as Europe's fourth largest bond market—surpassed only by the government markets of Italy, Germany, and France—had an outstanding volume of well over €400 billion as of year-end 2001. Prior to the arrival of the first issue of this nature, a DM 1 billion Frankfurter Hypothekenbank bond, the Pfandbrief market had been an illiquid and highly fragmented sector comprising of some 17,000 individual issues with a very small average volume of around €80 million. Investors in these "Traditional" Pfandbriefe were almost exclusively domestic.

---

[2] Supervision conducted by the German Financial Supervisory Authority (BAFin).

EXHIBIT 29.1   Pfandbriefe versus Euro-In Government Bonds (End 2001)

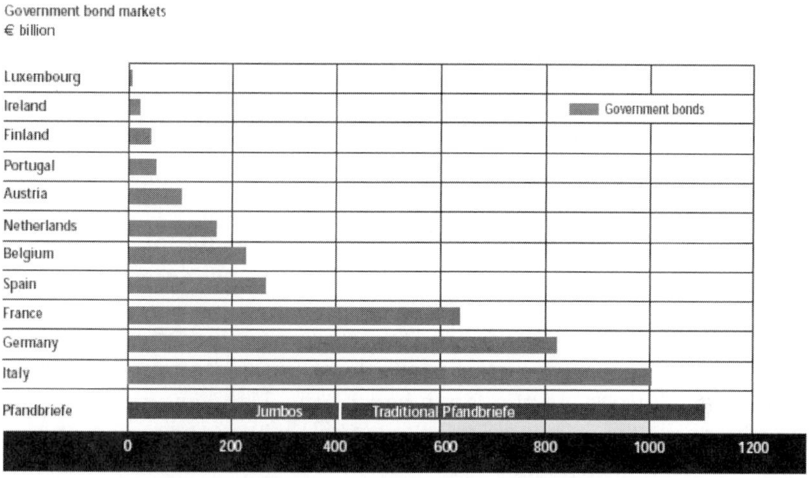

Source: Association of German Mortgage Banks. Used with permission.

In this light, the main focus of this chapter shall be on the jumbo sector as this has the most relevance to the investment community at large.

Exhibit 29.1 shows the size of the market compared to European sovereign government markets.

HISTORY OF THE PFANDBRIEF

The origins of the German Pfandbrief system are widely regarded to lie within the "cabinets-ordre" of Frederick II of Prussia on August 29, 1767—the basis of which concerned the introduction of the of the Pfandbrief system in an attempt to remedy the aristocrats' shortage of credit in the areas of Prussia that had been ravaged during the Seven Years War (1756–1763).

On the basis of this royal decree, the Silesian Landschaft, an association of estates belonging to the aristocracy, churches, and monasteries, was set up in 1770. In time, more of these cooperations were set up throughout the individual provinces of Prussia, as compulsory law associations to the aristocratic landowners. These so-called "Landschaften" facilitated the refinancing of loans to their members by issuing debentures. Purchase of this paper ensured the creditor acquired a direct charge over the estate, which the landowner had put up as collateral. In the event of default, the estate named in the Pfandbrief, the Landschaft, and all of the landowners belonging to the Landschaft served the Pfandbriefe holder as security. Understandably, this paper was also known as "estate Pfandbrief" and largely corresponds with today's mortgage Pfandbrief.

The Pfandbrief system rapidly gained popularity throughout Europe and the development of the present day format was given a decisive boost from the foundation of organisations outside of Prussia, such as *Crédit Foncier de France* in 1852. Issuers of this second generation Pfandbriefe were not law associations but private real estate credit institutions, which adopted the system for the refinancing of loans to the public sector borrowers and loans guaranteed by public sector institutions and agencies (public sector loans).

Whereas in the early days Pfandbrief were used to finance agriculture, this new variation was used to finance the then rapidly expanding towns and cities of Europe. In the latter half of the 19th century, one of the major priorities facing European governments was the provision of housing to meet the widespread exodus from rural areas and the corresponding growth in urban population levels. Concentration from the outset was on real estate financing and, above all, the financing of construction of housing and commercial properties. In this respect, today's mortgage banks were among Europe's first large-scale financial intermediaries and can very much be regarded as a by product of the industrial age.

The first German mortgage bank of the type familiar today was established, by the decree of the senate, on 8 December 1962 (*Frankfurter Hypothekenbank* in Frankfurt). From this moment, numerous other mortgage banks emerged in quick succession in almost all of the German federal states until, by the beginning of the twentieth century, a total of 40 private mortgage banks existed. Throughout the ensuing years of economic "boom and bust," the business sector occupied by these real estate credit institutions, understandably, became one of the biggest sectors in banking.

These developments led to the promulgation of the *German Mortgage Banks Act* (Hypothekenbankgesetz–HBG) of 1900, which was the first uniform law in the field of banking for the entire German Reich. This act provided a legally prescribed, uniform organization framework for this group of institutions that has stood the test of time, right up until the present day.

The new generation of Pfandbrief had spread across Europe from France, through Germany to the United Kingdom, Italy, and Spain among others. In this respect, it is interesting to note that in the annex to the preamble to the act contained the laws from Germany's neighbouring countries, evidencing the influence of foreign laws on the lawmakers of Germany. However, during the 20th century with the onset of two World Wars, global economic crisis, inflation and the currency reform in 1948 resulted in a curbing of cross border influence. This in turn caused the mortgage banks throughout Europe to develop in sharply divergent ways. Some countries chose to abandon the whole Pfandbriefe concept altogether, whereas others turned the mortgage banks into state monopoly institutions.[3]

In Germany, no other group in the whole of the banking sector was as impacted by these factors as the mortgage banks, which had seen their business volumes fall drastically by the time of the currency reform. Nevertheless, Pfandbriefe proved an invaluable tool in the reconstruction programs that were set up to deal with the aftermath of the war and their popularity grew with each successive decade. The reunification in Germany after the fall of the Berlin Wall highlights this resurgence, as a demand for both commercial and residential property construction as well as for public infrastructure renewal had to be met in the new federal states in East Germany. With the advent of the euro and the recent amendments that were made to the German Mortgage Bank Act, new avenues of cross-border lending have opened up in Germany for the mortgage banks. They now have the ability to market Pfandbriefe internationally.

The market has grown considerably from the lowly position it found itself in, midcentury, a period when mortgage banks reported business volumes down to levels of 5% of those quoted just 30 years earlier, to it current status as one of the largest bond markets in the world.

KEY FEATURES OF INVESTOR INTEREST

Reduction of Credit Risk

The tight legal framework within which the participants of the Pfandbrief market must operate is one of the foremost reasons why Pfandbriefe appeal to both domestic and international investors. In addition to being bound by the general provisions set out in the German Banking Act (KWG), the law by which all German banks are governed, German mortgage banks are also subject to the requirements of the Mortgage Bank Act.

The *Hypothekenbankgesetz* (Mortgage Bank Act) states that mortgage banks may only be engaged in two types of business:

■ Lending to public sector entities.

---

[3] *100 Jahre Hypothekenbankgesetz, Textsammlung und Materialen,* Verband Deutscher Hypothekenbanken (*100 Years Mortgage Bank Act, A Collection of Texts and Material,* Association of Mortgage Banks, Frankfurt/Main), Frankfurt, 1999.

■ The financing of mortgage-backed loans for residential and commercially used properties (i.e., mortgage loans).

In addition to what could be considered low-risk fields of activity; a strict regional restriction is added in order to reduce risks in connection with cross-border business. Under this restriction, loans may only be granted to borrowers situated within the member states of the European Union, the EEA, the European OECD countries as well as the non-European G7 countries.

Further security is provided to the investor by the fact that Pfandbrief bonds are required to be covered by assets, which have at least the same value and bear the same interest rate.

It is necessary for these underlying assets to be segregated into two separate cover pools, one for mortgage loans and the other public sector loans, thus reflecting the two types of business within which the mortgage banks are involved. In the case of mortgage Pfandbriefe, covering assets are "first-charge" mortgages.

In the event of a mortgage bank becoming insolvent, the Pfandbriefe creditor would receive a preferential claim over the assets in the respective cover pool, which is there solely to protect them. They would not be required to participate in the insolvency procedures, but instead have any claim satisfied on schedule in accordance with the terms of the respective issue out of the cover assets. However, if the claim cannot be satisfied on time, in respect of coupon payments and redemptions because the cover pool is insolvent, separate proceedings will then commence in regard to the pool affected.

It is worthwhile noting that there has not been a bankruptcy proceeding against a mortgage bank since the enactment of the Mortgage Bank Act over 100 years ago.

The Mortgage Bank Act contains further protective measures to safeguard investors in mortgage Pfandbriefe. Namely, a limit imposed on those mortgages being used as cover to a maximum of 60% of the "prudently" calculated mortgage lending value. This provides a safety cushion against the potential cyclical fluctuations in the market value of the cover pool asset.

The comparatively low risk that a portfolio of both residential and commercial mortgages entails is also expressed in the equity weighting of 50% for mortgage loans with a lending limit of up to 60%.

These elements obviously offer exceptional safety to investors in the Pfandbrief market and should therefore limit the impact of any adverse market movements on the back of any detrimental news in regard to the parent companies.

Liquidity

The jumbo Pfandbrief market—on its own it is Europe's fourth largest bond market, surpassed only by the government markets of Italy, Germany and France. The name is derived from the large issue volume, with the size requirement of €500 million. In comparison, the average size of the traditional Pfandbriefe is approximately €150 million, which tends to prohibit the trading-orientated investor and favour the "buy and hold" types.

The minimum issue size requirement for the jumbos is only of theoretical significance as the majority of issues are launched in considerably larger sizes (the average volume is currently around €1.5 billion, however, some jumbos have a volume of up to €5 billion). It can therefore be seen that the volume of jumbo Pfandbriefe is equal to that of the bonds brought by medium-sized sovereign issuers within the Eurozone. The overall Pfandbrief market, with a volume outstanding of more than €1.1 trillion, is the biggest bond market within Europe. Of course, this figure includes *structured* Pfandbriefe, the smaller traditional variety as well as the jumbo sector.

The market-making obligations further enhance the liquidity of the jumbo Pfandbriefe. Namely, that jumbo Pfandbrief are syndicated by at least three market makers who pledge to quote two-way (bid/offer) prices simultaneously, for lots up to €15 million during the usual trading hours—9.00 A.M. to 5.00 P.M. (GMT + 1) for the life of the issue. The issuer itself may also perform the function of market maker and should obtain an undertaking from the assigned market makers not to exceed the following bid/offer spreads when quoting:

Up to and including 4 years	5 cents
Over 4 years up to and including 6 years	6 cents
Over 6 years up to and including 8 years	8 cents
Over 8 years up to and including 15 years	10 cents
Over 15 years up to and including 20 years	15 cents
Over 20 years	20 cents

The maximum bid/offer spread is adjusted according to the remaining life of the bond.

There are further nuances to the market that should be noted. Admission to either the official or the regulated market at one German stock exchange is compulsory for jumbo Pfandbriefe; an official listing must be obtained immediately after issue or not later than 30 days after the settlement date. However, only a fraction of Pfandbrief trading is settled through the stock exchange. By far the greater share of trading is executed off the floor, for the most part via the telephone or, to an ever-greater extent, through the numerous electronic trading systems including the EuroCreditMTS. To be eligible to trade on this platform, bonds must fulfil stringent credit criteria. They must have a triple-A rating from either Moody's or Standard & Poor's and a minimum volume outstanding of €3 billion. jumbo Pfandbriefe are responsible for more than 80% of the issues traded on EuroCreditMTS.

Over and above this, there are certain recommendations in place regarding the issuance of jumbos:

■ The coupon should be expressed in fractions of not less than a quarter percentage point.
■ In the event of an issue being tapped, the tap amount should not be less than €125 million per add-on.
■ In the case of new issues or taps, a maximum of five days should separate pricing date and settlement date.

In addition, all jumbo Pfandbriefe with a volume outstanding of €1.25 billion or greater and with a residual life of more than two years are greatly assisted by the market making pledge, given by 17 institutions, to provide a repo market in these issues.

Yield and Yield Spread

In addition to the safety and liquidity aspects, Pfandbriefe also offer investors an attractive yield pickup over government bonds. For instance, the spread in the 10-year sector is as of March 2003 between 30 to 50 basis points above the relevant Bund issue. In 2000, this spread ballooned out to a high of almost 70 basis points, reflecting the uncertain environment in the credit markets, due to the decline in the equity markets witnessed around the world. As one might imagine, during these phases of increasing yield spreads, the Bund/Pfandbrief spread tends to widen to a considerably lesser extent than say the Bund spread versus "uncovered" bank bonds.

Exhibit 29.2 illustrates recent Bund/Pfandbriefe spread history from June 2000 to September 2002.

MARKET INSTRUMENTS

The Pfandbrief market is comprised of several types of issues; in addition to the aforementioned traditional and jumbo Pfandbriefe, there are global issues and a variety of structured issues and the latest enhancements to the product range by the way of medium-term note (MTN) and commercial paper (CP) programs.

EXHIBIT 29.2   5-Year/10-Year Jumbo Pfandbrief/Bund Spread

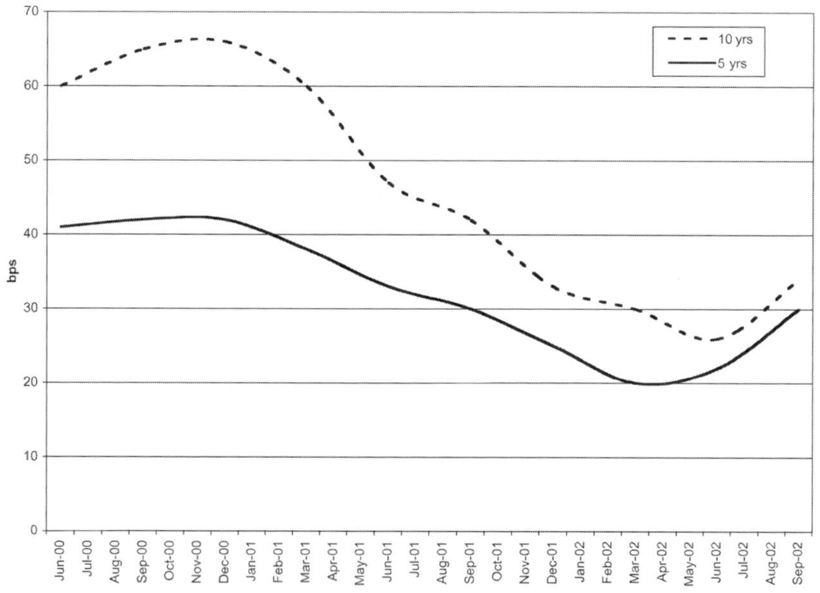

Source: Association of German Mortgage Banks (VDH). Used with permission.

As previously discussed, the major difference between traditional and jumbo Pfandbriefe is the issue volume. Further distinctions are also evident in the issuing procedures of the two. Traditional Pfandbriefe are brought to the market in tap form and individual series feature within one issue. jumbos, on the other hand, are issued via syndicates using the *fixed price reoffer* method. To guarantee the liquidity, jumbos must have at least three market makers willing to make prices throughout normal trading hours. Some time ago, a book-building procedure with a premarketing phase was put in place, in line with standard practices within the international markets. A so-called "pot procedure," similar to the auction procedure, has been introduced as well. With this method, syndicate banks can put together an order book from which the respective issuer can decide on allocation. This places the issuer in a position to allot investor demand among the syndicate banks in the runup to the issue, thus enabling greater control over the book and, of course, more precise pricing.

Traditional Pfandbriefe may be issued in either bearer or registered form, whereas jumbos are only issuable as bearer bonds. For several years now, there has been a considerable shift in favour of the bearer paper, an indication of the growing share of jumbo issues brought by the mortgages banks and their willingness to provide fungible bonds to their investors. Today, approximately 75% of all Pfandbriefe are bearer instruments.

As a rule, Pfandbriefe are issued with maturities of one to 10 years, and currently the most predominant incidence of issuance occurs in the medium term maturities of five to seven years. However, this predominance has been on the wane over the last few years and more and more bonds are appearing on the market with lives of less than one year or more than 10 years.

Global Pfandbriefe

These issues are aimed specifically at the large financial centres around the world. For example, in order to facilitate investor access to the market, particularly in the United States, the first Globals were issues almost exclusively in accordance with SEC Rule 144a. This prevents the need for investors to go through the costly SEC registration procedure and avoids the need for annual accounts in line with US accounting regulations. It does, however, restrict sales to so-called "qualified investors" with a portfolio of at least $100 million. A number of mortgage banks have gained a frequent issuer status in the United States, in accordance with Rule 12g 3-2 (b), which grants exemption from the extensive registration and reporting requirements. Under this rule, the publishing of a separate US prospectus is not required; the standard documents presented in the issuer's home country are sufficient. Despite these helpful measures, the process of marketing Pfandbriefe in the United States is still very much in its infancy and the competition for the attention of investors is huge.

By definition, jumbo Pfandbriefe are always plain vanilla structures: jumbos are fixed-interest bullet bonds, the coupon on which is payable annually in arrears. The calculation of interest accrued is done uniformly using the actual/actual method in line with international practice. While this standardisation helps to enhance the transparency of the market, it inhibits the ability for these issues to be targets to an investor's specific needs and this is where the structured issues come into their own.

Structured Pfandbrief

Aside from the traditional and jumbo Pfandbriefe, the mortgage banks also offer structured Pfandbriefe for those investors that seek a more individually tailored product to suit their portfolios. These products are structured to particularly suit the investors' interest rate expectations and their desired risk/return profiles. Structured Pfandbriefe allow the mortgage banks to combine the asset quality of the Pfandbrief with the advantages offered by derivatives.

MTN and Commercial Paper Programs

A recent important addition to the range of refinancing tools has arrived in the form of medium-term note and commercial paper programs. Pfand-briefe issued under these programs offer a greater range of maturities and can be denominated in different currencies. For the mortgage banks they offer a superior degree of flexibility in refinancing, as a variety of bonds can be issued as and when required. They offer a reduction in costs as the workload involved in issuance is much less and finally, they open the market to an increased range of investors with specific investment criteria.

Clearing

Transactions in Germany are usually settled through Clearstream Banking AG, Frankfurt, a subsidiary of Deutsche Börse AG, formed as a result of the merger of Deutsche Börse Clearing AG and Cedel International. The remainder are settled via Euroclear or Clearstream International.

KEY DIFFERENCES BETWEEN COVERED BONDS AND ABS OR MBS

While covered bonds are often regarded as similar to asset-backed securities (ABS) and mortgage-backed securities (MBS), many noteworthy differences exist between them:

- The assets behind the covered bonds assets remain on the originator's balance sheet, even though they may be maintained in distinct pools or lodged in special purpose affiliates. However, in the case of ABS or MBS, the assets are segregated from any other assets and are usually off balance sheet and placed in a special purpose vehicle (SPV).
- The covered bond issuer is the source of the principal and interest cash flows, whereas the actual assets provide those payments in the case of the ABS/MBS.
- In certain jurisdictions, covered bondholders have some recourse to "noneligible" assets and, in the case of the special purpose affiliates, may also rely on some form of parental support for the issuer. For ABS/MBS, in the event of insufficient proceeds from the pool assets to cover the claim, holders have no recourse above and beyond the collateral contained within the pools and the original ABS/MBS structure.
- Eligible assets for covered bonds are clearly defined by law and are substitutable. Therefore the asset mix varies over time and is relatively heterogeneous. For ABS/MBS, the assets are of the originator's

discretion and once the structure is finalised, no asset adjustments can generally be made. The mix of assets can usually be regarded as quite homogeneous.

■ Asset quality is a measure of the strengths of the specific structure created for the ABS/MBS. However, it is a function of the issuer and underwriting standards of the covered bond, as well as the features of each issues framework.

■ Covered bondholders, in the event of issuer insolvency and provided that the covering assets continue to meet regulator requirements, will still receive interest and principal payments according to the contractual dates (with the exception of Spain). However, certain credit events such as deterioration in the quality of the underlying assets for example, would trigger the acceleration of ABS/MBS payments.

MARKET PARTICIPANTS

In August 2002, the real estate and public-sector-lending operations of Commerzbank Frankfurt (Rheinische Hypothekenbank AG), Deutsche Frankfurt (Deutsche Hypothekenbank AG), and Dresdner Frankfurt (Europäische Hypothekenbank der Deutschen Bank AG) merged to form Eurohypo AG, Germany's largest mortgage bank, and in doing so, reduced the number of issuers of German Pfandbriefe to its current total of 40 institutions.[4] This number consists of 20 private mortgage banks, 18 public sector credit institutions, and two private ship mortgage banks. Nineteen private mortgage banks and one private ship mortgage bank form the *Verband Deutscher Hypothekenbanken* (Association of German Mortgage Banks) and issue approximately 60% of the outstanding total volume in the Pfandbrief market.

Exhibit 29.3 is an outline of the structure of market participants. Of the 20 private mortgage banks, 17 are classed as "pure" mortgage banks and, as the name suggests, their lending operations are limited essentially to mortgage loans for commercial and residential property and to public sector lending. The latter includes loans to the federal government, the federal state governments or *Länder*, local authorities and public sector institutions.

Alongside these "pure" mortgage banks are three "mixed" mortgage banks (Eurohypo, HVB RE, and DEPFA). The difference between the two is that the "mixed" banks, in addition to conducting the same business conducting as the other mortgage banks, they are also licensed to

---

[4] The main shareholders continue to be Deutsche Bank (approximately 34.6%), Commerzbank (approximately 34.5%), and Dresdner Bank (approximately 28.7%).

EXHIBIT 29.3   Outline of Market Participants

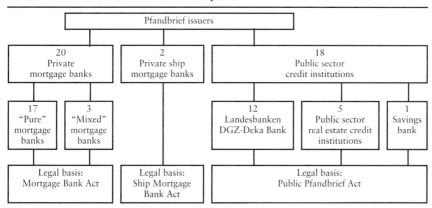

Source: Association of German Mortgage Banks. Used with permission.

engage in universal banking operations. Currently, only one mixed institution operates outside the regular remit of a German mortgage bank.

The three mixed mortgage banks are now the exception; mortgage banks founded today may only be done so as pure mortgage institutions. The existing mixed institutions retain their status as they were engaged in other banking activities prior to the Mortgage Bank Act of 1900.

As mentioned previously, the mortgage banks are monitored by BAFin, in close collaboration with the Deutsche Bundesbank and are bound under the requirements of both the Mortgage Bank Act (HBG) and the German Banking Act (KWG).

The next group of Pfandbriefe issuers are classified as public sector credit institutions. The most significant of these are the *Landesbanks* and the DGZ-DekaBank (an umbrella organisation).

The state banks, or Landesbanks, are legally independent public sector entities. At present they benefit from the principles of *Gewährträgerhaftung* (guarantee obligation) and *Anstaltslast* (maintenance obligation). That is to say, that both the respective federal state and the regional savings banks or their regional associations guarantee them. This extra "guaranteed" status ensures that the issues brought by these institutions trade at a premium to their counterparts (see the relative value analysis discussion later in this chapter). However, under an agreement concluded between the European Union commission and the German federal government (on 18 July 2001), the Gewährträgerhaftung must be abolished by mid-2005, while the Anstaltslast support mechanism has to be modified. The European Union commission felt these guarantees from the public sector were anticompetitive and effectively amounted to a state subsidy, allowing the Landesbanks to fund themselves more cheaply.

EXHIBIT 29.4   The Ten Most Active Jumbo Issuers (as of 23 January 2003)

Issuer	Issues	Volume (€ millions)	Average Size (€ millions)	Market Share
Eurohypo	38	73,282	1,928	17.98%
AHBR	27	49,088	1,818	12.05%
DEPFA	16	39,715	2,482	9.75%
HypEssen	19	34,380	1,809	8.44%
HVB	18	29,453	1,636	7.23%
DG HYP	18	29,075	1,615	7.13%
HVB RE	16	16,636	1,040	4.08%
LB NRW	7	16,250	2,321	3.9%
LB Bad. Württ	5	10,750	2,150	2.64%
WestHyp	7	10,500	1,500	2.58%
Sum top 10	171	309,130	1,808	75.85%
Overall Market	252	407,538	1,617	100%

Source: DZ Bank. Used with permission.

In order to protect investors, outstanding bonds will stay guaranteed through a "grandfathering" agreement.

Completing this group of issuers are the public sector real estate lenders and one savings bank, the Public Pfandbrief Act (ÖPG) governs all. The regulations set out in the ÖPG are not comparable to the stringent legislation laid down in the HGB.

Deutsche Schiffsbank AG in Bremen and Schiffshypothekenbank zu Lübeck, the two ship mortgage banks, complete the list of Pfandbriefe issuers. They issue long-term credit against ship mortgages and fund their lending by issuing ship Pfandbrief and are regulated by the Ship Mortgage Act.

Exhibit 29.4 shows recent issue size from selected participants.

AMENDMENT TO THE MORTGAGE BANK ACT

On 1 July 2002, the amendments to the German Mortgage Bank Act finally came into force. The main ambition of these changes was to allow the Pfandbrief market to compete on a more level playing field with their up-and-coming foreign rivals.

The principal changes made were threefold. First and foremost, they allow the mortgage banks to engage in lending operations in previously restricted areas, namely outside of Europe in countries such as the United States, Canada, and Japan. Under the old law, German mortgage banks were only allowed to use public sector loans made in the European Union and euro-currency area as collateral for their bonds. This increasingly placed them at a distinct disadvantage when competing with banks in countries such as Luxembourg, which can use loans to any OECD country to cover their *Lettres de Gage*.

Secondly, German mortgage banks are now allowed to provide a broader range of services related to real estate and public sector lending, opening up new, fee-paying business opportunities.

The third major component of the new legislation related to the inclusion of derivatives in the cover pools and the net present value calculation of the respective pools. The total volumes of these derivatives are limited to 12% of both the total pool and Pfandbriefe outstanding and to maintain the Pfandbrief reputation for safety, the banks are still prohibited from assuming too much risk, by writing open-ended options and the like.

Collateral cover is now calculated with reference to market value as well as nominal value, enabling greater transparency and precision in the calculation of cover. Both these amendments benefit the Pfandbrief investor; in the event of the insolvency of a mortgage bank, there would be no netting of derivatives, which would therefore continue to protect the cover pools and allow the banks to hedge against adverse market conditions that could cause their paper to suffer credit deterioration.

HEDGING PFANDBRIEFE HOLDINGS

Players within the market have several options available to them when it comes to hedging their exposure to the jumbo Pfandbrief. By far the simplest is to merely enter into an offsetting trade using the most relevant German government bond or futures contract and in periods of relative calm this can work reasonably well. There is a close correlation between Pfandbriefe and futures and the underlying Bunds have a well-developed repo market. For investors looking to capitalise on the pickup in yield between Bunds and Pfandbriefe, then this method would certainly seem to be ideal, it is not without one major inherent problem: basis risk. It is difficult if not impossible to calculate one's basis risk in this scenario.

In 1998, with the global fixed income crisis that occurred after Russia's devaluation, the ensuing "flight to quality" caused the spreads to balloon some 30 to 35 basis points and this strategy proved to be ineffective and extremely costly. Many investment fund managers that use this hedging approach tend to wait to see extensive spread widening between the Bund and the Pfandbrief market before entering the market in anticipation of tightening.

In an attempt to attract foreign investors to the market by providing a truly homogenous hedging vehicle, Eurex launched the jumbo Pfandbrief future on 6 July 1998. This followed a period of sustained issuance in jumbos and it was felt at the time that this would provide a critical mass of underlying bonds of a size, around €50 billion, that would underpin sufficient volumes of deliverable paper. Eurex at the introduction, felt that the criteria for such a contract had been fully met and were quoted as saying that "a delivery commitment under a short position in a Pfandbrief futures contract can be fulfilled only by certain jumbo Pfandbriefe, namely mortgage Pfandbriefe and public Pfandbriefe with a residual life on the delivery date of at least three and a half years and not more than five years, and a minimum issue size of DM 1 billion. Further, the jumbo Pfandbriefe must be rated AAA and structured in straight bond format. Also, at least three institutions must be named in the syndicate agreements of the issuers as market makers for the cash market."

The initial reaction to this new contract greatly exceeded most market participants' expectations with between 6,000 and 8,000 contracts being traded per day, but the enthusiasm was short-lived and by the end of July the volume traded had halved. The emerging market turmoil that began in the late summer dealt the faltering confidence in the new contract a further blow and as *Euroweek* reported in its 1998 Year End Review, "on one average day in October (1998), 214 jumbo contracts were traded—a paltry figure compared to 133,000 Bobl contracts traded that day."

And so the jumbo Pfandbrief contract had failed at its first major hurdle, and on 1 March 1999 Eurex suspended trading in both the Deutschmark- and euro-denominated contracts. It did however; indicate at the time, that the door remained open for a possible relaunch of the contract at a future date.

Several reasons as to why the liquidity in the contract failed to live up to expectations were offered. One, which many adhered to, was that the timing was extremely unfortunate, with the Russian crisis occurring so soon after the launch (although this type of situation is precisely the type of test that a genuinely liquid contract must be able to meet and surpass). In practice, however, the "flight to quality" proved this strategy very costly.

As at the start of 2003, no moves have be made to reinstate the jumbo contract and presently the only way to effectively hedge ones exposure to the Pfandbrief market is via the swaps market, although many still favour the peripheral government bond route, particularly for trades conducted on a short-term horizon.

Exhibits 29.5 and 29.6 show relevant spreads for market participants who use Bunds or interest rate swaps to hedge their holdings.

EXHIBIT 29.5   Jumbo–Bund Spreads

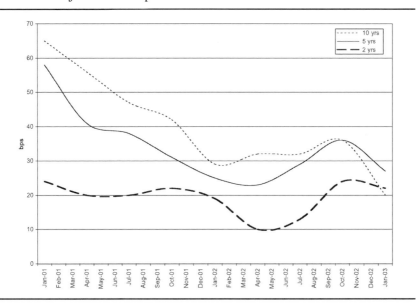

Rates Source: Bloomberg L.P.

EXHIBIT 29.6   Jumbo–Swap Spreads

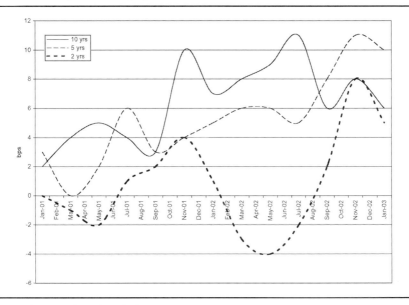

Rates Source: Bloomberg L.P.

THE CREDIT RATING APPROACH TOWARDS PFANDBRIEFE

With regard to credit rating, the jumbo market has developed considerably from its inception in 1995. In that year, only three of the issuers were formally rated. During 2003 all issuers were rated by one or more of the public rating agencies.

The two main international ratings agencies, Moody's and Standard & Poor's, adopt different methodologies when approaching Pfandbriefe and this has caused some confusion among investors.

Moody's generally assume a strong link between the credit quality of the bonds and that of the issuer and this has lead to a "notching" approach. This method mirrors Moody's general opinion that the credit quality of a covered bond is a "function of the quality of the assets originator rather than that of the assets themselves." As a concession to the fact that these are "covered" bonds and as recognition of the tight legal framework within which these issues are bound, Moody's add three or four notches (for mortgage and public sector Pfandbriefe respectively) to the senior unsecured rating.

The approach applied by Standard & Poor's is somewhat different. Although they too recognize the link between the creditworthiness of the issuer and its covered bonds, Standard & Poor's operates on the basis that any potential weakness of the issuer can be overcome by the provision of a higher degree of overcollaterisation.[5] As a result, Standard & Poor's's ratings are based essentially on an analysis of the collateral pool and therefore tend to be higher than those of Moody's.

This distinction between the two translated, until recently, into very little in practice. However, as the mortgage banks, in common with all German banks in the latter half of 2002, experienced significant credit deterioration these different approaches have become far more apparent. Pfandbrief paper from the same issuer is now rated differently by the two main rating agencies; for example, Moody's now rates AHBR's mortgage-backed bonds A1 whereas Standard & Poor's still maintains a triple-A outlook.

The VDH consider this disparity to be unsatisfactory as it makes the job of marketing the product to an investor base, with ever-increasing risk awareness, more difficult. Their view is that the rigid notching approach adopted by Moody's creates a certain asymmetry as one moves down the credit scale, as it does not recognize the high quality of the assets in Pfandbrief cover pools.

At present any change in approach from Moody's is unlikely, given their view that Pfandbriefe are not bankruptcy-proof entities. Though

---

[5] The increasing of nominal cover for the Pfandbriefe outstanding, by way of appropriate assets to a level higher than the minimum required by law.

none has gone bankrupt yet, this does not mean that such an event is impossible. In the event of bankruptcy, investors will be exposed to a loss.

RELATIVE VALUE ANALYSIS

The yields of a single covered bond within one maturity band currently vary by as much as 20 to 25 basis points. This is a sharp increase from the 6 to 8 basis points variations seen in 1999 and preceding years. We now focus on the factors that can cause such differences.

As discussed in the previous section, a differential exists between the methods used by the two main ratings agencies to rate Pfandbriefe and this obviously has an impact on how the fair value of an issue is perceived. Also, given several prominent downgrades witnessed within the German market in the latter half of 2002, it is understandable to see that the level of yield spread variations has increased throughout the curve.

The type of issuer is naturally a major influence and as an example of the impact this can have, covered bonds issued by the Landesbanken, which profit from state guarantees and from the fact that they are eligible assets for the covered bonds of the private mortgage banks, trade on average 6 to 8 basis points more expensive than the other issues.

Under the tax legislation in Germany, domestic investors tend to favour low coupon bonds that are trading below par. Therefore one would expect to see these issues to trade rich to the curve. However, the impact of this has become more and more muted in recent years, perhaps a clear indication of a reduction in the influence of tax-driven domestic investors on the overall flows in the market. On this note, interest income earned in Germany by nonresidents is generally not subject either to income tax or to corporation tax. By analogy, withholding tax is not retained on interest income that nonresidents earn on Pfandbrief investments.

One could also assume that the size of issue may be a determining factor in the curve spreads; larger size would usually imply greater liquidity. The fact that volume has an almost negligible effect on spreads is testament to the market making obligations that are present in the jumbo market.

Another factor to play its part is the collateral element of covered bonds. Mortgage loans are generally regarded as riskier than loans to the public sector, and hence, it has been noted that mortgage Pfandbriefe tend to trade some 1.5–2.5 basis points cheaper than public sector Pfandbriefe as investors tend to demand a slightly higher risk premium. The influence of collateral quality is obviously well covered by other aforementioned measures, such as the type of issuer and, of course, the bond's credit rating. These two variables have significantly increased their influence on curve spreads over the last couple of years and explain the majority of credit and spread differentiation in the world of covered bonds.

There is, therefore, a rationale behind the yield spread differential witnessed between two "like" issues occupying the same maturity band, and the above points must be factored in when assessing the fair value of a particular Pfandbrief. As of early 2003, it is generally felt that the market has found its echelon in regard to curve spread and that current relative valuations should remain to a large extent intact in the near term. In this context, any short-term deviations from fair value could represent profitable trading opportunities for investors.

THE EUROPEAN COVERED BOND MARKET

As more European countries aim to establish their own covered bond markets with updated legislation, investors are getting a larger choice of Pfandbrief-like products. Most of the laws are based on the established German framework and aim to provide the same high quality of asset, but slight differences still remain. Here we look at the differences between the main runners in the covered bond arena.

The European market volume share is shown in Exhibit 29.7.

France

The mortgage bond market in France dates back to 1852 when, on 28 February, the Decree of 1852 established mortgage banks that were authorized to lend funds to property owners. These loans were repay-

EXHIBIT 29.7 European Covered Bond Market as of 24 January 2003

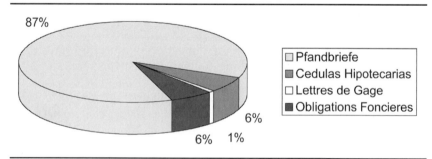

87%

6%

6%   1%

☐ Pfandbriefe
■ Cedulas Hipotecarias
☐ Lettres de Gage
■ Obligations Foncieres

able by long-term annual instalments. However, it was not until June 1999 when modifications to this law broadened the appeal of *Obligations Foncières* (OFs) for international investors. These modifications to the Mortgage Act had two main objectives: to lower refinancing costs for the issuer and to offer investors secure and liquid products.

France had seen Germany's mortgage banks, with the success of the Pfandbrief market, being able to raise refinancing facilities at considerably lower costs than their French counterparts. They wanted quickly to follow suit. The French banks realised that failing to do so could result in their domestic market share being eroded by aggressive competition from across the border.

Another major reason for amendments to the Mortgage Act was to attempt to restore a widespread confidence in the French mortgage-lending sector after the real estate crisis that occurred in the early 1990s. The new requirements set in place were successful in doing just that.

1999 saw the creation of a new type of financial institution in France, the Société de Credit Foncier (SCF) or mortgage loan company, provided for under the new law. Their creation sets the Obligations Foncières aside from other newly created European mortgage-backed sectors such as Spain's *Cédulas Hipotecarias* by the fact that their issuance is restricted solely to these Sociétés de Credit Foncier.

SCFs have the sole purpose of refinancing eligible assets, mainly through the issuance of OFs. While they have the legal status of banks, they are prohibited from engaging in traditional banking activities and from holding equity stakes in any subsidiaries, which mean that they operate very similarly to a SPV. French issuers also manage only one asset pool comprising both types of loans and whether the pool consists of public sector loans, mortgage loans or a mix of the both depends on the business model of the issuer.

Their bankruptcy remoteness is greatly enhanced through one of the most reassuring features of the French law and that is its specific exclusion of the SCF from any bankruptcy proceedings initiated at the level of its parent(s). The SCF is therefore less vulnerable to the default of its parent credit institution.

However, these legal provisions do not completely isolate the creditworthiness of the SCF from external factors, but only limit the extent to which credit risk contamination may occur. For this reason Moody's, when granting ratings, begin their analysis by assessing the creditworthiness of the SCF itself. They achieve this by principally analyzing:

- The strategic importance of the SCF to the refinancing of its parent credit institution(s).

- The support extended to the SCF by its shareholder(s) whether in terms of liquidity or capital.
- The nature and quality of the SCF's assets, underpinned by conservative loan-to-value thresholds.
- The capacity of the institution managing the SCF to adequately perform this role.
- Its asset and liability management practices, notably regarding interest rate mismatches.

The fact that the bankruptcy of a parent cannot be extended to an SCF is welcome, however, as a Moody's report published in October 1999 states

> ... the fact that OFs are issued by special purpose subsidiaries means that OF holders have no direct recourse to assets outside the SCF although they could reasonably expect some parent support. This is notably different from *Pfandbriefe* where bondholders have an eventual direct recourse to non-eligible assets if cover assets are insufficient to cover their claims and become *pari passu* with other senior unsecured creditors. Along similar lines, in case of insolvency of an originating credit institution, asset replenishment and/ or substitution is no longer possible, which leaves the SCF fully exposed to asset quality deterioration and repayment, and ensuing cashflow mismatches.

Although Moody's continues, "We consider that this element of weakness is mitigated by the strong likelihood that the French regulator would exert pressure on an SCF's shareholder(s) to extend support to this subsidiary."

Having thus arrived at a senior unsecured debt rating for the SCF, Moody's then turns its attention to the specific characteristics of the Obligations Foncières issued by the mortgage loan company. Given that the OFs exhibit a reduced frequency of default, a reflection of the bankruptcy-remote element of SCFs in regard to parent(s), and the lower loss potential due to their secured nature, Moody's grant a rating to Obligations Foncières of "up to three notches above the senior unsecured debt rating of the SCF."

Like Pfandbriefe, Obligations Foncières bondholders retain preferential rights with regard to the event of bankruptcy over any other claims. The similarities do not stop there. Issuers and market makers have agreed that the minimum size of issuance should be €500 million, that the issue is supported by a market making commitment from at least three banks, quoting continuous prices with bid/offer spreads of between 5 and 20 cents. Also, it almost goes without saying, all OFs must be rated by at least two of the internationally recognised ratings agencies.

While currently lacking in size in comparison to its German neighbour, the Obligations Foncières are rapidly proving to be a worthy competitor.

As of January 2003, there were 17 jumbo OFs outstanding with a maturity greater than two years, totalling €29.2 billion.

Spain

The year 1999 also witnessed, again due to a modification of legislation, the debut of the first international issue of the Spanish *Cédulas Hipotecarias* or "mortgage notes."

Like other covered bonds, their initial existence dates back many years previous, in the case of Spain's offering, to 1869. A considerable number of cédulas have been issued in the domestic retail market since that time.

In 1981, the introduction of the "Ley del Mercado Hipotecario" (Mortgage Market Law) and its subsequent amendments allowed Cédulas Hipotecarias to be issued by almost any credit institution.

The first jumbo-style issue was brought to the market in March 1999 and since then 12 more bonds have been launched. However, despite the enthusiastic start, only one bond was issued in 2000 and one of the existing issues was tapped. 2001 showed more promise, with a total of five new issues and the number of issuers increased from two to five.

Spanish cédulas are, so far, exclusively backed by mortgage loans; the legal framework for the issuance of "Cédulas Territoriales," public sector loans is still in the preparation stage.

Unlike the Obligations Foncières, cédulas do not possess the protection of bankruptcy remoteness in regard to their issuing entity; the probability of default between them is inextricably linked. Understandably, the ratings of these issues are therefore determined by the creditworthiness of the issuer and the whole process of rating is conducted on a case-by-case basis; analysing both the issuing institution as well as the specific characteristics of the security itself.

Under Spanish law, the underlying assets for the Cédulas Hipotecarias do not count as special assets. They are not separated from the bankrupt's assets in the event of the issuer becoming insolvent, as is the case with the German and French Pfandbrief-style bonds, and this obviously places the holder of cédulas in a much weaker position by comparison. However this weakness is considered to be largely offset by the fact that cédulas have the highest level of surplus cover (overcollateralisation) in Europe of at least 11%, which is imposed by law.

Cédulas have a "bond issuing ceiling" of up to 90% of the volume of "eligible mortgages" (loan-to-value ceiling of a maximum of 70% for commercial properties and 80% for residential properties). Even in the event of a full use of this ceiling, Cédulas Hipotecarias have an overcollaterisation of over 11%, as the mortgage loans also serve as collateral, although they cannot be included in the calculation of the maximum volume outstanding because of the higher loan to value levels. If this limit is exceeded at any time, the issuer has to restore the overcollateralisation limits by:

■ Depositing cash collateral of government bonds with the Bank of Spain within 10 working days.
■ Buying back/amortising early outstanding cédulas.
■ Adding new qualifying mortgages to the existing ones (e.g., by purchasing *Participaciones Hipotecarias*).[6]

It should be noted that due to the limited use of Cédulas Hipotecarias so far, the actual degree of overcollateralisation is at least within triple digits and this mandatory requirement is a major strength of the cédulas system.

The quality and size of the mortgage portfolio and the surplus cover are also subject to regular monitoring by the Bank of Spain.

All in all, the secured nature of this type of product strongly reduces the loss potential in a default scenario and to date, since their inception back in 1869, no Cédulas Hipotecarias has ever defaulted. In Moody's opinion these factors justify a rating of two notches above the senior unsecured debt rating for the issuer.

Although market makers provide a similar degree of liquidity for this product as for French and German jumbos, the overall turnover in the cédulas has been somewhat limited. This is something that is likely to change in the near future. As of January 2003, the amount of jumbo Cédulas Hipotecarias, with maturities exceeding two years, equals 16 with an outstanding volume of €30.05 billion.

Luxembourg

In November 1997 the Grand Duchy passed a new law that authorised the creation of a brand new financial entity known as the *Banque d'Emission de Lettres de Gage*, a mortgage-bond-issuing bank.

The Luxembourg law was modelled closely on the German Mortgage Bank Act governing the issuance of Pfandbriefe. Like Germany, the *Lettres de Gage* are subdivided into two categories: one backed by public sector loans (*Lettres de Gage Publiques*) and the other by mortgages (*Lettres de Gage Hypothecaires*). The bondholders also enjoy the same

---

[6] *Mortgage participations* are used for the securitisation of mortgages.

preferential rights over the covering assets which rank above all other existing claims, while the matching principal familiar in the German market also applies to the Luxembourg law.

There are, however, some key variances from Germany's mortgage law and perhaps the most important arises from the different geographical restrictions on lending business between the two. In the case of Luxembourg, public sector loans from the whole OECD area are eligible for refinancing via covered bonds without restrictions.

There are two diametrically opposing views as to the effect this difference has on the security aspect of the Lettres de Gage; the first is that the Luxembourg could be considered to be more secure than its German counterpart. This is thought to be due to the fact that in their search for diversified assets to use as collateral for their Pfandbrief-like product, Luxembourg banks will diversify their exposure to top-rated OECD sovereigns such as Australia and Japan.

However competition among the mortgage banks to deliver superior returns on investments will lead them to pursue assets in lower-rated OECD member countries such as Turkey and Mexico.

In the market we observe that German banks are keen to be involved in this wider business opportunity. This is borne out by the German mortgage bank involvement in the three main Luxembourg Pfandbrief banks. Pfandbriefbank International (PBI) is part of the HVB group, Europäische Hypothekenbank S.A is a 90%-owned subsidiary of the Eurohypo group and Erste Europäische Pfandbrief und Kommunalkreditbank (EPB), the third specialist bank to receive a Pfandbrief licence is owned jointly by Hypothekenbank in Essen AG, Düsseldorfer Hypothekenbank AG and a Geneva-based holding company of the financier Dr. Wolfgang Schuppli. The latter also holds a 49% stake in HypoEssen and, through another holding, a 100% stake in Düsseldorfer Hypothekenbank AG.

The Luxembourg market is still relatively small in comparison to its European cousins and has three jumbo issues outstanding, as of January 2003, with a volume of €3.25 billion. With no issue with an individual volume of €3 billion, the Lettres de Gage are currently precluded from trading on the EuroCreditMTS platform.

Ireland

The Irish covered market is the most recent in Europe. When Ireland sought to create their covered bond market, they looked at all the relevant laws already in place throughout Europe, and cherry-picked the most attractive factors from an investor's perspective. What made this initiative even more impressive was the fact that Ireland has no history in issuing mortgage bonds.

Towards the end of 2001, the Irish Asset Covered Securities Act was passed allowing banks recognised by the Central Bank of Ireland as "Designated Credit Institutions" (DCIs) to issue *Irish Asset Covered Securities.*

When the legal framework was first put forward in early 2000, some of the proposed features of these issues were considered to be unique attractions from an investor's perspective. Their impact, however, has been somewhat nullified by progresses made in other markets, for example, the recent amendments to the German Mortgage Bank Act. Nevertheless, the concept of Irish covered bonds still represents an improved version of the German Pfandbrief. Ireland's rules for investor protection are the most stringent in the market—with strict supervision,[7] controls on assets eligible for cover pools and no possibility of risk from duration mismatching.

The Irish steering committee decided against adopting a policy such as that used by Luxembourg's Lettres de Gage with regard to "eligible-assets." They felt that allowing loans made in any OECD country as collateral for their bonds would compromise the credit quality of their Irish Asset Covered Securities. Instead, Ireland has limited the asset pool to the EEA, along with G7 countries and Switzerland.

A maximum of 10% of the cover pool can be commercial property loans and substitution assets cannot exceed 20%. To limit cash flow mismatching risk, the Irish bonds exhibit tight matching requirements. For example, the nominal value of the cover assets must at all times exceed the value of the corresponding securities. The aggregate interest from the assets must also exceed that of the covered bond and the currency of the cover assets must be similar to the related bonds. In addition to this, the duration of the cover assets must be greater than the duration of the bonds.

Critically, it is only in Ireland where the regulator has further stipulated that "the weighted average duration of the cover assets should not exceed the weighted average duration of the Irish covered bonds by a period greater than three years."

There is a loan-to-value limit imposed of 60% for residential mortgages and 100% for public sector loans and hedging contracts against interest rate risk are permitted in the collateral pool.

This new Irish product provides an interesting enhancement to the range of high quality products available in this sector. The legal framework combines all the traditional elements of covered bonds from existing European markets with innovative augmentations that serve to strengthen credit quality further.

The first issue in the Irish Asset Covered Securities market is due in March 2003 and will be brought by a well-known German name, the

---

[7] Supervision by the Central Bank of Ireland and an Independent Cover Asset Monitor approved by the regulator.

Deutsche Pfandbrief bank (DEPFA) under the guise of their Irish subsidiary, DEPFA ACS Bank.

Investors will thus benefit from a high degree of liquidity coupled with professional expertise in the placement and trading of these bonds.

CONCLUSION

Covered bonds offer high safety while at the same time granting the investor an enhanced yield in comparison to government bonds. The sheer size of the Pfandbrief market with its market-making obligations has the potential to offer good liquidity and it is gradually breaking away from its reputation as a German "closed shop." However, it still has some way to go to catch up with the very markets that it purports to challenge, the aforementioned government markets, in terms of professionalism and ability to provide a credible liquid marketplace. Mortgage banks have now been given the opportunities to operate beyond European borders and truly market their product globally. Failure to take advantage of this situation could prove extremely detrimental to their standing. One issuer in particular, DEPFA, has already tapped into the United States with a Pfandbrief issue denominated in US dollars. This offers US investors a high-quality investment alternative to US agencies and triple-A ABS and can give them much sort after diversification.

New and sophisticated covered bond laws, offering significant improvements to the original Pfandbrief model, have been introduced in France, Spain, Luxembourg, and now Ireland. Germany has responded with its amendments to the Mortgage Bank Act.

The development of these other markets comes at a time when the Pfandbrief market is experiencing a difficult period, featuring several prominent downgrades, as the whole German banking system has become embroiled in an economic crisis. Their introduction is, for the first time, representing increased competition for the German market, albeit still some way off posing a serious threat.

The legislation changes throughout the European covered bond markets, also bring another possibility a step closer—a European Pfandbrief.

It is not unforeseeable for further adaptation to take place that would create a truly homogenized product; an idea originally envisaged back in the 1980s. Currently, investors have to research the slight differences between the various covered bonds and although these can offer up some interesting opportunities, they require greater analysis. In the absence of any further concerted efforts to create such an attractive instrument, the different national laws seem likely to prevail for some time.

Collateralised Debt
Obligations

Structured Credit:
Cash Flow and Synthetic CDOs

Oldrich Masek
MD, Global Structured Credit Origination, Repackaging and Solutions
JPMorgan Securities Ltd.

Moorad Choudhry
Head of Treasury
KBC Financial Products UK Limited

The advent of collateralised debt obligations (CDOs) was a natural evolution in the ever-growing and increasingly global securitisation market. A CDO is an area of structured finance whereby a distinct legal entity known as a *special purpose vehicle* issues debt and equity-like instruments secured against a portfolio of assets, or more generally, credit risk. The credit risks behind a CDO can be sourced directly from the marketplace (a key distinction from traditional ABS secutitisation) or identified by reference (that is, transferred from an existing bank, corporate, or other balance sheet). The first CDOs were developed principally as vehicles to accumulate and repackage financial instruments that, when evaluated on an asset by asset basis, were relatively

The authors would like to thank Tim van den Brande, Dorothee Fuhrmann, Sandra Wong, Vicki Lamb, and Ketul Tanna at JPMorgan, and Edwin Noomen at Robeco for their input and constructive review comments. Any errors remain the responsibility of the authors.

illiquid or too complex for some investors to consider (for example, high-yield debt).

With that objective in mind, CDO vehicles were used to selectively aggregate individual credits within an asset class in attempt to construct portfolios with very specific investment themes as well as risk/return profiles. By doing so, structured financiers would seek to make these new asset classes more appealing to investors that could not prudently or practically invest into the asset class directly. Direct-investing challenges can arise when an investor is deprived of the necessary credit selection skills in the desired asset class and/or lacks the sufficient risk management or operational infrastructure to surveil the ongoing quality of the asset portfolio. Furthermore, the investor may be unable to satisfactorily diversify its obligor and industry concentration risk due to limited investable funds or the investor is simply precluded by geography (i.e., limited local knowledge or cross-border investing barriers such as tax, regulatory, or legal constraints).

Hence, in very simple terms, the *pooling* concept that a CDO provides can attract scalable liquidity to an asset class that on its own would be limited for the aforementioned reasons. Again, the high-yield market serves as a good example in this regard; without the capacity made available to high-yield issuers through CDOs, the market would not have been able to develop as rapidly as it has in terms of size and breadth. This is best evidenced by the fact that today it is estimated that approximately two-thirds of all US high-yield new issuance is intermediated to end investors through CDOs globally. The significance of this should not be understated: The ability to enhance overall market liquidity for an asset class is a key value proposition of CDOs. This feature alone secures CDOs a critical role in the global financial marketplace (if not a major driver of its expansion). With that said, although the market initiated with high-yield debt, the scope of asset classes being repackaged today is extensive both in terms of type and risk characteristics (for instance, hedge funds, credit derivatives, real estate, ABS, and CDOs themselves). Various asset class case studies will be offered for discussion later in this chapter.

Expanding on this theme, the barriers that CDOs help investors overcome are not limited to providing diversified asset class access alone. More fundamentally, they provide a means to diversify into an asset class with the optional benefit of expert advice. Although static portfolios (and more recently indexation-based portfolios) can be constructed, most CDOs formally contract an asset manager with a unique specialization in the targeted asset class to administer the portfolio. In such fiduciary capacity, the asset manager selects the initial portfolio and has an ongoing responsibility to manage and maximize the value of the portfolio for the investor. Given that a CDO's liabilities are directly linked to the cash flows realized by the underlying portfolio, the choice of asset manager can significantly enhance or damage the overall ability of the CDO to repay its debt and equity obligations. Consequently, investors will spend considerable time evaluating an asset manager's capabilities and performance track record before investing. (A CDO is no different from a simple mutual fund in these respects.)

Another service a CDO affords investors is an ability to select the *degree of risk* an investor takes to an asset class (and, if applicable, the asset manager) depending on where in the CDO's capital structure the investor invests. An investor participating at the equity level, for instance, has more exposure to the management and ultimate performance of the asset-side activities of a CDO's balance sheet than a senior debt investor would—in this regard, it is no different than any other financial entity investment. This point is worth expanding upon, by overlaying rating technology to CDO vehicles, investor capacity can now be sourced from across the risk spectrum of investing clients (AAA through equity investors) creating investing options in virtually any asset type. The impacts of combining securitisation rating technology with portfolio theory are profound: The ability to tailor risk/return exposure to an asset class radically alters the scope of investible assets an investor has to choose from in order to manage and maximize its broader asset allocation/return objectives.

Consequently, CDOs have developed into sophisticated investment management vehicles in their own right. Therefore, it is not surprising that through the 1990s, CDOs were the fastest growing asset class in the asset-backed securities market. The 1990s were a period where the complexity in financial markets increased significantly due to the globalization of investable opportunities. Many credit markets have *come of age* in the last decade: European, Asian, emerging markets. Acknowledging the increasing complexities of the collateral markets in light of the industry trends facing the investor and asset manager community, one would expect the CDO market to continue its pace of growth. In many ways, a CDO's value creation is very transparent; this is illustrated in Exhibit 30.1. In a global context, CDO technology has and continues to be a major factor in reducing the global investing barriers between risk originators and risk consumers worldwide. Said differently, the market functions as an efficient conduit between the suppliers of capital and those who require capital accelerating the flow and recycling of the global money supply.

EXHIBIT 30.1   Illustration of CDO Value Creation

CDO business objective: to create efficient platforms for intermediation that respect these developments

STRUCTURED CREDIT: A TOOL FOR FINANCIAL INTERMEDIATION

As highlighted, the discipline of structured credit in its broadest characterisation is principally focused on creating new approaches to more efficiently intermediate borrowers and savers (i.e., *risk* originators and *risk* consumers). While structured credit had its genesis in the United States, the business has quickly globalised and become an essential component of global financial market development. Much of this growth is attributable to the flexibility and customisation CDOs provide in terms of product offerings. In many ways, financial products are no different than tangible goods; opportunities for market expansion are created by delivering new product options to end users. Equally, like most tangible goods, the ability to tailor CDOs rapidly while maintaining scale economies was only made possible through the advent of computing technology (portfolio analytics, risk frameworks, and so on).

Although the products typically identify with structured credit seem extensive and often confusing, reflecting the numerous underlyings that are possible: bonds, loans, credit default swaps, and so on *versus* CBOs, CLOs, CSOs, and so on. They all achieve a very similar value proposition: They are vehicles to pool and redistribute risk. In many ways, all these products are best classified as derivative instruments given that they employ techniques to either reference, repackage, or reconstitute risks in order to enhance the overall liquidity in the *underlying collateral* markets. It would be incorrect to assume that the concept of risk used here in as limited to credit risk: like the underlying instruments, CDOs can encapsulate many different forms of risk (interest rate, currency, market, and so on) albeit either reduced, enhanced or eliminated through product structuring (*tailoring*). Again, this will be explored further in the case studies.

If we adopt the premise that a CDO is nothing more than a customised intermediary, the easiest way to consider its mechanics is by drawing analogy to existing financial intermediary models. For instance, a CDO can be viewed as a limited purpose *minibank*, albeit more efficient than a bank given its focused nature in terms of the scope of its asset mix and the fact that CDOs have a limited life (they are not ongoing concerns). A CDO's limited purpose aspects makes them much more easier to understand—and value—from an investor point of view. Necessarily, the asset pool securing a bank's liabilities will be very diverse (loans, real estate, private equity, and so on) given the wide variety of customers/constituents a bank serves. CDOs, on the other hand, rarely commingle different asset types. In many ways, the benefit that this creates goes back to basic finance principles. Market efficiency is best achieved when the investor can choose the scope and composition of their asset allocation. Investors can achieve their targeted risk/return goals by investing in a series of different CDOs. For instance, an investor can replicate the types of exposures found in our bank example above, by investing in three different CDOs each uniquely secured by one of the three asset types identified. Interestingly, not only can the investor manage its percentage allocation across the various asset classes, the investor can also increase or decrease the amount of risk taken to each sector depending on where in the CDO capital structure the investor has chosen to participate (i.e., how much *leverage* is taken to the asset class).

The risk and return taken to any asset class will increase as an investor moves lower down the CDO's capital structure. Conversely, as the investor participation moves up the capital structure, its risk/return to the particular asset class decreases (in fact, the risk associated with a senior tranche can be less risky than the underlying asset class itself). This should not be surprising, given that the investor in this case is taking second, third, and so on, loss risk. Said differently, each class of notes benefits from the class of notes subordinated to them. The equity in a CDO, for instance, is in the first loss position, meaning the first unit of realised loss (or gain for that matter) on the underlying portfolio accrues to the equity investors. Relative seniority, in fact, is the basis upon which the credit rating agencies assign their ratings to the various tranches once they have assessed the range of cash flow expectation (assuming various stress scenarios) the underlying portfolio could generate. Not surprisingly, the cash flow outcomes under these different scenarios depend significantly on the type of asset class being considered, the diversity achieved within the asset class portfolio and, of course, the capability of the asset manager.

Coming back to our *minibank* analogy, we have established that investors are best served by constructing/controlling their own portfolio asset allocation. In many ways, direct investing into a series of CDOs affords the investor absolute transparency. Some banks, by virtue of their complexity, are often too opaque for some investors. Forcing them to value the bank based on a lowest common denominator principle. For example, if an investor was adverse to emerging market exposure and a bank had 10% of its assets held in such asset class, the investor would discount the value of any securities issued by such bank relative to one that did not have these types of exposures. Alternatively, the investor may like emerging market risk but feels the bank is not *best-in-class* in terms of originating or managing such risk resulting in a similar dilemma. In the extreme, the investor may never invest, depriving that bank (or more generally, the financial markets) of the liquidity that would otherwise be made available to the other asset pools being originated by the bank. Ultimately, the end result is the same, the velocity of the global money supply is reduced unless the investor can find a bank that meets his or her specific investing needs.

Stepping back, the analogy being drawn here has purposefully been exaggerated—banks have many differentiating features, not to mention the fact that they are ongoing concerns with broader societal importance. Nonetheless, it highlights the point: CDOs can fill the practical gaps that exist between borrowers and savers in the global economy.

Building a CDO: Basic Principles

The best and, perhaps, most durable opportunities for CDO creation arise when investable funds in a particular jurisdiction begin to outgrow the investment options historically available. Under such circumstances, investors begin searching elsewhere to invest their excess liquidity. The skilled structured financier will, in partnership with his or her distribution channels, recognise this liquidity disparity and begin his or her work.

For illustrative purposes, it is worth considering the German experience of the 1990s in conjunction with the high-yield debt example mentioned previously. During this period, German institutional investors were seeking to diversify and increase their overall returns. This need arose due to, among other things, the fact that prior to the advent of the euro (or more generally, a European credit market), there were limited investing alternatives other than domestic German Pfandbrief (secured AAA bank notes with a commensurate low yield). Simultaneously, the US high-yield market had reached a reasonable critical mass such that itself was looking for new capacity or liquidity. As a result, CDOs became the tool by which these two trends intermediated. The German institutional investor achieved its goals by gaining indirect access to an asset class that for reasons such as geography would have been impractical. For most of the early cross-border participants, direct investing would have been imprudent given the practical inability to select and monitor the individual high-yield issuers from afar, let alone any overall market subtleties. Conversely, the US high-yield market benefited by the fact that this new capacity introduced a broader bid for their issues, which, in turn, afforded high-yield issuers increased market access at acceptable issuance spreads.

Development of the Structured Asset Management Business

With that said, a new group of beneficiaries had been generated as well, the high-yield bond CDO manager or, more generally, the CDO asset management business. The asset management industry was, in many ways, transformed with the advent of structured credit. The *best-in-class* asset managers were afforded a unique opportunity to efficiently expand their asset gathering activities globally. In fact, many specialty asset manager brands have built their businesses almost exclusively through structured asset gathering. For most that participate in this space, their structured asset gathering platforms fit equally among their various other distribution options. The potential for scale economies are significant. Not only do CDOs bring sizable portfolios of assets under management at once with each issue ($300–500 million), they are *locked up* for seven to 12 years (the average maturity of a CDO) as well.

For an asset manager, this compares favourably to having a series of smaller, yet separate discretionary management mandates, each with different strategies and objectives since the requirements for credit infrastructure, systems and, of course, portfolio managers can be prohibitive. Not only are they more expensive to administer, discretionary funds tend to have more flight risk in periods of market volatility. The operational/scale benefits are clear; perhaps less obvious is the efficient global brand recognition it provides the asset manager. For smaller asset management brands, CDOs allow equal visibility in the global investing community with larger, more established global brands. This will certainly bear influence over the structure of the global industry as it continues to consolidate.

Shifting back to building a CDO, we will assume we have identified the existence of the German investor/high-yield bond CDO opportunity and have selected an asset manager that is *best-in-class* in terms of managing and trading high-yield bonds. Equally, we will assume that the portfolio manager is sufficiently exercised in a management style consistent with the constraints set out in the CDOs' management guidelines such that the asset manager is not encumbered in his efforts to maximise the value of the portfolio. A CDO's operating parameters or *bylaws* are imposed jointly by the credit rating agencies, as part of achieving the desired debt rating on the CDO notes and the investors, as investor sophistication has evolved, who have gained more influence over a CDO's operating construction.

Building a Minibank: Illustration of CDO Mechanics

Firstly, we must establish the corporate existence of our new limited purpose *minibank*: CASH CDO I—or *CCDO I*. CCDO I will be the vehicle by which we will attempt to intermediate the US high-yield market with the German institutional investor base. Exhibit 30.2 illustrates the mechanics described in this hypothetical example.

Specifically, we will look to domicile CCDO I in a jurisdiction such as Cayman Islands, Netherlands, and so on that introduces no or limited incremental risks or friction costs to the broader transaction being contemplated. Risks or friction costs would include things such as weakened legal perfection over the underlying assets or double taxation, for instance. Provided that CCDO I is now legally functioning with all

EXHIBIT 30.2   A CDO as a Minibank

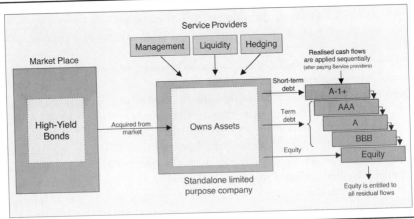

its necessary licensing and regulatory authorisations, CCDO I will next need to engage its service providers in order to begin building its balance sheet as well as developing and implementing its asset/liability management strategy.

Engaging CDO Service Providers

The first, and perhaps most important, service provider that CCDO I will engage is the asset manager, effectively the CDO's management. In our example, a speciality US high-yield manager is contracted to administer CCDO I helping to define and then execute on the investment theme of our CDO. Equally, we will look to outsource the operational/ financial reporting aspects of the CDO vehicle. Other service providers would include third parties such as trustees, custodians, and paying agents. Among other things, they will provide services to CCDO I like validating payment calculations, administering disbursements, affecting underlying collateral sales/transfers, as well as ensuring general compliance with the CDO's management guidelines. In terms of other services sought, CCDO I will engage one or more credit rating agencies to evaluate and pass its credit opinion upon the debt securities that CCDO I plans to issue, thus making them more placeable with investors. At the same time, CCDO I will be considering, to the extent necessary, its various hedging or risk-taking counterparties. These counterparties may provide, for instance, interest rate or currency swaps to CCDO I if its asset and liability strategy warrants such hedging tools. Another form of counterparty CCDO I may employ is a credit enhancement provider— market participants willing to accept a range of different risks in a CDO's complex architecture in exchange for a fee or premium. Often external credit enhancement mechanisms (e.g., bond insurance, letters of credit, liquidity facilities) are sourced when certain risks become too complicated for the rating agencies or investors to comfortably and fairly assess. In such cases, it is often easier to educate and convince one party of a unique risk's particulars than a broad syndicate of investors. Credit enhancement providers are specialised in valuing, pricing and accepting nonstandard or illiquid risks. Consequently, it may simply be that the market price for a particular risk is just more efficiently offered by third parties than born by CCDO I's capital structure directly. CCDO I, by construction, is a rational participant in the financial community and will source comparative advantage from others no differently than any other market participant.

Now that CCDO I has its asset manager employed and its operational infrastructure outsourcing in place, let's assume the following CDO strategy is identified. Firstly, the asset manager (and investor) sees value in the B–BB rated bond sector spread across all industries. Equally, the strategy contemplates significant trading to maximise portfolio value in what are expected to be volatile markets. We begin the practical implementation of the strategy by focusing on the asset accumulation tactics.

Building the Asset Side of the CDO Balance Sheet

The physical activity of purchasing the actual securities underlying a CDO (the *raw material*) is principally about collateral access and market timing. In our example, efficient access to high-yield new issues and the secondary market are important. There are situations when the underlying portfolio for a CDO is accumulated or *warehoused* well in advance of a CDO's debt issuance. Under such arrangements, the collateral is warehoused on a third party's balance sheet until the CDO's liabilities are sold, the proceeds from which are then used to purchase (or *take out*) the warehoused portfolio from the third party. In our case, the high-yield market has a relatively consistent new issuance calendar, and most importantly, a deep secondary market to purchase existing issues. Not only does this permit CCDO I to acquire and finance (i.e., issue the CDO's liabilities) the target portfolio almost simultaneously, it also allows for better blending of assets—seasoned securities will perform differently from new issues in terms of credit performance offering investors diversification by year of origination or *vintage*. Appreciative of the flexibility afforded by the market in terms of rapid collateral access (asset building), CCDO I must still evaluate the timing of its purchase in the context of its overall liability strategy, not to mention its deliverability (i.e., is the market open to financing a CDO with CCDO I's high-yield theme, and if so, at what cost).

Irrespective of collateral availability, the timing of portfolio acquisition is important. As part of its overall portfolio maximisation strategy, the asset manager attempts to accumulate the portfolio (i.e., the asset-side of our *minibank*) when it is *cheap* relative to historical values. The initial purchase price combined with the cash flow (or *revenue*) expectation of the acquired portfolio will determine the amount of debt financing CCDO I's balance sheet can support and, for that matter, the value of any residual or equity interest available in CCDO I. The value of a CDO's equity at any point in time is simply the value of its assets, the portfolio's mark-to-market value after defaults or losses, *less* all its outstanding liabilities: remaining debt obligations, service provider expenses, unreimbursed credit enhancement borrowings.

This general relationship, asset class yield *minus* cost of financing, is what defines the expected equity value (or *enterprise value*) of CCDO I upon its launch. This relationship is dynamic given that value of the portfolio moves overtime, as does the cost and availability of debt financing for particular combinations of asset classes and/or speciality asset managers. This relationship (*market opportunity* measure) is closely monitored by all market participants as a barometer to when a CDO becomes the most efficient tool for leveraging up a particular asset class. (Incidentally, this is why the CDO market demonstrates cyclical issuance patterns around asset class themes.) In practice, when a *market opportunity* is identified, the first parties approached are repeat CDO equity buyers, who themselves are aware of this dynamic relationship.

Building the Liability Side of the CDO Balance Sheet

Accepting that the *market opportunity* for high-yield debt is positive, CCDO I must now shift its focus to the liability structure of our *mini-bank*. In developing the liability strategy, we must optimize around four influential factors: the asset manager style, cash flow dynamics of high-yield bonds, investor customisation or *repackaging*, and, of course, the credit rating agencies.

In terms of fitting the liability structure around the style of the asset manager in our example, CCDO I will focus on financing mechanics that complement its high turnover trading approach. We have already established that CCDO Is chosen asset manager has a developed, proven track record in generating consistent excess returns (*alpha*) through high-yield trading. It is this unique capability our asset management brand possess that CCDO I will use to attract investors to its note offerings *versus* the invariability of competing CDOs that will follow, each attempting to exploit the same *market opportunity*.

Anticipating the high trading turnover, CCDO I decides to adopt a *market value* operating framework (cash flow *versus* market value operating models are further described later in the chapter). By construction, a market value approach will afford the asset manager the most flexibility with respect to portfolio composition. Counter to the more prevalent cash flow-based structure, investors and rating agencies depend mainly on daily valuation measures as opposed to asset mix constraint when evaluating a CDO's creditworthiness. In exchange for asset mix flexibility, however, the *CDO management team* will be subject to a more dynamic, and hence more complicated, liability structure featuring *less* permanent financing. The notes issued by CCDO I provide permanent financing as long as the current mark-to-market value of the portfolio, *less* all outstanding liabilities, is above a predetermined cushion. This cushion (*market value trigger*) is analogous to the CDO *enterprise value* concept mentioned earlier. Mechanically, if the value of our high-yield bond portfolio deteriorates such that the market value trigger is breached, the asset manager is obligated to commence portfolio liquidation in order to raise the proceeds necessary for the orderly repayment of the outstanding debt, which is now manditorily redeemable. This process will continue until the asset/liability relationship is back in compliance with those set out for CCDO I at inception.

Although a CDO's permissible leverage ratio is principally ascribed by the credit rating agencies, CCDO I's asset manager must understand well the circumstances that can drive an unwind of its operations. A CDO's portfolio can deteriorate for many reasons other than poor asset selection or default avoidance. For instance, by employing a market value-based structure, a significant change in asset spreads, or interest rates generally, can reduce the notional value of the portfolio sufficiently to trigger an unanticipated call on its debt financing. The seasoned and prudent asset manger will understand the various sensitivities that impact a CDO's asset/liability flexibility and often operate at leverage ratios safely below those permitted by the rating agencies. This highlights the importance of engaging a CDO asset manager who has developed the skills, infrastructure, and general appreciation of managing the liability-side of a CDO balance sheet. Managing the liability side of a CDO warrants the same importance that is placed on managing the asset side. In our *minibank* example, a CDO's asset manager has a fiduciary responsibility similar to a bank's treasurer or CFO in this regard.

There is more that the CDO structure can do to facilitate the needs of the asset manager's trading style and the market-value-based, prepayable financing arrangement. For instance, CCDO I could complement its term debt financing strategy with the issuance of short-term liabilities such as rated commercial paper (or *CP*). By staggering the term structure of our CDO's financing, the asset manager can more readily match the market value dynamics of the underlying collateral portfolio. For example, CCDO I can increase its CP issuance as short-term relative value purchase opportunities arise while repaying CP once the trading opportunities are exited or monetized. This approach provides a means to maintain some of the benefits core term funding offers, yet managing the liquidity needs necessary to fund our dynamic asset strategy. That is, short/long liabilities strategies are common for most financial institutions; there is no reason why it should be different for our *minibank*.

Focusing on the specifics of the collateral and it's bearing on the way CCDO I should be administered, another technique our CDO will most likely employ is the use of interest rate swaps. US high-yield bonds almost always carry a fixed-rate coupon. As highlighted earlier, asset-side duration risk does not fit well with our market-value-based structure given the impact it can have over the portfolio value over time. One way to immunize CCDO I against this potential for higher portfolio volatility is by swapping the portfolio's fixed-rate coupon streams in exchange for a coupon benchmarked to a floating-rate index (LIBOR). Not only does this dampen the portfolio's volatility, it also better matches the coupons payable on the CDO's notes; in practice, most of the CDO debt issued is offered with a floating-rate coupon and the CP portion of our financing structure is floating rate, by definition. Hence, another ordinary banking risk management type of activity.

Hopefully, at this point, one has gotten a flavour as to how our *minibank* can be shaped to accommodate the particulars of the underlying collateral and an asset manager's style. We shift our discussion to the investor and rating agencies, each of which also have influence on CCDO I's construction.

Influence of Rating Agencies and the Investor

As a general matter, once the basic aspects of CCDO I's asset and liability strategy is established and the vehicle's existence, domicile, legal form is identified, the credit rating agencies are approached for a debt rating on the notes. They are presented with an information package detailing CCDO I's mission statement, intended operating approach/constraints, as well as supporting analytics. Information around the contemplated asset manager is also provided; in fact, the rating agencies will visit the asset manager's facilities (*due diligence*) in order to gain comfort that the particular asset manager has the sufficient skills and infrastructure to manage the actual CDO on behalf on the investors. The actual analytical process around rating a CDO's liabilities is relatively complicated and probably warrants a chapter onto itself (separately, the rating agencies offer their criteria and rating analytic tools freely to market participants). In our high-yield example, they will assess the cash flow impacts on the portfolio under different patterns of default. In general terms, the path dependency of the default stresses being applied are based on a series of factors such as historical default probabilities on individual assets given their initial rating, pairwise correlation across rating categories and industry sectors, as well as expected recoveries on any defaulted assets once they have been worked out. More perspective on the roles and areas of focus for rating agencies are offered later in the chapter.

An important constituent that we have not mentioned lately is the German institutional investor, for those who remember, the catalyst behind the overall transaction. Now that we have built the basic product or tool (CCDO I) to help intermediate the high-yield market to the investor, we should explore any tailoring the CDO can provide to the end investor. The vehicle thus far has been customised principally around the collateral and asset manager.

We begin by presenting the German institutional investor the current value of the *market opportunity*, that is, the potential value an equity investment in the CCDO I can yield given current asset yields, expectations around defaults and the cost of financing). Assuming it has remained attractive, despite the time we have used in assessing the feasibility of the CDO, the equity investor either agrees to invest or not. Once sufficient equity interest is *circled*, then the process of sourcing debt investors begins. In practice, the equity investments are typically subject to certain conditionalities. The most obvious condition is that a minimum absolute *market opportunity* threshold must be achieved (so that a minimum yield on the CDO equity can be realized.

Investor-Specific Repackaging

In addition to expected yield thresholds, the investor may seek features that are highly customized around requirements typical to his or her jurisdiction of residence as well as risk/return goals. In our German example, for instance, the investor may appreciate the necessary flexibility a market value-based structure affords the asset manager (i.e., the investor's contracted management team), but not the mark-to-market volatility it introduces to his potential CCDO I equity investment. As a result, we will look to *repackage* the equity in a form that will help immunize the equity investment against certain downside scenarios. Investor *repackaging* is an important and regular element of the CDO intermediation process; repackaging allows customisation for investors outside the CDO without complicating the core operating vehicle. By bifurcating the tailoring in this way, the mechanics required by the asset manager and the collateral can be satisfied at the same time multiple investor customisation can be achieved—that is, introducing scalability to the specialized intermediation being sought. This is illustrated at Exhibit 30.3.

For reference, a repackaging vehicle employs similar techniques to a CDO in terms of establishing its legal and operational existence. However, the assets securing the repackaging vehicle notes tend to be single instruments (CDO equity). This should not be surprising given they tend to be single-investor specific.

In terms of reducing the equity volatility concerning the German investor, we can repackage CCDO I's equity with a zero-coupon government bond in a separate vehicle. Specifically, the investor will invest in the notes of the newly created vehicle, rather than CCDO I directly. In effect, the investor will be purchasing notes secured by a blended portfolio of two investments: one *risky* and one *riskless*. The ratio of risky to riskless—the amount of CCDO I equity purchased relative to the amount of AAA zeros—is determined such that the initial value of the

EXHIBIT 30.3 Illustrating Repackaging

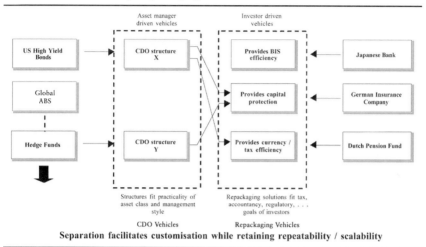

Asset manager driven vehicles | Investor driven vehicles

Structures fit practicality of asset class and management style | Repackaging solutions fit tax, accountancy, regulatory, . . . goals of investors

CDO Vehicles | Repackaging Vehicles

Separation facilitates customisation while retaining repeatability / scalability

riskless zero accretes overtime to the investors targeted total initial investment. Given that the maturity value of the riskless zero coupon instrument is equivalent to the initial total investment (i.e., the initial capital), at a minimum; the investors' capital is protected against any loss that may arise on the equity portion of our two-asset portfolio. The investor will at least get his or her principal back.

Under this strategy, it should not go unnoticed that by investing some of his or her initial capital in the AAA zero, the German investor has purposefully diluted some of the absolute yield (and risk) a pure equity investment might return. In fact, the investor will be returned the realized combined weighted average yield of the equity and zero instruments. From the investor's perspective, however, the yield reduction relative to what the *naked* equity investment could yield can be viewed as the necessary premium payable in order to insure against the loss of capital (to buy the AAA zero). In conclusion, the net result of our repackaging is an investment with a payout profile consistent with the German investor's initial intentions: meaningful upside participation in a new, diversifying asset class while maintaining meaningful downside protection (immunizing against high volatility). The German investor's risk/return has been tailored.

With that said, investor-driven repackaging is not limited to risk/return customisation only. In many cases, the physical form (or *format*) of the repackaged equity is altered. For instance, the aforementioned capital protection structure can be complemented by the fact that the repackaging vehicle can issue a loan rather than a note to the investor.

In Germany, a privately placed loan instrument, a Schuldschein, has much more acceptance than an investment in note format. By structuring a Schuldschein, German insurance companies, for instance, can tap the larger pools for investment available in their general accounts rather than from the more limited funds otherwise available for CDO equity.

In summary, a CDO is a very powerful tool that facilitates the needs of many market constituents. Like all tools, however, they have to be used properly. A CDO structured where the unique particulars of the collateral, the asset manager, and investor are considered, and most importantly balanced, begins to define the minimum standard of excellence that all good structured financiers should respect.

Credit Derivatives: A New CDO Asset Class

The advent of credit derivatives has radically altered the way credit risk is originated, managed, and transferred in the global financial economy. Similar to the way interest rate swaps have decoupled duration risk management from fund raising, credit derivatives have further bifurcated funding into liquidity sourcing and *pure* credit risk management. The impacts are profound; not only have they allowed pure credit risk an ability to trade (efficiently price) independent of the cash market's technical factors (i.e., new issue supply and demand), they have created comparative advantage opportunities between end-credit risk takers and funders. To appreciate such subtlety, one must understand the nature of these instruments.

What Is a Credit Derivative

A credit derivative in many ways is nothing more than an insurance policy on the credit performance of a particular asset. For example, a protection buyer pays a premium in exchange for a contingent payment payable upon an asset-related credit event defined principally around asset default, payment suspension, or restructuring. Credit derivatives on portfolios of credit risk take the analogy one step further in that they often have a deductible (i.e., the first loss or *equity* in the reference portfolio). This means the contingent payment is only triggered once the cumulative notional amount of defaults on a series of individual assets in the reference portfolio exceeds the deductible notional. Consequently, comparative advantage opportunities can arise between end credit risk takers based on their ability to finance or accept credit risk in its newly expanded forms (cash-based or synthetically). For instance, when a cash investor purchases a bond from an issuer, that investor is providing that issuer financing as well as accepting that issuers credit risk, that is, the ability of the issuer to repay on the borrowed funds received from the investor's investment. From an investor's point of view, the *income value* of this cash investment will depend in part on his or her cost of funds to purchase the instrument.

To be specific, assume a bond with a risked-adjusted yield (i.e., the net anticipated yield after default expectations) of LIBOR plus 50 bps; an investor with a cost of funds of LIBOR flat will find more *income value* in the bond than an investor who borrows at LIBOR plus 25 given the different levels of margin that can be secured (i.e., 50 bps in the first instance, 25 bps in the second). However, the investor with the higher cost of funds, now has an alternative in terms of sourcing the credit risk-based investment. He or she can invest in the bond *synthetically* by writing a credit derivative on the bond, becoming a protection seller on the bond. As a general matter, the credit derivative will pay a premium to the investor roughly equivalent to the bond spread (50 bps in our example). In effect, the high-cost-of-funds investor has replicated the margin realizable by the cash-instrument investor. This is made possible by the fact that the investor does not need to raise cash in order to enter into this agreement. The only time the synthetic risk taker will need to borrow cash and trigger his or her funding comparative disadvantage is when a credit event arises, obligating the investor to either take receipt of the underlying (now defaulted) bond or cash settle the difference between the bond's par value and its current distressed value. Hopefully, this example illustrates how comparative advantages in funding impacts the amount of liquidity that can be made available to the cash or synthetic market for credit risk. And more broadly, what credit derivatives have done in terms of increasing the overall opportunity set for credit risk intermediation in the financial marketplace (not to mention, its efficiency).

In-depth coverage of credit derivatives is given in Chapter 4.

The Advent of Synthetic CDOs

It is the aforementioned features that have made credit derivatives a unique element of the CDO market, making it the fastest growing CDO segment in terms of volume. The category of CDOs utilizing credit derivatives as an underlying have come to be known by practitioners as *synthetic CDOs*. The concept of synthetic CDOs was first pioneered by JPMorgan through its BISTRO program in 1997. As an alternative to the cash securitisation approach prevalent at the time—*balance sheet CDOs* further defined later—these programs used portfolio-based credit derivatives as an alternative to transfer credit risk from a bank's balance sheet without the associated asset transfer complications, that is, client relationship management, asset retitling/assignment, altered collections administration/processing. More specifically, these programs were designed to retain the benefits of cash securitisations (credit risk management and capital efficiency) without, however, a securitisation's most prohibitive friction: *expensive funding*.

Cash securitisations are premised on the fact that the assets are *sold* to, and in effect financed by, the securitisation vehicle. As a consequence, by employing cash securitisation methods, a bank is replacing its on-balance sheet cost of financing a portfolio with the funding levels realizable by the securitisation vehicle. Not surprisingly, banks generally achieve lower funding costs than structured vehicles can on a ratings equivalent basis. (As in our cash *versus* synthetic bond investor example earlier, the bank has a funding comparative advantage.) Prior to the advent of portfolio-based synthetic risk transfer, this incremental cost was a necessary friction in order to achieve the other benefits already described, and on balance, not sufficiently prohibitive to offset them (economically nor strategically). The use of portfolio credit derivatives have allowed banks or any asset originator for that matter to separate the funding component inherent in administering a credit portfolio from the credit risk component. More specifically, this new technology means a bank can continue financing and servicing its portfolio on balance sheet, effectively monetizing its comparative funding advantage without foregoing the other benefits it may have otherwise been seeking with a more traditional cash securitisation approach.

Interestingly, the balance sheet version of synthetic CDOs was embraced mostly by European bank participants; given that their comparative funding advantages have been uniquely more pronounced relative to their global competitors. From a cost of funds perspective, banks in Europe have been more structurally advantaged. They tend to be more highly rated and some of the few remaining beneficiaries of *cheap* retail deposits, each of which are changing given poor performance issues as well as increased self-directed investing by individuals.

Evaluating synthetic CDOs in a broader context, it is worth clarifying a general misconception: Synthetic CDOs are not an asset class onto themselves. A synthetic CDO (or SCDO) is no different that any other CDO except for the uniqueness of the underlying collateral: *unfunded credit risk*. It is true that SCDOs can reference all the various asset classes that are offered in cash-flow-based CDOs; but the true point of distinction is the fact that their different *forms* of collateral warrant very different liability structures. The contingency of cash flow exchange inherent in the underlying collateral for an SCDO (i.e., credit derivatives) results in radically different cash flow repayment dynamics than those observed with physical securities.

It is worth emphasizing, absent of the building or *structuring* challenges faced on the SCDO's liability side, all other basic CDO building principles apply. An SCDO, like a traditional CDO, also engages service providers to administer its operational, compliance, and management requirements. Relative to our traditional CDO, however, we are charged with identifying an asset manager that has a combined capability; it is not sufficient to have credit selection, surveillance and trading skills in the underlying reference asset alone. In fact, an SCDO warrants a trading capability in the asset class in credit derivative form as well. Although linked, the two markets—cash versus derivative—will interact differently around certain technical factors warranting cross-market knowledge. In practice, it is difficult to source this combined capability; in part, it is a function of the market's maturity. There are many participants who are skilled in using credit derivatives for hedging purposes (i.e., buying *insurance* on an asset once it has fallen out of favour as an alternative to *selling*), but very few can in fact trade the instrument for value and generate *alpha*. Coming back to our CDO basic building-block analogy, the SCDO will also seek a credit opinion from the rating agencies, provide risk/return customisation through credit tranching, as well as facilitate investor idiosyncratic needs through repackaging. It is the SCDO's liability structure where the similarities fade.

Building a Synthetic CDO's Liability Structure

In order to best understand the appropriate CDO liability structure, one should draw comparison of an SCDO to a *mini-insurance company* (or *mini-inco*). This should not be surprising given the fact that we have already established that a credit derivative is similar in nature to credit insurance. Conceptually, an SCDO's primary purpose is to *write* credit insurance to the financial marketplace, albeit in a much more standard, tradable, and hence, liquid form. Like a *mini-inco* then, an SCDO's liability strategy should not contemplate raising capital to fund or secure 100% of its credit insurance commitments. Specifically, as a seller of protection to the market, an SCDO's needs for cash (amounts and timing) are contingent upon the cumulative number of credit events that can be expected on its designated reference portfolio. In other words, an SCDO must be sufficiently liquid to either fund physical delivery of the underlying asset or cash settle the contract as credit events arise. In fact, as part of its credit assessment, an SCDO's *regulator* (i.e., credit rating agencies) will stress the claims-related liquidity needs of the vehicle under various rates and patterns of credit events. In broader terms, any third party—bank, insurance company, dealer)—that accepts protection from the SCDO will also evaluate its claims paying ability based on its *funded* collateralisation. In other words, the SCDO's counterparty value as a protection seller will depend on the overall quality of the portfolio protection written relative to the total capital (debt and equity) raised to support its performance.

It is worth noting that the capital raised in SCDO is, in some instances, itself an *unfunded* commitment. Meaning, as an alternative to investing in an SCDO note (i.e., raising cash upfront for the vehicle), an investor can *write* protection to the structure in the form of a *portfolio swap*. These swaps are structured to reproduce the same risks and ratings that are offered in funded or note form. For example, the credit risk embedded in an A rated note with a notional of 4% and subordinated equity of 5% can be replicated as a portfolio swap that has a *risk layer* of 4% attaching to the reference portfolio at 5%. As observed in the single-asset credit derivative market, comparative advantage opportunities can also arise between portfolio swap and note investors depending on their cost of funds and their own credit quality, that is the vehicle is taking counterparty credit risk to the investor under the swap format. In the extreme, the entire capital structure can be synthetically sourced. Under those circumstances, the value of the SCDO's claims-paying ability is exclusively dependent on the credit quality of the synthetic investors. Consequently, the value of an investor portfolio swap relative to a funded note (or *cash*) will depend on the credit rating of the investor as well as where in the capital structure the investor is attached. In other words, the *cash value* of a portfolio swap will reflect the joint probability that (1) the investor's risk layer gets called because portfolio credit events have been severe enough to *call* on the investor's protection; and (2) that the investor is still in existence—not in default—to honour the protection payment due at such time.

In practice, an SCDO vehicle will utilize both forms of liability: note and swap. Swaps are typically used higher up in the capital structure reflecting the lower risk and, therefore, reduced dependency upon the counterparty, while notes or cash are secured upfront for the riskier portions of the vehicle's risk layers (e.g., BBB–BB mezzanine debt or equity). Another reason why swaps are used at the higher end of the capital structure is that they facilitate efficient risk-adjusted pricing. If we assume the top 80% of a portfolio is tranched and rated AAA (the highest possible rating), as a note or cash investor there is no way to distinguish the difference between the first unit of loss on the tranche from the last. (The last 1% of loss on a portfolio is virtually risk free.) Given there is no real concept of AAA+++ rated risk, the investor accepts the average risk/return available across the tranche; in effect, the vehicle is underpaying for the first unit of loss embedded in the AAA tranche and forced to overpay for the last unit of protection. Portfolio swaps can be used by investors to further tranche the blended AAA into its true risk components affording more exact risk-based pricing. For instance, a blended AAA tranche might pay 50 bps across its entire notional, while an isolated top 20% tranche may warrant only 3 bps and the bottom 20% perhaps 100 bps (evidencing its increased leverage).

For illustrative purposes, refer to Exhibit 30.4. This diagram demonstrates the conceptual differences of an SCDO *versus* a cash flow-based CDO under our *mini-inco* and *minibank* model, respectively. Following this framework, the traditional CDO necessarily issues funded liabilities in order to raise cash from the market such that the target portfolio can be purchased (i.e., acquire the physical securities). As the underlying physical assets mature or repay, the cash received is then used to retire the liabilities outstanding. Conversely, the SCDO issues liabilities in an amount less than its total insured amount—the notional amount of credit protection written—yet sufficient enough to satisfy the requirements of the rating agencies and vehicle's protection buyers. In this case, the top 90–80% may not need to be hedged by either a note or swap; in fact, it may be a *naked* exposure that the vehicle's protection buyers are willing to accept. (The probability of actually exceeding 10–20% losses in our example is low.) Again, the SCDO's contingent claims-paying ability will depend on the robustness of its capital base relative to unanticipated increases in historical loss expectations. It is worth highlighting, the *naked* exposure an SCDO may be permitted to run is a significant driver of value for an equity investor in terms of the cost of leverage he or she is realizing, which is almost free.

EXHIBIT 30.4 Comparing Cash and Synthetic CDOs in Terms of Risk Intermediation

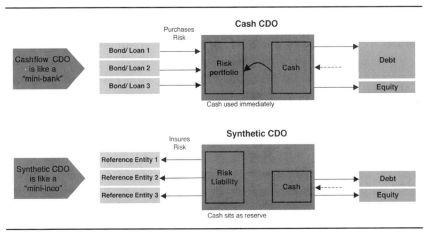

Variations on the Synthetic CDO Theme

We have identified that an SCDO's liability structure can adopt two forms: note and/or swap (i.e., cash and/or synthetic risk transfer). Along the same lines, the collateral securing an SCDO can also include cash instrument. As already indicated, an SCDO typically raises cash in order to manage its own credit quality as protection writer; hence, there is no reason why that cash cannot be deployed into physical securities. This makes possible *hybrid* cash/synthetic structures where the asset side of the CDO's balance sheet is mixed across bonds and credit derivatives and the liability side is mixed between note and swap issuance. Of course, a significant aspect of designing this type of CDO rests on building an appropriately matched asset/liability architecture. By construction, these types of CDOs are designed to exploit fully the anomalies that exist between the cash and derivative market for credit, or *basis* trading, as well as the comparative funding advantages that exist among end credit risk takers.

One unique value proposition afforded by credit derivatives that we have not highlighted yet is the ability that they give an asset manager to *short* individual credits. Prior to credit derivatives, short selling as means of generating trading value was, in practice, not executable on illiquid credits given the difficulty that can arise in sourcing the bonds in order to cover. The ability to use cash settlement with credit derivatives has helped to overcome this problem. Consequently, some CDOs have the faculty to use some of their net margin (i.e., net asset yield after liabilities and expenses) to short individual credits as a means to hedge existing bond positions or make *naked* directional bets on a particular credit. CDO vehicles that employ long/short capabilities can be viewed as *minihedge funds* (rounding out and completing our various financial institution analogies: bank, inco, and hedge fund). Under the *minihedge fund* model, an asset manager with the appropriate skills has significant ability to create trading value for the SCDO's equity investors.

CDOS: VARIATIONS AND MORE DETAILS

As already discussed, collateralised debt obligations are a form of security whose interest and principal payments are linked to the performance of a specific pool of assets (sourced either directly or by reference). These underlying assets act as the *collateral* for the issued notes, hence the name. In terms of basic principals, there are many similarities between CDOs and their predecessors: asset-backed securities (ABS) (see Exhibit 30.5). The major difference between CDOs and other ABS securities is

EXHIBIT 30.5   CDOs as ABS Products

The mechanics involved in structuring a cash flow CDO are similar in many respects to more traditional ABS securities. The following areas of commonality have been identified by Satyajit Das:

- The originator of the transaction establishes a bankruptcy-remote legal entity known as a special purpose vehicle (SPV) that is the formal issuer of the notes.
- It is the SPV that formally purchases the assets and their associated cash flows from the originator, thus taking the assets off the latter's balance sheet.
- Funds used to purchase the assets are raised through the issue of bonds into the debt capital market, which may be in more than one *tranche* and include an equity piece that is usually retained by the originator.
- Tranched securities are generally rated by a rating agency, with the rating reflecting both the credit quality of the underlying assets as well as any measures put in place to reduce credit risk, known as *credit enhancement*.
- Investors purchasing the issued notes can expect to receive interest and principal payments as long as the underlying asset pool does not experience default to any significant extent.

Source: Satyajit Das, *Structured Products and Hybrid Securities* (Singapore: John Wiley and Sons, 2001).

that the collateral pool (or reference risk) is principally sourced from the marketplace and managed by an independent asset manager. Like ABS, CDOs feature a multitranche, sequential-pay note reimbursement structure, with most of the notes being rated by one or more of the public credit ratings agencies. The payment priority of the issued securities is commensurate with the credit rating for each note, with the most senior note being the highest rated. The term *waterfall* is used to refer to the order in which cash flow receipts are applied.

In most cases, a CDO's debt securities offer investors a floating-rate coupon indexed to LIBOR (payable on a semiannual, quarterly or monthly basis) with a broad range of credit qualities (where the senior notes are rated from AAA to A and the junior/mezzanine notes are rated BBB to B). Investors are attracted to the senior notes of a CDO because they allow them to earn relatively higher yields when compared to other similarly rated securities. (Much of the pickup is a function of their complexity and relative illiquidity.) Other advantages for investors include: exposure to a diversified range of unique credits (often credits that are not easily accessible in public markets); access to the origination, fund management, and credit analysis skills of the portfolio manager; as well as risk/return customisation afforded through credit tranching and repackaging.

In addition to debt, there may be unrated subordinated—or *equity*—interests issued. Although the equity interest in a CDO is structured like a bond, it does represent the residual interest in the CDO vehicle; its return is variable and linked to the residual value of the collateral pool after all debt liabilities have been extinguished. Given that the equity resides in the first loss position, it carries the greatest risk and warrants the highest return—and represents a leveraged exposure to the asset class. More is offered on CDO equity later in this chapter.

CDOs can be broken down into two main categories: *balance sheet* CDOs and *arbitrage* CDOs. Balance sheet CDOs are most akin to a traditional securitisation. They are designed to remove assets from a sponsor's balance sheet (usually a bank) in order to diversify funding sources, manage credit risk and improve regulatory capital efficiency. An arbitrage CDO is created when the sponsor, who may be a bank or as asset manager, in conjunction with the investors wishes to exploit a margin differential that can materialize between the underlying asset yields and a CDO's cost of financing/debt. This differential can be enhanced by active management of the underlying portfolio. Arbitrage CDOs are bifurcated further into *cash flow* and *market value* CDOs. Almost invariably, balance sheet CDOs utilize cash-flow-based technology. As mentioned earlier in the chapter, a cash-flow-based CDO is one where the underlying collateral is expected to generate sufficient cash flow to repay the principal and interest on the notes. In a market value CDO, the collateral manager actively manages the portfolio and, by means of this trading activity, is expected to generate sufficient returns (i.e., increase its value) to repay the CDO obligations. The underlying securities are marked-to-market on a daily basis in a manner similar to a trading book.

Variations on the CDO Theme

As discussed, CDOs are generally categorised as either *balance sheet* CDOs or *arbitrage* CDOs depending on their intended purpose. In terms of operating mechanics, balance sheet CDOs are almost exclusively cash-flow-based; while, arbitrage CDOs are structured either as cash-flow-based or market-value-based. A later development, *synthetic* CDOs, now account for a growing number of transactions.

Balance Sheet CDOs

As stated, balance sheet CDOs are almost exclusively cash-flow-based, and on that basis, cash flow CDOs are similar in nature to other asset-backed securitisations involving a special purpose vehicle (SPV). Like asset backed securities, assets are pooled together in order to collateralise the liabilities of the SPV. As the underlying assets are sold to the

EXHIBIT 30.6 Generic Cash Flow CDO

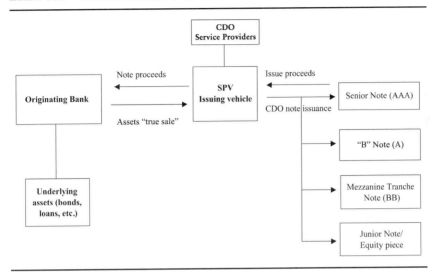

SPV, they are removed from the originator's balance sheet; hence, the credit risk associated with these assets is transferred to the holders of the issued notes. The originator also obtains funding by issuing the notes. The generic structure is illustrated with Exhibit 30.6.

Banks and other financial institutions are the primary originators of balance sheet CDOs. Sponsors/originators utilize balance sheet CDOs as a means to pool, repackage, and redistribute their wholesale assets. Historically, the predominate banking assets underlying these securitisations have been commercial loans in the investment grade or subinvestment grade rating categories, hence the nomenclature: CLOs. The main motivations for banks as sponsors of these types of transactions are credit risk management, capital efficiency, and alternative funding capacity.

Investors are often attracted to balance sheet CDOs because they provide investors with a higher return relative to more traditional ABS when compared on a rating equivalency basis, that is, the incremental spread is attributable to the fact that CDOs tend to be less liquid and more complex. Investors also see value in the diversification they offer when included as part of a broader, more traditional structured finance portfolio. For reference, a typical bank balance sheet CLO has the following capital structure characteristics:

- Senior note, AAA rated, and 90–95% of the issue.
- Subordinated note, A rated, 3–5%.

■ Mezzanine note, BBB rated, 1–3%.
■ Equity note, nonrated, 1–2%.

Like ABS, the cash flows realised on the underlying assets are the primary source of funds used to extinguish the CDO's liabilities. These realised collections are applied to each class of notes pursuant to a *priority of payments* that is commensurate with the rating seniority. Pursuant to this payment *waterfall*, the most senior payment obligation must be satisfied in full before the next payment can be addressed, this continues sequentially until the most junior liability is discharged. For the avoidance of doubt, if there are insufficient funds available, the payment obligations of the most junior liabilities will be suspended and payable in the future to the extent subsequent collections become available.

The waterfall process for interest payments is shown at Exhibit 30.7. Before paying the next priority of the waterfall, the vehicle must pass a number of compliance tests designed to measure the overall robustness of cash flow being generated by the collateral portfolio. These metrics include tests such as interest coverage and principal (par) coverage, which is similar in concept to bank loan covenants and explained more fully later.

During the life of a CDO, a portfolio administrator is obliged to produce a periodic report detailing the quality of the collateral pool. This report is known as an Investor (or *Trustee*) Report. This report details the results of the compliance tests and is used by the rating agencies, the CDO's regulator, to monitor the CDO's performance relative to its currently assigned rating.

Arbitrage CDOs

Arbitrage CDOs employ two types of operating models: cash flow and market value. Arbitrage CDOs differ from balance sheet CDOs by virtue of the fact that the assets are generally sourced from third parties or the marketplace. As the name suggests, they are utilized for the sole purpose of taking advantage of *market opportunities* as defined previously that arise between asset yields and the cost of CDO financing the assets (the cost of leverage).

The appropriateness of either model (cash-flow-based *versus* market-value-based) will depend on the asset manager's trading style as well as the particulars of the asset class: the asset's market liquidity, duration profile, and credit spread volatility. In terms of mechanics, *cash flow arbitrage* CDOs are no different than balance sheet CDOs—again, the only difference being their intended purpose and asset sourcing strategy. Consequently, one should see the section on "Balance Sheet CDOs" for further details. Now, we shift the discussion to *market value* CDOs.

EXHIBIT 30.7 Interest Cash Flow Waterfall for Cash-Flow-Based CDO

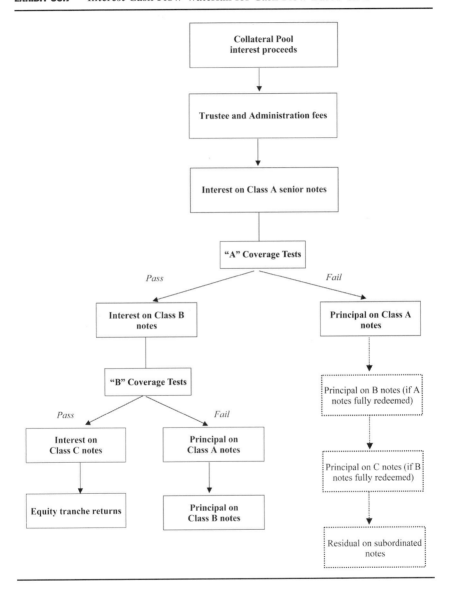

Market Value CDOs

The sponsors of market value CDOs are predominantly asset managers in partnership with investors. By construction, these transactions provide the asset manager with much more freedom to actively trade assets in and out of the collateral portfolio, as well as less restrictive asset eligibility criteria overall. This flexibility, in turn, requires that the assets are marked-to-market by the portfolio administrator on a regular basis (possibly as frequently as daily) in order to ensure the value of the portfolio is at least greater than the CDO liabilities outstanding. Investors are attracted by these types of structures based on a asset manager's trading credentials as well as the trading flexibility the structure provides to better manage losses when the market is experiencing a correction.

Market value transactions aggressively use *ramp-up* periods to acquire assets when accumulating the collateral pool. There is typically a liquidity facility, which is in place prior to the closing of the transaction, to help bridge the acquisition of assets. The principal repayment of liabilities are extinguished when the underlying assets are sold (traded) out of the portfolio, rather than when they mature.

Synthetic CDOs

Synthetic CDO's are a subclass of CDOs where the underlying collateral represents a portfolio of credit derivatives. Compared with conventional balance sheet CDOs, which feature an actual transfer of ownership or *true sale* of the underlying assets to a separately incorporated legal entity, *balance sheet synthetic* CDOs are engineered so that the credit risks of the assets are transferred from the sponsor to the CDO by means of a portfolio credit swap. Therefore, the sponsor is a credit protection buyer, and the CDO is a credit protection seller. In some cases, the credit risk may be transferred to investors directly without an intermittent SPV, that is, the investor becomes the credit protection seller in stead of the SPV. By using synthetic risk transfer, the underlying (*reference*) assets are not removed from the sponsor's balance sheet. This technology is employed whenever the primary objective is to achieve risk transfer rather than balance sheet funding.

There are two types of CDO liability structures utilized in synthetic transactions: completely *unfunded* structures that use portfolio swaps exclusively to transfer the entire credit risk of the reference portfolio to investors and *partially funded* structures which transfer only the highest credit risk segment of the portfolio.

The first synthetic deals were observed in the US market, while the first deals in Europe were observed in 1998. Market growth in Europe has been rapid; the total value of cash and synthetic deals in Europe in

2002 approached $120 billion, and a growing share of this total has been synthetic-based transactions.

The first European synthetic transactions were driven by bank originators with the underlying reference assets being commercial loans on the originator's balance sheet. *Arbitrage synthetic* CDOs have also been sponsored. Within the synthetic market, arbitrage-based transaction were the most frequently issued during 2001.

Arbitrage synthetic CDOs are originated generally by asset managers focusing on increasing their fee income and by investors who wish to exploit the difference between the underlying asset yield and financing cost payable on the CDOs. These structures source their credit risk from the market via single-name credit derivatives or from a third party's balance sheet warehousing (or *financing*) the assets and the risk is transferred subsequently to the SPV using a portfolio specific credit derivative. The second technique is used when certain assets such as ABS are not available in credit derivative form.

Credit Enhancement and Compliance Testing

Common to all the CDO themes are the use of various forms of credit enhancement. In addition to the natural credit enhancement afford through subordination of sequential pay notes, the following methods are also employed:

- *Overcollateralisation.* Protection created by the contribution of excess collateral above and beyond the face value of notes; for example, $250 million nominal of assets are contributed to secure $170 of CDO liabilities.
- *Cash reserve accounts.* Protection in the form of cash providing periodic liquidity and loss reimbursement; the funds can be sourced from the transaction's initial proceeds, and if drawn, replenished overtime with excess spread in order to maintain its requisite balance.
- *Excess spread.* Protection afforded intraperiod by the availability of excess interest income on the portfolio after discharging all service provider and interest expenses payable for the period.
- *Insurance wraps.* Protection provided by third parties in the form of a insurance policy guarantying the ultimate repayment of the notes pursuant to their stated terms.

As a matter of CDO surveillance, the quality of a CDO's collateral portfolio is monitored regularly and reported on by the portfolio administrator by way of a *trustee report*. This report details the results of various *compliance tests*, which are performed on an asset-by-asset level as well as on an aggregate portfolio level. Compliance tests are designed to monitor:

■ *Weighted average spread and weighted average rating.* Measures the average interest spread and average credit rating of the assets (i.e., portfolio income and credit quality), which must remain at a specified minimum.

■ *Concentration.* Establishes a set maximum share of assets that can be exposed to any particular asset class, single obligor, industry sector, and so on.

■ *Diversity score.* A statistical value that is calculated via a formula developed by the rating agencies and designed to measure the level of diversity in the asset portfolio, thus minimizing pairwise correlation in terms of each asset's probability of default.

These tests are calculated on a regular basis as well as each time the composition of the portfolio is altered, that is, each time assets are sold, purchased, or paid off ahead of their legal maturity date. If the test results fall below the required minimum, trading activity is restricted to only those trades that will improve the test results. Certain other compliance tests are viewed as more critical in terms of maintaining note repayment integrity; therefore, if any of them are *failed*, the cash flows will be diverted from the normal priority of payments and begin sequentially paying off the notes based on seniority until the test results improve. These include:

■ *Overcollateralisation.* The overcollateralisation level vis-à-vis the issued notes must remain above a specified minimum; for instance, it must be at 120% of the nominal value of the senior note.

■ *Interest coverage.* The level of net interest income on the portfolio (i.e., after defaults) must be sufficient to cover interest due on the liabilities.

Compliance tests are specified as part of the CDO's credit-rating process. The ratings analysis is comprehensive and focuses on the asset type/quality, liability/capital structure, as well as the sponsor's performance track record and reputation.

Analysing the Risks in a CDO's Underlying Portfolio

The risk analysis for CDOs performed by potential investors is necessarily different to that undertaken for other securitised asset classes. For CDOs, the three main factors to consider are default probabilities, default correlations and recovery rates. Analysts make assumptions about each of these with regard to individual reference assets, usually with recourse to historical data. We introduce each factor in turn.

Default Probabilities

The level of default probability will vary with each transaction depending on the underlying asset class. Analysts such as the rating agencies will use a number of methods to estimate default probabilities, such as individual reference credit ratings and historical probability rates. Assuming a statistically significant number of assets, a common approach is to use the average rating of the underlying or reference portfolio.

Correlation

The correlation between assets in a specified portfolio is an important aspect in CDO risk analysis. Challenges exist in terms of determining what precise correlation values to use; these can be correlation between default probabilities, correlation between timing of default, and correlation between spreads. The *diversity score* value of a portfolio attempts to measure and encapsulate these concepts by way of simplification. The higher the score, presumably the less correlated the default likelihood of each asset becomes.

Recovery Rates

Recovery rates for individual obligors differ by issuer and industry classification. Rating agencies publish data on the average prices of all defaulted bonds, and generally analysts will construct a database of recovery rates by industry and credit rating for use in modelling the expected recovery rates of assets in the collateral portfolio.

By using the aforementioned variables, analysts undertake simulation modelling to generate scenarios of portfolio return. For instance, they may model the number of defaults up to maturity, the recovery rates of these defaults and the timing of defaults. All these variables are viewed as random variables, so they are modelled using a stochastic process.

CDO Equity

Equity is the most junior note in the capital structure of a CDO. For this reason it is also known as the *first-loss* piece of the CDO, carrying the highest risk of payment delays and losses due to credit events or defaults. The equity, which actually takes the legal form of a debt instrument, receives all residual portfolio cash flows after all other liabilities and claims have been paid. In a cash flow structure, the return to the equity holder will be a function of defaults and payment delays of assets in the collateral portfolio; the level of trading or credit rating downgrades do not have an impact on the equity unless they affect the expected cash flows. Although the equity piece receives all residual cash flows generated by the structure, there is a distinction between coupon cash flows and principal cash flows. The residual coupon is paid out as it is received, while the residual principal cash flows are not paid out until all the outstanding notes have been extinguished.

Given all this, we see that CDO equity is a *leveraged* exposure to credit risk, taken on by the equity investor. The holder of CDO equity takes a view that the cash flows generated by the underlying assets are sufficient to bear expected credit losses and provide enough surplus to pay sufficient return on the equity given its risk. This risk/return assessment must take into account the amount of leverage being taken in the structure.

The timing, as well as extent, of defaults is critical to equity return. As a general matter, equity holders receive a significant part of their return early in the life of a transaction. This is because the initial excess spread tends to be highest given that defaults are unlikely to occur until later on in the deal's life. The later in a CDO's life that defaults occur, the less the return to the equity holder will be affected. Examples of equity returns patterns and their sensitivity to default will be demonstrated later in case studies.

CDO equity is not a straightforward instrument and must be assessed carefully by investors due to their complexity and limited liquidity. The asset manager, the quality of the collateral pool and the amount of leverage are very important issues for consideration. In addition, potential investors must consider how the equity investment fits with his or her broader portfolio.

CASE STUDIES

In this section we will attempt to complement the theory and approaches discussed so far with actual transaction examples. Specifically, we will highlight Euro Zing I CDO as a further example of the flexibilities a CDO's liability structure can adopt. Equally, we will explore the use of indexation in CDO structures with the Rosetta CBO I transaction. And finally, Robeco CSO III will be examined as the first fully managed, standalone CDO backed by credit derivatives.

Euro Zing I CDO

Euro Zing I is a cash flow CDO that presents several features of novelty and interest. It is the first true arbitrage CDO of European asset-backed securities in that, 100% of the assets were sourced from the marketplace rather than an existing balance sheet. It is also the first CDO to use a unique, innovative dual-currency liability structure in sterling and euro to access the sterling ABS market in a cost-efficient way as opposed to currency swapping each asset individually to a common currency.

EXHIBIT 30.8   Euro Zing I CBO Structure

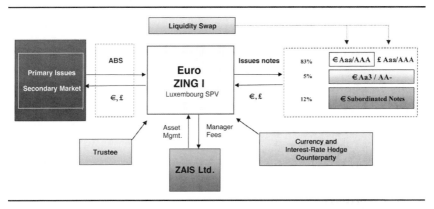

EXHIBIT 30.9   Euro Zing I CBO Tranching

Tranche	Structure	Currency	Sub-ordina-tion	Moody's/ S&P Rating	Spread	Coupon Frequency	WAL/ Maturity
Class A-1	60%	€	29%	Aaa/AAA	E + 50	6 months	8.0/38 yrs
Class A-2[a]	23%	£	17%	Aaa/AAA	L + 55	6 months	8.0/38 yrs
Class B	5%	€	12%	Aa3/AA–[b]	E + 90	6 months	9.5/38 yrs
Sub. Notes	12%	€	N/A	BBB–[c]			NA/38 yrs

[a] Delayed draw-down note.
[b] Fitch rating.
[c] Principal only (Fitch rating).

The originator of Euro Zing I CDO is Zais plc. The transaction structure diagram is shown at Exhibit 30.8. The overlying note tranching is shown at Exhibit 30.9.

Investor interest in this deal was spurred by a variety of factors:

- *Defensive asset class.* European ABS securities benefit from embedded structural subordination and credit enhancements, with excellent credit performance and stability in ratings despite a market environment that was volatile at the time of marketing the issue such that a variety of investors sought access to this specialty asset class.
- *Portfolio quality and inherent diversification.* The portfolio of European ABS represents credit exposure to different consumer and corporate sectors, across multiple countries and multiple asset managers/servicers. The portfolio on closing had an average rating of Baa2/BBB.

■ *Conservative structure*. The use of prudent leverage (only 8-times leveraged) and the stability of the asset class allow the subordinated notes to receive an investment-grade rating (BBB– by Fitch). The reduced leverage affords the asset manager greater flexibility to manage the portfolio over time.

Transaction Terms

Name:	Euro Zing CBO I S.A.
Manager:	Zais Group Investment Ltd.
Arranger:	JPMorgan Securities Ltd.
Closing date:	23 August 2002
Legal Maturity:	23 August 2040
Size:	€300 million
Number of Issuers:	70
Portfolio Administrator:	JPMorgan Chase Bank Institutional Trust Services

The expected returns of the subordinated notes are shown at Exhibit 30.10, under specified assumptions.

EXHIBIT 30.10   Euro Zing I CBO Returns

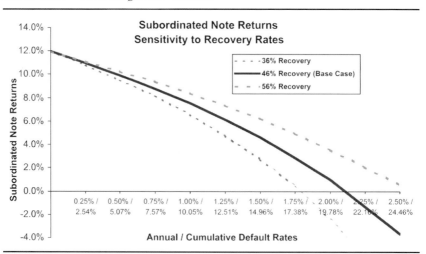

Note: No assurance can be given with respect to the returns. The assumptions underlying the return analysis illustrated above are unlikely to be consistent with actual experience.

EXHIBIT 30.11   Rosetta I CBO Structure

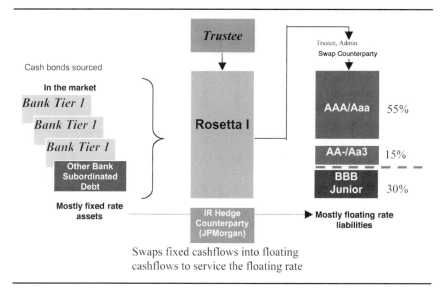

Case Study: Rosetta CBO I

Rosetta CBO I is the first leveraged credit transaction based on an index of European financial institutions subordinated debt[1] (specifically, JPMorgan's SUSI index[2]). Indexation was the asset selection tool of choice as investors were unwilling to pay an asset manager due to quality and stability of the underlying but wanted to ensure a nonbiased selection of the underlying portfolio. Rosetta I's key structural innovation was to transform a portfolio of predominantly perpetual debt into a leveraged instrument with a fixed 10-year maturity. In the case of Rosetta I, assets that extend beyond their call date will generally be sold through an auction procedure. While the first transaction was based on a static portfolio of cash bonds, next generation products are being developed using credit derivatives on subordinated debt as a means to source the risk and are likely to include some substitutability.

The transaction structure is shown at Exhibit 30.11, and overlying note tranching at Exhibit 30.12.

[1] Deeply subordinated exposures at the Tier 1 and Upper Tier 2 level.

[2] JPMorgan's SUSI index focuses on the largest (issues size >= €400 million) and most liquid issuances in the European subordinated debt market. The SUSI subindices cover Bank Lower Tier II, Banker Upper Tier II, Bank Tier I, Insurance Subordinated as well as Landesbanks Lower Tier II and Tier I. With the exception of the Landesbanks subindices, all SUSI indices are available in € and £. The composition of each index is revisited every six months.

EXHIBIT 30.12   Rosetta I CBO Tranching

	Notional	Percent	S&P/Moody's Rating	Spread	WAL	Legal Final
Class A	€220,000,000	55%	AAA/Aaa	45 bp	8 yrs	11 yrs
Class B	€60,000,000	15%	AA–/Aa3	80 bp	10 yrs	11 yrs
Junior	€120,000,000	30%	BBB/Baa2		NA	11 yrs
Total		100%				

Investor interest was spurred by a variety of factors:

■ *Asset class*. Focus on European subordinated debt because of the yield pickup for what is perceived as little incremental risk compared to senior debt.
■ *Portfolio diversification*. Immediate access to most of Europe's highly rated financial institutions; static nature of the portfolio-allowed investors to conduct a name-by-name review.
■ *Structure*. The introduction of moderate leverage allowed junior notes (only 3-times leveraged) to receive enhanced returns while still achieving an investment-grade rating (BBB by S&P; Baa2 by Moody's).

Transaction Terms:

Name: Rosetta CBO I S.A.
Manager: N/A, based on JPMorgan's SUSI index
Arrangers: JPMorgan Securities Ltd.
Closing date: 28 October 2002
Maturity: 28 October 2012
Size: €153.5 million
Number of Issuers: 27
Number of Issues: 37
Portfolio Administrator: JPMorgan Chase Bank Institutional Trust Services
Auction Administrator: JPMorgan Chase Bank Institutional Trust Services

The expected return of the junior note (the shaded piece in Exhibit 30.12) is shown at Exhibit 30.13 as a spread over LIBOR.

EXHIBIT 30.13   Rosetta I CBO Returns

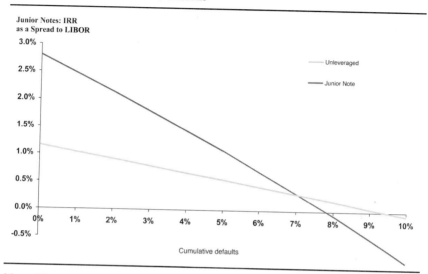

Note: No assurance can be given with respect to the returns. The assumptions underlying the return analysis illustrated above are unlikely to be consistent with actual experience.

Case Study: Robeco CSO III B.V.

Robeco CSO III was the first standalone, managed synthetic CDO and closed in December 2001. Its structure has since been replicated by a number of fund managers and arrangers. The transaction is in the form of a risk intermediation vehicle that transfers exposure to a portfolio of corporate US and European credits from the credit derivatives dealer market into the cash investors market through rated, tradeable cash instruments. Robeco III CSO is innovative in the sense that it brings together for the first time structural and asset management features from the traditional CDO market with risk transfer technology from the credit derivatives market. The transaction has not created a new asset class in its own right. It is still based on the application of portfolio diversification theory to create different layers of risk from a pool of credit risk as any other form of CDO. However, the utilisation of credit derivatives technology has impacted the industry with a few fundamental evolutions:

■ *Impacts on the credit derivative market.* Introduction of a new type of risk counterparty in the credit derivatives market that has the capacity to sell protection on large portfolios of risk, increasing the capacity and the efficiency of the credit derivatives market. Along the same lines, it has helped intermediate credit risk away from the bank market into a new investor base, making it an efficient risk spreading tool for credit risk.

■ *Impacts on the asset manager community.* Expanded access to credit risk through the utilisation of CDS, rather than the multiple forms of cash instruments available. The asset manager benefits from a broader universe of credits to choose from given that the credit derivatives market has the largest number of different credit entities available. Consequently, the asset manager's ability to perform is enhanced; the scope of credits and their liquidity provide more ability to extract value through trading rather than by up-front credit selection alone. As a general matter, these type of programs offer a new asset management model, as synthetic CDOs allow for rapid and efficient asset accumulation over a short period of time as well as a new flexibility entirely: the ability to short credits (i.e., buying protection on reference names).

Investor interest was spurred by a variety of factors:

■ *Access to CDS market dynamics.* The CDS market provides the structure with liquidity and exposures which are not available in either the loan or the bond market, across a diversity of currencies and maturities.

■ *Managed transaction.* In case some of the credit quality of some of the exposures in the portfolio change, the manager is able to trade in and out of the exposure.

■ *Cheap leverage.* The structure benefits from cheap leverage as it issues only a portion of the CDS portfolio under a funded cash format. The leverage is provided by the CDS counterparties.

■ *Portfolio quality and diversification.* The portfolio of CDS represents exposure to a pool of 100 different corporate and financial entities representing over 20 industries across multiple countries. The exposures are principally investment grade, which offers a diversification from cash CDO portfolios.

The structure diagram is shown at Exhibit 30.14. The note tranching is shown at Exhibit 30.15, while the expected return of the subordinated notes is shown at Exhibit 30.16.

Transaction Terms

Name:	ROBECO CSO III BV
Manager:	Robeco AM

Arrangers:	JPMorgan Securities Ltd.
Closing date:	7 December 2001
Maturity:	17 September 2008
Credit Portfolio Size:	€1,000,000,000
Notes Issued:	€300,000,000
Number Reference Entities:	100
Portfolio Administrator:	JPMorgan Chase Bank Institutional Trust Services

EXHIBIT 30.14   Robeco CSO III Structure

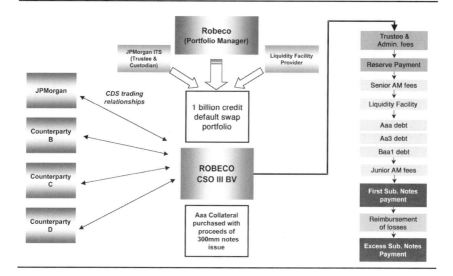

EXHIBIT 30.15   Robeco CSO III Tranching

Tranche	Moody's Rating	Tranche Size ($ million)	Available Subordination (%)	Spread	Final Maturity
A	Aaa	213.0	8.70	55 bp	7 yrs
B	Aa3	15.5	7.15	85 bp	7 yrs
C	Baa1	31.5	4.00	275 bp	7 yrs
Sub	NR	40.0	0.00	NA	7 yrs
P[a]	Baa1[b]	7.5	NA	NA	7 yrs
Total		300			

[a] Combination note.
[b] Principal rating only.

EXHIBIT 30.16 Robeco CSO III Returns

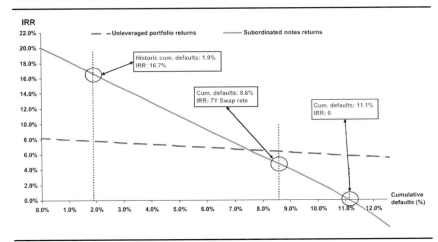

Note: No assurance can be given with respect to the returns. The assumptions underlying the return analysis illustrated above are unlikely to be consistent with actual experience.

CHAPTER 31

Single-Tranche Synthetic CDOs

Barnaby Martin
Assistant Vice President
Credit Strategist
Merrill Lynch

Alexander Batchvarov, Ph.D., CFA
Managing Director and Head
International Structured Credit Research
Merrill Lynch

Atish Kakodkar
Vice President
Credit Derivatives Strategist
Merrill Lynch

Single-tranche synthetic CDOs, although in existence for a while, are only now rapidly becoming a hot product in the credit markets. In this chapter we provide a guide to the product basics, mechanics, valuation and risk factors.

We, Barnaby Martin, Alexander Batchvarov, and Atish Kakodkar, hereby certify that the views each of us has expressed in this chapter accurately reflect our respective personal views about the subject securities and issuers. We also certify that no part of our respective compensation was, is, or will be, directly or indirectly, related to the specific recommendations or views expressed in this chapter.

WHY INVEST IN SINGLE-TRANCHE SYNTHETIC CDOS?

With sources of value in the credit markets rapidly disappearing as yields are chased, investors are faced with a conundrum of generating yield and return targets whilst maintaining an acceptable level of credit risk. One way of boosting yields and beating yield hurdles might involve moving down the credit curve and investing in higher beta (β) crossover credits and other "outliers." While this strategy may appeal to actively managed investors, such strategies may be too risky for those not wishing to hold highly volatile portfolios. The distribution of credit spreads is now more concentrated and credit, on the face of it, trades much more like a 'homogenous' asset class than bottom-up fundamentals would suggest. Should volatility rear its ugly head again, the relative richness of some BBB sectors of the credit market may prove just the catalyst for some sharp spread widening and volatility in excess returns.

What alternative strategies can credit investors employ in the current environment to boost return? One potential answer to this credit conundrum may be to assume structural complexity rather than moving aggressively down the credit curve. By focussing on a portfolio of core credits that have been carefully screened and selected by the investor, and tailoring the required risk and reward profile, these products can offer a significant yield pickup whilst maintaining investment grade ratings. It is in this context that we view the latest entrant into the credit markets—the bilateral single-tranche synthetic CDO.

Problems with Multitranche CDOs

The developments in the corporate bond sector have made their indelible impact on the multitranched CDO sector—in many respects the CDO sector should be viewed as "derived" from the corporate sector. As a result, investing in fully-tranched CDOs presents some challenges.

Firstly, the composition of the CDO markets has evolved to reflect the realities of the corporate bond market and investor preferences. With the tightening of corporate credit spreads throughout the course of 2003, many types of multiple-tranche ("full-blown") CDO transactions on high-grade names are not economically feasible as of this writing. As can be seen in Exhibit 31.1, the funding gap (excess spread) has shrunk to a degree where generally economically viable CDOs are now only those based on ABS, leveraged loan and high-yield collateral. Due to investor preference, CDOs of ABS and CLOs of leverage loans have accounted for the biggest chunk of CDO issuance in 2003, while CDOs of high-yield bonds have barely been seen.

EXHIBIT 31.1 European Collateral CDO-Funding Gap Based on Fully Tranched CDO

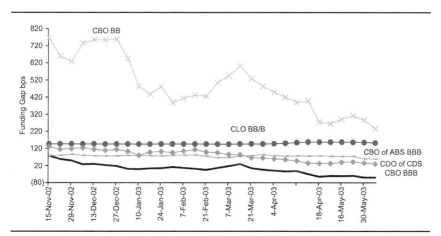

Source: Merrill Lynch.

Secondly, investors at different levels of the capital structure have different, often conflicting interests—particularly in the motivations of debt versus equity investors. While structural and other enhancements have been put in place in more recent transactions to mitigate such interests, these solutions are far from perfect.

Thirdly, while opportunities in the CDO primary market for investors seeking exposure to corporate credit pools may have diminished, they seem to be more readily available on the secondary market. But, analysing secondary market deals is often perceived to be more complex than analysing newly issued deals, and some of them may have the "smell" of being "distressed," which is often a no-go zone for many investors, despite the opportunities they may offer.

Reasons for Popularity of Single-Tranche Synthetic CDOs

The single-tranche synthetic CDO is gaining widespread appeal not only within the traditional CDO investment community but also from credit investors who have traditionally focussed only on straight bond investments. The single-tranche variation is a particularly rapidly growing subset of the synthetic CDO. Some of the factors behind the growth of this product are:

■ The dynamically managed, single-tranche CDO investment offers an innovative, *tailor-made*, leveraged, synthetic credit investment to meet the specific risk and reward requirements of investors. An investor determines the credit risk of the desirable exposure by deciding the attachment points (tranche) in the portfolio-loss distribution. Such a tranche can be rated at request.

■ Moreover, the investor has ultimate flexibility in determining the parameters of the investment and whether to sell portfolio protection or invest in a credit-linked note (CLN)—in other words, there is flexibility associated with the execution of the liability side of the CDO, providing an opportunity to investors facing different constraints.

■ Where transactions are dynamic, substitution rights managed by either the investor or by a selected CDO manager (according to predefined criteria) with experience in the bond and credit derivatives market. These products facilitate access to the credit markets for investors who may not have the capacity to manage a large portfolio of names, but who are essentially bullish on the asset class. They may choose to hire a manager to manage a portfolio for them or alternatively seek exposure through a mezzanine single-tranche CDO investment.

■ The single-tranche synthetic CDO is a bilateral contract between the investor and dealer. This can often lead to quicker execution of deals than with traditional synthetics where the whole of the capital structure will be placed. This may offer greater scope for investors to capitalise on arbitrage opportunities between the CDS and cash markets. Furthermore, the bilateral nature of the investment significantly mitigates the perceived, and often real, conflict between debt and equity in a CDO capital structure.

■ The asset side of the single-tranche CDO is executed synthetically. No physical purchase of assets is required—the portfolio can be created through CDS both on individual corporate names and on ABS. This eliminates the need for a ramp-up period (portfolio building phase), which is often a long process and requires additional management.

PRODUCT OVERVIEW

In this section we provide a product overview which includes a description and mechanics of the product, leverage and tranche returns, defaults and loss valuation, and portfolio construction and management ratings.

Description and Mechanics

In our description of the product, we begin with the basics of synthetic CDOs and then go on to explain single-tranche versus multitranche synthetic CDOs and the basic structure of a single-tranche synthetic CDO.

EXHIBIT 31.2   Prioritisation in a CDO Capital Structure

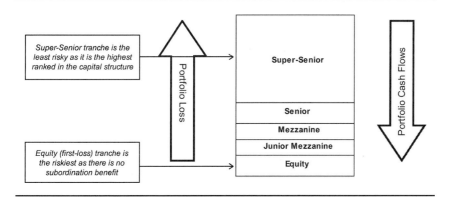

Source: Merrill Lynch.

Synthetic CDO Basics

A synthetic CDO is an investment where the underlying collateral is a portfolio of credits as opposed to a just a single bond or loan. Importantly, in a synthetic CDO transaction, the underlying collateral pool is a collection of single-name credit default swaps, which synthetically transfer the credit risk of the names that they reference. In contrast, traditional cash CDO structures have funded physical portfolios of bonds or loans as the underlying collateral pool, while the CDS assets of a synthetic CDO are typically not funded.

The CDO structure redistributes the credit risk of the underlying portfolio through *tranching*, and cash flow and loss prioritisation. For example, all cash collections (interest and principal payments from the underlying portfolio in a cash CDO structure, or credit default swap (CDS) premiums and CLN collateral yield in funded or partially funded synthetic structures) are distributed to the CDO notes on a priority basis—from senior to junior, sequentially (in most cases). Shortfalls in the cash flows in cash structures due to losses or credit events crystallised in losses in a synthetic structure, are allocated first to the lowest CDO tranche, known as the equity tranche, and then upwards in a reverse priority to the cash flow allocation mentioned above (see Exhibit 31.2).

The capital structure of a CDO, that is its tranching, is determined by assessing the risks of its asset side and allocating those risks in priority on the liability side, so that the risks of each liability tranche are consistent with a desired rating level, expressed either in expected loss or in probability of default.

Every CDO has an asset side, generating its revenue, and a liability side, whose obligations need to be satisfied. The difference between the two is usually termed the *funding gap* or *excess spread*. One of the reasons that synthetic CDOs have risen in popularity is that they are able to pass on any positive benefits of the CDS-cash basis, thus generating more excess spread for investors.

Furthermore, the asset and liability sides need to be carefully matched. One of the advantages of using credit default swaps as the underlying collateral is the ability to facilitate better matching (in terms of currency and maturity, etc.) of the assets and liabilities of a CDO.

Synthetic (and cash) CDO structures are commonly used by banks (balance sheet CDOs) as a means of reducing regulatory capital requirements on their portfolios of risky assets, and so improving the return on equity. In addition, banks can use CDOs to better manage the risks of their balance sheets in terms of exposures, credit lines, diversification, etc. Depending on the yield of their portfolios and their funding needs, they may choose to execute either a cash or a synthetic CDO transaction.

By purchasing the tranches issued from a CDO, an investor can gain exposure in varying degrees to the credit risk of the underlying portfolio. Specifically, the investor can gain exposure to the risk of *specific losses* on the underlying portfolio due to default. That risk is defined by the *attachment point* of the tranche, which defines the point at which losses on the underlying portfolio begin to reduce the notional of the tranche. A lower attachment point implies a riskier tranche than a higher attachment point, other things being equal. The full risk exposure to the investor is defined by the notional amount of the investment, which lies between the lower and the upper attachment points—the boundaries of the trade.

For example, suppose that we have a €1 billion portfolio comprising 100 default swaps each transferring €10 million notional of credit risk. The first loss, or equity tranche might absorb the first 4% of losses (€40 million) on the portfolio due to default. The second loss tranche might absorb losses from 4–8% on the portfolio due to default, and so on until 100% of the losses on the portfolio have been tranched.

Exhibit 31.3, details a hypothetical tranching of a €1 billion portfolio into 5 tranches. Losses in the portfolio up until 5% (€50 million of losses in total) would result in a write-down of principal of the equity tranche. Further losses in the portfolio in excess of 5% and up until 6.5% (€65 million of losses in total) would then result in a write-down of principal in the junior mezzanine tranche. This process of loss allocation would continue bottom-up sequentially through the tranches.

The level of losses in the portfolio (and hence tranche loss) depends on the timing of defaults and the subsequent recovery rate following

EXHIBIT 31.3 An Example of Tranching Portfolio Credit Risk

Collateral Pool	Characteristics
Collateral Pool	
No. of reference entities	100
Notional amount of protection on each credit	€10 million
Total portfolio size	€1 billion
Tranches	*% of Credit Losses*
Equity tranche	0–5%
Junior mezzanine tranche	5–6.5%
Mezzanine tranche	6.5–9.5%
Senior tranche	9.5–12.8%
Super-senior tranche	12.8–100%

Source: Merrill Lynch.

each default of credits in the underlying portfolio. For instance, if each credit in had a 50% recovery rate, each default in the underlying portfolio would result in a €5 million loss. Accordingly, it would take 10 defaults to write-down the equity tranche. We talk more about recovery rates and tranche pricing later in this chapter.

Tranches across the capital structure of a deal can be viewed as an "option" on the performance of the underlying portfolio (Exhibit 31.4). For instance, the super-senior tranche is effectively "short a call option" on the performance of the underlying portfolio. Alternatively, the mezzanine tranche payoff can be viewed as a mixture of a call and a put on the pool loss.

Single Tranche Synthetic CDOs versus Multitranched Synthetic CDOs

In a synthetic CDO, the issued tranches are typically purchased by different investors, according to their different risk and reward preferences, and often there is syndication of the deal. Investors in the equity portion, being the riskiest, are often hedge funds or dedicated structured finance investors. Conversely, investors in the super-senior tranches, which attract very high credit ratings, tend to be insurance companies and monolines.

A single-tranche synthetic CDO is crucially different in that just one of the tranches is placed with one investor and the remaining tranches are retained by the broker/dealer. The risks of these tranches are dynamically

EXHIBIT 31.4 Tranche Loss Can Be Thought of as an "Option" on the Total Portfolio Loss

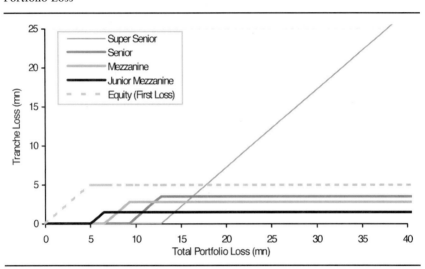

Source: Merrill Lynch. Tranching as in Exhibit 31.3.

managed (delta hedged) by the dealer.[1] A single tranche synthetic is non-syndicated, simply being a bilateral contract between the broker/dealer and *one* investor. This provides the most flexible option for the investor in terms of constructing the underlying portfolio, attachment point of the tranche, and desired tranche rating (which may well be higher than the average rating of the underlying collateral pool). Furthermore, with just two parties to a deal, tranches can be efficiently and speedily placed, providing opportunities to capitalise on arbitrage between the CDS and cash markets. Exhibit 31.5 compares some common features of single-tranche synthetic CDOs and traditional synthetic CDOs.

Basic Structure of Single-Tranche Deals

The basic structure of a single-tranche synthetic CDO is shown in Exhibit 31.6. Credit risk is synthetically transferred via single-name default swaps by the dealer selling protection into the market place on each name. The portfolio is tranched into three simple pieces of equity, mezzanine and senior risk and the investor purchases (via a CLN in this

---

[1] Although it may be more advantageous for a dealer to place the remaining tranches with other investors at a later date, instead of delta hedging them. For example, originating numerous mezzanine deals would result in a concentration of senior and equity risk for the dealer.

EXHIBIT 31.5   Comparison Between Single-Tranche Synthetic CDOs and Traditional Synthetic CDOs

Single-Tranche Synthetic CDO	Multitranche Synthetic CDO
Synthetic risk transference via single-name credit default swaps is used to create the underlying collateral pool.	Synthetic risk transference via single-name credit default swaps is used to create the underlying collateral pool.
Usually between 50 and 100 high-grade names in the collateral pool.	Typically around 100 high-grade names in the collateral pool.
Only one tranche is placed with an investor. The remaining tranches are retained by the dealer and the associated risk is actively managed ('delta hedged').	A majority of the tranches are placed with different investors and hedging is more straightforward than in single-tranche deals. Syndication may be involved.
Bilateral contract between protection buyer and protection seller. No reliance or dependence on equity tranche investor or other parties as in traditional CDOs. Client has ultimate flexibility in determining the underlying portfolio, investment size, tranche structure and desired rating.	Different investors will be attracted to different tranches depending on risk/return preference. Less flexibility in determining underlying collateral pool depending on the type of investor.
Investor-driven, single-investor.	Issuer-driven in traditional securitisation or equity investor/portfolio manager driven in case of arbitrage CDO.
Potentially faster execution than full capital structure deals, allowing the investor to capitalise on arbitrage opportunities between the CDS and cash markets, as well as sweet spots in the capital structure.	Typically slower execution as all tranches need to be placed. Deals can collapse if the entire capital structure cannot be placed.

Source: Merrill Lynch.

example) the mezzanine tranche referencing losses on the underlying portfolio between 4% and 8% of the total portfolio notional. However, the investor can gain exposure to various tranches of credit risk in both funded and unfunded form:

■ *Unfunded form.* The investor directly enters into a *portfolio default swap,* selling portfolio protection. A portfolio default swap is a credit derivative instrument that allows the transfer of exposure to specific losses in the underlying portfolio due to default. The dealer (protec-

EXHIBIT 31.6   Example Transaction Diagram for a €1 billion Portfolio

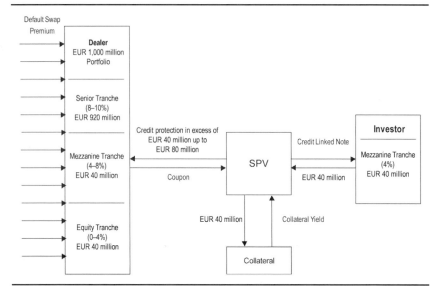

Note: Investor purchases €40 million CLN tied to losses on the mezzanine tranche.
Source: Merrill Lynch.

tion buyer) pays a spread on the remaining notional of the tranche,
and the investor (seller of protection) compensates the buyer for any
losses in the tranche due to default.

■ *Funded form.* The investor purchases a CLN issued by a Special
Purpose Vehicle (SPV). In this instance, the dealer buys mezzanine
protection from the SPV in return for default payments following
losses on the tranche. The SPV issues coupon-paying notes to the
investor and the proceeds of the note issuance are used to purchase
preagreed collateral which (1) forms the default payments to the protection buyer and (2) provides an enhanced coupon for the investor.

The CLN can pay either a fixed or a floating coupon (depending on seniority) and the currency can be tailored to meet the demands of the investor.
Importantly, both the CLN and the credit default swap can be rated.

If rated, the rating process is similar to that used in rating public
CDO transactions based on investment grade names executed either in
cash or synthetic forms. Ratings will focus on both the quantitative and
qualitative aspects of the transaction. Typically, this will involve an
analysis of the composition of the underlying portfolio, its diversification, any single-name concentrations, the average rating of the underly-

ing portfolio, substitution rights, trading guidelines, assessment of any CDO manager, legal review of the transaction, default swap documentation, and the like. We address certain aspects of the rating process further in the next sections.

Leverage and Tranche Returns

Single-tranche synthetic CDOs offer a leveraged exposure to the underlying portfolio above the attachment point. Any tranche subordination effectively acts as a "buffer" against defaults (i.e., there is room for defaults on the underlying portfolio without suffering a loss of notional and return.) For some mezzanine tranches that achieve investment grade ratings, the subordination implies that the internal rate of return (IRR) will likely be much higher compared to the IRR on a straight investment in the underlying portfolio (which will have a weighted-average rating similar to the rating of the mezzanine tranche). This can present a compelling investment opportunity. For example, at the time of this writing, a portfolio of BBB+ credits currently yields about 70 basis points, while the single-A tranche of a single-tranche CDO would likely yield 120 basis points.

Below we analyze the dynamics of a leveraged investment in a mezzanine (single) tranche of a synthetic CDO. We need to emphasise, though, that a mezzanine tranche position is actually "deleveraged" up to the attachment point, and then more leveraged than an investment in the underlying portfolio.

The return on the investment is a function of the level of leverage, number of defaults in the underlying portfolio and the level of recoveries in the case of defaults.

Leveraged Tranche Returns as a Function of Defaults

We can describe the leveraged tranche dynamics as a function of the number of defaults under a 40% recovery assumption (Exhibit 31.7). We have assumed a portfolio of 100 names with an average spread of 100 basis points and tranched this portfolio into a first-loss piece of 4% and a mezzanine piece of 4%. For a direct investment in the portfolio ("100% tranche"), each default contributes to a loss in the IRR as there is no subordination. For the mezzanine tranche, subordination means that the IRR is constant until the seventh default, following which the IRR falls much quicker than for the portfolio. After the attachment point, each default contributes to a greater loss (as a % of initial investment) in the case of the mezzanine tranche than in the case of the whole portfolio. Naturally, the timing of defaults and recoveries will also have an impact on returns.

EXHIBIT 31.7 IRR Analysis for Tranches versus IRR for Underlying Portfolio

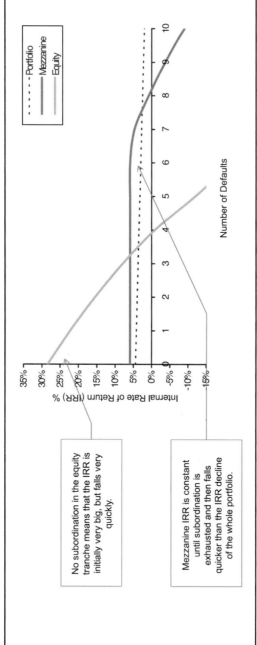

Note: Assuming 5-yr swap rate of 3.5%, coupon of Mezzanine tranche of 2.5%. Coupon on Equity tranche of 25%.
Source: Merrill Lynch.

Leveraged Tranche Returns as a Function of Recovery Rate

We can also describe the leveraged tranche dynamics of the mezzanine tranche as a function of the recovery rate while keeping all other factors constant (see Exhibit 31.8). For a greater recovery rate assumption, more defaults in the underlying portfolio are needed before the subordination benefit of the mezzanine tranche is exhausted. Consequently, for higher recovery rate assumptions, the IRR of the tranche remains constant (and higher than the IRR of the underlying portfolio) for longer. The reverse is true for lower recovery rate assumptions.

Defaults and Loss Valuation

Below we discuss cash settlement following a default and the definition of a default/credit event.

Cash Settlement Following a Default

Typically, following the default of a name in the underlying portfolio, the loss amount will be determined by a cash settlement process. This involves polling the market place for the price of the relevant security following the default. While the mechanics of such a process vary from deal to deal and vary between dealers, the following factors play an important role in the overall robustness of determining the loss amount:

- *The number of firms participating in the auction process.* Prices will typically be sourced from major dealers in the specific debt obligation being valued. Usually the minimum required is five.
- *Method of price discovery.* Valuation could involve bid or mid-price calculations. Moreover, the highest price or an average of the prices may be used. Typically, the highest bid is used.
- *Time period for loss to be determined and how long after default this process is begun.* Immediately after a credit event, an obligation's value may not be representative of recovery rates as there may not be enough information available for the market to price the obligation reasonably. Rating agency recovery studies are based on a minimum period of time after default. Standard & Poor's, for example, requires a minimum of 60 days, while market practice is 72 days.
- *The number of readings involved in determining the loss amount and the frequency between these.* This prevents the final loss amount being artificially low should a poll produce too few prices. Rating agencies require at least two prices.
- *Obligation (s) used for reference pricing.*
- *Calculation agent, usually the dealer, and maybe a third-party verifier, if any.*

EXHIBIT 31.8 IRR Analysis for Mezzanine Tranche for Varying Recovery Rates

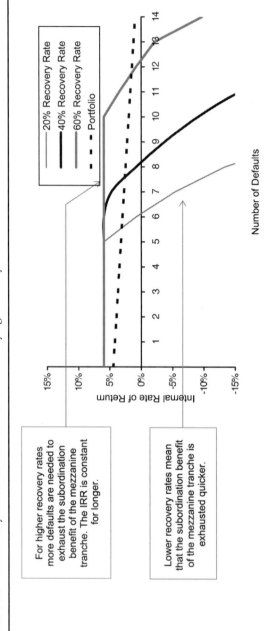

For higher recovery rates more defaults are needed to exhaust the subordination benefit of the mezzanine tranche. The IRR is constant for longer.

Lower recovery rates mean that the subordination benefit of the mezzanine tranche is exhausted quicker.

Note: Coupon on mezzanine tranche of 2.5%
Source: Merrill Lynch.

"Default" and Credit Events

Throughout this chapter we interchangeably use "default" and "credit event." In reality, "default" as captured by rating agency statistics may sometimes be a more severe test than certain credit events. Moody's, for example, notes three categories of default for the purposes of its ratings and historical default statistics:

- Missed or delayed interest or principal payments.
- Bankruptcy or receivership.
- Distressed exchange either leaving investors with a diminished financial obligation or an exchange for the apparent reason of avoiding default.

Credit events for corporates are bankruptcy, failure to pay, and restructuring. Restructuring can sometimes be considered a "soft" credit event. Rating agency recovery rate statistics reflect events of "hard default" whereas the expected recovery following a "soft" restructuring credit event, for example, would likely be significantly higher than for a liquidation.

Current market consensus is for *modified-modified restructuring* to be applied to European reference entities[2] and *modified restructuring* to be applied to US reference entities. If the underlying portfolio of the single-tranche CDO consists of both European and US reference entities, then the respective restructuring alternatives would still apply to those credits.

Portfolio Construction and Management

Prior to the investment decision, the investor and dealer will agree upon the choice of underlying reference entities in the portfolio. The portfolio composition will typically involve decisions based on:

- *Number of reference entities.* Single-tranche deals typically reference portfolios of between 50-100 names.
- *Type of reference entities.* They are usually corporate credits, but ABS credits can also be added under some circumstances.
- *Credit quality of reference entities.* Both investment grade and high yield credits can be selected, although typically portfolios are constructed of solely investment grade credits.
- *Subordination.* Credit risk can be transferred into the portfolio at both the senior and subordinated level. In Europe, subordinated contracts tend to be most liquid on banks and insurance companies. Typically, the market assumes a recovery rate of 35% for senior unsecured debt

---

[2] Although some sectors, such as the subordinated insurance sector, trade with *restructuring* documentation.

and 20% for subordinated debt, but actual recovery rates following default are likely to vary around these averages.

- *Maturity.* Default swaps tend to be most liquid in the 5-year part of the curve with the issued tranches having a similar maturity.
- *Domicile of Reference Entity.*
- *Notional Amount.*

When constructing the underlying portfolio, investors should be mindful of the impact of portfolio diversity on deal tranching. Diversification in a synthetic CDO pool serves to avoid the risk of excessive losses relating to a single name, country or industry category. All other things equal, higher diversity would mean larger higher-rated tranches. The benefit gained from the diversification of the underlying collateral pool varies though between risk tranches in the deal structure. Most of the benefits of diversification in the pool are actually allocated to the senior tranches, while the mezzanine tranche, depending on its size may lie on the "inversion point" in the diversification benefits.

Adverse Selection

One of the key determinants to the overall performance of a single-tranche deal is the initial portfolio selection, regardless of any credit substitutions permitted during the transaction. Credits that trade wide for their respective rating category may well be reflecting negative credit trends, and while cheap for the respective rating, may well result in portfolio losses further down the line. Given that the maturity of single-tranche transactions tends to be five years, the choice of underlying collateral should be based on not only current credit quality, but also expectations about future credit quality.

Structural models of credit risk can be used to help assess adverse selection. Market-based indicators of credit risk, such as total debt to total market capitalisation and implied equity volatility are popular methods of assessing the market-implied credit quality of an issuer. Moreover, fundamental analysis can be used to gauge future rating trends of issuers.

Static and Dynamic Transactions

Synthetic CDOs can be both static and dynamic transactions. In static transactions, the underlying portfolio is agreed up-front between the investor and dealer and is fixed throughout the life of the transaction. Should a credit experience a negative trend before maturity of the transaction, there is no scope to substitute this name and prevent potential portfolio loss. In this type of structure, there is also no possibility of trading gains (or losses) from active management of the portfolio.

Transactions can also be dynamic in nature. In this structure the underlying portfolio may be modified throughout the life of the deal, by either the investor or an elected manager. While the investor gives up some yield on the invested tranche for the right to have substitution (the investor can be thought of as long an "option" to restructure the portfolio), credits that deteriorate may be substituted with less risky alternatives to prevent credit loss.

Deals may be "lightly managed," as all single-tranche CDOs tend to be, where a small element of defensive trading is permitted or more fully managed, where the manager has the right to enter into hedging transactions to mitigate the credit risk of earlier trades or buy protection for arbitrage purposes. The trend towards dynamic transactions has been bolstered by the credit volatility and CDO ratings downgrades in recent years. Conversely, proponents of static transactions argue that substitution rights are of limited value in a well-diversified portfolio, as market risk is much more difficult to mitigate. That value also depends on the actual ability to trade the selected credit exposures.

Degrees of Management in Synthetic CDOs

Where active management is permitted, the choices for substitution rights are typically threefold:

- *Investor managed.* The investor has ultimate flexibility as to the initial composition of the portfolio and the ongoing substitutions into the portfolio.
- *Third party managed.* The investor delegates the management of substitution rights to a third-party asset manager, typically with experience in managing synthetic CDOs. The manager may well invest in a portion of the first-loss piece. The manager is responsible for the credit performance of the collateral portfolio and for ensuring that the transaction meets the diversification, quality and structural guidelines specified by the rating agencies. Part of the credit analysis may focus on the capabilities of the CDO manager and the way the manager is compensated. This option may be appealing to new entrants into the credit markets who may not have the capacity to monitor a large portfolio of credits. However, they should keep in mind that in return for managing the collateral portfolio, the manager receives a fee. Such a fee is usually paid on the nominal value of the portfolio rather than on the notional of the investor's tranche.
- *Dealer managed.* The dealer pays the investor an enhanced coupon to retain the substitution rights (although this option is much less common and was originally used to facilitate dealer hedging).

Credit Substitutions

Credit substitutions (replacing one credit with another) are allowed in the portfolio subject to certain conditions. Such conditions are set in place to ensure that the initial portfolio criteria remain in place. We note that single-tranche deals do not allow removal without replacement as it leads to deleveraging on a fixed income investment. Substitutions will typically be for reasons of:

- *Credit deterioration.* Spreads on the underlying reference entity have widened and the investor believes that a possible default is much more likely. These substitutions may be subject to constraints such as spread widening tests on the outgoing credit, as well as tests on the incoming (substituting) credit similar to the ones mentioned below.
- *Credit improvement.* Substitutions due to credit improvement may be subject to a minimum spread tightening test as well as constraints meant to protect the credit quality of the portfolio: rating of incoming credit, industry and obligor concentration limits, concentration of certain rating categories, and so on.

There may also be restrictions on the number of substitution trades permitted, typically 5–10 per annum (depending on the trading account). Generally, there will be restrictions on the level of spread of the incoming credits versus that of the outgoing credits, enforced through spread tests. Rating agencies tend also to stipulate that to maintain ratings, the credit rating for the incoming credit should be better or should not be of any worse credit quality than the outgoing credit.

Where substitutions are allowed, a *trading account* may be created with the dealer on day one of the transaction. In the absence of such an account, all trading losses must be paid for by the investor. The size of the trading account will depend on the investment size, tranche subordination, average spread of the portfolio, and the like. Trading losses from substitution would be debited from the trading account whilst trading gains from substitution would be added to the trading account. Such an account is for the benefit of the investor and it may choose to withdraw available funds or add funds at any time.

Trading out of "deteriorating names," generating a loss, will be allowed to the extent that the balance in the trading account is sufficient to cover the loss (where the account cannot cover the loss, trading may still be permitted with the mark-to-market payment settled immediately between the investor and dealer). Higher trading accounts would generally mean more trading flexibility but a lower running spread on the tranche.

The loss or gain from substitution will be a function of two factors. First, the mark-to-market on the outgoing credit is a function of its spread change since trade inception and remaining duration. This calculation needs to be adjusted for the characteristics (spread, duration, etc.) of the incoming credit. The second factor is the the delta of the credit. A transaction may or may not adjust the gain/loss for deltas of the incoming and outgoing credits. Importantly, the delta, which is less than 100%, has the impact of "dampening" trading losses and dampening any profit from trading gains.

In the absence of a trading account, changes in P&L may be reflected in a modification to the running coupon on the tranche. In this case, the net present value (NPV) of the substitution is converted into a coupon value (the coupon value of a 1 basis point annuity is needed to determine this).

Furthermore, any trading gains or losses can also be added or subtracted from subordination beneath a mezzanine tranche. This requires converting the trading gain/loss into a mark-to-market change in the tranche by changing the subordination. Such a conversion is done through an adjustment factor.

Overall, the trading gain/loss can be reflected in cash (trading account), coupon change or subordination change. In any of these cases a different adjustment factor is applied.

Ratings

Most CDO transactions are rated either on the entire capital structure or only for a part of it. When rating the entire capital structure in a fully tranched CDO, issuers and rating agencies try to improve the economics of a transaction by achieving the highest possible rating on each tranche, or alternatively put, by maximising the size of the seniormost tranches. In a single-tranche CDO, the tranche size and related attachment points are determined by the investor, who may or may not require a specific rating level.

In either case, however, the rating process is similar and involves the evaluation of the credit quality of the portfolio, determination of the expected performance of the underlying credits, the expected level of defaults and recoveries (should such defaults occur), their timing, the default correlations among the credits in the pool, and determining the level of protection (subordination) needed for each tranche, given the structural features of the tranche and the transaction as a whole in order to achieve the desired rating.

In Exhibit 31.9, we summarise the key inputs used by the rating agencies, when modelling CDO transactions for rating purposes.

EXHIBIT 31.9 Key Inputs Used by the Rating Agencies, when Modelling CDO Transactions for Rating Purposes

Heading	Fitch	Moody's	Standard & Poor's
Methodology, models, monitoring	Vector—Monte Carlo simulation.	Binomial expansion, double and multiple binomial expansion CDO navigator (for monitoring only).	CDO evaluator—Monte Carlo simulation.
Default probabilities for corporate and ABS	Default statistics over the past 20 years, through the end of 2002 (update in July 2003) are used to derive asset default probabilities. Default behaviour of an asset is modelled on the basis of the default probabilities particular to this assets, its actual size, and amortisation schedule, which in turn allows for the integration of the conditional annual default probability for each year that the asset is outstanding. This is a departure from old methodology of basing default probabilities on the average life of an asset. Weighted average rating is used to convey portfolio's average default probability, all derived from a CDO default matrix. While no specific default matrix for ABS has been published, the default probabilities for ABS are generally assumed to be lower than for equally rated corporates. For older deals, a sector score based on concentration by ABS sector was calculated and then converted into a default rate multiple (ranging from 1.5 times to 0.8 times) to stress the base corporate ± default matrix.	"Idealised" expected loss rates for each asset were established in the mid-1990s. The expected loss is based on a historical review of defaults (about 20 years of data) and recovery rates for different classes of debt. The same idealized expected loss rates are applied regardless of the asset type so long as the same Moody's rating is applied, and in this respect, ABS is not an exception. Binomial expansion transforms real portfolio assets and maturities into one or more idealised asset portfolios, each of them representing an "asset" with a given size, maturity, and default probability—all such "assets" sum up to the average characteristics of the portfolio (weighted average default probability, weighted average life, etc.).	Default probabilities are derived from default statistics covering the 10-year period ending in 1997. Default probabilities for ABS are assumed to be lower than for corporates. The ABS default assumptions are based on 7-year probability of default, but applied across the board for all ABS notes regardless of their term.

612

EXHIBIT 31.9 (Continued)

Heading	Fitch	Moody's	Standard & Poor's
Recoveries for corporates (Recoveries are not modelled as a function of default.)	Recovery rates are based on empirical evidence for US and UK debt up until early 2001. Given minimal European historical data, those rates are also applied for continental Europe, but adjusted to reflect the insolvency regimes in the different European jurisdictions. Recovery rates also depend on the a given asset's position in the capital structure of the respective company. On the CDO asset side, recovery assumptions are independent of default frequency. However, instead fixed recoveries for all scenarios, recovery rates are decreased for higher rated tranches in the CDO liability structure. Fitch uses 16 recovery rates, and within its simulation, runs each recovery rate for defaulting assets according to a probability distribution. Weighted average recovery rate is used to convey the loss given default of a CDO portfolio. Under the "postsimulation" approach, Fitch runs the simulation, in which lower-rated assets will default more frequently and higher-rated assets will default less frequently. Using the results of the simulated, total recoveries are divided by total defaults to arrive at the weighted average recovery rate for the pool, thus taking in to account both the default frequency and the par value of the asset that has defaulted.	Recovery rates depend on the position of the respective debt instrument in the capital structure of a company, as well as on the given jurisdiction. They are derived from years of empirical observations primarily in the US. Similar to other rating agencies, Moody's also doesn't model recovery rates as a variable, whose value depends on general default levels, except in the case of nth-to-default baskets. Loan defaults and bond defaults are assumed to have different recoveries, and Moody's uses 11 recovery rates between 0% and 100%. Further adjustments are made for CDS. Portfolio measure of weighted average recovery rate is based on a presimulation approach—each asset's recovery rate is weighted by the par value of the asset in the portfolio, and then this figure is reported as the weighted average recovery rate for the portfolio.	Fixed recovery rates are applied for each tier of debt in a company's capital structure. Such recovery rates are used as constant on the asset side regardless of the CDO liability tier. Recently, the different recovery rates used for each region (e.g., the US, Southern Europe, Northern Europe) were further detailed and developed into different recoveries for each country. Similar to the other rating agencies, recovery assumptions for non-US assets were based on legal reviews of various insolvency regimes. Specific recovery assumptions are also established for leveraged loans and CDS. The portfolio measure of weighted average recovery rate is calculated and expressed as each asset's assumed recovery rate weighted by the asset's weight in the portfolio.

EXHIBIT 31.9 (Continued)

Heading	Fitch	Moody's	Standard & Poor's
Recoveries for ABS assets	Base recoveries for ABS are the same as for corporates, but may be further reduced for sub-investment grade ABS tranches included within a CBO, in particular when stressing for the AAA liabilities. Some level of differentiation is introduced for the different tranches of ABS, given their position within the capital structure—their rating and "thickness."	ABS recoveries are arrived at by adjusting corporate recoveries specifically looking at the position of the ABS tranche in the capital structure as well as its size as a proportion of the total capital structure. The asset sector is also taken into consideration. Five different recovery matrices are used in the models.	Recoveries for ABS assets within CDOs are tiered both by seniority of the ABS tranche, and by the seniority/desired rating of the relevant CDO liability.
Corporate asset/ default correlation	Using US and European corporate equity price data from the 6-year period 1997–2003, correlation matrices are derived. In addition, correlations between corporates and ABS are established. ABS correlations ranging from 15–55% are applied. A single portfolio correlation measure is used to convey the idea of diversification in the CDO pool.	Diversity score methodology is the way to reflect correlations in CDOs. Allegedly, it assumes default correlation of 20% intraindustry and 0% between industries. For ABS, a range of correlations between ABS asset classes is assessed with a lower number of "industry groups." The correlation could be as low as 0.15 and as high as 0.4. Correlation factors are adjusted on the sector relationship, ratings (investment grade vs. non-investment grade) and the seniority of the tranche within an ABS structure. The diversity score is a single number that reflects the level of diversification in a portfolio (inversely, its industry concentration levels). Typical corporate CDO diversity scores are between 40 and 70, whereas typical ABS CDOs are between 15 and 30.	Static correlation assumptions are used: 30% correlation between two corporates within any one industry, and 0% between corporates in different industries. These assumptions are 30% and 10% respectively for ABS. Additional assumptions may be made for correlation for corporates (15%) and ABS (20%) within both the same sector and the same region. In the absence of a single measure, industry concentration and single obligor concentration limits evidence diversification.
Manager impact on enhancement levels	Managers are rated on a scale of 1 (best) to 4 (worst). Such rating is then incorporated in the determination of the credit enhancement of a CDO—credit enhancement is modified by prescribed multiples.	Via CDO navigator performance figures for CDO managers are published and measure manager performance, based not on any qualitative assessment, but ultimately on gain or loss of par for rated CDO tranches for each such manager. There is no clear formulaic approach.	Manager's quality is taken into consideration in different ways—for example, by increasing level of recovery rates in a transaction for a high quality manager (indicating defensive ability to minimise losses).

Source: Rating Agencies, Merrill Lynch.

614

Ratings and Portfolio Loss

Here we attempt to illustrate the rating process and some of its pitfalls on the basis of the expected loss approach.

A rating agency would model a loss distribution of the portfolio using a specific model (as shown in Exhibit 31.9) and on that basis determine the amount of credit enhancement for a given tranche(s) to achieve the respective credit rating. For the purposes of this illustration we have run a simulation and presented the results in Exhibit 31.10—the two graphs represent the expected loss distributions of a portfolio assuming two different recovery rates.

In case of an expected loss approach to credit ratings, the credit enhancement for a tranche (left of the vertical line) should be consistent with an expected loss a tranche of that rating may sustain (right of the vertical line or "the tail").

A risk to the rating and the investor in the respective tranche is that the tail is 'fatter' than originally anticipated for a number of reasons. For example, actual recovery rates are significantly lower than the initially assumed ones. If that is the case, all other conditions being equal, the respective tranche would experience more losses than consistent with its rating and should be credit-wise weaker than anticipated.

CORRELATION AND PRICING FACTORS

In this section we introduce the concept of default correlation, explain how this can be estimated in practice, and show how default correlation plays a fundamental role in the pricing of single-tranche CDOs.

Pricing Factors

The loss profiles of portfolio credit derivative products can be complex but are essentially influenced by the following factors:

- The number of credits underlying the portfolio and their granularity.
- The individual default probabilities of each credit.
- The recovery rate assumptions of the underlying credits.
- The *default correlation* assumption between the credits.

Importance of Default Correlation

Default correlation assumptions estimate the tendency of credits in a portfolio to default together over a given time horizon. While in practice there is a lack of historical data that can be used to reliably extract default correlations, empirical evidence shows that default correlation is linked to credit

EXHIBIT 31.10 Impact of Recovery Assumption on Loss Distribution and Rating of a CDO Tranche

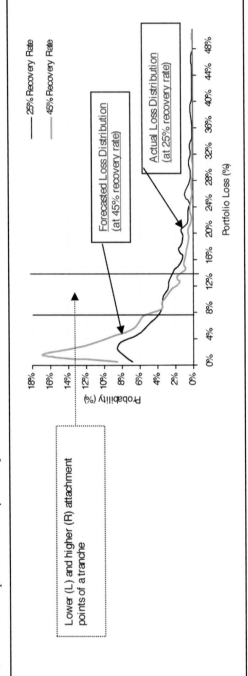

Source: Merrill Lynch.

616

rating and varies with time. In a negative economic environment, lower-rated companies that are generally more leveraged are likely to default together and hence default correlation is expected to be higher. Conversely, in a positive economic environment, default correlation is expected to be lower.[3]

Proxies for default correlation might include looking at the asset correlations of companies. These models, called "structural models" consider a firm in default when the value of its assets fall below a certain threshold amount, such as the face-value of its debt. As such, the probability of two firms defaulting is simply the probability that the market value of each firm's assets falls below their corresponding default threshold amounts. Stock market data is usually used to derive asset correlations as equity market information tends to be readily available and have a longer history from which to perform analysis. The asset correlation derived in this manner is deterministically related to the default correlation, that is, one can be transformed into the other.

Another approach is spread "jump" models. In these models, credit spread correlation is used to determine the expected spread widening (or mathematically, a jump in the annualised default rate) of the non-defaulted credits in case one credit in the portfolio defaults.

Finally, rating transition studies can also be used to imply default correlation. In such cases, the assumption is that the correlation of two bonds being downgraded more or less at the same time is an indicator that they may default at the same time.

Relationship Between Default Rates and Recovery Rates

A further corollary to the above is that there is a relationship over time between default rates and recovery rates of corporate bond issuers. In particular, there is an inverse correlation between the two: An increase in the default rate, defined as the percentage of issuers defaulting, is generally associated with a decline in the average recovery rate. In other words, default severity will be highest when defaults are at their most severe. Exhibit 31.11 plots average yearly recovery rates against associated default rates for speculative-grade issuers and highlights the negative correlation between the two.

Correlation and Portfolio Loss

We can examine how default correlation assumptions can have a significant impact on the *distribution of losses experienced by a portfolio of*

---

[3] It can be argued that default correlation could be negative between companies in the same industry sector. This is because the default of one company may free up capacity and reduce competition, leaving the remaining companies in a stronger financial position.

EXHIBIT 31.11　Inverse Correlation of Speculative-Grade Default Rates and Recovery Rates

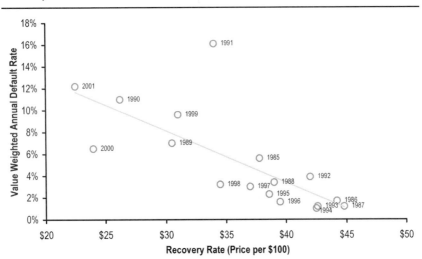

Source: David Hamilton, "Default & Recovery Rates of Corporate Bond Issuers, 1920-2002," *Moody's Special Comment*, February 2003.

credits. It is the loss distribution that encapsulates the default character-istics of a portfolio of credits and ultimately drives pricing of the vari-ous tranches. Understanding the shape of the loss distribution and what factors influence it provides intuition as to the pricing and risk of tranched portfolio credit products.

In the following example, we have created a hypothetical portfolio to examine the influence of correlation. For the purposes of illustration, we have assumed that the portfolio is constructed of *identical* credits with respect to spread, recovery rate assumption and maturity.

We assume the following about the portfolio:

■ Number of credits in the portfolio: 50
■ Spread level for each credit: 100 basis points
■ Recovery assumption for each credit: 50%
■ Maturity of each credit: 5 years

We examine three scenarios, one of very low correlation assumption between the credits, one of medium correlation assumption and one of high correlation assumption. In all cases we examine the shape of the expected loss distribution from holding this portfolio to maturity.

EXHIBIT 31.12   Distribution of Losses for 1% Correlation Assumption

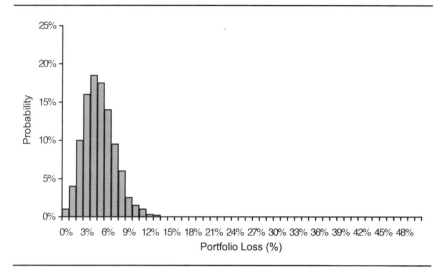

Source: Merrill Lynch.

Case 1: Low default correlation assumption (1%). With an extremely low default correlation assumption, the distribution is almost "symmetric." There is a high probability of experiencing a few losses but almost no probability of experiencing a very large number of losses. Furthermore, there is also a low probability of experiencing zero losses. Exhibit 31.12 plots the loss distribution for the 1% correlation case.

Case 2: Medium correlation assumption (45%). With a medium default correlation assumption, the distribution begins to look more "skewed." Compared to Case 1, we now see that there is a higher probability of experiencing no defaults but also a higher probability of experiencing a large number of losses. As a result, there is now a "tail" developing in the loss distribution profile, as there is a greater likelihood of assets defaulting together. Exhibit 31.13 plots the loss distribution for the 45% correlation case.

Case 3: High correlation assumption (99%). With an extremely high default correlation assumption, the portfolio behaves almost like a single credit and there is *no diversification*. The loss distribution has virtually disappeared apart from two peaks at 0% and 50% loss. The assets either all survive, or they all default with recovery rate equal to our assumption of 50%. Exhibit 31.14 plots the loss distribution for the 99% correlation case.

EXHIBIT 31.13   Distribution of Losses for 45% Correlation Assumption

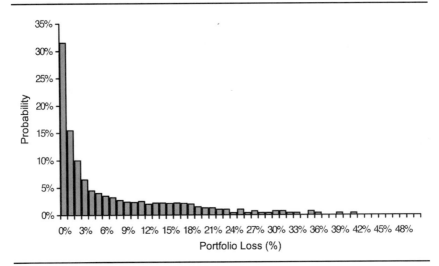

Source: Merrill Lynch.

Correlation, Recovery, Spread, and Tranche Pricing

We now examine the sensitivity of single-tranche CDO pricing as we adjust some of the fundamental inputs into the pricing equation.

Tranche Pricing as a Function of Correlation

We can now analyse how the different outcomes in the above three cases can provide intuition as to the pricing dynamics of the various tranches of a synthetic CDO. To aid the analysis we tranche a 50-name portfolio into a simple structure of equity, mezzanine and senior pieces, all of 4% size, with subordination of 0%, 4%, and 8% respectively. Exhibit 31.15 details transaction specifics. The tranche premium for each of the three tranches as a function of correlation is shown in Exhibit 31.16.

For all levels of correlation, the premium on the equity tranche is the highest, the premium on the senior tranche is the lowest and the premium on the mezzanine tranche lies between the two. This reflects the subordination of the various tranches. The equity tranche, being the first-loss tranche, has no subordination and is inherently the riskiest tranche to own. Conversely, the mezzanine and senior tranches are protected by 4% and 8% subordination respectively and command a lower risk premium than the equity tranche. It should be noted that tranche premia are very sensitive to the average level of spread in the underlying portfolio. Whilst we are

EXHIBIT 31.14   Distribution of Losses for 99% Correlation Assumption

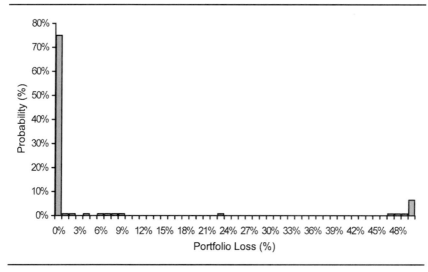

Source: Merrill Lynch.

EXHIBIT 31.15   Hypothetical Portfolio: 3-Tranche Example

Portfolio and Tranche Characteristics	Assumption
Portfolio Summary	
Number of credits	50
Notional size per credit	$15 million per name
Total portfolio size	$750 million
Maturity	5 years
Default swap premium	Each name trading at 100 bp
Recovery assumption	35% for each name
Tranche Summary	
Equity tranche	0–4%
Mezzanine tranche	4–8%
Senior tranche	8–12%

Source: Merrill Lynch.

EXHIBIT 31.16 Tranche Premia versus Correlation

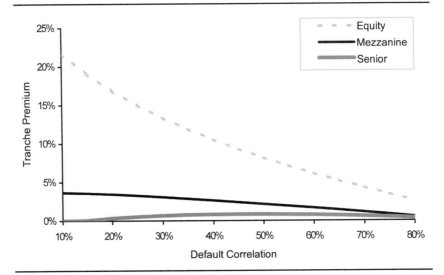

Source: Merrill Lynch.

assuming a 100 basis points spread for each credit in the portfolio, we note that the asset-swap spread on Merrill Lynch's ER30 Index (single-A Euro Corporates) is currently 53 basis points at the time of this chapter.

At *low* correlation, the assets are virtually independent. Exhibit 31.16 shows that the probability of a large number of losses is small. As a result, the probability of losses reaching the senior tranche is low and therefore the spread required to hold this tranche is small (or buying protection on the senior tranche is less valuable). Similarly, Exhibit 31.12 also shows that the probability of zero losses is small and hence there is a high probability that the equity tranche will suffer losses. The spread required to hold this tranche is high. The spread of the mezzanine tranche lies between the two.

At medium correlation, the assets in the portfolio become more likely to default together, and the tail of the portfolio loss distribution is pushed out, pushing more of the risk into the senior tranche. Exhibit 31.13 shows that the probability of a large number of losses has increased. As a result, the probability of losses reaching the senior tranche is higher and therefore the spread required to hold this tranche has increased (buying protection on the senior tranche is now more valuable). Similarly, Exhibit 31.13 also shows that the probability of zero losses has increased making the equity tranche less risky to hold. The spread required to hold this tranche has decreased. Again, the spread of the mezzanine tranche lies between the two.

A *high* correlation, the portfolio virtually behaves like *one asset*, which either defaults or survives. Exhibit 31.14 shows that the probability of a large number of losses is high. As a result, the probability of losses reaching the senior tranche is high and therefore the spread required to hold this tranche is high. Similarly, Exhibit 31.14 also shows that the probability of zero losses is high making the equity tranche less risky to hold. The spread required to hold this has decreased further (buying protection on the equity tranche is less valuable). Again, the spread of the mezzanine tranche lies between the two.

Correlation is highly important for standalone tranches. However, except in the extremes, the mezzanine tranche tends to be less sensitive to correlation than the senior or equity tranches.

An investor's view on correlation can be summarised as follows:

- The equity tranche holder (i.e., protection seller) can be viewed as *a buyer of correlation*.
- The senior tranche holder can be viewed as a *seller of correlation*.
- The mezzanine tranche holder can be characterised as more *neutral* with regards to correlation (although this will depend on transaction specifics).

Tranche Pricing as a Function of Recovery Rate

We can also look at how the premium of the various tranches changes as recovery rate assumptions are changed, keeping spreads constant (see Exhibit 31.17). Increasing the recovery rate means that for a fixed credit spread, the annualised probability of default increases.[4] However, if default does occur, the payment received by the protection buyer is lower.

The break-even coupon on the equity tranche rises as recovery rate is increased. This at first may seem somewhat counterintuitive but the reasoning lies in the dominating impact of rising default probability (which is ultimately what buyers of protection on a first-loss piece care most about). Buying protection on the equity tranche is more valuable as recovery rates are increased (for fixed spread) and so the premium of the equity tranche rises.

The break-even coupon on the senior tranche falls as recovery rate is increased. For the senior tranche, the dominating effect is the higher recovery rate. Increasing the recovery rate means that less and less of the losses on the portfolio hit the senior tranche. Buying protection on the senior tranche is less valuable as recovery rates increase, and so the tranche premium falls.

---

[4] We estimate the annualised probability of default (λ) from the CDS spread S and recovery R: $\lambda \approx S/(1 - R)$. Over five years, the default probability is $1 - \exp(-\lambda \times 5)$

EXHIBIT 31.17   Tranche Premium Versus Recovery Rate

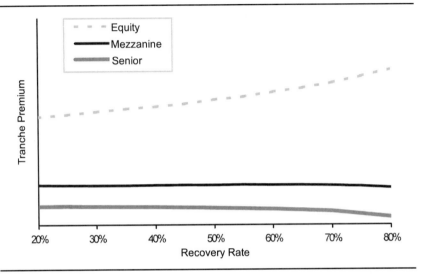

Note: Credit Spreads for underlying portfolio constant at 100 bps.
Source: Merrill Lynch.

The mezzanine tranche is the least sensitive to recovery rates.

Tranche Pricing as Credit Spreads Shift

From our base case of 100 basis points spread for all credits in the underlying portfolio, we show the impact on tranche premiums as all credits spreads are shifted wider (parallel shifts). Exhibit 31.18 shows the premia of the three tranches as credit spreads are increased (keeping correlation and recovery constant). As spreads widen, all break-even coupons increase, and vice versa.

Senior tranche protection only pays out if a large number of individual defaults occur: The likelihood of this occurring increases significantly if credit spread—and hence the probability of default—is increased. Protection on the equity tranche is likely to pay out over the life of the trade, irrespective of whether spreads are increased or not. Increasing credit spreads makes it likely that defaults in the underlying portfolio will happen sooner, but the impact of rising credit spread is more significant on the senior tranche premium.

In summary:

EXHIBIT 31.18   Tranche Premium Versus Credit Spread Shift

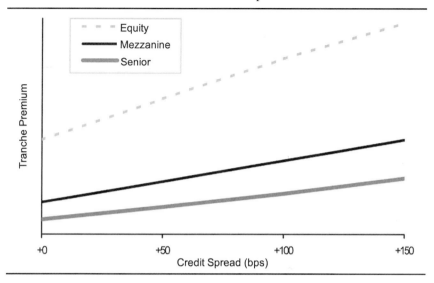

Note: Constant recovery and correlation assumptions. Shifts are from base case of a 100 bp spread for all credits.
Source: Merrill Lynch.

- For the equity tranche, premium increases with a *decrease* in correlation and with an *increase* in recovery rate.
- For the senior tranche, the converse holds. Premium increases with an *increase* in correlation and a *decrease* in recovery rate.
- The mezzanine tranche demonstrates *reduced sensitivity* to correlation and recovery rate, behaving in a similar fashion to the senior tranches for certain ranges of recovery and correlation and behaving in a similar fashion to the equity tranche for other ranges of recovery and correlation.
- All tranches have higher coupons as the spread on the underlying portfolio increases, and vice versa.

Tranches of Default Swap Indices

Despite the problems associated with estimating default correlation, for credit derivative indices, a small but growing market has developed for trading single tranches across the capital structure. Brokers can use quoted premiums on these tranches to infer implied correlation to get an indication of the ranges in which correlation has been trading, although the bid-offer spreads are very wide for some of the tranches as liquidity is low.[5] Implied correlation will also reflect market sentiment and can be influenced by supply and demand flows for particular tranches.

DELTAS AND TRANCHE HEDGING

In a classic CDO structure where all tranches are placed, the dealer would buy protection on all the tranches and hedge the risk on these positions by selling protection on each of the individual credits in the portfolio in the *same* notional amount. When a dealer buys protection on just a single tranche of a portfolio, the risk position, and therefore hedging strategy, is typically much more complicated. This is because in full capital structure deals, the senior tranches tend to hedge the correlation risk of the subordinated tranches.

Buying and selling protection on a portfolio of credits incurs three major types of risk:

■ *Default risk.* The probability that an individual credit will default.
■ *Recovery risk.* The uncertainty of the loss amount in the event of default.
■ *Correlation risk.* How the credit quality of the issuers affect one another.

By buying protection on a tranche and simultaneously selling protection on all the individual names in the underlying portfolio, one can reduce the default and recovery risk whilst isolating the correlation risk. In other words, the dealer seeks to manage default and recovery risk on a risk-neutral basis, and this process is run dynamically over the life of the transaction.

We define the *delta*, or *hedge ratio*, for a dealer who has bought tranche protection, as the amount of protection sold on each credit in the underlying portfolio. In practice, valuation models are used to compute the appropriate deltas, which are rebalanced throughout the life of the trade. However, when hedging ABS names, constant deltas are more likely to be used. Deltas for individual names depend on the following parameters and will change as these parameters change through the life of the transaction:

■ Relative default premiums of the individual credits.
■ Subordination beneath the tranche.

---

[5] This is similar to the equity options market, for instance, where prices of traded options can be used to back-out implied equity volatility and the results can be applied to a current estimate of historical volatility to calculate richness or cheapness and so on.

- Size of the tranche as a percentage of the portfolio.
- Correlation assumption of the individual credits.
- Recovery assumptions of the individual credits.
- Maturity of the transaction.

For example, suppose that an investor has purchased (sold protection on) a mezzanine tranche of a portfolio of 100 names, with each name having a €10 million notional. For a delta of 35% for each credit, this implies that the dealer has to sell €3.5 million of protection on each credit into the market to hedge its position taken via this tranche. The delta for each credit will be less than 100%.

The credit derivatives market has grown exponentially in recent years and liquidity in the CDS market has improved substantially. As infrastructure has become more advanced, dynamic risk management of portfolio credit derivatives and single-tranche CDOs is now much more practical. The potential to dynamically manage the risk of synthetic CDO tranches has increased the scope of products that can be offered to investors.

Deltas vary for each name (depending on the relative default swap premiums and recovery rates of the underlying credits) and will also vary for each tranche depending on which tranche the investor has bought. The dealer will hedge its position in the retained tranches according to delta measures. For example, if a dealer has bought mezzanine protection, the dealer retains the risk of the equity and senior tranches (assuming that these tranches are not placed with investors). The hedging behaviour of the dealer provides important intuition into the pricing of the various tranches.

The dealer needs to rebalance the portfolio hedges on the individual names as changes in the portfolio occur. The extent to which the dealer incurs costs in this re-balancing process depends on actual spread movements. In addition, another potential risk for the dealer is a change in the portfolio correlation away from dealer's original assumptions. Another potential exposure for the dealer is the risk of overnight default in which case the delta drops to a zero, but the dealer has had no time to hedge out.

Delta Sensitivities

We can look at how the deltas change as we adjust some of the above mentioned factors. In our examples, we stick with the hypothetical portfolio outlined in Exhibit 31.15. We examine the behaviour of deltas for different tranches in the capital structure, how delta changes over time given static spreads and no defaults, and we look at how deltas change for individual credits according to which tranche the dealer has bought protection on.

Delta as a Function of Tranche Subordination

As single-tranche synthetics are leveraged trades, tranche deltas should reflect that leverage. Other things remaining equal, deltas are therefore higher in more subordinate tranches (deltas can essentially be viewed as reflecting the probability of losses in each tranche and, therefore, are higher in subordinated tranches). In Exhibit 31.19, we show how the delta changes when the dealer buys protection on different tranches. The delta is greatest for the equity tranche (47%), lower for the mezzanine tranche (30%), and is the lowest for the senior tranche (19%).

EXHIBIT 31.19   Delta Declines for Higher Rated Tranches

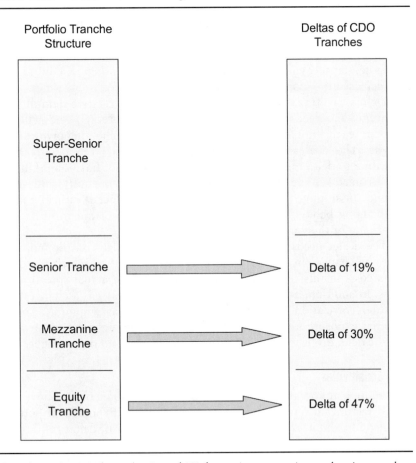

Note: Assuming equal tranche sizes of 4% for equity, mezzanine, and senior tranches.
Source: Merrill Lynch.

EXHIBIT 31.20   Equity Delta Rises over Time Whilst Mezzanine and Senior Deltas Falls

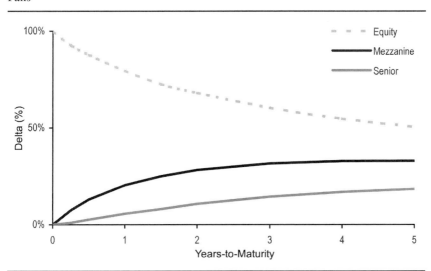

Note: Assuming equal tranche sizes of 4% for equity, mezzanine, and senior tranches.
Source: Merrill Lynch.

Delta as a Function of Time

Assuming that spreads remain steady during the life of the transaction, and there are no defaults, deltas "migrate" as the maturity of the transaction approaches. For instance, the delta on the equity tranche increases as the transaction approaches maturity and tends to the limit of 100% (see Exhibit 31.20). Conversely, delta falls for mezzanine tranches and above, and approaches a 0% limit at maturity of the transaction.

In practice though, hedging shorter dated exposures may be more difficult, depending on liquidity.

Deltas for Individual Credits as Spreads Disperse

For a portfolio of identical credits (spread, recovery, maturity, correlation, etc.), the delta would be identical for every credit in the portfolio. In reality, a typical portfolio would not be so homogenous, consisting of credits at different spreads, and so the delta would likely be different for each name. We can examine how the delta for individual credits would change as spreads disperse in the portfolio (see Exhibit 31.21).

In general:

EXHIBIT 31.21 Name Spread and Delta: Higher Spread Implies a Higher Delta for an Equity Tranche but Vice Versa for Senior Tranches

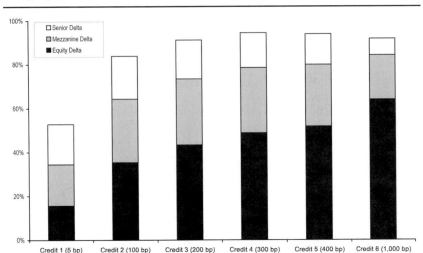

Note: Assuming tranche sizes of 4% for equity, mezzanine, and senior tranches.
Source: Merrill Lynch.

- A rising credit spread will cause a credit's delta to rise for the equity tranche and a credit's delta to fall for the senior tranche. The dynamics of the intermediate tranches will be a combination of the two, depending on the capital structure of the deal.
- A falling credit spread will cause a credit's delta to fall for the equity tranche and a credit's delta to rise for the senior tranche. Again, the dynamics of the intermediate tranches will be a combination of the two, depending on the capital structure of the deal.

Therefore, the dealer's hedging behaviour depends on which tranche the dealer is short.

In Exhibit 31.21, we show the relationship between credit spread and delta for different tranches of the portfolio. We have chosen a broad range of credit spreads with extremes of 5 and 1,000 basis points. In this example, a rising credit spread corresponds to a higher delta for the lower-rated tranches. In the example, Credit 3 (200 basis point spread) has a delta of approximately 43%, whilst Credit 4 (300 basis point spread) has a delta of approximately 50%, if the dealer buys protection on the equity tranche.

As we approach the senior tranche though, this relationship is reversed and a rising credit spread corresponds to a falling delta. If the dealer has bought protection on the senior tranche, Credit 3 has a delta of approximately 18%, whilst Credit 4 has a delta of approximately 15%

For a pool of varying credit spreads, the equity tranche becomes more dependent on the worst names in the portfolio and the senior tranche less dependent on the worst names. Once credit spreads deteriorate and scatter, individual tranches depend on different names.

CHAPTER 32

Rating Methodology for Collateralised Debt Obligations

Henry Charpentier
AVP–Analyst
Moody's Investors Servive

Hernan Quipildor
AVP–Analyst
Moody's Investors Service

As with all Moody's long-term ratings, ratings for collateralised debt obligations (CDOs) are based on the "expected loss" concept. In order to determine the expected loss of an obligation, Moody's calculates the average loss incurred by holders of the obligation (the noteholders) under any possible default scenario, weighted by the probability of each default scenario occurring. In this chapter we explain the rating methodology and then illustrate how the described methodology is applied by means of a case study.

RATING METHODOLOGY: THE BINOMIAL EXPANSION TECHNIQUE

In the first section, we will describe (1) the methodology used by Moody's to determine the probability distribution of default scenarios; (2) how the loss of a noteholder is calculated for a given loss scenario; and (3) how the expected loss (and therefore the rating) of the notes is determined.

Defining the Probability Distribution of the Default Scenarios

In defining the probability distribution of the default scenario, we describe the following:

- The underlying concept
- The theoretical portfolio
- The diversity score
- The weighted average probability of default
- The weighted average recovery rates

The Underlying Concept

The difficulty in analysing CDOs lies in determining the probability of each default scenario according to the number of assets considered, their heterogeneity in terms of ratings and magnitude, and the degree of correlation between them. The Monte Carlo approach is inarguably an accurate tool for this kind of analysis. However, in this chapter, we will focus on the so-called *binomial expansion technique* (BET), an alternative method also used by Moody's that will help us to outline the main credit issues for this kind of transactions.

The underlying concept is to create a "theoretical portfolio"—consisting of identical (in terms of amount, ratings, maturity, and recoveries) and uncorrelated assets—that has a similar default behaviour to the actual portfolio to be securitised. As it comprises homogeneous and independent assets, the theoretical portfolio enables the use of a binomial distribution in order to determine the probability of each default scenario. Specifically, the outcome of each theoretical asset can be viewed as a Bernoulli random variable, with a p probability of defaulting (a success) and a $1 - p$ probability of nondefaulting. Therefore, the probability of having i defaults out of D theoretical assets is equal to the probability of having i "successes" out of D Bernoulli trials, which is given by the binomial distribution:

$$P_i = \frac{D!}{i!(D-i)!} p^i (1-p)^{D-i}$$

The Theoretical Portfolio

As an initial step in its quantitative analysis, Moody's determines the theoretical portfolio given the actual portfolio to be securitised. The defining parameters of such a theoretical portfolio are as follows:

■ The number of theoretical assets included in the theoretical portfolio is D, where D is the diversity score.

■ All the theoretical assets represent an identical amount, which is the amount of the actually securitised portfolio divided by D.

■ All the theoretical assets have the same probability of default, which is the weighted average probability of default of the actually securitised assets.

■ All the theoretical assets are assumed to have a bullet profile, with a maturity equal to the weighted average life of the actually securitised assets.

■ All the theoretical assets have the same recovery rate, which is the weighted average recovery rate of the actually securitised assets.

The Diversity Score

The diversity score of an actual portfolio to be securitised can be seen as the equivalent number of independent and homogeneous assets included in such portfolio. The diversity score calculation primarily takes the following two factors into account:

■ *Heterogeneity in terms of amount.* If a portfolio of $100 is composed of two obligations, one of $99.9 and another of $0.01, the diversity score will be close to 1, regardless of the correlation between the two obligations, as a single theoretical asset with the same defining parameters as the first obligation will accurately recreate the default behaviour of the portfolio.

■ *Correlation between the obligations.* If a portfolio is composed of two perfectly correlated obligations (i.e., if one obligation defaults, the other one will as well), the diversity score will once again be 1, regardless of the amount of each obligation, as a single theoretical asset will accurately recreate the default behaviour of the portfolio.

In practical terms, the diversity score is calculated as follows:

1. An *obligor par amount* is calculated for each obligor represented in the portfolio by summing the notional amount of all bonds or loans in the portfolio issued by that obligor.[1]

2. An *average par amount* is calculated by summing the obligor par amounts and dividing by the number of obligors represented.

3. An *equivalent unit score* is calculated for each obligor by taking the lesser of (i) 1 and (ii) the obligor par amount for the obligor divided by the average par amount.

---

[1] Any obligors affiliated with one another will be considered as a single obligor.

4. An *aggregate industry equivalent unit score* is then calculated for each of the Moody's industry groups (see Appendix 1) by summing the equivalent unit scores for each obligor in that industry.
5. An *industry diversity score* is then established by reference to the diversity score table (as shown in Appendix 2) for the related aggregate industry equivalent unit score provided that, if any aggregate industry equivalent unit score falls between any two such scores, the applicable industry diversity score will be the lower of the two industry diversity scores in the diversity score table.
6. The *diversity score* for the portfolio is then calculated by summing each of the industry diversity scores.

For example, suppose we have the portfolio shown in Exhibit 32.1. The portfolio is composed of 15 assets, issued by 15 different obligors, each appertaining to industry groups A, B, C, or D:

EXHIBIT 32.1   Diversity Score Calculation

Obligor	Amount	Industry	Equivalent Unit Score
1	15	A	0.87
2	10	A	0.58
3	10	A	0.58
4	20	A	1.00
5	10	A	0.58
6	15	B	0.87
7	25	B	1.00
8	30	C	1.00
9	10	C	0.58
10	10	C	0.58
11	15	D	0.87
12	20	D	1.00
13	25	D	1.00
14	30	D	1.00
15	15	D	0.87
TOTAL	260		
Average Par Amount	17.33		

Industry	Aggregate Equivalent Unit Score	Industry Diversity Score
A	3.5962	2.17
B	1.8654	1.40
C	2.1538	1.55
D	4.7308	2.57
	Diversity Score	7.69

The Weighted Average Probability of Default

In order to determine the weighted average probability of default of the portfolio, Moody's uses the ratings of the securitised obligations. As mentioned above, a Moody's rating reflects the expected loss of an obligation. The Moody's Idealised Expected Loss Table (Exhibit 32.2) gives the expected loss of any rating for a given time horizon.

In order to determine the default probability of an obligation of the securitised portfolio, Moody's will first map its expected loss in the idealised expected loss table (considering a time horizon equal to the weighted average life of the securitised portfolio). As the expected loss of an obligation is the product of its default probability times the average severity of its default, one can deduce the default probability of an obligation dividing its expected loss by the average severity. In the framework of corporate debt securitisation, Moody's assumes a 55% average severity.

The Weighted Average Recovery Rates

When modelling recovery rates, Moody's tends to use different assumptions mainly based on the jurisdictions where the assets are located. The rationale behind this procedure is twofold. Firstly, there are jurisdictions, such as the US, for which substantial historical data are available to drive uni-modal recovery rate assumptions. Secondly, other geographical areas, such as Europe, may represent a variety of jurisdictions, leading us to conclude that the volatility around a mean assumption is a crucial factor. In light of this issue, Moody's has refined its modelling of European CDOs to take into consideration recovery rates volatility instead of a fixed unique assumption. The rationale for this modelling refining is linked to the very nature of European markets, where several sources of volatility can be identified. Firstly, the heterogeneous legal environment represented by particular countries' jurisdictions, secondly, the different possible outcomes of defaults among them (liquidation, restructuring, etc.) and last but not least, the ranking of the obligation and the security arrangements, which may vary depending from obligation to obligation.

Furthermore, when modelling recovery rates, Moody's is faced with the issue of estimation (the recovery rate distribution is not known with certainty, as the availability of historical data is often limited).

In order to include the variability of recovery rates within the BET framework, Moody's models recovery rates as following a discrete distribution, in which they take values of 0%, 10%, 20%... up to 100%, in the aim of determining a probability distribution of recoveries.

This distribution has a four-phase construction process, as follows:

EXHIBIT 32.2 Moody's Idealised Expected Loss Table

					Time Horizon (in year)					
Rating	1	2	3	4	5	6	7	8	9	10
Aaa	*	0.0001%	0.0004%	0.0010%	0.0016%	0.0022%	0.0029%	0.0036%	0.0045%	0.0055%
Aa1	0.0003%	0.0017%	0.0055%	0.0116%	0.0171%	0.0231%	0.0297%	0.0369%	0.0451%	0.0550%
Aa2	0.0007%	0.0044%	0.0143%	0.0259%	0.0374%	0.0490%	0.0611%	0.0743%	0.0902%	0.1100%
Aa3	0.0017%	0.0105%	0.0325%	0.0556%	0.0781%	0.1007%	0.1249%	0.1496%	0.1799%	0.2200%
A1	0.0032%	0.0204%	0.0644%	0.1040%	0.1436%	0.1815%	0.2233%	0.2640%	0.3152%	0.3850%
A2	0.0060%	0.0385%	0.1221%	0.1898%	0.2569%	0.3207%	0.3905%	0.4560%	0.5401%	0.6600%
A3	0.0214%	0.0825%	0.1980%	0.2970%	0.4015%	0.5005%	0.6105%	0.7150%	0.8360%	0.9900%
Baa1	0.0495%	0.1540%	0.3080%	0.4565%	0.6050%	0.7535%	0.9185%	1.0835%	1.2485%	1.4300%
Baa2	0.0935%	0.2585%	0.4565%	0.6600%	0.8690%	1.0835%	1.3255%	1.5675%	1.7820%	1.9800%
Baa3	0.2310%	0.5775%	0.9405%	1.3090%	1.6775%	2.0350%	2.3815%	2.7335%	3.0635%	3.3550%
Ba1	0.4785%	1.1110%	1.7215%	2.3100%	2.9040%	3.4375%	3.8830%	4.3395%	4.7795%	5.1700%
Ba2	0.8580%	1.9085%	2.8490%	3.7400%	4.6255%	5.3735%	5.8850%	6.4130%	6.9575%	7.4250%
Ba3	1.5455%	3.0305%	4.3285%	5.3845%	6.5230%	7.4195%	8.0410%	8.6405%	9.1905%	9.7130%
B1	2.5740%	4.6090%	6.3690%	7.6175%	8.8660%	9.8395%	10.5215%	11.1265%	11.6820%	12.2100%
B2	3.9380%	6.4185%	8.5525%	9.9715%	11.3905%	12.4575%	13.2055%	13.8325%	14.4210%	14.9600%
B3	6.3910%	9.1355%	11.5665%	13.2220%	14.8775%	16.0600%	17.0500%	17.9190%	18.5790%	19.1950%
Caa2	14.3000%	17.8750%	21.4500%	24.1340%	26.8125%	28.6000%	30.3875%	32.1750%	33.9625%	35.7500%

* 0.00003%

638

1. Moody's defines assumptions of recovery rate by country and by type of asset. These definitions are based on a variety of information collected from banks and expertise from analysts and practitioners.
2. Based on the modelling of the portfolio (which will then be treated as D (diversity score) independent and identical assets), a mean and a standard deviation of the recovery rate of one such D identical asset is determined from the recovery rate assumptions by country and by type of assets.
3. From the mean and standard deviation (as described above), Moody's sets up a shape for the recovery rate probability distribution for one asset, which is assumed to be bimodal (opposed to the observed unimodal US shape). This means that this distribution is likely to have two main peaks of probability: one corresponding to low recovery rates, the other to high recovery rates. Historical data suggest indeed that once a default has occurred, recoveries are either high or low. There are few "intermediary" cases. These levels can be correlated with the default scenario (arrangement or liquidation scenario, for instance).
4. Finally, Moody's extends this recovery probability distribution to two defaulting assets in the pool, and then to three defaulting assets in the pool, and so on, up to D defaulting assets in the pool.

We note that the more defaults there are in the pool, the closer the recovery distribution resembles a single-peak distribution (rather than a bimodal distribution) centred on the asset mean, and the more the volatility decreases. This tendency is illustrated in the graph shown in Exhibit 32.3.

EXHIBIT 32.3   Recovery Rate Probability Distribution

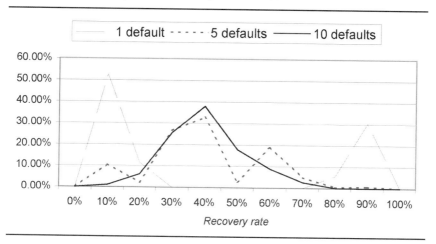

Having obtained these conditional probabilities (conditional on the number of defaults), the final step is to multiply these probabilities by the probabilities of occurrence of the default scenario (as determined in the binomial expansion method).

The final default probabilities, taken into account for calculating the expected loss, and thus the rating, are the probabilities of the scenarios with N defaults, and $x\%$ recoveries, where $N = 0$ to *diversity score*, and $x = 0\%$ to 100%.

If we assume that defaults and recoveries are independent, the probability of a given scenario with N defaults and $x\%$ of recoveries is the product of the default probability calculated with the binomial method and the recovery probability calculated with the recovery distribution.

The total expected loss for a given class of notes is thus,

$$\text{Expected loss} = \sum_{\substack{N = 0 \\ x = 0\%}}^{\substack{N = D \\ x = 100\%}} \begin{aligned} &\text{Probability(scenario } N \text{ defaults)} \\ &\times \text{Probability(scenario } x\% \text{ recovery)} \times S(N, x) \end{aligned}$$

where $S(N,x)$ is the severity of the loss for the class of notes under the scenario (N,x).

Determining the Noteholders' Loss Under a Given Default Scenario

After defining the probability distribution of default scenarios, the next step is to determine the loss incurred by the noteholders under each default scenario. This is done using a cash flow model that recreates the cash flow allocation as described in the legal documentation of the contemplated transaction. Such a model enables us to anticipate the cash flows to be received throughout the transaction by each class of noteholders given a default scenario.

The loss incurred by a class of noteholders under a given default scenario is

$$L_{A_{i_x}} = 1 - \frac{NPV_{A_{i_x}}}{PP_A}$$

where

$L_{A_{i_x}}$ = the loss (expressed as a percentage) incurred by a Class A noteholder when i theoretical assets default, with $x\%$ recoveries;

$NPV_{A_{i_x}}$ = the net present value of all the cash flows received by a Class A noteholder when i theoretical assets default, with $x\%$ recoveries, discounted at a rate equal to the interest rate borne by the Class A notes; and

PP_A = the initial purchase price of a Class A note.

Determining the Expected Loss and the Rating of a Note

The first step provided the probability P_{i_x} of each default scenario and the second step provided the loss $L_{A_{i_x}}$ incurred by each class of notes under each default scenario.

The third step consists in calculating the expected loss on each class of notes, which is the average loss incurred under each default scenario weighted by the probability of each default scenario occurring:

$$EL_A = \sum_{\substack{i = 0 \\ x = 0}}^{\substack{x = 100\% \\ i = D}} P_{i_x} L_{A_{i_x}}$$

where EL_A is the expected loss on a Class A note.

The expected loss on a class of notes associated with its average life directly yields the rating of such notes according to Moody's Idealised Expected Loss Table (see Exhibit 32.2).

The BET: An Adaptive Approach

The previous sections describe the methodology used by Moody's to assign its expected loss ratings for CDOs. However, given the complexity and variety of this asset class, several characteristics related to the specific type of asset and structure also need to be incorporated into the analysis. Thus, Moody's BET methodology is adjusted to accurately account for these complexities.

Although an in-depth description of the binomial expansion method implementation in such cases is beyond the scope of the present chapter, we provide below a brief introduction to the main analytical concerns in rating two structures that are currently particularly popular in Europe.

Synthetic CDOs [2]

Credit derivatives allow investors to have exposure to an entity without actually buying a security or loan issued by that entity. Because the expo-

---

[2] For more details on Moody's methodology see "Moody's Approach to Rating Synthetic CDOs," *Moody's Special Report*, July 2003.

sure is synthetic, the transaction can be tailored to meet investors' needs with respect to currency, cash flow and tenor, among other things. However, if the transaction is not structured carefully, it may expose investors to additional risks in comparison to holding an equivalent cash position.

The credit event definitions under a credit default swap are typically a source of additional risks to be borne by the noteholder. As the credit event definitions published by the International Swaps and Derivatives Association (ISDA) are, in some respects, broader than the common understanding of default, they imply a higher probability for the noteholder to incur a loss. Moody's takes into account this feature by applying a stress on the weighted average default probability of the theoretical portfolio, thus translating a default probability into a "credit event probability" in accordance with the terms of the credit default swap.

Another sensitive feature in synthetic transactions is the procedure used to determine the recoveries once a credit event has occurred. Moody's may, in some instances, adjust its recoveries assumptions accordingly.

Multisector CDOs: CDOs of Structured Securities [3]

The inclusion of an increasingly broad range of assets in CDO collateral pools poses several analytical challenges. To analyse diversification within a multisector CDO (also called *CDO of ABS* or *resecuritisation*), Moody's has established asset-backed securities (ABS), mortgage-backed securities (MBS), and CDO sector classifications in addition to those for existing corporate industries.

Within this classification scheme, Moody's makes explicit assumptions about the default correlation between assets to calculate the diversity score ("alternative diversity score"). In addition, Moody's recognises that the loss severity of a structured security varies by asset type, credit rating, and position within the capital structure. For asset types that are prepayment-sensitive, maturity shortening or extension risk due to faster or slower prepayment speed must be examined. Finally, the introduction of synthetic technology into resecuritisations raises additional analitical issues.

CASE STUDY: A SYNTHETIC CDO OF CORPORATE EXPOSURES

In this section, we illustrate how the rating methodology described in the previous section is applied to a synthetic CDO of a pool of corporates.

---

[3] For more details on Moody's methodology, please see "Moody's Approach to Rating Multisector CDOs," *Moody's Special Report*, September 15, 2000.

Transaction Overview

In this transaction, the Arranger purchases credit protection against losses of over €78,500,000 on a €1.0 billion portfolio of corporate reference entities (see Exhibit 32.4) through a credit default swap (CDS) entered into with a special purpose vehicle (SPV). Under the CDS, should a "credit event" occur in respect of a reference entity, the arranger will have to go through a valuation process for this reference entity in order to determine its final price. The notional amount of the reference entity minus its final price will be deemed to be a net loss. Should the aggregate amount of all the net losses incurred in respect of the reference portfolio increase to over €78,500,000, the SPV will pay such excess to the arranger (a credit protection payment). The CDS documentation also provides that the arranger will pay to the SPV a premium of 1.00% p.a. on the reference portfolio's notional amount.

In order to be able to meet its obligations under the CDS, the SPV issues €921,500,000 of credit-linked notes to investors. The proceeds of such issuance constitute the collateral of the CDS and is initially invested in a risk-free overnight deposit yielding EURIBOR minus 0.20%. Should the SPV have to make a credit protection payment to the Arranger, it will use the collateral to fund such payments and will write off the credit-linked notes accordingly (so that the outstanding amount of the credit-linked notes is, at any time, equal to the amount of remaining collateral). On the maturity date of the transaction (five years after closing), the SPV will use the remaining collateral to redeem the credit-linked notes at 100% of their then current outstanding amount. During the life of the transaction, the SPV will pay EURIBOR plus 0.80% on the credit-linked notes out of the premium received under the CDS and the remuneration of the overnight deposit.

Determining the Theoretical Portfolio

As a first step, Moody's determines the parameters of the theoretical portfolio consisting of homogeneous (in terms of amount, rating, maturity and recovery rate) and independent assets that display a similar default behaviour to the actual portfolio.

Diversity Score

Given that all the reference entities have the same notional amount, they all have an *equivalent unit score* equal to 1. The *aggregate industry equivalent unit score* (AIEUS in Exhibit 32.5) of each industry is therefore equal to the number of reference entities included in that industry, and the *industry diversity score* (IDS in Exhibit 32.5) is deduced by reference to the Diversity Score Table shown in Appendix 2. Finally, the diversity score of the reference portfolio is determined by summing the *industry diversity scores*.

EXHIBIT 32.4   The Reference Portfolio

Reference Entity	Notional Amount (€)	Rating	Domicile	Industry
Reference Entity 1	25,000,000	Baa1	UK	Aerospace & Defense
Reference Entity 2	25,000,000	Baa2	Italy	Aerospace & Defense
Reference Entity 3	25,000,000	A2	Germany	Banking
Reference Entity 4	25,000,000	Aa2	Spain	Banking
Reference Entity 5	25,000,000	Aa2	France	Banking
Reference Entity 6	25,000,000	Aa2	UK	Banking
Reference Entity 7	25,000,000	A2	Germany	Beverage, Food, & Tobacco
Reference Entity 8	25,000,000	Baa1	UK	Beverage, Food, & Tobacco
Reference Entity 9	25,000,000	Baa1	France	Buildings & Real Estate
Reference Entity 10	25,000,000	Baa1	UK	Buildings & Real Estate
Reference Entity 11	25,000,000	A2	Switzerland	Chemicals, Plastics, & Rubber
Reference Entity 12	25,000,000	A3	Germany	Chemicals, Plastics, & Rubber
Reference Entity 13	25,000,000	A3	Netherlands	Chemicals, Plastics, & Rubber
Reference Entity 14	25,000,000	A2	France	Containers, Packaging, & Glass
Reference Entity 15	25,000,000	A3	France	Diversified/Conglomerate Manuf.
Reference Entity 16	25,000,000	Baa2	Switzerland	Diversified/Conglomerate Service
Reference Entity 17	25,000,000	Baa1	Sweden	Diversified/Conglomerate Service
Reference Entity 18	25,000,000	Aa3	Germany	Electronics
Reference Entity 19	25,000,000	Baa1	UK	Hotels, Motels, Inns, & Gaming
Reference Entity 20	25,000,000	Baa2	UK	Hotels, Motels, Inns, & Gaming
Reference Entity 21	25,000,000	A2	Switzerland	Insurance
Reference Entity 22	25,000,000	A2	France	Insurance
Reference Entity 23	25,000,000	A3	Sweden	Machinery (Nonagriculture, ...)
Reference Entity 24	25,000,000	Baa1	France	Mining, Steel, & Iron
Reference Entity 25	25,000,000	Baa2	Spain	Oil & Gas
Reference Entity 26	25,000,000	Aa1	UK	Oil & Gas
Reference Entity 27	25,000,000	Baa2	Sweden	Oil & Gas
Reference Entity 28	25,000,000	Aa3	Italy	Oil & Gas
Reference Entity 29	25,000,000	Baa1	Germany	Printing & Publishing
Reference Entity 30	25,000,000	A3	UK	Retail Stores
Reference Entity 31	25,000,000	Baa1	Germany	Retail Stores
Reference Entity 32	25,000,000	Baa1	UK	Retail Stores
Reference Entity 33	25,000,000	Baa3	Germany	Telecommunications
Reference Entity 34	25,000,000	Baa2	Finland	Telecommunications
Reference Entity 35	25,000,000	A1	Finland	Telecommunications
Reference Entity 36	25,000,000	A2	UK	Telecommunications
Reference Entity 37	25,000,000	A1	Germany	Utilities
Reference Entity 38	25,000,000	Baa2	Spain	Utilities
Reference Entity 39	25,000,000	Baa1	UK	Utilities
Reference Entity 40	25,000,000	Baa3	UK	Broadcasting & Entertainment

EXHIBIT 32.5 Determining the Diversity Score

Industry	AIEUS	IDS
Aerospace & Defense	2	1.50
Banking	4	2.33
Beverage, Food, & Tobacco	2	1.50
Buildings & Real Estate	2	1.50
Chemicals, Plastics, & Rubber	3	2.00
Containers, Packaging, & Glass	1	1.00
Diversified/Conglomerate Manuf.	1	1.00
Diversified/Conglomerate Service	2	1.50
Electronics	1	1.00
Hotels, Motels, Inns, & Gaming	2	1.50
Insurance	2	1.50
Machinery (Nonagriculture, ...)	1	1.00
Mining, Steel, & Iron	1	1.00
Oil & Gas	4	2.33
Printing & Publishing	1	1.00
Retail Stores	3	2.00
Telecommunications	4	2.33
Utilities	3	2.00
Broadcasting & Entertainment	1	1.00
Reference portfolio diversity score		29.00

Weighted Average Probability of Default

The time horizon to be considered in this transaction is five years. Based on the *Moody's Idealized Expected Loss Table* shown in Exhibit 32.2, the expected loss of each reference entity can be determined. By assuming a 55% average severity, the default probability of each reference entity can be calculated as its expected loss divided by 55% (Expected loss = Default probability × Average severity).

However, credit events applicable to this CDS are (1) bankruptcy, (2) failure to pay, and (3) restructuring as defined in the 1999 ISDA Credit Derivatives Definition. In Moody's views, the "Restructuring" credit event definition is in some respects broader (and therefore has a greater probability of occurrence) than the situations of default captured by a Moody's rating. In order to capture such increased probability of occurrence, Moody's applies a 1.125 stress to the weighted average default probability of the reference portfolio.

Therefore the credit event probability used for this transaction is 1.04681% (0.93050% × 1.125).

EXHIBIT 32.6 Determining the Weighted Average Default Probability

Rating	5-Year Expected Loss	5-Year Default Probability	Notional Amount per Rating
Aaa	0.0016%	0.0029%	—
Aa1	0.0171%	0.0310%	25,000,000
Aa2	0.0374%	0.0680%	75,000,000
Aa3	0.0781%	0.1420%	50,000,000
A1	0.1436%	0.2610%	50,000,000
A2	0.2569%	0.4670%	175,000,000
A3	0.4015%	0.7300%	125,000,000
Baa1	0.6050%	1.1000%	275,000,000
Baa2	0.8690%	1.5800%	175,000,000
Baa3	1.6775%	3.0500%	50,000,000
Weighted average default probability:		0.93050%	

EXHIBIT 32.7 Determining the Weighted Average Recovery Rate

Country	Recovery Rate Assumption	Notional Amount per Country
Finland	20%	50,000,000
France	20%	150,000,000
Germany	25%	200,000,000
Italy	15%	50,000,000
Netherlands	20%	25,000,000
Spain	20%	75,000,000
Sweden	25%	75,000,000
Switzerland	25%	75,000,000
UK	20%	300,000,000
Weighted average recovery rate:	21.50%	

Weighted Average Recovery Rates

Although Moody's would usually use a bimodal distribution of recovery rates—for the sake of simplicity and as a good approximation of the expected loss of the credit-linked notes to be rated—a fixed weighted average recovery rate can be assumed for the reference portfolio based on the assumptions shown in Exhibit 32.7.

Determining the Noteholders' Loss Under a Given Default Scenario

This part of the analysis is performed through a cash flow model that replicates the transaction structure, as the one shown in Exhibit 32.8.:

1. This first line represents the amount of net losses incurred during each year of the transaction. This amount is equal to (i) the number of theoretical assets assumed to default (4 in this example), multiplied by (ii) the notional amount of a theoretical asset, multiplied by (iii) one minus the assumed recovery rate, divided by (iv) five (losses are assumed to be evenly distributed over the transaction life). In Exhibit 32.8, the net loss was calculated as follows:

$$4 \times (1,000,000,000/29) \times (1 - 20.5\%)/5 = 21,655,172$$

2. This is just the sum of all the net losses incurred at each point in time.

3. This is the amount that is due to be paid by the SPV to the arranger. According to the terms of the CDS mentioned above, this amount is equal to any new aggregate net loss that is in excess of €78,500,000.

4. The credit-linked notes' outstanding amount is equal to their initial outstanding amount (€921,500,000) reduced by the amount of any credit protection payment made by the SPV.

5. The amount of interest is equal to EURIBOR plus 0.80% applied to the outstanding amount of the credit-linked notes (here EURIBOR is assumed to be constant at 2.20%).

6. This is the amount of principal redeemed to the noteholders which is equal to the credit-linked notes outstanding amount at the end of year five.

7. This is the sum of lines (5) and (6), that is, the actual cash flows received by the noteholders.

8. The NPV is based on the string of cash flows established in (7), discounted at EURIBOR plus 0.80%.

9. The loss is calculated as one minus the NPV calculated in (8) divided by the initial investment of the noteholders.

EXHIBIT 32.8 Cash Flow Analysis[a]

	Year				
	1	2	3	4	5
1. Net losses	21,655,172	21,655,172	21,655,172	21,655,172	21,655,172
2. Aggregate net losses	21,655,172	43,310,345	64,965,517	86,620,690	108,275,862
3. Credit protection payment	0	0	0	8,120,690	21,655,172
4. Credit-linked notes outstanding	921,500,000	921,500,000	921,500,000	913,379,310	891,724,138
5. Interest	27,645,000	27,645,000	27,645,000	27,401,379	26,751,724
6. Principal	0	0	0	0	891,724,138
7. Cash flow to noteholders	27,645,000	27,645,000	27,645,000	27,401,379	918,475,862
8. NPV	894,828,078				
9. Loss	2.9%				

[a] Number of theoretical assets assumed in default: 4.

EXHIBIT 32.9   Expected Loss Calculation

Defaults	Loss	Probability
0	0.00%	73.6994%
1	0.00%	22.6100%
2	0.00%	3.3486%
3	0.26%	0.3188%
4	2.89%	0.0219%
5	5.58%	0.0012%
6	8.30%	4.9069%
7	11.02%	1.7056%
8	13.76%	4.9619%
...	...	...
29	63.33%	3.7687%
Expected loss:		0.00154%

Determining the Rating of the Credit-Linked Notes

Thanks to this simple cash flow model, the noteholders' loss can be determined for each default scenario. Then the probability of occurrence of each scenario is provided by the binomial distribution $B(n,p)$, where n is the diversity score and p the credit event probability, as shown in Exhibit 32.9.

Mapping the 0.00154% expected loss in the Moody's Idealised Expected Loss Table over a 5-year horizon, we find that the rating to be assigned to the credit-linked notes should be Aaa.

APPENDIX 1: MOODY'S INDUSTRY GROUPS

1. Aerospace and Defence
2. Automobile
3. Banking
4. Beverage, Food and Tobacco
5. Buildings and Real Estate
6. Chemicals, Plastics, and Rubber
7. Containers, Packaging, and Glass
8. Personal and Nondurable Consumer Products (manufacturing only)
9. Diversified/Conglomerate Manufacturing
10. Diversified/Conglomerate Service
11. Diversified Natural Resources, Precious Metals, and Minerals
12. Ecological
13. Electronics
14. Finance
15. Farming and Agriculture
16. Grocery
17. Healthcare, Education, and Childcare
18. Home and Office Furnishings, Housewares, and Durable Consumer Products
19. Hotels, Motels, Inns, and Gaming
20. Insurance
21. Leisure, Amusement, and Entertainment
22. Machinery (nonagriculture, nonconstruction, and nonelectronic)
23. Mining, Steel, Iron, and Nonprecious Metals
24. Oil and Gas
25. Personal, Food, and Miscellaneous
26. Printing and Publishing
27. Cargo Transport
28. Retail Stores
29. Telecommunications
30. Textiles and Leather
31. Personal Transportation
32. Utilities
33. Broadcasting and Entertainment

APPENDIX 2: MOODY'S DIVERSITY SCORE TABLE

Aggregate Industry Equivalent Unit Score	Industry Diversity Score	Aggregate Industry Equivalent Unit Score	Industry Diversity Score
0.10	0.10	5.10	2.70
0.20	0.20	5.20	2.73
0.30	0.30	5.30	2.77
0.40	0.40	5.40	2.80
0.50	0.50	5.50	2.83
0.60	0.60	5.60	2.87
0.70	0.70	5.70	2.90
0.80	0.80	5.80	2.93
0.90	0.90	5.90	2.97
1.00	1.00	6.00	3.00
1.10	1.05	6.10	3.03
1.20	1.10	6.20	3.05
1.30	1.15	6.30	3.08
1.40	1.20	6.40	3.10
1.50	1.25	6.50	3.13
1.60	1.30	6.60	3.15
1.70	1.35	6.70	3.18
1.80	1.40	6.80	3.20
1.90	1.45	6.90	3.23
2.00	1.50	7.00	3.25
2.10	1.55	7.10	3.28
2.20	1.60	7.20	3.30
2.30	1.65	7.30	3.33
2.40	1.70	7.40	3.35
2.50	1.75	7.50	3.38
2.60	1.80	7.60	3.40
2.70	1.85	7.70	3.43
2.80	1.90	7.80	3.45
2.90	1.95	7.90	3.48
3.00	2.00	8.00	3.50
3.10	2.03	8.10	3.53
3.20	2.07	8.20	3.55
3.30	2.10	8.30	3.58

MOODY'S DIVERSITY SCORE TABLE (CONT.)

Aggregate Industry Equivalent Unit Score	Industry Diversity Score	Aggregate Industry Equivalent Unit Score	Industry Diversity Score
3.40	2.13	8.40	3.60
3.50	2.17	8.50	3.63
3.60	2.20	8.60	3.65
3.70	2.23	8.70	3.68
3.80	2.27	8.80	3.70
3.90	2.30	8.90	3.73
4.00	2.33	9.00	3.75
4.10	2.37	9.10	3.78
4.20	2.40	9.20	3.80
4.30	2.43	9.30	3.83
4.40	2.47	9.40	3.85
4.50	2.50	9.50	3.88
4.60	2.53	9.60	3.90
4.70	2.57	9.70	3.93
4.80	2.60	9.80	3.95
4.90	2.63	9.90	3.98
5.00	2.67	10.00	4.00

CHAPTER 33

CLOs and CBOs for Project Finance Debt: Rating Considerations

Arthur F. Simonson
Director
Standard & Poor's

William H Chew
Managing Director
Standard & Poor's

Henry Albulescu
Managing Director
Standard & Poor's

Project financing has long been focused on two chief ways of raising debt capital: project loans backed by the revenue of individual project facilities and project developer debt backed by cash flow from leveraged and unleveraged ownership interests in a number of projects. At the present time, lenders and sponsors are increasingly looking to a third way to raise debt and equity capital for project financing in the form of securitised project collateralised loan obligations (CLOs) and collateralised bond obligations (CBOs).

Bonds are now being issued to fund closed-end-defined pools of project loans made by banks and multilateral/expert credit agencies. To date, several types of securitisation structures and features have been used. These include closed-ended defined pools of project loans and open-ended financings. Sponsors have used both true sale of assets and setting up a portfolio where credit risk has been synthetically transferred to the CLO securities.

Under a CLO or CBO structure, capital market bonds are paid by cash flow generated from a pool of project loans or bonds. The credit strength of the bonds generally will be stronger than the credit strength of any individual loan, to the extent that the pooled cash flows diversify the default risk and principal loss potential inherent in the loan making up the pool. In addition, the bonds may benefit from overcollateralisation by loans and loan cash flows. Typically, these bond issues use tranching to give separate series of bonds priority claims on the pools' cash flows. Standard & Poor's stresses that this type of securitisation does not constitute any credit alchemy—rating elevation results only from specific credit strength provided by diversification, subordination, and overcollateralisation. However, Standard & Poor's believes that CLO/CBO securitisation does represent one of the most significant ways that borrowers likely will tap the broader market for project debt. It brings significant advantages for borrowers, capital market investors, and bank lenders.

- For borrowers, it offers a way to raise debt capital at lower costs and with more attractive terms and tenor than those available for individual projects.
- For investors, it represents an efficient way to diversify the risks inherent in individual project loan or bond investments. In addition, CLOs may offer substantially greater liquidity than single-asset project investments, especially those that do not carry credible ratings.
- For bank and agency lenders, project CLOs provide a way to liquefy one of the largest illiquid components of bank loan portfolios. Thus, lenders benefit from regulatory capital relief, as well as expanded lending capacity. One of the chief motivations for many bank lenders is the immediate opportunity to improve profitability by redeploying capital.

Standard & Poor's believes the growth of project CLOs and CBOs will be an important step in expanding the participation of portfolio investors in the broader infrastructure debt markets. However, potential issuers should recognize that effective use of rated project CLO and CBO structures will require sponsors to address key credit questions inherent in this type of securitisation as it applies to infrastructure, notably:

■ How do postdefault recovery rates compare for projects, especially in the emerging and developed countries, where project loans are increasingly being originated?

■ How diverse are project risks really likely to be across sectors and regions—particularly, should project debt experience some generic challenges such as construction, operating, or political risks across a number of countries?

■ How does default likelihood change over the life of a loan? For amortizing loans, there is evidence, for example, that loans are less likely to default after they have amortized a substantial amount of debt.

Initial information indicates that answers to these questions are favorable for pooled project debt issues. For example, recovery rates may be higher than those on comparable corporate loans, where project loans are appropriately secured and economic incentives strongly support project debt. However, much will depend on the ability of project sponsors and sponsors of project portfolios to document the key project data on which credit assessment of portfolios will necessarily rest, in particular, project-specific information on default timing, duration, and recovery rates.

For many types of project loans, default and loss severity experiences are still fairly limited. This is especially true for cross-border project loans, such as infrastructure projects raising capital in hard currency and repaying the loans from local currency tariffs or governmental support payments. Because the data on default timing, recovery, and loss severity does not have a statistically significant track record, ongoing surveillance is important to maintain ratings on the CLO securities, especially for the ratings on the subordinated and junior tranches. Standard & Poor's expects the ratings on the junior and subordinated tranches of project finance CLOs to be more dynamic than typical structured finance securities. Until statistically significant data are available, any assessment of default rates and loss severity and how they affect the ratings on the CLO securities needs to be monitored closely on an ongoing basis. Standard & Poor's believes it will be some time before actuarial assumptions will be established for the key credit risk factors that drive a project finance CLO rating.

In view of these uncertainties, lenders and borrowers who are contemplating this type of financing will be well served to focus on the specific pool of assets supporting a given transaction, as Standard & Poor's does in establishing its CBO and CLO ratings. It is the credit profile of the loans supporting a given asset-backed debt issue rather than any generic assumptions about global loan performance that will determine whether a project CLO or CBO issue will pay out.

Project finance debt can be very specialized. This chapter outlines how Standard & Poor's will tailor general criteria to address asset characteristics, which differ from established norms.

STANDARD & POOR'S PROJECT FINANCE CLO RATING CRITERIA

In a CLO transaction, payments to the CLO noteholders are derived from the cash flows realized from the underlying pool of loans in the securitised portfolio. While most of the CLO transactions rated to date involve the repackaging of corporate loans, the rating process for a transaction with project loans as the underlying asset class is similar.

Rating any CLO transaction requires a linear approach with distinct levels of analysis. The first level of analysis is an assessment of the credit quality of the underlying assets. The second level of analysis focuses on the default and loss severity characteristics of the pool. The third level of analysis involves cash flow forecasts, and the last level examines the structural features of the transaction.

In preparation for rating CLOs with project loans as the underlying assets, Standard & Poor's researched the loan structure and behavior of project loans and concluded that project loans have different fundamental characteristics than corporate loans. As a result, the criterion inputs needed to perform the analysis of a CLO transaction with project loans as the underlying assets will differ from those for transactions with corporate loans. Through internal studies and conversation with external parties, Standard & Poor's has concluded that the key differences between project loans and corporate loans result from:

- Different credit profiles
- Different loan structures
- Different behavioral characteristics

DIFFERENT CREDIT PROFILES

Project financing is normally used for large, capital-intensive assets. Usually, the inherent risks of an asset using this financing structure are easily identified. Through the rating process, Standard & Poor's can determine if the project's risks are mitigated and to what extent the risks are residing with the lenders. The types of assets that have availed themselves of this financing technique include power plants, pipelines, toll roads, mines, energy facilities, and infrastructure projects. These types of assets are rated by Standard & Poor's following an established criteria framework.

The analysis of any project financing takes a bottom-up approach, focusing on project-level risks, institutional risks, currency risks, sovereign risks, and any credit enhancements structured into the transaction. Typically, the financial profile of a rated project appears weaker than that of a similarly rated corporation in the same industry. For example, the initial debt leverage for a BBB rated power project is generally higher than that of a BBB rated utility company. Despite the weaker financial measures, Standard & Poor's may be able to assign the same rating to the project as it does to the corporation if the predictability of the project's cash flows is greater.

Project finance transactions are usually made up of a single asset, are owned by the private sector, and are dependent solely on the performance of the project (nonrecourse to the owners) for repayment of any debt issued at the project level. In addition, the structural, legal, and financial features incorporated into most project transactions to protect and enhance the cash flow make it easier to predict a project's cash flow stream and to determine the project's ability to service its debt obligations.

DIFFERENT LOAN STRUCTURES

Project loan structures differ from corporate loan structures in that projects typically have amortizing debt, tailored debt service payments, stricter covenants, and cash traps. Amortizing debt mitigates refinancing risk. Refinancing risk is usually present in corporate financings and forces Standard & Poor's to look beyond the tenor of the debt to assess the ability of the corporation to repay its obligations. In contrast, the lack of refinancing risk in most project financings allows Standard & Poor's to focus purely on the project in relation to the tenor of the rated debt. Amortizing debt also leads to decreasing debt leverage over time, which is beneficial from a credit perspective.

Tailored debt service payments are also a strength of project financings. Project financings usually pay down principal as time progresses. However, there is no limitation on how the schedule of principal repayments can be designed. Therefore, projects can match repayment of debt with cash flows expected from project operations.

Covenants and cash traps within the financing documents of the transaction also lead to a better ability to monitor projects. The better ability to monitor transactions can help the lenders be more active in their dealings with the project's owners and management. While differences in the loan structure can affect the underlying rating on a project, these differences are also the primary reasons why corporate and project bonds behave differently as stress situations develop and as defaults and restructurings take place.

DIFFERENT BEHAVIORAL CHARACTERISTICS

Most corporate financings typically issue unsecured debt. In contrast, most project financings pledge to lenders both the physical assets and the revenues to be derived from operations. The secured nature of project loans provides the lenders with a different type of claim on a borrower's assets, which, in the event of a stress scenario, may be a better incentive to project sponsors to carry or fund a project's obligations through a short-term anomaly. In addition, the project financing structure is generally used for infrastructure and other essential assets.

The type of assets that avail themselves to a project finance structure has led Standard & Poor's to conclude that defaults with ensuing restructurings, rather than liquidations, will likely be the norm for project finance transactions experiencing stress. This assumption is based on an analysis of troubled project finance transactions in both the bank and capital markets.

While construction, technical, operating, or market difficulties have caused projects to experience problems, overleverage is usually the primary reason for a project financing to get into financial trouble. Most project financings are highly leveraged transactions, and therefore, the debt-expense component of total expenses will likely be higher when compared to that of a similarly rated corporate financing. Excess leverage has caused many defaults of both projects and corporations. However, Standard & Poor's believes that project financings have a larger capacity than corporations to carry high leverage. Although high debt levels will negatively affect the underlying rating on a project financing, most projects generate higher cash flows than cash expenses from operations, which means that some level of debt can be supported. Therefore, in a stress scenario, a restructuring can take place that lowers the yearly debt service requirements but extends the maturity of the project loan.

Due to the differences in credit profile, loan structure, and behavioral characteristics, Standard & Poor's has concluded that project loans act differently and are structurally different from corporate loans. As a result, Standard & Poor's has modified the necessary inputs in the CLO-rating process to better reflect the characteristics of project loans. Each stage of the established CLO-rating criteria has been modified to properly reflect the underlying fundamentals of project finance loans. Specifically, the areas that have been modified include:

- Credit assessments of a pool's underlying assets
- Default model characteristics
- Cash flow analysis characteristics
- Diversity characteristics

CREDIT ASSESSMENT OF A POOL'S ASSETS

The primary change in this stage of the CLO analysis has to do with the credit assessment of the loans in the proposed pool of loans. Due to the uniqueness of each individual project, Standard & Poor's will perform credit assessments for each loan in the proposed pool. If the size of the proposed pool of project loans makes an actual analysis unwieldy, Standard & Poor's may rely on sampling techniques.

If the number of project loans in the pool is approximately 25 or less, Standard & Poor's will assign an actual credit assessment to each individual loan. Generally, if the number of loans in the pool is more than 25, Standard & Poor's will assign credit assessments to some subset of the portfolio, as long as a sampling technique can be utilized.

As part of the sampling process, Standard & Poor's interviews the lending institution's personnel to gain insight into its credit origination, surveillance, and workout procedures. The sampling process will also place constraints on the lending institution to avoid "cherry-picking" and the substitution of weaker credit quality loans for stronger credit quality loans once the portfolios have initially been designed. Standard & Poor's requires the lending institution to provide the documentation needed to properly assess the credit quality of the underlying loans.

DEFAULT MODEL CHARACTERISTICS

The result of the credit assessment process will give a rating distribution on all the assets in the portfolio. The default frequency of a project and corporate loan with the same rating is statistically equivalent. Therefore, the proprietary Standard & Poor's default model used for other CLO transactions can be used for portfolios with project loans as the underlying asset. The default model estimates how many loans in the portfolio will experience a default based on each loan's credit rating and payment characteristics.

As with other types of CLO transactions, Standard & Poor's employs either a "traditional" single-jurisdictional default model or a multijurisdictional default model to assess the default probability of a pool of project finance loans. The specific version of the model used is dependent on the characteristics of the asset portfolio. The single-jurisdictional model is used for transaction that do not have a significant level of projects concentrated within the same sovereign country. The multijurisdictional model is used when multiple projects are concentrated within the same country. The multijurisdictional model factors into the default probability the likelihood of default on all the projects situated in the same country, caused by the actions of the sovereign government (for example, exchange controls affecting all projects). Standard & Poor's will work with the issuer to establish which default model must be used, based on the characteristics of the project portfolio.

One critical area in the default analysis is the assessment of diversification penalties. Diversification penalties are reductions in a loan's implied ratings due to high degrees of correlation between assets in the portfolio. The correlation analysis between individual project finance loans in a pool will be done at the beginning of the rating process to give the sponsor the ability to alter the portfolio to make it as efficient as possible. The correlation between the same type of infrastructure assets will depend on the specific characteristics of each individual loan and the interplay of each loan within the overall pool. The correlation between similar types of project loans could actually be minimal because of the unlikely chance of experiencing credit deteriorations. Two examples illustrate this point.

First, the financing of a toll road in Arizona will have very little positive correlation to a toll road financing in Florida. Second, a power plant selling power to a New York utility has very little positive correlation to a power plant selling power to a Brazilian utility. In both cases, the reason for the default would be specific only to that asset. Standard & Poor's, however, believes that diversification penalties should be assessed for project loan CLO transactions that have high degrees of obligor and/or geographic correlations. The current Asian crisis and the Latin America crisis of the 1980s show that geographical correlation extends to entire regions and is not limited to single country correlations.

Standard & Poor's has divided the world into 13 regions, as shown in Exhibit 33.1.

The economic environment of countries situated in each region are likely to be correlated, and as such, economic difficulties may be experienced by a number of the countries at the same time. This correlation

EXHIBIT 33.1 Standard & Poor's Geographic Regions for CBOs/CLOs

Latin America and the Caribbean	Eastern and Central Europe, Turkey
Chile and Colombia	The Gulf States
Southeast Asia and Korea	Africa and the Middle East
India and Pakistan	Sub-Saharan Africa
Sri Lanka, Bangladesh, and Nepal	South Africa
China, Hong Kong, and Taiwan	Pacific Islands
Russia and the CIS	

EXHIBIT 33.2 Rating Notch Down by Regional Concentration

Regional concentration	Notch down
Less than 15%	0 notches
15% to less than 25%	1 notch
25% to less than 30%	2 notches
30% to less than 35%	3 notches
Above 35%	Case-by-case analyses

may lead to increased pressure on the projects and lead to higher defaults. To account for this correlation in determining the default probability, Standard & Poor's will notch down the rating of each project in a given region as shown in Exhibit 33.2.

In addition to diversification penalties for obligor and geographic concentrations, these penalties will also be assessed if there are significant concentrations and correlations in critical project finance aspects. Critical aspects include a purchaser of projects' products, key suppliers to projects, technology supporting projects, and a provider of project-level credit enhancements. Standard & Poor's analysis will explore these relationship types for any proposed CLO project loan transaction. If there is a significant concentration (for example, a high portion of the projects sell electricity to one utility), Standard & Poor's will assess additional diversification penalties for all the noncomplying project loans.

The level of a correlation penalty will be determined on a case-by-case basis. However, Standard & Poor's will use the criteria already established as a guideline. The severity of diversification penalty is based on the overall level of concentration and normally ranges from a one- to three-notch downward adjustment from the original project loan credit assessment.

CASH FLOW ANALYSIS CHARACTERISTICS

In a CLO transaction, Standard & Poor's assumes a certain number of the underlying pool's assets will default. The amount of defaulted loans will be specified by the default model. Therefore, assumptions surrounding loan restructurings are critical to the rating analysis of the CLO transaction. Specifically, for CLOs with project loans as the underlying pool assets, Standard & Poor's must determine how the underlying loans will act in terms of timing of default, timing of recovery, and loss severity.

Default Timing

To rate a CLO made up of project loans, Standard & Poor's will run a number of sensitivity analyses, varying default timing. The standard default scenarios include concentrations of defaults throughout the transaction. In each of these cases, the rating will be determined by the transaction's ability to make every scheduled debt service payment. Standard & Poor's has concluded that when there is a pool of amortizing loans, running backend stress scenarios, typical for corporate loans, may be unnecessary. In the case of a pool of amortizing loans, a project loan nearing the end of its term is probably less likely to default when compared to a loan facing a bullet or balloon payment due to the amount of equity accretion in the project. Similar to a mortgage on property, it is in the owner's interest to make scheduled loan payments on project debt to avoid the loss of a project that has been significantly paid for. Consequently, given the lower likelihood of default late in the project loan life, the need for a backended loss scenario is minimal.

Recovery Timing

The established CLO criteria states that there is a one-year, no-pay period followed by two successive years in which 50% of the total amount to be recovered is received at the end of each year for the loans chosen to default in the cash flow analysis. After researching project finance loans, Standard & Poor's concluded that the timing of recovery on project loans will, on average, be shorter than the recovery timing on comparable corporate loans. While Standard & Poor's still anticipates a period where no interest or principal is received, the recovery of the estimated recovery percentage may occur faster than for corporate loans, depending on the structure of the projects and where they are domiciled. A faster recovery is generally due to the structural protections incorporated into project financings and the fact that borrowers are more likely to be aware of and can react to the negative situations in a more timely fashion. These protections include:

- Distribution/dividend blocks.
- The need to use the debt service reserve.
- Items that trigger an event of default, even when there may be enough cash flow to pay debt service.
- The ease of monitoring these transactions.

Severity

Standard & Poor's has identified a number of items that illustrate why project finance loans are fundamentally different from corporate finance loans in the area of loss severity. These items include:

- Project debt secured by both physical assets and the contracts underlying the transaction.
- Larger step-in rights of lenders to projects.
- Clear contractual obligations, penalties, and remedies incorporated into project transactions.
- Decreasing leverage over time.
- Essential nature of many infrastructure projects.
- Linked inputs and outputs.
- Vested interests of counterparties.

The presence of these items causes Standard & Poor's to conclude that the recovery rate for project loans on average will be higher than that of corporate loans. However, empirical evidence on the actual history of loss recovery for project loans is lacking, and it is likely that the actual recovery rates will differ based on the asset type and where the asset is domiciled. Therefore, Standard & Poor's will assign a recovery value for each loan that has received a credit assessment in an effort to determine an average pool recovery rate. The range of recovery rates assumed for individual project loans in a CLO transaction is expected to fall in the 30–70% range.

STRUCTURED FINANCE ISSUES

Once Standard & Poor's completes its analysis of the underlying pool of loans and determines the total amount of losses required to support each rating level, an analysis of the transaction's cash flow and structure is performed. Factors such as the priority of payments, servicing fee, interest coverage, the transaction's liquidity, and the legal final payment date of the rated securities are all considered in the analysis.

Priority of Payments

The priority of payments or cash flow "waterfall" refers to the manner in which the transaction pays its obligations under the governing indenture. In most CLO transactions, cash flows are allocated to pay the senior class of notes before the subordinated or junior classes are paid. Shutting off principal payments to the junior notes in favor of the senior notes acts as credit enhancement. Credit enhancement in a structured financing is a mechanism that protects a class of notes against a payment default. Consequently, those notes in the senior position in the priority of payments will receive a higher rating, since junior securities and/or overcollateralisation assume a first loss position.

Servicing Fee

The servicing fee must be sized and quantified to ensure that not only the initial servicer is adequately compensated, but also that a successor servicer or backup servicer would be able to service the pool of project finance loans given the level of compensation. Standard & Poor's will require either a "hot" backup servicer that can immediately assume the role of servicer or the submission of a detailed plan that can readily be implemented if the initial servicer is unable to carry out its required responsibilities. As part of Standard & Poor's servicer review, the successor or backup servicer must provide a detailed history of its experience in servicing project finance loans. During this review, the potential successor servicer must demonstrate to Standard & Poor's satisfaction that it has the capability to service not only project loans, but also the relevant industries that encompass these financings.

Among its duties, such as ensuring that all investors receive their payments, it is the responsibility of the servicer to manage the restructuring process for troubled loans. Since the servicer's role is the linchpin in ensuring repayment of the debt securities, Standard & Poor's believes that servicing and administrative fees should be paid prior to any payment to noteholders. This will protect investors against potential disruption of payments caused by workouts on problem project loans.

Interest Coverage

The timely repayment of interest must be ensured by structural features that protect against a mismatch of interest earned on the project finance loans compared with the interest owed on the CLO liabilities. Therefore, an interest coverage covenant must be incorporated into the transaction that states that the interest earned on the assets (project loans) is greater than or equal to the interest on the securities plus servicing fees. If an interest rate swap were to be incorporated in a transaction to cover the risks associated with a pool of fixed rate loans paying floating rate interest or vice versa, then the cost of the swap must be included in the interest coverage test.

Transaction Liquidity

While a transaction may be tranched sufficiently to ensure noteholders' repayment of their investment, the transaction may not have sufficient internal liquidity to make such payments on a timely basis. Therefore, a liquidity reserve funded either at the inception of the transaction or over time, if there is sufficient cash generated or excess spread during the initial life of the transaction, can be utilized to ensure timely repayment of principal and interest in a liquidity squeeze.

Once the transaction's structure and cash flows are reviewed, Standard & Poor's will then stress losses, determined by the CLO model, over the tenor of the transaction. As mentioned earlier, Standard & Poor's will focus the stress analysis on front- and middle-end scenarios for a pool of amortizing project loans. However, if balloon or other nonamortizing loans were included in the portfolio, a backended stress scenario would be more heavily weighted. After reviewing the various stressed cash flows, Standard & Poor's will determine if the proposed capital structure or credit enhancement is sufficient to meet the desired rating. Credit enhancement usually takes the form of subordinated securities (tranching) and/or overcollateralisation, but does not preclude other forms of enhancements such as an LOC.

Setoff Risk

Setoff risk arises when the project obligor may have other contractual relationships with the sponsor or lender. If the sponsor or lender goes insolvent or can not perform, the obligor may chose to set off or reduce the balance of the project loan by the amounts on which the sponsor or lender have not performed.

Depending if the loans documents contain provisions against setoff, Standard & Poor's will examine the enforceability of the provisions and size a commensurate amount of credit support or sellers interest in master trust structures to cover such risk.

Legal Final

The legal final payment date for the rated debt must either be the date on which the last payment of the last loan outstanding is paid or some subsequent point. The importance of having an extended legal final payment date should not be understated. It is expected that defaults will occur over the life of the transaction. Those loans that do default will either be liquidated or restructured in such a way as to provide cash payments to the transaction, although likely at reduced levels. The terms of this restructured loan must have repayment occurring before the termination of the transaction. Any project loan restructuring that would extend the life of the loan beyond the final payment date of the transaction, and not structurally mitigated, would cause a reduction in the transaction's cash flows and be considered a representation and warranty violation with the potential of causing a default on the rated securities.

Interest Rate Basis

Many project finance loans allow the obligor to select and change the index on which interest accrues. For example, the obligor may have the option of selecting 3-month LIBOR or 6-month LIBOR, or perhaps any other index, as the index. This option can create a basis risk in the transaction if the Liabilities of the trust pay interest based on a different index than that of the assets.

The level of risk presented by this is based on the characteristics of the assets included in the trust and the transaction structure employed. To overcome this risk, the transaction sponsor should consider including in the transaction a basis swap or matching the interest basis characteristics of the liabilities with the assets.

When the interest basis of the assets and the liabilities is different, Standard & Poor's will stress the transaction by running multiple cash flow scenarios under different interest rate paths.

Alternate Loan Amortization Schedules

Some project finance loans allow the obligor the option of deferring principal payments or changing the principal payment amortization schedule. If such loans are to be included in the securitisation, the sponsor must notify Standard & Poor's of these features and provide the appropriate details. Standard & Poor's will analyze these loans and assume that the obligor will chose the payment options that will maximize the default probability of the loan. Clearly, a 10-year level pay amortizing loan has a different probability of default as compared with a 10-year bullet amortization.

Modified and Restructured Loans

During the life of the securitisation, it is possible that some project finance loans are modified or restructured. The loans may be restructured with respect to payment terms, interest rates, and tenor. Because the new terms might not be consistent with the structure of the securitisation, any variance in the maturity and payment characteristics of the loans will be addressed during Standard & Poor's surveillance of the transaction rating. The transaction structure must be sufficiently robust to allow some potential changes in the nature of the collateral. Standard & Poor's will work with the sponsor in addressing these risks in the proposed structure.

CLOSED AND OPEN COLLATERAL POOL CONSIDERATIONS

The majority of project finance CLO transactions that Standard & Poor's has been asked to evaluate so far consist of a closed pool of assets, where all loans have already been originated and fully funded. Standard & Poor's has also evaluated a few "open-ended" transaction structures that expect to add additional project loans into the pool over time. In these open-ended transactions, sponsors have a critical core of assets but wish to structure a transaction that is larger than the current asset pools. By over-issuing liabilities, such transaction may offer more efficient execution and the opportunity to fund future projects.

Regardless of which approach is used, Standard & Poor's must evaluate and rate each project as is included in the asset pools. Additionally, Standard & Poor's must establish a specific recovery estimate for each project, should it default.

Establishing the capital structure for a closed asset pool transaction is relatively straight-forward since the uncertainty regarding the characteristics of the assets has been removed. Standard & Poor's analyzes the pool of project finance loans to establish the rating on each project, its post-default recoveries, and the expected default rate for the pool. The capital structure for the transaction is then established by running cash flows proving that the notes can withstand the level of stress commensurate with the rating.

Structuring open asset pool transactions is possible but must incorporate features to control how far the collateral pool characteristics may migrate.

As in all structured transactions, Standard & Poor's main concerns with open asset pools are driven by how subsequent asset additions will affect the following features of the final asset pool:

- Default frequency
- Recovery rate
- Cash flow characteristics

In closed pool transactions, all of the characteristics of the assets are essentially locked in at closing and are used to establish the capital structure needed to achieve the required rating In open pool transactions, the characteristics of the collateral will change. Hence, the capital structure for the transaction must be sufficiently robust to withstand such potential changes.

Most CBO/CLO transaction structured with corporate loans and bonds incorporate an open pool concept. The transactions typically start with 50–60% of the asset pool already purchased at closing and typically have a 30- to 90-day ramp-up period to fully acquire all the collateral assets. The transaction then enters a reinvestment period during which any principal collected is not used to repay the investors, but rather is held and used to purchase new collateral assets. Following the end of the reinvestment period, the transaction enters an amortization period during which principal collections are used to repay the investors.

The same approach may be employed in project finance CLOs. However, since the universe of project finance loans is less broad and less liquid than the universe of corporate loans, the risks associated with open asset pools may be more acute since they also include the following risks:

- The sponsor may not be able to underwrite or purchase project loans eligible for inclusion in the transaction.
- Principal collections may not be able to be reinvested quickly in new projects.

The inability to quickly invest the issuance proceeds from the bond offering or the principal collections from performing projects creates a negative carry on the transaction. The funds not invested in project loans are typically held in other types of eligible deposits generally yielding less than the project loans, and possibly less than the interest payable on the bonds.

To overcome these risks, the sponsors have proposed longer ramp-up and reinvestment periods than traditionally seen in corporate loan CLO transactions. To rate such structures, Standard & Poor's must not only be convinced that the capital structure is sufficiently robust, but must also get comfortable with the sponsors' ability to continue participating in the project finance market and to underwrite transactions in the future. The longer the ramp-up period and reinvestment period, the more likely it is also that market conditions would change and not allow the sponsor to fully acquire all the needed assets.

Sizing Capital Structure for Open Asset Pools

The first step in establishing the capital structure for a project finance CLO transaction is to size the default frequency expected for an open pool of assets. To do so, Standard & Poor's used the following two approaches:

- Active use the default model with cash flow modeling.
- Sizing the capital structure of the transaction assuming a "worst-case portfolio."

Standard & Poor's will work with each sponsor to customize one of the above two approaches based on the transaction requirements and the sponsor's capabilities and area of operations. Discussed in the next sections is a general description of each approach.

Active Use of the Default Model with Cash Flows

Under this approach, the issuer gets credit for the quality of the existing asset portfolio. The default model is run prior to setting the capital structure of the transaction by using a combination of the actual existing portfolio ratings and an estimate of the ratings and cash flow characteristics of the future projects, which will be added. This establishes an expected default frequency. The same is done to establish an expected recovery rate for the portfolio, based on the actual and expected. Standard & Poor's will work with the sponsor to make sure that the characteristics of the future projects are realistic and achievable by the sponsor.

The capital structure of the transaction is then set based on the cash flow results achieved using the expected default probability and recovery rates. Obviously for this to work, the default frequency and recovery rate of the loan portfolio available at closing must be better than the expected rates, otherwise interim credit support solutions must be incorporated in the transaction.

After the transaction closes, projects may be added to the transaction as long as the resultant expected default and recovery rates are not violated. The collateral manager must run the default frequency model using the existing portfolio and substituting the details of the planned acquisitions for the ones inputted as the expected projects. If the results of the default model are at or below the default frequency used in sizing the capital structure, then the acquisition can take place. Additionally, recovery rates and the cash flow characteristics of the planned acquisition are reviewed to insure that they do not violate the earlier assumptions.

The main advantage of this approach is that it generally results in more cost-efficient capital structures for the issuer. The main disadvantage is that it may exclude certain projects from being added because the resultant expected default frequency and recovery rates would violate the assumptions under which the capital structure for the CLO transaction was formulated. Additionally, the sponsor must be able to run cash flow simulations to confirm that the planned acquisition does not breach the capital structure of the transaction.

For this approach to work, the collateral manager must be fairly certain that it can fund or acquire loans that meet the expected characteristics, and Standard & Poor's must be comfortable that the procedure and underwriting standards employed by the originator will fund projects that are eligible for inclusion in the CLO asset pool.

Worst-Case Portfolio

Under the worst-case-portfolio approach, the CLO collateral pool at the end of the ramp-up period is assumed to be one of the worst possible pools of assets, as allowed under the project CLO collateral pool eligibility criteria detailed in the transaction documents. Under this approach, Standard & Poor's must still rate and assign a recovery rate to each project. But projects may be included into the asset pool of the transaction as long as the "worst-case" collateral pool criteria is not violated.

This approach is viewed as being a worst-case scenario because it does not take into account that the actual expected project portfolio, at the end of the ramp-up period, will likely have characteristics that yield a lower default frequency. The benefit of this approach is that it gives maximum flexibility to adding projects as long as the worst-case collateral debt security parameters are not violated. The drawback is that it typically results in a higher level of credit support needed for the CLO transaction since it assumes that all projects additions have effectively brought the portfolio to the worst possible portfolio, as allowed by the transaction eligibility criteria. Some issuers may find capital structures achieved by this approach to be more costly. Additionally, this approach is difficult to implement in transactions that require the use of the multi-jurisdictional default model, since additional specifications must be made in regards to the sovereign ratings and maximum concentrations allowed within any one country.

To model this worst-case portfolio, the collateral eligibility criteria must incorporate a Standard & Poor's ratings distribution, a maturity distribution, a maximum obligor concentration, and a minimum recovery percentage. The Standard & Poor's ratings distribution specifies the maximum amount of collateral allowed at each rating level. The maturity distribution specifies how much of the collateral matures during each year in the future. The maximum obligor concentration specifies the amount of loans that may be due from the same borrower.

Standard & Poor's would then build a worst-case theoretical portfolio assuming that the obligor with the highest concentration will also be the one that is the lowest rated and have a loan out with the longest maturity. These assumptions would be repeated on a loan-by-loan basis to construct a portfolio that meets the ratings distribution, maturity distribution, and maximum obligor concentration as specified by the eligibility criteria. This theoretical portfolio would then be run through the Standard & Poor's default model to establish a worst-case default frequency.

The capital structure of the transaction would then be set by running cash flows using the above worst-case default frequency and the minimum recovery percentage specified for the pool.

Reinvestment Period

During the reinvestment period of the transaction, principal collections are held and used to fund or purchase new project finance loans. Such reinvestment is generally permitted as long as the transaction performs as expected and meets certain structural covenants and triggers. Typical covenants include interest coverage ratios, asset overcollaterization ratios and total loss triggers. If these covenants or triggers are breached, reinvestment is stopped and principal proceeds are used to pay down the rated tranches either in full or until the covenants are brought back into compliance.

Surveillance

Regardless of which approach is used to size that capital structure, Standard & Poor's will maintain active surveillance not only on the underling project loans, but also on all CLO transactions involving such loans. The main concern is that the default frequency, recovery rates, and cash flow characteristics used to establish the commensurate ratings are still valid.

As ratings migrate and the collateral changes, Standard & Poor's may request that additional cash flow runs be made to determine that the transaction still performs at its assigned ratings. Because statistically significant data on default timing, timing of recoveries, and loss severity are still being gathered, ongoing surveillance is important to maintain correct ratings on the CLO securities, especially for the ratings on the subordinated and junior tranches. Standard & Poor's expects the ratings on the junior and subordinated tranches of project finance CLOs to be more dynamic than typical structured finance securities due to the nature of the loans and structure of the CLO transactions.

Standard & Poor's will look at the trustee reports and monitor the default probability and the cash flow characteristics of the assets, the structural covenants, and the ability of the transaction to perform as structured.

Hybrid Project Finance CLOs

To overcome some of the concerns surrounding long ramp-up periods and negative carry on the transaction, some sponsors have proposed combining high-yield corporate loans or bonds with project finance loans. The liquidity of the corporate market and the known cash flow characteristics of the assets make this attractive. Nevertheless, Standard & Poor's has some general concerns with this approach. The primary concern focuses on the ability of the sponsor to manage both type of assets. Project finance loans market is substantially different than the high-yield corporate loan market. Success in one does not guarantee success in the other. Thus, this approach must be viewed with caution.

Second, if the strategy is to hold the high-yield corporate loans and bonds until project loans become available then to redeploy into such, this concept introduces market risk into the transaction. The sponsor may not be able to redeploy because market conditions would may not allow the sale of corporate loan or bond assets and reinvestment into project finance loans without breach of the transaction covenants and triggers.

MASTER TRUST CONSIDERATIONS

To securitise project finance loans, some sponsors are interested in structuring transactions using a master trust structure. This structure is attractive to some issuers because it is potentially more cost effective to issue an additional series of bonds, rather than creating a new trust. Depending on the issuer, securities issued out of a master trust may be backed by one large, diverse pool of assets containing a mix of seasoned and newly originated loans. Master trusts may contain other features that benefit investors, such as sharing of excess cash flows and reserve accounts among the different series of issued bonds.

In structuring master trust transactions backed by project finance loans, the sponsors should consider the factors described below.

Seller's Interest

The seller's interest is equal to the amount of trust assets that are not matched by the correspondent trust liabilities. The sellers interest provides a buffer against two major potential risks: amounts that may be set-off and amounts that exceed obligor and industry concentration limits.

Depending on whether or not the loans documents contain provisions against set-off, Standard & Poor's will examine the enforceability of the provisions and size a commensurate amount of sellers interest to cover such risk. The sellers interest is also used to protect noteholders from obligor and industry concentrations. If certain projects exceed obligor or industry concentration limits, such overconcentrations are allocated to the sellers interest to limit the potential exposure.

Collateral Additions

Master trust structures for different asset types typically have a number of ways in which collateral can be added to the trust. They include required additions, automatic additions, and permitted additions. Since project finance loans are not homogenous assets, such required and automatic additions of collateral can not be used in project finance CLO. Standard & Poor's must rate and give expected recovery values for each project finance loan included in the master trust.

In master trust structures there are two important payment dates for each series: the expected final payment date and the series termination date. The *expected final payment date* is when a series of notes are expected to be paid out. The *series termination date* is the date after which the series of notes has no legal rights to any additional cash flows. Since project finance loans are not homogenous in nature, care must be used in setting the payment date for each series to cover extension risk on the loans. Standard & Poor's will work with the sponsor to set these dates to mitigate such risk.

SUMMARY

The ability to issue debt collateralised by project finance loans and bonds highlights that the CLO market and its participants are becoming more sophisticated. Project finance loans can vary as to industry, security, asset type, and location, but assumptions can be made that establish a cash flow profile for these types of loans. Securitising project finance loan cash flows in CLO structures is an obvious next step and provides project finance lenders a number of efficiencies. Standard & Poor's has rated a number of CLOs that have project finance loans as the primary asset. The methodology follows the established CLO rating criteria; however, some alterations had to be made to reflect the assumed behavioral characteristics of these types of loans. This chapter points out the key characteristics Standard & Poor's views differently and how these differences are incorporated into the CLO rating process. Standard & Poor's only rated its first project financing in the early 1980s and therefore cautions that its assumptions about the behavior and characteristics of project loans will likely change as more actual data points are obtained.

CHAPTER 34

Independent Pricing of Synthetic CDOs

Farooq Jaffrey
Head of Structured Credit Trading, Europe
CreditTrade

David Jefferds, CFA
Head of Structured Credit Trading, Americas
CreditTrade

S ynthetic Collateralised Debt Obligations (sCDOs) face all of the valuation difficulties that can confront any capital market instrument. Yet the regulatory and accounting requirements of market participants, as well as their economic welfare, require accurate and periodic price benchmarking. Until recently, however, there have been no third-party, independent pricing services that could provide the required transparency. In this chapter, we discuss the dynamics and challenges of pricing in the rapidly evolving sCDO market as well as the methodology of our third-party solution: CreditTrade's CDO Independent Pricing Service (IPS).

OVERVIEW OF PRICING CHALLENGES

The problems confronting the pricing of sCDOs comprise the entire laundry list of capital market challenges.

675

■ *OTC nature.* Because they are privately negotiated, sCDOs are subject to the lack of transparency that is typical of many over-the-counter (OTC) markets. This lack of transparency is exacerbated because sCDOs are themselves composed of underlying assets that are OTC instruments: corporate or asset-backed securities-linked credit default swaps (CDSs). Moreover, the ultimate placement of risk in this young OTC market is often unknown, and migration to offshore centres is encouraged. Ultimately, these issues increase the need for diligence regarding counterparty risk and the friction associated with any transaction.

■ *Legal uncertainty.* Because these underlying instruments are relatively new to the capital markets, they bear residual legal uncertainty that bleeds into any analysis of the sCDO structure. Apart from any uncertainty pertaining to the underlying instruments, the packaging structure itself is a heavily negotiated contractual arrangement that is only semistandardized and creates direct documentation risk. And because all of these transactions are unregulated, uncertainty regarding basic "rules of the road" requires additional caution and negotiation. Last, evolving guidance from banking regulators regarding "Basel 2," "Fin46" and other pending matters adds to the overall murkiness.

■ *Modeling risk.* In addition to these documentary and legal risks, sCDOs have complicated cash flows requiring sophisticated analytics, and the lack of a fully accepted unified approach creates modeling risk for market participants. As the underlying CDS are "tail-risk" instruments, complicated issues arise regarding the correct statistical distribution to utilize in predicting credit events. In addition, correlation is notoriously unstable, particularly for tail events, yet this is the key input for analyzing the tranching and pricing of portfolios of risk. A variety of simplifying assumptions underlie the approaches used by the major rating agencies in approaching correlation, while major players in the market add layers of sophistication in customizing their own approaches. Last, basic assumptions such as assumed constant default rates (CDR) and expected sell prices of assets if sold today make material differences in resulting quotes. As a consequence all of these assumptions must be made explicit in order to fully understand sCDO valuations.

There is little reason to expect that the risks enumerated above are offsetting, and so it is reasonable to postulate that these factors contribute in cumulative ways to the lack of pricing clarity in the product.

NEED FOR TRANSPARENCY

In recent years, demand for such clarity has grown exponentially with the market's evolution. An explosion of activity in sCDOs has coincided with extremely difficult credit markets—and this combination has underlined the need for improved sCDO pricing visibility. Over $50 billion notional of sCDO transactions are estimated to have been downgraded between 2000 and 2002. Fitch estimates that in Europe alone over 161 sCDO deals were downgraded in 2002.

Many original purchasers of these transactions sought and continue to seek liquidity in the secondary market for these trades, or at least accurate marks for their books. But it has historically been difficult to source this liquidity because potential counterparties must do a large amount of diligence up-front on the trade, and are still likely to face several of the uncertainties listed above even after having done their modeling work. The result is pricing that can vary widely from theoretical models, often even when such pricing is provided by the original counterparty. Such counterparties are generally understood to bear a reputational consequence when they do not support deals they have originated, but in practice investors can be frustrated by the actual pricing support given.

In addition to any market-related need for accurate pricing and valuation, sCDO market participants have accounting, regulatory, and mark-to-market needs for a consistent and transparent approach to sCDO pricing. Insurance companies and commercial banks are subject to both external pressures and internal risk management imperatives in this regard. But even unregulated, absolute return accounts such as hedge funds almost always have clauses in their investor agreements that require periodic and verifiable third-party marks.

SOLUTIONS AND RESOURCES

In this environment, there are only limited tools available to investors for verifiable third-party pricing. In this chapter we explore the background of sCDO valuation as well as some of these tools. We conclude with a discussion of IPS—a comprehensive service that meets the need of the market.

The tools available fall into several categories, including deal databases, rating agencies, counterparty quotes, and independent third-party services like CreditTrade's IPS. The relative feature sets available are summarized in Exhibit 34.1.

EXHIBIT 34.1 Relative Feature Sets Available

Service Feature	Pricing Issue/ Requirement	Providers			
		Deal Databases	Credit Trade IPS	Rating Agencies	Counterparty Quote
Live CDS input	Single-name CDS uncertainty		x		x
Cash flow modeling	Structural documentation risk	x	x		
Implied tranche rating	Modelling risk	x	x	x	
Monte Carlo analysis	Modelling risk	via partners	x	x	
Deal database	Deal structure	x	deal specific	x	
Formal rating	Formal rating			x	
Fair value	Nonadversarial	x	x	x	
Secondary quotes	Liquidity, docs, modelling		x	x	x
Corporate		x	x	x	x
MBS		x		x	x
ABS		x	x	x	x

Deal Databases

Investors are able to access cash flows and basic documentation describing a variety of deals, particularly on the cash flow side, from certain providers of deal databases. However, such sources of information, while useful, provide only a start in making it possible to value CDOs and sCDOs in the secondary market.

As an initial matter, many cash flow CDOs are private deals whose registration requirements impose hurdles on the facile distribution of such information. Moreover, sCDOs as bilateral contractual arrangements are only available for pricing when one of the counterparties privy to the contract shares the documentation.

Additionally, the mere provision of background documentation on particular deals, even when some rudimentary analytics accompany such materials, is not sufficient to enable accurate pricing. For this goal, more direct market inputs and feedback (including acknowledgments of changes in liquidity, spread levels, documentation standards, and ultimately actual quotes where possible, etc.) are practically necessary.

Rating Agency Models

A second aid to the pricing of sCDOs arises from the existence of rating agency models. Indeed, the ability of rating agencies to provide somewhat uniform principles to the analysis of these innovative pooled instruments provided a chief impetus for the development of the market in the first place. Arbitrage CDOs (and sCDOs) as an asset class were driven from the outset by the ability of investors to create assets and liabilities with "ratings" that exploited the inefficiency of the markets at that time.

The various agencies, though differing in the specifics of their approaches, all examine the correlations of performance among assets in the pool to derive expected losses and returns. Ultimately, these probabilities, when compared with the performance of other rated assets such as cash bonds, allow for them to be rated. The standardization of these approaches has in itself been an aid to liquidity in the secondary market for sCDOs.

In the end, however, the application of a rating to an asset can only provide an indication for what its pricing should be. Rating agencies do not themselves price. Moreover, even the indication suggested by a particular rating can be problematic. For instance, in the last several years "rated" sCDO tranches have particularly underperformed their expected levels. Many participants attribute this underperformance to fundamental adverse selection on the part of those who structured, offered and sold those deals to customers who, on the other hand, approached the investments with more purely statistical, expected loss "ratings" methodologies. In short, the deals were filled with assets that, while apparently solid from a ratings point of view, were subject to risks individually or in the aggregate that were not sufficiently captured by "playing the rating odds." More generally, it can be noted that, even in the single-name CDS market, rating agency downgrades have tended to lag the actual performance of deteriorating credits.

Counterparty Quote

On the occurrence of a credit event for an asset underlying a particular sCDO, the method often mandated by the terms of the synthetic trade is the requirement of receiving a set number (typically three) quotes from participating dealers in order to determine the recovery value of the defaulted asset. And typically the first call for the refreshing of pricing of entire sCDOs for mark-to-market purposes is usually the dealer who was counterparty to the trade. This entity will be most familiar with the deal, will be maintaining marks for its own risk management as well as for collateral risk management, and should in theory be incentivised to assist the client in order to build goodwill. Thus for both individual credit pricings and for pricing of the entire deal, market practice encourages a reliance on the dealing community for pricing.

In practice, however, the adversarial nature of the relationship of clients with dealers undermines the accuracy of such quotes. It should go without saying that in such cases pricing is a zero-sum game, and any gain on the mark-to-market by an investor is a loss on the mark for any counterparty pricing the deal. Even in the case where no trade results, this conflict of incentives has a hard dollar impact in terms of the amount of collateral that may need to be posted against the trade. Moreover, because of the relatively high hurdles of effort necessary for pricing these deals, it is relatively difficult to call on disinterested parties to provide timely "reality checks." To some extent this effect is being addressed by the initiation of "global" syndicated deals that have the participation of many dealers (up to a dozen or more) at the outset. As they resemble bond deals with wide sponsorship, these global sCDOs should be expected to have better performance in the secondary market from the mere fact that a larger number of participants will be familiar enough with the deals to price them regularly. However, the appearance of more deals of this type will only mitigate, but not eliminate, the adversarial hazards of relying on counterparty quotes.

KEY PRICING COMPONENTS AND UNCERTAINTY

Prior to describing the CT IPS approach and its utility in filling the market gap for third-party pricing, it is worth reviewing the basic structure and advantages of synthetic sCDOs. This review will facilitate a better understanding of the sources of risk associated with each of the relevant components.

CDS Benefits

The term synthetic in synthetic CDOs refers to underlying assets, typically corporate CDSs, which are not cash instruments. As an asset class CDSs have significant benefits compared to bonds or other cash instruments because of their flexibility and implied funding costs; these benefits translate directly into the comparative advantage of sCDOs versus cash CDOs.

Ramp-Up

The flexibility benefit arises from several sources. Because actual cash bonds do not have to be sourced as assets for the CDO over the course of weeks or months, a significant cost in terms of optionality can be avoided. A portfolio of CDSs can be "ramped" in an afternoon or an hour, rather than over weeks or months. Therefore investor orders need not be held firm while the arranger enjoys a free option on the deal. Depending on the volatility of the assets underlying the transaction, this type of option can be worth tens of basis points.

Larger Theoretical Universe

A second related benefit is that investors can draw from a larger group of potential credits when accessing the CDS market as opposed to the bond market. Geographic, regulatory, liquidity or other limitations can be made irrelevant by the use of CDSs. Because a wider universe of assets can be invested, a greater return should be available to investors for similar risk. The ability to draw from a larger universe of assets can have a material effect on a sCDO portfolio referencing 100 names, often allowing for the substitution of superior names (that is, names with incrementally greater yield or lower risk) for 10% or more of the total portfolio as compared with what would have been available using cash bonds only.

Basis

Third, and also related to the first two flexibility benefits, is that CDS frequently trade with a basis to corporate bonds on the same credit. As opposed to the benefit gained by expanding the universe of investable credits, this basis relates to a greater yield available for the same credit. The basis at times results from the fact that a CDS carries implied LIBOR funding, whereas a cash bond purchase must be funded at the internal funding rate of the investor. Technical trading dynamics of the cash bonds may also impact the basis. In general, however, because investors will naturally migrate to credits with an advantageous basis, the effect on a portfolio may be significant, especially for wider trading credits where the basis has been known to expand to 50 basis points or more.

CDS DRAWBACKS

Despite these benefits, from a pricing perspective there are several challenges that remain endemic to the CDS asset class.

Documentation

Although there has been great progress in standardizing terms, geographic differences continue to evolve among Europe, Asia, and the Americas. This geographic basis risk increases the expertise requirement of any investor in one region that invests in a multiregion structure. In recent years numerous cases have been brought related to interpretations of CDS language. For instance, there are at least four options for treatment of restructuring of debt as a credit event (no restructuring, old restructuring, modified restructuring, and modified modified restructuring) as well as customized language put forth by certain end-users. To cite another example, there have been variations in the definition of what is allowed to qualify as a deliverable obligation. The result, in a market of evolving standards, is a liquidity penalty for secondary trades on seasoned CDS or pooled transactions that trade under "old docs." In fact, the market discounts a quantifiable basis risk for certain types of documentation differences. The basis for trading between "NoR" and "ModR," for instance, has often been quoted at between 5% and 15% of the total spread. Similarly, the cost of bearing "doc risk" for certain types of basket trades recently has been observed on the order of 5 to 10 basis points.

Limited Liquid Universe

Despite a great increase in trading, the universe of liquid names in corporate CDS is limited and presents an additional pricing challenge. Indeed, despite the fact that a theoretically very large universe of credits exists, the liquid set is generally considered to include only about 2,000 names, of which only 200 to 300 trade with regularity. Trading histories even for these names tend to be sporadic as troubled names or new issues can trade with great activity in one period only to then remain quiescent for months afterward.

Limited Yield Curve

Corporate CDSs also suffer in comparison to bonds with regard to pricing that is available along the yield curve. Although limited activity exists on the 1-year, 3-year, 7-year, and 10-year points, an estimated 80% or more of notional CDS single-name trading still occurs at the rolling 5-year point. The result is that subsequent hedging of deals that were originally issued at the 5-year point will automatically entail a penalty as investors roll down the illiquid curve. Recently, CDSs have traded to quarterly expiration dates, which has the beneficial effect of aggregating liquidity. Nevertheless, with only one "on-the-run" point of the curve, CDSs remain at a disadvantage compared to corporate bonds when it comes to curve trading.

sCDO STRUCTURE

As alluded to above, sCDOs are leveraged spread arbitrage and/or balance sheet regulatory structures. Arbitrage CDOs capitalize on the difference in rating and spread of the assets versus the rating and spread of the liabilities. Balance sheet CDOs capitalize on the difference in the capital requirements associated with assets on balance sheet versus the same assets repackaged into highly rated debt tranches. sCDOs repackage the gamut of asset classes including investment-grade and high-yield credits, either referenced to bonds or loans, quasi-equity, and even private equity or hedge fund interests. Among this diversity of asset classes addressable by the sCDO vehicle is a similar diversity in documentation terms used by various counterparties. Finally, each rating agency has its own proprietary ratings methodology, which reflects its particular views on ratings, default rates, default timings, recovery rates, and interest rates. It is the foolish investor that does not approach investments in sCDOs without the assistance of legal experts. Exhibit 34.2 illustrates a sample capital structure of a sCDO. Exhibit 34.3 illustrates the cash flow waterfall of a sCDO.

Documentation

The documents that govern a sCDO are prepared by securities lawyers in conjunction with investment bankers and address the operational, marketing, and legal issues of the transaction. In order to correctly understand how a CDO can be marked, it is important to review the main operating documents:

- Offering memorandum
- Indenture
- Trust deed

EXHIBIT 34.2 Capital Structure

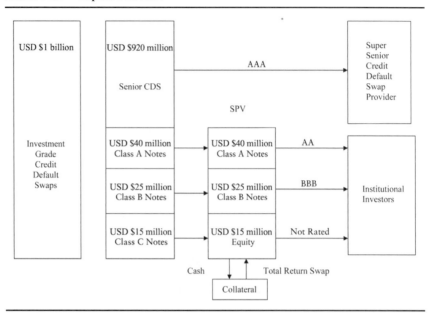

■ Senior credit default swap agreement
■ Credit default swap confirmations
■ IDSA schedule

Documentation is a key element of determining the value of the CDO as it raises the case of whether the CDO is "market standard." Investment banks and lawyers have traditionally promoted proprietary methodologies in structuring and documenting CDO transactions. Clearly, given the complexities of a sCDO, it is natural for individual teams at banks and law firms to have different solutions to client projects, especially with market-driven structures such as sCDOs as markets change. However, the problem with this differentiation is that it has become a source of illiquidity of CDOs making it difficult to compare sCDOs or to create a benchmark.

CT IPS

In light of these many factors illustrating the problematic nature of pricing of sCDOs, CT has crafted a methodology for third-party pricing tailored to addressing these difficulties. Although certain features of the

EXHIBIT 34.3   Priority of Payments

Proceeds Prior to Enforcement (PPE)	Proceeds at Maturity Date/Enforcement
Administrative fees and expenses, amounts due on senior credit default swap and hedge agreements	Administrative fees and expenses and any outstanding amounts due to credit default swap counterparties on credit default swaps
Interest payments on Class A notes	Unpaid items in PPE waterfall through to amounts due to senior credit default swap
Interest payments on Class B notes	
Deferred Interest payments on Class B notes	Payment for losses on senior credit default swap, if any
Payment of collateral management fees (if any)	Redemption of Class A notes
To collateral account if reinvestment test not satisfied	
Payment of collateral management incentive fees	Redemption of Class B notes
Payments to Class C notes	Redemption of Class C notes, plus excess proceeds

Decreasing Priority of Payments →

685

EXHIBIT 34.4 Values Under Various Methods

	MTM Method	Cash Flow Method	Secondary Spread Method
Senior CDS	100.00%	99.82%	99.20%
AA	12.50%	80.36%	77.20%
BBB	0.00%	71.63%	54.90%

valuation methodology remain proprietary, in the second part of this chapter we outline the basics of the approach.

The valuation methodology of IPS draws on the benefits of three accepted approaches to valuation. They are the mark-to-market method, the cash flow method, and the secondary spread method. Only by utilizing the insights that can be drawn from these three differing but complementary approaches is it possible to create an accurate picture of the correct pricing of sCDOs. In Exhibit 34.4 we illustrate the possible initial pricing indications for various tranches of a sCDO using the three methods.

Mark-to-Market

The mark-to-market method for valuation is a key component of the portfolio of valuation techniques that are validated in the sCDO marketplace. It compares the market value or market price of the assets within an sCDO at issuance to the market value of the assets at valuation date. Assets in the sCDO include the portfolio of credit default swaps, bonds or ABS, any cash collateral accounts, total return swaps, interest rate or foreign exchange hedges. The valuation is a static analysis of the improvement or deterioration of the assets during the period of time elapsed since issuance. If the value of the assets of the sCDO is less than the value at valuation date, then there is a mark-to-market loss, equivalent to the difference in values. There is a mark-to-market gain if the converse is true. Essentially, the mark-to-market value is what the investor receives if the sCDO was unwound or called, and its individual components sold off. As can be seen this value can differ dramatically from the other methods and can be understood as analogous to the valuation of an operating company that is being liquidated. The value differs from the value of the business as a "going concern" but is nevertheless highly relevant to understanding the relative safety of the bonds, preferred shares, and common equity.

For this valuation method to be accurate, it is important that the valuation of the assets be completed on an arms' length basis. In order to achieve this, the investor effectively will have to solicit an independent

EXHIBIT 34.5   Liquidation Impact on Tranches

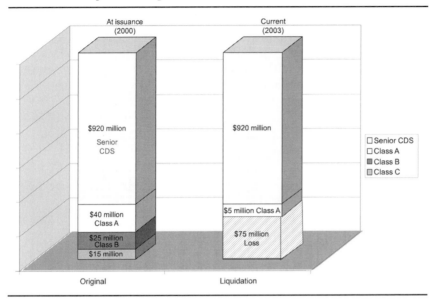

mark from the marketplace for each single security in the portfolio, each swap and each hedge. This solicitation is somewhat similar to the unwind scenario where each of the assets will have to be sold off independently.

The value of the underlying assets is offset against the principal and accrued interest obligations on the sCDO liability tranches. Losses and gains are offset in reverse priority of the tranches. A loss will offset the most subordinate (or equity) tranche, first, then the mezzanine tranche, and so on. Thus, in our example the BBB tranche has undergone the greatest percentage loss, as is appropriate given its more leveraged position in the capital structure. Exhibit 34.5 illustrates the possible impact of an unwind on the differing layers of a transaction: Typically junior tranches can be wiped out while the most senior are preserved. In this example, accumulated mark-to-market losses of $75 million means that 100% of Class C notes, 100% of the Class B notes, and $35 million (or 87.5%) of the Class A notes are written off. In this scenario, it is expected only $5 million in principal of the Class A notes will be redeemed.

However, there are certain limitations to using this technique. First, it would be rare to have a situation where each asset in the sCDO can be independently sold off, without there being an effect on the value of the other assets in the portfolio. Second, trying to solicit a mark for all the assets often proves very time consuming and laborious, given that the investor often must approach more than one market maker to obtain prices. Third, by going to the market, the investor is sharing private information in a public domain, which may have an adverse impact on the price of the sCDO, the perception of the deal, or the reputation of the investor. Last, the sum of the elements of the sCDO maybe worth less than the sCDO itself due to the liquidity premium placed on complex financial structures. This approach in fact bears the greatest cost in terms of liquidity premium of the three described in this chapter.

Cash Flow Method

The cash flow method for valuation utilises the calculation of the *net present value* (NPV) and *internal rate of return* (IRR) of the future expected cash flows. Unlike the mark-to-market method valuation, which looks at a spot-sale type scenario, the cash flow method presumes a longer-term view, where value is obtained by holding the sCDO to maturity.

Cash flow models are used to calculate the inflows and outflows of a sCDO. Cash inflows include interest and principal on the assets, with an adjustment for realised principal gains or losses due to trading of the assets, amounts received from any interest rate, and foreign exchange hedges. Cash outflows include interest and principal to be paid on the liabilities, amounts to be paid on any interest rate or foreign exchange hedges, and administrative costs. Cash flow models are usually developed by the investment bank structuring the CDO and reflect the details of a particular CDO and differ significantly from deal to deal.

A common practice is to use the Monte Carlo method to simulate default rates, default timings and interest rates to generate expected cash flows. By using this technique, it is possible to stress test a CDO by subjecting the cash flows to extreme variations in assumptions. A variety of scenarios for default rates and timings will be undertaken to evaluate the probabilities of loss for the tranche and finally create the probability-weighted expected cash flows.

Although it is impossible to predict defaults with certainty, rating agencies have compiled historical default rate statistics that provide a context for the likelihood of future defaults, based on the particular credit rating of the asset. Rating agencies use these statistics to generate default analysis and expected loss scenarios, which they use to attach ratings to CDO liabilities. It is possible to either use the average historical default rate, or a proxy future default rate, to forecast the likely number of defaults over the remaining life of the CDO. Although, as described above, rating agency models are not without drawbacks, historical rating agency data can provide a beneficial input to dynamic modeling.

Predicting the timing of defaults is similarly challenging. It is important to look at rating agency historical analysis to determine when defaults occurred and what factors contributed to these defaults (i.e., economic recession, interest rates, etc.). To the extent there is any basis for predicting future economic recessions, it is important to adjust the timing of defaults in the cash flow analysis.

The waterfall can be subdivided into the proceeds prior to enforcement and proceeds at maturity date. Proceeds are used to pay for ongoing fees and expenses of the transaction, premium on the senior credit default swap, interest on the notes and finally, dividends to the equity investors. Proceeds at maturity date are used to pay for any outstanding amounts due on the senior credit default swap or notes, any additional fees, principal on the notes and par amount to the equity investors.

Interest rates play a very important role in CDOs. The assets in a CDO are interest bearing securities where the interest received is partly based on the floating or fixed nature of the basis. Similarly, the liabilities are interest bearing securities where the interest paid is partly based on the basis. The difference in interest basis between the assets and liabilities create an interest rate mismatch that either needs to be hedged, or taken into account in the cash flow modeling. For example, it is possible to have assets that pay on a fixed rate basis and liabilities to pay in a floating rate basis. In this case, if interest rates increase during the life of the CDO, cash outflow increases while the cash inflow is constant.

CDO structures often use interest rate hedges, such as interest rate swaps, caps and options. Valuing these hedges is essential in deriving the cash flow value.

An additional factor to consider is the reinvestment period; substitutions of collateral during this window can have a substantial effect on cash flows. Given that a certain element of subjectivity to trading assets exists, predicting changes in the portfolio during the reinvestment period is challenging. Asset managers are able to use their judgment on how to change the portfolio to maximize return. Depending on the number of years left in the reinvestment period, the assumptions used in predicting the cash flow or change in credit rating of the assets will have a substantial impact on the valuation.

Actively managed CDOs have a reinvestment period of several years where the asset manager is able to trade the underlying collateral, to either (a) sell any credit deteriorated or credit improved asset, and (b) trade on a speculative basis, usually limited to 10–20% of the portfolio per year. After the reinvestment period, the collateral amortises according to its maturity schedule. The quality of the trading decisions during the investment period depends on the experience and credit analysis of the asset management team controlling the investment decisions of the CDO. CDO valuation

EXHIBIT 34.6   Expected Cash Flows

Date	Tranches		
	Senior CDS	Class A	Class B
15-Mar-03	($920,000,000)	($40,000,000)	($25,000,000)
15-Jun-03	4,469,536	231,087	304,151
15-Sep-03	4,937,191	231,087	304,151
15-Dec-03	4,826,938	228,575	300,845
15-Mar-04	4,736,956	228,575	300,845
15-Jun-04	4,626,958	231,087	304,151
15-Sep-04	4,661,117	231,087	304,151
15-Dec-04	4,900,282	228,575	300,845
15-Mar-05	4,954,614	226,063	297,539
15-Jun-05	4,692,581	231,087	304,151
15-Sep-05	4,692,712	236,110	310,763
15-Dec-05	4,478,324	228,575	300,845
15-Mar-06	4,440,094	221,039	290,927
15-Jun-06	4,708,728	236,110	310,763
15-Sep-06	4,804,115	228,575	300,845
15-Dec-06	4,330,078	228,575	300,845
15-Mar-07	4,357,032	228,575	300,845
15-Jun-07	5,196,329	228,575	300,845
15-Sep-07	4,658,749	228,575	300,845
15-Dec-07	888,723,859	29,894,946	13,421,730

based on the net present value method thereby involves certain assumptions on how the asset manager is able to trade the portfolio during the reinvestment period. This assumption can create differences in valuation given its subjectivity. The cumulative impact of all of these cash flow considerations can lead to accruals that resemble those shown in Exhibit 34.6.

Secondary Market Method

The secondary market for CDOs and sCDOs has grown tremendously over the past several years. Previously, these pooled deals were primarily buy-and-hold instruments with very little liquidity. As mentioned above, the very nature of a CDO being uniquely developed by a particular issuer and dealer created an illiquidity premium that cautioned investors against selling their positions (at a potentially large loss versus the fair mark). Furthermore, dealers that were unable to fully sell the CDO structures they developed preferred to hold onto the positions in order to avoid large losses on their balance sheets. A direct result of this was that the actual market price of a particular CDO was very difficult to determine, especially when the CDO documents were not available in the public domain.

However, in 1999, with the advent of the CDO of CDO transactions, asset managers realized the value of purchasing, at a discount, secondary CDOs and repackaging them into new CDOs. This development caused dealers to provide documents on CDO transactions structured by them to listing agents and data compilers. Today, there are numerous CDO of CDO asset managers that regularly trade secondary CDOs on the back of this additional information and liquidity.

Using the secondary market method (sometimes called "mark to model") an active presence in the trading market is necessary to provide an accurate contextual snapshot to investors. A value for the sCDO can then be determined by quoting bid or offer levels from dealers or investors in the marketplace not only for the deal in question but also with reference to deals that share similar structural features. Essentially, supply and demand forces on both new issuance and secondary sCDOs drive this valuation technique, and thereby collapse the uncertainty associated with all of the theoretical and practical factors we have previously described into the narrower parameter of actual liquidity. Given the general efficiency of new information in the market place, secondary market levels can usually reflect the perceived performance of the transaction, the reputation of the asset manager (if any), rating agency surveillance reports and statistics, as well as the overall performance of the asset classes contained within the sCDO. More than this, however, the process provides a diligence around the process of finding the true clearing price of a sCDO investment, rather than gauging the interest available from just a limited set of (adversarial) counterparties. Exhibit 34.7 illustrates the iterative process that comprises the IPS approach to incorporating secondary market quotes into sCDO valuation.

Deriving a market price from indications in the secondary market in certain respects has features that are more art than science. A secondary market price looks at the previous two valuation techniques—mark-to-market and cash flow valuation methods—while also taking into consideration other factors such as vintage, the reputation of the asset manager, current ratings, new issue spreads and general information from financial news reports. Market pricing may be affected by the performance of the credit environment and the debt markets in general. Other macro-dynamics enter into the consideration as well; for instance, the downturn in equity markets in 2000 and 2001 generated additional demand for sCDO assets as investors sought suitable returns outside of the stock market. And layered onto these analyses of market conditions is a widespread polling technique that utilizes the credibility and extent of a trading network not necessarily available to the investor.

EXHIBIT 34.7   Iterative Process for Secondary Market Approach

Open market CDO auctions by banks have become relatively common as a technique for increasing liquidity. In early 2003, a large U.K. bank utilized an open market auction to generate interest among market players to its USD $10 billion book of senior CDO tranches. The bank used the services of an experienced third party asset manager with relevant CDO experience to act as a selling agent. The asset manager provided credibility to the auction process by making it an arm's length and independent auction where all potential bidders were provided with full disclosure of information on the CDO inventory. The bank's appointment of a selling agent immediately generated interest among major investment banks, who were seeking well priced collateral to ramp up CDO of CDO transactions they were arranging for their own clients. In order to maximize the sale prices of the CDO tranches, the asset manager sold the portfolio over several months, and distributed new auction lists on pre-determined data. Over several months, the asset manager was able to trade USD $4 to $5 billion (perhaps more) of the CDO inventory.

Block trading of CDO tranches has become more common as a result of these auctions. Clips of CDO tranches of up to USD $100 million or more can typically trade at one time. This is partly due to the fact that investors originally purchased large quantities of tranches and, related to the first point, partly due to economies of scale associated with a CDO investment. Given the amount of time required to perform the appropri-

EXHIBIT 34.8   Primary Issuance Spreads

Tranche Rating	HY Bond	HY Loan	Inv. Grade CDS	ABS	EMG
CDS	—	—	15	—	—
AAA	65	58	80	70	55
AA	125	110	175	150	150
A	200	185	300	225	275
BBB	350	300	500	375	400
BB	900	825	1,000	950	n.a.

ate credit analysis, investors would rather purchase a substantial size in order to generate an adequate return.

New issue spread levels have a large impact on the supply/demand factors for secondary sCDOs, and the levels will be dramatically different for different asset classes, as shown in Exhibit 34.8. Like any other products, sCDOs are subject to the laws of supply and demand. A large supply of new issue sCDOs depresses the market prices for sCDOs in general, and secondary sCDOs in particular. However, it is important to note that interest rates also play an important role. In a low interest rate environment, fixed rate liability tranches have traded at a premium to par.

CreditTrade uses its professional brokers to source pricing for secondary CDOs by regularly being in contact with buyers and sellers of secondary CDOs. By trading secondary CDOs between dealers, its brokers are able to determine the pricing matrix for all rated tranches of liabilities. In recent periods, for instance, great liquidity has been available for senior tranches (ratings of AAA to AA), with more limited liquidity available for A-rated and BBB-rated tranches. Even in cases where there is limited liquidity for certain parts of the capital structure, however, it is still possible to imply the pricing levels for illiquid tranches based upon a relevant factor. This factor is calculated by CreditTrade based on rating, vintage, and asset class.

CONCLUSION

The market experience in recent years leaves little doubt that a pressing need exists for investors to have an arm's length method to mark their CDO investments. Regulatory capital and accounting bodies have become aware of the fact that many investors are inadequately valuing their investments, a danger that can have a significant impact on the state of the financial markets. In 2000, a large U.S. financial services firm caught the market by surprise by reporting several hundred million dollars in mark-to-market losses on a large risk position of CDO investments, which called into question the financial strength of the firm. Similarly in 2002, a well known U.K.-based bank reported heavy losses due to a large portfolio of CDO investments that had deteriorated in credit quality over a number of years. As a result of this news, its management team was revamped, and subsequently, the largest well-known CDO auction process was initiated.

Unfortunately, these events are not uncommon. Given the opaque nature with which internal pricing/mapping is conducted at institutions and the lack of a proper accounting method for marking CDO investments, it is impossible to determine the exact number of parties that may be underreporting CDO losses. Turnover in management and staffing often can create institutional confusion regarding the correct management of sCDO positions, often because new staff did not participate in the initial investment decision.

In order to avoid these types of situations, it is important that investors maintain a written, independent and transparent valuation methodology, which remains consistent over the life of a CDO investment.

ANNEXES OF IPS OUTPUTS

While certain aspects of the CT IPS methodology remain proprietary, the following section provides some sense for the different components of the IPS service.

Collateral

The collateral in a sCDO usually consists of investment grade credit default swaps that are chosen to fit into a diversified portfolio of credits, with a target yield and rating. The credits are selected based on the expected default rate of the portfolio and the ability to pay the premium, interest and principal on the liabilities at maturity. A snapshot of the collateral underlying an investment-grade corporate sCDO is detailed in Exhibit 34.9.

With the increasing popularity of the credit default swap market and its applications to transferring or investing in risk, default swap technology is being applied to more asset classes. Apart from the investment grade asset class, high yield and emerging market sovereign credit sCDOs have also come to prominence in recent years. Increasingly, asset backed securities are being repackaged into credit default swaps. IPS accommodates a wide range of these evolving assets.

EXHIBIT 34.9 Sample Portfolio

Portfolio	
Deal	Synthetic Investment Grade CDO

Portfolio summary	
Number of issues	100
Notional	$1,000,000,000.00
Avg. Spread	130 bp
Avg. Mat.	15-Dec-07
Avg. Rtg.	BBB/A-
Agg. Principal Bal. (excluding defaults)	$10,000,000.00

Portfolio Breakdown

	Issuer	Security Type	Region	Seniority	Amount	Spread	Cpn. Type	Maturity	Industry
1	Adecco SA	CDS	Europe	Senior secured	10,000,000.00	0.650%	Fixed	15-Dec-07	Diversified/Conglomerate Service
2	Albertsons, Inc.	CDS	North America	Senior secured	10,000,000.00	0.690%	Fixed	15-Dec-07	Grocery
3	Allianz AG	CDS	Europe	Senior secured	10,000,000.00	0.270%	Fixed	15-Dec-07	Banking
4	Altria Group, Inc.	CDS	North America	Senior secured	10,000,000.00	2.150%	Fixed	15-Dec-07	Beverage, Food, & Tobacco
5	American Honda Finance Corp.	CDS	North America	Senior secured	10,000,000.00	0.250%	Fixed	15-Dec-07	Banking
6	American International Group	CDS	North America	Senior secured	10,000,000.00	0.270%	Fixed	15-Dec-07	Insurance
7	AMP Group Holdings	CDS	Australia	Senior secured	10,000,000.00	2.850%	Fixed	15-Dec-07	Finance
8	ANZ Banking Group	CDS	Australia	Senior secured	10,000,000.00	0.100%	Fixed	15-Dec-07	Banking
9	AOL Time Warner, Inc.	CDS	North America	Senior secured	10,000,000.00	0.660%	Fixed	15-Dec-07	Electronics
10	Arcelor	CDS	Europe	Senior secured	10,000,000.00	1.060%	Fixed	15-Dec-07	Diversified/Conglomerate Manufacturing
11	AT&T Wireless Services, Inc.	CDS	North America	Senior secured	10,000,000.00	0.720%	Fixed	15-Dec-07	Telecommunications
12	AXA SA	CDS	Europe	Senior secured	10,000,000.00	0.270%	Fixed	15-Dec-07	Insurance
13	Banca Di Roma SpA	CDS	Europe	Senior secured	10,000,000.00	0.270%	Fixed	15-Dec-07	Banking
14	Banca Monte Dei Paschi di Siena SpA	CDS	Europe	Senior secured	10,000,000.00	0.180%	Fixed	15-Dec-07	Banking
15	BHP Billiton, Ltd.	CDS	Australia	Senior secured	10,000,000.00	0.220%	Fixed	15-Dec-07	Banking
	...	...	...	...	...	...	...	...	...
100	Vivendi Environnement	CDS	Europe	Senior secured	10,000,000.00	1.500%	Fixed	15-Dec-07	Telecommunications

EXHIBIT 34.10   Industry Diversification
Deal: Synthetic Investment Grade CDO

Detail

Industry	Percent
Broadcasting and Entertainment	8.97%
Chemicals, Plastics, and Rubber	8.06%
Telecommunications	8.00%
Retail Stores	7.79%
Healthcare, Education, and Childcare	7.54%
Leisure, Amusement, Entertainment	6.17%
Containers, Packaging, and Glass	6.15%
Finance	5.29%
Hotels, Motels, and Gaming	4.28%
Machinery	4.06%
Utilities	3.91%
Personal Transportation	3.91%
Farming and Agriculture	3.67%
Electronics	3.39%
Personal, Food, and Miscellaneous Services	3.22%
Automobile	3.00%
Beverage, Food, and Tobacco	2.43%
Grocery	2.29%
Textiles and Leather	2.09%
Diversified/Conglomerate Manufacturing	2.04%
Oil and Gas	0.85%
Cargo Transport	0.81%
Printing, Publishing	0.81%
Personal and Nondurable Consumer Products (manufacturing only)	0.58%
Mining, Steel, Iron, and Nonprecious Metals	0.51%
Diversified Natural Resources	0.14%
Total	100.0%

Certain inputs related to ratings by the various agencies can also be calculated as part of the IPS service. Exhibit 34.10 provides an industry breakdown for the portfolio described previously.

Tranching

The average sCDO capital structure includes one layer of credit default swap and several layers of funded debt notes (super senior credit default swap, senior notes, mezzanine notes, and equity). The priority of these notes is reflected in their ratings. Usually, the most super senior credit default swap and senior notes are rated.

The sCDO applies the proceeds raised through the issuance of the notes (i.e., super senior credit default swap exchanges risk to the investor, but raises no cash) to payment of fees and expenses associated with the CDO issuance, with the balance being deposited into a reserve account ("Reserve Account"). Amounts in the Reserve Account are used to reimburse the counterparties, with which the sCDO has entered into credit default swaps on the collateral, on credit defaults swaps which have suffered a credit event. Through the super senior credit default swap, the issuer buys protection on the collateral.

Required Assumptions

Exhibit 34.11 provides an overview for the types of assumptions that must be input into the CDO model to generate cash flows as described above.

EXHIBIT 34.11   CDO Model

Assumptions

STRUCTURE

Term (periods)	20			
Ann Periods	4			
		Seniority	Layer	Notional (millions)
Unfunded		CPS	92.0%	920
Funded		A	4.0%	40
Funded		B	2.5%	25
Funded		C	1.5%	15

RATES

Int Rate Term Structure		Default Swaps		Timing of Losses		
1	2%	Pfolio Avg Spread	75	20%	1	5.0%
2	2%	Collateral Yield (Spd to LIBOR)	0		2	5.0%
3	2%	Default Rate (cum)	4%		3	5.0%
4	2%	Recovery Rate	30%		4	5.0%
5	2%			20%	5	5.0%
6	2%	# Names	100		6	5.0%
7	2%	Notional per Name	10		7	5.0%
8	2%	Total Notional	1,000,000,000		8	5.0%
9	2%			20%	9	5.0%
10	2%				10	5.0%
11	2%				11	5.0%
12	2%				12	5.0%
13	2%			20%	13	5.0%
14	2%				14	5.0%
15	2%				15	5.0%
16	2%				16	5.0%
17	2%			20%	17	5.0%
18	2%				18	5.0%
19	2%				19	5.0%
20	2%				20	5.0%

Credit-Linked Notes and Repacks

CHAPTER 35

Credit-Linked Notes

Moorad Choudhry
Head of Treasury
KBC Financial Products UK Limited

Frank J. Fabozzi, Ph.D., CFA
Frederick Frank Adjunct Professor of Finance
School of Management
Yale University

redit derivatives are grouped into funded and unfunded variants. In an unfunded credit derivative, typified by a credit default swap, the protection seller does not make an upfront payment to the protection buyer. In a funded credit derivative, typified by a credit-linked note (CLN), the investor in the note is the credit protection seller and is making an up-front payment to the protection buyer when buying the note. Thus, the protection buyer is the issuer of the note. If no credit event occurs during the life of the note, the redemption value of the note is paid to the investor on maturity. If a credit event does occur, then on maturity a value less than par will be paid out to the investor. This value will be reduced by the nominal value of the reference asset that the CLN is linked to. In the European market, CLNs make up a greater share of credit derivatives by volume than in the U.S. market. Exhibit 35.1 shows the proportions during 2002 as reported by the BBA. In this chapter we discuss CLNs.

The authors would like to thank Abukar Ali at Bloomberg L.P. in London for assistance with preparing this chapter.

EXHIBIT 35.1   Share of Euro-Denominated Credit Derivatives Market, 2002

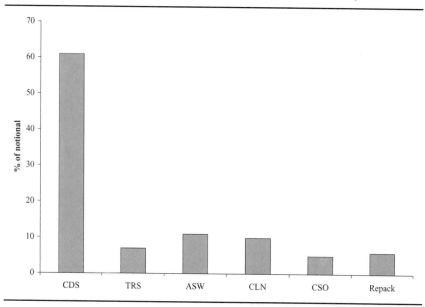

Source: BBA.

DESCRIPTION OF CLNS

Credit-linked notes exist in a number of forms, but all of them contain a link between the return they pay and the credit-related performance of the underlying asset. A standard CLN is a security, usually issued by an investment-graded entity, that has an interest payment and fixed maturity structure similar to a vanilla bond. The performance of the CLN, however, including the maturity value, is linked to the performance of a specified underlying asset or assets as well as that of the issuing entity. CLNs are usually issued at par. They are often used as a financing vehicle by borrowers in order to hedge against credit risk; CLNs are purchased by investors to enhance the yield received on their holdings. Hence, the issuer of the CLN is the protection buyer and the buyer of the note is the protection seller.

Essentially CLNs are hybrid instruments that combine a pure credit risk exposure with a vanilla bond. The CLN pays regular coupons, however the credit derivative element is usually set to allow the issuer to decrease the principal amount, and/or the coupon interest, if a specified credit event occurs.

EXHIBIT 35.2 Bloomberg Screen SND: Definition of Credit-Linked Note

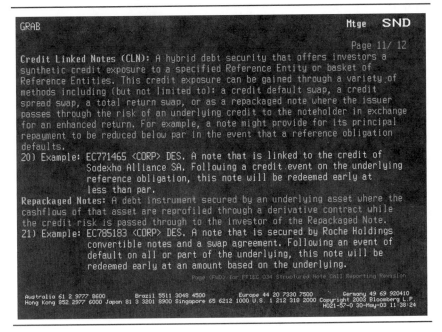

GRAB   Mtge **SND**

Page 11/ 12

Credit Linked Notes (CLN): A hybrid debt security that offers investors a synthetic credit exposure to a specified Reference Entity or basket of Reference Entities. This credit exposure can be gained through a variety of methods including (but not limited to): a credit default swap, a credit spread swap, a total return swap, or as a repackaged note where the issuer passes through the risk of an underlying credit to the noteholder in exchange for an enhanced return. For example, a note might provide for its principal repayment to be reduced below par in the event that a reference obligation defaults.

20) Example: EC771465 <CORP> DES. A note that is linked to the credit of Sodexho Alliance SA. Following a credit event on the underlying reference obligation, this note will be redeemed early at less than par.

Repackaged Notes: A debt instrument secured by an underlying asset where the cashflows of that asset are reprofiled through a derivative contract while the credit risk is passed through to the investor of the Repackaged Note.

21) Example: EC785183 <CORP> DES. A note that is secured by Roche Holdings convertible notes and a swap agreement. Following an event of default on all or part of the underlying, this note will be redeemed early at an amount based on the underlying.

Page <FWD> for FFIEC 034 Structured Note Call Reporting Revision

Australia 61 2 9777 8600   Brazil 5511 3048 4500   Europe 44 20 7330 7500   Germany 49 69 920410
Hong Kong 852 2977 6000 Japan 81 3 3201 8900 Singapore 65 6212 1000 U.S. 1 212 318 2000 Copyright 2003 Bloomberg L.P.
                                                                        H021-57-0 30-May-03 11:38:24

Source: © Bloomberg L.P. Used with permission.

Exhibit 35.2 shows a screen Bloomberg screen SND and their definition of the CLN.

To illustrate a CLN, consider a bank issuer of credit cards that wants to fund its credit card loan portfolio via an issue of debt. The bank is rated AA−. In order to reduce the credit risk of the loans, it issues a 2-year CLN. The principal amount of the bond is 100 (par) as usual, and it pays a coupon of 7.50%, which is 200 basis points above the two-year benchmark. The equivalent spread for a vanilla bond issued by a bank of this rating would be of the order of 120 bps. With the CLN though, if the incidence of bad debt amongst credit card holders exceeds 10% then the terms state that note holders will only receive back 85 per 100 par. The credit card issuer has in effect purchased a credit option that lowers its liability in the event that it suffers from a specified credit event, which in this case is an above-expected incidence of bad debts. The cost of this credit option to the credit protection buyer is paid in the form of a higher coupon payment on the CLN. The credit card bank has issued the CLN to reduce its credit exposure, in the form of this particular type of credit insurance. If the incidence of bad debts is low, the CLN is redeemed at par. However, if there a high incidence of such debt, the bank will only have to repay a part of its loan liability.

Investors may wish purchase the CLN because the coupon paid on it will be above what the credit card bank would pay on a vanilla bond it issued, and higher than other comparable investments in the market. In addition such notes are usually priced below par on issue. Assuming the notes are eventually redeemed at par, investors will also have realized a substantial capital gain.

As with credit default swaps, CLNs may be specified under cash settlement or physical settlement. Specifically:

- Under cash settlement, if a credit event has occurred, on maturity the protection seller receives the difference between the value of the initial purchase proceeds and the value of the reference asset at the time of the credit event.
- Under physical settlement, on occurrence of a credit event, the note is terminated. At maturity the protection buyer delivers the reference asset or an asset among a list of deliverable assets, and the protection seller receives the value of the original purchase proceeds minus the value of the asset that has been delivered.

Exhibit 35.3 illustrates a cash-settled CLN.

CLNs may be issued directly by a financial or corporate entity or via a Special Purpose Vehicle (SPV). They have been issued with the form of credit-linking taking on one or more of a number of different guises. For instance, a CLN may have its return performance linked to the issuer's, or a specified reference entity's, credit rating, risk exposure, financial performance or circumstance of default. Exhibit 35.4 shows Bloomberg screen CLN and a list of the various types of CLN issue that have been made. Exhibit 35.5 shows a page accessed from Bloomberg screen "CLN", which is a list of CLNs that have had their coupon affected by a change in the reference entity's credit rating. In the European market, many practitioners view a bond as beig a CLN only if it is issued by an SPV as part of a structured finance transaction (such as a synthetic CDO). However we define any bond as a CLO if its return is linked to the credit performance of a named entity.

Many CLNs are issued directly by banks and corporate borrowers, in the same way as conventional bonds. An example of such a bond is shown at Exhibit 35.6. This shows Bloomberg screen DES for a CLN issued by British Telecom plc, the 8.125% note due in December 2010. The terms of this note state that the coupon will increase by 25 basis points for each one-notch rating downgrade below A–/A3 suffered by the issuer during the life of the note. The coupon will decrease by 25

EXHIBIT 35.3   Credit-Linked Note

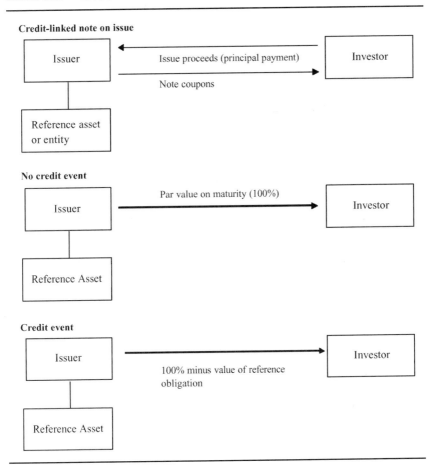

Credit-linked note on issue

No credit event

Credit event

basis points for each ratings upgrade, with a minimum coupon set at 8.125%. In other words, this note allows investors to take on a credit play on the fortunes of the issuer.

Exhibit 35.7 shows Bloomberg screen YA for this note, as at 29 May 2003. We see that a rating downgrade meant that the coupon on the note was now 8.375%.

Exhibit 35.8 shows Bloomberg screen DES for a fixed-coupon, sterling-denominated CLN issued directly by Southern Water plc, a UK utility company. The credit-linking on this note is to the credit rating movement of the issuer company. This is noted at the bottom of Exhibit 35.8, where we see that the bond may have its coupon reset with a downward rating

EXHIBIT 35.4 Bloomberg Screen CLN

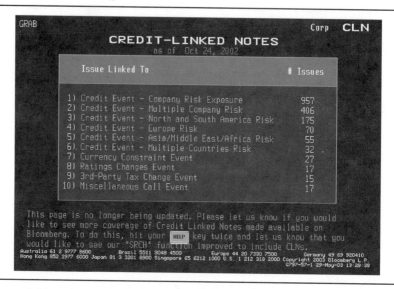

GRAB Corp CLN

CREDIT-LINKED NOTES
as of Oct 24, 2002

Issue Linked To	# Issues
1) Credit Event - Company Risk Exposure	957
2) Credit Event - Multiple Company Risk	406
3) Credit Event - North and South America Risk	175
4) Credit Event - Europe Risk	70
5) Credit Event - Asia/Middle East/Africa Risk	55
6) Credit Event - Multiple Countries Risk	32
7) Currency Constraint Event	27
8) Ratings Changes Event	17
9) 3rd-Party Tax Change Event	15
10) Miscellaneous Call Event	17

This page is no longer being updated. Please let us know if you would like to see more coverage of Credit Linked Notes made available on Bloomberg. To do this, hit your HELP key twice and let us know that you would like to see our "SRCH" function improved to include CLNs.

Australia 61 2 9777 8600 Brazil 5511 3048 4500 Europe 44 20 7330 7500 Germany 49 69 920410
Hong Kong 852 2977 6000 Japan 81 3 3201 8900 Singapore 65 6212 1000 U.S. 1 212 318 2000 Copyright 2003 Bloomberg L.P.
G797-57-1 29-May-03 13:28:38

Source: © Bloomberg L.P. Used with permission.

EXHIBIT 35.5 Bloomberg Screen Showing a Sample of CLNs Impacted by Change in Reference Entity Credit Rating, October 2002

GRAB Corp CLN

Page 1/ 1

RATINGS CHANGES EVENT

Issuer	Settle Date	Cpn	Crncy	Maturity Date	Rating Changes Exposure
1) BHFBK	04/28/1998	6.25	DEM	04/28/2006	Govt of Ukraine
2) BSPIR	03/21/2000	7.00	EUR	02/20/2010	B-Spires
3) CATTLE	10/21/1999	8.63	GBP	12/07/2007	Cattle PLC
4) CNTCNZ	09/14/2000	FRN	AUD	09/14/2007	Contact Energy
5) CNTCNZ	09/14/2000	FRN	USD	09/14/2007	Contact Energy
6) HI	11/13/1997	FRN	USD	11/13/2013	Household Fin Co
7) IFCTF	08/04/1997	7.88	USD	08/04/2002	Indust Fin Corp
8) IFCTF	08/04/1997	7.75	USD	08/04/2007	Indust Fin Corp
9) KPN	06/13/2000	FRN	EUR	06/13/2002	KPN NV
10) KPN	06/13/2000	FRN	EUR	06/13/2002	KPN NV
11) KPN	06/13/2000	6.05	EUR	06/13/2003	KPN NV
12) METALF	07/25/2000	6.75	EUR	07/25/2005	MetallGesell Fin
13) METALF	07/25/2000	6.75	EUR	07/25/2005	MetallGesell Fin
14) OSTDRA	02/16/2000	Var	EUR	02/16/2007	Oester Draukraft
15) SIRSTR	06/25/1998	FRN	USD	10/06/2006	Bk Tokyo-Mitsub
16) SOWLN	03/26/1998	6.89	GBP	03/26/2008	Southern Water
17) SPIRES	01/26/1998	FRN	DEM	10/24/2007	Greece

Australia 61 2 9777 8600 Brazil 5511 3048 4500 Europe 44 20 7330 7500 Germany 49 69 920410
Hong Kong 852 2977 6000 Japan 81 3 3201 8900 Singapore 65 6212 1000 U.S. 1 212 318 2000 Copyright 2003 Bloomberg L.P.
G797-57-1 29-May-03 13:29:32

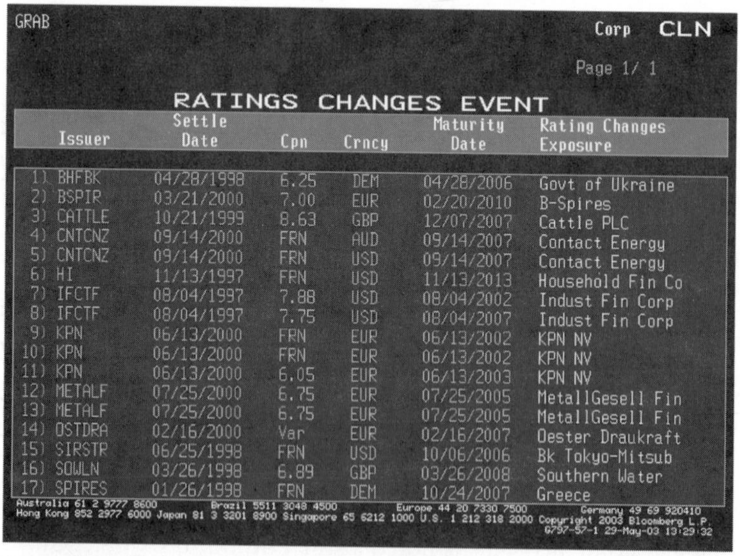

Source: © Bloomberg L.P. Used with permission.

EXHIBIT 35.6   Bloomberg Screen DES for British Telecom plc, 8.125% 2010 Credit-Linked Note, Issued on 5 December 2000

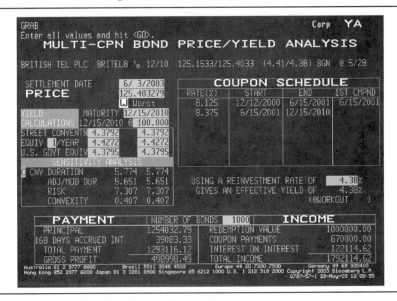

Source: © Bloomberg L.P. Used with permission.

EXHIBIT 35.7   Bloomberg Screen YA for British Telecom CLN, as at 29 May 2003

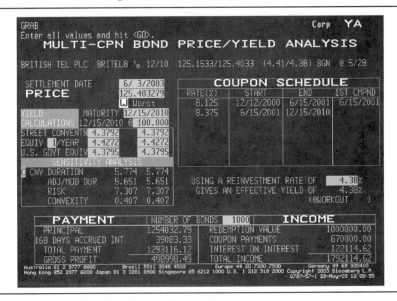

Source: © Bloomberg L.P. Used with permission.

EXHIBIT 35.8   Bloomberg Screen DES Issued by Southern Water plc

```
GRAB                                                        Corp   DES
STRUCTURED  NOTE  DESCRIPTION Page 1/ 2
REPURCH-03/26/03 SOWLN6.842 03/08      N O T   P R I C E D
ISSUER INFORMATION             IDENTIFIERS              1) Additional Sec Info
Name SOUTHERN WATER SRVCS FIN  Common    008531773      2) Multi Cpn Display
Type Water                     ISIN    XS0085317732     3) Identifiers
Market of Issue EURO NON-DOLLAR BB number  TT3379589    4) Ratings
SECURITY INFORMATION           RATINGS                  5) Fees/Restrictions
Country GB       Currency GBP  Moody's    WR            6) Sec. Specific News
Collateral Type COMPANY GUARNT S&P        A-     *-     7) Involved Parties
Calc Typ( 133)MULTI-COUPON     Composite  A3            8) Custom Notes
Maturity   3/26/2008 Series    ISSUE SIZE               9) Issuer Information
CALL/PUT                       Amt Issued             10) ALLQ
Coupon     6.842   FIXED       GBP 100,000.00   (M)   11) Pricing Sources
S/A          ISMA-30/360       Amt Outstanding        12) Related Securities
Announcement Dt  3/ 5/98       GBP            (M)
Int. Accrual Dt  3/26/98       Min Piece/Increment
1st Settle Date  3/26/98         1,000.00/ 1,000.00
1st Coupon Date  9/26/98       Par Amount   1,000.00
Iss Pr 100.0000 Reoffer    100 BOOK RUNNER/EXCHANGE
SPR @ FPR   75.0 vs UKT 7 '4 07  HSBC                 65) Old DES
NO PROSPECTUS                   LONDON                66) Send as Attachment
CPN RESETS WITH RATINGS MVMTS, GTD BY SOUTHERN WATER SRVCS. UNSEC'D, UNSUB. CALL
FROM 3/01 @HIGHER OF UKT 7¼% 12/07 OR 100%. PUT @100% IF RATINGS ARE DOWNGRADED
Australia 61 2 9777 8600    Brazil 5511 3048 4500     Europe 44 20 7330 7500     Germany 49 69 920410
Hong Kong 852 2977 6000 Japan 81 3 3201 8900 Singapore 65 6212 1000 U.S. 1 212 318 2000 Copyright 2003 Bloomberg L.P.
                                                          G926-802-0 19-Aug-03 10:33:19
```

Source: © Bloomberg L.P. Used with permission.

movement. A rating move below investment grade will enable investors to put the bond at 100%. Exhibit 35.9 is the YA screen for this bond, we see that the coupon was indeed reset on two occasions after issue, as the issuer rating was downgraded.

A different type of credit linking is illustrated by the bond described at Exhibit 35.10. This shows a euro-denominated CLN issued by an SPV as part of a repackaging transaciton. The bond is credit linked to a basket of reference entities, as described at the bottom of the screen. The reference entities are the following names, and their successors:

- ABB International Finance Ltd.
- BASF AG
- Commerzbank AG
- Roche Holding AG

In the event of a credit event on any of these names, the bond is called immediately. Exhibit 35.11 shows the yield analysis page for this bond as at 19 August 2003.

EXHIBIT 35.9   Bloomberg YA Screen for Southern Water plc

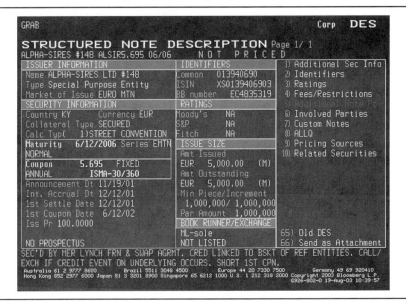

Source: © Bloomberg L.P. Used with permission.

EXHIBIT 35.10   Bloomberg Screen Showing Euro-Denominated CLN

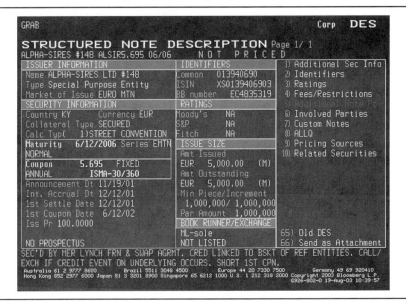

Source: © Bloomberg L.P. Used with permission.

EXHIBIT 35.11 Bloomberg YA Screen for Euro-Denominated CLN

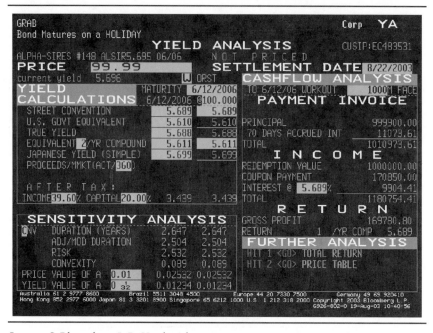

Source: © Bloomberg L.P. Used with permission.

EXHIBIT 35.12 CLN and Credit Default Swap Structure on Single Reference Name

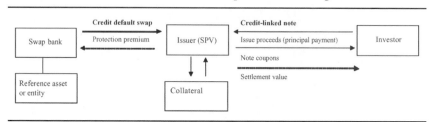

Structured products such as synthetic collateralised debt obligations (CDOs) described in Chapter 30 may combine both CLNs and credit default swaps, to meet issuer and investor requirements. For instance, Exhibit 35.12 shows a credit structure designed to provide a higher return for an investor on comparable risk to the cash market. An issuing entity is set up in the form of a special purpose vehicle (SPV) which issues CLNs to the market. The structure is engineered so that the SPV has a neutral position on a reference asset. It has bought protection on a single reference name by issuing a funded credit derivative, the CLN,

EXHIBIT 35.13   Progression of CLN Development

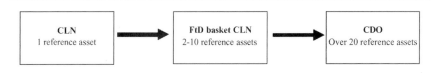

and simultaneously sold protection on this name by selling a credit default swap on this name. The proceeds of the CLN are invested in risk-free collateral such as Treasury bills or a Treasury bank account. The coupon on the CLN will be a spread over LIBOR. It is backed by the collateral account and the fee generated by the SPV in selling protection with the credit default swap. Investors in the CLN will have exposure to the reference asset or entity, and the repayment of the CLN is linked to the performance of the reference entity. If a credit event occurs, the maturity date of the CLN is brought forward and the note is settled as par minus the value of the reference asset or entity.

THE FIRST-TO-DEFAULT CREDIT-LINKED NOTE

A standard CLN is issued in reference to one specific bond or loan. An investor purchasing such a note is writing credit protection on a specific reference credit. A CLN that is linked to more than one reference credit is known as a *basket credit-linked note*. A development of the CLN as a structured product is the first-to-default CLN (FtD), which is a CLN that is linked to a basket of reference assets. The investor in the CLN is selling protection on the first credit to default.[1] Exhibit 35.13 shows this progression in the development of CLNs as structured products, with the *fully funded synthetic CDO*, described in Chapter 30, being the vehicle that uses CLNs tied to a large basket of reference assets.

An FtD CLN is a funded credit derivative in which the investor sells protection on one reference in a basket of assets, whichever is the first to default. The return on the CLN is a multiple of the average spread of the basket. The CLN will mature early on occurrence of a credit event relating to any of the reference assets. Settlement on the CLN can be either of the following:

■ Physical settlement, with the defaulted asset(s) being delivered to the noteholder.

---

[1] "Default" here meaning a credit event as defined in the ISDA definitions.

EXHIBIT 35.14   First-to-Default CLN Structure

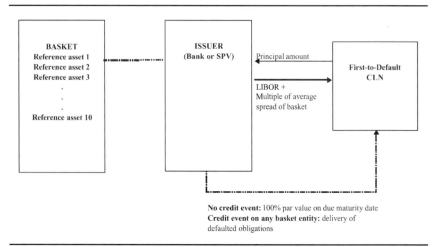

No credit event: 100% par value on due maturity date
Credit event on any basket entity: delivery of
defaulted obligations

▪ Cash settlement, in which the CLN issuer pays redemption proceeds to the noteholder calculated as (Principal amount × Reference asset recovery value).

In practice, it is not the "recovery value" that is used but the market value of the reference asset at the time the credit event is verified. Recovery of a defaulted asset follows a legal process of administration and/or liquidation that can take some years, and so the final recovery value may not be known with certainty for some time. Because the computation of recovery value is so difficult, holders of a CLN may prefer physical settlement where they take delivery of the defaulted asset.

Exhibit 35.14 shows a generic FtD credit-linked note.

To illustrate, consider an FtD CLN issued at par with a term-to-maturity of five years and linked to a basket of five reference assets with a face value (issued nominal amount) of $10 million. An investor purchasing this note will pay $10 million to the issuer. If no credit event occurs during the life of the note, the investor will receive the face value of the note on maturity. If a credit event occurs on any of the assets in the basket, the note will redeem early and the issuer will deliver a deliverable obligation of the reference entity, or a portfolio of such obligations, for a $10 million nominal amount. An FtD CLN carries a similar amount of risk exposure on default to a standard CLN, namely the recovery rate of the defaulted credit. However its risk exposure prior to default is theoretically lower than a standard CLN, as it can reduce default probability

EXHIBIT 35.15   Diversified Credit Exposure to Basket of Reference Assets: Hypothetical Reference Asset Mix

	Automobiles	Banks	Electronics	Insurance	Media	Telecoms	Utilities
AAA							
Aa1							
Aa2				SunAlliance			
Aa3		RBoS					
A1							
A2							Powergen
A3	Ford					British Telecom	
Baa1			Philips		News Intl		
Baa2							
Baa3							

through diversification. The investor can obtain exposure to a basket of reference entities that differ by industrial sector and by credit rating.

The matrix shown in Exhibit 35.15 illustrate how an investor can select a credit mix in the basket that diversifies risk exposure across a wide range—we show a hypothetical mix of reference assets to which an issued FtD could be linked. The precise selection of names will reflect investors' own risk/return profile requirements.

The FtD CLN creates a synthetic credit entity that features a note return with enhanced spread. Investors receive a spread over LIBOR that is the average return of all the reference assets in the basket. This structure serves to diversify credit risk exposure while benefiting from a higher average return. If the pool of reference assets is sufficiently large, the structure becomes similar to a single-tranche CDO. This is discussed in Chapter 31.

CHAPTER 36

Structured Credit Products and Repackaged Securities

Alessandro Cocco

Vice President and Assistant General Counsel

JPMorgan Chase

S tructured credit products represent a significant portion of the credit derivatives market. This market continues to grow at remarkable speed. *Structured credit products* involve the blending of credit derivative, repackaging, and securitisation technology to create investment products that allow investors to gain exposure to a wide variety of credit-related risk and benefit from related returns. In order to understand structured credit products it is essential to have a good grasp of credit default swap technology. We refer the reader elsewhere in this book, which touches on fundamental notions regarding credit default swaps and other credit derivatives.[1] In this chapter we examine certain different types of structured credit products. The common link between these different types of products is apparent from their name: The underlying exposure of an investor in structured credit products is exposure to credit risk. The term "credit derivative" can be used to refer to a number of transactions involving the transfer of credit risk, including credit default swaps, credit-linked notes, and total return swaps. In the

---

[1] For a further discussion, see Chapter 4.

The views and opinions expressed in this chapter are the author's own in a private capacity and not the views of JPMorgan Chase. This chapter does not constitute legal or other advice. The author would like to thank Don Thompson and Alex Hunt for their comments.

context of this chapter we will use the term *credit derivative* to refer to credit default swaps and credit-linked notes. Total return swaps are currently less frequently used than credit default swaps and credit-linked notes in the context of structured credit products.

We begin with a look at the concept of credit risk.

CREDIT RISK

Credit risk may be defined as the risk that a debtor will not meet its payment obligations as they become due. In a credit default swap the seller of protection agrees with the buyer of protection that if certain specified credit events occur with respect to one or more specified reference entities, the seller will make a payment to the buyer. Credit events are certain preagreed strong indicators of serious financial difficulties affecting the reference entity. The party buying credit risk protection pays a predetermined amount to the seller of protection. The entity or entities that constitute the point of reference in determining the value of a credit derivative are referred to as the "reference entities."

The current documentation standard for single name credit default swaps is set by the *2003 ISDA Credit Derivatives Definitions*, as supplemented from time to time by additional supplements. The definitions are published by the International Swaps and Derivatives Associations (ISDA), the association of leading participants in the privately negotiated over-the-counter (OTC) derivatives market. An earlier version of the definitions was published in 1999. The definitions and subsequent supplements have been drafted through inclusive consultation of market participants. By the end of 2001, between 91% and 98% of the active credit derivative portfolios of respondents to a global survey conducted by the British Bankers Association were based on standard documentation. (See the BBA *Credit Derivatives Report* 2002, www.BBA.org.uk.)

CREDIT EVENTS

The parties specify in the transaction documentation for a credit derivative transaction which credit events apply to that transaction. Current market standard for credit default swaps where the reference entity is an investment grade corporate is to specify as credit events the *bankruptcy* of the reference entity and its *failure to pay* in respect of certain types of obligations specified in the documentation for the credit derivative (for example: all borrowed money issued or guaranteed by the reference entity). *Restruc-*

turing in respect of certain types of obligations specified in the documentation for the credit default swap is also often specified as a credit event. Typically the parties to a physically settled credit derivative (see below) specify slightly different criteria to identify deliverable obligations following a restructuring credit event, depending on whether the reference entity is organised in Europe, the US or Asia. For reference entities that are sovereign states *repudiation/moratorium* and *failure to pay* are often specified, and bankruptcy is regarded as not applicable. Repudiation/moratorium is a credit event triggered by an entity disclaiming, rejecting, or imposing a moratorium on its external debt obligations. In the case of all but the bankruptcy credit event, it is market standard to specify a materiality threshold by agreeing a payment requirement or default requirement that has to be reached before the credit event is triggered. For example, typically, a failure to pay credit event will be triggered only if it consists of a failure to make a payment in an amount of €1 million or more.

CONDITIONS TO PAYMENT/CONDITIONS TO SETTLEMENT

A credit derivative is *triggered* when a credit event has occurred and certain preagreed *conditions to settlement,* in some case referred to as conditions to payment, have been satisfied. Credit derivatives can be structured as either credit default swaps or credit-linked notes, depending on the needs of different investors. It is very common for these products to be issued as cash settled credit-linked notes. This makes the product more accessible as it can be purchased by investors who are not organized to enter into collateralized credit default swaps or to receive physical settlement of distressed bonds, loans, or other assets following a credit event. The inter-dealer single name credit derivatives market relies largely on physically settled credit default swaps.

In a *funded credit derivative,* such as a *credit-linked note,* the seller of protection makes an upfront payment to the buyer of protection. In the case of a credit-linked note, this upfront payment is the purchase price of the notes, paid by the buyer of the credit-linked note to the issuer of the credit-linked note. It is important here to grasp the somewhat counterintuitive jargon: the buyer of a credit-linked note is the seller of protection. The issuer of the credit-linked note is the buyer of protection. If no credit event occurs, the principal amount of the note is returned by the buyer of protection to the investor at maturity. If a credit event has occurred, and cash settlement applies, at maturity the holder of the credit-linked note (seller of protection) receives the value of the original principal amount of the note minus an amount which reflects any drop in market value of the reference asset following the credit event. We will call this amount *credit event amount* as it is an amount which represents payments related to the occurrence of credit events. If a credit event occurs, and physical settlement applies, at maturity the seller of protection receives the value of the original principal amount of the note minus an amount which reflects the face value of certain pre-agreed debt instruments delivered by the buyer of protection. In this case the holder of the credit-linked note (seller of protection) also receives delivery of the deliverable obligations.

Market standard conditions to payment are the delivery by the calculation agent to the trustee for the notes (or, in the case of a credit default swap, by the notifying party to the other party to the credit default swap) of a credit event notice and a notice of publicly available information. For physically settled credit derivatives (see below for a distinction between physical settlement and cash settlement) delivery of a notice of physical settlement typically is an additional condition to settlement. The main function of a *credit event notice* is for the notifying party to alert the other party to the credit derivative that a credit event has occurred. The notice also contains a description of the circumstances which constitute a credit event. A *notice of publicly available information* states that publicly available information exists regarding the credit event. As its name suggests, the principal purpose of the notice of publicly available information is to provide confirmation from public sources that the credit event that is the subject of the credit event notice has indeed occurred. This is also a means of ensuring that no confidentiality obligation is being breached by one party informing the other of the occurrence of circumstances that constitute a credit event as these circumstances are public knowledge. The transaction documentation specifies which information will be eligible to constitute publicly available information. Typical examples of publicly available information are articles published in financial newspapers or internet news sources, official filings with judicial or regulatory authorities, or public statements made by or posted on the website of the reference entity itself.

Only the *notifying party* can trigger a credit event by delivering a credit event notice and notice of publicly available information to the other party. The transaction documentation will specify who can act as the notifying party. Typically the buyer of protection is a notifying party, and in some transactions both buyer and seller of protection are notifying parties. When both buyer and seller are notifying parties, either the seller or the buyer can trigger a settlement of the credit derivative following a credit event. A seller of credit derivative protection will be incentivised to trigger a credit event to limit its exposure if the seller takes the view that the market value of the obligations of the reference entity will decrease with time, thereby increasing the settlement amount payable by seller to buyer pursuant to the credit derivative.

CREDIT DERIVATIVES AND INSURANCE CONTRACTS

One of the main characteristics of a credit derivative is that following the trigger of a credit event the buyer of protection need not have suffered an *actual loss* as a result of that credit event and need not have an *insurable interest* related to such event in order to qualify for a settlement payment by the seller of protection. Assume that A enters into a cash-settled credit derivative with B in which A buys credit derivative protection from B with respect to company X as the reference entity and specifies *bankruptcy* and *failure to pay* as credit events. In other words, A buys from B the right to receive from B an agreed payment in case company X is subject to bankruptcy proceedings or does not repay its debt. If company X undergoes bankruptcy proceedings or fails to repay its debt, a credit event occurs. This, assuming any other conditions to payment specified in the contract are satisfied, gives A the right to receive from B the agreed payment. Payment does not depend on whether A had any credit exposure to company X, or suffered any losses as a result of that bankruptcy or failure to pay.

The absence of a requirement for an actual loss or an insurable interest is also the main technical difference between a credit derivative and an insurance contract from a legal point of view. In our example, in order to receive payment under the credit derivative following a credit event, A is not required to have suffered any losses, and is not required to have any credit exposure to company X. Generally, a claim by the insured in an insurance contract is only valid if the insured has an insurable interest in the asset insured: I cannot insure against the risk that somebody else's bicycle is stolen. An insurance claim is usually also subject to the insured having suffered an actual loss as a result of a covered event. Imagine that my bicycle has been stolen at night while I sleep, but it is returned intact before I wake up. In that case I have not suffered an actual loss and I will not be able to receive a payment under my insurance contract.

Before proceeding, readers should familiarise themselves with the content of Chapter 4 on credit derivatives.

PORTFOLIO CREDIT PRODUCTS

From Chapter 4 readers will be familiar with the distinction between single name and portfolio credit derivatives. The latter comprises credit derivatives where the parties trade credit risk of more than one reference entity. There are several different types of portfolio credit derivatives. Let us examine some of the types currently used in the European credit markets. Some variations apply to the market standard for single name credit default swaps depending on whether the reference entity is an investment grade corporate or a sovereign entity, and on the geographical area of the country of organisation of the reference entity (US, Europe, Asia). Notwithstanding these differences, it is accurate to say, however, that there is a widely accepted market standard with respect to single name credit default swaps. The same is not true at this stage for portfolio credit derivatives and other structured credit products. Consequently, in the context of this paper, when we refer to certain characteristics of certain types of transactions, please bear in mind that these can change from transaction to transaction.

ISOLATING CREDIT RISK WITH SPECIAL PURPOSE VEHICLES

Exhibit 36.1 shows a CLN issued by an SPV. In this case, the seller of protection is the investor who buys the note. The investor pays principal upfront to the issuer of the note, who is the buyer of credit derivative protection. The investor also expects to receive a coupon during the life of the transaction and, at maturity, principal minus any credit event amounts. One relevant aspect of this structure is that by purchasing the credit-linked note the investor is acquiring exposure to two types of credit risk: (1) the credit risk represented by the reference entity or entities that are the subject of the credit derivative; and (2) the credit risk of the issuer of the credit-linked note. If the issuer of the credit-linked note becomes insolvent, the investor may lose some or all of the coupon and principal invested.

EXHIBIT 36.1   Credit-Linked Note and Swap Hedge

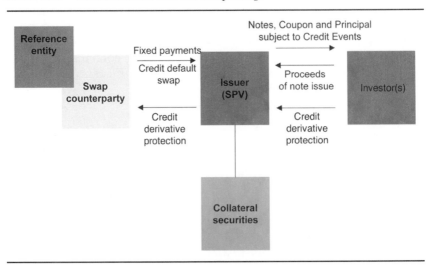

An issuer's failure to pay coupon or principal could be linked to matters completely unrelated to the specific credit derivative risk represented by the portfolio of reference entities, such as a bankruptcy of the issuer following a downturn in the markets where the issuer operates. In this case the investor is exposed to risks that affect the general commercial activity of the issuer of the credit-linked note.

Let us imagine an investor purchasing a credit-linked note from A, a European bank. The portfolio of reference entities comprises reference entities that are active in the US automotive industry. Let us say that Bank A subsequently becomes insolvent for reasons completely unrelated to the US automotive industry. Following the insolvency of Bank A, the investor will rank as an unsecured creditor in the insolvency proceedings of Bank A and may receive a recovery value of less than 100 cents on the dollar. By purchasing the credit-linked note the investor has taken on two levels of credit risk: (1) the credit risk of the portfolio of US automotive industry reference entities and (2) the credit risk of Bank A.

Credit-linked notes, a funded instrument, can be contrasted with the position in an unfunded credit product, such as a credit default swap. In the case of the latter the buyer of protection is exposed to the credit risk of the seller of protection. In a credit default swap, unlike in a credit-linked note, there is no up-front payment from the seller of protection to the buyer. In that case the buyer of protection is exposed to the credit risk of the seller for payment of the settlement amount following a credit event. The seller of protection is exposed to the buyer for payment of the protection fee. It is therefore the case that in both funded and unfunded credit products one of the parties is exposed to the credit risk of the counterparty. The natural solution to this problem is to collateralise that credit risk. *Collateralisation* is the process by which a party that has credit exposure to a counterparty acquires rights over an asset or portfolio of assets to secure its exposure to that counterparty so that the party bearing the risk can satisfy itself on those assets in case of insolvency of the counterparty.

In the case of an unfunded credit default swap the parties can collateralise their reciprocal exposure by entering into a *collateral agreement*.[2] Participants in the privately negotiated derivatives market generally rely on a standard form of collateral agreement published by ISDA, such as the ISDA Credit Support Annex.

A distinguishing feature of structured credit-linked notes is the use of *special purpose vehicles* (SPVs), also called *special purpose entities* (SPEs).

---

[2] A collateral agreement is a legally binding document governing the transfer of ownership of or a security interest in cash, securities or other valuable assets between the parties to secure one party's credit exposure to the other.

This technology was initially used in securitisation and repackaging. This consists of creating a new corporate entity whose purpose is to serve as a conduit for the issue of one or more series of notes. This has the benefit of resolving the issue of the exposure of the investor to the risk of the issuer. Each issue of notes is collateralised and the SPV is bankruptcy remote.

The basic architecture of a structured credit transaction involving an SPV is as follows: The SPV issues credit-linked notes to the investors. The investor pays the purchase price of the credit-linked note to the SPV. The SPV uses the sale proceeds to purchase collateral securities, that meet certain eligibility criteria preagreed with the investor. Typically, the SPV also enters into a swap with a dealer, who is referred to in this context as the swap counterparty. The swap with the swap counterparty is usually composed of a credit default swap element and an asset swap element. The credit default swap constitutes a hedge for the SPV issuer of the credit-linked note as it transfers to the swap counterparty the credit protection purchased by the SPV from the note investor. The SPV buys protection from the investor and sells protection to the swap counterparty. The SPV receives protection payments from the swap counterparty and pays a coupon to the holders of the credit-linked note. Typically, under the terms of the asset swap the SPV pays to the swap counterparty all amounts received by the SPV under the collateral securities and the swap counterparty pays to the SPV a pre-agreed amount. This is typically sufficient to enable the SPV to meet its cash flow obligations, including payments of coupon and principal under the notes.

With the proceeds from the issue of the credit-linked note the SPV purchases collateral. The purpose of the investment in collateral is twofold: firstly, to secure the obligations of the SPV, secondly, to produce a positive cash flow into the structure. The SPV has no assets other than the collateral. If the issuer fails to pay under the terms of the note, the noteholders, or a trustee acting for all noteholders, can access the collateral, sell it in the marketplace and recover all or part of the amounts owed to the investor by the SPV. In addition, as mentioned, the collateral usually produces a yield, and this yield can be used to boost the return to the investor of the credit-linked note. However, if the yield of the collateral is lower than the yield of the relevant credit-linked note, the structure will produce a loss. Transaction documents may provide that any losses on collateral are deducted from the amounts payable to investors, either during the life of the transaction (losses deducted form the coupon payable by the note) or at maturity (losses deducted from principal at redemption). In other structures, under the terms of the asset swap the SPV pays to the swap counterparty any cash flows under the collateral, and the swap counterparty undertakes to make fixed payments to the SPV irrespective of the amount of coupon and principal, if any, yielded by the collateral. In this case the swap counterparty takes the mark to market and credit risk of the collateral.

In the case of an investor buying a credit-linked note issued by an entity that has been trading for several years, the capacity of the issuer to repay that investor will depend on its ability to repay all its debt. If the same investor buys a credit-linked note issued by an entity created for the purpose of issuing credit-linked notes and to do no other business, that investor's only exposure is to the portfolio of reference entities in the credit derivative, and to any collateral held by the SPV to secure repayment of the notes. The effect is to isolate the exposure of the investor to each particular issue of notes.

One of the most important provisions in the trust agreement which establishes the SPV is a clause usually referred to as the *waterfall*.[3] The waterfall provisions list the order of priority in which each party is entitled to receive payments of coupon and principal. The transaction documentation will specify which party is entitled to which payments at each coupon payment date and on the notes reaching maturity or earlier redemption. By way of example, a typical maturity date principal repayment waterfall would provide that any amounts available at maturity would be used to pay the parties in the following order: first, any amounts due to the swap counterparty, such as payment of settlement amounts pursuant to the credit derivative swap between the SPV and the swap counterparty. If any principal is available after satisfaction of the swap counterparty's claim, that principal would be used to pay the noteholders. In tranched structures where more than one class of noteholders is present, the waterfall provisions reflect the different order of priority agreed between noteholders (discussed below). Similar waterfall provisions govern the priority of payments at each coupon payment date and in the case of an early termination of the structure. Transaction documentation typically provides for early termination of a structure following a default by the SPV or by the swap counterparty, or unforeseen circumstances. The waterfall is one of the most important provisions in the structure as it determines who is paid first when funds are not sufficient to pay 100% of the claims of each party in the structure.

Collateral

As mentioned, prior to receiving payment of the purchase price for the notes, an SPV has no assets of its own, and for this reason the transaction documents of credit-linked notes issued by an SPV invariably provide that the SPV must invest the proceeds of each issue of notes in collateral, which meets certain preagreed eligibility criteria, and hold that collateral

---

[3] Waterfall priority of payments are also discussed in Chapter 30.

to secure its obligations to the noteholders. The most widely used type of eligible collateral is represented by securities such as highly rated government or corporate bonds or asset-backed notes. A second type of eligible collateral is a cash deposit with a bank. A third type of eligible collateral is the credit and asset swap with the swap counterparty. This swap will have a mark to market value which will be positive or negative for the SPV. A positive mark to market swap value will be an asset for the SPV, a negative mark to market value will be a liability of the SPV. The *mark to market value of the swap* is usually calculated on the basis of the standard ISDA provisions, and it relates to the amount a third party would pay or expect to be paid to step into the shoes of the swap counterparty to enter into a swap with the SPV, which replaces the existing swap and reproduces its economics as closely as possible.

BANKRUPTCY REMOTENESS

From the perspective of the noteholder, in its capacity as investor in a credit-linked note, an SPV structure allows the investor to ring-fence the noteholder's exposure to the specific characteristics of that credit-linked note, rather than exposing the investor to the risk of a default of the issuer due to the general commercial activity of the issuer. This is aimed at allowing the investor to concentrate its risk and reward analysis on the characteristics of the structured product itself, such as the soundness of the structure and the economics of each transaction, including the credit derivative terms and the credit quality of the collateral securities. In the case of a note issued by an SPV that has no commercial activity other than its role in the credit derivative structure, the investor does not need to investigate the credit risk of the SPV itself and can look through to the collateral held by the SPV to secure its obligations pursuant to the notes. Needless to say, the investor would be well advised to analyse the transaction documentation to ensure that it achieves the intended purpose.

The use of an SPV with the purpose of isolating the investor from risks that are unrelated to the economics of the credit derivative at hand is also achieved by adding the bankruptcy remoteness feature to the structure. The transaction documentation often makes the SPV bankruptcy remote from the originator of the credit portfolio, the swap counterparty or any other entity involved in the structure. Bankruptcy remoteness is a concept developed in the context of asset securitisations such as credit card receivables and mortgage-backed obligations. It is used as shorthand for a structure where the existence of the SPV is independent of the continued existence of the swap counterparty or any other entity related to the transaction. All entities that deal with the SPV do so at arm's length. All cash flows are calculated at the outset so that if one party defaults or ceases to exist, it can be substituted with other market counterparties. Typically the transaction documentation also provides that the SPV cannot engage in any business, assume obligations or dispose of collateral in a manner not contemplated by the transaction documentation.

LINEAR BASKET PORTFOLIO STRUCTURES

An example of a credit contract that references multiple names is a *linear basket portfolio structure*, illustrated at Exhibits 36.2, 36.3, and 36.4. In this the buyer and seller of protection agree on a portfolio of

EXHIBIT 36.2   Linear Basket Structure: Portfolio of Reference Entities on Day One

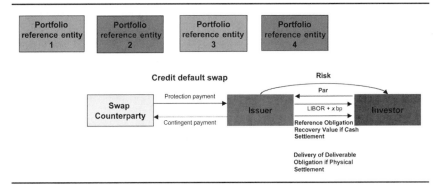

EXHIBIT 36.3   Linear Basket Structure: One of the Reference Entities Experiences a Credit Event

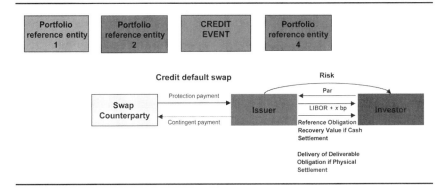

EXHIBIT 36.4   Linear Basket Structure: Transaction Continues Following
Settlement with Respect to Reference Entity 3

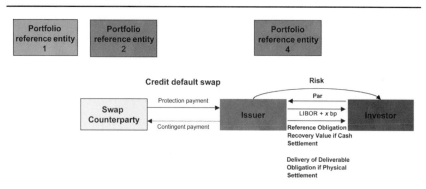

reference entities. For each credit event affecting one of the reference
entities in the portfolio during the life of the transaction, the buyer will
have the right to receive a payment from the seller. A notional amount is
specified with respect to each reference entity and the settlement amount
is calculated on the basis of that notional amount. In most structures of
this type the parties agree that once a credit event has affected a reference entity, that reference entity is deleted from the portfolio and no further credit events can be triggered in relation to that reference entity.
Further settlement with respect to that linear basket credit derivative
can be triggered in relation to credit events affecting the remaining reference entities comprised in the portfolio.

Let us imagine that a buyer of protection issues a credit-linked note
to a seller of protection. The portfolio comprises a basket of corporate
reference entity names: Reference Entity 1, Reference Entity 2, Reference Entity 3, and Reference Entity 4. Cash settlement applies. The
transaction has a notional amount of €10 million per reference name,
resulting in a total notional amount, or portfolio amount of €40 million. The effective date is 25 February 2003 and the maturity date is 25
February 2008. In our example this credit derivative takes the form of a
credit-linked note, the protection seller will be the investor in the note
who has paid upfront €40 million to the issuer of the credit-linked note.
Assume a credit event is triggered with respect to Reference Entity 3 on
25 June 2004. If the market value of the reference obligation determined
by the calculation agent is 65%, the credit event amount with respect to
the related reference entity will be equal to the credit position of the reference entity specified in the transaction documentation multiplied by
100% minus that market value: €10 million × (100% – 65%) = €3.5

million. Assuming there is no further credit event at maturity, the investors will receive in the aggregate a cash settlement amount equal to the full notional of each reference entity which was not affected by the credit event plus the notional of the reference entity affected by the credit event minus any credit event amount for the reference entity affected by the credit event. In the example above the credit event amount is €3.5 million. The investors in the aggregate would receive at maturity €40 million − €3.5 million = €36.5 million. Each investor would receive a pro rata amount of the total principal available depending on the notional amount of note held by that investor. This is different from a tranched structure, examined below, where investors are divided into different classes, some of which have priority over the others in the repayment of principal.

If the credit derivative referred to above were structured as a credit default swap, the cash flows would be slightly different, but the economic substance would remain the same. In a portfolio credit default swap, if the recovery rate of the reference obligation is 65% following a credit event, the seller of protection will pay to the buyer an amount equal to the notional amount for the reference entity affected by the credit event (Reference Entity 3 in our example above) × market value of credit event reference entity. In our example above, this would be €10 million × (100% − 65%) = €3.5 million.

In the case of a portfolio credit default swap as in the case of a portfolio credit-linked note, the portfolio transaction will continue to exist with a portfolio notional of €30 million and collateral assets of €36.5 million. No further credit events can be triggered with respect to Reference Entity 3, but if a credit event occurs with respect to another reference entity contained in the portfolio, settlement will take place in the same way as we illustrated above in relation to Reference Entity 3. The affected reference entity will be excluded from the portfolio going forward, and the transaction will continue to exist until the maturity date agreed by the parties, or, if earlier, the date on which all reference entities have been affected by credit events, followed by settlement.

Our credit derivative would have terminated following settlement with respect to Reference Entity 3 if it had been a single-name credit default swap. However, the credit derivative in our example is a linear basket portfolio structure. In this case, following the credit event affecting Reference Entity 3, the portfolio trade in our example will continue to exist, with a portfolio amount equal to the original portfolio amount minus the notional amount applicable to the reference entity that has been triggered.

Linear portfolio structures are popular with buyers of protection who wish to buy wholesale protection on a large portfolio of names, usually at a better price than it would cost to buy protection by entering into separate single-name swaps in relation to each single name comprised in the portfolio.

Linear portfolio structures are popular with sellers of protection who wish to acquire exposure to a portfolio of names that they can customise to acquire a more or less diversified risk profile. A portfolio composed exclusively of airline companies is likely to have a different risk/reward profile from a portfolio tracking composition of the most liquid corporate and financial names. A linear portfolio structure can also be viewed as a series of single name credit default swaps.

FIRST-TO-DEFAULT PORTFOLIO STRUCTURES

First-to-default structures are similar to linear basket portfolio structures because buyer and seller trade credit risk relating to a portfolio on a list of reference entity names. They differ, however, from linear basket portfolio structures in that the transaction terminates with respect to its whole notional amount following the first credit event affecting one of the reference entities, hence the name *first to default*. In a first-to-default portfolio structure, the parties agree on a portfolio of reference entities, and provide that following a credit event and settlement relating to one the reference entities, the whole credit transaction terminates. By contrast, as we have illustrated above, in the case of a linear basket the credit derivative continues to exist with respect to the reference entities unaffected by credit events. The structures are illustrated at Exhibits 36.5 to 36.7.

EXHIBIT 36.5   First-to-Default Structure: Portfolio of Reference Entities on Day One

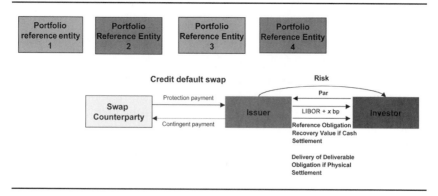

EXHIBIT 36.6   First-to-Default Structure: One of the Reference Entities Experiences a Credit Event

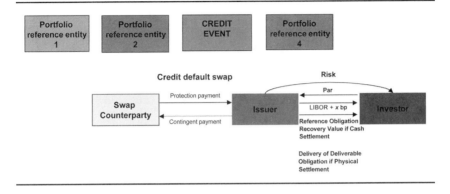

EXHIBIT 36.7   First-to-Default Structure: Early Termination

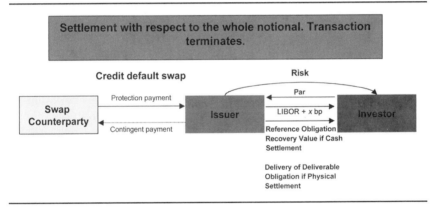

Going back to the example of a portfolio credit derivative referred to above with a notional of €40 million we have seen that in the case of a linear basket portfolio structure referenced to four reference entities, a trigger with respect to one reference entity does not constitute a trigger of the whole credit derivative. This is the case, however, for a credit event with respect to a first to default portfolio credit transaction. In the case of a first to default credit derivative referenced to four reference entities and with a notional of €40 million, the first credit event to occur and to be followed by satisfaction of the condition to settlement will result in settlement of the whole structure with respect to the full €40 million. A characteristic risk factor involved in a first to default structure is the correlation between reference entity names. Correlation can be assessed by reference to industry sector, geographical region or otherwise. In most types of investments, diversification is thought to reduce the level of risk of an investment. By contrast, in a first to default structure diversification increases the likelihood of a default, because the first reference entity to experience a credit event will trigger the whole structure. Investors in a first to default structure usually are attracted by higher coupons to compensate them for increased risk when compared with a linear portfolio structure. Protection buyers usually benefit from buying protection on an aggregate basis with respect to several reference entity names as an alternative to buying protection on each name separately.

TRANCHED STRUCTURES

Credit risk tranching is a risk management technology based on the distribution of probability of default risk within a given portfolio on the basis of actuarial principles. Let us consider a hypothetical portfolio of 100 loans issued by a bank, that we will call the *originator*. Let us assume that based on historical default data an actuarial study of default probability for that type of portfolio tells us that the most likely outcome is that in the next five years 4% of these loans will default. The same actuarial analysis indicates to us that there is some likelihood that in the same period of time a further 7% of these 100 loans will default in addition to the 4% mentioned above, resulting in a total of 11% of defaults. Finally, let us assume these studies indicate to us that there is an extremely low probability that more than 11% of those loans will default over the next five years. To summarise, the actuarial analysis indicates that 4% of portfolio defaults are likely, a further 7% of portfolio defaults may occur but are less likely to occur than the first 4%, and it is very unlikely that defaults will exceed 11% of the portfolio.

By following the actuarial principles referred to above and based on the probability of credit events given a certain portfolio of reference entity names, separate levels of risk are expressed as percentages of the notional amount of the whole portfolio, and allocated to tranches of the portfolio. The concept of first loss is introduced and the portfolio of reference entity names is divided into tranches, providing a number of levels of risk that can be sold to different investors. The transaction documentation will identify different classes of notes, each reflecting a tranche, or level, of risk. This is one area where the waterfall provisions in the documentation acquire even greater importance than in other structures. By purchasing the notes, investors consent to specific rules for the distribution of principal and interest on interest payment dates and at maturity or early redemption of the notes. The waterfall provision in the documentation will identify different classes of notes, each bearing a different coupon and exposing the holder to a different level of risk. The key to the structure, which is illustrated at Exhibit 36.8, is to identify appropriate levels of projected defaults and reward each level with an appropriate coupon payment.

The notes linked to the first level of risk (4% of a portfolio of €40 million in our example) are often referred to as the Class C notes, or *equity tranche*. The coupon paid by the issuer on this tranche will most likely be higher than the coupon paid on the tranches ranking higher in the capital structure. This coupon reflects the higher level of risk of the equity tranche. This is also sometimes referred to as the "first loss." The notes linked to the second, or mezzanine level of risk (between 4% and 11% of a portfolio of €40 million in our example) are often referred to as the Class B notes, or *mezzanine tranche*. Finally, the notes linked to the third level of risk (in excess of 11% of a portfolio of €40 million in our example) are often referred to as the Class A notes, or *senior tranche*. At each interest or principal payment date, any assets held by the SPV for the purpose of paying interest or principal will be allocated to pay the Class A holders, up to the full amount of the coupon or principal amount expected to be paid with respect to Class A. Any excess will be paid to the Class B holders up to the full amount of coupon or principal expected to be paid with respect to Class B. Any excess will then be allotted to the Class C noteholders. These principles are contained in the waterfall provisions in the transaction documentation.

Let us refer back to the fictional portfolio highlighted above. In this case the waterfall section in the transaction documents will provide that the first class of notes will be impacted for the first 4% of credit event

EXHIBIT 36.8 Tranched Portfolio Structure

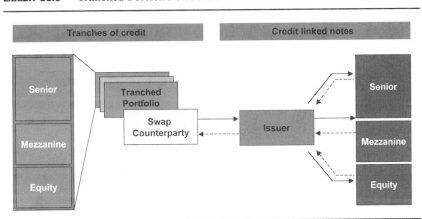

amounts affecting the portfolio. On a portfolio notional of €40 million this would be €40 × 4% = €1.6 million. If credit events affect this portfolio they will be allocated as follows: The calculation agent will calculate a credit event amount; and the SPV will sell collateral securities and make a payment to the swap counterparty under the credit default swap in amount equal to such credit event amount. This will result in a decrease in the funds held by the SPV to pay principal and coupon to the investors. The waterfall provisions will say that the equity tranche investors (the Class C investors) will bear that first loss. No money is lost by the mezzanine tranche investors (the Class B investors) or the senior tranche investors (the Class A investors) at this stage.

In fact, the equity level investors will bear the first loss and all losses on the structure up to €1.6 million (4% of the capital structure). This is referred to as the first loss position. If that level is reached, the equity level investors have lost all their initial capital. If that credit event amount level is exceeded, the Class B investors, or mezzanine investors, will bear all losses that exceed 4% of credit events affecting the capital structure, up to 11% of the notional amount of the transaction. This corresponds to credit event amounts in excess of €1.6 million and up to €4.4 million. The 4% level is the point at which mezzanine tranche investors begin suffering losses. This is also referred to as the *attachment point* of the mezzanine tranche. This is the minimum credit event amount that must be reached by the structure for the mezzanine investor to suffer a loss. Again, the senior tranche investors do not bear any losses until the credit event amount reaches 11% of the notional amount of the transaction. The senior tranche would bear losses if the credit event amount exceeds 11% of the capital structure, equivalent to a credit event amount in excess of €4.4. million. This is the maximum loss that can be borne by the mezzanine investor.

The mezzanine and senior tranches are said to benefit from the subordination below them. This is shorthand to describe the process by which a specified level of portfolio defaults need to be incurred (4% in our example) before the investors in the mezzanine and senior tranches are affected and begin to lose money. Given the same portfolio, the higher the level of subordination below a tranche, the safer the investment in that tranche. Consequently the senior tranche is regarded as the most secure level of investment as it benefits from the subordination of both the mezzanine tranche and the equity tranche below it. In some cases some or all of the tranches will be rated by a rating agency. The rating is intended to reflect the ability of the issuer to meet its payment obligations with respect to coupon and principal of the notes. Senior tranches are structured with the aim to receive a AAA rating. The equity tranche is not always rated. Some structures feature a *super senior tranche*. Investors in a super senior tranche only incur losses after all of the equity tranche, all of the mezzanine tranche and all of the senior tranche have incurred losses for their respective full notional amounts.

SYNTHETIC MEZZANINE TRANCHES

The mezzanine tranche often offers a higher coupon than a senior tranche and a lower level of risk than an equity tranche. Some of the most advanced credit derivatives structures consist of the creation of a *synthetic mezzanine tranche*. In these structures an investor purchases a mezzanine credit-linked note on a portfolio tailored to that investor's needs. There is no equity investor and no senior investor, just the mezzanine level. This allows the investor to customise a transaction by choosing the reference entity names in the portfolio, the minimum credit event attachment point and the maximum credit event attachment point, and identifying an adequate level of coupon for that level of risk. The arranger structuring the transaction on the other side will absorb or hedge separately the equity level risk and the senior level risk.

LEVERAGED STRUCTURES

It is possible to increase the level of risk and the related reward of a transaction by *leveraging* the risk. This is achieved by entering into a credit derivative that references a portfolio of reference entity names that exceeds the notional amount of the credit-linked notes issued.

By way of example let us compare two fictional structures, Structure 1 and Structure 2. Let us assume that (1) credit-linked notes are issued for an amount of €100 million; (2) defaults occur at a rate of 1% of portfolio reference entities in both Structure 1 and Structure 2; (3) cash settlement applies; and (4) all valuations of reference obligations following a credit event will result in a market value of 65% for the purpose of cash settlement.

In the case of Structure 1, let us assume the reference entity portfolio comprises 10 reference entity names having a notional of €10 million each. The portfolio notional amount of Structure 1 is €100 million. Structure 1 is not leveraged. A 1% default rate will result in *one credit event* affecting the portfolio. Investors in Structure 1 will incur tranche losses for an amount of €3.5 million (10 × 100% − 65%). Let us now turn to Structure 2, the leveraged structure. The reference entity portfolio comprises 20 reference entity names for a notional of €10 million each.

The portfolio notional amount of Structure 1 is €200 million, and credit-linked notes are issued for an amount of €100 million. A 1% default rate will result in *two credit events* affecting the portfolio. Investors in Structure 2 will incur credit event amounts for an amount of €7 million (2 × 10 × 100% − 65%). A leveraged structure would normally command higher levels of coupon than an unleveraged structure due to the higher level of risk involved.

DYNAMIC PORTFOLIO STRUCTURES: SUBSTITUTION AND MANAGEMENT

We have examined so far portfolio structures where both the portfolio of reference entity names and the collateral portfolio is static during the life of the transaction. These are referred to as static portfolio transactions. Some more complex structures have emerged in recent years, in part due to the recent downturn in the credit markets, in part due to a desire for greater flexibility. These structures provide for substitution or management features that apply to either the reference entity names in the portfolio, the pool of collateral securities, or both.

DYNAMIC PORTFOLIO STRUCTURES: SUBSTITUTION OF PORTFOLIO AND COLLATERAL

The distinguishing substitution feature of a substitutable portfolio credit derivative is that one of the parties to the credit derivative, or both, can request that during the life of the transaction some of the reference entities in the portfolio or some of the collateral securities held by the SPV are taken out of the portfolio or collateral pool and substituted with a different reference entity or asset. As mentioned above this can apply to the portfolio of reference names, the pool of collateral securities, or both. The substitution of a reference entity will affect the risk profile of the transaction. It is possible to make the transaction riskier for the seller of protection by removing from the portfolio a reference entity name with a high credit quality and adding a reference name with a lower credit quality. By inverting the process the transaction can be made less risky for the seller of protection. The same is true in the case of substitution of an asset in the collateral pool. The main function of collateral is to secure the obligation of the issuer to pay coupon and principal on the notes. In transactions where the investor is exposed to the market value or credit risk of the collateral, the removal of a lower credit quality collateral asset and its substitution with a higher credit quality asset would reduce the likelihood of the investor experiencing a loss. Conversely, this likelihood would be increased by the substitution of a higher credit quality collateral asset with a lower credit quality asset.

Exhibit 36.9 illustrates substitution in a dynamic structure. Substitution is a useful feature where the buyer of protection wants to have the flexibility of tracking its exposure to a portfolio of names that could change over time. This feature would be of interest to a lender managing a portfolio of loans that have different maturity dates. Substitution is also a useful feature for a seller of protection who wishes to have the means of contrasting portfolio credit quality deterioration over time by taking out of the portfolio assets that have deteriorated and adding assets with a better credit quality.

Specifying the appropriate eligibility criteria allows the investor to provide for substitutions and for the risk profile of the transaction to remain consistent with the risk profile at the time of issue of the credit derivative instrument, or to alter such risk profile if necessary and agreed between the parties.

Let us assume that an investor sells protection on a portfolio of 10 reference names that are all rated AA at the issue date of the relevant credit-linked note. The transaction documents may provide that if certain conditions are satisfied, it may be possible to substitute one of the reference names in the portfolio with another reference entity, provided that the new reference entity meets the eligibility criteria specified in the deal documentation. Usually the parties specify individual eligibility criteria as well as portfolio eligibility criteria. Individual eligibility criteria

EXHIBIT 36.9 Dynamic Structures: Substitution of Portfolio and Collateral

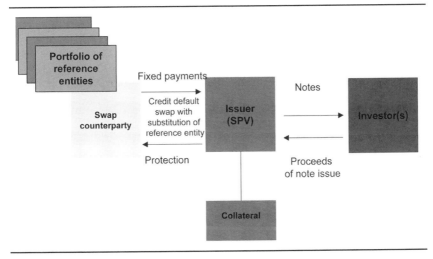

are the criteria that a particular name must satisfy in order to be eligible to be added to the portfolio. These criteria may be based on the rating of the reference name, the currency of denomination of the debt issued by that reference entity, the industry category of the reference name or currency of denomination of a particular reference asset. Portfolio eligibility criteria usually refer to the concentration of risk within the whole portfolio. Limitations may apply to the number of assets that may originate in a particular country or region, on the currency of denomination, or on the industry sector. Almost invariably the seller of protection will require that in order for any substitution to occur, the *weighted average rating* (WAR) of the assets within the portfolio must be kept within a certain preagreed range. The weighted average rating of the portfolio is an indication of the overall credit quality of the assets comprised in the portfolio, calculated on a weighted average basis by reference to the notional amount of each loan or bond in the portfolio. The weighted average component is intended to adjust the rating data to take into account the size of each asset relative to other assets in the portfolio. A substitution that deteriorates the weighted average rating of the portfolio is valuable to a buyer of protection and unattractive to a seller of protection because it implicates a lower average credit quality of the portfolio and an increased likelihood of credit events affecting the portfolio. This makes the portfolio riskier from the perspective of the seller of protection.

By way of example, the parties may agree that a substitution may be allowed only if as a result of the substitution: (1) no more than 20% of reference entities will be organised under the laws of Country X; (2) no more than 5% of reference entities will be operating in the field of commercial airline carriers; (3) no more than 10% of reference obligations will be denominated in a currency other than the Euro; and (4) the weighted average rating of the portfolio will be kept within a certain preagreed range.

DYNAMIC PORTFOLIO STRUCTURES: MANAGEMENT OF PORTFOLIO AND COLLATERAL

A further step from substitution is the provision of an investment management element. As in the case of substitution, a management feature can be adopted with reference to the portfolio of reference names or the pool of collateral. Issuer and investor will appoint a portfolio manager to manage the portfolio of reference names, or the pool of collateral obligations according to preagreed investment criteria.

The power to substitute reference entity names or collateral obligations usually rests with one of the parties. Active management is usually

EXHIBIT 36.10   Dynamic Structures: Management of Portfolio and Collateral

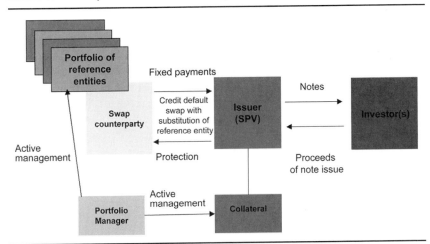

carried out by a portfolio manager who is independent from the parties. This is because the management element provides a more direct influence on the risk profile of the investment. The involvement of the investor and the other parties is usually limited to setting the parameters to be followed by the portfolio manager in managing the portfolio during the life of the transaction. The parties also retain the power to substitute the portfolio manager in case of a failure by the portfolio manager to perform its function. Exhibit 36.10 illustrates the process.

CONCLUSION

The notion of structured products and the use of special purpose vehicles have come under intense scrutiny in recent times. While it is advisable to analyse with particular attention the economic impact of complex transactions such as structured credit products, a structured element and the use of an SPV do not automatically imply that a transaction carries with it an increased level of risk. Structured credit products represent a sophisticated tool which, if used and disclosed appropriately, can assist in allocating risk and reward between market participants. In this respect, structured credit products share a particularly important virtue with other types of financial derivatives: they allow risk precisely to be identified and transferred to those most willing to bear that risk and receive the related reward.

Index